EUROPEAN HISTORY IN A WORLD PERSPECTIVE

Modern Times

VOLUME III

Shepard B. Clough
Columbia University

Otto Pflanze
University of Minnesota

Stanley G. Payne
University of Wisconsin

Robert E. Frykenberg
University of Wisconsin

G. Wesley Johnson
University of California – Santa Barbara

D. C. HEATH AND COMPANY
Lexington, Massachusetts   Toronto   London

THIRD EDITION

EUROPEAN HISTORY
IN A WORLD PERSPECTIVE

Modern Times

Cartography by Norman Adams.

Cover design by Daniel Thaxton.

Preface to the Third Edition

The great success of the first and second editions of this work has encouraged the authors and the publisher to present this third edition. The text has found enthusiastic users literally around the world and has elicited from them a demand that our story include the happenings of the last few years. Indeed, we realize that textbooks must be renewed frequently to bring the record up to date, to include new findings of scholarship, and to introduce the best of the new pedagogical devices.

This new edition has been thoroughly revised, and much of it has been rewritten to obtain greater fluency and clarity. The bibliographies have been simplified and reduced in bulk to indicate more precisely where students may best go for additional reading. Each part now contains an illustrated section on the major contributions received from the past. Charts and tables have been used to assist the student in fixing events in their complex relationships in time. All the maps have been revised and replotted in two colors for greater clarity, and many new maps have been added. A great effort has been made to introduce illustrated material that will add to the comprehension of styles, techniques, personalities, and physical conditions. Lastly, sections have been added on the history of Africa and the East, for the effects of these regions on the western world have been so great and their history so neglected by Europeans and Americans that we believe our readers should have this material at their disposal.

The Third Edition is available in two bindings—a two-volume paperbound edition: *Ancient Times to 1715* and *1715 to the Present;* and a three-volume paperbound edition: *Ancient and Medieval Times, Early Modern Times,* and *Modern Times.*

The authors who have collaborated in the writing of *European History in a World Perspective* are specialists in their respective fields with broad experience not only in research and writing, but also in teaching. It seems appropriate to list here all the authors even though they may not have contributed to this particular volume. The division of writing is as follows: Nina G. Garsoian, Professor of Armenian Studies and Byzantine History and Chairman of the Department of Middle East Languages and Cultures, Columbia University: Parts I–IV and Chapter 3 in Part V; David L. Hicks, Associate Professor of History, New York University: Part V, Chapters 1–2 and 4–5 and Parts VI–VIII; David J. Brandenburg, Professor of History, The American University: Part IX, Chapters 1–4, Part X, Chapters 1–3, Part XI, Chapter 1 and Chapters 3 and 4, and Part XII. Peter Gay, Professor of History, Yale University: Part IX, Chapter 5, Part X, Chapter 4, Part XI, Chapter 2; Shepard B. Clough, Professor Emeritus of European History,

Columbia University: the Introduction on "The Nature of History" and portions of Chapter I, Part XI; Otto Pflanze, Professor of History, University of Minnesota: Part XIII and Chapter 5 of Part XIV; Stanley G. Payne, Professor of History, University of Wisconsin, Madison: Part XIV, Chapters 1–4, Part XV, Chapter I, and Parts XVI and XVIII; Robert E. Frykenberg, Professor of History and South Asian Studies, University of Wisconsin, Madison: Chapters 2–4 of Part XV and Chapters 1–3 of Part XVII; G. Wesley Johnson, Associate Professor of History, University of California, Santa Barbara: Chapter 5 in Part XV and Chapter 4 in Part XVII. Professor Brandenburg wishes to state that Millicent H. Brandenburg is, in fact, co-author with him and that she did most of the picture research and caption writing for his sections of this edition.

Any endeavor like this one involves a great number of persons to whom thanks for their generous help are due. The authors are particularly grateful to the late Garrett Mattingly, Miriam Haskett, Albert Mott, Robert Shipkey, Josef L. Altholz, Theophanis G. Stavrou, Hans Rogger, and Eugen Weber. For their help in preparing the Third Edition the authors would particularly like to thank Linda C. Rose, Robert J. Scally, Thalia Cosmos, Carl G. Anthon, O.B. Hardison and the helpful staff at the Folger Shakespeare Library, Ira N. Klein, James A. Malloy, Jr., Renate Shaw and her colleagues in Prints and Photographs at the Library of Congress, and Kathleen Wilson.

CONTENTS

Introduction
The Nature of History

At the beginning of every scientific investigation and, indeed, at the beginning of every attempt to increase our knowledge and understanding, it is essential to state as precisely as possible what the object of the investigation is, what steps will be taken in the process of analysis and synthesis, and what methods will be employed in furthering the undertaking. Such a statement is particularly necessary in the study of history, for this subject is used to encompass so much and so wide a variety of concepts that the uninitiated frequently become confused and then lost in its labyrinthian twists and turns.

The Study of History In essence, history is the total recorded past of humankind on this earth—the totality of human experience. Inasmuch as all aspects of this great experience are not of equal importance either to an understanding of how the world of the present got the way it is, or in comprehending how men lived in the past, or in learning how changes were made that got us from primitive society to the present complex societies, the historian has to make selections from the total record for special study. These selections, based upon the major categories of man's behavior in society, provide the historian with his orienting themes. Thus the historian endeavors to explain how man has provided for his material wants at various times in the past and how our present economic system came into being (economic history); he tries to describe how men have organized their social relationships for continuing the society, for procreation, for training the youth, and for establishing rules of conduct (social history); he makes an effort to analyze the way people in society create a government to bring together all members for collective action, to effect compliance with

common rules, and to determine policies to be followed (political history); and he aspires to ascertain what the basic values of the society are—what people strive for, be it a place in the hereafter or some goal on this earth, and by what means they hope to achieve their ends, whether through the intercession of a divine being or beings or reliance on their own resources (intellectual history).

This division of man's activities through time for study provides one essential means for making sense out of the vast record of the past, but it is obvious that all mankind in all parts of the world cannot be treated at once. Consequently, the historian selects segments of mankind for study. On the largest scale, mankind is divided into *cultures* or *civilizations,* each with distinctive ways of making a living, of organizing socially, of governing, of thinking, of creating esthetic works, and of establishing basic values. Thus historians and other social scientists recognize such cultures as the Greek, the ancient Egyptian, western European, the Eskimo, the Chinese, and the Russian Communist. Parts of these cultures may, in turn, be set apart for study in order to get further understanding of some particular phase of life, such as the city of recent times, the philosophy of the Greeks, or the art of the Egyptians. And, by the same token, the historian may legitimately study relations among cultures or their parts and how one culture has been influenced by others. Indeed, in recent times one of the great developments in the world has been the way in which nearly every culture has attempted to take on some aspects of western European civilization, especially the economic.

Once the historian has selected his segment of human society for study, he then has to make a decision regarding the time-span over which he intends to trace and analyze behavior. Indeed, the historian must not only select periods for study, but he must also divide his period into sections of time for purposes of clarity and effect, much as the dramatist separates his play into acts and scenes. To some extent such divisions will be determined by major changes in development, but sometimes they may be arbitrary and mere literary conveniences. Thus, the student, as well as the historian himself, should never forget that changes in the stream of human experience are seldom so abrupt as represented in history books and that always some parts of former ways of doing things and formerly held values continue to be held by some members of a society when other ways and values have been adopted by a majority.

Finally, the historian needs some criterion for deciding what are the important things he should isolate for study and what are the unimportant and the insignificant, which he may ignore. Obviously the Battle of Waterloo was more important in the Napoleonic period than the head cold of Josephine in 1799; the invention of the steam engine was more important than the curling iron; and World War II was more important than the Spanish-American War. To handle this problem of what is important the historian should, although he not always does, select for study those subjects (things and men) that have affected *most* men *most* profoundly for the *most* time. The historian should observe the rule of the *three mosts*—he should eschew the ephemeral.

The Character of European Culture In the economic phase of man's activity, western Europe developed a system of production based upon the use of composite mechanisms, which stretch all the way from the fulcrum and lever and the bow and arrow down to the most complex computing machines and giant metal presses of the present, and upon intricate processes that reach from the use of friction to create fire to, let us say, the catalytic method of refining petroleum. This system of production has made increasing use of inorganic materials, which were stored over millions of years in the earth's crust and which were infinitely more abundant than organic materials produced in relatively short periods of time. Furthermore, the processes of production have been moved by power or energy largely from inorganic resources and sometimes transformed by power mechanisms, like the waterwheel, the steam engine, the internal combustion engine, the electrical dynamo, and the atomic pile. Western man has had at his disposal power sources never equalled in any previous culture. Then, too, man was able to conquer space by rapid means of transportation and thereby bring large quantities of materials together from very distant parts for the use of men in the West. Lastly, western man has made enormous improvements in strains of growing things and in the breeds of animals, as well as in soil fertility, so that what he grew yielded many times more per acre and per unit of human input than that obtained by his ancestors of ancient times.

The great productive systems of the present depend in large part upon the ability of individuals to specialize in some aspect of economic activity—in what economists usually refer to as the division of labor. Individuals nowadays seldom endeavor to be economically self-sufficient in the sense of themselves's producing everything they may need for consumption; they rely, instead, upon the exchange of goods and services with others. This reliance upon the market has been made possible, in part, by cheap and rapid transportation and by communication of information about goods and their supplies, and also, in part, by the institution of money, which is a medium of exchange, a measure of value, and a store of wealth. Indeed, money is one of the most important inventions of man, ranking with fire and the wheel, because of its role in establishing a division of labor.

On the social side of European culture the great characteristic of our present day is the enormous complexity of groupings compared with the rather simple family and tribal organizations among primitive peoples. Peoples now fall into groups determined by their families, fortunes, professions, religions, political affiliations, education, and even physical characteristics. Human relations are regulated in large part by the standards set by the groups to which people belong and relations become anarchic when individuals are torn from their groups by some disturbance like war. Nevertheless, within European culture a basic ethic persists—an ethic which comes from the Christian-Jewish tradition—based upon the Golden Rule of doing unto others as you would have others do unto you, and upon the Ten Commandments. In time this ethic became written into law codes and the laws came to be more nearly the same for all groups in society. In the past, the family was a central institution for regulating procreation, for educating the youth in the fundamentals of the culture, and in caring for the aged and the infirm. More recently, as the task of training has come to be more technical and as relations among men have become more impersonal, because of the division of labor, the schools have taken on more of the training task and state organizations have assumed many of the responsibilities for the aged and the infirm (the welfare state).

Other important characteristics of present-day social existence pertain primarily to the increase in population, the lengthening life span of man, and to ever-greater concentrations of population in cities and their suburbs. In the last three and a half centuries, the population of Europe has grown sevenfold, which has been made possible, in part, by access to the resources of overseas areas. The average length of life of individuals, technically called "expectation of life at birth," has gone up from the twenty-five or thirty years that it was from Roman times to the middle of the eighteenth century to nearly seventy years in the majority of European countries. This has meant that more people can make use of technical training over long periods, and put that training to greater use, but it also means that a larger percentage of the population lives beyond the productive ages and becomes dependent upon society.

Today, in the more economically advanced countries of Europe, some 65 percent of the population lives in cities of 2,500 or over, whereas at the end of the eighteenth century, only some 15 percent of the population lived in such agglomerations. This means that the lives of more and more people are regulated by city customs and values. Among such values are a desire for a higher standard of living, which has led to the curtailment of size of families, a demand for more man-made works of art and spectator entertainment, and a drive for more popular participation in the affairs of government.

In the political realm of human activity, the trend in European history has been toward the establishment of larger states, to endow these states with a sovereignty that implied no other power existed over them, to extend their functions until they invaded every phase of life, and to have these states coterminous with "nationalities," or subcultures of western culture, to which individuals came to attach great emotional loyalties. Many of the traditional histories of Europe have, indeed, concentrated their attention primarily on these issues and upon relations among states, which is an indication of how important they loom in the public life of European peoples. In the present work, emphasis will be placed upon them, but always with the end in view of making clear the long and arduous process by which our present-day political system came into being. Furthermore, an effort will be made to show what social groupings controlled political organizations, which ones wanted change, and how those in power used the machinery of the state for advancing the policies they favored. Lastly, considerable attention will be given to the tensions that arose among states in the process of state-building and to the strife that developed among national states—a strife that in the twentieth century seriously threatened the very continuation of European culture and greatly lessened the position of Europe in the world.

In intellectual life, the outstanding achievement of western culture has been the development of science, for it has permitted man to extend his control dramatically over the physical universe. The basic principle of scientific thought has been the ascertainment of the various factors, including their quality and their magnitudes, and the manner and timing in which they came together, which were necessary to produce event "x" and which invariably did produce event "x". The more accurate and precise the data resulting from the application of this principle were and the more thoroughly the explanation for event "x" could be established through repetitive experimentation or observed experience, the more "scientific" the knowledge was considered to be.

Even though in some fields of activity, as in the social sciences, it is recognized that the investigator cannot control all the forces at work, is largely an observer, and cannot know even all of the factors involved, as for example the functioning of Napoleon's endocrine glands during the Battle of Waterloo or what Brutus had for breakfast before he turned sourly against Julius Caesar, the theory of knowledge employed in the name of science in all fields is essentially the same. How this epistemology, or theory of knowledge, came into being over millennia of time will be a recurring theme in the pages ahead. So, too, will be the uses to which scientific knowledge has been put in conquering the physical world. It has made possible the practical elimination of famine; it has freed man from many of the scourges of pestilence and disease; and it has given him so much confidence in himself and his methods that he believes he can accomplish almost any physical task he may set for himself. Western man has from this confidence developed a firm conviction in "progress" toward a more ample fulfillment of his goals. This confidence has, in turn, led to a great optimism regarding the future, albeit that this optimism is mitigated from time to time by man's realization that he has not been able yet to control relations among men according to the culture's values.

On the esthetic side of man's life, the West has tended to glorify the arts. By his oft-repeated use of the expression—"the finer things of life"—western man indicates how highly he esteems works of art. Moreover, in spite of the fact that he places the appreciation of esthetic productions high in his scale of values, he rates creativity in the arts above passive enjoyment. In fact, he invariably places the activist above the passivist in all efforts in conformity with the culture's values.

About the respective merits of the various arts and of the multitudes of artistic styles western men differ very widely. Esthetic judgment seems to be a highly individualistic thing and esthetes have been at a loss to establish an objective measure for determining excellence. This is embarrassing for the historian, who has to rely so heavily upon specialists for forming his own conclusions. He knows, to be sure, that men learned in the arts do set standards that establish some criteria for judging craftsmanship and accomplishment. In the final analysis he is forced to acknowledge that he must accept as esthetically great what most competent judges have most consistently and most universally considered great.

Finally, students of history should have before them one other major consideration—that is, a general conception of the goals of our culture, for it is in terms of these goals that judgments about various historical trends or events are made; and contrary to what is often contended, historians are forever making judgments, and in the opinion of many quite properly so. Be that as it may, however, the values that the West attaches to achievements in various categories of human existence constitute our present-day conception of levels of civilization. These levels are determined, so far as those in western European culture are concerned, by the degree to which men establish control over their physical universe, are able to regulate human relations among all mankind according to the Golden Rule, and succeed in producing generally recognized masterpieces in architecture, painting, literature, sculpture, music, philosophy, and science. The more a people realizes both qualitatively and quantitatively these tenets of civilization without exception, the more civilized it is. And conversely, the less it realizes them, the less civilized it is.

Some Problems in Historical Study: Evidence, Causation, and Change The historian, much like the lawyer, proceeds to describe human behavior through time by collecting evidence. Sometimes this evidence is scanty, as in the case of population statistics when no censuses were taken. In such instances, the historian has to rely upon subsidiary data like baptismal and death records, or he has to infer size by the walls of cities, the height of buildings, and the number of persons using dwelling units. At other times, evidence may be overwhelming, as for example, the records of World War II. In such cases, selection and condensation are necessary and the historian has to guard against falsifying the story, by choosing what is most representative and what is the most relevant to the immediate issue he is investigating.

Both in the amassing of evidence, as well as in the selection of segments of history for study, in the subsequent analysis of why events took place, and in passing judgment as to the desirability of certain behavior, the historian is confronted with the danger of being influenced by his personal likes and dislikes, or his own subjective set of values. The Parisian writing about the Franco-Prussian War of 1870 may produce a very different account of the war than the German; the anti-Catholic may regard the seizure of the Papal States in the nineteenth century in another manner from the members of the Vatican; and the social reformer may look upon the industrial revolution in quite another way from the economist interested in economic growth. The historian acts, like all the rest of us, on the basis of the set of values he has acquired in his maturing, and what he writes is related to these values. This is the problem of relativity. Its dangers can be minimized by keeping judgments about the desirability of an event or of a development relevant to the values of the culture rather than to the values of the individual and by making whatever values are brought into play clearly explicit.

Once the historian has managed to keep his own prejudices and hopes from coloring his work (or makes clear what his prejudices and hopes are), and has amassed evidence regarding the character of events, he is then concerned with an explanation of how and why these events took place. Here he comes face to face with the knotty question of causation. What were the causes of the event—the war, the invention, the style of art, or the way of thought. In trying to ascertain the "causes" for any event, a temptation exists to seek a simple explanation, a single cause. In fact, some his-torians have tried to explain all of the past on the basis of geography, or of climate, or of economic forces, or of patterns of thought, or of the action of a supernatural power. Unfortunately, monocausal explanations are *ipso facto* inadequate for explaining what is very complex.

The task of the historian is, then, to establish what are the multiple and necessary factors involved in any development or in the background of any event. This is not an easy affair, for so many and such varied kinds of forces come into play that the historian has to exercise his own judgment and has to have very broad competences. He has to know something of psychology, something of economics, and something about sociology, politics, law, art, philosophy, and the physical sciences. And in addition, he must know the languages of the area he is treating, and the techniques for measuring quantities of evidence (statistics), and he must be able to present his materials and his conclusions in effective speech or writing. His task is, indeed, formidable, but not impossible, especially if he has begun early enough in his life to acquire proper training. At all events, the historian finds immense satisfaction in trying to understand human behavior so that man may adopt those policies that will help establish more readily than would otherwise be the case the kind of a world that is in conformity with the basic values of his culture. And there is a great sense of achievement in attempting to provide a synthesis of the various aspects of human activity that go to explain the world in which we live.

In the process of attempting to explain how humans have developed the kinds of cultures that exist today or have existed at various times in the past, the historian inevitably becomes involved in the phenomena of *change*. This is a subject of such great importance in historical study that a few words about it here may prove useful to the student, for the historian, *perforce,* is primarily concerned with periods of change rather than with periods in which things remain static.

Change is always the result of something new being introduced into a given situation—a platitude that has been raised to what might seem to some a great height of erudition by an elaborate theory of innovation. Contrary to what many observers have said, change may come from any one of the aspects of human existence. It may be initiated by an increase in population, or, for that matter, by a decrease. It may come about from the invention of a new machine, like the steam engine. It may be started by a new pattern of thought, like that of science or Christianity. It may get its original impetus from the appearance of a great leader, like Alexander the Great or Napoleon. It may begin with an alteration in climate, like a long period of drought or flood. Or it may result from a change in the alignment of groups in society and a consequent shift in the locus of power, as in the French Revolution. It may come from within a society (autonomous change), or it may come from without the society (adaptive change). In any case, change is always impending, if for no other reason than that the actors on the stage of life are always being renewed. The more gradual change is, the more easily societies seem to be able to adjust to it.

The facility with which change is effected in any society depends in large part upon the range of opportunities for alternative decisions open to the members of the society in question. The greater the range, the more extensive change may be; and the less the range, the less the change to be expected.

The extent of the range of opportunities for alternative decisions will depend upon the degree of rigidity in the case under analysis. If a society's culture, institutions, groups, ideologies, and leadership are rigidly fixed in traditional patterns, change will occur more slowly and with greater travail than in a society characterized by flexibility in values and institutions and by mobility of people up and down the social scale.

Rigidity will depend to a considerable degree on the extent to which a proposed change affects favorably the status of those segments of society that possess influence, authority, and power. This proposition represents a drastic modification of the traditional belief that underprivileged classes are the breeding ground of change. It seems clear that the upper groups of society are responsible for a large measure of change, especially that which does not at once threaten their positions, for they have the means of initiating new undertakings and their positions of power give them some immunity from social sanctions when breaking with tradition.

Secondly, rigidity will depend on the extent to which there is a fear of change in society and conversely will be weakened when *progress*, which implies change, is glorified. Thirdly, rigidity is increased if a society has little surplus energy or resources for experimentation—if it lives from hand to mouth and can run no risks. And fourthly, rigidities in society depend in part on physical environment and in part on the biological characteristics of members of the group. Thus, change in desert cultures has been less than in the rich valleys of navigable rivers; and it has been less among bodily weak and inactive peoples, like the Pygmies, than among the physically strong and active like the western Europeans.

Finally, attention should be drawn to the fact that change will vary in rate, size, and direction according to the nature of the innovation, the nature of the environment in which it is introduced, and the leadership that is given it. It will almost certainly affect some phase of life more rapidly than others, so that some phases will seem to be *leading* in the process of change while others will be *lagging*. Among those who favor change, criticism will be directed toward the *lags*; and among the reactionaries who oppose change, criticism will be directed toward the *leads*. Rate of change will depend in large part upon the urgency with which the society feels a need for what is new and upon its ability to adopt it. And the magnitude and direction of change will likewise be determined primarily by social need, awareness of that need, and ability to do something about it.

In the vast panorama of the past, change as effected by people is of fundamental importance. Only by understanding it in relation to goals toward which society should strive can they form public and private policies that will give them more nearly the kind of world they want. The study of the past has a very practical side—it is at the bottom of most human decisions, whether it be the purchase of an automobile or the defense of one's religious belief. From this it should follow that the better the understanding of the past, the better will be everyday decisions.

FURTHER READING

A great many introductions to the study of history exist for the use of students. See especially Homer C. Hockett, *The Critical Method in Historical Research and Writing* (1955); Jacques Barzun and Henry F. Graff, *The Modern Researcher* (1970); and Marc Bloch, *The Historian's Craft* (1953).

The study of history involves a number of philosophical problems, particularly those having to do with a theory of knowledge (epistemology), the selection of issues for study, the choosing of data relevant to these issues, and the personal preferences and prejudices of the historian. These matters are discussed in W. H. Walsh, *An Introduction to Philosophy of History* (1964); Herbert Butterfield, *Man on His Past: The Study of the History of Historical Scholarship* (1955); Pieter Geyl, *Use and Abuse of History* (1970); and Ernst Cassirer, *The Problem of Knowledge: Philosophy, Science, and History since Hegel* (1950). Excerpts from many of the recent writers on the philosophy of history are to be found in Hans Meyerhoff, *The Philosophy of History of Our Time* (1959). Also, Ronald H. Nash, ed., *Ideas of History*, 2 vols. (1969).

For an understanding of the philosophy of history represented in the present work, see *Theory and Practice in Historical Study*, Bulletin 54 of the Social Science Research Council (1946) and *The Social Sciences in Historical Study*, Bulletin 64 of the Social Science Research Council (1954).

Various historians of the relatively recent past, their methods, and their points of view have been discussed by G. P. Gooch, *History and Historians of the Nineteenth Century* (1959); Bernadotte Schmitt, *Some Historians of Modern Europe* (1942); Trygue Tholfsen, *Historical Thinking, An Introduction* (1967); Felix Gilbert and Stephen R. Graubard, eds., *Historical Studies Today* (1972); and Samuel William Halperin, ed., *Essays in Modern European Historiography* (1972). Different interpretations of certain periods and different types of history are found in collections of passages from well-known historians. Shepard B. Clough, Peter Gay, and Charles K. Warner, *The European Past*, 2 vols. (1970); Fritz Stern, *The Varieties of History* (1972); and in the series *Problems in European Civilization*, edited by Ralph W. Greenlaw and Dwight E. Lee.

Every student of history should have a good English dictionary and an encyclopedia, at least of desk size, *The Columbia Encyclopedia* (3rd ed., 1963), or *Le Petit Larousse*. He should also have a guide to names, dates, and events, such as William L. Langer, ed., *An Encyclopedia of World History* (1972); and an historical atlas, such as William R. Shepherd, *Historical Atlas* (1964), or Edward W. Fox, *Atlas of European History* (1957).

PART XIII

Beginning with the French Revolution of 1789, European civilization entered an era of turbulence and conflict which did not cease with the "restoration" of 1815 but has continued until our own times. The relative homogeneity of European society, government, and intellectual life in the eighteenth century steadily disintegrated under the impact of economic development, the appearance of new social classes, the growth of class conflict, the emergence of hostile political ideologies, and the rise of nationalism and national discord.

Although the dominant trend of European civilization in the last two centuries has been toward division and conflict, political and cultural bonds still existed at the beginning of the nineteenth century which resisted this trend. One bond was the political system variously known as the "European balance of power," "European equilibrium," and "Concert of Europe." During the Napoleonic period, the European balance of power had been nearly destroyed by French conquests. Napoleon's defeat, however, made possible its reconstruction at the Congress of Vienna in 1815, and thereafter it regulated the struggle among the European great powers.

In pursuing their own objectives, statesmen were usually compelled to consider how those objectives affected the vital interests of other states. At critical moments in the nineteenth century some even recognized that there was a common European interest transcending the self-interest of individual states. Imperfect though it was, this "Concert of Europe" gave the continent the longest period of relative peace it had known.

Europe was also united by strong cultural ties. Although they emanated primarily from England and France, the ideas of the Enlightenment became the common property of educated Europeans. After 1800, the Enlightenment gradually gave way to the age of Romanticism which, although most at home in Germany, affected the cultural life of every European country.

In other respects, nevertheless, Europe was internally divided into at least three great regions: western Europe (England, France, and the Low Countries), central Europe (Germany and the Habsburg empire), and eastern Europe (Russia and the Balkans). Since the sixteenth century, the economic development of central and eastern Europe had lagged behind that of western Europe. The initial consequence of the industrial revolution in the late eighteenth and nineteenth centuries was to accentuate these differences. Beginning in Great Britain, the factory system spread slowly across the continent from west to east.

This irregular economic growth produced significant contrasts in social structure and political life. In western Europe, the commercial and industrial revolutions accelerated the growth of towns and of the capitalistic system. Both meant an expansion in the number of artisans, laborers, merchants, entrepreneurs, professional people, and other occupational groups which constitute the lower and middle classes. From the seventeenth to the nineteenth centuries, the middle class emerged as a factor in English political life; and, in France, it overthrew the nobility in the revolutions of 1789 and 1830. In central Europe, and, to a still greater degree, in eastern Europe, the aristocratic social and political order remained intact, despite French attempts, in the period 1792–1815, to export revolutionary social and political ideals. There, society and government remained under the domination of a conservative nobility whose wealth was based on large landed estates tilled by a subservient peasantry. Lagging economic development in these areas delayed the growth of a middle class capable of grasping and applying revolutionary doctrines. The revolutions of 1848 and 1905 demonstrated the weakness, more than they did the strength, of the middle class in central and eastern Europe. When industrialization began to transform these regions, it proceeded so rapidly that middle-class liberalism had little chance to mature. The political effects of this uneven economic and social development are still with us.

DETAIL OF "THE BARRICADES" BY EDOUARD DETAILLE. (French Embassy & Press Information Division.)

RESTORATION, REVOLUTION, AND REALISM, 1815-1870

LEGACY OF THE PAST

(Above) *A Ball at Mansion-House, Official Residence of the Lord Mayor of London.* During "the season" London society enjoyed a steady round of such entertainments.

(Opposite) *How the Poor of White-chapel, a Working-Class Region of London, Spent their Days.* Artisans and peddlars display their wares and hope for customers, while their children play in the streets.

During the first seventy years of the nineteenth century the industrial revolution, which had begun earlier in Britain, reached the continent of Europe. With it came a "population explosion" that greatly increased the number of people inhabiting Europe and their concentration in large cities. What these developments meant in the daily lives of the people was brilliantly depicted by the French artist Gustave Doré who visited London in the 1870's. His drawings portrayed with malice tempered by humor and compassion the overcrowded streets and the contrasting lives of rich and poor in Europe's largest city. Ultimately the factory system provided vast new opportunities for employment and a higher standard of living that mitigated some of the ills that Doré saw. Railways and steamships brought fast and cheap transportation for people and freight, while machines produced goods in huge quantities at lower cost. The spread of education and literacy improved the lives of millions, but it also initiated a new and at times destructive age of ideological politics. Europe and the world entered a far more complex stage in the development of civilization than any previously recorded. Governments are still trying to cope with the new realities and multiplying problems produced by this "modernization."

MAJOR EVENTS, 1815-1870

1815– Maturation of Industrial Capitalism in England (1815–1850)
Congress of Vienna (1815)
Quadruple Alliance (1815)

Economic Depression (1818–1819)
Congress of Aix-la-Chapelle (Aachen) (1818)
"Peterloo" Massacre and Six Acts in Britain (1819)
Karlsbad Decrees in Germany (1819)

1820– Revolts in Spain and Italy (1820–21)
Congress of Troppau (1820)

Congress of Laibach (1821)
War for Greek independence (1821–29)

Congress of Verona (1822)

1825– Decembrist Insurrection in Russia (1825)
Economic Depression (1825–1830)

1830– Industrialization in France and Belgium (1830–1860)
Railway Construction begun (1830's)

Revolutions in France, Belgium, Germany, Italy, and Poland (1830–31)

First British Reform Act (1832)
First War between Egypt and Turkey (1832–33)
Completion of German Zollverein (1834)

1835–

Second War between Egypt and Turkey (1839)

1840– Industrialization in Germany and Austria (1840–1873)

1845– Economic Depression (1845–1848)
Repeal of Corn Laws in Great Britain (1846)

Revolutions in France, Italy, Germany, and Austria (1848)

1850–

Crystal Palace Industrial Exhibition (1851)
Founding of Second Empire in France (1852)

Crimean War (1853–56)

1855–

Invention of Blast Furnace introduces Age of Steel (1856)
Economic Depression (1857–1859)

Italian War (France and Sardinia against Austria) (1859)

1860– Cobden Treaty (Britain and France) introduces Era of Free Trade (1860)

Founding of the Kingdom of Italy (1860)
February Patent in Habsburg Empire (1861)
Emancipation of Serfs in Russia (1861)
Constitutional Conflict in Prussia (1862–66)
Insurrection in Poland (1863)
War over Schleswig-Holstein between Denmark, Prussia, and Austria (1863–64)

1865– Economic Depression (1865–1868)
War of Austria against Prussia and Italy (1866)

Establishment of the Dual Monarchy (Austria-Hungary) (1867)
Second Reform Act in Great Britain (1867)

1870– War of France against Prussia and other German states (1870–71)

1 The European Balance of Power, 1815-1847

"History teaches us, and invariably we disregard her lesson, that coalitions begin to disintegrate from the moment that the common danger is removed," wrote Harold Nicolson. This observation, which applies equally well to 1918 and 1945, is particularly apt for the fate of the great allied coalition which brought about the defeat of Napoleon in 1813–1814. The "grand alliance" had been formed only with difficulty. Even before Napoleon's defeat, the first divisions had appeared in its ranks, divisions which, after Napoleon's exile to Elba, were to bring the allies themselves to the brink of war.

Although many of the soldiers who fought in the ranks were motivated by patriotism and the desire to liberate Europe from the tyrannical Corsican, the generals who commanded them and the rulers and ministers who formulated the objectives of the campaign belonged to Europe's traditional ruling class. These aristocrats had been trained in the old classical school of diplomacy and statecraft, which taught that the primary concern of the statesman must be *raison d'état:* the needs of the state. While hostile to the ideals of the French Revolution, which had threatened the traditional social order throughout Europe, their immediate interest was in the redistribution of power that would follow victory. What were to be the future frontiers of the European states? How were the victors to be compensated for their sacrifices and their contributions to the common cause?

THE PEACE
SETTLEMENT
OF 1815

Russia's primary role in Napoleon's defeat naturally led Tsar Alexander I to expect a significant territorial gain in Poland. His aim, however, was not the incorporation of more Polish soil into Russia, but the creation of a satellite kingdom. This strange, ambivalent man hoped to satisfy both the self-interest of his state and the liberal idealism which as a youth he had imbibed from his Swiss tutor, La Harpe. In Poland, he would grant the liberal constitution that he rejected for Russia itself. Abroad, he would act the benevolent despot, fulfilling the ideals of the *philosophes;* while at home he continued to rule as a conservative autocrat over a subservient nobility and an enserfed peasantry. But Poland could only be gained at the expense of

Austria and Prussia. These powers had participated with Russia in the three partitions (1772, 1793, 1795) which had liquidated the Polish state. Defeated by the French in 1806 and 1809 they had been compelled to surrender their segments of Poland to the Grand Duchy of Warsaw established by Napoleon. But now they expected either to regain what they had lost or be compensated for its permanent surrender.

Prussia Frederick William III, the mediocre and melancholic King of Prussia, was willing to consider the latter possibility. His goal was not the return of the alien Poles to Prussian sovereignty, but the total incorporation of his prosperous neighbor, the Kingdom of Saxony. After his defeat by the French in 1806, King Frederick Augustus I of Saxony had collaborated with Napoleon. Now he was held captive and the independence of his kingdom was in jeopardy. By acquiring it, his Hohenzollern neighbor hoped to round out the Prussian frontiers. Such a gain would have added significantly to the wealth and power of Prussia. For this very reason the Austrian government felt compelled to object.

Austria The Habsburg monarchy was the last major European power to join the "war of liberation" against Napoleon. Badly crippled by previous defeats, the government in Vienna was wary of the Corsican genius. For nearly four years Prince Clemens von Metternich, who became Austrian foreign minister in 1809 at the age of thirty-six, accepted a secondary role in Europe. Not until the armies of the grand alliance were on German soil and Napoleon's star was obviously waning did the prince commit the forces of Austria to the struggle.

Metternich's aim was the restoration of a stable balance of power in Europe, a balance in which Austria would once again be one of the primary weights. France, he realized, was also important to the European equilibrium; to weaken her too much would only strengthen the power of Russia. To the Habsburg monarchy, in fact, Russia was as serious a threat as France. By setting up a puppet kingdom in Poland, Tsar Alexander would in effect extend the frontiers of Russia nearly to the Oder River. The acquisition of Saxony by Prussia, furthermore, would remove an important buffer on the frontier of Bohemia; it would strengthen the power of Berlin within Germany and hence threaten the traditional dominance of Austria in German affairs.

Great Britain Great Britain likewise had an interest in the re-establishment of the European balance of power. With but one brief interruption, the British had been at war with revolutionary and Napoleonic France since 1793. Napoleon's attempt to destroy Britain commercially through the Continental System had demonstrated once more the mortal danger to the British Isles should France or any other European power permanently control the continent. While sympathetic to the expansion of Austria in Italy and of Prussia in northern and western Germany (except for Hanover), Lord Castlereagh, the British Foreign Secretary, was firmly determined not to permit France

EUROPE IN 1815

—— Boundary of the German Confederation

Miles
0 _____ 300

ATLANTIC
OCEAN

SCOTLAND
Edinburgh•
NORTH
SEA
IRELAND UNITED KINGDOM OF
Dublin• GREAT BRITAIN
AND IRELAND
WALES ENGLAND
London•

KINGDOM OF
NORWAY AND SWEDEN
Oslo•
Stockholm•

FINLAND
(To Russia, 1808)

ÅLAND
IS.

BALTIC SEA

St. Petersburg•

RUSSIAN   EMPIRE

Moscow•

Volga R.

Don R.

Riga•

Kiev•

Dnieper R.

Dniester R.

BESSARABIA
(To Russia, 1812)

Odessa•

CRIMEA

Sebastopol•

BLACK   SEA

Kars•

SYRIA

Beirut•
Acre•

CYPRUS

Alexandria•

Cairo•
Nile R.

EGYPT

DENMARK
Copenhagen•
SCHLESWIG
HOLSTEIN

Hamburg•
Berlin•
Elbe R.

EAST
PRUSSIA
Danzig•
Vistula R.
Warsaw•
POLAND
Cracow•
Oder R.

Moscow

THE
NETHERLANDS
HANOVER
P R U S S I A
Cologne•
Aix-la-Chapelle•
BELGIUM
(Ind. 1831)
Lux.
Metz•

THURINGIAN
STATES
SAXONY
Prague•
Trappau•

AUSTRIAN   EMPIRE

Pressburg•
Vienna•
Budapest•
HUNGARY

TRANSYLVANIA

MOLDAVIA
(Aut., 1829)

WALLACHIA
(Aut. 1829)

Danube R.

SERBIA
(Aut. 1829)
Belgrade•
BOSNIA
CROATIA
DALMATIA

BULGARIA

Sofia•

MONTENEGRO

OTTOMAN   EMPIRE

Adrianople•
Constantinople•

Salonika•

AEGEAN
SEA

Smyrna•

ANATOLIA

BADEN
WÜRT.
BAVARIA
Munich•
AUSTRIA
TYROL
Danube R.
Rhine R.

SWITZ.
Berne•
Milan•
LOMBARDY
VENETIA
Verona•
Po R.

GREECE
(Ind. 1829)
Athens•
CRETE

MEDITERRANEAN   SEA

Strasbourg•
Lyons•
Rhône R.

FRANCE
Paris•
Rouen•
Seine R.
Tours•
Loire R.
Bordeaux•
Garonne R.
Toulouse•
Marseilles•

PARMA
MODENA
LUCCA
TUSCANY
Genoa•
PAPAL
STATES
Rome•
ADRIATIC SEA
Laibach•

KINGDOM OF THE
TWO SICILIES
Palermo•
SICILY
MALTA
(Br. 1800)

CORSICA
SARDINIA

BALEARIC
IS.
(Sp.)

Barcelona•

Valencia•

SPAIN
Madrid•
Burgos•
Tagus R.
Seville•
Cadiz•
Gibraltar
(Br.)

PORTUGAL
Lisbon•

MOROCCO

ALGERIA
(Fr. 1830)

TUNISIA

to retain control over any part of the Netherlands. The coastline opposite England must be in the possession of a weak power dependent upon Britain for the preservation of its independence.

In the end, the question of France's future borders was settled by Napoleon himself. His insistence on keeping the Rhine frontier gave the allies no other choice than to march on Paris and dictate peace. But this also meant that Napoleon had to be deposed and exiled to the island of Elba off the Italian coast. After some uncertainty about his successor, the allies reluctantly chose the oldest surviving brother of Louis XVI, who assumed the French throne as Louis XVIII. As was noted earlier (1053–1054), the allies gave him an easy peace in the first Treaty of Paris (May 1814). France was to keep the border she had possessed in 1792 and was to pay no reparations. The desire to restore and to effect a durable peace outweighed the desire to punish.

The Congress of Vienna   There remained the more difficult problem of drafting a peace settlement for the rest of the continent, and for this purpose the powers were summoned to Vienna. It was a brilliant gathering. From September 1814 until June 1815, most of the rulers and all of the leading

A Session of the Congress of Vienna. Metternich stands prominently at the left. The seated figures in the foreground are (seated left to right) Hardenberg, Nesselrode, Castlereagh, Talleyrand, and Stackelberg (Russian ambassador to Vienna).

statesmen of Europe were assembled in the Habsburg capital: for Russia, Tsar Alexander I and Count Nesselrode, supported by Baron Stein, the former reform minister of Prussia; for Austria, Emperor Francis I and Metternich; for Great Britain, Lord Castlereagh; for Prussia, King Frederick William III and Prince Hardenberg; for France, the ubiquitous Talleyrand, who had deserted Napoleon just in time to make himself indispensable to Louis XVIII. Also present were the representatives of Spain, Portugal, Sweden, and Holland, and most of the petty princes of Italy and Germany.

The successive fetes, balls, and banquets helped to distract the rulers and ministers of the smaller states while the five great powers—Russia, Prussia, England, Austria, and France—set about the task of redrafting the map of Europe. In the beginning it was not their intention to admit France to this conclave, but the astute Talleyrand quickly confounded them by introducing the "sacred principle of legitimacy." Napoleon, he pointed out, was on Elba; Louis XVIII, who had never made war on anyone, now reigned in France. It was the quarrel over Poland and Saxony, however, that gave this slippery Frenchman his great chance to rehabilitate France. Tsar Alexander remained adamant in his plans for a satellite Polish kingdom and was joined by Prussia, which needed Russian support for its intended spoliation of Saxony. On January 3, England, Austria, and France signed, on Talleyrand's initiative, a secret treaty of alliance to resist these demands. "France," Talleyrand exulted, "is no longer isolated in Europe."

For a few days, the danger of war was acute; but Tsar Alexander and Frederick William III decided to compromise. Prussia received the Polish district of Posen, Austria that of Galicia; the disputed town of Cracow was made a free city. Out of what was left, Russia created the kingdom of Poland, often called "Congress Poland." King Frederick Augustus of Saxony was restored to his throne in Dresden, but two-fifths of his country was acquired by Prussia, which also gained Swedish Pomerania, Westphalia, and most of the left bank of the Rhine. In addition to Galicia, Austria regained Illyria, the Tyrol, and Lombardy and was granted Salzburg and Venetia.

The rest of the settlement was not so difficult. The former republic of Holland was converted into a kingdom under the house of Orange, to which was joined the former Austrian Netherlands (later Belgium). England returned the Dutch colonies it had seized in the Indies, but kept Ceylon and the Cape of Good Hope, as well as Malta, Helgoland, and some minor French colonies promised in the Treaty of Paris. Germany was reorganized into the German Confederation, composed of thirty-nine sovereign states. Switzerland regained its independence. Sweden received Norway, which was given its own constitution; and Denmark was compensated with tiny Lauenburg. In Italy, the "legitimate" dynasties were restored in the kingdom of Sardinia (which received Genoa), in Modena, in Tuscany, in the Papal States, and in Naples. The Bourbon family was returned to power in Spain.

From this it is evident that what has popularly been called the "restoration" of 1814–1815 was not a restoration of the Europe that had existed in 1789. For all their conservatism, the statesmen at Vienna were aware that this was impossible. They followed the principle of legitimacy where convenient, but tempered it with two other principles: the mutual compensation of the victors and the re-establishment of a balance of power. By preserving France as a European great power, strengthening Prussia in northern Germany, and reducing the size of Congress Poland, Metternich and Castlereagh gained support against any possible future expansion of the Russian colossus into Europe. By uniting the northern and southern Netherlands, giving Prussia most of the Rhineland and creating the German Confederation, they created new barriers against future attempts by France to expand toward the Rhine. The same effect was achieved in Italy by making Austria the dominant power on the peninsula and by enlarging the possessions of the House of Savoy, which commanded the passes over the Alps.

Because it flouted the principle of national self-determination, the settlement of 1814–1815 was attacked by liberals and nationalists during the century that followed. It was denounced as reactionary and unprogressive. Yet the distribution of power achieved at Vienna gave Europe a long period of relative stability in international affairs.

"The European Equilibrium," a caricature by Honoré Daumier. Statesmen at the Congress of Vienna saw the balance of power as a guarantee of peace. To Daumier and his public it seemed based more on mutual fear than on mutual accommodation.

Napoleon's Return and the Hundred Days While the princes and ministers debated and intrigued, Napoleon sat on his Mediterranean isle, impatient and calculating. After abdicating at Fontainebleau he had attempted suicide but the poison made him nauseated and thereby saved him. On his way to captivity, in fear of his former subjects, he had disguised himself as a postillion. But now his belief in his star revived. Observing the bitter dispute in Vienna and the general disillusionment in France under the corpulent and gouty Louis XVIII, he resolved to give the wheel of fortune another whirl. On March 1, 1815, he landed at Cannes at the head of 1,500 men.

At first he was very successful. The forces sent against him deserted to him, and on March 20 he entered Paris on the heels of the departing Louis to be carried into the Tuileries on the shoulders of rejoicing Parisians. Yet the news of his escape created immediate unanimity, rather than heightened confusion at the Congress in Vienna. The allied armies were hurriedly regrouped for a new campaign. On June 18, occurred the decisive Battle of Waterloo. In vain Napoleon hurled his regiments upon the Duke of Wellington's army, until the arrival of the Prussians under Blücher turned the tide. This time the treatment of the French was less generous. Napoleon, who surrendered to the British, was shipped off to St. Helena in the south Atlantic to remain in captivity until his death in 1821. Louis XVIII regained his throne, but his government was compelled to pay an indemnity of 700,000,000 francs, to return the looted art treasures and to cede important border fortresses to Holland, Prussia, and Sardinia. Napoleon had undone the work of Talleyrand; France was again isolated, a pariah in Europe.

THE FORCES FOR CHANGE AND STABILITY

In the decades that followed, the potential threats of the stability of the Vienna settlement were chiefly two: (1) aggression by European powers in pursuit of their own interests, and (2) subversion of the dominant aristocratic-monarchical order by popular movements. Since the equilibrium devised by the Congress proved to be fairly effective in restraining the ambitions of the great powers, the greatest danger came from the threat of subversion.

Liberalism Ideas are more difficult to destroy than armies and governments. Despite the successive failures of the French republic and the Napoleonic empire, the spirit of liberty, equality, and fraternity lived on in the European movements known as "liberalism" and "nationalism." Those who called themselves liberals were men of progressive viewpoint who were opposed to monarchical absolutism and aristocratic privilege. They desired constitutions that would state the basic rights of man, limit the power of the executive, establish a Parliament equipped with real legislative authority, and create an independent judiciary capable of impartial and equitable judgments. In economics, the liberals generally stood for the abolition of mercantilism and for free enterprise. Following the doctrine of laissez faire, developed by the Physiocrats and Adam Smith, liberals argued that governmental interference in the economic process could only harm the businessman, that maximum economic growth was only possible where the entrepreneur had the freedom to make his profit or suffer his loss in accordance with his own insight and the chances of the market place.

In other matters, however, there was disagreement among liberals throughout Europe. Two basic tendencies are discernible: moderate liberalism and democratic liberalism. Moderate liberals had serious doubts about the merits of popular sovereignty. What they desired was a constitution with "mixed powers": that is, concentration of the executive power in the hands of the monarch and division of the legislative power between the monarch and a parliament chosen by a restricted suffrage based upon wealth. Democratic (or radical) liberals, on the other hand, accepted the principle of popular sovereignty. They favored universal suffrage and popular control over the executive power. Some wished to copy the English system, placing the cabinet under the control of Parliament, while others preferred the American design, a republic with a popularly elected president.

The moderates were men of wealth or of professional standing, who feared the lower classes; though they demanded the transfer of political power from the nobility to themselves, they denied it to those beneath them. The democrats, on the other hand, wanted political power for the masses: that is, the lower middle class, the artisans, peasants, and proletarians. Reflecting the divisions of Europe, the democrats were strongest in western Europe while the moderates dominated the liberal movement in central Europe. In eastern Europe, liberalism was not a popular movement until the third quarter of the nineteenth century.

Nationalism Nationalism was another popular movement that threatened to subvert the established order. While the spirit of nationalism had been present in Europe since the decay of feudalism in the late middle ages, it did not become a genuinely popular force until the French Revolution. Nationalism is a sentiment or loyalty arising from an awareness of belonging to a cultural community formed by common institutions and traditions or by common language, religion, customs and the like. This awareness can only flourish in a society whose economic and social development permits some degree of popular education. It can be greatly stimulated, moreover, by the creation—through evolutionary or revolutionary means—of a political order which grants to the masses the right, or at least the illusion, of participation in public affairs. Patriotic fervor generated in this way enabled republican and imperial France to conquer the greater part of Europe. Those countries which France attacked used the same weapon in bringing about her defeat.

Johann Gottfried Herder. A Lutheran minister by profession, Herder grew up in East Prussia, and it heightened his awareness of nations. While inhabited by Germans, Prussia was surrounded by Poles, Lithuanians, Russians, and many other ethnic groups. (Brown Brothers.)

The growth of nationalism was assisted by the work of a German philosopher, J. G. Herder (1744–1803). Herder believed that his fellow Germans were insufficiently aware of their cultural heritage. They slavishly adhered to the intellectual standards propagated by the French *philosophes* and the literary and artistic norms imposed by French classicism; many educated Germans, including Frederick the Great, even thought of the German tongue as barbaric and preferred French. Attacking the absolute norms and static concepts of the Age of the Enlightenment, Herder taught men to value what was unique and original in their own cultures and to think in terms of organic growth.

Herder's great work, *Ideas on the Philosophy of History of Mankind* (1784), exerted a strong influence. In Germany, it nourished a cultural renascence, a period of great intellectual achievement which for a few decades gave to the Germans a leading position in European thought and literature. In translation it was avidly read by the educated people among the other nations of central and eastern Europe, where it promoted the growth of national consciousness.

Herder's views had impact because they articulated the new aspirations of the reading public in these regions. His aim was the maximum development of humanity as a whole rather than merely of Germany or any other nation. Never did he assert that political unity or independence was necessary for the cultural growth of a people. Yet the new awareness of national individuality led, with seeming inevitability, to a demand for "national self-determination." In this form, nationalism became a revolutionary force threatening the existing order in Europe.

At the beginning of the nineteenth century, liberalism and nationalism appeared to be inseparable movements. The liberals were usually nationalists, and the nationalists were usually liberals. The achievement of national independence or national unity did not appear possible except under liberal auspices. Similarly, those European progressives who lived in submerged or divided nations did not think it possible to achieve constitutions and make secure the rights of man except by the path of national self-determination. Only time would show that these twin forces of subversion were separable and even capable of mutual hostility.

Edmund Burke (1729–1797). One of the ablest publicists of his time, Burke was a vigorous critic in parliament of British policy toward the American colonies. While opposing the extremes of rationalism and revolution, he favored political reform.

Conservatism The dominant aristocratic-monarchical order in Europe found in conservatism a political and social philosophy with which to combat the attacks of the liberal nationalists. In 1790, Edmund Burke had supplied the foundation upon which the conservative philosophy was to be built in his *Reflections on the Revolution in France.* Society is not based, he maintained, upon a "contract"—which can be torn up or redrafted at will; it is a partnership between the dead, the living, and the unborn. No generation has the right to destroy that partnership; instead it has the sacred duty to transmit the heritage of the past to posterity. New liberties can be achieved by molding traditional rights into new forms rather than by attempting to reconstruct society and government according to the abstract norms of natural law.

The philosophy of conservatism assumed several forms. Following Burke, moderate conservatives insisted on evolutionary rather than revolutionary change, striving to preserve the continuity of social and political institutions. In France, Joseph de Maistre maintained that the absolute authority—of the monarch over the state and of the pope over the church—was the only effective barrier against revolution. Romantic conservatives, like the German Adam Müller, were as much opposed to absolutism as they were to liberalism. Their ideal society was the corporate one of the middle ages, which had been governed by the nobility rather than the monarch; society should be regarded as an organism composed of estates, or occupational groups, each performing its separate function for the welfare of the whole. They praised the feudal system with its contractual rights, services, and dependencies. Naturally, this doctrine found favor among French *émigrés* and the nobility of central and eastern Europe.

The Holy Alliance and the Concert of Europe In addition to the treaties already discussed, the victors of 1815 negotiated two other diplomatic instruments with which they hoped to buttress the political stability of Europe. After Waterloo, the great powers signed (November 20, 1815) a Quadruple Alliance providing for military cooperation in the event of a resumption of French aggression. In the final clause they agreed to meet "at fixed periods" to "consult upon their common interests," and to consider measures "for the maintenance of the peace of Europe." It was the first such compact in the history of international politics. In the past, it had been customary to hold a European congress only to negotiate peace after a general war. Now it was agreed to meet in peacetime in order to avert war. This "Concert of Europe," as it came to be known, was the forerunner of the League of Nations and United Nations.

Tsar Alexander I of Russia, Emperor Francis I of Austria, and King Frederick William IV of Prussia. Fear of subversion led the three monarchs who formed the Holy Alliance and their successors to cooperate in European politics until the revolution of 1848. (Staatsbibliothek, Berlin.)

In the popular mind, the Quadruple Alliance came to be overshadowed by an earlier agreement signed on September 26, 1815. This was the Holy Alliance proposed by Tsar Alexander I. The impressionable Alexander had lately undergone a religious conversion under the influence of Baroness von Krüdener, a mystical occultist, adventuress, and general charlatan. In this mood, he asked his fellow monarchs to sign a document guaranteeing that in the future they would be guided in the government of their countries and in their relations with each other only by the "precepts of that holy religion, the precepts of justice, charity, and peace." Privately, the rulers and statesmen received this proposal with derision and cynicism. Castlereagh called it "a piece of sublime mysticism and nonsense," Metternich a "loud-sounding nothing." Its very harmlessness enabled most European monarchs to sign; only two refused: the sultan of Turkey because of his Moslem faith, and the king of England because only an absolute monarch could enter into such a compact.

Metternich, however, soon realized that the Holy Alliance might have utility for Austrian policy. He amended one of the clauses to imply that the signatory monarchs would render each other "fraternal" assistance in putting down internal disturbances. In this way the Concert of Europe came to look less like a compact between states for the adjustment of mutual differences than a conspiracy among monarchs for the suppression of the popular forces of liberalism and nationalism.

EUROPEAN POLITICS IN THE RESTORATION ERA

In conformity with the agreement for periodic consultations the European powers held four congresses: Aix-la-Chapelle (1818), Troppau (1820), Laibach (1821), and Verona (1822). At Aix-la-Chapelle, it was already apparent that, once the common danger of French imperialism had disappeared, the conflicting interests of the great powers took precedence over their common purposes. With each succeeding conference the breach widened until by 1822 it could no longer be bridged. Europe's first feeble attempt at some kind of international government collapsed.

The Conference System By 1818, the Bourbon regime in France had succeeded in stabilizing itself. Cabinet and Parliament were under the control of moderate royalists who accepted the Charter of 1814 as the constitution of France. Hence the powers met at Aix-la-Chapelle in order to settle the reparations problem, terminate the allied occupation of French soil, and receive the Bourbon regime back into the community of European states. All this was accomplished, and the conference was outwardly successful. Behind the scenes, however, ominous differences of policy had developed. Tsar Alexander proposed a "general alliance" for the "solid guarantee" of the territorial settlements of 1815 and support for "legitimate" governments. But the British delegates, Castlereagh and Wellington, protested that "nothing would be more immoral or more prejudicial to the character of government" than a European alliance for the perpetuation of corrupt and tyrannical governments merely because of the antiquity of their dynasties. Although Alexander withdrew his proposal, the exchange of views had its consequences. Convinced that the cooperation of Britain was not to be obtained, the governments of Russia, Austria, and Prussia began to consider the possibility of acting without her.

Indeed it was soon evident that the conservative monarchies had to cooperate, if the principle of legitimacy was not to be seriously damaged by the forces of subversion. Throughout Europe there were signs of popular ferment against the settlement of 1815. Students, intellectuals, and idealistic bourgeois, who had fought in the recent wars, found that their sacrifices and hopes had been laid on the altar of aristocratic privilege and monarchical authority, rather than upon the altar of freedom and national unity. In their frustration they combined into radical groups, conspired and demonstrated, and vowed the destruction of reactionary governments.

The first blow was struck in Spain. In January 1820, an uprising occurred among the troops assembled in Cadiz for service against revolutionists in Latin America. The soldiers were motivated not by liberalism, but by anger over such matters as bad food, poor quarters, and infrequent pay. Rioting and demonstrations followed in the larger cities. The Bourbon ruler Ferdinand VII, whom the allies had placed on the throne, was compelled to restore the liberal 1812 constitution he had revoked in 1814.

The events in Spain were an inspiration to the discontented throughout Europe. In the Italian Kingdom of Naples, a military insurrection in July 1820 compelled another restored Bourbon king, Ferdinand I, to grant a constitution like that of Spain. During August, Portugal was the scene of another rebellion, and in March 1821 an uprising in Piedmont led to the abdication of Victor Emmanuel I and the grant of another constitution based on the Spanish model. To conservative rulers and statesmen, it appeared that, unless some preventive action were taken, the fires of revolution might spread to the whole of Europe. In May 1820, Tsar Alexander expressed his wish to send a Russian army to intervene in Spain, and in October the powers met at Troppau to confer on the problem.

Even before the diplomats convened it was evident that the issue of intervention had destroyed what remained of the Grand Alliance. On May 5, 1820, the ailing Castlereagh issued what was to be a famous memorandum in which he contrasted the differences in "outlook and method between the autocratic, or eastern powers, and the democratic, or western powers." "The principle of one state interfering in the internal affairs of another in order to enforce obedience to the governing authority is always a question of greatest moral, as well as political, delicacy. . . . To generalize such a principle, to think of reducing it to a system, or to impose it as an obligation, is a scheme utterly impracticable and objectionable." At Troppau in October, Metternich presented a protocol, previously accepted by the three eastern powers, in which it was declared that any state succumbing to revolution thereby sacrificed its membership in the Holy Alliance. Moreover, the remaining members had the right to take armed action to restore it "to the bosom of the alliance." Castlereagh, who had refused to attend, replied through the British delegate that the powers had no right to assume the armed guardianship of thrones and to deny to the peoples of Europe the right to determine their own destiny.

The eastern powers, however, were undeterred. Meeting at Laibach in January 1821, they implemented the Troppau protocol by intervening in Italy. By March, eighty thousand Austrian troops had placed Ferdinand I back upon his throne in Naples. Returning northward they suppressed the Piedmontese rebellion and secured the throne for the absolutist Charles Felix. Because of its geography, Spain was more difficult to handle. Meeting at Verona in October 1822, the three eastern powers commissioned the French government to invade the peninsula. France, the land that had given birth to the great revolution, whose imperial armies had carried the cause of social and political reform throughout the continent, now became the instrument of the conservative reaction. Crossing the Pyrenees, a force of 100,000 men swept the peninsula within six months; Bourbon France succeeded where Napoleonic France had failed. Restored to power, Ferdinand VII proceeded to inflict brutal reprisals upon the defeated rebels. Once more "order" had been restored in Europe.

George Canning, who succeeded Castlereagh as British Foreign Minister, was determined that the Spanish "restoration" should not cross the Atlantic. He proposed to the United States a joint declaration against the re-establishment of Spanish control over her rebellious colonies in Latin America. But John Quincy Adams, the American Secretary of State, decided upon independent action and the result was the presidential message to Congress which came to be known as the "Monroe Doctrine." Canning's boast that he had "called the new world into existence to redress the balance of the old" was idle, for the new world, including the United States, had as yet no power with which to influence the course of European politics. The threat that ended the possibility of intervention in Latin America was that of British sea power, rather than the brave words uttered by President Monroe.

The Eastern Question Even while French and Austrian troops marched through Italy and Spain to suppress revolutionary governments, the events taking place in the East were soon to prove the hollowness of the Holy Alliance. The internal difficulties of the Ottoman Empire compelled the European powers to re-examine their principles in the light of their own interests. By 1827, Britain, the opponent of intervention, had allied with Russia and France, the defenders of legitimacy, to support the Greeks in their war for independence from Turkish rule.

During the nineteenth century, the Ottoman Empire appeared so often on the verge of dissolution that it earned the sobriquet "the sick man of Europe." The sources of its difficulties were misgovernment, maladministration, and the rising tide of nationalism among Balkan peoples. In the region of the Balkans the Sultan ruled about 8,000,000 people of varying nationality, but mostly of Christian (Orthodox) faith. In the past, Turkish rule over this region had not been very oppressive. Though the Turks were Moslems, they permitted their Christian subjects a large degree of local autonomy. Since Islamic law could not be applied to them, the Christians were allowed their own legal systems, a measure of self-government, freedom from military conscription, and freedom of religious practice and education. Nevertheless, the Turkish government was in general decadent, inefficient, and often corrupt. The tax system was discriminatory, and no efforts were made to further economic progress. The central government, moreover, had lost control over its local officials and garrison troops.

As the hand of the Sultan weakened, the grievances of the people grew and likewise the opportunity for revolt. In 1804, the Serbs had risen under the leadership of Kara George. Defeated by 1813, they returned to the attack two years later under the resourceful Milos Obrenovich. By 1817, the Serbs, despite bitter feuds among themselves, had succeeded in driving off the Turks; though it was not until 1829 that the Turks officially recognized Obrenovich as the hereditary ruler of an autonomous principality. In return, they received the right to maintain certain garrisons on Serbian soil along with the payment of annual tributes. Meanwhile, the Serbian example was being followed by the Greeks.

The Greek Revolt Ottoman rule had never been complete on the mountainous Greek mainland. While exacting tribute, the Turks did not succeed in occupying or pacifying the entire peninsula. Protected by armed bands, the Greek villages were like miniature republics controlling their own local affairs. Toward the end of the eighteenth century the Turks undertook the task of suppressing these bands. Greek resistance soon took on the character of a national rebellion. A seafaring nation, the Greeks were in closer contact with western Europe than were other Balkan peoples. Under the influence of the French Revolution, secret societies were formed in Greece for the purpose of propagating liberal and national ideas. Established in 1814 with headquarters at Odessa on Russian soil, the Philike Hetaireia (Friendly Association) soon extended its leadership over the rebellious movement.

In 1821, the Greeks revolted, proclaiming their independence under a constitution. The struggle was carried out with great barbarity on both sides. While the Greeks slaughtered the Turks who came into their hands, Sultan Mahmud II sought to terrorize the insurgents into submission. On Easter Sunday in 1821 the Greek Patriarch and three archbishops were butchered in the cathedral at Constantinople. In the beginning, the rebels were successful, but the tide turned against them in 1825 when the Sultan called upon the services of his powerful vassal, Mehemet Ali of Egypt, and a systematic reconquest of the Greek peninsula was begun.

While the Serbian revolt had passed largely unnoticed in the West, the Greek war for independence engaged the attention of Europe almost from the start. Greece was the original home of western civilization, and its people, while Orthodox rather than Roman Catholic, were nonetheless Christian. To European intellectuals, who had been educated in the classical tradition, the Greek cause was that of the cultured West against Moslem barbarism—of light against darkness. In France and Britain, the Philhellenes staged public meetings and demonstrations; money was raised and volunteers dispatched.

European statesmen regarded the Greek revolt with uneasiness. The Austrians feared that Russia would exploit the Greek situation in order to expand into the Balkans. Naturally, the Russians were interested in the fate

Lord Byron in Greek Costume. One of the greatest English poets of the romantic age, Byron volunteered to fight for Greek independence. He died in 1824, not long after arriving in Greece, and became a martyr for the cause. (National Portrait Gallery, London.)

of Orthodox Christians struggling against Moslems. While Tsar Alexander listened to Metternich's plea that Russian intervention would violate the principle of legitimacy, his successor, Nicholas I, who came to the throne in 1825, was less impressed. He found willing partners for intervention in Britain and France. While Castlereagh had held to the principle of non-intervention in Greece as well as in Italy, Canning took a more opportunistic view of the question. He was concerned about the Ottoman inability to protect British commerce, and he felt the pressure of Philhellene sentiment in Britain. Furthermore, he feared that Greece might become a satellite of Russia if she owed her independence entirely to Russian intervention. The French government likewise felt the pressure of educated opinion on the

Greek question. When Russia and Britain took the initiative, the French felt constrained to join.

On July 6, 1827, Britain, France, and Russia agreed in the Treaty of London to blockade Turkey and compel her to accept their mediation. Seemingly by accident, on October 20 a combined French and British fleet engaged the Turco-Egyptian fleet at Navarino Bay and destroyed it. Lest the western powers gain the initiative, the Russian government declared war on April 26, 1828; and London and Paris felt compelled to follow suit. Crossing the Danube, a Russian army took Varna, but met unexpected resistance and was forced to halt for the winter. Next year the Russians

Battle of Navarino Bay. The destruction of his fleet forced Ibrahim Pasha, son of Mehemet Ali, and his Egyptian army to retreat from the Greek peninsula. Since this was the most effective force fighting for Turkey, his departure greatly aided the Greek rebels. (The Mansell Collection.)

resumed the offensive and crossed the Balkan mountains to seize Adrianople. Meanwhile, another Russian force operating in the Caucasus had reached the upper Euphrates, and a French expeditionary force had occupied the Morea in the wake of the retreating Egyptians. Their empire on the verge of collapse, the Turks sued for peace.

Through the Treaty of Adrianople (September 14, 1829) Russia received the mouth of the Danube and a segment of the Black Sea coast. While nominally under Turkish suzerainty, the Rumanian provinces of Moldavia and Wallachia were given independent governments under a Russian protectorate. All Turkish fortresses in the provinces were to be razed, their garrisons withdrawn, and all Moslems deported. In addition, the Sultan was to pay a large indemnity over a period of ten years, during which Russian forces were to occupy the two conquered provinces. Impressed by these Russian gains, Britain and France hastened to secure an independent Greece under western influence. Seconded by Austria, who had stood nervously by throughout the war, they negotiated a new London Protocol (February 3, 1830) which established Greek independence under a monarchy. As king, they ultimately chose a Bavarian prince, Otto I, of the house of Wittelsbach.

The Revolutions of 1830–1831 and the Renewal of the Holy Alliance In July 1830, the focal point of European politics suddenly shifted from the Near East to western Europe. A revolution exploded in Paris on July 28, producing a chain reaction elsewhere in Europe. The reactionary Charles X, who had succeeded Louis XVIII in 1824, lost his throne to Louis Philippe, the Duke of Orleans, who had once fought in the armies of the first French Revolution. On hearing the news, Tsar Nicholas is said to have exclaimed: "Saddle your horses, Gentlemen; revolution rules again in Paris!" The fissure that had opened between Vienna and St. Petersburg concerning Greece was quickly closed. Only one week after Louis Philippe became king, Metternich and Nesselrode met at Carlsbad and signed an agreement stating that their governments intended to preserve the existing European order against French subversion; soon afterward Prussia adhered to the compact. Europe's three great conservative monarchies appeared united before a continent threatened with revolution. In September, an uprising in Belgium subjected their alliance to a crucial test.

In handing over the Austrian Netherlands to Holland, the Congress of Vienna had followed the needs of the European balance of power rather than the wishes of the inhabitants. The Belgians resented Dutch rule for a number of reasons. They were Catholic, while the Dutch were mostly Calvinist. Since the sixteenth century, their development had been separate from that of Holland. While the Dutch were farmers and merchants who thrived on free trade, the nascent industry of Belgium needed tariff protection if it were to survive. The Dutch administration was blamed for the economic distress that stemmed from a series of bad harvests in the 1820's, a rise in living costs that squeezed the incomes of urban workers, and a sharp business recession that struck early in 1830. Inspired by the news from Paris, the Belgians rioted in the streets of Brussels on August 25. In September, the Dutch troops were expelled, and on October 4 a provisional government declared Belgium an independent state.

King William I of Holland appealed to the conservative monarchs of Europe for aid against the rebels. But Louis Philippe warned that France could not sit idly by while the eastern powers intervened so close to her frontiers. In Britain, there was no sympathy for the cause of King William, only fear that the eastern threat would trigger a French occupation and eventual annexation of Belgium. Hence the British government proposed a conference. Meeting in London in November, the European powers agreed to recognize Belgian independence. On January 21, 1831, they signed a protocol which guaranteed Belgian neutrality in perpetuity and established that the ruler of the new state might not come from any of Europe's leading dynasties. Eventually, the Belgians chose Leopold of Saxe Coburg, a German principality.

Nicholas I had favored intervention in Belgium; but, in November 1830, he was distracted by an uprising in Poland. His predecessor as tsar, Alexander I, had granted the Poles all the institutions and liberties he denied to his own people: a constitution, bicameral legislature, and freedom of press and religion. In addition, it was stipulated that only Poles could hold posts in the civil service and that a separate Polish army was to be officered by Poles. Nevertheless, the final power of the state was wielded by the tsar's representative, and the army commander was a Russian. This was resented by Polish nationalists: mostly army officers, petty noblemen, and intellectuals. Meetings of the Polish Diet produced sharp criticism of Russian rule, and secret clubs and societies conspired against the regime. On November 29, 1830, the conspirators struck and were supported by the excited citizens of Warsaw. The insurrection spread across the land; and on January 25, 1831, the Diet declared Poland independent. Unlike the Belgians, the Poles were isolated in eastern Europe, surrounded by hostile conservative powers. For all their patriotic bravery, they could not hold back the Russian army. In September 1831, the Russians took Warsaw, crushed the rebellion, and deprived the Poles of the liberties they had recently enjoyed.

The Paris revolution also sent its shock waves into Germany and Italy. In September 1830, the rulers of Saxony, Brunswick, and Hesse-Cassel were compelled to abdicate and constitutions were adopted. This was accomplished without foreign intervention because the constitutions were limited in character and because Europe was distracted by the Belgian and Polish rebellions. In Italy, however, the revolutionists were not so fortunate. Beginning in February 1831, the insurrection spread from the duchies of Modena and Parma to the Papal States. France, however, did not send the expected aid since Louis Philippe had no intention of following a revolutionary policy in Europe. Metternich acted quickly, and in March, Austrian troops dispersed the rebel levies and once more stamped out the Italian revolution.

EUROPEAN POLITICS BETWEEN THE REVOLUTIONS

The revolutions of 1830–1831 shocked the conservative rulers and statesmen and restored something of the mood that had existed in the years 1815–1823. Obviously, the lack of solidarity among European monarchs had encouraged the liberals and nationalists to undertake their insurrections. The Italian conspirators had, in fact, hoped for Russian assistance, in view of the friction between Russia and Austria over Turkey. In September 1833, the Russian and Austrian emperors and the Prussian crown prince met at Münchengrätz and renewed the Holy Alliance, pledging their determination to preserve the European order created by the Treaty of Vienna.

For a time there was a real possibility that Europe would divide into two hostile blocs separated by differing social and political systems, as well as by conflicting interests. In France the revolution of 1830 had brought to power a liberal monarchy based primarily on the wealthy entrepreneurial and land-owning classes, in contrast to the aristocratic elements that had supported the regime of Charles X. The French thought of their revolution as accomplishing that which Britain had achieved by the Glorious Revolution of 1688. In terms of their ruling classes and political structures, the two countries appeared to be much closer than they had been since the middle ages. Hence it seemed natural to many that Britain and France should form an entente to protect their interests and their political systems from the conservative bloc in the east. Before long, however, the reaction of the European powers to events taking place in the Near East demonstrated that the two blocs were an illusion. Once again, self-interest triumphed over ideological solidarity.

The Egyptian Crises Behind the Russian desire to renew the Holy Alliance lay an ulterior motive hardly in keeping with its ideological character. The tsar hoped to find in Prussia and Austria support for his ambitious policy in the Near East. He and his ministers thought that the recent military triumph over Turkey had made the Porte dependent upon Russia. Nesselrode exulted in the belief that Turkey "could now exist only under the protection of Russia and must comply with her wishes." But it was soon apparent that, if Russia should undertake to extend her control over Asia Minor, she would encounter considerable opposition on the part of the other powers.

The sultan's Egyptian vassal, Mehemet Ali, expected a handsome reward, indeed the whole of Syria, for his services in the war against the Greeks. When the sultan refused, the Egyptian forces once again took the field and gained a series of victories over the Turks. When Anatolia itself was invaded, the sultan was compelled to turn to the Russians for assistance. "A drowning man," said an Ottoman official, "clings to a serpent." In February 1833, a Russian squadron arrived at Constantinople; and, in April, Russian troops landed on the Asiatic shore of the Bosphorus. These actions produced intense excitement throughout Europe. Not only France and Great Britain but also Austria and Prussia exerted diplomatic pressure to restore the situation. Finally the sultan surrendered the whole of Syria to the Egyptian pasha, and the pretext for the Russian occupation was gone.

Before withdrawing, however, the Russians secured from the Sultan the Treaty of Unkiar Skelessi (July 8, 1833). Concluded for a period of eight years, the treaty provided mutual support in the event that either power was attacked. Turkish assistance to Russia, it was declared in a secret clause, was to consist of the closing of the Dardanelles to foreign warships. In St. Petersburg, it was believed that the treaty would lead in "a year or two" to the dispatch of another expeditionary force to the Bosporus where, this time, it would remain. Britain and France remonstrated against the treaty,

Mehemet Ali (1769–1849) began as a common soldier. Through political and military skill he became the governor (pasha) of Egypt, making it virtually independent of the Ottoman Empire. He accomplished important reforms in government, education, and public works. (Photo by Charles Phelps Cushing.)

and for many months there was some danger of war. Although conflict was avoided, the Treaty of Unkiar Skelessi left in the minds of British statesmen an abiding distrust of Russian ambitions in the Near East which was to last throughout the century. Britain became committed to a policy of shoring up the tottering Ottoman Empire as a barrier against Russian expansion toward the Mediterranean. In a few years this policy nearly brought her into conflict with France.

When a second Egyptian crisis arose in 1839, the Russians made no effort to exploit the advantage they had gained at Unkiar Skelessi. The sultan, alarmed by the military preparations of Mehemet Ali, precipitated war by sending his own forces over the Syrian border. In June, they came reeling back after a smashing defeat at the hands of the Egyptians. On July 1, the day on which the unhappy sultan died, the entire Turkish fleet sailed into Alexandria and surrendered to the Egyptians. "In three weeks," summarized the French statesman Guizot, "Turkey had lost her sultan, her army, and her navy." Once again, the threat to the Ottoman Empire engaged the foreign policies of the European powers. France alone wished to see Mehemet Ali retain his conquests. In a dramatic reversal of alignments, the Quadruple Alliance of 1815 was revived. Russia, Prussia, Austria, and Great Britain joined hands to rescue the Turks. In September, British forces landed in Syria; and the Syrians rose in revolt against Egyptian rule. Beirut and Acre were taken after heavy bombardments, and the Egyptians were compelled to retreat southward.

In Paris, these actions produced an angry reaction. Crowds demonstrated on the boulevards; Foreign Minister Adolphe Thiers threatened war. During 1840, it appeared possible that the Orleanist monarchy, frustrated by the failure of its eastern policy, would challenge the reborn Quadruple Alliance by marching toward the Rhine. But Thiers was forced to resign, and on November 27 Mehemet Ali signed the Convention of Alexandria, agreeing to return the Turkish fleet and to abandon Syria in return for recognition of his hereditary rule over Egypt. In July 1841, the European concert was reestablished when France joined the European powers in the Straits Convention, which established that the Bosphorus and Dardanelles were to be closed during wartime to all foreign warships. Afraid to exploit the Treaty of Unkiar Skelessi because it might unite the European powers against her, Russia obtained the internationalization of its "secret" clause. For a time, the troublesome problem of the Near East was laid to rest.

CONCLUSION   The shifting alignments of the European powers in the years 1815–1848 reveal that their foreign policies were based more on their respective interests than on social or political principles. Nevertheless, the result was hardly anarchical. As in the eighteenth century, before the French Revolution, the balance-of-power system once again imposed a degree of unity upon the European state system. In the pursuit of self-interest, the powers generally considered the consequences of their actions upon the European balance as a whole, mindful that any major aggression would arouse a hostile coalition and set off a general European war. For this reason, Austria did not oppose the other powers on the subject of Greece; Russia did not exploit Unkiar Skelessi; and France had to suffer a diplomatic defeat in Egypt. Likewise the moderate Louis Philippe refused to follow a revolutionary policy in support of the Italians and Poles and based his protection of the Belgians upon a consideration of power rather than ideology.

But the most striking evidence of the existence of a sense of unity in Europe can be seen in the operation of the European Concert at certain highly critical moments. When the peace of Europe was threatened by the Belgian revolution, the matter was settled by a European conference and a general guarantee. Similarly, the problem of the Straits was handled by a European pact through which the secret clause of Unkiar Skelessi on the closure of the Straits was made multilateral. For all their selfish aims and ambitions, statesmen felt a sense of responsibility for the peace of Europe, which compelled them at critical moments to follow a policy of mutual accommodation.

FURTHER   Two good general works on the period are B. Artz, *Reaction and Revolution,*
READING   *1814–1832* (1934); and E. J. Hobsbawm, * *The Age of Revolution, 1789–1848* (1962). The Congress of Vienna and the congress system have received a lot of attention in this century. Two members of the British delegation at

*Books available in paperback edition are marked with an asterisk.

Versailles wrote books on it: C. K. Webster, *The Congress of Vienna* (1937); and H. Nicolson, *The Congress of Vienna, A Study in Allied Unity, 1815–1822* (1946). Henry Kissinger found in the same events lessons for our times; see his *A World Restored, Metternich Castlereagh and the Problems of Peace, 1812–1822* (1957). Still valuable is W. Alison Phillips, *The Confederation of Europe, A Study of the European Alliance, 1813–1823* (1913).

Standard descriptions of the foreign policies of individual statesmen are: C. K. Webster, *The Foreign Policy of Castlereagh, 1815–1822* (2nd ed., 1937), and *The Foreign Policy of Palmerston, 1830–1841*, 2 vols. (1951); E. Kraehe, *Metternich's German Policy* (1963); P. W. Schroeder, *Metternich's Diplomacy at Its Zenith, 1820–1823* (1962); and A. A. Lobanov-Rostovsky, *Russia and Europe, 1789–1825* (1947). A classic work on its subject is J. A. F. Marriott, *The Eastern Question* (4th ed., 1940), which can be supplemented by P. E. Mosely, *Russian Diplomacy and the Opening of the Eastern Question in 1838 and 1839* (1934); and V. Puryear, *France and the Levant* (1941).

On nationalism, see particularly B. C. Shafer, *Faces of Nationalism* (1972); and the sociologically oriented works by K. Deutsch, *Nationalism and Social Communication* (2nd ed., 1966); and A. D. Smith, *Theories of Nationalism* (1971). Older works of merit are H. Kohn, *The Idea of Nationalism* (1944); C. J. H. Hayes, *Essays on Nationalism* (1926); and Royal Institute of International Affairs, *Nationalism* (1939). G. Ruggiero, *European Liberalism* (1927), is a classic study, which should be supplemented by L. Krieger, *The German Idea of Freedom* (1957). Comparable works on conservatism are lacking, but see R. Kirk, *The Conservative Mind from Burke to Santayana* (1953); and Peter Viereck, *Conservatism Revisited: The Revolt against Revolt, 1815–1849* (1949).

2 Industrialization, Social Change, and Social Protest

The nineteenth century witnessed the greatest and most rapid transformation of living and working conditions in history. This was the consequence of the shift from handicraft to machine production. Beginning in Great Britain, the "industrial revolution" spread across the continent of Europe from west to east as the century progressed. The same development occurred in America and by the end of the century in Japan. Today the transformation is affecting the rest of Asia and Africa.

While "revolutionary" in its ultimate consequences, the growth of machine production was not a sudden convulsion of the kind one associates with political revolutions. As we have already seen, it developed gradually over a long period of time, although with increasing velocity in the nineteenth century. Instead of working at home or in small shops with hand tools, the new generation of workers labored together in factories tending large machines powered first by water and steam and later by electricity and petroleum. The products, which earlier had been individually made, now came from assembly lines and were uniform in character. The rate of production was greatly increased by the whirling wheels and reciprocating pistons. In many regions, like northern England and the German Ruhr, sprawling cities and belching smokestacks took the place of rural villages and open fields. In a few decades, the population of most countries doubled and even tripled. Although the ultimate benefits were great, through the raising of the general standard of living, the immediate consequence of industrialization was the appearance of social ills of unprecedented character. The altered circumstances of life produced new attitudes toward society and government, and the changed relationship between the social classes created new tensions. Europe entered a long period of readjustment.

THE REVOLUTIONS IN INDUSTRY, TRANSPORT, AND AGRICULTURE

Construction of the Great Eastern *in 1859.* The largest ship of its time, the Great Eastern was outfitted with sidewheels propelled by steam; the vessel was considered an engineering marvel. It was used to lay the first Atlantic cable in 1866. (Institution of Mechanical Engineers, London.)

Great Britain Great Britain possessed numerous advantages that enabled her to lead the world in industrialization for many decades. She had large deposits of the most vital raw materials, especially coal and iron, which are indispensable for heavy industry. Since large-scale iron production is dependent upon coke made from coal, it was also important that these minerals were located in close proximity, in the region of Birmingham; the coal of Newcastle and South Wales, moreover, was close to the sea and could easily be transported to the iron smelters. The entrepreneurial spirit had flourished in Britain in the eighteenth century, and large sums of capital had been built up which could now be invested in mines and factories. Her insular position also gave Britain an initial advantage. Distances were short and transportation correspondingly easy; her domestic market was compact and easily served; through her merchant marine, which already dominated the sea lanes of the world, she had ready access to foreign markets and raw materials. Finally, Britain was extraordinarily productive in the field of technology;

an unending stream of inventions came from her workshops and drawing boards.

During the Napoleonic Wars, British progress in developing methods of mechanical production was especially rapid. Once the fighting was over, the goods that had been stored up in British warehouses were dumped on foreign markets. Cheap British products drove most competitors from the field, especially in backward areas like Asia and South America. By 1850, the London dock system was the largest in the world, transmitting great

Cotton Spinning Factory, Manchester, England, 1835. Textile manufacture was the leading sector of the British economy during the period of industrialization, a part played by railway construction in the United States and other countries. (Radio Times Hulton Picture Library.)

quantities of goods into and out of England. The cotton mills of Lancashire clothed much of the population of India and America. But Britain exported capital and technology as well as the bounty of her industrial system. The profits of industry and trade made London the financial center of the world. British capital built railroads in France and the United States; British engineers supervised their construction; and British mills supplied many of the rails. By the 1850's, Britain produced so many things that were beyond the capability of other nations that she was dubbed "the workshop of the world." In 1851, she advertised her supremacy by staging the first modern industrial fair, held in London.

Belgium Of all continental countries the economic history of Belgium in the nineteenth century most nearly approximates that of Great Britain. In the great basin of Mons, the Belgians possessed one of the largest coal resources in Europe. It was easy to mine, good for coking, and readily transported on her accessible waterways. Furthermore, Belgium had long been a leading producer of manufactured goods, particularly linen and woolen textiles. After 1815, Belgians began to adopt new technical methods from across the channel. Though the domestic system of production re-

INDUSTRIALIZED EUROPE, 1850

- ⊢⊣ Major Railroads
- ⊙ Cities Over 500,000 People
- ● Cities 200,000 to 500,000 People
- • Other Cities

Pig Iron Production, 1850
Shown in Percent of Total

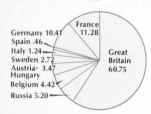

Germany 10.41
Spain .46
Italy 1.24
Sweden 2.72
Austria- 3.47
Hungary
Belgium 4.42
Russia 5.20
France 11.28
Great Britain 60.75

TOTAL: 5,761,000 LONG TONS

mained dominant, the introduction of steam power and machines brought about a fairly rapid development of the factory system. After 1830, Belgium was the most progressive of all continental countries in the construction of railways.

France Until the end of the eighteenth century, France was the chief producer of manufactured goods in Europe; but British progress in industrialization soon left her far behind. In contrast to Britain, her coal resources were few and scattered. Only in the region of Creusot were iron and coal found in close proximity. The great, though low-grade, iron deposits of Lorraine have little coal nearby, and the rich coal basin of Valenciennes (an extension of the Belgian Mons) was similarly isolated. The distances were great and unconnected by rivers and seaways. While their contributions to science were significant, the French had less interest in technological invention and innovation. A major exception was the Jacquard loom, finished in 1804, which permitted the weaving of cloth with intricate designs. Until 1791, there was no patent law and the survival of the guilds acted as a deterrent upon labor mobility. The wars of the eighteenth century cost France her colonies with their markets and raw materials. Capital accumulation, moreover, was much less rapid than in Britain; small businesses were the rule, and the entrepreneurial spirit was less well developed.

Nevertheless, France also soon began to experience the transformation of industrialism. The revolution of 1789 swept away many of the restraints imposed by the guilds and state regulations. While Britain could forbid the export of machinery to the continent, she could not prevent the emigration of technicians, who taught the French and Belgians the new methods of iron production and machine construction. Between 1825 and 1845, coal and iron production more than doubled. Steam engines became more numerous after 1830 and their horsepower rose. Great progress was made in the cotton and woolen textile trades. In the 1840's, railway construction began in earnest, easing the transport problem for heavy goods. While Britain left her far behind, France's production rose at a very respectable rate of nearly 3 percent per year.

Germany In terms of resources Germany possessed the greatest industrial potential of any European country. Coal was particularly abundant in the region of the Ruhr on the lower Rhine and in Upper Silesia. But there were also important deposits in the western valleys of the Roer and Saar and in Saxony. Not far from the Ruhr and connected to it by convenient waterways was an impressive iron deposit in the valley of the Sieg. Despite these extraordinary resources, industrialization began in Germany fairly late, for the Germans had much further to go to enter the industrial age than did Britain, Belgium, or France. Although her economic development had been as impressive as any in Europe during the late Middle Ages and the Renaissance, Germany had failed to progress thereafter. She had not been able to participate in the great commercial growth of the seventeenth and eighteenth centuries, which chiefly benefited the countries bordering on the Atlantic. Not until the development of the railway in the mid-nineteenth century did Germany again become the crossroads of European commerce.

Because of her economic backwardness, Germany lacked two of the most important prerequisites for early industrial growth: an aggressive entrepreneurial class and an accumulation of private capital available for investment. Furthermore, the guild system was still dominant, and there was no ready reservoir of workers that could easily be tapped. Compared with western Europe, the urban population was quite small. In the early nineteenth century, domestic production was still the rule, even in the metalworking trades. Wrought iron and steel, for example, were manufactured by peasants who worked part-time in the fields and part-time in the little shops of the wooded Siegerland where the ore was crushed and smelted and the metal hammered, drawn, and cut in a succession of small operations powered by water. Economic growth was further hampered by political disunity, which multiplied the tariff frontiers, legal systems, currencies, and weights and measures.

By the 1840's, nevertheless, the first signs of industrialization had begun to appear. Steam engines were introduced in 1820 and had become increasingly common after 1840. While still lagging behind Britain, Belgium, and France, coal and pig-iron production were on the rise. In the Ruhr, large-scale enterprises like the machine works of Krupp and Borsig, had been founded. While most textiles were still produced at home by peasant labor, power looms were being introduced. The bringing together of most of Germany in a Customs Union (*Zollverein*) by 1834 probably acted as a stimulus. Even more important was the construction of railways after 1840. It was not until the 1850's, however, that German industrial development really began to move forward. Thereafter pig-iron production grew at the fantastic pace of 9 percent per year, while coal production increased even faster at 11 percent per year. Other industries grew at comparable speeds. It was during this era that the modern industrial might of Germany was founded.

The Development of Industrial Technology The enormous growth of industrial production was made possible by the rapid invention of machines and new techniques for the working of raw materials. Particularly important was the development of steam engines and their application to mining and manufacturing. When coupled with other technical developments of the eighteenth century, the steam engine revolutionized the textile industry and created the factory system. The spinning jenny and power loom had prepared the way by greatly increasing the speed with which thread and yarn could be spun and woven into cloth. Numbers of spinning and weaving machines could now be placed in the same building and connected to a common source of power. An American invention, the cotton gin developed by Eli Whitney, also helped to speed the production of cotton cloth. In the southern part of the United States, where, after 1800, most of the cotton used in Britain was grown, one slave with a cotton gin could now do the work that once had required fifty. Whitney also organized one of the first assembly lines in his arms factory in Connecticut. Heretofore each gun had been made from start to finish by individual craftsmen. But Whitney standardized the parts and gave each employee a separate function in their manufacture. The total output of the factory soared as a consequence. In the course of the century, the assembly line became increasingly common in the production of machines and metal goods.

The advances of the late eighteenth century in the field of metallurgy, especially the development of a purer and harder iron, were followed after 1800 by rapid growth in the metal-working trade. The appearance of boring machines in England and Germany made possible the precision manufacture of cylinders and cannon. Turning lathes and machines for planing, cutting, milling, and stamping were invented to shape the metals into the precise forms needed for manifold industrial uses. Precision screws and ball bearings, circular saws, rotary planes and lathes, breech-loading guns and revolvers were among the many other products of the new metallurgical techniques. But the stronger and cheaper iron also made possible the construction of large bridges and buildings. For the industrial exhibition in 1851 the British erected in London the famous Crystal Palace, a building one-third of a mile long, made of ribs of iron intersticed with panes of glass.

The Crystal Palace, Which Housed the London Exhibition of 1851. The uniform parts of cast iron and glass were mass produced in distant factories and assembled on the site, a unique procedure. Six million visitors saw exhibits that ranged from art objects to massive machines.

Canal Building and the Railway Age Expanding production made it imperative that cheaper means of transportation be found to ship the needed raw materials to factories and the finished goods from factories to consumers. Before the invention and construction of railways the cheapest conveyance was by water. But nature had not always provided rivers to connect the new industrial towns with the mines and markets. Hence thousands of miles of canals were dug in Britain, France, Belgium, and the United States during the first half of the nineteenth century. By 1830, England and Wales had 3,200 miles of canals; and by 1850, France had almost as many. But considerable attention was also given to the improvement of roads. Two Scots, Telford and MacAdam, pioneered a new technique of construction. On a base of large stones they spread a layer of small rocks topped by fine gravel or clay which was rolled. It was the first major improvement in road construction since the Romans and is still in use today.

Even more significant was the application of steam to transportation. In 1807, the American inventor Robert Fulton successfully tested his steamboat, the *Clermont,* on the Hudson River. Inventors were soon busy experimenting with steam-powered land vehicles as well. Rails, the key to the problem, were already being employed in British coal mines. Iron tracks were laid down over which flange-wheeled vehicles carrying coal were pushed by hand or drawn by horses from the pits to the canal barges. The next step was to hitch the wagons together and mount a steam engine for propulsion. In 1814, George Stephenson developed the first practical locomotive, and sixteen years later his *Rocket* reached the phenomenal speed of fifty kilometers an hour on the new line from Manchester to Liverpool.

A network of iron rails spread across Europe from west to east in the 1830's and 1840's. From 835 kilometers of track in 1838 the British railways grew to over 11,000 kilometers in 1850, more than any other European country. Since it was left entirely to private initiative, however, the English system was in the beginning very chaotic. In 1844, the average line was only twenty-five kilometers in length, and there was no through service or standardized construction. Thereafter, consolidation began and Parliament intervened to require the adoption of a standard gauge. French construction did not begin in earnest until after 1840. As in Britain, many prejudices had to be overcome. The French feared that the puffing, clattering machines would frighten the horses and dry up cows; tunnels were criticized as unhealthy and unsafe for women who were advised to put pins in their mouths as a defense against male passengers. Private capital was limited and capitalists were reluctant to take risks. Hence the state intervened in 1842 with a master plan for a national network of interconnecting lines constructed by a combination of private and state capital. Six years later, 1,931 kilometers had been built and 8,000 more were either under construction or planned.

Belgium was the first continental country to enter the railway age. From the beginning, the state took the initiative by planning and constructing an interlocking system, which connected the major cities and ports and made Belgium a center of commerce between Germany, France and the channel ports. Despite the handicap of political disunion, Germany also made great strides in the 1840's. By 1850 she possessed 6,044 kilometers, financed by a mixture of state and private enterprises. Railways linked the major river basins and gave Germany, which had poor roads and few canals, an adequate system of long-distance transport for the first time. Berlin soon became a center of commerce and industry.

The "age of the railway" gave a great impetus to the general economic development of Europe. It introduced cheap transportation for all kinds of heavy goods in areas without navigable waterways. Remote regions were made accessible. Famines resulting from local crop failures could be prevented. Differences in prices between localities were greatly reduced or even eliminated. Production could be concentrated in larger plants, and less efficient enterprises were forced out of business. People could travel more easily for business or pleasure; what previously had been an arduous journey of days became a brief, if sooty, journey of hours. Troops could be mobilized and speeded to the frontiers with greater rapidity. The seemingly insatiable

First Class, Second Class and Third Class Coach. Londoners entrain for the horse races at Epsom in the 1840's. While the industrial age inaugurated an age of mass sports, the social classes were separated by the facilities they could or could not afford.

demand for rails, cars, and locomotives also stimulated the growth of heavy industry. Railways affected every aspect of economic and social life and were soon regarded as indispensable to every modern country.

The Growth of Capitalism   Industrialization provided another powerful stimulant to the development of capitalism. But the reverse is also true. Industrialization proceeded at the most rapid pace where supplies of capital (surplus funds available for investment) had accumulated and the capitalistic spirit (the willingness to take risks in the expectation of gain) was most highly developed. In the seventeenth and eighteenth centuries, British merchants had accumulated surpluses from the transport and sale of goods throughout the world. They were accustomed to risks and they found in the burgeoning factory system a frequently rewarding place to put their capital to work. Richard Arkwright, who was once a barber, borrowed merchant capital to build up his textile machinery enterprises; tobacco merchants financed the first factories of Glasgow; money originally gained in the slave trade by the merchants of Nantes and Bordeaux and in the cloth markets of Paris and Lyons played an important role in the financing of early industrialization in France.

Yet there were other significant sources of capital for industrialization: banking, mining, rent and profits from land, taxation, and manufacturing itself. Industrialists, who began with little capital, constantly reinvested their profits in order to expand their enterprises. The father of Robert Peel began as a cotton spinner and piled up a fortune in cotton textiles with little outside help; the founder of the great Krupp works in the Ruhr started as an iron-worker; William Cockerill, the founder of a great textile machinery, mining, and iron-making enterprise in Belgium, was the son of a mechanic of Lancashire and began as a workman himself. On the other hand, the Duke of Orléans invested a fortune gained from farming in French textile factories. Great banking concerns, like the Barings in London, the Hopes of Amsterdam, and the international house of Rothschild, provided investment capital. British capital promoted railway construction in France, Italy and the United States. And, as we have seen, the governments of Belgium, France, and various German states committed tax revenues to the support of domestic railway construction.

Corporations Yet commercial capitalism made its greatest contribution to the expansion of industrial capitalism by developing the forms of business organization, money, banking, and credit. While the partnership remained an important kind of business organization, it was soon overshadowed by the growth of joint stock companies or corporations. The latter had unique advantages in that ownership might be spread among a great number of people, some with very little capital to invest. Furthermore, it allowed the investor to invest his funds in many enterprises and hence avoid total loss in the event of a single business failure. But it also provided opportunities for unscrupulous promoters to pocket the resources of other people or to sell to trusting investors shares in enterprises of doubtful earning capacity. Spectacular failures, like the Mississippi and South Sea Bubbles of 1720, had discredited the joint stock companies in England and France. But the advantages were such that the laws passed against them in the eighteenth century were rescinded in the nineteenth. At the same time, the corporate form was improved and refined by the establishment of legal limits to the liability of stockholders and the issuance of preferred stock, which receives preference over common stock in the payment of dividends and in the liquidation of assets in case of bankruptcy. Corporations also began the practice of issuing bonds at fixed rates of interest instead of increasing the amount of common stock in order to raise capital. The steady increase in the buying and selling of securities led naturally to the organization of bourses, or stock exchanges, where brokers could execute the orders of their customers. In 1802, the London Stock Exchange moved from a coffee house into a building of its own, and the French Bourse, founded in 1724, attained its modern form in a reorganization of 1816. The stock exchange soon became a feature of every major financial capital in Europe. By the end of the eighteenth century, most European countries had already made considerable progress toward stabilizing currency.

The Currency Problem Coins had been improved by milled edges and minting imprints, which discouraged clipping and counterfeiting. Their metallic content, furthermore, was firmly fixed by law so that coins could not be secretly debased. But the problem of stabilizing the value of paper currency was even greater. The French assignat, backed by confiscated lands, had proved worthless and had finally been repudiated. Treasury notes frequently declined in value as governments resorted to the printing presses to solve their financial problems. But bank notes were also vulnerable if more were issued than the bank could redeem. Even the famed Bank of England had to suspend specie payments for a time in 1797. During the first half of the nineteenth century, earnest efforts were made to regulate the issue of paper money. A frequent solution was to abolish treasury notes and hand over the privilege of issuing notes to a central bank organized as a joint stock company in which the government was usually a prominent shareholder. What constituted suitable backing for the notes remained, however, a subject of controversy. A few argued for specie, some for government bonds, and others for discounted commercial paper as well.

The Business Cycle As the capitalistic system developed, so did its most perplexing problem: the business cycle. Between 1786 and 1850 there occurred a series of business recessions alternating with periods of prosperity. Generally, these seem to have been caused by a combination of crop failures, wars, and political revolutions, but also by factors within the capitalistic system. Poor harvests in 1787–1788 helped to bring on the French Revolution. Thereafter war, the Continental System, and the British blockade disrupted European commerce. Although peace prevailed after 1815, downward movements in the cycle occurred again in 1818–1819, 1825–1830, 1837, and 1845–1848. Usually the crises were set off by agricultural failures, which drove up food prices, diverting purchasing power from manufactured goods and hence bringing about a decline in business activity. But they were also attributable to the normal working of the capitalistic system. During periods of prosperity, prices rose faster than wages, drying up purchasing power. Credit became overextended as businessmen became too optimistic about future earnings. Periods of speculation ended in crashes of the stock market followed by runs on banks, bankruptcies, shutdowns, and unemployment. As industrial capitalism spread, the crises became increasingly European in scope. In 1857, came the first general crash attributable solely to the operation of the capitalistic system.

The Agricultural Revolution Great changes were simultaneously underway in agriculture. As in industry, the development of new techniques led to a rise in productivity, new forms of ownership and marketing, and the transformation of social relationships.

The transition from medieval to modern agriculture had already begun in Holland and Great Britain during the eighteenth century with the introduction of improved crop rotation, the seed drill, row cultivation, hoe plowing, and improved livestock breeding. New crops were planted, like the turnip, clover, and alfalfa, which could be stored for winter feed. Farmers who had slaughtered most of their cattle in the fall could now fatten them through the winter. People consumed more meat and benefited from the increasing cultivation of such new crops as potatoes and sugar beets.

Advances in metallurgy and machine manufacture soon affected the technology of farming. Iron plows came into use in the 1840's, and the same decade saw the invention of mechanical reaping. Other inventions speeded

Steam Plowing in Bohemia. The plow was attached to cables that were pulled back and forth across the field by two steam tractors in alternation. Only big landowners could afford such equipment, which gave them a competitive edge over the small farmer.

the labor of threshing and winnowing. The construction of railways and improved roads eased the problem of transport from farm to market.

As farming became more profitable, new lands were brought under cultivation. Wastelands were reclaimed through improved drainage, irrigation, and terracing. As a consequence, crop yields began to soar. Ultimately, the greatest improvement in yields, however, was attained through the use of fertilizers. In 1840, the German chemist Justus von Liebig published a monumental work on soil chemistry which explained how the addition of chemicals to the soil could increase its fertility. Soon Peruvian guano, phosphates, superphosphates, and Chilean nitrates were being imported and used to enrich the land.

These technical improvements brought about radical changes in economic and social relationships. Agriculture tended to be reorganized on a capitalist basis. Heretofore landowners and peasants had raised their crops largely for local consumption. Now they produced money crops for distant markets; and this required new book-keeping, banking, and credit arrangements. Since the new techniques required less labor and worked best on large plots, the landlords tried to remove peasants from the land. In response, the peasants strove to acquire clear titles to their holdings. The consequence of both actions was the dissolution of manorialism, of the traditional relationship of mutual obligation and service between lord and peasant. The lord became an agricultural capitalist who farmed for profit, and the peasant became a small landowner, a sharecropper, or a wage-earning laborer.

Once again the process of economic and social change was uneven. While Britain led, as she did in industrialization, France and the low countries followed and were soon joined by Germany. From west to east the new techniques spread across the continent of Europe until they reached the Russian steppes.

SOCIAL DISTRESS AND THE LIBERAL RESPONSE Economic changes of the magnitude of the industrial revolution inevitably affect the social order. They bring about a redistribution of economic functions and hence of wealth and status.

German Industrialist and His Wife, 1838. The evident pride of the subjects, their clothing and jewelry, as well as the factory and mansion in the background illustrate the appearance of a new élite class based on industrial rather than agrarian wealth. (Landesmuseum, Trier.)

By greatly expanding the possibilities for the accumulation of wealth, the industrial revolution increased the spread between the upper- and lower-middle classes. The owners and managers of the great industrial and banking enterprises became a new elite—apart from small merchants, white collar workers, and professional people. Another consequence was the rise of a new working class, the factory proletariat, and the decline of the artisan class. Under the old system, the articles of use had been produced largely in small shops by skilled artisans or handicraftsmen working with limited equipment. In some cases, like cloth manufacture, the stages of production were usually executed by artisans working in their own homes, often in the country where they could combine farming with manufacture. Industrialization changed this by introducing the factory system. Workers were now congregated in towns and labored in large numbers in a single building or complex of buildings, tending machines that required little skill on the part of the operator.

The Social Consequences of Industrialization The factory system tended to depersonalize the process of production. The gap between worker and employer widened. Under the old handicraft system at its best, an artisan might expect to rise from apprentice to journeyman, to master and owner. Under the factory system, some men like Krupp, Peel, and Cockerill did rise through inventive genius, shrewdness, and luck from the status of worker to employer, but this good fortune was barred to most. The average laborer was condemned to daily work at monotonous, repetitive tasks that required little skill and no initiative. Lacking any prospect of advancement, he had small interest in the enterprise that employed him. A sense of corporate harmony gradually gave way to a sense of class conflict.

From the vantage point of the mid-twentieth century, social historians have found much to criticize in the living and working conditions of the proletarian class of early industrialism. By our standards, these conditions were often wretched indeed. A working day of twelve to fourteen hours was common. Little attention was given to safety devices on the machines, with the consequence that the accident rate was high. The buildings were badly lighted and poorly ventilated, and there was scant concern for the comfort of the workers. Discipline was sometimes harsh. Workers were fined for infraction of factory rules or failure to perform their duties properly. Women and children were employed under the same conditions and for nearly the same hours as men. Often, children were preferred for tasks requiring smallness of stature, such as pushing loaded carts through narrow seams in coal mines or sweeping sooty chimneys. In some cases, indentured or orphaned children were housed in barracks and flogged by overseers. There was no social security in the form of disability pay, unemployment insurance, or old-age benefits.

Living conditions in the new factory towns were often miserable. Although most people still lived in rural areas, many migrated to the cities in search of work. In 1801, 40.5 percent of the population of England and

Child Labor in a Lancashire Coal Mine During the 1840's. Women and children often had to work because families could not support themselves on the wages earned by the father. Child and female labor were ultimately limited by law. (Radio Times Hulton Picture Library.)

Wales lived in towns of 2,000 or more; in 1851, this percentage had risen to 51.3, while during the same period the percentage of those living in cities of over 20,000 rose from 27.1 to 38.3. Between 1801 and 1831, Manchester expanded from 95,000 to 238,000 inhabitants, Leeds from 53,000 to 123,000, and Liverpool from 82,000 to 202,000. London grew from 958,000 in 1801 to 2,362,000 in 1851. The urban areas of other countries experienced similar increases in proportion to their industrialization. This rapid growth produced social problems of appalling character. Municipal governments were often unprepared to cope on such a scale with such elementary matters as sanitation and shoddy construction. Workers' families were packed into jerry-built tenements divided into cubicles and tiny apartments. As the factories mushroomed, so did the slums. Soot and grime from smoking chimneys drifted through the air and deadened the landscape.

The working conditions of the pre-industrial age, however, were by no means as idyllic as they have been described by social reformers and nostalgic romanticists. The picturesque villages and vine-covered cottages of the rural age were often the scene of famine, starvation, and disease. Not all of the new industrial towns were unhealthy and depressing; some were fairly well planned, with wide streets and space for yards and parks. By contrast, the villages often had inadequate sanitary facilities and contaminated water. If the atmosphere was healthier, the hours of labor were equally long and the standard of living low. There is evidence to show that in good times factory workers received wages at least as high as those employed on farms and in domestic manufacture. Probably the most distressed class in the new industrial society was that of the artisans, whose livelihood was being steadily undermined by the advance of the factory system. Some with mechanical skills became the elite of the new working class; others surrendered to proletarianization by becoming factory workers; a minority with skills that could not be replaced by the machine (such as jewelry manufacture and other luxury goods) continued to prosper. But many were ruined. In some cases, they attacked the factories and wrecked the machines which were the cause of their distress. They, more than the proletarians, were a force for change during the revolution of 1848.

Growth of Population According to one argument, the growth in population demonstrates that in general the conditions of life improved during the era of industrialization. Between 1800 and 1850, the population of Europe increased from 187,693,000 to 266,228,000. England and Wales expanded during this period from 8,893,000 to 17,928,000. Although the British increase was particularly rapid, most European countries experienced a considerable acceleration after 1800. Yet it is difficult to attribute this development entirely to industrialization, for those areas whose economies remained agrarian, like Ireland and Poland, also showed large increases, while France lagged despite moderate industrialization (from 27,349,000 in 1800 to 35,784,000 in 1850). Demographers are still uncertain whether the expansion in Europe's population that began in the eighteenth century was due to a higher birth rate or a lower death rate. Those who take the former viewpoint maintain that the changing pattern of social life led to earlier marriages and larger families, while adherents of the latter position argue that improvements in living standards and food supply produced a healthier population with more resistance to disease. It is generally agreed, however, that improvements in sanitation and medical services played a significant part only in the last half of the nineteenth century.

The Failure of Classical Economics Viewed from the standpoint of the twentieth century, nevertheless, it must be admitted that much more could and should have been done to mitigate the undesirable social consequences of early industrialism. But this would have required sacrifices which the entrepreneurs of that age were unwilling to make. Those who were piling up fortunes through the exploitation of labor were reluctant to sacrifice; those who were operating marginal businesses in a fiercely competitive market were unable to do so. It has also been argued that, without the sacrifices of this age, capital could not have been accumulated for the tremendous expansion of the next. In any event the amelioration of social distress in the early nineteenth century was only practicable through governmental intervention. But governments were usually dominated by precisely those groups whose interests would have been harmed by such an action. Intervention was forbidden, furthermore, by the theories of classical economics.

The "classical" or "liberal" economists dominated economic thought in the early industrial age. The heart of their doctrine was the concept of "laissez faire" conceived by the French Physiocrats and developed by Adam Smith. Laissez faire emphasized the initiative of the individual in economic activity, while mercantilism, the doctrine it was intended to refute, had emphasized that of the state. The theorists of laissez faire believed that businessmen must be free from governmental regulation and patronage; their unrestricted search for profit would in the end achieve the greatest good for the greatest number of people. The free exchange of goods between nations would lead to a "division of labor" enabling each country to produce in accordance with its natural and human resources. Economic growth and the general welfare, it was believed, could only proceed from the "natural" operation of the market-place in contrast to the "artificial" stimulus provided by tariff protectionism. Like other commodities, labor must find its price according to the "law of supply and demand." Following this doctrine, businessmen insisted that the state cease to regulate and direct private enterprise, and that it forbid workers from organizing in order to agitate, bargain, and strike for more pay and better working conditions.

Malthus One of the most popular classical economists was Thomas Malthus (1766–1834), whose *Essay on the Principles of Population* appeared in 1798. An Anglican clergyman, Malthus began by attacking the optimistic assumption of the Enlightenment that mankind is perfectible. The laws of nature, he maintained, made this impossible. Man's power to procreate is far greater than his power to produce. "Population, when unchecked, increases in a geometrical ratio. Subsistence only increases in an arithmetical ratio." Hence, there is a constant tendency for the human race to breed itself into starvation. Life is prodigal, but the means of sustaining it are meager. Certain "preventive" and "positive" checks operate to hold the population in balance with food supply. In contrast to plants and animals, man has the capacity to prevent starvation by restraining his urge to reproduce. This voluntary check, requiring chastity and late marriage, was not likely to be effective. Hence nature would impose the positive checks: "unwholesome

Working-Class Homes in Glasgow about 1870. At the lower right is the single spigot that supplied water for all who resided in the alley. (The Mansell Collection.)

occupations, severe labor and exposure to the seasons, extreme poverty, bad nursing of children, great towns, excesses of all kinds, the whole train of common diseases and epidemics, wars, plague, and famine."

Ricardo An English banker-economist, David Ricardo (1772–1823), developed further the views of Malthus as they applied to economic theory in his *Principles of Political Economy* (1817). His pessimism concerned the entire human race, including both capitalist and wage earner. Capitalists, he asserted, were subject to the "law of diminishing returns." As the population grew, landowners would be compelled, in order to feed the growing masses, to cultivate marginal lands increasingly poor in quality. Because of the scarcity of land, rents would soar and consume an ever larger proportion of the national income. Owing to the effort required to exploit the poorer soils, capital employed on land would yield a constantly smaller return. Capital invested in other fields would be similarly affected. On the other hand, workers were subject to the "iron law of wages." Their incomes would tend to fluctuate above and below the level of subsistence. In times of labor shortage, their wages would improve, which would lead them to beget larger families. This in turn would increase the supply of labor and drive down its price until starvation and disease killed off the excessive numbers.

The speculations of Malthus and Ricardo, and the school of writers whom they spawned, caused economics to be called the "dismal science." Those who read them could only conclude that social distress was beyond human power to cure. To the classical economists, the law of nature was harsh and ruthless, quite in contrast to the philosophers of the eighteenth century, to whom it was a benevolent force, the smiling guide to inevitable progress. While deploring misery and suffering, they were convinced that any effort at amelioration would merely accentuate the evil.

THE EMERGENCE OF SOCIAL PROTEST

Utilitarianism Not all British intellectuals of the early nineteenth century were as pessimistic as Malthus and Ricardo. One of the most important thinkers of that age was Jeremy Bentham (1748–1832), who expounded a doctrine known as "utilitarianism." Bentham was a reformer who believed that society and the conditions of life are primarily the result of human creativity. The notion of "iron laws" or "natural laws" he denounced as "simple nonsense," "rhetorical nonsense," "nonsense upon stilts." There was only one valid test by which human customs and institutions might be judged. This was the test of utility: did they add to or detract from the total happiness of mankind? Pain and pleasure, he argued, were the "two sovereign masters" of humanity. All human actions, whether by government or by an individual, must be judged according to whether they diminished the one or increased the other. Bentham enumerated the chief pains and pleasures of life and worked out a "calculus" by which humanity could chart its course and achieve the greatest felicity for the individual and for society at large.

Following the principle of utility, Bentham and his followers (variously known as utilitarians, Benthamites, and philosophic radicals) subjected the social and governmental institutions of their day to withering criticism. History and tradition, they declared, could not justify practices that failed to pass the test of utility. To this end they wished to reconstruct the judiciary, modernize the codes of law, reform the prison system, adopt universal suffrage, and rationalize the administration of poor relief. Yet even Bentham imposed severe limits upon governmental activity in economic and social matters. Like the classical economists, he concluded that arbitrary interference in the natural processes of economic life would jeopardize the attainment of the greatest good for the greatest number. Yet there was something inherently contradictory in this position, and even Bentham recognized that in times of distress the "omnicompetent" state might be compelled to intervene. It seems hardly accidental that his greatest disciple, John Stuart Mill (1806–1873), ended as a virtual socialist where the distribution, though not the production, of wealth was concerned.

Collectivist Socialism: Saint-Simon Other important thinkers of the early nineteenth century found in the doctrine of socialism the only solution to the problem of the social effects of industrialism. While differing radically in other respects, the early socialists possessed in common the conviction that private property and the competitive spirit were thoroughly evil. In their opinion, the struggle for survival between capitalists and between capitalists and workers brought out the worst in human nature. The classical economists believed that it conferred many benefits: the stimulation of individual initiative, the purging of inefficient enterprises, the most economical exploitation of resources, the development of a natural equilibrium of productive forces. But the socialists shuddered at a society which seemed to be based upon the law of the jungle rather than upon the Christian virtues of mutual help and harmonious cooperation.

The Comte de Saint-Simon (1760–1825), a French nobleman and veteran of the American Revolution, believed that industrialism itself would ultimately create a cooperative society which would render government unnecessary. In a famous parable he asked his readers to suppose that France should suddenly lose its most successful doctors, chemists, physiologists, bankers, merchants, agriculturists, ironmasters, and the many other technicians of modern society. The result, he declared, would be catastrophic. Yet suppose it should suddenly lose its king, royal family, ministers, civil servants, generals, judges, cardinals, archbishops, bishops, and the like. They would hardly be missed. To him this meant that industry, and the scientific technology upon which it is based, is all important. He envisioned a heaven on earth in the form of a society organized like a gigantic factory. This society would be a great cooperative enterprise whose goal was not the accumulation of private wealth, but the maximum development of the country's material resources for the benefit of all. Politics, he believed, would eventually

surrender to economics; government would be absorbed in economic organization. The new society would be divided into the idle and the industrious, not into owners and workers. For the idle there would soon be no place.

Saint-Simon did not attack the institution of private property and hence can be classified as a socialist only with difficulty. But this is not true of his disciples, who elevated his views to the status of a religious faith, which they confidently believed would ultimately replace Catholicism and liberalism alike. Capitalitsts, the Saint-Simonians argued, are idlers living only from the labor of others. Such exploitation can only be ended by the abolition of private property. They believed, nevertheless, that differences in capacity should be recognized by differences in reward. They also distinguished between capitalist and entrepreneur, regarding the former as a mere parasite and the latter as a leader and organizer entitled by his services to a high income. The Saint-Simonians were among the first social theorists of modern times to envision a collectivist society organized like an immense beehive, in which the whole of life would be coordinated to a common productive end.

Associative Socialism   Yet the collectivist approach was not the only solution to the social problem offered by socialist thinkers of the early nineteenth century. Others resorted to various schemes which have been lumped together under the term "associative socialism," for they believed in the practicality of voluntary associations that would demonstrate the benefits of cooperative as against competitive living. These voluntary associations were generally model communities in which property was held and profits shared in common by the members. In these communities, the associative socialists, whom Marx later branded as "utopian socialists," expected to build a new social environment which would correspond more closely to the "natural order" of society than the "artificial order" of capitalism.

Owen   A fascinating figure in this movement was Robert Owen (1771–1858). Beginning as a laborer in a cotton factory, he became by the age of thirty the manager and part-owner of New Lanark Mills in Scotland. Owen took an interest in the welfare of his employees and converted New Lanark into a model factory town. He reduced the working day from seventeen to ten hours, refused to employ children under ten, and abolished fines for the infraction of factory rules. Model homes were constructed for the workers and schools for their children. Despite the expense, the enterprise prospered, for productivity rose. Owen hoped that other manufacturers would emulate his example, but in this he was unsuccessful. Although he became a famous man, the correspondent and consultant of kings and statesmen, his social experiment remained unique.

Discouraged over the prospect of voluntary reform, Owen turned to legislation. Yet here, too, he was doomed to disappointment. Although the principles of New Lanark were to be the model for future laws, the British Factory Act of 1819 abolished child labor only below the age of nine and was easily evaded. Owen turned to associative socialism in the hope of improving the social environment by eliminating the profit motive. He drafted plans for a model community, to be called a "parallelogram" from its geometrical design. Evenly balanced between manufacture and farming, the community was to be a cooperative enterprise jointly owned and operated by its members. Its lack of tradition and its plenitude of land made America an obvious place for Owen's experiment. A number of communities were founded in the United States under his influence, the most famous being that at New Harmony, Indiana, but they soon failed.

In Britain, Owen turned restlessly to other experiments. When trade unions were made legal by an act of Parliament in 1824, he joined in the agitation for their formation. His ideal was a national organization to embrace unions in all trades and dedicated to his own social objectives. He advocated an eight-hour day, to be achieved if necessary through a general strike. But the Grand National Consolidated Trades Union, formed in 1834, aroused a hornet's nest of opposition from hostile employers and soon collapsed. In the end, Owen's only lasting achievement was that in which he placed the least stock. Beginning in 1832, a number of consumers' cooperatives were formed in which the members could purchase goods practically at cost. In the following years, the movement prospered and was imitated throughout the world.

Sketch of a Phalanstery as Proposed by Fourier. The central building surmounted by the tower was to house dining commons, assembly halls, library, and recreational facilities. Living quarters were to be on the upper floors of the wings above the workshops on the ground floor. (The Granger Collection.)

Fourier Another associative socialist was the Frenchman Charles Fourier (1772–1837), who developed a plan for model communities to be known as "phalansteries." A frustrated bachelor, Fourier concluded that men were dominated by certain passions, which he proceeded to enumerate and analyze, much as Bentham did his system of pains and pleasures. In Fourier's opinion the competitive system of modern capitalism and the urban centers produced by industrialism did not adequately satisfy these passions. Greater

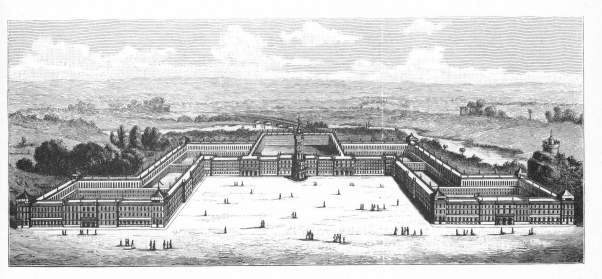

satisfaction could be achieved in a society organized into largely self-contained cooperatives composed of about 1,600 individuals or 400 families.

These phalansteries were to be housed in large hotels where manager, capitalist, and worker would live and work together for mutual gain. In the productive activities of the phalanstery, manufacturing was to be held to a minimum. Agriculture was the favored pursuit, particularly horticulture and arboriculture. Workers were to be relieved of the tedium of their tasks by frequent alternation of jobs, as often as eight times in one day. By abandoning the great cities and factories of the new industrialism, men would find a healthier environment, a hotel ringed by fields and forests, and a new harmony founded on mutual cooperation for the common good.

Fourier found disciples, but little support for his phalansteries. His impracticality aroused amusement, and his advocacy of free love shocked many in the Victorian age. Nevertheless, he had some effect upon later social theory. His view of social psychology was more fully developed by subsequent thinkers, and some of his individual recommendations bore fruit. Many admired the earnestness of his social criticism and the inventiveness with which he approached the difficulties of his age. Nevertheless, his phalanstery, like Owen's parallelogram, could hardly serve as a model for the future.

State Socialism: Louis Blanc In contrast to collectivist and associative socialism, state socialism was an attempt to solve the social problem through the instrumentality of existing goverments. Perhaps the first influential advocate of this approach was the French publicist, historian, and politician Louis Blanc (1813–1882). In 1841 Blanc published a short tract called *The Organization of Work,* which was immediately popular. Without developing an elaborate philosophy like those of Saint-Simon and Fourier, the author attacked the competitive system as the root of every moral and economic evil. Blanc found the solution in a society reorganized into producers' cooperatives or "social workshops." Unlike Owen and Fourier, he did not visualize these workshops as self-contained economic units, but as factories owned and operated by workers, and producing goods for existing markets. He believed, moreover, that the necessary capital could only be obtainable from the state, which should take the lead in financing and organizing the workshop before turning it over to the workers. By the gradual spread of this system, cell by cell, the entire productive capacity of the nation would be reorganized on a cooperative basis ending the competitive system.

It will be seen that Blanc played a role in the revolution of 1848, but that his attempt to introduce his workshop scheme during the early months of the Second Republic was abortive. In later years, other intellectuals like the German Ferdinand Lassalle wrote and agitated for state socialism in one form or another. But the actual experimentation in state socialism was carried out by two statesmen, Napoleon III and Bismarck, not in the interest of an economic or philosophic theory, but for the consolidation of monarchical power. What began as a democratic concept for the betterment of the lower classes became a technique for the perpetuation of authoritarian governments.

Anarchism: Proudhon and Bakunin The most radical of all the early reactions to social distress was that of anarchism. Distaste for existing governments led anarchists to the belief that all government should be abolished. They were inspired by confidence in the native goodness of the human heart, by the belief that in the absence of the state men would use their freedom to cooperate toward common ends.

The most famous anarchist was Pierre Joseph Proudhon (1809–1865). In a pamphlet published in 1840, he asserted that "property is theft." Proudhon was not, however, opposed to personal property as such, but to unearned income, that is, income received from investment or interest-bearing loans. In his view the money lender was the most destructive force in society. Proudhon's cure for the "leprosy of interest" was a People's Bank that would lend money to anyone without charging interest, and thus make it possible for everyone to work on his own. Unlike Karl Marx Proudhon was uninterested in revolutionizing the entire economy. He merely wanted to overturn the credit system and enable everyone to become an independent middle-class property owner. Marx wanted to create a one-class society of proletarians, Proudhon a one-class society of bourgeois. The latter opposed restraint on the individual and rejected the socialism of Blanc and Fourier as coercive. His own doctrine of "mutualism" proposed a loose federation of independent producers which could replace an impersonal government.

Proudhon's doctrines were most popular in France among small shopkeepers, with whose revolutionary tradition they harmonized. His anarchism was bourgeois individualism carried to the extreme; it was not geared for the working class. In fact, Proudhon opposed labor unions, for he was opposed to class division. Perpetuation of the propertyless proletariat was a moral evil, and exploitation of the workers should be avoided by having every man work for himself. Above all, Proudhon was a moralist who wanted to preserve the sanctity of the bourgeois family and moral self-responsibility. For this reason, he always stood somewhere apart from the revolutionary activists of the anarchist government.

The typical anarchist might be a moralist, like Proudhon, but his main interest was not the bourgeois family or a credit revolution, but the destruction of every existing institution in society. He believed that the best way to attain this end was to assassinate heads of state. The anarchist thus became the prototype of the wild-eyed, fanatical, knife-wielding, bomb-throwing assassin of nineteenth century radicalism. The true founder of the anarchist movement was the Russian nobleman Michael Bakunin (1814–1876). After being expelled from Russia, Bakunin lived in various western countries and won followers all over the continent. He advocated obliteration of all existing political and social institutions, as well as private property. His aim was to replace the state with loosely connected local confederations which would assure their members economic justice and individual freedom.

This vague utopia was to be achieved through violent action against existing governments by anarchist conspirators in every country.

FURTHER READING

Recent interest in economic development and social change has directed considerable attention to the epoch of industrialization. As a consequence, the classic study of P. Mantoux, *The Industrial Revolution in the Eighteenth Century* (1906, 1937) is now dated. The direction of the revision can be seen in T. S. Ashton, *The Industrial Revolution, 1760–1830* (1948); G. N. Clark, *The Idea of the Industrial Revolution* (1953); and W. W. Rostow, *The Stages of Economic Growth* (1960). For the latest views see P. Deane, *The First Industrial Revolution* (1965); and especially D. S. Landes, *The Unbound Prometheus* (1969), an expanded version of his contribution to the great *Cambridge Economic History of Europe*, vol. VI, *The Industrial Revolution and After* (1965).

The social consequence of industrialization is still controversial. The grim side in Britain was depicted by J. L. and B. Hammond, *The Village Labourer* (1911), *The Town Labourer* (1917), and *The Skilled Labourer* (1919). For revisionist views see the works by Ashton and Clark above and F. A. von Hayek, ed., *Capitalism and the Historians* (1954). More recent studies are E. P. Thompson, *The Making of the English Working Class* (1964); and E. J. Hobsbawm, *Labouring Men: Studies in the History of Labour* (1953). Explanations of the population explosion of the nineteenth century, another controversial topic, can be found in M. C. Buer, *Health, Wealth, and Population in the Early Days of the Industrial Revolution* (1926); and in D. V. Glass and D. E. C. Eversley, eds., *Population in History* (1965).

Bentham and the Utilitarians have been exhaustively studied by E. Halevy, *The Growth of Philosophic Radicalism*, 3 vols. (1901–1904, 1955). On the "utopian socialists" see G. D. H. Cole, *The Life of Robert Owen* (1930); and the works of F. Manuel, *The New World of Henri Saint-Simon* (1956) and the *Prophets of Paris* (1962); J. O. Hertzler, *History of Utopian Thought* (1926); E. Roll, *A History of Economic Doctrines* (3rd ed., 1963); and C. Gide and C. Rist, *A History of Economic Doctrines* (2nd ed., 1948).

3 Reaction and Revolution in Britain, France, and Germany

Through much of modern history, the political development of France and Great Britain offers contrasts that are both interesting and instructive. In the seventeenth century, the two countries followed opposite courses: France toward monarchical absolutism and Britain toward constitutional monarchy. During the nineteenth century, however, both countries progressed from limited parliamentary regimes based on a restricted suffrage to the status of parliamentary democracies based on universal and equal suffrage. Yet Britain attained this goal without violent changes in the structure of her system, while France suffered two coups and three revolutions, each of which altered the character of her political order. One of the purposes of this chapter is to determine some of the reasons for this difference in development.

Italy likewise achieved a parliamentary system of government during the nineteenth century, which brought her closer to the political tradition of western Europe. But Italian conditions and Italian political evolution were in other respects far different from those of Britain and France. In the sixteenth century, Italy had been the glory of Renaissance Europe; in the nineteenth century she was an impoverished land, backward in economic and social development and burdened with a largely illiterate population. Under these circumstances, popular sovereignty, whose effectiveness depends upon an educated public, was hardly realizable. For many decades, furthermore, Italy's fate was not in her own hands. Her revolutions had to be directed not merely against her own native reactionary governments, but against the military might of Austria.

GREAT BRITAIN IN REACTION AND REFORM — In 1815, Britain was governed by the land-owning class known as the "gentry," that dominated the two houses of parliament. The House of Commons was elected at least once in seven years by a restricted and unequal suffrage.

1109

Each English county elected two members, who since 1430 had been chosen by "freeholders" possessing land with an annual rental value of at least forty shillings. One did not have to be wealthy to have this much land. Nevertheless, the number of small freeholders was dwindling, and those who remained were frequently also the tenants of large landowners. Economic dependence resulted in political dependence, and the great landowners usually dictated which candidate would be chosen.

The urban, or "borough," franchise was also inequitable. In past centuries, the king had granted to the towns on an individual basis the right to representation in Parliament. The inequity arose not only from the indiscriminate way in which the grant had been given, but also from the fact that the British population had changed drastically during the eighteenth century both in size and distribution. The southern counties, which earlier had possessed the greatest town population, had long since been outstripped by the industrial north. Yet no changes had been made in parliamentary representation. Large cities like Birmingham, Leeds, Sheffield, and Manchester had no representatives in Parliament. But the most notorious aspects of the system were the "pocket" and "rotten" boroughs. Pocket boroughs had only a few dependent voters who were "in the pocket" of some wealthy landowner of the neighborhood; rotten boroughs were towns that had seriously declined in population and even disappeared. Two examples were Old Sarum, which was no longer even a village, and Gatton on the North Downs, which possessed six dwellings and a single elector. According to one estimate, the great landowners controlled 276 of the 658 seats in Parliament.

The landowning class was also dominant in the House of Lords whose hereditary membership included the titled nobility of Britain. Elevation to the peerage, however, had become a standard way to reward distinguished citizens and supporters of the government; thus many generals, admirals, and wealthy businessmen had reached the upper house. Lords was still important as a political force in the English system, and throughout the century cabinet ministers were drawn from both houses. Nor was the crown yet the powerless institution it ultimately became. The king chose the ministers, who theoretically were responsible both to the crown and Parliament. Through patronage, moreover, the crown could influence the election of the House of Commons. Yet in practice the power of the crown was in the hands of the ruling party. George III had gone insane in 1811, and a regency had been established by his witty and indolent son, who cared more for the art of good living than for that of good government.

From 1783 to 1830, the Parliament and Cabinet were dominated by the Tory party. The Prime Minister after 1812 was Lord Liverpool, a shy and amiable man whose talents were more those of a diplomat than a statesman. No formulator of policy, he governed through the skillful choice of ministers and the harmonization of their conflicting views and personalities. In general, the Tories had a paternalistic view of government. They were responsible for humanitarian reforms, such as prohibition of the slave trade (1807), abolition of the pillory (1816) and of the whipping of women (1820), and restriction of child labor in factories (1819). Nevertheless, they firmly believed in the necessity of preserving the supremacy of the landed interests, and they possessed little grasp of the social problems with which they were faced after 1815.

The social composition of the opposing Whig party was little different. While controlled by a few aristocratic families, the Whigs had been a little more sympathetic than the Tories toward the ideals, though not the methods, of the French Revolution. They stood for the emancipation of Catholics, who could not hold public office or sit in Parliament; the limitation of royal patronage; and a suffrage reform about which they were not specific. Like the Tories, they possessed no fixed party platform. Neither group had the organization of a modern political party, and neither was able to exert much discipline upon its members. For an opposition party, the Whigs were not very aggressive.

Tory conservatism and Whig lethargy compelled men of progressive viewpoint to seek their political goals outside the two political parties in the movement known as radicalism. Never a formal political party, the Radicals were businessmen, journalists, intellectuals, and political agitators who were inspired by Bentham's utilitarianism to criticize abuses in the existing system and to call for its reform. But like Benthamism itself they were drawn in contradictory directions toward both the contraction and expansion of governmental activity and responsibility. On the one hand, they stood for laissez-faire individualism and, on the other, for suffrage reform, judicial reform, the extension of public education, and greater efficiency in government. The manufacturers of the industrial north were particularly attracted to radicalism during the first half of the century. Through suffrage reform, they expected to establish their influence in Parliament and protect their interests. While some Radicals wished to exploit social unrest in the interest of their cause, others were suspicious of the lower classes and fearful of a social upheaval.

Social Distress and Repressive Government No sooner had the Tory government triumphed over the French in 1815 than it was compelled to deal with disturbances at home which at times verged on revolution. With the end of the war, British farmers were again subject to the competition of continental producers, and the price of grain fell to one-half its previous value. The landowners in Parliament responded with a tariff that was higher than ever. It included increases in the rates on grain, known as the Corn Laws, which aroused the ire of the Radicals and the urban classes, whose food costs rose. But manufacturing, too, was in difficulty. After a short boom, British exports fell off one-third, production dropped, and unemployment rose. Starvation stalked the slums of the industrial cities. In Nottingham, artisans attacked the factories and destroyed machines; strikes and riots occurred in the eastern counties; workers' deputations travelled through the country.

Even more shocking to the wealthy classes was the appearance of democratic agitators who sought to exploit popular unrest and give it a political orientation. One of these was the journalist William Cobbett, a fiery reformer though not a revolutionary, whose *Political Register* advocated parliamentary reform and a variety of other causes and frequently brought him into conflict with the law. Less reputable was Henry Hunt, a dynamic speaker capable of stirring large audiences. Other orators and pamphleteers also emerged who were obviously under the influence of the French Revolution. Like the Jacobins, they preached equality, denounced social privilege, and attacked both church and constitution. This propaganda, although of limited effect upon the distressed social groups, created anxiety in the upper classes and the government. Britain's police force was inadequate to deal with popular disturbances, and her army had been seriously reduced after 1815. In 1817, the government tried to cope with the situation by suspending the right of habeas corpus and prohibiting seditious assemblies.

"Peterloo"　　The unrest, however, reached a climax in the industrial city of Manchester in 1819. On August 16, more than 50,000 working-class

The "Peterloo Massacre" of 1819. At the time Britain had no national police force and depended on the army to handle civil disobedience. Untrained for the task and commanded by reactionary officers, they frequently bungled the job. (Radio Times Hulton Picture Library.)

citizens assembled on St. Peter's field to listen to Hunt and draw up a petition. Although the meeting was peaceful, the local magistrates lost their heads, and ordered the yeomanry, a local militia, to arrest Hunt. But the yeomanry could make no headway through the angry crowd, and cavalrymen of the 15th Hussars were ordered to extricate them. Swinging their sabres, the Hussars cleared the field at a cost of eleven dead and about 400 injured. Since the Hussars had served at Waterloo, this unheroic episode became known as "Peterloo."

Most Englishmen were horrified by the "massacre" at Manchester. To people of property and government officials, however, it was another sign of spreading public disorder. The cabinet secured Parliament's approval of the Six Acts, which limited the circulation of journals and pamphlets among the poor and further restricted public meetings for the drafting of petitions. Other clauses were directed against private military training and provided for speedy judicial action against subversives. But the real conspirators were undeterred. Shortly after passage of the acts, a band of assassins, led by the Jacobin Arthur Thistlewood, plotted to murder the entire cabinet and seize control of the government. They were surprised by the police in London's Cato Street and were hanged.

Better harvests and an upswing in the business cycle relieved public distress in 1820. The riots, mass meetings, and demonstrations ceased for a few years. Yet much bitterness remained against a regime that had failed in a time of crisis to provide for the public welfare. Castlereagh was a common target of public contempt. His role in defending the cabinet's domestic policy in Commons obscured his successes in foreign policy. Shelley expressed the common view in his *Mask of Anarchy:*

I met Murder on the way—
He had a mask like Castlereagh;
Very smooth he looked, yet grim;
Seven bloodhounds followed him.

All were fat, and well they might
Be in admirable plight,
For one by one, and two by two,
He tossed them human hearts to chew,
Which from his wide cloak he drew.

In August 1822, the overworked minister lost his mind and cut his throat. As his funeral procession wound through the streets, the London poor gathered at the curbside and cheered to see him gone. Some observers feared that the funeral of the regime itself might not be far off.

Tory Reform Britain was saved from a revolutionary convulsion like that of 1830 on the continent by the appearance of new leaders, in both the Tory and Whig parties, who understood the need for change and got the chance to undertake it. In 1820, Liverpool, the Prime Minister, brought new talents into the cabinet. He secured the appointments of "liberal" Tories—Robert Peel as Home Secretary, George Canning as Foreign Secretary, and William Huskisson as President of the Board of Trade—who shifted the balance within the government in the direction of reform.

Canning inaugurated a "liberal" foreign policy by breaking from the Holy Alliance and by supporting the cause of Greek independence. Huskisson brought about a reduction of tariffs on manufactured goods and raw materials, though not on agricultural produce. A vigorous administrator, Peel quickly set about the task of modernizing the archaic criminal code by abolishing the death penalty for more than a hundred offences and mitigating other punishments as well. The prisons, which had been breeding places for both crime and disease, were reformed. But Peel's most enduring achievement was the founding of an effective metropolitan police system. Established first in London, the "Bobbies" or "Peelers," as they were called, finally became the symbol of honest law enforcement throughout Britain.

Repeal of the Combination Laws   One of the most important reforms of the period, the repeal of the Combination Laws which prohibited trade unions, was not the work of Tory liberals, but of two clever Radicals, Francis Place and Joseph Hume. Place, a self-educated London tailor, and Hume, a member of Parliament, were convinced that these laws were a needless violation of the principle of laissez faire. If they were repealed, British workers would come to realize that what actually held down their wages was the law of supply and demand in the labor market. By deft parliamentary maneuvers the two Radicals succeeded in getting passed a very liberal Trade Union Act in 1824. But the result was not what they had expected. Instead of resigning themselves to their fate, British workingmen hastened to exercise their rights. Trade unions sprang up; strikes were called; some violence occurred. In 1825, Parliament hastened to pass a second act which, while reaffirming the right to organize and negotiate, jeopardized the right to strike, picket, and maintain a union treasury.

The Collapse of the Tory Party   Liverpool's retirement in 1827 left no one capable of holding together the conservative and liberal factions of the Tory party. The appointment of Canning as Prime Minister led to resignation of the conservative ministers. After his death the conservative Duke of Wellington assumed power, and the liberals resigned, except for Peel. Nevertheless, the Wellington cabinet was responsible for the passage of one of the most progressive measures of the entire era: the political emancipation of Catholics.

Since the seventeenth century, Catholics and Dissenters had been legally excluded from holding office in Britain. In practice, the Dissenters had been allowed to do so, and in March 1828 the inoperative law was repealed. Yet Catholics were still excluded, which meant that the Catholic voters of Ireland could vote only for Protestants. Since 1823, a brilliant lawyer and orator, Daniel O'Connell, had agitated against this situation. In 1828, he stood for Parliament despite his religion, and defeated a member of Wellington's own cabinet. Though personally opposed to emancipation, Wellington and Peel realized that to deny O'Connell his seat might easily result in civil war. Since this was abhorrent to both, they pushed through Parliament an act removing the restrictions upon Catholics. Loyalty to the Anglican Church was a basic tenet of Toryism, and Wellington was repaid for his realism

"The Great Wellington and the Little Napoleon." His military victories in Spain and at Waterloo over Napoleon made Wellington a national hero. In politics, however, he belonged to the extreme right of the Tory party which was highly unpopular with the lower classes.

by a torrent of abuse from his own conservative colleagues. But it was the issue of parliamentary reform that finally severed the torn ligaments of the Tory party.

Whig Reform For many years Benthamites, Radicals, and humanitarians had earnestly pointed out that the inequities of the parliamentary franchise were socially dangerous. Few reformers were ready to advocate the enfranchisement of the masses through universal suffrage, but they saw that the urban middle class had to be granted a political representation commensurate with its new economic and social importance. The defenders of the existing system, on the other hand, argued that it had provided excellent leadership, that the rotten and pocket boroughs had enabled young men of talent to enter Parliament who might otherwise have had difficulty in getting elected; the elder William Pitt, for example, was first "elected" from Old Sarum. But the real reason for the obduracy of the conservatives is evident in the words of Wellington: "I see in thirty members for the rotten boroughs thirty men, I don't care of what party, who would preserve the state of property as it is."

Yet it was increasingly evident that the lid could no longer be held so tightly upon the boiling kettle. In 1829, the harvest was bad. Social distress, which had already been serious in the north for two years, radiated over the south, accompanied by a fresh outbreak of rioting, rick-burning, and machine-breaking. The union movement surged ahead among the workingmen; and, in January 1830, the "Birmingham Political Union of the Lower and Middle Classes" was founded on a program of "manhood suffrage and paper money." The Radicals were seeking to forge an alliance with the unenfranchised urban classes against the landowners. An election in 1830 resulted in a Tory decline of about 30 seats, and many Tories and Whigs concluded that parliamentary reform could not safely be delayed much longer. But this was not Wellington's view. In the House of Lords, he declared that "the system of representation possessed the full and entire confidence of the country." The public reacted with fury, and this was the final nail in the Tory coffin. Deserted by liberal and conservative Tories alike, the Wellington cabinet had to resign.

The Whig government that took office in November 1830 was headed by Lord Grey and was pledged to parliamentary reform. Yet the ministers were motivated by the necessity of the situation rather than by democratic idealism. In composition, it was in fact the most aristocratic cabinet of the century; all but four members belonged to the House of Lords. Their intention was not to take the first step toward universal suffrage, but rather to settle the issue once and for all by a moderate reform. These landed aristocrats, some of whom were of the noblest lineage, were dimly aware of the social changes occurring in Britain and recognized the wisdom of coming to terms with the middle class. "It was," Grey told the king, "the spirit of the age which was triumphing . . . to resist it was certain destruction."

During the twenty months after Grey's appointment, Britain passed through a turbulent period in which there was a real threat of popular revolution. His chief lieutenant, Lord John Russell, introduced no less than three successive reform bills. The first failed in Commons and led to a dissolution and an election which was won by the reformers. The chief obstacle to reform was then the House of Lords, the stronghold of Tory conservatism. At one point, Grey resigned, and Wellington tried futilely to form a cabinet. Riots spread through the country; castles were burned and jails delivered; Francis Place organized a run on the banks; and many citizens refused to pay taxes. Finally, Lords gave way when King William IV (1830–1837) agreed to appoint fifty new peers, and a bill was passed on June 4, 1832.

The Reform Bill of 1832   The Reform Bill of 1832 disfranchised fifty-six boroughs, enfranchised forty-two new ones, and either reduced or increased the representation of many others. It nearly doubled the size of the electorate, from 478,000 to 814,000. Nevertheless, the property qualification for voting remained, and only one-thirtieth of the population was represented in Parliament. While the upper middle class of the new industrial towns was enfranchised, the lower middle, artisan, and proletarian classes were still

"The Reformers' Attack on the Old Rotten Tree; or The Foul Nests of the Cormorants in Danger." This cartoon depicts the campaign against the rotten boroughs in 1832. The king and queen look on from "constitution hill." To the gentry who owned rotten or pocket boroughs property rights were more sacred than human rights. (Radio Times Hulton Picture Library.)

denied the vote. About fifty pocket boroughs still remained, and the retention of open balloting made it difficult for tenant farmers to cross the will of the local landlords, upon whom they were dependent. Only the well-to-do could sit in Parliament, for the property qualification was high, campaigning was expensive, and no salaries were paid. Nevertheless, there is no denying that a significant step had been taken. The enlarged electorate was more difficult for the old ruling class to organize and dominate, and an important precedent had been established which eventually led to the electoral reform bills of 1867 and 1884–1885.

Reinforced by an electoral victory in 1833, the Grey Cabinet was responsible during the next three years for a number of additional social reforms. In 1833, slavery was prohibited in the colonies and the first effective Factory Act was passed. The latter prohibited child labor under the age of nine, restricted children under thirteen to nine hours work a day (forty-eight hours a week) and those under eighteen to twelve hours a day (sixty-nine hours a week). In contrast to earlier statutes, the law provided for a board of inspectors for enforcement.

The Poor Law of 1834 The Poor Law of 1834 was another example of the limited social outlook of the Whigs and of the Benthamite doctrine which inspired it. Abandoning the system of dole that had tended to pauperize British labor, this act established a system of workhouses in which the destitute were to be supported on a level lower than that of the poorest independent laborer of the community. The calculus of pain-pleasure was to assure that as few persons as possible would go on public relief. Families were separated; even children were committed, as readers of *Oliver Twist* will remember; those who wished to avoid the workhouse were often compelled to send their wives and children to work in the fields and factories.

The Repeal of the Corn Laws While the landowners and manufacturers who enjoyed the vote under the Reform Bill of 1832 agreed that no further extension of the suffrage was called for, they were bitterly at odds on other issues. Spurred on by popular unrest, the pleas of humanitarian reformers like Lord Ashley, and their feud with the manufacturing interests, the landowners assisted in the passage of three acts: the Mines Act of 1842, prohibiting the employment underground of boys under ten and women of all ages; the Factory Acts of 1842 and 1847, the last of which established a ten-hour day and a fifty-eight hour week for women and youths; and the Factory Act of 1850, which established a twelve-hour day and a sixty-hour week for adults. The manufacturers, on the other hand, became vitally interested in repeal of the high tariffs on agricultural products, which protected the interests of the landowners but drove up the cost of food for the urban classes and hence the wages that the manufacturers paid their workers.

Two earnest social reformers, Richard Cobden and John Bright, assumed the leadership of the movement for repeal of these protective tariffs. Heading the Anti-Corn Law Association founded at Manchester in 1838, they developed new techniques of popular agitation and political campaigning which were highly effective. Yet it was the conversion of Robert Peel from protectionism to free trade, and a famine in Ireland, which finally decided the issue. Peel, who formed a Tory cabinet in 1841, had concluded that protectionism hampered the economic development of Britain. In 1845, a potato blight spread over Europe and reduced the Irish peasants to the point of starvation and revolt. To ease the food crisis Peel introduced into Commons a bill drastically reducing the duties on imported grains of all kinds, and in the summer of 1846 it passed both houses of Parliament.

For Peel, the cost was great. The landowners, who were the bulwark of the Tory party, could not forgive him for betraying their interests. Inspired by the cutting and witty attacks of the young Benjamin Disraeli, the majority turned against the government. Peel resigned, and with his followers, including William Ewart Gladstone, he formed a separate faction. Even after Peel's death in 1850, the faction held together, usually cooperating with the Whigs against their former party colleagues, the Tories. For a time, Britain had four political groups: Whigs, Radicals, Tories, and Peelites.

The Failure of Chartism   The repeal of the Corn Laws was a victory for the urban middle and lower classes. Its accomplishment took some of the fire out of another contemporary movement known as Chartism, whose appeal was directed entirely at the proletarian class. Beginning in 1836, a group of workingmen had founded a political organization to fight for certain objectives listed in a "People's Charter": annual Parliaments, universal suffrage, the secret ballot, equal electoral districts, the abolition of property qualifications for membership in Parliament, and the remuneration of members. The objective, of course, was to attain political power for the

Pillage of the Workhouse at Stockport in 1842. Unemployment and reductions in wages produced strikes, demonstrations, and rioting in the area of Manchester. The *Illustrated London News,* which printed this depiction, attributed the disorder to agitation by chartists and anticorn-law leaguers.

working class and to gain by this route what trade unionism had failed to achieve. In the years of greatest economic distress, 1839, 1842, and 1848, the Chartists sent petitions to Parliament with as many signatures as they could assemble; the last was so massive that it had to be carried across London in three carriages. They also planned a general strike and hoped for popular uprising, but neither materialized. Rioting occurred, but was speedily suppressed. On examination, the petition of 1848 proved, moreover, to have many bogus signatures: e.g., "Sir Robert Peel," "Victoria Rex," and "Mr. Punch." The ensuing laughter was more damaging to the Chartist cause than the vigor of the troops and police.

The year 1848, which produced revolutions over most of Europe, passed without a major crisis in Britain. On the continent, the middle class assumed leadership of the revolutionary forces. But in Britain, the middle class had been appeased by the Reform Act of 1832 and the repeal of the Corn Laws in 1846; and without its help, the British proletarians could accomplish nothing, as the failure of Chartism showed. During the fifties, Europe entered a period of rapid economic growth, rising wages, and greater opportunity— all of which relieved the pressure of social discontent in Britain.

FRANCE IN REACTION AND REVOLUTION
The man who ascended the restored Bourbon throne as Louis XVIII (1814–1824) did not cut a very kingly figure. He was fat, gouty, and indolent. Yet he was not lacking in shrewdness. Having lived many years in exile, he was anxious not to have to travel again, a feeling that Napoleon's return and the Hundred Days only confirmed. While a believer in absolutism and divine right, he understood that the clock could not be turned back to 1789. On arriving in Paris, he issued a royal charter, which, despite its limited character, was for many years the most advanced constitution on the continent of Europe.

The Charter of 1814 It created a government of "mixed" powers. The king was granted the executive power, including the right to appoint cabinet ministers, command the armed forces, and conduct foreign affairs. He was to share legislative power with a bicameral legislature: an hereditary Chamber of Peers and a Chamber of Deputies elected by a restricted suffrage. Whether the lower chamber had the power to overthrow the cabinet was not established, but certainly not intended. Neither chamber was given the right of legislative initiative. Only the crown could introduce bills for parliamentary consideration.

The Charter of 1814 was an uneasy compromise between the Bourbon, revolutionary, and imperial traditions. While asserting the divine right of kings, it accepted the principle of constitutionalism. It guaranteed the basic rights of man (freedom of speech and press, equality before the law, trial by jury, and the possession of property), but left loopholes for their subversion. Although freedom of faith was guaranteed, the Catholic Church was declared to be the state religion. Political power was monopolized by men of wealth or aristocractic birth. The Chamber of Peers was the stronghold of the nobility; its members enjoyed a handsome salary of 30,000 francs yearly. The deputies of the lower chamber, on the other hand, received no remuneration for their parliamentary services. Under the electoral law, candidates had to be at least 40 years of age and worth 1,000 francs in direct taxes per year. Voters were limited to men over 30 years who paid annual direct taxes of 300 francs. This last restriction meant that only about

The French Royal Family of the Restoration. Seated are King Louis XVIII and the Duchess of Angoulême. Standing (left to right) are the Count of Artois (the future Charles X) and his sons, the Dukes of Angoulême and Berry. The latter was assassinated in 1820. (Musée Carnavalet, Photo Bulloz.)

88,000 persons in a population of 30,000,000 could vote. The deputies were elected indirectly through an electoral college, another conservative feature designed to shield the government from the masses.

From the start, the Charter of 1814 had powerful enemies in France. Many of the returning *émigrés* and those of the rural nobility who had escaped the revolutionary purges were severely disappointed by the readiness of Louis to compromise. The king, one of them bitterly remarked, had not restored the Bourbon throne but merely occupied that vacated by Napoleon. They were antagonized by his appointment of a cabinet composed of former Napoleonic ministers, including Talleyrand and the notorious Fouché, Napoleon's chief of police; by his willingness to allow the Napoleonic aristocracy to sit with noblemen of ancient lineage in the Chamber of Peers; and by his retention of the Napoleonic codes and the centralized administrative system of the empire. They were also angered by his guarantee that the purchasers of confiscated and nationalized property could expect to retain it. These royal extremists, or Ultras, were led by the king's own brother and heir, the Count of Artois.

In romantic conservatism, the Ultras soon found a political philosophy sympathetic to their interests. Their program was similar to that of the French nobility in 1789. Many wished to restore the social and political structure as it had been before Richelieu. They wanted a decentralized monarchy based upon estates that were to be dominated by a landed aristocracy. The nobility were to be protected by the restoration of primogeniture and enriched by an indemnification for their confiscated properties. By abrogating the Napoleonic Concordat with the papacy, they hoped to restore the church to its former position of wealth and influence. Once again the Catholic clergy was to dominate the educational system and become the guardian of social order.

At the opposite end of the political spectrum from the Ultras were the "Independents," whose aims were equally incompatible with the Charter of 1814. During twenty-five turbulent years, France had made the swift transition from constitutional monarchy to republic to empire; and each of these regimes had left behind its adherents, men who could not be reconciled to a restored Bourbon monarchy. The activities of the Ultras and the terrorism that followed the Hundred Days served to confirm them in the belief that both Louis and his Charter had to go. Yet the Independents could not form a cohesive party. While joined by mutual hostility toward the Ultras and the existing dynasty, they were intensely divided over what was to replace it: a constitutional monarchy under the Duke d'Orléans of the collateral Bourbon line, a republic of either Girondist or Jacobin character, or another empire under a liberal constitution. Only on social issues did the Independents generally agree with each other. They favored the bourgeoisie in the conviction that only men of wealth and property could be made responsible for public policy. They were contemptuous of the nobility and clergy and the democratic rabble alike.

Between the two extremes there was a group known as "Constitutional Royalists," who alone accepted the Charter. They were the moderates who believed that the Charter was an adequate compromise between the old regime and the revolution and wished to use it to establish in France a stable and conservative government. Many were noblemen of the old regime who understood that it could not be reconstructed; some were bourgeois who were weary of revolution and war; others were men of the Empire who did not believe in its re-establishment. The Constitutional Royalists looked upon the Charter as striking the correct balance between authority and freedom. Upon them the future of the regime depended.

While the Charter of 1814 was modeled after the English constitutional system, it is apparent that a wide gulf existed between the political situations of the two countries in 1815. The British constitution was the product of centuries of evolutionary development, punctuated by a revolution that had occurred more than a century before. But the French charter was not yet sanctified by tradition, and its acceptance was not yet a matter of habit or patriotism. It was a contrived attempt to bridge the three mutually hostile systems that had been successively overturned during the preceding twenty-five years. Its defense was not yet a matter of moral obligation for the great majority of Frenchmen. On the contrary, two of the three dominant factions in French politics were bent on its destruction. The history of the Bourbon restoration is the story of the growth of the extremes at the cost of the moderate center.

The White Terror and Moderate Rule In 1814–1815, the Ultras were the most politically active group in France. After Waterloo, royalist mobs massacred liberals, Bonapartists, and Protestants in many southern cities. Under pressure from the Ultras, Louis violated his promise of fair treatment for Napoleonic generals and officials, who were punished whether or not they had actually betrayed the Restoration. Eighteen generals were court-martialed; twenty-nine peerages were revoked; men were held for weeks without trial; many of the accused were executed, including the famed Marshal Ney, who was condemned by the Chamber of Peers. Almost all of the Napoleonic prefects were replaced by royalists.

In 1815, while suspicion and fear dominated the land, the first elections were held for the Chamber of Deputies, and the result was victory for the Ultras. Nevertheless, Louis appointed a new cabinet of moderates headed by the Duke de Richelieu, a descendant of the famous cardinal. Cabinet and chamber soon came into conflict, for neither Louis nor Richelieu could accept the kind of repressive laws the Ultras sought to impose upon the country. The Ultra majority was so reactionary, in fact, that the European powers, fearing a revolution, advised Louis to dissolve the chamber. New elections in 1816 produced a majority for the Constitutional Royalists. During the next four years the king, Cabinet, and both chambers of Parliament were in agreement; and France had a stable and effective government. A new suffrage law abolished the electoral college and strengthened the bourgeoisie at the polls; the finances were reorganized and the war indemnity paid; the army was reformed and promotion was made a matter of service and seniority; France was re-established as a great power and restored to the European concert; a more liberal press law was enacted, which reduced censorship. In 1818, the capable Richelieu was replaced by Decazes, another moderate, who had endeared himself to Louis as a purveyor of gossip.

By 1820, nevertheless, the attempt of Louis and the moderates to steer between reaction and revolution had run into difficulty. The elections of 1817, 1818, and 1819 were mostly won by Independents, who appeared likely soon to become the majority in the chamber. In 1820, a radical fanatic assassinated the Duke of Berry, son of the Count of Artois, in the expectation that his death would end the dynasty for lack of an heir. The murderer miscalculated, for the duchess was already pregnant and within a few months gave birth to a son. Furthermore, the effect of this action was to bring about the fall of Decazes. Fearful of the revolutionary current, Louis recalled Richelieu, who sought for two years (1820–1822) to govern with the support of both Ultras and moderates. It was an uneasy and insecure coalition. The political atmosphere in France and Europe as a whole was unfavorable for men of moderate viewpoint. They were driven either to the right or left. Under pressure from the Ultras, indirect election was restored, press censorship tightened, and machinery provided for the suppression of secret societies. In late 1822, French underground associations patterned after the Italian Carbonari were responsible for a number of insurrections, which the government suppressed. But this success was not enough to satisfy the Ultras and they obtained Richelieu's dismissal.

The Rule of the Ultras With the fall of Richelieu, the pendulum swung to the far right. Once more the Ultras had the chance to show whether they could actually reverse the course of French history. While still convinced of the rightness of the moderate course, Louis no longer had the strength of will to follow it. The current in Europe was flowing in the direction of reaction, and he drifted with it. During the two years of life that remained to him, he nearly withdrew from the affairs of state, devoting himself to the witty companionship of Madame du Cayla, who was actually an agent of the Ultras. For all practical purposes, the Ultras and the Count of Artois dominated the government. When Louis died in 1824 and was replaced by the Count as Charles X (1824–1830), no essential change in the cabinet was necessary.

King Charles X in Coronation Robes. Charles looked more kingly than the obese and immobile Louis XVIII; yet he was inferior in political judgment. To Frenchmen his insistence on dynastic tradition and absolute power seemed anachronistic. (Brown Brothers.)

While a more kingly figure than Louis XVIII, Charles X was devoid of all political sense. He had himself crowned at the cathedral in Rheims with all the pomp and circumstance of a medieval coronation. Miraculously, the clergy rediscovered for the occasion the container of holy oil that had been used to anoint the kings of feudal France. Afterward, the king undertook, like St. Louis, to cure by his touch several cases of scrofula. His first prime minister was Villèle (1822–1827), an able financier and administrator, but not a statesman. While a staunch royalist, even he doubted that he could execute some of the measures thrust upon him by the extremists.

Charles X and his Ultras were bent upon a social and religious reconstruction that would have amounted to the restoration of the old regime in France. In order to secure control over the chamber, they pushed through the septennate law, providing for elections only every seventh year. Another key measure was a bill indemnifying the dispossessed nobility for their losses during the revolution. Villèle hit upon the clever expedient of refunding the public debt at a lower rate of interest in order to pay the interest on new bonds which were issued to the former *émigrés* as compensation for their losses. The landowners were reassured; no new taxes were required; only the old bondholders, whose incomes suddenly sank, were unhappy. Other measures were less successful. A bill to strengthen the landed class by reintroducing primogeniture was too much even for the Chamber of Peers, which rejected it. A similar fate met a bill that would have abolished all but a few newspapers. In Paris, there was general rejoicing and cries of "Down with the ministry!"

It was the clerical policy of the Ultras, however, which aroused the greatest popular indignation. Supported by the government, the clergy began to interfere in educational and political matters. A bishop became grand master of the University of France, and liberals were hunted out of the faculty. Civil marriages, which had predominated in France since the revolution, were declared null and void; middle-aged couples found themselves living in a state of sin, their grown children branded as illegitimate. But the climax came with the "Law of Sacrilege," which declared it a felony punishable by death to desecrate an altar. Desecration was hardly a problem in France, and the passage of such a bill merely demonstrated the fanaticism of the regime.

In 1827, an election revealed how hollow was the assertion of the Ultras that they represented the majority of Frenchmen. Frightened by the gains made by the Independents, Charles X dissolved the chamber; but the following new election produced an even greater liberal triumph. Villèle resigned, and for a year Charles suffered a moderate cabinet under Martignac. But this experiment was doomed to failure, for the Constitutional Royalists were no longer an effective group in French politics. The efforts of Martignac to appease the Independents were rejected by them as insufficient and attacked by the Ultras as too far-reaching.

The king, believing that he had demonstrated the impossibility of a government of moderates, now felt free to appoint a cabinet of his own liking. The enthusiasm with which he had recently been received on a tour of France deceived him into thinking that his was actually a popular government. The Prince of Polignac, whom he chose as prime minister, belonged to the most extreme wing of the Ultras. Worst of all, Polignac was devoid of any political talent. He claimed to be acting on the advice of the Virgin Mary who appeared to him in visions. Throughout France, his appointment was believed to be the prelude to the destruction of the constitution. When the chamber that convened in 1830 proved uncooperative, Charles dissolved it and appealed to the electorate. But the result was a victory for the opposition.

The Revolution of 1830   Again the comparison with Britain is instructive. In contrast to the Whig aristocrats of Grey's Cabinet, the Ultras were insensitive to the actual state of popular opinion in the country. In contrast to William IV, Charles X deliberately flouted the will of the parliamentary majority and the electorate. He made the fatal tactical error of identifying the crown with a particular political faction. In rejecting the latter, the Parliament in effect rejected the king himself.

Attack on the Royal Palace, the Louvre, during the Revolution of 1830. The king and his court were at another palace, St. Cloud, on the outskirts of Paris. From there Charles fled to England without attempting to raise the provinces against the rebels in Paris. (Musée Carnavalet, Photo Bulloz.)

On July 26, 1830, the government published four ordinances designed to put an end to the opposition. Newspapers were required to renew their licenses every three months; the new chamber was dissolved before it met and fresh elections ordered; the number of deputies was cut and the size of the electorate reduce to 25,000. In Paris, popular excitement ran high. The shops and factories closed, and thousands of men poured into the streets. Following the familiar ritual of revolution, paving blocks were ripped up and carts overturned to form barricades. The king and his cabinet had made no preparations for the suppression of an uprising. The few available troops were soon driven from the streets, and on July 29 a group of republicans set up a provisional government in the Hôtel de Ville.

But the republicans were quickly outmaneuvered by the liberal monarchists. Once again the versatile Talleyrand called the turn. He persuaded Louis Philippe, the Duke of Orléans, to come to Paris and head a government. During the night of July 29–30, the liberal monarchists, headed by Adolphe Thiers, were hard at work plastering the city with placards praising the duke's virtues. Mounted on a horse and bearing the revolutionary tricolor, Louis Philippe made his way through the sullen crowds to the Hôtel de Ville. The republicans, of whom Lafayette was the most prominent, recognized that they had been outflanked. To reject the duke now meant civil war, which no one desired. After embracing the duke, Lafayette presented him to the crowd: "Here is the king we need; it is the best of republics." Charles X, meanwhile, had fled to England and exile.

The July Monarchy The ambivalence of Lafayette's statement to the crowd at the Hôtel de Ville is indicative of the character of the new regime. Louis Philippe was both a Bourbon and a former revolutionary. A cousin of Louis XVIII, he was the son of Philippe d'Orléans, who in 1789 had joined the revolutionists and ended on the scaffold. As a youth the new king had fought at Valmy and participated in the Jacobin Club, but had fled France during the Terror. As a refugee in England he had taken great care not to identify himself with the *émigrés,* and during the Restoration, he had kept his distance from Charles X and the Ultras. He was a cautious man, and it took considerable persuasion to get him to mount the throne.

Those who placed him there expected the new regime to represent their own interests. They were men of wealth and status, capitalists, well-to-do landowners, and professional people (lawyers, journalists, and professors) who feared that a republic would mean universal suffrage and the democratic rule of the masses. They denied the uprising that had boosted them into power. "There has been no revolution," declared the minister Casimir Périer, "there has simply been a change in the person of the chief of state." They compared their actions to those of the British in deposing James II and inviting William and Mary to ascend the throne in 1688. They pictured themselves not as revolutionists, but as the defenders of the proper constitutional order against the usurpations of a tyrannical king. Hence they retained the Charter of 1814 with few changes. The most significant change was made in the electoral law. Candidates had to be only thirty instead of forty years old and pay only 500 instead of 1,000 frances in direct taxes. The requirements for voters were reduced from 20 to 25 years and from 300 to 200 francs. As a result, the size of the electorate doubled from 100,000 to 200,000 in a population of 33,000,000. The Chamber of Peers ceased to be the monopoly of the nobility; the seats were no longer hereditary, and many of the peers created by Villèle were removed. The result of these amendments was that a wider circle of the wealthy gained political power, but the lower classes (peasants, proletarians, artisans, and lesser bourgeois) were still excluded.

The regime of Louis Philippe has often been called the "bourgeois monarchy" in view of the source of its political support. The king and his court seemed proof of its middle-class character. Abandoning military dress, Louis Philippe clothed himself like a well-to-do merchant and could be seen walking about the streets of Paris carrying a green parasol. His figure lent itself to caricature and earned him the sobriquet "Louis the Pear." Like a proper bourgeois, he was parsimonious, saving and investing his funds with

Caricature of Louis Phillipe. During his trial for *lese majeste* the artist Charles Philipon drew this cartoon to demonstrate the hazards under the censorship laws of caricaturing not only the king, but even a pear. Punishment for such "crimes" was up to five years in prison and 5,000 francs fine. (The Bettmann Archive.)

considerable acumen until he became a very rich man. Ultra aristocrats boycotted his court, but their places were taken by businessmen, intellectuals, and nobles sympathetic to the regime. Despite his bourgeois exterior, Louis Philippe was proud of his Bourbon heritage. "I am not a usurper!" he cried at those who denied the legitimacy of his claim to the throne. Yet at the same time he was conscious of the revolutionary origin of his power and of the necessity for popular approval. He found himself in the ambiguous position of claiming both a legitimate and a popular basis for his authority. Secretly, he aspired to assume full control of the government and worked with considerable astuteness toward this end.

In contrast to the preceding regime, the "July monarchy" began with a favorable political situation in Parliament. Neither of the two groups into which the lower chamber divided was fundamentally opposed to the government. The Party of Movement and the Party of Resistance, as they were popularly called, were both parties of center orientation representing the wealthy capitalist and land-owning classes that possessed the vote. What divided them primarily was a matter of personalities and temperament rather than fundamental issues. Under the leadership of the historian François Guizot, the Resistance advocated, in both domestic and foreign affairs, a conservative policy the principal objective of which was the stability of the established order. The Movement was led by another historian, the brilliant and ambitious Adolphe Thiers, who pushed for an active foreign policy with the aim of restoring France to her accustomed predominance in Europe.

Neither of the rival parties was cohesive or well organized; factionalism was rife, and personal rivalries frequently took precedence over issues. Although the average life of the cabinet was less than a year, the Party of Resistance was usually in power. In Casimir Périer, the party produced the only effective minister of the era; he suppressed disorder and compelled Louis Philippe to let his ministers rule. After Périer died of cholera in 1832, there was no one of equal stature to take his place.

The international crisis of 1840 enabled Louis Philippe to end parliamentary government in France. He dismissed Premier Thiers, whose adventurous foreign policy in Egypt had brought France to the brink of a disastrous war, and summoned Guizot, who held the premiership to the end of the regime in 1848. In this arrogant man, Louis Philippe found a perfect instrument for his plans, for Guizot was quite willing to accept the fact that the cabinet was responsible to the king rather than to Parliament. By appointing as many as one-third of the deputies to salaried posts in the government, Guizot systematically undermined the chamber's independence. But aside from political stability the government of Louis Philippe and Guizot achieved little. As could be expected of a bourgeois regime, it devoted itself primarily to the encouragement of business expansion. Although this meant some extension of state aid to business enterprise, the dominant policy was that of laissez faire. Only in the field of public education was Guizot responsible for any notable legislation; the elementary school system was reorganized and greatly expanded.

During the Orléans monarchy, the main currents of dissatisfaction and opposition developed outside the chamber. The first five years were marked by repeated outbreaks, which usually began with strikes and often ended as insurrections such as that of 1831 in Lyon, where 15,000 workers battled the National Guard. Their failure discouraged the republicans, who turned away from revolutionary to political agitation. In so doing they alienated many proletarians, who began to interest themselves in socialist doctrines. A cleavage began to develop between the middle and lower classes, which was to become glaringly evident in 1848. But the Bonapartists were also active, and were aided by a changing popular attitude toward the deceased emperor. The adverse side of his regime was forgotten; its achievements were remembered and romanticized. Of all the opposition movements, nevertheless, that of the Bonapartists seemed to have the least prospects. The pretender, Louis Napoleon Bonaparte, appeared to have none of the talents of his famous uncle and his attempt to invade France in 1836 and 1840 aroused no public response.

Outwardly, the July monarchy appeared safe. Its leaders congratulated themselves on having mastered the secret of social order and political stability. Like England, France appeared to have experienced her last revolution. In 1848, this illusion was to be suddenly and rudely shattered.

THE RESURGENCE OF ITALY

Since her remarkable achievements during the Renaissance, Italy had declined in vitality. The development of the Atlantic sea lanes had left her in the backwash of European commerce. Since the mid-sixteenth century her cities, once so dynamic, had ceased to grow, and her cultural life, once the marvel of Europe, had lost much of its creativity. Politically divided, she was ruled or fought over by the European great powers. Except for a relatively small middle class, located mostly in the northern towns, the population was composed of an impoverished and illiterate peasantry dominated by landlords. Napoleon brought major changes to this inert country. After the conquests of 1797 and 1800, he reconstructed the Italian map, swept away feudalism, and imposed a modern code of law and a uniform administrative system. Nevertheless, French rule was also exploitative. The country was heavily taxed; its art galleries were looted; and its men were conscripted for foreign wars.

The Congress of Vienna substituted Austrian for French domination of Italy. The Habsburgs received the two rich northern provinces of Lombardy and Venetia and secured control over a number of satellite states. Branches of the Habsburg family ruled the duchies of Parma, Modena, and Tuscany. The Bourbon rulers of Lucca and the kingdom of the Two Sicilies were dependent upon Austria. The only native rulers in the entire peninsula were the Pope, who regained control over the Papal States of central Italy, and King Victor Emmanuel I, who ruled over Savoy, Piedmont, Genoa, and Sardinia. In the years that followed, only the latter managed to assert his freedom from Vienna. Austrian agents, informers, spies, troops, and bribes kept the satellite states in line.

Generally the masses received the returning rulers with enthusiasm. Their reward was reactionary government. Victor Emmanuel I tried to restore the old order by revoking laws issued since 1770; Pope Pius VII reimposed a backward priestly rule in the Papal States; King Ferdinand I re-established his stagnant and oppressive regime in Naples; the other rulers, with the notable exception of the Duke of Tuscany, followed suit.

The Risorgimento The social changes already underway in Italy were soon to subject the settlement of 1815 to severe pressures. Napoleon's reconstruction had weakened local loyalties by wiping out old frontiers. Service in the imperial armies had awakened many Italians to the new ideas abroad in Europe. Furthermore, there had been some economic growth in both commerce and agriculture. Merchants, manufacturers, and capitalistic landowners saw the financial advantages of unification. Disunity in such matters as tariffs, currencies, weights, and measures hampered trade.

During the Napoleonic period the *risorgimento* (resurgence) of Italian national sentiment began. Secret societies, the Carbonari, were formed by middle-class citizens on the pattern of the Masonic Order. In 1817, an uprising in the Papal States was badly bungled and brutally suppressed. In 1820, news of the revolution in Spain set off a Carbonari insurrection in Naples; and Ferdinand I quickly granted a constitution, which he solemnly swore to uphold. But this cowardly monarch soon deserted to the Austrians, whose army invaded and occuped the country. The rebel forces quickly disintegrated, and Ferdinand indulged in an orgy of revenge. While the Austrian troops were thus engaged in southern Italy, a military mutiny occurred in Piedmont. Backed by the popular agitation of the Carbonari, the insurgents forced the abdication of Victor Emmanuel; but the returning Austrian army soon scattered the rebels and placed his heir, Charles Felix, on the throne. In 1831, the conspirators again had their chance. Organized into a common front by a lawyer, Enrico Misley, they accepted Duke Francis IV of Modena as their candidate for the throne of a united Italy. Although the duke, afraid of failure, betrayed the plot, and the expected assistance of France under Louis Philippe failed to materialize, the uprising began in Bologna and soon spread to other cities. Again Metternich acted swiftly. Austrian troops marched in and stamped out the rebellion.

The failures of 1820–1821 and 1831 revealed the inadequacy of the Italian movement for national unity and independence. The rebels were either army officers or middle-class Carbonari. They were but a small minority of the Italian people, most of whom remained unaffected by their aspirations. The Italian peasants were too ignorant and unlettered, too involved in the daily struggle for economic survival, to concern themselves with national and political ideals. The brave bands of middle-class patriots paid the price of their isolation: that of betrayal, imprisonment, death, and exile.

Plans for Unity For seventeen years after the debacle of 1831, Italy was again relatively quiet. The restlessness of the dissatisfied found an outlet in intellectual activity of political import. Nationalism and romanticism combined to produce a literary revival. Manzoni's masterpiece, *The Betrothed*, published in 1826, set the style. During the 1830's and 1840's, there appeared many works of historical fiction which celebrated the periods of Italian greatness and the deeds of patriotic rebels against alien rule. In poetry and drama, the message was repeated. Poverty and censorship had severely limited the number of journals and newspapers published in Italy during the first half of the century. In the periodical *Annali*, Italy finally acquired a national journal of significance. Its economic news was interspersed with patriotic messages.

During this period, Italian intellectuals began to think more clearly about the future structure of the united Italy for which they yearned. Three possibilities were advanced: a unitary republic, a monarchical federation, and a constitutional monarchy. They were championed respectively by Giuseppe Mazzini (1805–1872), the Abbé Vincenzo Gioberti (1801–1851), and Count Cesare Balbo (1789–1853).

Mazzini was one of the foremost apostles of modern nationalism. In him, there was something of the fanaticism that was to characterize national movements in the twentieth century. After witnessing the miserable failures of the Carbonari, Mazzini concluded that they lacked moral inspiration and were too restricted in their appeal. The goal of national unity, he believed, must become an ethical ideal capable of infusing the Italian masses with a spirit of dedication and a readiness to sacrifice. Nationalism must become a religious faith and an apostolate. Only through revolutionary action by the people themselves could the unitary republic be created which alone could revitalize the nation. He envisioned a reorganization of Europe into national republics which would inaugurate a new era of peace and democracy.

Driven into exile in 1831, Mazzini spent most of his remaining years abroad in France, Switzerland, and England. Wherever he went he became a focal point of political agitation and conspiracy. Throughout Europe his name was synonymous with revolutionary nationalism. Yet the Young Italy movement which he founded has to be regarded as a failure. While he succeeded in giving to the *risorgimento* an ethical content, his movement never really aroused the Italian masses. His message reached the middle class, in particular its professional segment, but it did not affect the peasants, "who took their politics from the parish priest." The revolutionary insurrections he fostered all ended in failure, for they had no adequate popular backing.

Gioberti published in 1843 a work, *On the Moral and Civil Primacy of the Italians,* which voiced the views of moderate nationalists and loyal Catholics who disliked the insurrectionary, democratic, and anticlerical views of the Mazzinians. Obviously one of the central problems in uniting Italy concerned the Papacy. A unitary republic would cost the pontiff his rule over the Papal States. It might also threaten his freedom as the spiritual ruler of the world-wide Catholic Church. Gioberti's solution was a federal Italy headed by the pope, with a college of princes acting as the executive. By this solution the Italians, whose "civil and moral primacy" he exalted, would lead the way for a federal reorganization of all Europe. The major shortcoming of the Abbe's work was his failure to explain how Austria could be brought without war to accept such a union and to surrender Lombardy and Venetia.

Balbo, whose *The Hopes of Italy* was also published in 1843, desired the expulsion of Austria and the unification of Italy under the House of Savoy. Charles Albert (1831–1849), who ascended the Sardinian throne on the death of Charles Felix, was an absolutist and a legitimist, but he also hated Austria. With the help of able ministers this cold, relentless autocrat brought efficient government to Sardinia; economic and military reforms enabled him to assert his independence from Vienna. Nevertheless, his foreign policy remained an enigma. If the opportunity came, would he throw his army into the scales and assume the leadership of the national cause? Would the House of Savoy become the ruling house of united Italy? Until 1848, the Italian patriots had no certain answers to these questions.

Giuseppe Mazzini about 1860. By his tireless agitation and propaganda Mazzini made Italian unity a European cause among liberal republicans. That Italy was ultimately united under a monarchical constitution was for him a severe disappointment.

FURTHER READING The literature on nineteenth-century Britain is rich. Authoritative and highly readable is Anthony Wood, *Nineteenth Century Britain, 1815–1914* (1960). For the early period, the best study is E. L. Woodward, *The Age of Reform, 1815–1870* (1938). For greater detail, see E. Halevy, *History of the English People in the Nineteenth Century,* 6 vols. (2nd rev. ed., 1949–1952). On social unrest, see D. Read, *Peterloo: The Massacre and Its Background* (1958); C. Woodham-Smith, *The Great Hunger* (1963); J. L. and B. Hammond, *The Age of the Chartists, 1832–1854* (1930); G. D. H. Cole, *Chartist Portraits* (1941); C. R. Fay, *The Corn Laws and Social England* (1932). The movement for political reform can be followed in N. Gash, *Politics in the Age of Peel* (1953); J. R. M. Butler, *The Passing of the Great Reform Bill* (1914); G. M. Trevelyan, *Lord Grey and the Reform Bill* (1920).

Excellent one-volume histories of modern France are P. A. Gagnon, * *France Since 1789* (1972), J. B. Wolf, *France, 1814 to 1919* (1940, 1963); and Gordon Wright, *France in Modern Times, 1760 to the Present* (1960). The early part of the century can be studied in greater detail in F. B. Artz, *France under the Bourbon Restoration 1814–1830* (1931); G. L. Dickinson, *Revolution and Reaction in Modern France* (2nd ed., 1927); and J. Plamanetz, *The Revolutionary Movement in France, 1815–1871* (1952). Biographies of significant figures are those by J. M. S. Allison on Thiers (1932); D. Johnson on Guizot; T. Howarth on Louis Phillipe (1961); and V. Beach, on Charles X (1973). Illuminating for Guizot, Thiers, and others is S. Melon, *The Political Uses of History, A Study of Historians in the French Restoration* (1958).

Brief histories of Italy in the age of unification and after are A. J. Whyte, *The Evolution of Modern Italy* (1944); L. Salvatorelli, *A Concise History of Italy* (1940). Earlier works that still have merit and more information are B. King, *A History of Italian Unity,* 2 vols., (1912); and G. and J. Berkeley, *Italy in the Making, 1815–1848,* 2 vols. (1932–1940). The connection between economics and politics has been studied by K. R. Greenfield, *Economics and Liberalism in the Risorgimento* (1934). Other useful works on the Risorgimento are W. K. Hancock, *Ricasoli and the Risorgimento in Tuscany* (1926); and R. Grew, *A Sterner Plan for Italian Unity* (1963). G. Griffith, *Mazzini* (1932), is the best biography; but see also E. E. Hales, *Mazzini and the Secret Societies* (1956).

*Books available in paperback edition are marked with an asterisk.

4 Reaction in Central and Eastern Europe

To travel eastward across Europe in the early nineteenth century, it has been said, was to progress laterally in space, but backward in time. The further east the traveller went the more closely the circumstances in which most people lived and worked resembled those of the feudal age. After the Rhine and Upper Danube were left behind, the towns became increasingly infrequent, the wide stretches of open farmland more common. On the great plains of Hungary, Poland, and northeastern Germany the peasants were no longer serfs, but most possessed no land and they remained subservient to noble landlords. In Russia, serfdom still existed and the authority of the landlord over the peasant was greater than it had ever been in the west.

As the economic and social circumstances changed from west to east, so did those of political life. Although central Europe was still dominated by autocratic monarchs and their bureaucracies, reforms had occurred under the influence of the Enlightenment, the French Revolution, and Napoleonic hegemony. As the decades progressed, there were increasing signs of middle-class unrest. In eastern Europe, on the other hand, the dead hand of reactionary rule prevented all but the most superficial changes in the tsarist regime. Except for occasional peasant revolts, the Russian masses were untouched by popular protest. The only Russian attempt at violent overthrow, in 1825, had the character of a conspiracy rather than a revolution.

GERMANY UNDER THE VIENNA SETTLEMENT

The German Confederation The Congress of Vienna replaced the defunct Holy Roman Empire with a German Confederation composed of thirty-nine states. The largest were the "dual powers" (Austria and Prussia), followed by the "middle states" (Bavaria, Württemberg, Baden, Saxony, and Hanover), and the "small states," some of which were only a few square miles in size.[1] The confederation was neither sovereign nor entirely German. Its central organ, the Confederate Diet, which met in Frankfurt, was an assembly

[1] A map of Germany after 1815 see page 1225.

of diplomats rather than legislators. They voted according to instructions from their governments. Two foreign states had membership: Denmark through its possession of the German duchy of Holstein, and the Netherlands through its possession of Limburg and Luxemburg. Both of the dual powers, furthermore, had possessions lying outside the frontiers of the Confederation; East Prussia was excluded and likewise the whole eastern half of the Habsburg Empire.

The purpose of the German Confederation was not to govern Germany, but chiefly to provide a means of common defense against foreign attack. This was a considerable disappointment to those German patriots who had been inspired by the war of liberation against Napoleon to hope for the creation of a unified German state. Yet the majority of Germans were probably satisfied. After centuries of deterioration, the Holy Empire had proved impotent to protect Germany from foreign invasion. The Confederation promised to give greater cohesion without destroying local loyalties, which were dearer to most Germans than the ideal of national unity. Although the French conquests had destroyed hundreds of sovereignties, this drastic surgery had not excised the spirit of "particularism" in Germany. After 1815, the states of Baden, Württemberg, and Bavaria—all three of which emerged from the Napoleonic wars with expanded frontiers— succeeded in developing a sense of dynastic patriotism among their newly incorporated subjects. The same was true of the Hohenzollern monarchy; by the 1840's it had absorbed the population of the Rhineland (acquired in 1815), whose economic, social, and religious (mainly Catholic) composition differed radically from that of the old Prussian state.

Yet the chief bulwark of the settlement of 1815 was the dominance of the landowning class and the conservative political philosophy in Germany. Because of the backwardness of Germany's economic development, the landowners remained unshaken in their social and political hegemony. While the four "free cities" of the German Confederation—Bremen, Hamburg, Lübeck, and Frankfurt—were ruled by patrician oligarchies, the other governments were all principalities whose rulers and ministers depended primarily upon the support of the nobility, to whose ranks they themselves belonged. The conservative creed, which defended their interests, emphasized the antirevolutionary doctrine of legitimacy. Monarchical governments were considered to be part of the divine order, and their preservation a moral imperative. Naturally, this meant the perpetuation of Germany's disunion.

The possibilities for change were threefold: (1) the growth of German national sentiment ending in a popular revolution, (2) the establishment of Prussian hegemony over the lesser states at the cost of Austria, and (3) agreement by the governments to reorganize Central Europe along federal lines.

The Possibility of Prussian Leadership It was only logical that some German nationalists should have looked to Prussia for leadership. During the eighteenth century, Frederick the Great had, by his genius as a soldier, statesman, and *philosophe,* elevated his dynasty to a position of leadership in Germany. Although the catastrophic defeat of 1806 dimmed the luster of Hohenzollern prestige, the reforms of the Prussian ministers, Stein and Hardenberg, had brightened it once more. By abolishing serfdom, establishing municipal self-government, and adopting military conscription and a popular militia, the reform government was able in a few years to modernize and regenerate the Prussian state. While Austria delayed, the Prussian forces joined the assault on Napoleon at the earliest opportunity in 1813.

The settlement of 1815 strengthened further the possibility of Prussian leadership in Germany. The Habsburg monarchy surrendered its outlying possessions in the west: the Austrian Netherlands to Holland, the Breisgau to Baden. This naturally weakened her traditional interest in Germany and strengthened her absorption in the Danubian area, Italy, and the Balkans. By contrast, Prussia surrendered most of her Polish possessions in return for German soil in the Rhineland. The Habsburg monarchy remained a multi-national empire ruled by a German minority, while Prussia became a largely German state with a Polish minority. Prussia, furthermore, was left in a divided condition with territories in the east and west. Should an aggressive statesman of the character of Frederick the Great ever come to power in Berlin, his natural goal would be to annex the intervening states. Inevitably this would be a step toward German unity.

The man who occupied the Prussian throne, Frederick William III (1797–1840), was not a Frederick the Great. He was a man of mediocre talents who had been rescued from disaster in 1807 by talented ministers and generals. Once the foreign crisis was over in 1815, he lapsed into a conservative policy, and Prussia lost her position of moral leadership in Germany. By 1820, there was no longer any possibility that Frederick William would fulfill his promise to promulgate a constitution for Prussia. In foreign policy as well, Prussia was largely inactive after 1815. The king and his successor, Frederick William IV (1840–1861), were content to follow the leadership of Metternich in German and European affairs. The one independent achievement of Prussian foreign policy in this era did not arise from imperialistic or German national motives. This was the creation of a German Customs Union known as the *Zollverein.*

The Zollverein Naturally political disunion meant economic fragmentation for Germany. After 1815 there were thirty-eight tariff boundaries, which hampered commerce and increased the price of goods. Between the port of Hamburg and Austria, shipments of goods crossed ten states and were taxed ten times. "Whoever is so unfortunate," wrote Friedrich List, "as to live where three or four states come together, spends his whole life amidst hostile customs officials and is a man without a fatherland." This situation was contrary to the doctrine of laissez faire and to common sense. In 1818, the Prussian government adopted the policy of free trade by issuing a law that wiped out all internal tariffs within the Prussian state. The advantages this gave to commerce inside Prussia threatened the economic welfare of neighboring states. Hence, they signed commercial treaties with Prussia creating a common tariff frontier. By 1834, almost all German states had joined the system. The major exception was Austria, whose infant industries would have suffocated without protective tariffs. Prussia's success in organizing the *Zollverein* seemed to German nationalists further proof that it was her destiny to lead Germany. Without actually willing it, the Hohenzollern monarchy had taken the first step toward national unity.

The Possibility of National Revolution During the period 1750 to 1830, Germany experienced an intellectual revival which gave a richer cultural content to the German nation. So great was the achievement of these years that the period has been called the "Augustan age of German culture." While the movement received some impetus from the Enlightenment, it soon revolted against the artificial standards of French classicism. Under the influence of Herder, Germany's poets and dramatists turned to their native Germany, to its folklore, history, and traditions for their literary themes and forms of expression. Through the achievements of Immanuel Kant (1724–1804), Georg W. F. Hegel (1770–1831), and others, German philosophy became the most influential in Europe.

This great cultural achievement made educated Germans increasingly aware of their national heritage and laid the groundwork for the future growth of German nationalism. Yet the German intellectuals themselves were more cosmopolitan than national in viewpoint. Most pictured themselves as citizens of the world rather than as Germans and thought of their views as universal rather than national. They were concerned only secondarily with political matters. While most were of burgher origin, they were not the intellectual vanguard of a power-hungry middle class. Until the 1840's, the

Festival at the Wartburg in 1817. Here the Burschenschaften celebrated the 300th anniversary of Luther's revolt against the Catholic Church by calling for national unity and freedom. They also burned reactionary books—an ominous precedent. (Archiv Gerstenberg.)

German middle class was too weakly developed to assume, or even to aspire to leadership in Germany.

During 1812–1815, the Prussian government sought to whip up German national sentiment as a political and military weapon against France. But the response was limited. German society had not yet reached a level of development that could make possible spontaneous popular movements. For the same reason liberal reform did not make its first appearance in Germany on the crest of a popular revolution, but was either imposed from without by the conquering French or from above by native governments.

The liberal and national movements that emerged after 1815 were limited in the beginning to professors and students. The dual issues of freedom and unity, which the recent wars had raised, continued to be discussed and debated within the universities. Among the students, this agitation led to the formation of a new kind of student club (*Burschenschaft*). The members disdained the carousing and duelling characteristic of the older student fraternities; their motives were political rather than social. At the University of Giessen, the *Burschenschaft* came under the leadership of Karl Follen, a radical revolutionary who advocated a German republic based on popular sovereignty. In 1819, a fanatical follower of Follen, Karl Sand, murdered August von Kotzebue, a conservative writer and Russian agent.

The Karlsbad Decrees The subversive agitation of the *Burschenschaften*, climaxed by the assassination of Kotzebue, aroused the German governments to action. Under the leadership of Metternich and Frederick William III they issued the famous Karlsbad Decrees which prohibited the *Burschenschaften*; introduced a severe censorship of the press; and placed the universities, their faculties, and students under close supervision and control. Through the Karlsbad Decrees, which were accepted by the confederate Diet in Frankfurt, the German Confederation became an instrument of reaction. Projected constitutions, promised in Article 13 of the treaty of 1815, were abandoned. In the Final Act of the Congress of Vienna, signed in 1820, the confederation was given the power of "execution" against any member state that might surrender to subversive doctrines.

The success of the Karlsbad Decrees in suppressing radical agitation shows again the weakness of the liberal-national movement in Germany. Although the *Burschenschaften* lingered on into the 1830's, their members were never able to agree on a single program, much less a course of action. Radical liberalism was represented after 1820 by a group of writers known as the "Young Germans," of whom Ludwig Börne and Heinrich Heine, Germany's greatest lyric poet, were the most important representatives. After 1830, there appeared the "Young Hegelians," the left-wing disciples of Hegel who protested against the religious and intellectual attitudes of the age. Most were philosophical rather than revolutionary radicals; they rebelled against established ideas rather than against established institutions. Those who rebelled against both differed in their objectives; Arnold Ruge favored a democratic republic, while Karl Marx was a convert to socialism. Although

DER DENKER=CLUB
Auch eine neue-deutsche Gesellschaft

the Young Germans and Young Hegelians were significant for their literary and philosophical achievements, they too were isolated intellectuals without a great popular following. Many, like Heine and Marx, were driven into exile.

The Revolution of 1830 and Its Aftermath   The July revolution in Paris echoed through Germany. Yet Metternich's judgment that the "dam has been broken in Europe" was but partly justified. Neither Austria nor Prussia was affected and, there was no revolutionary attempt to unify Germany. Only one minor state, Brunswick, experienced a genuine revolution; the reigning duke abdicated and his heir granted a constitution. In Saxony, Hanover, and Electoral Hesse, there were public demonstrations which resulted in the granting of constitutions. But none of these constitutions conceded the principle of popular sovereignty. They were based on the familiar system of mixed powers.

Despite its limited effect, the Revolution of 1830 aroused a wider circle of the German population to the issues of unity and freedom. During the 1830's and 1840's, the liberal and national movement gained nourishment from the growth of commerce and industry, the expansion of capitalism, and the development of the middle class. The confusion in weights, measures, currency, and commercial law which was the consequence of political disunion was increasingly galling to the emerging groups of merchants, bankers, and industrialists. Self-interest made common cause with German national sentiment. But these groups were also easily influenced by liberal professors, who maintained that autocratic governments should be limited by constitutions and that well-to-do bourgeois should have the right through elected parliaments to make their interests known in the legislative process.

Liberalism and nationalism seemed to be inseparable, mutually reinforcing concepts. Despite their other differences, moderate and radical liberals appeared to be united in demanding the unification of the German nation. Yet there was a significant difference in emphasis. While the moderates wished Germany to be "first united and then free," the radicals maintained that freedom was the prerequisite of unity.

AUSTRIA IN THE AGE OF METTERNICH

Of all the major dynasties in Europe, that of the Habsburgs was the least successful in building a sense of unity among its subject peoples. Having gotten off to a late start in the eighteenth century, the Hapsburgs had had less time than others to erase local traditions of autonomy and independence. In western Europe, royal governments carried out their unifying function at a time when the national consciousness of the masses was only weakly developed; the Habsburg monarchy was compelled to undertake this task in the era of rapidly developing cultural nationalism.

The Habsburg monarchy also had a far greater ethnic problem than any other great European power. Within the borders of the empire lived no less than eleven peoples of differing national origin. Some (the Czechs, Slovaks, Slovenes, and Magyars) were totally contained within the empire, while others (the Germans, Poles, Ruthenians, Rumanians, Serbs, Croats, and Italians) lay astride the frontier.[2] The Germans were the leading people of the empire. The dynasty was German; German was the official language of the state administration; it was also the language of commerce. This leadership did not arise from a conscious policy of cultural imperialism; rather it was the natural consequence of the fact that the German population was economically the most advanced. Throughout the empire, towns such as Prague and Budapest were German speaking, regardless of the ethnic character of the surrounding countryside. Their commercial dominance made possible for the Germans a higher educational level and greater cultural achievement. The Austrian Germans participated in the German cultural revival of the period 1750–1830, particularly in the field of music. Haydn, Mozart, and Beethoven made their careers in Austria.

Although there was some manufacturing in Lombardy, Austria, and Bohemia by the 1840's, the economy of the empire as a whole was overwhelmingly agricultural. Hence the middle class was but thinly developed; Austrian society was dominated by a relatively small class of high nobility. The latter was an imperial class of great wealth based on large landed estates; its families had largely lost their local connections. From this favored class, the emperor drew his army officers, diplomats, ministers, and high civil servants. The petty noblemen, many of whom had little or no land, preserved their status by entering the imperial civil service. A major exception was

---

[2]For an ethnic map of the Habsburg monarchy see p. 1161.

Hungary, where the landowning Magyar gentry were the dominant social class.

The Habsburg monarchy was held together by certain centripetal forces: the dynasty, the imperial civil service, the imperial army, the Catholic Church (which embraced about 65 percent of the population), and the imperial class of high nobility. The centrifugal forces that increasingly threatened its cohesion during the nineteenth century were the growth of ethnic nationalism and the demand for territorial autonomy.

Hungary was the most pressing problem of the monarchy early in the century. The Magyar landowners had successfully resisted all efforts of the Habsburg government to abolish the Hungarian diet and the autonomous county diets (the *comitats*). As the nineteenth century progressed, the gentry discovered in Magyar nationalism a valuable force with which to reinforce and preserve the historic rights and institutions that served their interests.

Prince von Metternich in 1818. Metternich was despised by German historians who blamed him for blocking German national unity before 1848. More recently he has had a better press. He is given some credit for the fact that for a century after 1815 Europe did not experience another general war. (Bildarchiv d. Ost. Nationalbibliothek.)

Metternich The man who for four decades was to guide the destinies of the Habsburg monarchy was not an Austrian by birth. Prince Clemens von Metternich was born a "free knight" of the Holy Roman Empire. His family home was on the Rhine. Entering the Austrian foreign service in 1803, he became foreign minister in 1809 at the age of thirty-six. With great skill he maneuvered his defeated country through the difficult years of French supremacy to a commanding position in Europe after 1815. More than any other figure he epitomizes the era of the Restoration, which has often been called the "Age of Metternich."

Metternich is frequently considered to have been a black reactionary. While an aristocrat to the core, he was never a doctrinaire. He was a product of the eighteenth century, a rationalist rather than a romantic. He believed that monarchical governments based on a wealthy aristocracy offered the best guarantee of social and political stability in Europe; this was the natural order of society and government. To weaken or destroy that order would unleash again the destructive forces of democracy and nationalism that had recently brought havoc to Europe. As a student at Strassburg and Mainz, Metternich had witnessed the French Revolution and formed a life-long hatred for the doctrine of popular sovereignty. Civilization's greatest evil, he declared, was that presumption which led men to try to overthrow traditional institutions and seek to erect a new society based on abstract ideals. It was chiefly the middle class, he charged, that was infected by this "moral gangrene."

In order to prevent the spread of this disease, Metternich supported repressive government at home as well as abroad. Austria has been called the "classic example of the police state." The newspaper press and publishing industry were closely controlled. Police agents regularly steamed open, read, and resealed letters passing through the mails. Not even the correspondence of the imperial family was immune. Passports were required for those travelling from one province of the empire to another or between town and country. University professors and students were spied upon and denounced for unorthodox views. Subjects suspected of subversion were imprisoned and held without trial. Yet absolutism was tempered by inefficiency. The Austrian bureaucratic system never worked with the precision of the Prussian, much less that of the modern totalitarian state.

Francis I Metternich never identified conservatism with immobility. He was aware of the need for moderate reforms within the empire, yet he never gained as much influence in domestic as in foreign affairs. While a conscientious man devoted to the tasks of government, Emperor Francis I was also an autocrat who jealously guarded his inherited power; worse still, he also hoarded it, permitting his ministers little independent initiative in internal matters. He had neither the capacity to govern, nor the wisdom to let others govern for him. After 1826, Metternich had a strong rival in Count Kolowrat, whose achievements in balancing the budget had impressed the emperor. Kolowrat was a career bureaucrat, who strove for centralization of authority and function. The emperor's incapacity, his unwillingness to delegate power, and the rivalry between his two chief ministers prevented the pursuit of any consistent governmental policy. Except for some economic achievements, particularly in railway construction, the country stagnated. "Administration," remarked one official, "has taken the place of government."

Stagnation under Ferdinand the Simple With the death of Francis I in 1835, the situation worsened, for his successor, Ferdinand, was an epileptic simpleton. Metternich hoped now to become the sole power behind the throne. As Francis lay on his deathbed, the slippery diplomat obtained from him a testament enjoining the feebleminded Ferdinand to rely on Metternich and the Archduke Lewis, the least competent of the Habsburg princes. But Kolowrat and the Archduke John succeeded in frustrating this scheme. Imperial affairs were placed in the control of a Council of State composed of Lewis, Metternich, and Kolowrat. The result has been nicely summarized by A. J. P. Taylor: "Kolowrat and Metternich hated each other, and Lewis hated activity of any kind. There was therefore always a majority against action; the stoppage was complete. Not only had administration taken the place of government; even the administration was not working." That the system survived until 1848 was due to the sheer momentum of the bureaucratic machine and the absence of any organized opposition or critical press.

If the government was stagnant, this was not true of the population. Industrialization reached the Habsburg Empire in the 1840's. The textile industry, particularly the production of cotton goods, made great progress in the provinces of Bohemia and Lower Austria. Railway and steamboat construction spurted ahead, and rapidly growing Vienna became a center for the production of machine tools. Businessmen became more numerous, wealthy, and conscious of their lack of social status; the factory workers were concerned about rising prices, shrinking incomes, and wretched working conditions; the artisans declined in number under competition from the machine, and many became proletarianized. Yet the Austrian economy was still overwhelmingly agricultural, and the most vital question was the attitude of the peasantry. Although their situation was considerably better than it had been in the eighteenth century, the peasants in some parts of the empire were increasingly conscious of social inequities. While freed from personal bondage, they still owed their landlords certain dues and obligations including the Robot, a compulsory and unpaid labor service. The landlords retained, furthermore, some political and judicial authority over peasant tenants.

Even more ominous for the Habsburg Empire was the growth of nationalism. The educational reforms of Maria Theresa and Joseph II had significantly enlarged the number of people who could read and write. The peoples of the empire became increasingly aware of the virtues of their own language, literature, and history. This awareness was nourished by native writers, philologists, and historians. Being the most economically advanced, the Czechs, Poles, Italians, and Magyars were the first to feel the surge of national pride. This development foreshadowed the end of German cultural predominance, but its effect was soon evident in the political sphere as well. In Bohemia and Hungary, public agitation for greater rights of self-government began to grow during the 1840's, preparing the way for the explosion of 1848.

RUSSIA UNDER ALEXANDER I AND NICHOLAS I

Stretching from the Baltic Sea to the Pacific Ocean and from the Arctic Circle to the Caspian Sea, the Russian Empire was much larger than any other European state. Yet size and resources did not make Russia the dominant power in the nineteenth century that she became in the twentieth. Her population of 31,000,000 in 1800 was not much larger than that of France (27,800,000), and it was spread over a much wider area. But the chief limitation to Russian power in the nineteenth century was her economic and social backwardness. While industrialization came to Russia in the nineteenth century, it did not flourish until after 1890. Nor had Russia been greatly affected by the commercial revolution of the previous epoch. Few people lived in urban areas, and the middle class was insignificant. The country was largely rural and agrarian.

The Russian Peasant It was also largely feudal in social organization. Most of the arable land was owned by a small class of noble landlords and tilled by serfs, who formed the great majority of the Russian people. While many nobles were poor, the average landowner enjoyed a fair livelihood from the labor of 100 to 500 serfs. A few great noblemen were extremely wealthy, owning and exploiting tens of thousands of serfs. From local government to the central bureaucracy in St. Petersburg the nobility dominated the machinery of government.

The Russian peasants were the most exploited working class in Europe. Only the "state peasants" living on secularized church lands enjoyed rea-

sonably tolerable conditions. Privately owned serfs, unlike the former serfs of western Europe, could be bought and sold. Many of the infant industries of Russia were manned by serfs who were herded into the factories and mines by their noble owners. Except for capital punishment, which was denied them, the nobles had almost complete authority over their serfs: they could order them flogged, sentence them to hard labor, exile them to Siberia, and condemn them to military service for twenty-five years. The use, and threat, of such punishments was intended to keep the peasants from rebelling against economic exploitation. Peasant labor kept the nobility afloat, and peasant taxes were the principal source of state revenue. Although peasant revolts were frequent, they were local, spontaneous, and unorganized.

Thoughtful Russians of the early nineteenth century were aware of the terrible cost of serfdom for Russia. That the great bulk of the population lived in poverty, ignorance, and bondage was not only morally objectionable, it was also an almost insuperable obstacle to economic progress. And yet even those who understood this were compelled to recognize that the abolition of serfdom would mean a reversal of the recent course of Russian history. In the seventeenth and eighteenth centuries the tsars had increased their autocratic powers at the cost of the feudal nobility, but in return they had permitted the nobles to enserf the peasantry. By furthering emancipation, the state would upset this arrangement and might even jeopardize the autocratic principle. Liberation without land would create an immense agricultural proletariat which might easily get out of hand. But if the freed peasants were granted land, the nobility would suffer and conceivably turn against the monarchy. This was the dilemma that frustrated reform.

The Power of the Tsar The tsar was absolute, holding his position by divine right and responsible to God alone for his conduct of public affairs. The autocratic tradition of the Russian monarchy was Byzantine rather than western, and the personal authority of the monarch over his subjects was correspondingly greater. The tsar was pope as well as emperor, for the Russian Orthodox Church was controlled by the Holy Synod appointed by him and headed by one of his functionaries, the Over Procurator. There was no cabinet in the western sense, only ministers individually responsible to the emperor, who was his own prime minister. In this he was assisted by his "personal chancery." The effectiveness of the system depended upon the wisdom and efficiency of the tsar himself. Beneath him, the state civil service was notoriously inefficient and venal. It moved laboriously if at all, ground out endless reports, and buried itself under a mountain of paper. Poorly paid, the bureaucrat had to depend upon graft to eke out his livelihood.

The Liberal Alexander The man who guided Russia's destiny during the turbulent years 1800 to 1825 was, as has been noted, an ambivalent personality, capable of espousing liberal causes, even while pursuing a reactionary course. In France, he advised Louis XVIII to grant the Charter of 1814; in Poland, he himself granted a constitution which created a Polish diet with autonomous powers. Yet his promise of "free institutions" for the rest of the empire never materialized, for Alexander was an autocrat whose liberal deeds were acts of imperial benevolence rather than a genuine recognition of popular rights. He had no intention of fostering popular movements and was easily disillusioned when they appeared in Europe.

Alexander's accession in 1801, after the murder of the hated Emperor Paul, was greeted enthusiastically by most Russians. The nobility expected the restoration of those privileges curtailed during the tyrannical regime of his predecessor, and this was in fact done. But the small group of educated people who were aware of Russia's social and political backwardness also expected reforms, and they too were gratified by the new tsar's first decrees. He declared a general amnesty, liberalized trade, lifted prohibitions against travel abroad, mitigated the severity of the penal code, and abolished the security police. In 1802, two laws reorganized the central administration of the empire and sought to revitalize the senate, an appointive body created by Peter the Great. In 1804, the new ministry of education was responsible for a statute providing for a system of public education open to all regardless of social class; but primary schools remained scarce and only the sons of the well-to-do reached the universities.

The Russian defeats by Napoleon in 1805–1807 aroused enough discontent in Russia to cause Alexander to consider once more the problem of reform. He found in Michael Speransky (1772–1839) an able collaborator. The son of a village priest, Speransky had risen through brilliance, personality, and aristocratic patronage to a high position in the civil service, a most unusual career in tsarist Russia. In 1809, Speransky completed, at Alexander's request, a proposal for constitutional reform, whose principal feature

In his *The Rare and Extraordinary History of Holy Russia* Gustave Doré satirized Russian social conditions, including this drawing of nobles wagering their serfs, having already gambled away money and land. (Culver Pictures.)

was a pyramid of elective dumas ascending from the lowest governmental unit, the canton, to a State Duma in St. Petersburg. While Alexander was highly impressed with Speransky's plan, the only aspect of it that he put into effect was the most innocuous: the creation of a State Council—a body of ministers and high officials chosen by the emperor—whose function was to draft legislation and advise the crown. But even this mild innovation was too much for the nobles, who were further antagonized by Speransky's financial reforms and his introduction of civil service examinations. Speransky was probably the ablest mind to serve the Russian state in the nineteenth century, but his rise from nowhere to the status of an intimate adviser to the tsar had created jealousies and antagonisms at court and in the government. In 1812, his enemies obtained his dismissal.

Speransky's fall shows what obstacles lay in the way of reform. In contrast to the English gentry, the Russian nobility clung to every shred of power and privilege. As the career of Peter the Great had demonstrated, the autocratic system of government offered great opportunity for change to a resolute monarch. But the latter-day Romanovs lacked either the wisdom, interest, or firmness of will to do what had to be done.

The Conservative Alexander   Although he continued to espouse liberal causes abroad and in Poland until 1820, Alexander ceased to toy with the idea of reform within Russia after Speransky's dismissal. This was the time of his religious conversion. Alexander became convinced that true government must be based upon religion and that he had a special mission to demonstrate the validity of this assumption. To him this meant reactionary, rather than progressive, government, for liberalism was the product of the age of reason and was identified with skepticism and anticlericalism.

Speransky, the civil servant, was soon replaced in the emperor's favor by Count Alexis Arakcheev, an artillery officer. The career of Arakcheev had begun under the Emperor Paul and had carried him to the office of minister of war by 1810. He was an efficient administrator, but thoroughly reactionary in his political views and a martinet in his insistence upon military order and precision. There was also a streak of cruelty in the man, which bordered on the sadistic; the murder of his mistress by outraged serfs on his estate, Gruzino, in 1825 was followed by shocking reprisals. After 1815, he assumed the position of an unofficial prime minister of the cabinet, through whom the other ministers transmitted their proposals to the tsar. Nevertheless, he did not act independently and endeared himself to Alexander by his readiness to carry out his master's projects, the most significant of which was the creation of military colonies.

His experiences in the Napoleonic wars had convinced Alexander that Russia must maintain an army at least equal to those of Austria and Prussia combined, if she were to play an effective role in European politics. But this was made difficult by the perennial weakness of the imperial treasury. He therefore conceived the idea of founding self-supporting military colonies in the frontier regions. Regiments of the army were quartered in these regions from which all inhabitants except serfs had been removed. Soldiers and serfs were fused into soldier-serfs who worked the land, received military training, and lived under military discipline. Their sons were educated in military schools and automatically inducted into the regional military units at the age of eighteen. By 1825, these military colonies included about 375,000 men. In his strange way Alexander thought of this system not only as an act of expediency which would relieve the treasury, but as a way of improving the lot of both soldier and peasant; the former would have a healthier existence on the land and a more settled family life, while the latter would receive the benefits of military discipline. But the system was harsh and arbitrary for those who were consigned to this kind of life by imperial order. Furthermore, the colonies did not prove to be self-sustaining and were an additional drain on the treasury. Under Alexander's successors the system was gradually abandoned.

The retreat from liberalism was also evident in the fields of education and censorship. Acting on the premise that the dominant rationalist influence in the schools and universities was the source of godlessness, liberalism, and revolution, the authorities hunted out and dismissed the more enlightened teachers and professors. The educational system became an instrument for indoctrination in the conservative creed and the orthodox faith. Editors, writers, and publishers received similar treatment. Censorship, relaxed in the first years of Alexander's reign, was restored to its former stringency. The security police (revived in 1807) and the Ministry of Education competed in applying restrictions and ferreting out violators. The repression was severe, but, even worse, it was arbitrary and capricious. It was impossible to predict what would bring down the heavy hand of official displeasure.

By increasing the number of schools and universities, the regime promoted the development of a class of educated people known in Russia as the "intelligentsia." Yet this was a class which the regime basically did not trust and which, through the denial of academic freedom and freedom of the press, it progressively alienated. From the intelligentsia were ultimately to come the ideas and the leadership of the revolutionary movements that doomed the monarchy and aristocratic order.

The Decembrist Insurrection   Just such a group within the officer corps undertook the first organized attack upon the autocratic system immediately after the death of Alexander in 1825. The tsar's support of constitutionalism abroad, the activities of his reform committee, and the work of Speransky had stimulated discussion of Russia's ills among a thoughtful minority of the nobility. This was particularly true of aristocrats from impoverished families who had kept their status by becoming army officers and who, having no estates, were not wedded to the institution of serfdom by self-interest. Many of these noblemen had served abroad during the Napoleonic wars and had been infected with the ideals of liberalism and democracy. They were also patriots who were deeply distressed by the backwardness of their own country. At home they formed discussion groups which grew into conspiratorial secret societies. After 1820, the two most important of these clubs were the Northern Society at St. Petersburg and the Southern Society in the Ukraine.

In November 1825, Alexander died suddenly and, since none of his children was by the empress, there was confusion about the succession. Before his death, Alexander had designated his youngest brother, the Grand Duke Nicholas, as his heir rather than the older Grand Duke Constantine, for the latter had a wife of nonroyal blood. But this arrangement was unknown to the public and Nicholas, fearing to appear a usurper, waited for Constantine to renounce the throne. For three weeks the latter, who was in Warsaw far away from the capitol, failed to act. During this interregnum the conspirators struck.

The rebellion was predestined to failure, as the most realistic participants realized, including the leader, Prince Trubetskoy. The plotters were too few in number and, being junior officers, they could not command the soldiers to act, but only persuade them. They were, furthermore, the victims of their own limitations. As aristocrats they distrusted the masses and did not appeal to them. What they planned was a military coup, not a revolution. In the end they failed because they could not bring enough of the army into the revolt and they had no active popular support.

The tragedy began on December 14 in St. Petersburg when 700 men of the Moscow regiment refused to take the oath to Nicholas and marched shouting to the Senate Square, where their ranks soon swelled to 3,000 men and 30 officers. Deserted by Trubetskoy and his staff, they found a commander in Prince Obolensky, who waited aimlessly while Nicholas marshaled his loyal troops for the attack. Toward evening of that wintry day, Nicholas, having failed with a cavalry assault, unlimbered his artillery. On the third volley, the rebels broke and ran, leaving seventy to eighty corpses in the square. The premature arrest of its leaders apparently prevented the Southern Society from acting until early January when a small band of insurgents met a similar fate.

Those rebels who escaped capture hastened to give themselves up and there followed an unedifying spectacle of repentance, confession, and self-condemnation. Five men were hanged, and over one hundred sentenced to hard labor or deportation to Siberia. Speransky, who had learned his lesson well, was one of the judges.

Nicholas I   In contrast to Alexander, Nicholas I was a completely integrated personality. He was an autocrat to the core and firmly believed in the doctrine of divine right. While he had received a good general education (including the arts, ancient and modern languages, law, jurisprudence, public finance, and political economy), it was the military life that aroused his greatest enthusiasm. Political theories were alien to his mind, and everything "abstract" aroused his contempt. He regarded the state and its bureaucracy as an army to be drilled, disciplined, and organized according to a hierarchical system of command ascending to himself. But instead of becoming a well-ordered machine, the bureaucracy remained unwieldy, corrupt, backward, inefficient, and strangulating.

Tsar Nicholas I (1825–1855). Despite his oppressive government and rigid censorship, intellectual life flowered during his reign. This was the age of Pushkin, Lermontov, and Gogol. (The New York Public Library, Astor, Lenox, and Tilden Foundations.)

Like Alexander, Nicholas was a handsome man, but he lacked his brother's charm. His manner was cold, displaying firmness of will mixed with cruelty. Yet he was driven by a strong sense of duty; no other Romanov of the century took such an active part in the daily administration of the state. Insofar as he was able to conceive it, he probably wished the best for Russia. He participated personally in the investigation of the Decembrists in order to determine the causes of their unrest and read closely the letters they wrote to him from prison and exile. Yet he was deeply shocked by the fact that the army, particularly the elite guard regiment, could harbor treason. His fears of subversion were further aroused by the western European revolution of 1830 and the Polish revolt of 1831. Every loosening of the social fabric through basic reforms, he concluded, would only open the way to greater ills. Hence he opposed the abolition of serfdom, although he knew it to be a "flagrant evil."

Characteristic of the regime was the notorious Third Section of the Imperial Chancery, a new and more efficient police organization, which symbolically was created on the tsar's birthday, June 25, 1826. Under the leadership of Count Alexander Benckendorff, this new body was given a variety of functions, such as the hunting down of grafters, counterfeiters, religious dissenters, political malcontents, secret societies, and any happenings of which the government was suspicious. The Third Section operated on two levels: the visible and invisible. Its visible arm was the gendarmery, a uniformed force organized into five districts (later eight) covering the whole of Russia. But Benckendorff also controlled a network of secret agents whose function it was to pry into the lives and thoughts of the citizenry in all strata of society. Most sinister of all, Benckendorff and his successor, Count Alexis

Orlov, attained an influence throughout the government almost equivalent to that of a prime minister. The Third Section, moreover, often assumed judicial as well as police functions; it investigated, arrested, tried, and condemned.

In their quest for social control Nicholas and his minister of education naturally turned their attention to the schools. The tsar scrapped Alexander's plan for a one-class system of public education; under a new statute, only the children of nobles and officials could enter the secondary schools. Here the curriculum stressed classical languages, which were believed to have a disciplinary value. The five universities were ultimately limited to three hundred students each. The students were drawn from the upper classes and were to be trained for the state service. Such dangerous subjects as history, philosophy, and constitutional law were dropped from the curriculum. Through censorship of the press and lecture platform, limitations on foreign travel, and the prohibition of foreign literature believed subversive, the government sought to insulate Russia against the circulation of dangerous ideas. In the end, all it succeeded in doing was to alienate the educated class of "intelligentsia," which could have been, as in Germany, a source of support for the regime, but which was eventually to be its nemesis. By identifying itself with ignorance, the tsarist government drove the educated into subversion.

Yet some efforts at reform were undertaken during the reign of Nicholas. Under the leadership of Speransky, the Second Section of the Imperial Chancery succeeded in codifying Russian law, a major achievement that was to last until 1917. In Count Yegor Kankrin, Nicholas inherited from Alexander an able minister of finance who temporarily stabilized the currency and halted inflation; but his cautious policies were abandoned with his dismissal in 1844; and once again the printing press began to turn out inconvertible paper notes. Through another minister, Count Paul Kisilev, Nicholas tried, on the imperial domains, to inaugurate a social reform he hoped would be copied by the private landowners. Attempts were made to equalize the land holdings of the state peasants, to make their taxes more equitable, to improve agricultural techniques, and to expand the school system and the facilities for medical care. While inimical to serfdom, Kisilev was an ingrained bureaucrat who frustrated his own sincere efforts with the throttling hand of bureaucratic control. Furthermore, the squires did not copy the government's reform to any degree, and peasant unrest continued to grow.

The Rise of the Intelligentsia   The reign of Nicholas is notable for the beginning of an intellectual conflict in Russia that was to last for the rest of the tsarist regime. The government made an effort to attract the intelligentsia through a doctrine known as "Official Nationality." "Orthodoxy, autocracy, and nationality" formed the trinity of this creed, which maintained that tsarist absolutism conformed to the Russian national tradition and was sanctified by the Orthodox faith. While Official Nationality did find influ-

Alexander Herzen (1812–1870). Herzen left Russia in 1847 and lived out his life in exile in Paris and London. While believing in political liberty, he was more inclined toward associate socialism than laissez-faire. (The Bettmann Archive.)

ential proponents among writers and professors sympathetic to the regime, it had little appeal for the intelligentsia as a whole.

The dominant schools of Russian thought during this era were those of the Slavophiles and the westernizers. The former taught the superiority of Russia's Slavic culture and its historical mission to the world. Its adherents preached an emotional doctrine of love, harmony, and cooperation, which they believed to be native to Russia and the Orthodox faith, in contrast to the rationalism and authoritarianism of western culture and its principal religions—Catholicism and Protestantism. While they justified tsarist authoritarianism on practical grounds, the Slavophiles advocated the abolition of serfdom and other reforms. Their opponents praised the process of "westernization" begun by Peter the Great. They took a positive view of western culture, recognizing its political and social achievements and advocating the further integration of Russia into European civilization.

Out of the camp of the westernizers came most of the revolutionaries who were to trouble the reign of Alexander II. The signs of their alienation were already evident in Nicholas' time. Discouraged from political action by the failure of the Decembrists, many westernizers like Nicholas Stankevich and his circle devoted themselves to philosophical radicalism. Vissarion Belinsky found in literary criticism a vehicle for social and political protest. But the most significant of the westernizers was Alexander Herzen, sometimes regarded as the father of Russian liberalism. Because of the lagging economic development of the country the westernizers were an isolated group, deeply disturbed by the social and political conditions of their country, yet without the popular backing necessary for a successful effort to change them.

FURTHER READING The best general history of Germany is H. Holborn, *History of Modern Germany,* 3 vols. (1959–1968), whose second volume deals with the period 1648–1840. Other works dealing with the nineteenth century are A. Ramm, *Germany, 1789–1914* (1967); W. Carr, *A History of Germany, 1815–1945* (1969); G. Mann, * *History of Germany Since 1789* (1968), and W. M. Simon, *Germany: A Brief History* (1966). H. von Treitschke, *History of Germany in the Nineteenth Century,* 7 vols. (1915–1919), is a translation of a famous work which, despite the title, does not go beyond 1847. For a valuable study of the political influence of the generals see G. Craig, *The Politics of the Prussian Army, 1640–1945* (1955). Good monographs on special topics are W. Simon, *The Failure of the Prussian Reform Movement, 1807–1819* (1955); W. O. Henderson, *The Zollverein* (1939); T. Hamerow, *Restoration, Revolution, Reaction* (1958); and R. H. Thomas, *Liberalism, Nationalism, and the German Intellectuals, 1822–1847* (1952).

*Books available in paperback edition are marked with an asterisk.

On Austria, the best general history in English is C. A. Macartney, *The Habsburg Empire, 1790–1918* (1969). A. J. P. Taylor, *The Habsburg Monarchy, 1815–1918* (2nd ed., 1948), contains interesting, though tendentious judgments. Useful for its analysis of the nationalities problem is O. Jaszi, *The Dissolution of the Habsburg Monarchy* (1929). Biographies of Metternich have been attempted with limited success by A. Cecil (1933), R. du Coudray (1935), and C. de Grunwald (1953). Other biographies of important figures are P. R. Sweet, *Friedrich von Gentz* (1941); G. Mann, *Secretary of Europe, The Life of Friedrich Gentz* (1946). A study of social relationships is J. Blum, *Noble Landowners and Agriculture in Austria, 1815–1848* (1948).

One-volume histories of Russia are countless. Perhaps the most successful are those by N. Riasanovsky (1963); B. Pares (rev. ed., 1955); and S. Harcave (1952). The second volume of M. T. Florinsky, *Russia, A History and an Interpretation*, 2 vols. (1953), is valuable for the nineteenth century. A Russian classic in translation is V. Kliuchevskii, *A History of Russia*, 4 vols. (1911–1926). The most important social problem of the tsarist regime is dealt with in J. Blum, *Lord and Peasant in Russia* (1961); and G. T. Robinson, *Rural Russia under the Old Regime* (1932). A classic study of Russian intellectual history is that of the Czech statesman T. G. Masaryk, *The Spirit of Russia.* Important monographs have been written by N. Riasanovsky on *Russia and the West in the Teaching of the Slavophiles* (1952), and *Nicholas I and Official Nationality in Russia, 1825–1881* (1959). Other works of merit are A. G. Mazour, *The First Russian Revolution, 1825* (1937); and M. Raeff, *Michael Speransky* (1957).

5 The Revolutions of 1848

In February and March 1848, a tidal wave of revolution, rising in France, raced across the continent of Europe. Various explanations have been given by historians for this dramatic event. Some see it as a "revolution of the intellectuals," produced by the rise of liberal and national idealism. Others explain it in terms of the progress of economic development and the emergence of new social classes eager to advance their interests.

The revolutionary surge did not affect all areas alike. We have seen that the same circumstances did not prevail throughout the continent. Western, central, and eastern Europe were in differing stages of economic and social development. Furthermore, the political and ethnic structures of the areas were dissimilar. Two major European states, Great Britain and Russia, escaped revolution—for opposite reasons. Although Britain was in the midst of an economic and social revolution, she avoided the political one by acting in time to accommodate the interests of the new social classes. In Russia, still largely unaffected by economic and social change, no new social groups had yet arisen capable of challenging the immobile autocracy of the Romanovs. Russia's revolutionary crises lay in the future.

Where revolution did occur, there is no evidence of a widespread conspiracy. That the uprisings were spontaneous shows the depth of popular dissatisfaction. Businessmen of growing wealth wanted to share in political power; artisans were restive because of the increasing competition of machine production and the decay of guild protectionism; workers were critical of the conditions under which they lived and worked; in central Europe peasants yearned for the abolition of the remnants of feudalism; members of the professional groups—lawyers, journalists, professors, students, and intellectuals—were eager to put abstract political views into practice; nationalists wanted either national unity or national autonomy for their ethnic groups.

The ground for revolution was prepared by a depression. It began in 1845 with the failure of the potato crop through blight and continued in 1846 with the failure of both the potato and grain crops. Famine, disease, and death stalked the rural areas of Europe in a broad path from Ireland to the Danube. In the cities, the cost of food rose sharply; the market for manufactured goods dried up; production declined and unemployment increased. Simultaneously there was a decline in new investments following a recent railway construction boom. Hunger riots occurred. In many cities, at least one-third of the inhabitants were destitute; crime and prostitution flourished; hundreds of thousands emigrated.

The bottom of the depression was reached in the summer of 1847; thereafter economic conditions began to improve. By February and March 1848, when the revolution came, the cost of food was nearly back to normal, and industrial production was again on the rise. Nevertheless, the misery of the preceding years had created a mood of unrest and protest, which was easily converted into revolt. The effect of economic recovery was not to prevent revolution, but progressively to weaken it, once it had occurred.

THE REVOLUTION OF 1848 IN FRANCE

The revolution of 1848 began in Paris on February 23 and spread like a chain reaction to Austria, Italy, and Germany. In all probability, the Paris insurrection could have been averted by shrewder actions on the part of Louis Philippe and his ministers. Although there was considerable popular discontent, the opposition leaders aimed at the fall of the cabinet or the abdication of the king, but not at the overthrow of the monarchy.

The Revolution of Contempt Forbidden the right to hold public meetings, the opposition deputies resorted, in July 1847, to the strategy of the political banquet. As many as 3,000 guests dined at 500 tables at Macon on July 18 and, with 3,000 others looking on from bleachers, listened to the poet and historian Lamartine denounce the regime and even predict a "revolution of contempt." Thereafter, political banquets were held throughout France in almost every town. The banqueteers were generally well-dressed bourgeois; their motto was "reform," not "revolution." By January 1848 the campaign of food, wine, and politics had lost momentum, for the government simply ignored it. Then suddenly the situation changed dramatically when a group of radicals announced its intention to hold a banquet in a volatile working-class district of Paris. The moderate leaders of the banquet movement were embarrassed, for they feared a rowdy gathering and wanted no part of it. They wrested control of the affair from the radicals and were busy converting it into a harmless farce, when the minister Guizot blundered by forbidding it.

For three days, Paris seethed with unrest. On February 22, the date on which the banquet was to have been held, crowds demonstrated in the streets and were dispersed by the police. Next day, barricades appeared, and the National Guard was called out by the government. But nine of the twelve battalions of this citizens' militia refused to obey.

Louis Philippe, who had previously scoffed at this "tempest in a teapot," now yielded by dismissing the unpopular Guizot. That ought to have sufficed, but the radicals and the hungry were unappeased by the prospect

François Guizot (1787–1874). Guizot was a professor of history who first became involved in politics as a parliamentary deputy and opponent of Charles X. After the revolution of 1848 he returned to his profession and became one of France's most eminent historians. (Brown Brothers.)

of a liberal cabinet. In the evening, a column of demonstrators came face to face with a line of troops in the Boulevard des Capucines. A musket went off, probably by accident, and the soldiers fired into the crowd. Fifty-two corpses littered the bloody pavement. They were taken up by the mob and borne through the city in a grisly torchlight parade. Next day the loyal troops could make no progress along the barricaded streets. Still, Paris was not France, and the king might well have summoned his regiments from the provinces and reconquered the city. But he lacked nerve and zest for bloodshed. Instead he abdicated and took the long road to exile which the Bourbons had so often trod.

The Emergence of Class Conflict   The abdication of Louis Philippe left France with two choices: a regency or a republic. While the Chamber of Deputies debated the former possibility, it was invaded by a mob demanding a provisional government that would prepare the way for a republic. The deputies yielded. The provisional government that took office was composed of two republican factions with different programs, fostered by two Parisian newspapers, *Le National* and *La Réforme.* The former advocated a moderate bourgeois government; the latter desired a program of social reform. The executive included men of various shades of republican opinion, from Alexandre Marie on the right to the Jacobin Ledru Rollin and the socialist Louis Blanc on the left. Lamartine was foreign minister, and it was his oratorical ability that tided the new government over its first internal crises.

In the beginning, there was no obvious cleavage within the cabinet on the social issue. The Right as well as the Left voted for the decrees of February 25, 26, and 28, which guaranteed a minimum income for labor, created "national workshops" for the unemployed, and established the Luxembourg Commission under Blanc to recommend labor legislation. Nevertheless, the commission ended in complete frustration, and the workshop scheme, administered by Marie as Minister of Public Works, was a far cry from the system of cooperative factories envisioned by Blanc. It became mere unemployment relief, the men spending their time in leaf raking and ditch digging. In April, the social radicals, who lacked leadership and a cohesive program, were badly beaten in a general election conducted under universal suffrage. The peasants and villagers, who still composed the great majority of the French population, voted mostly for local notables, who were usually moderates. Of 900 seats, 500 were won by moderate republicans, 300 by monarchists, and only 80 by the radicals. Even in Paris, the radicals, including Louis Blanc, came in well behind the moderate candidates.

On May 15, a largely proletarian throng sought to overthrow the government, but it was unorganized and unarmed, and was dispersed by the National Guard. By-elections on June 5–6 increased the number of Monarchists and Bonapartists in the chamber. Meanwhile, depression and revolution had combined to create a major financial crisis in France. The treasury was empty and unemployment relief expensive; between March

Workers Invading the French National Assembly in Paris on May 15, 1848. Their banners identify the radical clubs that participated and some of their causes. This was one of the episodes that weakened the republic by arousing fears of class conflict and socialist subversion.

and June, the number on relief had grown from about 6,100 to over 100,000. On June 21st, the government announced the closing of the workshops.

The result was another insurrection, beginning on June 23, 1848. This time, the barricades were manned mostly by proletarians, including women and children. For four days, there was bitter fighting, until the forces of the government, reinforced from the provinces, prevailed. Although workers and peasants also fought in the loyalist ranks, the struggle had the character of a class conflict between the poor and the well-to-do, which accentuated its ferocity. At least 1,500 revolutionaries were slain; 12,000 were arrested, many of whom were transported to Algeria. This fateful clash left behind a legacy of bitterness among the urban workingmen and of fear among the bourgeois and aristocrats, which was soon to destroy the republic.

France Moves to the Right As a result of the "June days," as the insurrection was called, the executive commission was replaced by a military dictatorship under General Cavaignac, who had commanded the loyalist forces. Cavaignac was an earnest republican who had no intention of perpetuating his power. But he was also determined to preserve order, and his political orientation was toward the right. He imposed censorship of the press, placed the radical clubs under surveillance, and purged the National Guard of rebels and the government of radicals. An attempt was made to appease the unemployed by a dole, public works, and the stimulation of private construction.

Meanwhile, the assembly hurriedly drafted a republican constitution designed to perpetuate the power of the moderates. It provided for a president elected by universal suffrage for a term of four years, who appointed the ministers. The unicameral legislature of 750 seats was elected by universal suffrage for three years and was indissoluble. No practicable way was provided to amend the constitution, and the document was not submitted to the public for approval. Furthermore, the deputies did not seek a renewal of their mandates from the electorate when the constitution went into effect. They continued in office and only the president was chosen in the first election of the Second Republic.

This unwillingness of the moderate republican majority to face the voters was not without cause. The June days had shifted public sympathy away from the republican system, which appeared synonymous with chaos. Despite his republicanism, Cavaignac was cordially hated by the radicals and the lower classes for the brutality with which the insurrection had been suppressed. In December, the moderate republicans, who were his supporters, discovered what a grievous mistake they had made in submitting the choice of a president to the vote of the people rather than to the vote of the chamber. Of the seven million votes cast, only 1,500,000 went to Cavaignac, 370,000 to Ledru-Rollin, and a mere 17,000 to Lamartine. To the astonishment of France, the winner was Louis Napoleon with 5,500,000 votes. France had chosen a Bonaparte to head a republic!

THE REVOLUTION OF 1848 IN GERMANY

In Germany, the economic crisis was particularly acute, and the rising current of dissatisfaction was very evident during 1847. A "United Diet" summoned in Prussia by King Frederick William IV (1840–1861) produced a majority opposed to the government despite the fact that most of its representatives were noblemen. After seven weeks of fruitless debate, Frederick William, shocked and angered by this outcome, sent the deputies home. In southern Germany, liberals agitated for national unity under a constitution. Yet there would probably have been no revolution in Germany had there not been one in Paris.

The "March Days" In February 1848, the news of the battles at the barricades and the flight of Louis Philippe created great excitement throughout Germany. Peasant insurrections and artisan uprisings occurred; the liberals demonstrated and petitioned. Beginning with Baden, the rulers of the smaller states replaced their conservative ministers with members of the liberal opposition. In the Habsburg monarchy, demonstrations in Budapest, Prague, and Vienna led to the dismissal of Metternich on March 13.

At Berlin, Frederick William IV strove to avert disaster by recalling the United Diet on March 14. The news from Vienna impelled him to dismiss his conservative ministers, promise internal reforms, and call for the reorganization of the German Confederation. But he was already too late. On March 18, a great throng massed in front of the royal palace in Berlin. As the soldiers attempted to clear the square, two shots were fired. Angered by what they believed was an unprovoked assault, the mob put up barricades and battled fiercely against the attacking troops. On March 19, the king disengaged his forces and withdrew them from the city. Owing to a mistaken order, even the palace was denuded of protection, and the king became a

Attack of the Revolutionaries on the Berlin Arsenal on the Night of March 18, 1848. As in Paris, no one knows who fired the shots that ignited the uprising in Berlin. From the arsenal the mob acquired weapons with which to fight the troops.

virtual prisoner of the rebels. He humbled himself by donning the revolutionary tricolor, and by reviewing a funeral parade for the fallen. A liberal cabinet took office; and, in May, a Parliament chosen by universal manhood suffrage assembled in Berlin to draft a constitution for Prussia.

Meanwhile, the first steps had been taken to unite Germany under a single government. On March 30, the Diet of the German Confederation in Frankfurt voted for the election of a National Parliament; on the following day about 500 delegates of the liberal-national movement convened in the same city. This "preparliament," as it has been called, prepared the way for the election of a National Parliament, which assembled in St. Paul's Church in Frankfurt on May 18, to draft the constitution for a united Germany.

On the surface, Germany appeared in a matter of only three months to have swept away the settlement of 1815 and to have removed the obstacles standing in the way of national unity under a liberal constitution.

The Failure of the Prussian Revolution   The liberals who were boosted into power in Berlin by the revolutionary uprising of March were ill-equipped to lead a revolution. Socially they belonged to the upper bourgeoisie and the enlightened minority of the aristocratic class; politically they belonged to the category of the moderate liberals. Their social origin made them suspicious of the lower classes and reluctant to depend upon them for support against the monarchy and conservative nobility. While they desired to limit monarchical power and to deprive the nobility of some of its privileges, they had no intention of destroying either. They had never advocated or wanted revolution and feared the social chaos that might result from it.

During their first weeks in power, the liberal ministers witnessed further signs of unrest among the urban and rural masses. Distressed artisans invaded factories to destroy the machines that threatened their livelihoods; teamsters tore up railway tracks and wrecked locomotives; boatmen attacked the new steamboats on the Rhine with muskets and cannon. Even factory workers, who were more secure, struck for higher pay and an end to guild restrictions. In some areas, peasants plundered the castles of wealthy noblemen, rioted against forest and hunting privileges of the aristocracy, and demanded the abolition of manorialism. What the rioters and demonstrators wanted was not the constitution so dear to the hearts of the liberals, but the redress of concrete social grievances.

These pressures increased the dependence of the cabinet upon the monarchy. Fearful of further social disorder, the ministers hesitated to tamper with the king's power over the armed forces. In the end, this proved to be their undoing. Throughout the revolution, the army remained under royal control and was commanded by noble officers of unquestioned loyalty to the old regime. Frederick William IV was surrounded by a "camarilla" of reactionary noblemen (including the youthful Otto von Bismarck) who urged him to use the army to overthrow the liberal cabinet and Parliament. He procrastinated until the fall of 1848 when, angered by Parliament's attack on the theory of divine right, he finally acted. On November 9, the king appointed a conservative cabinet under Count Brandenburg and Otto von Manteuffel; and, on December 5, he dissolved the Prussian Parliament and decreed a constitution for Prussia.

The revolution was at an end in Prussia. Nothing remained of the popular excitement and enthusiasm of the preceding spring. Economic conditions had steadily improved; many social grievances had been rectified; and the ranks of those who yearned for order and stability had steadily grown. The appeal of liberal principles was far too weak to surmount these changed conditions. Hence the reactionary coup was accomplished without bloodshed.

The Failure of the Frankfurt Parliament Meanwhile, the German revolution was following a course similar to the Prussian one. The first clash between the moderate and democratic factions occurred in the preparliament of April. A group of extremists, led by Gustav von Struve and Friedrich Hecker, demanded a German republic and profit sharing for workers. But the moderate majority promptly voted down this Jacobin program, with the consequence that forty deputies withdrew and appealed to the German masses for a new popular rebellion. Only a few responded, and the uprising which occurred in Baden was quickly crushed. Nevertheless, the experience left its mark upon the moderates. Their fear of Jacobinism and the social radicalism of the lower classes increased their dependence upon the old German governments and dynasties.

Although the Frankfurt Parliament that followed was supposed to be elected by universal suffrage, various devices were used to disfranchise the lower classes which, in any case, displayed very little interest in the election. The result was that most of the elected deputies came from the middle class, particularly from the professions.

While the revolutionary ardor of the public cooled and the counter-revolution gathered strength, the Frankfurt Parliament proceeded at a measured pace to draft a German constitution. The result was a system of mixed powers, the traditional aim of moderate liberals. The draft constitution left executive authority to an emperor, while the law-making power was given to a bicameral legislature. The upper chamber represented the federal states, while the lower chamber was to be elected by universal suffrage.

In drafting the constitution, the deputies in Frankfurt were compelled to decide whether united Germany was to include or exclude Austria. The issue created two parties which cut across other political divisions in the chamber. The "Great-Germanists" wished to preserve the historic connection with Austria, while the pro-Prussian "Little-Germanists" wished to sever it. In the final vote, the latter won.

Their victory meant that the German crown was to be offered to the Hohenzollern dynasty. But Frederick William IV was not at all pleased by the offer of this "pig crown," as he contemptuously called it. His legitimist soul was repelled by the prospect of occupying a revolutionary throne "by the grace of butchers and bakers." In April 1849, he rejected the offer. The Parliament now had no other recourse than to disband. It possessed no army with which to enforce its will, and the moderate majority was unwilling to summon the people once more to the barricades. The radical minority chose to resist. There were demonstrations in Bavaria, Württemberg, and the Rhineland, but the only serious fighting occurred in Dresden and the Palatinate. In a brief campaign the rebels were crushed by the Prussian army. The German revolution was over.

THE REVOLUTION OF 1848 IN THE HABSBURG EMPIRE

In early March 1848, the news of the fall of Louis Philippe and of the demonstrations in southern Germany caused intense excitement in the Habsburg Empire. Like a shower of sparks, it ignited the many grievances that had accumulated during the reign of Kaiser Ferdinand.

The "March Days" In Hungary, the nationalist leader Louis Kossuth quickly grasped the initiative. On March 3, he demanded in a tumultuous session of the Hungarian Diet the grant of a constitution. On March 11, an assembly met in Prague to demand constitutional reform and local autonomy for Bohemia. Two days later, the revolution reached Vienna. A great throng gathered in front of the building housing the provincial Diet of Lower Austria. Kossuth's speech was read and, as radical agitators harangued the crowd, the excitement grew. Rumors of betrayal set the mob in motion and the building was stormed. Workers streamed from the suburbs, forcing the city gates. When troops were ordered to clear the streets, they were stoned by the mob and opened fire. The maddened crowd threw up barricades, and fighting began in earnest. At the imperial palace, there was panic and indecision. By evening it was apparent that Metternich had to be sacrificed. Reluctantly, the man who for more than four decades had guided the destiny of the empire wrote out his resignation and departed in the night to end his years in exile.

Metternich's fall accelerated the revolution in Hungary. Although radical students demonstrated and appealed to the peasantry with democratic doctrines, the brilliant Kossuth took charge of the revolution in the interest of the gentry. By demanding national autonomy and a constitution for Hungary, he kept the social issue in the background and made the turbulent Magyar noblemen the major force behind the Hungarian revolution. In the March Laws passed by the Hungarian Diet and accepted under duress by the crown, he achieved his aims. Henceforth, Hungary was to be linked with Austria only through a common monarch; it was to have its own government in Budapest with full control over the army, budget, and foreign relations. The feudal Diet was to be replaced by a modern Parliament (elected by a restricted suffrage favorable to the gentry) to which the cabinet was to be responsible. The Robot was abolished, and the nobles were no longer exempted from paying taxes.

What had been conceded to the Hungarians could not long be denied to the Bohemians. Emboldened by the collapse in Vienna and the success of Kossuth, another assembly met in Prague on March 29 to demand a Parliament and a responsible cabinet. On April 8, the demoralized imperial government in Vienna capitulated to the demand. The Habsburg Empire, already split into two segments, had divided yet again.

South of the Alps, the vital question of 1848 was whether another segment of the Empire was to be lost altogether. The news from Paris and Vienna ignited five days of rioting and street fighting in Milan (March 18–23) at the end of which Radetzky, the Austrian commander, withdrew his troops from the city. In Venice, the republican lawyer Daniele Manin, rescued from prison by popular action, led his Italian compatriots with such audacity that this city was also cleared of Austrian troops. Throughout the peninsula, reactionary governments fell and revolutionists assumed power. On March 26, Charles Albert of Piedmont launched his forces across the Austrian frontier, and Radetzky was compelled to retreat to the fortresses of the Quadrilateral at the southeastern end of Lake Garda.

By the end of March 1848, the rebels appeared to be triumphant in all of the four crucial centers of the Austrian revolution: Vienna, Budapest, Prague, and northern Italy. As in Berlin and Frankfurt, the vital task of the revolutionaries was to unite their disparate forces. If their efforts to sweep away the old regime were to be successful, the moderates and radicals had to cooperate and, furthermore, they had to preserve the revolutionary ardor of the peasant, artisan, and proletarian classes whose dissatisfactions had provided the tinder for the sparks from Paris. But the Austrian problem was even greater than the German. In Germany, cultural nationalism was a synthetic force which favored the revolution, but in the Habsburg monarchy it was a divisive force which contributed more than any other single factor to the revolution's ultimate defeat.

The Course of the Viennese Revolution Even while they rejoiced over the fall of Metternich on March 13, the bourgeois citizens of Vienna experienced a tremor of fear. Not all of the violence on that day was directed at the troops and the government of the old regime. In a city of 400,000 inhabitants, about 10,000 men were out of work because of the depression; vice and crime had been on the rise. During the uproar, while the crowd in the city shouted and fought for liberty, unruly mobs of artisans and proletarians burned and looted in the industrial suburbs. Food stores, butcher shops, bakeries, and tobacco shops were sacked. Artisans stormed the factories, destroyed the machines, and set fire to the buildings. Tax-offices, parsonages, and houses were plundered and demolished. During the days that followed, the imperial court and property-holding citizens co-operated to restore order. The Civic Guard, in which many hastened to enroll, and the Academic Legion, formed by university students, patrolled the streets. Hundreds of suspected rioters, plunderers, and arsonists were arrested and thrown into the crowded jails.

The Nationalities of
THE HABSBURG MONARCHY

Magyars
Germans
Rumanians
Ruthenians
Italians
Czechs
Slovaks
Slovenes
Poles
Friulians
Croats and Serbians

Struggle at the Barricade in St. Michael's Square, Vienna, on May 26, 1848. Continued uprisings after major concessions had been made by the government in March weakened the revolutionary front by driving moderates into the arms of reactionaries.

In order to quiet the masses and retain the support of the middle classes, the imperial court was compelled to make a series of concessions, including the promise of a constitution. An interim government was established under a prime minister. Faced by constant unrest, marked by intermittent riots and demonstrations, the imperial court strove during the following months to keep the revolution in hand. Yet the task was increasingly difficult. Radical journalists attacked the aristocracy, monarchy, court, bureaucracy, and cabinet. Capitalists, employers, landlords, and the wealthy were denounced for their failure to tend to the needs of labor. Proletarians were urged to look upon themselves as "worthy of the rank of princes. Freedom gives proof that all of you are descendants of the gods!" On May 15, a fresh insurrection compelled the government to agree to summon a constituent assembly elected by universal suffrage to draft a democratic constitution. On May 26, still another revolt struck the city, which now came under the control of student radicals backed by artisans and workers.

The revolt of May 15 shocked the court, the aristocrats, and the moderate liberals of the upper middle class. On May 17, the court fled Vienna for Innsbruck in the mountain fastness of the loyal Tyrol. The nobility and the bourgeoisie were driven together by the menace of the lower classes. All that the moderate liberal burghers had wanted was a parliament of property owners capable of advising the monarchy and checking absolute government. Now they found popular sovereignty and the rule of the masses.

But the most damaging consequence of May 15 for the future of the Austrian revolution was the reaction of the peasantry. Although the news of the March insurrection had been joyfully received in the provinces, the Emperor's promise to abolish compulsory labor (the Robot) had appeased the peasants, to whom liberal doctrines were either unknown or unimportant. The Emperor was popular with his rural subjects, to whom he was fondly known as "Ferdinand the Good." His simplicity aroused affection, while his idiocy was masked by the court faction (composed of the Empress, archdukes, and ministers) that managed him. On September 7, the Constituent Assembly in Vienna passed an Act of Emancipation abolishing the Robot and ending the administrative and juridical powers of the landlords. This final liquidation of manorialism completed the work begun by Emperor Joseph II in the eighteenth century. It satisfied the peasants and made them lose interest in the revolution.

Triumph of the Monarchy in Bohemia, Italy, and Vienna The first major victories of the counter-revolution, however, stemmed from divisions in the revolutionary ranks produced by national, rather than social, conflict. These victories were the conquest of Prague by General Windischgrätz in June and the defeat of the Sardinian army by General Radetzky in July of 1848. Both generals acted only in the interest of restoring monarchical authority, yet their successes were applauded by revolutionaries who were antipathetic toward the Czechs and Italians.

In Bohemia, the March revolution had aroused a sharp antagonism between Czechs and Germans. Among the demands raised by the Czech rebels was one for Czech control over "the lands of St. Václav" (Bohemia, Moravia, and Silesia), large areas of which were populated by Germans. Under the leadership of Francis Palacký, they summoned a pan-Slav Congress which met in Prague on June 2 and demanded the conversion of the Empire into a "federation of nations all enjoying equal rights." This manifesto alarmed Germans everywhere; they began to fear for the future of German leadership in the Empire. In Prague, Czechs and Germans brawled in the streets until June 11, when Czech students staged an insurrection and seized control. Five days later, the commander of the imperial garrison, Prince Windischgrätz, laid seige to the city, which surrendered after a fierce bombardment. Hundreds were arrested; the March concessions were abrogated; and Habsburg authority was re-established. The Viennese radicals hated the Czechs so fiercely that they too cheered the triumph of the imperial forces. They did not realize that they, too, had lost a crucial battle.

The Viennese liberals were more divided concerning the cause of the Italians. While some radical democrats loudly protested the attempts of the monarchy to suppress the rebellion in Lombardy and Venetia, many Austrian Germans looked upon the revolt as an act of treachery and ingratitude on the part of the Italians. When Sardinia attacked, the war became more popular. Volunteers flocked to the colors, and the Viennese gathered supplies for the Empire's defense. As the Habsburg forces grew in strength, those of the Italians weakened. The Italian patriots who had rallied from the whole peninsula to the cause of the Lombard rebels had lost their fervor. Believing that the Austrians were already defeated, detachments from central and southern Italy headed for home, and even the Lombards failed to support Charles Albert and the Sardinian army facing Radetzky on the river Mincio. On July 22, the Austrians attacked, and four days later thay drove the Italians from the field at Custozza. Falling back upon Milan with half his army gone, Charles Albert was compelled to sue for an armistice.

The triumph of the Hungarians in March had created other tensions among the peoples of the Empire, a fact that also speeded the counter-revolution. The lands of the crown of St. Stephen, which the Magyars claimed, contained Croats, Serbs, Ruthenians, Slovaks, and Rumanians who bitterly resented Magyar rule. Because they possessed a Diet and a long political tradition, the Croats led the resistance. They found an able leader in Josip Jellačić, an imperial general, who in late March had been appointed governor of Croatia by the Viennese government. During the summer, the

The National Guard and Academic Legion Drilling in Vienna. The withdrawal of the regular army and flight of the court from the city left these units to maintain order. (Bildarchiv d. Ost. Nationalbibliothek.)

imperial court finally undertook to exploit the Magyar-Croat conflict. Plentifully supplied from the west, Jellačić was able to march on Budapest, September 11. His invasion tumbled the moderate government in the Hungarian capital and brought the radical Kossuth to power. On October 3, the imperial government repudiated the March laws and declared war on the Kossuth regime. The first victim of the struggle, however, was not Budapest but Vienna.

Although the imperial cabinet had remained in Vienna after the May 15 insurrection and the departure of the court to Innsbruck, it was dominated until August by a body known as the Security Committee. As the summer progressed, the revolutionary front which had produced the Committee steadily disintegrated. On August 23, the proletarians of Vienna, many of whom were out of work because of the growing economic paralysis, rioted over unemployment relief and were bloodily suppressed by the bourgeois National Guard. A few weeks later (September 11–13), the bitter laborers refused to support middle-class citizens who demonstrated against the financial policy of the government. These frictions ruined the Academic Legion, which by the end of September had degenerated into an undisciplined mob.

In early October, however, the radicals were galvanized into one final action by news of the government's action against the Hungarians. On the 6th, a throng prevented the march of a regiment to the front, attacked the

Taking Down the Corpse of the Murdered Count Latour, October 6, 1848. To moderates the Viennese revolution appeared to be out of control, following the same path as the Jacobin terror during the first French revolution. (Bildarchiv d. Ost. Nationalbibliothek.)

few loyal troops remaining in the city, and butchered the Minister of War, Count Latour. In a scene reminiscent of the French Terror, a drunken horde of men, women, and even children reveled insanely about his mangled corpse as it dangled from a lamp post. The court, which had returned to Vienna in August, fled once more, this time to Olmütz in Moravia. Vienna fell under the control of radical students, artisans, shopkeepers, and proletarians. The aristocrats, capitalists, and other property owners fled the city. Bereft of leadership and without support anywhere in the empire except Hungary, the radicals manned the city walls and barricaded the suburbs. From the east, the Croat legions of Jellačić, which had been compelled to retreat from Hungary, moved toward the capital, and from the north Windischgrätz seized the long-awaited moment to conquer Vienna, as he had conquered Prague. While Jellačić repelled the attacking Hungarians, the imperial troops bombarded and took the city on October 31. West of the river Leitha, the counter-revolution was complete.

Ferdinand's Abdication and the Reconquest of Italy and Hungary The fall of Vienna was followed by a complete change in imperial leadership. A new cabinet of "strong men" assumed office under the leadership of Prince Felix Schwarzenberg. Schwarzenberg was an army officer and diplomat, who belonged to the high nobility. Assisting him were Alexander Bach, a lawyer and former liberal, who had participated in the recent cabinet; Count Stadion, a career civil servant who had brought reform to Galicia; and Baron Bruck, the developer of the port of Trieste. Unburdened by any loyalty to the Metternich regime, the new ministers were political realists who thought in terms of power rather than ideas. One of their first acts was to persuade Ferdinand to abdicate in favor of his eighteen-year-old nephew. The new ruler, who had been christened Francis, chose to be called Francis Joseph in order to identify himself with his progressive ancestor, Joseph II. It was the beginning of a reign that was to last sixty-eight years.

The most pressing problem of the new regime was the restoration of Habsburg power in Italy and Hungary. With the bulk of its forces committed to operations against Hungary, the imperial army had failed to exploit its great victory at Custozza on July 24, 1848. Venice and Tuscany remained in rebel hands, and in November 1848, an insurrection compelled the pope to flee Rome in disguise. A Roman republic was established under the leadership of Mazzini. On March 20, 1849, the Sardinian government again went to war against Austria, only to be decisively beaten at Novara in a campaign lasting but six days. Charles Albert abdicated, leaving to his son, Victor Emmanuel II, the dismal task of signing a peace which cost Sardinia an indemnity of 65,000,000 francs. The reconquest of Tuscany and Venice by Austrian troops followed, but the French took on the task of suppressing the radical republic at Rome. On April 24, 1849, a French expedition landed on the Italian coast and, despite the daring and resourceful defense by Garibaldi, the city fell at the end of June. The Italian revolution was at an end.

Against the Hungarian rebels the imperial army was less successful. In December 1848, the forces of Windischgrätz did occupy Budapest. Like Washington at Valley Forge, Kossuth was magnificent in adversity, and he found a remarkable general in Arthur Görgey, formerly a lieutenant in the imperial army. The war, furthermore, had become a national crusade for the Magyar people; peasantry and gentry, men and women, flocked to the Kossuth standard and harassed the attacking armies in guerilla bands. By May 1849, the Austrian forces had been driven back across the frontier. The Diet in Budapest declared Hungary an independent republic.

In Hungary, the revolutionaries succeeded in solving the problem of social synthesis which had defeated the revolution everywhere else in Central Europe. Here nationalism acted as a centripetal force binding to-

Louis Kossuth (1802–1894). A lawyer by profession, Kossuth was a fiery orator. After the failure of the Hungarian revolution he visited England and the United States and was widely acclaimed as a champion of liberty. (Bildarchiv d. Ost. Nationalbibliothek.)

gether peasants and landowners in a united front against the reaction. In order to defeat Kossuth's republic, the imperial government was compelled to take the humiliating step of appealing for outside help. Tsar Nicholas I committed 140,000 Russian soldiers to the struggle. On August 13, 1849, the advancing Russian and Austrian armies forced Görgey to surrender and drove Kossuth and his ministers to seek asylum in Turkey. Hundreds of soldiers and civilians were hanged or imprisoned; women who interceded for their husbands were stripped and publicly flogged.

The Restoration of Austrian Power in Germany With the crushing of the Hungarian revolt and the final re-establishment of order in Italy, the Schwarzenberg government could turn its attention to Germany. Here the threat to Habsburg power was no longer the Frankfurt Parliament, long since dissolved, but the schemes of Frederick William IV and his adviser, Josef Maria von Radowitz, for the reorganization of Germany at the cost of Austria. While the Habsburg armies were engaged in Italy and Hungary, Prussia might have succeeded in imposing its will upon the German lesser states. But Frederick William was averse to coercing his fellow princes and chose instead the route of persuasion. He even summoned a second German parliament to the Thuringian city of Erfurt to deliberate upon the proposed constitution.

By the time these steps had been taken, the Habsburg monarchy was once more in the saddle in Austria and Hungary. Schwarzenberg had no intention of abandoning the position of primacy enjoyed by the Habsburg monarchy for centuries in Germany. The states divided into rival factions headed by Austria and Prussia, each pursuing a different program for Germany. In November 1850, the two great powers mobilized and came close to war. At Bronzell, near Fulda, a skirmish occurred in which the only casualty was a white horse. But Frederick William IV finally yielded. At Olmütz, on November 29, he agreed to demobilize; and at Dresden, in May 1851, he consented to revive the German Confederation.

THE REVOLUTIONS
IN PERSPECTIVE

By the summer of 1851, Europe appeared to be largely what it had been in January 1848. In Vienna and Berlin, the Habsburgs and Hohenzollerns were back in the driver's seat; in the German and Italian minor states, the sovereignty of the traditional dynasties had either survived or been restored. In Italy, Austrian power was again triumphant over the cause of national unity; and in Germany, the Confederation so despised by German nationalists had been re-established under the presidency of Austria. Only in France had a new regime come to power, and its durability was already in question.

Yet Europe was not the same. The revolutionary paroxysm had shown that new forces were at work in European society which even conservative governments could no longer ignore. In every country, the revolution had revealed the plight of the artisan class in its struggle against the emerging factory system. In France, the proletarian class of factory workers had acted for the first time in Europe as an independent force capable of revolutionary action. Beyond the Rhine in central Europe, the proletarians also played a role; but here they were led by students and petty bourgeois and sacrificed themselves for the interests of others.

In Paris, one bourgeois regime replaced another; and the revolution demonstrated again that the landed aristocracy was no longer a political force in France. Yet in central Europe, the nobility emerged from the revolutionary fire scathed but still dominant. By sacrificing the remnants of manorialism, the large landowners of Austria and Prussia removed the greatest source of dissatisfaction which had made the rural masses a force for change. As a consequence, the peasants turned conservative and became a bulwark for the existing order. Still another result was that the landowners themselves were free to reap the benefits of the new agricultural technology and to adapt capitalistic techniques to agricultural production. But the most striking fact about the revolutions of 1848 in central Europe was the political weakness of the middle class. Its moment had come too soon, for the industrial revolution had not yet laid, either in Germany or in the Habsburg Empire, the necessary social foundation for the lasting victory of the liberal ideal.

If France's proletarian and central Europe's middle classes failed in their quest for political power, they did succeed in shocking the ruling elite into an awareness of their needs. In France, the June days made the propertied classes, in their search for order, willing to accept Napoleonic authoritarianism and state socialism. In Prussia, the counter-revolutionaries embraced constitutionalism and adapted it to authoritarian purposes. By granting a constitution of mixed powers, the Hohenzollern monarchy stole another vital plank from the liberal program and constructed with it a facade behind which the old aristocratic-monarchical system remained intact. In Austria, the somnolent government of the Habsburgs had been rudely awakened to the necessity of governing. Schwarzenberg and Bach were active ministers who strove to cope with the Empire's problems by an aggressive policy of centralization at home and expanded influence abroad. In Italy, as will later be shown, the attempt of Charles Albert to assume the leadership of the Italian people had left behind in defeat the memory of an heroic effort and, more concretely, the famous Statuto which converted Sardinia into a constitutional state. Both were to bear good fruit a decade later for the cause of Italian unity.

From the perspective of the twentieth century, however, the most depressing revelation of the continental revolution was the selfishness inherent in the idea of nationalism. It had been assumed that the growing awareness of national individuality and the compulsion it aroused either for national unity or national independence was a progressive force which could only benefit humanity as a whole. The concept of national self-determination was regarded by liberals as the most viable principle for the reorganization of Europe. Once the artificial frontiers, which either divided peoples or bound them unnaturally together, were gone, it was believed that Europe would enter a new era of peace and harmony. But the experience of 1848 in central Europe revealed that this was a pitiful illusion, that a recognition of the virtues of one's own culture led almost automatically to the assumption of its superiority and of its greater right to exist at the cost of others.

FURTHER READING Few attempts have been made to study the revolutions of 1848 as a whole. The best general study of the era is W. L. Langer, *Political and Social Upheaval, 1832–1852* (1969), a volume in the *Rise of Modern Europe* edited by the same author. Readable but lacking in depth is P. Robertson, *Revolutions of 1848, A Social History* (2nd ed., 1960). Leading participants are described in A. Whitridge, *Men in Crisis* (1849). Anthologies giving the views of many scholars are F. Fejtö, ed., *The Opening of an Era: 1848* (2 vols., 1948); M. Kranzberg, ed., *1848: A Turning Point?* (1959); and O. Pflanze, *The Unification of Germany, 1848–1871* (1968).

The best study of the French revolution is G. Duveau, *1848: The Making of a Revolution* (1966), a French work in translation. Chapters on 1848 are to be found in R. Arnaud, *The Second Republic and Napoleon III* (1930), which is Vol. 9 of F. Funck-Brentano, ed., *National History of France.* J. Plamenatz, *The Revolutionary Movement in France, 1815–1871* (1952); and G. Dickinson, *Revolution and Reaction in Modern France* (2nd ed., 1938). D. C. McKay, *The National Workshops* (1933) is an important monograph. Biographies of important figures are H. Whitehouse, *The Life of Lamartine* (2 vols., 1918); and A. R. Calman, *Ledru-Rollin and the Second French Republic* (1922). Important for its subject is B. Gooch, *Belgium and the February Revolution* (1963).

On the German revolution see V. Valentin, *1848: Chapters in German History* (1940), an abridgement of an exhaustive two-volume work in German. The social aspect of the struggle is ably described by T. S. Hamerow, *Restoration, Revolution, Reaction* (1958) and the national aspect by L. B. Namier, *1848: The Revolution of the Intellectuals* (1945). P. Noyes, *Organization and Revolution* (1966), studies the artisans and F. Eyck, *The Frankfurt Parliament, 1848–1849* (1968), the center of political debate.

The complicated story of the Habsburg revolution has not inspired many Anglo-Saxon authors or translators. Still valuable is C. E. Maurice, *The Revolutionary Movement of 1848–1849 in Italy, Austria–Hungary, and Germany* (1887). A fine study of the most important center of the revolution is R. J. Rath, *The Viennese Revolution of 1848* (1957), which weaves together the social and political aspects of the event. G. M. Trevelyan has described important episodes of the Italian revolution in *Garibaldi's Defense of the Roman Republic* (1909), and *Manin and the Venetian Republic of 1848* (1923). Diplomatic aspects of the revolutions are treated by W. E. Mosse, *The European Powers and the German Question 1848–1871* (1958); and A. J. P. Taylor, *The Italian Problem in European Diplomacy, 1847–1849* (1934).

6 From Romanticism to Realism and Materialism

The dynamic character of European culture is nowhere more evident than in the restless shift of its educated minds, in successive generations, from one body of intellectual assumptions to another. During the eighteenth century, when the Enlightenment seemed unassailable, there appeared the first signs of a reaction which ultimately prevailed and became known after 1800 as "Romanticism." Like the Age of Reason, the Age of Romanticism affected every aspect of intellectual life—including philosophy, literature, art, religion, and politics. But the same was true of the age of realism and materialism which had begun to replace Romanticism by the middle of the nineteenth century. While each of these movements has left an enduring mark upon European culture, all were outgrown and superseded as men groped for new answers to the eternal questions of life and coped with new needs produced by a society in a constant state of evolution and change.

THE AGE OF ROMANTICISM The concepts of the romantic movement varied from person to person and group to group. The most basic viewpoint, however, was the rejection of reason and a new reliance upon emotion and imagination as sources of understanding. Gone was the assumption of the rationalists that reason alone could unlock all the secrets of nature and of human existence. Whereas the rationalists had believed in the existence of natural laws that were universally valid in every age and circumstance, the romanticists thought in terms of the growth and development of institutions and cultures. Discarding the quest for what was uniform and general, they valued what was unique and individual. Instead of decrying cultural diversity, they deliberately cultivated it for the enrichment of humanity as a whole.

The New Attitude Toward Sentiment and Individualism Jean Jacques Rousseau (1712–1778) was the first philosopher to argue that man's feelings are more important than his reason. But the religious revivals of the eighteenth century were also important in emphasizing the emotional side of human nature. In Britain evangelicalism, and in Germany pietism, reawakened popular interest in religion. The evangelical movement, from which Methodism came, sought the spiritual rebirth of all classes and emphasized the necessity for moral and social reform. German pietism was a movement within the Lutheran Church, a reaction against rationalistic theology, which exhorted Christians of all classes to seek a sense of union with God. Both movements appealed to man's inward nature and endeavored to evoke powerful religious feelings.

Johann Wolfgang Goethe (1749–1832). Goethe departed from the romantic mode in favor of classicism after 1786 and disapproved of the excesses of romantic writers whom he had inspired. This portrait was sculpted by David d'Angers in 1828. (Brown Brothers.)

Romanticism in Germany Although Romanticism was European in scope, it prospered most in Germany. The rediscovery of emotion brought forth that grand outburst of poetic exuberance during 1767–1787 known as the "Storm and Stress" (*Sturm und Drang*) during which Goethe, Schiller, and other leading poets and dramatists produced some of their greatest works. The period of Storm and Stress was brief, but the seed had been sown, and after 1800 it prospered. Outsiders first became aware of what was developing in Germany through a gifted French writer, Madame de Staël, who coined the term "Romanticism" in her *On Germany* (1813). She was struck by the naturalness of the new German writers in contrast to the artificiality of French classicism. While the characters in classical epics were moved only by "external events," those in German romantic poetry acted according to their inner natures. What they did depended upon the sentiments and passions they felt rather than what their environment forced upon them. These were the qualities romanticists everywhere found in Shakespeare, who after two centuries of relative neglect was rediscovered and became the vogue.

Having rediscovered sentiment, many romanticists carried it to the same absurd extreme to which the rationalists had carried reason. In their novels and poems they dissected the secret sorrows and passions of their characters in endless detail. Goethe's *Sorrows of Werther* (1774) depicts a young man tragically in love and at odds with society who ends his life in suicide. Every great writer usually inspires dozens of imitators, and this work set a style in romantic literature. In popular novels and dramas, frail and fainting heroines were carried off by disease (tuberculosis preferred) to the frustration of lovesick swains. The romanticists also loved the heroic. Their characters dared and sacrificed themselves for great causes, struggling against fate and yet drawn to destruction as inevitably as the moth to the flame. In his *Heroes, Hero-Worship, and the Heroic in History* (1841), Thomas Carlyle concluded that the course of history is determined by the works of great men.

Typical also of the romanticists was an intense individualism, a powerful urge to seek the fullest possible development of men's talents and potentialities. Whereas the Enlightenment had been more concerned with what was universal in human nature, the romanticists were concerned with what was unique in each personality and how that uniqueness might be nourished to the maximum benefit of the individual and hence of humanity as a whole.

The drive for self-realization was a powerful impulse behind the German literary renascence. Its great symbol was Goethe's *Faust* (1808), the learned man who exhausted all rational paths to truth and turned to the occult in the form of Mephistopheles in order to attain those ultimate experiences necessary if he were to fulfill himself.

The compulsion for self-realization caused many romanticists to lead unorthodox lives, to defy law and convention, placing their complete trust in their own insight and intuition rather than in the existing standards of society. Outwardly, this revolt often expressed itself in garish or sloppy clothing, long beards and uncut hair, uncouth manners and loose living. But it also resulted in artistic radicalism, the demand of the artist for freedom from all traditional standards. Friedrich Schlegel's *Lucinde* (1789) produced a sensation by arguing that free love and inconstancy are natural to man and hence good. By using unorthodox stage techniques in his play *Hernani* (1830) Victor Hugo outraged the traditionalists and delighted the romanticists of Paris.

The New Attitude Toward Religion Like the rationalists, the romanticists were fascinated with nature. Their constant quest was for the attainment of a greater harmony between nature and man. Yet the natural world in which they gloried was not that of scientific phenomena and mathematical laws; it was the untamed nature of forests, streams, and cataracts. Here they discerned a mysterious force—some called it "will" or "spirit"—with which the poet could commune in his search for truth.

> *One impulse from a vernal wood*
> *May teach you more of man,*
> *Of moral evil and of good,*
> *Than all the sages can.*

This thought from William Wordsworth's *The Tables Turned* appeared again in *Tintern Abbey* and many other poems of his *Lyrical Ballads* (1798–1800). Many romanticists identified the great force in nature as God and ended in pantheism. God was not simply the creator of the world-machine as the Deists had taught; he was everywhere, immanent in all nature. Through Friedrich Schleiermacher, pietism and pantheism were synthesized with Lutheran theology. His *Speeches on Religion* (1799) sought to revive Protestantism as a vital personal faith, freed from the arid dogmas of the Enlightenment. Yet Catholicism, rather than Protestantism, was the chief beneficiary of Romanticism. In the eighteenth century, the Catholic Church had lost its hold upon the educated classes. But the romantic emphasis upon emotion, the renewed interest in the supernatural, the return to tradition—all of these tendencies favored a revival of Christianity's oldest faith. In his famous *Genius of Christianity* (1802) François René Chateaubriand presented a powerful defense of the Catholic faith based not upon logic or reason in the tradition of the medieval theologians, but upon romantic sentiment. The work is a long reverie in which the author meditates eloquently on the mysteries of Christianity, the beauty of its art and liturgy, the emotions that faith evokes, and the glories of the Christian past.

The New Attitude Toward the Past One of the most important fruits of Romanticism was a renewed interest in, and understanding of, history. Again, Herder's contribution justifies the assertion that he was the "father of romanticism." In teaching his generation to value what was unique and individual in human culture, he also stressed that this uniqueness and individuality were the consequence of organic growth. Every culture is in a constant state of becoming. Institutions, languages, beliefs, customs, and the like are forever in the process of realizing the ideals they embody. Hence their character can only be understood by discovering how they came to be what they are. This realization meant the abandonment of all the conceptions stemming from Locke and Newton. The analytical and mechanical methods were replaced by the genetic and historical. Beginning in the studies devoted to human affairs, the new approach eventually influenced the natural sciences as well. We shall see that it was no accident that the concept of evolution transformed the study of biology in the nineteenth rather than the eighteenth century.

The first of the human disciplines to be affected was philology, the study of language and literature. Romantic scholars discovered in popular ballads, legends, and folk tales a neglected and exciting form of literature. Two examples were the fairy tales collected and published by Jakob and Wilhelm Grimm and by Hans Christian Andersen, which are still widely read. While the Romantic Age spawned a number of important historians, the most significant was Leopold Ranke (1795–1886). Following the techniques developed by the philologists, Ranke dedicated himself to the ideal of historical objectivity. The purpose of the historian, he declared, is not to judge the past in order to instruct the present, but only to show "what actually occurred." For the historian, it was no longer plausible to praise one epoch and condemn another; each period is necessary to the next, like the acorn to the oak, "Every age," wrote the devout Ranke, "is immediate to God."

Literature, too, was influenced by this new historical mindedness. Everywhere in Europe poets and novelists turned to the past for their themes. The medieval novels of Sir Walter Scott (1771–1832) probably had the largest reading public in Europe and were universally imitated by lesser writers. Another example was Alexander Pushkin who based his *Boris Godunov* (1831) and *Evgeni Onegin* (1833) on two great figures from the Slavic past. Naturally the new reverence for history, emphasis upon emotion, and quest for the heroic had a strong influence on the growth of nationalism. Pride in the past stirred new hopes for the future.

The Romantic Age was prone to extremes and history did not escape. Writers tended to glorify the Middle Ages as much as the rationalists had tended to deprecate it. They were attracted by its religious faith, its seemingly organic character, and its spontaneous folk literature. But they were particularly drawn by the tales of chivalry. Instead of an age of darkness and ignorance as the Enlightenment had conceived it, the medieval period suddenly became an heroic era of chivalrous knights and damsels in distress. After a lapse of nearly two centuries, the Gothic style returned to architecture. Churches were once more constructed with flying buttresses; lofty towers; and soaring, pointed arches. Houses and public buildings displayed turrets, pinnacles, and crenellations. German princes erected castles or "artistic ruins" as works of art rather than dwellings.

St. Pancras Railway Station in London. Built in 1868, it typifies the Gothic revival under the influence of Romanticism. But it also symbolizes nostalgia for a simpler past in an age being transformed by railways and factories. (Radio Times Hulton Picture Library.)

Romanticism in Politics Earlier it has been shown that the romantic view of the past was a powerful force for conservatism. Particularly in central Europe, the glorification of the Middle Ages, the emphasis upon the traditional, the concern for the organic tended to justify the aristocratic-monarchical system. The revival of religious faith reinforced the alliance of throne and altar. Yet liberalism and even socialism were also inspired by romantic idealism. The stress on individualism, the revolt against the conventional, the development of national feeling—all of these tendencies promoted the growth of liberalism. In the revolutions of 1830 and 1848, the romantic liberals found a chance to make sacrifices in behalf of great causes and lofty ideals for which they yearned.

In western Europe, Romanticism also expressed itself as a revolt against industrialism and an increasingly materialistic society. Social criticism—the condemnation of economic competition, of slums and exploitation, and of the complacency of the bourgeoisie—was a common theme in romantic literature. The "Utopian" socialism of Saint-Simon, Owen, and Fourier was an outgrowth of this mood. Romanticism also revived the tradition of aristocratic paternalism—i.e., the obligation of a feudal lord to look after his peasants—and caused some conservatives to interest themselves in the problems of social welfare. Disraeli and Bismarck were two notable examples. Naturally they were also moved by the political wisdom of winning labor support for conservative parties and institutions being attacked by middle-class liberals.

The Fine Arts The revolt against classicism was also evident in the fine arts. Romanticists rejected the classical view that beauty was a timeless, universal concept, arguing that it varied from culture to culture and age to

The Raft of Medusa by Géricault. The classical style can be seen in the carefully balanced composition, Romanticism in the drama of the shipwreck and emotions of its victims. Géricault also liked to paint horses, one of which threw him and ended his brilliant career at age 32. (The Louvre.)

age. They exalted light and color over form and composition. Whereas the classicists preferred to paint the human figure, the romanticists revived landscape painting. Classical restraint was abandoned for warmth, emotion, and movement. Beginning in Britain with the works of Lawrence, Constable, and Turner, the new style spread to the continent. Although romantic painters were eventually to be found in every country, the most significant school developed in France. Important French artists, like Ingres, continued to paint in the classical style and were supported by the academies, but they found competition from such painters as Géricault and Delacroix whose canvasses were in the romantic mood.

In music, the transition from classicism to Romanticism was foreshadowed in the greatest musical genius of the age, Ludwig van Beethoven. While Beethoven's rhythms are closely controlled and balanced in the classical tradition, his compositions have a grandiose character typical of the Romantic Age. The vastness of his conceptions, his warmth and fervor, the power with which he developed his themes, the complete independence and high status he demanded for the artist are all characteristic of the new outlook. After him, romantic composers abandoned the classical rules in favor of uncontrolled rhythms that flowed in "natural" patterns. They strove for richness and warmth of color, often sacrificing unity and cohesion in their preoccupation with individual effects. Perhaps the most characteristic composer in the romantic style was Hector Berlioz whose *Symphonie Fantastique* (1830) reveals all the extravagant emotionalism of the era. By developing new techniques on the violin and piano, Nicolò Paganini and Franz Liszt set new standards for the performing arts. Paganini, in particular, caught the romantic imagination with his flowing black hair, brilliant improvisations, and the seemingly demonic skill of his bow.

Nicolò Paganini (1782–1840). The Italian virtuoso extended the range of the violin by employing harmonics, double and triple stops. His compositions are still among the most difficult in musical literature for that instrument. (Radio Times Hulton Picture Library.)

German Idealism In philosophy, the greatest achievement of the Romantic Era was that of the German idealists. Characteristic of German idealism was a belief in abstract forces that lie behind the phenomena of existence. These forces provide the movement that determines the development of nations, states, institutions, laws, customs, and all other aspects of life. These are the forces that produce the infinite variety, the uniqueness and individuality in human culture.

The most powerful mind among the idealist philosophers was Georg W. F. Hegel (1770–1831). Hegel was one of the towering figures in European philosophy; his doctrines were influential for generations to come. There was a dualism in western thought, he observed, which had to be overcome. Whereas the rationalist was concerned with the world as it ought to be, an ideal society ordered by reason in accordance with the laws of nature, the romanticists focused upon the world as it is, the historical world characterized by endless variety and individuality. Hegel's philosophy of history was designed to overcome this dualism through the discovery of a rational process in historical development. The course of history is determined, he maintained, by an objective force he called the *Weltgeist* ("world mind" or "world spirit'"), which acts through all men, but particularly through the great men in history. The evolution of the *Weltgeist* is a dialectical process, for the world mind has an irresistible tendency to create opposites. Every thesis gives rise to its antithesis and their conflict leads to a reconciliation in the form of a new synthesis. Just as the evolution of the world mind is the subject of universal history; so the evolution of the *Volksgeist*, or national mind, is the subject of national history. States are the manifestation of the national minds, and conflicts between them are the inevitable clash

Hegel Lecturing to his Students at the University of Berlin. His voice was weak, his delivery poor, his style complicated. Yet his profundity brought him a following. His posthumous *Philosophy of History* was published from student notes. (The Bettmann Archive.)

of the "ideas" they represent. The conquests of revolutionary France, for example, were but the manifestation of the momentary supremacy of French rationalism. Napoleon was simply a "world-historical individual" acting out his role in the grand dialectic of history.

In Hegel's view the state was a vital part of God's plan for mankind. It was "the divine idea as it exists on earth." This deification of the state was one of the peculiarities of German political thought and gravely heightened the power of the state at the cost of liberty. While the German idealists were vitally concerned with the problem of freedom, it was the freedom of the human, creative spirit rather than political freedom or the rights of man they had in mind.

THE DEVELOPMENT OF REALISM AND MATERIALISM

By the middle of the nineteenth century, the Romantic Age had begun to wane. In Hegelian terms the thesis of Romanticism created its own antithesis in realism and materialism. The last great age of metaphysics gave way to science. Abstract speculation was replaced by empirical research, philosophical systems by scientific theories. In the 1820's and 1830's, the philosophy of Hegel had dominated western thought; but in the 1860's and 1870's, it was the evolutionary theory of Darwin. Hegel had sought to combine in a single system the realms of reason and reality, but his successors, Comte and Marx, dealt only with the latter. In literature and art the emotional effusions and historical outlook of Romanticism went out of style. The interest of writers and artists shifted to the contemporary scene and the drama of everyday life. In politics, men lost their faith in the supremacy of principle: power rather than ideas appeared to be the decisive force in human affairs.

The Advance of Science   During the first half of the nineteenth century, while philosophers were soaring to new heights of abstraction, scientists were steadily adding to the store of concrete factual information about nature. Not until the metaphysicians had overreached and spent themselves did the scientists again turn to theory in the effort to find meaningful patterns in accumulated knowledge. At mid-century, scientific generalization again became respectable. During the next twenty-five years, experimentation declined, while the former experimentors tried to make sense out of what they had learned.

The results were impressive—not only to the scientists, but to the public at large. General concepts began to emerge ("matter, energy, ether, organism, environment, evolution") under which the available facts could be subsumed. Simultaneously, progress was made in discovering the interrelationships between the sciences: physics and chemistry, chemistry and biology, geology and biology, physiology and psychology. "Thus they developed a system of thought," declares the historian Robert Binkley, "that exceeded in scope the world of Newton, as it exceeded in experimental certainty the world of Goethe. While the age looked on and marveled, the different parts of the structure of science were falling into position."

With mounting excitement scientists throughout Europe pieced together many of the missing links in their knowledge of the physical world. Once the relationship between atomic weights and molecular proportions had been clarified, for example, it was possible to discern the atomic structure of the molecule and to construct a chart showing both the known elements and those yet to be discovered. In spectrum analysis, scientists found a valuable tool for analyzing the chemical content of various substances. The invention of the steam engine stimulated speculation on the nature of energy, leading to the great synthesis known as thermodynamics. The general laws of thermodynamics were derived from the study of many fields: mechanics, heat, electromagnetism, chemical reactions, and the molecular action of gases. Charles Darwin provided the most dramatic synthesis of all by explaining the process of evolution through natural selection.

The Advance of Technology   Similar advances were made in technology. In the past, technological achievements had only rarely been the consequence of growth in scientific knowledge. They were the work of practical men who worked out mechanical problems without the help of the scientist. Henry Bessemer, the developer of the blast furnace (1856), was an inventor and mechanic rather than a scientist. Thereafter, the great improvements in metallurgy (e.g., the development of alloys) stemmed from the laboratory rather than the machine shop. Another significant adaptation of science to technology came with the discoveries by André Ampère and Michael Faraday of the relationship between magnetism and electricity. There followed the development of the dynamo, the invention of the electric telegraph, and the first commercial use of electricity. By the 1840's, the telegraph was in general use, and in 1858 the first attempt was made to lay an Atlantic cable. Although it failed, further research made possible a successful cable in 1866. From the chemistry laboratories came synthetic (aniline) dyes for the textile industry and new chemical fertilizers for agriculture. In 1854, the chemist Louis Pasteur began his study of germs which in the 1860's enabled the doctor Lord Lister to introduce antiseptic surgery.

The daily lives of the people were most affected, however, by the continued application of earlier technical discoveries, especially in the transportation field. In the period 1850–1870, the length of the world's railways grew from 38,000 to 204,000 miles. During the same decades, steam engines became common on ocean-going vessels, first as a supplement to sails and later as the sole means of propulsion. The screw propeller came into use in the 1850's and the compound engine a decade later.

These advances in scientific knowledge and technology caught the imagination of the reading public. Scientific theories were still relatively uncomplicated and within the grasp of the average person. At the same time the spread of public education was rapidly increasing the number of individuals who could read, while the rising standard of living increased the number of those who had the leisure to do so. Popularizers followed on the heels of the scientists, explaining the new theories to the general public in books and articles. The consequence was a rapid shift of interest away from the metaphysical systems and the passions and enthusiasms of the Romantic Age. Ludwig Büchner's *Force and Matter*, which explained the new conception of matter with almost missionary zeal, went through nine editions. In Germany and Russia, students deserted the lecture halls of the philosophers and took up avidly the new fad of science. The new theories on matter, energy, and evolution became the common topics of general conversation.

The "Negation of Philosophy"   The advance of science, the development of technology, the rising standard of living—all of these factors form the background for the transition in European thought toward realism and materialism. The shift was evident in the thought of the most powerful intellects of the mid-century era as well as in the popular mind. During the middle decades, the conviction spread that metaphysical philosophy had reached its end with Hegel. Doubts arose that truth could be found in abstract, transcendental systems remote from the mundane facts of man's daily life. The conviction grew that truth was rather to be found in the concrete material existence of man. Furthermore, many were dissatisfied with the negative character of Hegelian thought, the fact that his dialectical system meant that nothing could ever be permanent, that the present would inevitably be negated by the future. There was a need, it was argued, for a more positive philosophy.

Comte   Perhaps the most significant thinker who sought to satisfy this need was Auguste Comte (1798–1857). The volumes of his *System of Positive Philosophy* appeared during the years 1830–1842 and became one of the most influential works of the nineteenth century. In its development, he maintained that every branch of knowledge passes through three stages of development: (1) the theological, or fictitious, in which events are explained in terms of the arbitrary acts of gods or spirits; (2) the metaphysical, or abstract, in which they are explained in terms of the movement of transcendental forces; and (3) the scientific, or positive, in which phenomena are explained in terms of general laws based upon observation, experiment, and the careful comparison of facts. Comte's purpose was to introduce the third stage in the study of society by teaching men to regard society as a valid subject of scientific inquiry. He was the founder of the modern discipline of sociology.

Comte's call for discovery of the "laws" of society is reminiscent of the Enlightenment. Yet there was an important difference. Whereas the rationalists had believed that the laws of nature could be discerned by reason alone, Comte maintained that they could only be discovered through extensive research. Of all the scientific disciplines (mathematics, astronomy, physics, chemistry, biology) sociology, being the latest to develop, was in his opinion the most complex. The general laws of society would never be understood until the sociologists had gathered and collated a great variety of data concerning man and his social environment. The most astonishing aspect of Comte's work was his vain attempt to found a new religious faith. The priests of the new faith were not to be mediators between man and god, but specialists in sociology; the saints were the benefactors of mankind, the devils those who hindered progress.

Marx The writings of Karl Marx (1818–1883) also illustrate the transition at mid-century from metaphysics to materialism. As a student at the University of Berlin in the late 1830's, Marx naturally became acquainted with Hegelian doctrine. While he was greatly influenced by the structure of Hegel's philosophy, he rejected its content. The course of history, he reasoned, is determined by material rather than spiritual forces. "Wholly in contrast to German philosophy, which comes down from heaven to earth,"

Karl Marx in London, 1861, When He Was Still Relatively Obscure. His first volume of *Capital* was published in 1867 and he was soon known as the "red terrorist doctor" who helped organize the First International.

he wrote in *The German Ideology,* "we here ascend from earth to heaven." It is not, in other words, the movement of the *Weltgeist* that establishes the condition of society, but the changing way in which men make their living. Whether one lives under a predominantly agricultural, commercial, or industrial economy determines whether one will have a feudal, capitalistic, or socialistic system. From the mode of production stems the class structure; from the class structure comes the political and institutional structure of society and the beliefs that men hold. "With the change in the economic foundation, the whole immense superstructure is slowly or rapidly transformed."

Like Hegel, Marx believed that the process of change was one of conflict. Yet in his view the conflict was not between ideas produced by spiritual forces, but between social classes produced by the mode of economic production. For the Hegelian dialectic, Marx substituted the philosophy of "dialectical materialism." Unlike Hegel, Marx was no ivory-tower philosopher, but an active propagandist and a social revolutionary. The *Communist Manifesto,* published in January 1848, by Marx and his collaborator Friedrich Engels, was a call to action rather than a philosophical treatise. "The history of all hitherto existing society," it asserted, "is the history of class struggles." What had been true of the preceding feudal society was also true of modern bourgeois society. The conflict between lord and vassal, noble and serf, master and journeyman had become one between the bourgeoisie and proletariat.

Marx argued that the bourgeois class cannot exist without digging its own grave. Through the expansion of industrial capitalism it must create an ever-larger proletarian class; by appropriating the wealth produced by the working class, the bourgeoisie would steadily increase the gap between the wealthy few and the impoverished masses. Out of this contradiction and the periodic crises of the business cycle would come the ultimate collapse of the capitalistic system, the fall of the bourgeoisie, and the introduction of a classless society. But the proletarians must not be content to wait for the ultimate collapse. The *Manifesto* ended with a call for the "forcible overthrow of all existing social conditions." Since governments are merely the means by which the dominant class consolidates and preserves its power over the exploited, the state will wither away once the proletariat has achieved its triumph. Universal harmony and mutual cooperation will prevail, replacing the competitive and exploitative system of capitalism.

With the background supplied in previous chapters it is easy to see why Marx should have come to some of these conclusions. As we have seen, the aristocracy and wealthier bourgeois of the 1830's and 1840's did tend to monopolize economic wealth and political power in those areas where each was dominant. The early years of industrial capitalism did tend to produce social inequities of a serious kind. The doctrine of laissez faire and the writings of the classical economists did tend to justify the self-interest of the capitalistic bourgeoisie. In many countries, the established churches were but arms of the state and religious faith was deliberately exploited as a means of social control. Yet ideas are not always the reflection of class interests, and the later history of Marxism is itself one of the clearest demonstrations of this fact, for the industrialized nations have been the most resistant to Marxian socialism. Marx underestimated, furthermore, the power of humanitarianism and liberal idealism, the capacity of industrialism to elevate the general standard of living, and the potentiality of trade unionism to improve wages and working conditions. Nor did he foresee that the competition between the dominant social groups and political parties, and their mutual search for political support in the lower classes, would lead to the extension of the suffrage in Britain, France, and Germany and to the passage of needed social legislation.

The advance of materialism brought with it a weakening of religious faith. Comte rejected the traditional religions, while Marx was openly atheistic. Religion he denounced as the "opiate of the masses." In Germany, the Young Hegelians crusaded against what they regarded as religious superstition. Christianity, they believed, was an obstacle to man's understanding of history as the progress of the world spirit. Works published in Germany and France created a sensation by describing Jesus as a historical rather than a divine figure.

REALISM IN
PAINTING,
LITERATURE, AND
MUSIC

Painting At Paris, the quarrel between the classical and romantic schools of art was still unresolved at mid-century, when both were rudely shocked by the attack of a new movement of independents who rejected both traditions. Calling himself a "realist" (the first use of the term in the new sense), Gustave Courbet (1819–1877) abandoned the themes and styles of the classical and romantic artists. Having never seen an angel, he declared, he couldn't paint one. Instead of the classical, allegorical, or historical scenes, he preferred those from everyday life. His *Stone-Breakers* (about 1850) represented two workmen repaving a road. Other typical subjects were the wife of a saloon keeper, a railroad station, and a factory. "Realism," he asserted, "is essentially a democratic art." No subject was too mundane, too harsh or ugly, to interest him. Realism did not mean to him the exact graphic reproduction of nature. Instead he wished to depict the essence of what he saw, the living reality, which the artist must interpret rather than merely describe. To this end, he chose a simplified style, planes of color sharply delineated from each other, with heavy strokes of pigment often applied with the palette knife rather than with the brush.

Other independents followed Courbet's lead. Honoré Daumier, whose satirical cartoons and posters enlivened Paris for over forty years, also did a number of paintings in the realistic style. After Courbet, however, the most important rebel was Edouard Manet, whose *Déjeuner sur l'Herbe* was excluded from the official Paris exhibition of 1863 by the traditionalists. The uproar that followed led Napoleon III to authorize a second exhibition ("Salon des Réfusés") of excluded paintings. In contrast to the lifelessness and artificiality of the first salon, the second was fresh and exciting. Manet's painting shocked both the public by its seeming immorality, and the academic artists by its bold disregard of all previous standards in the handling of color. To the new generation of artists, however, it represented a liberation from outworn traditions and pointed the way to new adventures with palette and canvas.

The Novel The word "realism" was soon applied also to a new trend in literature. Foreshadowed in the works of Stendhal (1783–1842) and Honoré de Balzac (1799–1850), the new school definitely arrived with Gustave

Dejeuner sur l'Herbe by Edouard Manet. What shocked the public was not that Manet painted nudes, but that they appeared to be prostitutes rather than the nymphs and goddesses depicted in allegorical paintings of the romantic school. (The Louvre.)

Flaubert's *Madame Bovary* (1856). Eschewing the artificiality and sentimentality of Romanticism, the realists dealt with characters from actual life. They did not write of chivalric knights and heroic battles, of great loves and rending passions, but of men and women in scenes and situations credible to every reader. Typical of the new realism was a searching interest in social questions. In Russia Ivan Turgenev's *Sportsman's Sketches* (1852) handled the problem of serfdom; in America, Harriet Beecher Stowe's *Uncle Tom's Cabin* (1852) indicted slavery. The greatest of the English novelists to be concerned with the problem of poverty in the early industrial age was Charles Dickens (1812–1870). With intense compassion he etched portraits of the urban poor and described the brutalization and moral degeneracy which breeds in slums.

Music Music was less influenced by the new trend than the other arts. Berlioz lived until 1869, and after him Johannes Brahms kept alive the romantic tradition in symphonic composition. The era was most significant for the development of the opera. The years 1851–1853 saw the production of Giuseppe Verdi's *Rigoletto, Il Trovatore,* and *La Traviata.* Verdi grew as an artist to the very end. *Aïda* (1871) saw the maturation of his style; yet he reached new heights with the *Requiem Mass* (1874) and *Otello* (1887). The continuance of the romantic tradition in the era of realism is best seen, however, in Richard Wagner (1813–1883), whose themes were drawn from Celtic and Germanic mythology, as in *Der Ring des Nibelungen,* and *Tristan* *und Isolde,* or the Middle Ages as in *Tannhäuser, Die Meistersinger, Lohengrin,* and *Parsifal.* The somber, brooding quality of much of his music was romantic in mood; the "love-death" passage from *Tristan und Isolde*—a long, swelling, and highly erotic crescendo—has been described as the final great achievement of the Romantic Age. In other respects, however, Wagner belongs to the realists. Unlike the romanticists, he was driven by the ambition to realize a total conception: that of uniting all of the arts into a single art form (*Gesamtkunstwerk*). Poetry, drama, and the plastic arts were to join with music in one great universal work. In his subjection of every detail to a total plan, in his use of the *Leitmotiv* or single theme which, though ever changing, ties together the entire composition, and in his resort to stage tricks such as the fire that envelopes Brünnhilde in *Die Walküre,* Wagner belongs to the age of realism.

THE EMERGENCE
OF REALPOLITIK

In European politics, the advance of realism is to be seen in the growth of power politics (*Realpolitik*) at the cost of political idealism. It is true that conservatives everywhere were shocked by the revolutions of 1848. To romantic conservatives it was a matter of dogma that the three great legitimate monarchies of central and eastern Europe—Russia, Austria, and Prussia—must stand together to preserve the old order against political and social subversion. Hence Nicholas I sent Russian troops in 1849 to suppress the Kossuth republic and restore Habsburg power in Hungary.

Yet the din of revolution had hardly died away when the politics of self-interest began to take precedence over that of conservative solidarity even in central and eastern Europe. The near collision between Prussia and Austria in 1850, which was resolved at Olmütz and Dresden, left a legacy of distrust in both countries. The Prince of Prussia, heir to the throne, was incensed over the "humiliation" suffered by Prussia at Olmütz. In Frankfurt, the Prussian delegate to the Diet of the German Confederation, the young Otto von Bismarck, argued unceasingly for a policy of Prussian self-interest against Austria. "In politics," he maintained, "no one does anything for another, unless he also finds it in his own interest to do so." The Holy Alliance, he believed, was an unnecessary handicap to Prussian policy.

During the 1850's, nevertheless, Bismarck was unable to persuade his government to adopt a policy of *Realpolitik.* The first breach in the conservative phalanx was opened between Russia and Austria rather than between Austria and Prussia. It was the Crimean War which finally destroyed the Holy Alliance and ended, for a time, the Concert of Europe as well.

The Crimean War Despite repeated crises the European powers had avoided war over the "eastern question" for nearly thirty years. Yet the new generation of diplomats that assumed power after 1848 dismally failed to solve problems that arose in that area and stumbled into a war no one apparently wanted. The issue which led to war began as a dispute between the priests and monks of the Latin and Orthodox Catholic Churches over their respective rights in certain "holy places" in Palestine: the reputed sites of Jesus' birth, his vigil at Gethsemane, and his tomb in Jerusalem. The Greeks, it was complained, had progressively encroached upon the rights of the Latins in all three places. In order to curry favor with Latin Catholics and heighten the prestige of his new regime, Napoleon III pressured the Turkish government to use its authority for the restoration of the usurped rights. As head of the Russian Orthodox Church, Tsar Nicholas I felt compelled to take up the Greek cause, but he also feared, and rightly so, that Napoleon's intention was to replace Russian with French predominance in Constantinople. Confronted with bellicose threats from both sides, the Sultan decided that the French navy was a greater danger than the Russian army. In 1852, he gave the upper hand in the holy places to the Latins.

Faced with the prospect of a diplomatic defeat, Nicholas decided upon a counter-attack. He demanded the right to intervene in the Ottoman Empire to protect Orthodox Christians and, when the Sultan refused, he ordered the Russian army to prepare for action. Nicholas did not intend to precipitate a European war. He was confident that Prussia and Austria would stand by Russia for the sake of the conservative cause, and he believed that he had bought off the British with a suggestion that the Ottoman Empire should be divided among the interested powers.

But Nicholas miscalculated badly. Britain's ambassador in Constantinople, Lord Stratford de Redcliffe, actually encouraged the Turks to resist the Russian demand. In June 1853, the French and British fleets were ordered to the Dardanelles, and during July Russian troops entered the Danubian Principalities. Russia's invasion of what was nominally Turkish soil produced a violent public reaction in Constantinople, and on October 4 the Sultan declared war. At Sinope in late November, a Turkish fleet was attacked while at anchor and annihilated by Russian squadrons. British public opinion was inflamed by this assault of "autocratic Russia" upon "helpless Turkey." If the Ottoman Empire was to be saved and likewise their own prestige, Britain and France had only one recourse—war. This was declared on March 28, 1854.

The Crimean War, which cost the lives of half a million men, was not the result of a calculated plan, nor even of hasty last-minute decisions made under stress. It was the consequence of more than two years of fatal blundering in slow motion by inept statesmen who had months to reflect upon the actions they took. It arose from Napoleon's search for prestige; Nicholas's quest for control over the Straits; his naive miscalculation of the probable reactions of the European powers; the failure of those powers to make their positions clear; and the pressure of public opinion in Britain and Constantinople at crucial moments.

The war was fought with equal ineptitude. Lacking a better place to campaign, the struggle took place on the Crimean peninsula, where British and French forces (later joined by Sardinia) disembarked in September 1854 to invest the fortress of Sebastopol. For a full year, the Russian garrison held out. The allies, led by untrained and bickering officers, lost more men

Effect of Allied Bombardment on the Russian Fortress of Redan During the Crimean War. The capture of Redan and Malakhov in 1855 led to the fall of Sebastopol, after which the Russians sued for peace. (The Mansell Collection.)

through disease (chiefly cholera and dysentery) and inadequate medical care than in combat. Only the heroic efforts of Florence Nightingale succeeded in creating some order out of the British hospital service. The charge of the Light Brigade, celebrated in Tennyson's poem was an unnecessary slaughter brought on by incompetent officers. On the Russian side, there was similar mismanagement. Although the troops fought well, the generalship was poor and the services of supply totally inadequate. Fighting on its own soil, the tsarist regime was unable to exploit its superiority in manpower to push the enemy back into the sea.

To the Russians, the most shocking revelation of the war was the conduct of Austria. Far from supporting the Russians against the western powers (or the "European revolution" as Nicholas chose to call the opposition), Vienna came close to joining the latter in the attack. Count Buol, foreign minister since the death of Schwarzenberg in 1852, was alarmed by the Russian occupation of the Danubian Principalities, but he also hoped to exploit the crisis to establish Austrian power in the Balkans to the exclusion of Russia. An ultimatum from Buol forced the Russians to withdraw their troops from the lower Danube in August 1854.

The bungling Tsar Nicholas had intended to act in harmony with the European powers in his action against Turkey; but instead, an isolated Russia suffered a humiliating defeat. In March 1855, Nicholas died, bitter and disillusioned; and his heir, Alexander II, accepted the terms imposed by the western powers. At the Congress of Paris in 1856, Russia abandoned her claims on Turkey, to whom she ceded the mouth of the Danube. She also ceded southern Bessarabia to the Danubian Principalities and surrendered her right of intervention in the latter. In addition, she was compelled to disgorge the captured Turkish fortress of Kars, to guarantee the demilitarization of the Aaland Islands in the Gulf of Finland, and accept the neutralization of the Black Sea. The latter provision meant that both Russian and Turkish warships and fortifications were forbidden. The Turks promised to prevent the passage of warships of other powers through the Dardanelles and Bosporus.[1]

The Triumph of Realpolitik   On the surface, the Congress of Paris appeared to strengthen the European Concert. For the first time since Verona in 1823, the major powers had met to settle significant issues. They solemnly admitted the Ottoman Empire to the Concert and entered into commitments which did, or could, require joint action in the future. The Danubian Principalities were placed in effect under their wardship; this was a significant step toward the creation of the future Kingdom of Rumania. The great powers agreed to mediate disputes between Turkey and other states, to supervise the autonomy of Serbia, and to guarantee the Ionian Isles. But the most significant responsibilities assumed by the powers were the neutralization of the Black Sea and the guarantee of free navigation on the Danube. A "Declaration of Paris" sought to limit the rights of belligerents in maritime wars.

Nevertheless, the European Concert had failed to prevent the war in the first place. After the Congress of Paris, moreover, there was no major force in Europe fully committed to the preservation of the status quo. While Napoleon III. continued to seek the overthrow of the settlement of 1815, Alexander II and his foreign minister, Prince Gorchakov, wished to end the neutralization of the Black Sea. But the Holy Alliance had also disappeared as a stabilizing force in European politics. There was no longer the possibility of a solid front by conservative monarchs against liberal and national subversion. Even Nicholas had toyed, in 1853, with a plan to proclaim the independence of all Balkan peoples as a war measure against the Turks. More important, the war engendered a lasting hostility between Habsburg and Romanov.

Austria's hostile actions in 1854–1855 were a betrayal which shocked and embittered the Russians. The blundering Buol congratulated himself on having accomplished "nothing less" than a revolution in Austria's foreign relations. This was true, but it was hardly an occasion for elation, since the possibility now arose that Russia would ally with France. For seven years—until the Polish revolt of 1863—this possibility created anxiety in the chancelleries of Europe. Although the alliance did not materialize, the assurance of Russia's benevolent neutrality enabled Napoleon III in 1859 and Bismarck in 1866 to attack and defeat Austria. The politics of self-interest triumphed over the doctrine of conservative solidarity and the concept of a common European interest.

[1] For a map which includes the Balkans and the Middle East see Part XIII, Chapter 1.

FURTHER READING The difficult task of tracing in detail the development of European thought and literature has been undertaken in a few major works: T. Merz, *History of European Thought in the Nineteenth Century*, 4 vols., (1896–1914); G. Brandes, *Main Currents in Nineteenth Century Literature*, 6 vols. (1901–1905); and E. Friedell, *A Cultural History of the Modern Age*, 3 vols. (1932). Attempts at a single-volume synthesis are G. L. Mosse, * *The Culture of Western Europe* (1961); and J. Bowle, *Politics and Opinion in the Nineteenth Century* (1954). Romanticism has enjoyed much attention from scholars. Representative studies are C. E. Vaughan, *The Romantic Revolt* (1923); O. F. Walzel, *German Romanticism* (1932); N. H. Clement, *Romanticism in France* (1939); H. A. Beers, *A History of English Romanticism in the Nineteenth Century* (1929); and C. Brinton, *The Political Ideas of the English Romanticists* (1926).

Standard works on their respective subjects are P. Lang, *Music in Western Civilization* (1941) and W. Dampier, *A History of Science and Its Relations with Philosophy and Religion* (1932)—too broad a title for the content—and A. P. Usher, *A History of Mechanical Inventions* (2nd ed., 1954). All aspects of the transition to realism and materialism are described in R. C. Binkley, *Realism and Nationalism, 1852–1871* (1935). Important monographs on aspects of it are D. G. Charlton, *Positivist Thought in France 1852–1870* (1959); S. Hook, *From Hegel to Marx* (1936); and H. Marcuse, *Reason and Revolution* (3rd ed., 1954). Best on their subjects are W. Kaufmann, * *Hegel* (1966); and I. Berlin, *Karl Marx* (2nd ed., 1948).

On the Crimean War see V. J. Puryear, *England, Russia and the Straits Question, 1844–1856* (1931); G. Henderson, *Crimean War Diplomacy and Other Historical Essays* (1947); H. Temperley, *England and the Near East*, vol. 1, *The Crimea* (1936). How Britain fought the war has been described by C. B. Woodham-Smith, *The Reason Why* (1953); and O. Anderson, *A Liberal State at War: English Politics and Economics during the Crimean War* (1967).

*Books available in paperback edition are marked with an asterisk.

7 The Advance of Political Democracy in Britain, France, and the Minor States

The third quarter of the nineteenth century was a period of gestation in both British and French political development. By yielding before it was too late on the issues of suffrage reform and protectionism, the British gentry and nobility were able to preserve their control over both houses of Parliament, and hence over the cabinet. For three decades, their power remained uncontested and British constitutional development was at a standstill. Yet behind the scenes new social forces were gathering strength and by the late 1860's Britain's ruling class saw that further changes were necessary. The Reform Act of 1867 proved to be the decisive step in the development of political democracy in Britain.

In France, the period of gestation was that of the Second Empire. Louis Napoleon became the dictator of France by capitalizing upon the desire of most Frenchmen for the restoration of order after the disturbances of 1848. While his government was autocratic, he gave the masses the illusion of participation in government through universal suffrage. After 1860, the electorate began to get out of control and Napoleon, like the British ruling class, sought to retreat in time—before popular dissatisfaction could destroy the entire system. The budding parliamentary regime which he introduced failed to stand the test of war in 1870. In the end, the Second Empire proved to be only an interruption in France's progress toward popular sovereignty under a republic.

Among the minor states of northern Europe a similar development was underway. At the beginning of the nineteenth century, the Low Countries (the Netherlands and Belgium) and the Scandinavian countries (Denmark, Sweden, and Norway) all possessed monarchical constitutions of mixed powers with parliaments elected by a very limited suffrage. By 1914, all had become parliamentary democracies with constitutions like that of Great Britain. Switzerland achieved the same goal, but in the form of a federal republic. In the Iberian countries (Spain and Portugal), however, the story was different. Here the social foundation for the liberal ideal was lacking, and both countries were destined to be ruled by military dictatorships.

GREAT BRITAIN IN THE AGE OF PALMERSTON

There were several reasons why the gentry and aristocracy were able to retain their monopoly of British politics despite the fact that the upper middle class had acquired the vote in 1832. The distribution of seats in the House of Commons was still inequitable and favored the rural areas. Voice voting enabled the landlords to influence the votes of their tenants and other dependents, and some boroughs were still controlled by local magnates. The gentry were more experienced in the ancient art of political corruption than were the newly enfranchised. Furthermore, they had always been the ruling class, and voting for their candidates was in many areas a habit not easily broken. England, wrote Walter Bagehot, had a "deferential electorate."

The successive cabinets reflected the character of Parliament. Whether Whig or Tory (these party designations were giving way to "Liberal" and "Conservative"), they were usually composed of ministers drawn from the same landowning elite. Yet it would be wrong to assume that the government throughout this period represented exclusively the interests of the landowners. Many gentry and nobility had investments in industry and commerce. The motivations of political actions, moreover, are not always as simple or selfish as the materialists would have us believe. Humanitarianism, the requirements of political strategy, and many other factors can intrude.

The most striking result of the first Reform Act was not the social and political transformation of Parliament, but the reduced power of the crown. Before 1832, the crown, that is, the king and cabinet, had usually been able to control elections through the power of patronage, but after that date the electorate was too large to manage in this way. Parliament now held the final power over the cabinet and the legislative process. In 1850, however, this did not mean what it does today for Commons was not under the firm control of a disciplined majority.

The Party System The two-party system, which is almost a precondition of a disciplined majority, did not yet really exist in Britain. The two major parties were composed of groups, whose shifting relationships were responsible for the rise and fall of cabinets. Not until 1867 was the voice of the electorate usually decisive for determining what government would sit in Whitehall.

One of the reasons for this instability was the split of the Conservative Party after the repeal of the Corn Laws in 1846. The departure of the Peelites left the Party more homogeneous, but bereft of leadership and doomed numerically to a minority position. Its new leader, Lord Derby, lacked the dynamism of Peel. The young Benjamin Disraeli could have supplied this quality, but many were reluctant to accept him because of his brilliance and his Jewish origin. The conservative governments formed in 1852, 1858–1859, and 1866–1868 had no absolute majority in Commons. They were tolerated for a time because of the incohesion of the Liberals.

For two decades (1846–1866) the Liberal Party was usually in power. Many of its cabinets, nevertheless, were short-lived because the Prime Minister and his parliamentary whips were unable to hold the party members in line. The Liberal leadership, supplied by Anglican landlords, was dependent within the party upon the support of the Manchester Radicals, who represented the middle-class manufacturers. Outside the party they were usually dependent upon the Peelites, without whom no majority could be formed. This uneasy coalition of political forces was never firm. Frequently personal differences were enough to bring about the reconstruction of the cabinet. Only the greater weakness of the Conservatives permitted the continuance of Liberal power.

John Henry Temple, 3rd Viscount Palmerston. In a political career that lasted more than half a century, Palmerston became very popular with the British public, whose attitudes he seemed to embody. He was colorful, patriotic, somewhat arrogant, and fond of horses and feminine society. (Brown Brothers.)

Palmerston and Queen Victoria   During this period, the dominant personality in the successive Liberal governments was Lord Palmerston. Although he held other cabinet posts, Palmerston is chiefly known for his roles as Foreign Secretary (1830–1841, 1846–1851) and Prime Minister (1855–1858, 1859–1865). Being an Irish peer, Palmerston could sit in the House of Commons, to which he was elected sixteen times from five different constituencies. Convinced of Britain's superiority, he often lectured continental rulers and statesmen upon the virtue of following her example. On occasion he meddled unnecessarily in the diplomatic affairs of other states, blustering at the great powers and bullying the smaller ones. He despised autocratic governments and supported constitutional ones; yet he recognized the pursuit of Britain's interests to be his primary duty. To the British public he was affectionately known as "Lord Pumicestone."

Although the power of the crown had declined, its prestige among Englishmen grew during the reign of Queen Victoria (1837–1901). As Regent and King, George IV had, by his immorality and lack of integrity, brought the monarchy into grave popular disrepute. Although William IV (1830–1837) was more acceptable, his reign was short. Ascending the throne at the tender age of eighteen, Victoria took her task with great seriousness. Her judgments on political matters were often emotional, but she understood the limits of her constitutional position better than either of her predecessors. In Prince Albert of Saxe-Coburg she found a consort of considerable ability and political understanding. She bore him nine children and his death in 1861 left her inconsolable. Her intense devotion to duty and the exemplary character of her private life won Victoria the respect and affection of the nation. The high repute of the monarchy at the end of her reign, the longest in English history, was a great personal achievement, but it also demonstrated the wisdom of the British in removing the crown from the turbulence of politics.

Foreign Policy in the Middle Years   The great issues of the mid-Victorian era were all in foreign affairs. Almost all of the cabinet changes between

Queen Victoria, Albert, and All Nine of Their Children, 1857. The marriages of Victoria's children allied the British royal family with those of Germany, Russia, Greece, Denmark, Rumania, and a number of small German states. (Radio Times Hulton Picture Library.)

1846 and 1866 occurred over some crisis in foreign policy. The Whig-Peelite cabinet of Lord Aberdeen involved Britain in the Crimean War. Although the war was popular in Britain, the cabinet was discredited by the miserable record of British generalship, the failures of the military supply services, and journalists' accounts of the wretched conditions in British hospitals. Palmerston replaced Aberdeen and brought the war to a successful conclusion. It was hardly over when Britain was compelled to put down a major revolt in India (1857). Beginning with a mutiny among native troops (Sepoys), the revolt became a general protest against British colonialism. The rebels massacred man, woman, and child, and the British reprisal was brutal (burning, hanging, crucifixion, and torture). Meanwhile there was difficulty in China. The attempts of western merchants and governments to open China for commercial penetration had led to a long series of incidents, including the "Opium War" of 1839–1842. These episodes troubled the consciences of many Englishmen. In 1856, British bombardment of Chinese forts on the Canton River brought a vote of censure in Commons. Palmerston dissolved Parliament, and was returned with a comfortable majority by the voters. In April 1858, a joint British-French expedition reached Peking and dictated a favorable settlement.

Yet a few months later Palmerston, seemingly at the height of his prestige and power, stumbled and fell over the Orsini affair. In January 1858, an Italian conspirator, Felice Orsini, nearly succeeded in assassinating Napoleon III. Since the plot had been hatched in London and the bombs procured in Birmingham, the French government lodged a vigorous protest. In the interest of preserving the entente with France, Palmerston introduced a Conspiracy Bill, which made such acts punishable as a felony. But the public reacted with fury. The bill failed and Palmerston resigned.

After a short-lived cabinet under Lord Derby, "Lord Pumicestone" came back into power in 1859. His second cabinet was troubled by four major problems in foreign affairs: the unification of Italy (1859–1860), the American Civil War (1861–1864), the Polish revolt against Russia (1863), and the German war against Denmark (1864). Whereas Derby had followed a pro-Austrian policy in the Italian affair, (see pp. 1163–64), Palmerston favored the Italians and assisted in their triumph. In dealing with the American war he was not so lucky. Until Lincoln's Emancipation Proclamation raised the moral issue of slavery, Britain tended to favor the cause of the southern planters. Southern agents succeeded in outfitting in British shipyards two war vessels, the *Florida* and *Alabama*, which played havoc with federal shipping. Naturally the United States protested sharply and in 1872 succeeded in getting a settlement of $15,000,000 for the damage caused.

Palmerston was least successful in dealing with the Polish and Danish crises. Sympathetic on ideological grounds with the Polish rebels, he and his Foreign Minister, Lord Russell, meddled in the affair without accomplishing anything for the insurgents, who were suppressed by the Russians. When the German Confederation, led by Austria and Prussia, made war on Denmark in behalf of Schleswig-Holstein, the British threatened the German powers but did not intervene, and the Danes were defeated. Military intervention, whether in Poland or in Denmark, would have required an alliance with Napoleon III, whom the British did not trust. They suspected him of designs upon Belgium and the German Rhineland, whose acquisition by France would dangerously upset the European balance of power and damage the vital interests of Great Britain.

Domestic Affairs in the Middle Years The absorption of the government in foreign policy during the 1846–1866 period was possible because, after three decades of turbulence often bordering on revolution, Great Britain was relatively quiet.

The reason for this lull was prosperity. As has been shown, earlier political crises were usually the consequence of agricultural failures followed by business declines, unemployment, and social distress. But the two decades after 1846 were marked by rapid industrial progress, interrupted only by the brief depression of 1857. Coal production in Great Britain rose from 57,000,000 tons in 1850 to 112,000,000 tons in 1870, pig-iron production from 2,200,000 to 6,000,000 tons. Naturally this development was accompanied by a spectacular growth in the capitalistic system and an expansion in the size and wealth of the entrepreneurial class. But the working class also benefited. Wages climbed faster than prices, and the real income of the average working-class family improved about ten percent during the two decades.

The passage of new factory legislation and the progress of unionization also took some of the steam out of social protest. Although the Factory Act of 1833 had abolished child labor under nine in the textile factories, other industries were unaffected and adult labor of fifteen to sixteen hours a day was still common. The Mines Act of 1842 removed women and girls from the mines and prohibited the labor of boys under ten. The goal of the reformers, led by Lord Shaftesbury, was a ten-hour working day for adults; and in the Factory Act of 1850 they nearly attained it. The working day was limited to twelve hours, with an hour and a half for meals and a 2:00 P.M. closing on Saturdays. During these years, other measures made a beginning in the protection of the health and safety of miners and factory workers. The resistance of the employers to these bills was bitter, but they were compelled to give way before Britain's growing conscience and the desire of the landed interests to avenge their defeat in the battle over the Corn Laws.

After 1850, trade unionism absorbed the energies of the British working class. Turning their backs on socialistic theories and doctrines of violence, the leaders of the movement strove for respectability and public recognition of collective bargaining as a normal part of the economic process. After many local unions had been established, efforts were made to amalgamate them into national organizations on a craft basis. In 1851, the Amalgamated Society of Engineers was formed, which had a membership of 11,000 and became the model for similar organizations in other trades. Through membership dues, the union treasuries became strong enough to afford strike pay, sickness benefits, and lawyers' fees. Lockouts and strikes caused the leaders of the major unions to confer and cooperate for common ends. In typical English fashion, the movement grew empirically, without plan, according to the exigencies of successive situations.

These developments were highly depressing to Karl Marx, busy in the British Museum composing his denunciations of capitalism. Prolonged prosperity, he complained, had "demoralized the workers." "The revolutionary energy of the British workers has oozed away. . . . They totally lack the mettle of the old Chartists."

The Reform Bill of 1867 Although Britain was quiet on the surface, observers like Gladstone and Russell appreciated that the current of economic and social change was running swiftly and that the electoral system of 1832 could not endure. Early in 1865, the trade unions, disturbed over an adverse judicial decision, began to agitate for an extension of the suffrage. Without political power, it appeared, their interests were not secure. Later that year the harvest failed and cholera reappeared. Beginning in May 1866, the collapse of a number of banks and business enterprises aroused fears of unemployment.

The death of Palmerston in 1865 enabled Gladstone and Russell to assume leadership of the Liberal Party and the cabinet. As Prime Minister, Russell presented to Parliament (March 1866) a moderate reform bill that would have added only about 400,000 persons to the voting lists, including many laborers. But the Liberal Party divided over the issue, for many Liberals distrusted the lower classes. Russell resigned and the Queen turned to Lord Derby who formed a minority government with Disraeli as Chancellor of the Exchequer.

The news of Russell's fall produced demonstrations in the streets of London, and on July 23 an angry crowd, barred from Hyde Park by the police, tore down the iron railings and trampled the flower beds. John Bright led monster demonstrations in the northern and midland cities. Derby and Disraeli, while convinced by these disturbances of the necessity for electoral reform, also relished the prospect of undercutting the Liberals. By giving proletarians the vote, the Conservatives might win their lasting support.

The government's bill was somewhat more liberal than that of Russell and Gladstone. To appease his Conservative critics, however, Disraeli included a number of safeguards against democratic suffrage. In Commons, Gladstone's tactic was to strike out the safeguards in the hope of making the bill unacceptable to Disraeli's own party, but Disraeli calmly accepted the amendments one after the other. The consequence was that the bill that

Garden party at the London residence of Lord Holland (left). Backyards of tenements underneath the railway trestles in London's East End (right). In a novel *Sybil* published in 1845 Benjamin Disraeli wrote of the "two nations" in British society—the rich and the poor. These drawings from Gustave Doré's book on London show what he meant.

became law on August 15, 1867 was far more democratic than most members of Parliament, whether Liberal or Conservative, thought wise. Derby himself regarded it as a "leap in the dark." More than a million citizens gained the vote, doubling the size of the electorate. Included were the better paid members of the working class. Only the agricultural laborers and those miners who lived in the country were still excluded.

Once the bill had carried, the vital question was who would profit from it: the Liberals, who had introduced the issue, or the Conservatives, who were mainly responsible for the final outcome. The answer was not long in coming, for the next election was held in 1868. The retirement of Derby and Russell left the helms of the two parties in the hands of Disraeli and Gladstone, perhaps the most dynamic and capable political leaders in British politics during the century. Although Disraeli had shone at Gladstone's cost in the reform debates, the Liberal leader was always "terrible on the rebound." On election day, the Liberals won control of the house by a majority of 112 seats. For three decades labor generally supported the candidates of the Liberal Party.

The changes produced in British politics by the reform of 1867 were far greater than those produced by that of 1832. The enlarged electorate necessitated a new kind of politics, in which Gladstone particularly excelled. Heretofore, campaigning had been largely local, and the leaders of neither party had sought to appeal to the country at large. But Gladstone knew how to move large audiences and understood the appeal of mass meetings and torchlight parades. Eventually the Conservatives were compelled to follow suit. While the two political leaders who inaugurated the new age were of middle-class origin, aristocratic leadership was by no means finished. Until 1900 most British cabinets, whether Conservative or Liberal, were filled with men of title or status. The most significant change was the fact that henceforth the voters, rather than shifting party relationships, were decisive in determining who would reside in Downing Street. The new electorate spoke with greater clarity than the old, usually returning either the Liberals or Conservatives, in alternation, with workable majorities. The age of political democracy had dawned in Britain.

FRANCE UNDER THE SECOND EMPIRE

Louis Napoleon When elected President of France in December 1848, Louis Napoleon was forty years old and had spent most of his life in exile. Born of Hortense de Beauharnais, daughter of the Empress Josephine by her first marriage, and Louis Bonaparte, brother of the Emperor and King of Holland, he became in 1846 on the death of his father the only remaining heir to Bonapartism. Unfortunately for him, he did not resemble his famous uncle, and some even questioned his paternity (unfairly in all probability). The features of Napoleon I were round, those of Louis sharp and angular, accentuated by his pointed beard and waxed mustaches. The two men also differed radically in temperament. While ambitious and power hungry, Louis lacked the vulcanic personality and driving energy of Napoleon I. Instead, he achieved through tactical shrewdness, maneuverability, and a capacity for intrigue.

On three previous occasions he had attempted unsuccessfully to gain power. In 1830, at the age of twenty-two, he participated in a farcical coup against the Papal government in Rome. His efforts in 1836 at Strasbourg and 1840 at Boulogne to mount insurrections against Louis Philippe cost him six years detention in the fortress of Ham. Between coups, he devoted himself to building up the legend of Bonapartism and his own image as its living exponent. In articles and pamphlets he appealed to almost every element in the French population. Nationalists were reminded of the greatness of the Empire, liberals of its reforms, property owners of its internal order. Idealists were assured that Napoleon's wars had been fought for the creation of a European league based upon national states. Military men were given evidence of his knowledge of artillery, businessmen and farmers of his partiality for protectionism, scientists of his interest in the phenomenon of electricity. Perhaps his shrewdest stroke of all was a pamphlet called *The Extinction of Poverty* (1844), which outlined a socialistic scheme for the workers.

Yet this would have gained him little had not the revolution of 1848 given him his chance. From exile in London, he permitted his name to be entered in the parliamentary elections of June and September of that year and was elected each time in five constituencies. After these successes, he dared to go to Paris, despite a law of 1830 which prohibited his entering France. His first speech to the chamber was unimpressive. His nervousness, his foreign accent, his big nose and short legs made him appear insignificant to the deputies who had previously feared his ambitions. The ban was removed. In December, when Louis was elected President by an overwhelming majority, the deputies learned the magnitude of their mistake.

Napoleon as President Although he talked of "liberty" and swore to uphold the constitution, Louis planned from the outset to overthrow the republic and create a new empire. His election demonstrated the growing desire of the French peasants and bourgeois for "order" and their deepening distrust of radical republicanism. Yet he approached his goal with caution. Touring the provinces, he built up his popularity, appealing to every section and every interest in carefully worded speeches. He was a master of the moralistic, meaningless prose of the skilled political propagandist.

His first task was to rid himself of the republican majority in the chamber. To this end he appointed a conservative, Orleanist cabinet and defended it against the attacks of the republican deputies. In January 1849, he forestalled a Jacobin insurrection by investing Paris with troops and announcing that the revolution was at an end. Four months later the electorate chose a new chamber whose majority (500 out of 750) belonged to the "party of moral order," a loose coalition of legitimists, Orleanists, Bonapartists, Catholics, and moderate republicans. In June, Napoleon sent a French army to occupy Rome, to destroy the revolutionary Roman republic, and to restore the power of Pius IX. When French republicans rioted over this policy, they were quickly suppressed. The Second French Republic was no longer controlled by republicans.

The Orleanist cabinet, headed by Odilon Barrot, thought to use Napoleon—only to be used by him. By supporting the ministers against the republican chamber before the May election, Napoleon established the principle that the cabinet was responsible only to himself. This enabled him in October 1849 to dismiss the Barrot cabinet, even though it was now backed by a parliamentary majority, and appoint one manned by his own supporters. When the chamber, made panicky by republican victories in by-elections, deprived three million voters (out of nine and a half million) of their suffrage rights, Louis Napoleon acquired the propaganda weapon with which to destroy his opponents. Now he could pose as the protector of the masses against the selfishness of the Right by championing the cause of universal suffrage. In January 1851, a Bonapartist general, Saint-Arnaud, was made commander in chief of the army and soon afterward another supporter became Prefect of the Paris police. The stage was prepared for a coup d'état.

On December 2, 1851 (the anniversary of Austerlitz), Paris awoke to find itself occupied by Saint-Arnaud's troops. At every street corner, placards accused the dissolved chamber of "conspiracy . . . forging weapons for civil war . . . encouraging all kinds of evil passions." A presidential decree ("in the name of the people of France") declared martial law, restored universal suffrage, and called for a plebiscite. By December 4, the stunned republicans had recovered sufficiently to erect barricades. But in six hours of fighting, the valiant but ill-armed defenders (numbering only 1,200) were crushed by artillery, musket balls, and bayonet charges. Captured insurrectionists were executed on the spot. Throughout France, nearly 27,000 individuals whose opposition was feared were placed under arrest. They were of all classes and political viewpoints and many were the innocent victims of senseless denunciations.

Through a new constitution, Napoleon created a presidential dictatorship. His term extended to ten years, the president was given full control over the executive power; command over land and sea forces; the right to institute martial law in any part of the country; and the power to declare war, make peace, and carry out all other functions of foreign policy. Although the document provided for a bicameral legislature with a senate appointed for life by the president and a legislative body chosen for six years by universal suffrage, the president exercised the dominant role in legislative matters. He proposed all laws, which were drafted by a council of state appointed by him. The deliberations of the legislative body took place chiefly in committee, for the Parliament as a whole had no power to debate. All amendments introduced in the committee had to be approved by the council of state before the final bill could be reported to the Parliament. The senate could only review for constitutionality the laws passed by the lower chamber and deliver any dissenting opinion in the form of a *Senatus Consulta*, which required presidential approval. The officers of both chambers were named by the president. Justice was dispensed in the president's name, and he alone could pardon the convicted. The entire administrative hierarchy, from the provincial prefects to the village mayors, was appointed by the central government.

Only a stroke of the pen was required to convert this "republican" constitution into an imperial one. To no one's surprise this happened—on December 2, 1852. "Prince Louis Napoleon" became "Emperor Napoleon III."

The Authoritarian Empire The new constitution sought to create the illusion that the power of the President-Emperor was based upon the "general will." "The President of the Republic," it declared, "is responsible to the French people, to whom he has always a right to appeal." This "appeal" was conducted through plebiscites, only three of which were ever held (1851, 1852, and 1870). The first two, in which the voters were asked to approve the destruction of the republic and revival of the empire, produced overwhelming majorities in the affirmative (7,500,000 to 640,000 in 1851 and 7,800,000 to 250,000 in 1852). These plebiscites were hardly free, since the voting was conducted in public and the opposition press was severely handicapped. Yet it is probable that most Frenchmen did approve. Like the famous literary critic Sainte-Beuve, they had concluded that France needed a "strong and stable government." Republican institutions seemed to invite chaos and social revolution.

Napoleon III and Empress Eugenie in 1861. Louis spoke little and Eugenie much. This gave him the reputation of being "enigmatic" and "sphinx-like" and her that of spokesperson and policy-maker for the regime. Neither reputation was justified. (Radio Times Hulton Picture Library.)

Few monarchs have taken as great an interest as Napoleon III in the temper and tempo of public opinion. To be sure, he did not permit its free expression. The right of assembly was curtailed; cafes and wine-shops, where Frenchmen usually gathered to discuss politics, were licensed; political journals could be suppressed after two warnings. Yet the government ordered its prefects to report in great detail on public reactions to its measures. Recent research suggests that the shifting current of popular opinion was closely followed by Napoleon and may at times have influenced his decisions.

Nor did Louis neglect the window dressing so necessary to an authoritarian regime. Once again, the Tuileries and St. Cloud became glittering centers of French society. A perennial succession of balls, banquets, and fetes enlivened the social life of the capital. Only two elements were lacking: an empress and an heir. In the past, Louis had deliberately avoided marriage, for the wrong alliance could have handicapped his career. But his search for a wife among the legitimate dynasties ended in failure, and in 1852 he was attracted to Eugénie de Montijo, a Spanish girl of noble but not royal blood. By refusing to be his mistress, she became his wife. Deeply religious, Eugénie became the center of the Catholic faction in the government and often meddled in politics, for which she had no talent. In 1856, she gave birth to an heir, the Prince Imperial.

Economic Growth Napoleon sought to bind all classes to the regime by cultivating their interests. He aimed to "divert the attention of the French from politics to economics." Influenced apparently by the doctrines of the Saint Simonians, he hoped to stimulate general prosperity by encouraging industrial growth. A basic obstacle was lack of credit. Until now the French banks had specialized primarily in government loans rather than loans to industry. Napoleon encouraged the development of banks providing the latter service. Founded in 1852, the *Crédit Mobilier* expanded rapidly, paying dividends as high as forty percent until it collapsed in 1867. The *Crédit Foncier*, also founded in 1852, was a mortgage bank subsidized by the government which eased the pressing need of peasants and town dwellers for new financing. It survived to become one of the most significant of French financial institutions. During the Second Empire, the French money market expanded so rapidly that Paris came to rival London as a financial center. For the first time France exported capital in quantity.

Although the period of the Empire was one of rapid economic growth throughout western and central Europe, the policies of Napoleon III undoubtedly did much to enable France to participate in the general prosperity. Railway construction (in which France lagged behind Britain and Germany) was accelerated through government subsidies and guarantees. Mergers were encouraged and the entire system was rationalized to increase its efficiency. Harbors, roads, and waterways were likewise improved. Better transportation benefited the whole economy. During the period of the Empire industrial production doubled, coal and iron production tripled; the use of steam power increased fivefold, railway mileage sixfold. While less interested in agriculture than in industry, Napoleon became concerned that the farmers were being overlooked. He initiated a program for the improvement of livestock breeding, model farms, land reclamation, forest conservation, and increased yields of grain and wine. While rarely willing to back the interests of the urban working class against the employers, he did seek to encourage employer patronage of labor in the fields of housing, health, and education. Through confiscation of the property of Louis Philippe and his family, Napoleon obtained funds with which to improve the lot of the workingmen by endowing mutual-benefit associations, constructing public baths, clearing some slums, and erecting a primitive employment bureau. In 1863, a credit bank was founded to finance both producers' and consumers' cooperatives. Labor was granted the right to strike in 1864 and unions were tolerated after 1868.

Napoleon became an enthusiastic promoter of free trade. Beginning in 1852, some tariffs on agricultural and industrial products were reduced. Yet the free-trade policy was heavily attacked by industrialists and national economists who feared the competition of foreign producers. Thwarted in his attempt to get the legislative body to renounce protective tariffs, Napoleon bypassed that body by exercising his treaty-making prerogative. In 1860, Britain and France signed the Cobden Treaty providing for a gradual reduction of tariffs over a period of five years. Similar agreements were negotiated with Belgium, the German Zollverein, Italy, Switzerland, Sweden and Norway, the Hanseatic towns, the Netherlands, Spain, and Austria.

Segment of the Sewer System under Construction beneath the New Boulevards of Paris in 1858. Not since Roman times had Europe known a public works project on the scale of that executed by Baron Haussmann under Napoleon III.

Dictators are usually builders on a grand scale, for the public must be compensated for the loss of its liberties by the visible evidence of the regime's effectiveness. Napoleon's greatest achievement in this sphere was the reconstruction of Paris. In two decades Paris was converted from a medieval city into a modern metropolis with broad boulevards lined with trees, sidewalks, and new buildings of uniform height. She had a gigantic system of storm sewers that was the marvel of Europe, great public squares with grand vistas, magnificent parks, and a water supply that was approaching adequacy. For this work, the Emperor was fortunate to find an able subordinate, Baron Haussmann, who ruthlessly surmounted every opposition and every financial and technical obstacle. The purpose of this reconstruction was not only aesthetic and social but military. The open squares and radiating boulevards were more convenient for cavalry and artillery. Never again would barricades choke the streets of Paris and bring down the government of France.

Foreign Policy Under the Empire   Naturally the ascension to power of another Bonaparte in France aroused anxiety throughout Europe. Not many were reassured by his assertion that "the Empire means peace." Napoleon's ambition was to rid France of the shackles of the Treaty of 1815. Furthermore, he probably believed his earlier words that Europe's future tranquillity depended upon the reogranization of its frontiers along national lines. Yet he lacked the military genius, indifference to bloodshed, and unlimited ambition of Napoleon I. France, furthermore, was no longer the wealthiest and most populous country in Europe. Hence, what he achieved depended more on the quality of his diplomacy than upon France's military power.

His first major venture in foreign affairs, the Crimean War, proved to be astonishingly profitable. Although he did not seek the conflict, France gained the most from it. By going to war against Russia, Napoleon escaped from isolation, gaining the alliance of Great Britain and nearly that of Austria. The coalition that had destroyed the First Empire no longer existed; the Holy Alliance and Concert of Europe were broken instruments. At Paris, in 1856, Napoleon presided over the peace conference. In four years, he had brought France to the pinnacle of European politics.

After 1858, nevertheless, Napoleon steadily squandered the political capital he had gained in the Crimea by antagonizing every European power in turn. In 1859, he went to war against Austria in support of Sardinia and the cause of Italian unity. Despite victories over Austria at Magenta and Solferino, he hastily made a separate peace at Villafranca. While acquiring Lombardy for Sardinia, he promised the restoration of the reactionary princes of central Italy to their thrones. This earned him the enmity of Cavour and many other Italians. Yet the movement for unity could no longer be halted, and in 1860 the goal was achieved (except for Rome and Venetia) without French assistance. The result was a unitary monarchy rather than the four-part confederacy Napoleon had planned. Cavour bought Napoleon's acquiescence by ceding Nice and Savoy to France, but this event aroused the whole of Europe, for it was feared that the Emperor's next move would be toward the Rhine. Britain's anxiety ended the British-French entente formed in the Crimean War. As a consequence, France was without an ally in 1863 when Napoleon wanted to support the Polish uprising against Russia. His expressions of sympathy for their cause did not help the Poles, who were defeated, but did alienate Russia.

A MOVING SPECTACLE.

Certainly the most foolish venture of Napoleon III, however, was his ill-fated intervention in Mexico. Beginning in 1861 as an effort to force the Mexicans to respect foreign property rights, the intervention became an attempt to establish a monarchy in Mexico under the Austrian Archduke Maximilian. Once the American Civil War was over, the United States forced the French to withdraw their troops under the threat of war. Although he had no popular support, the valiant Maximilian remained, only to be seized and executed. His wife, the lovely Carlotta, failing in her appeal for succor in Paris, became mentally deranged. She lived on until 1927 to haunt the memory of Bonapartism.

Yet the greatest failures of Napoleon were still to come. In 1866, he encouraged Prussia to attack Austria in the expectation that the embroilment would mean a territorial gain for France on the Rhine. But the Prussian victory came with stunning speed, and the wily Prussian statesman, Otto von Bismarck, frustrated his demands for compensation. By permitting war with Germany in 1870, Napoleon committed the final mistake which destroyed his regime.

The Liberal Empire During its early years, the Napoleonic regime undoubtedly possessed much popular support. In building the political machine with which they controlled the elections to the legislative body, the Emperor and his ministers carefully avoided the pitfall of relying exclusively upon the small group of "pure" Bonapartists. Instead they drew heavily upon the old elites, particularly the Orleanists, whose loyalties they sought to attract—with considerable success. Catholics were pleased, moreover, by the French occupation of Rome in support of the Papacy and by Napoleon's acceptance of the Falloux Law of 1850, which in effect placed public education under the control of the clergy. Businessmen were happy over the rising prosperity. While they received fewer material benefits than the bourgeois, the peasants were moved by the glamor of the Napoleonic legend, by the regime's suppression of radicals, and by the new freedom they enjoyed from the domination of local magnates. The urban working class also received only limited benefits from the regime. Although wages increased, prices appear to have advanced faster. Public works provided employment; but the reconstruction of Paris drove the workers, who could not afford the new housing, out into the slums of the suburbs.

The first signs of urban discontent came in the election of 1857. Although the government captured nearly eighty-five percent of the popular vote, the lower classes of the great towns showed their "evil disposition," as Napoleon put it, by voting for republican candidates. By 1860, other classes and interests were also disaffected. Catholics were antagonized by the war of 1859, and by the progress of Italian unification in 1860 at the cost of

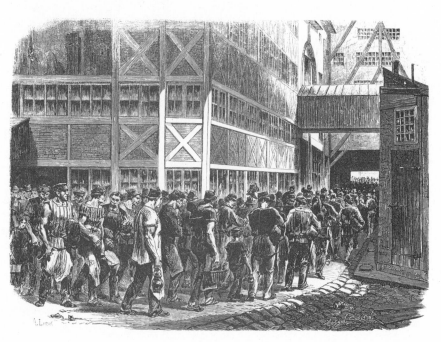

French Factory Workers Going on Strike in 1870. Although Napoleon sought to appease all classes, labor received the fewest benefits. In April 1870 there were many strikes in heavy industry for better wages and a ten-hour work day.

the Papacy. Many manufacturers were damaged by the free-trade treaty of 1860 and became critical of the regime. Depressions struck in 1857 and 1867. Although recovery was rapid, the marked industrial expansion of the 1850's tapered off in the following decade. The drifting and bungling in foreign policy in the 1860's also had its adverse effect upon public opinion. Napoleon appeared to have lost his grip on affairs. His intuition failed him; his sense of mission faded and likewise his will. Physically ailing, his main concern was to perpetuate the dynasty beyond his death.

It is difficult to say whether Napoleon's decision to liberalize the Empire after 1860 stemmed entirely from his desire to appease the dissatisfied. He had earlier insisted that liberty must one day "crown the edifice" after the Empire was secure. His half brother, minister, and adviser, the Duke de Morny, believed that liberalization would make the chamber more manageable. In 1860, came the first concessions to the legislative body: the right to vote an address to the crown; the right of ministers to defend their policies in Parliament; and the publication of the chamber's proceedings. Other concessions followed piecemeal: greater budgetary rights for Parliament in 1861, educational reforms in 1863, and the right to strike in 1864. Despite de Morny's death in 1865, the liberalization continued in 1867 when the deputies received the right to interpellate cabinet ministers; and the tribune, which favored political oratory, was reintroduced into the chamber. The censorship laws were relaxed and public meetings for political purposes permitted.

Meanwhile, the government's control over both the electorate and the chamber began to ease. In 1863, opposition candidates polled nearly 2,000,000 votes, as against 5,308,000 for official candidates, and carried all the major cities of France. During the next six years, however, the chamber witnessed a rapprochement between the two blocs. Émile Ollivier and his band of republican deputies moved toward acceptance of a liberalized empire, while many members of the government party came to accept the necessity of the Empire's liberalization. In the election of 1869, the government abandoned most of the pressures hitherto used to bring in official candidates. The result was 4,438,000 for the government and 3,355,000 for the opposition. Confronted with this, Napoleon took a long step toward parliamentary government by dismissing his own ministers and calling upon Ollivier to form a cabinet.

By introducing the parliamentary system, Napoleon hoped to remove the crown from the political struggle and make it independent of the shifting currents of public opinion. That the Empire was still popular, despite the election result of 1869, is evident from the results of the plebiscite of May 1870, in which the Emperor asked the public to endorse the constitutional changes of the last decade: 7,366,000 voted yes, 1,572,000 no. Yet only three months later the regime came to an abrupt end. It committed the one sin most Frenchmen could not forgive; it was decisively defeated on the battlefield.

The Low Countries Commercially, the Netherlands, or "Holland" as it is popularly known, was far more important than its size would indicate. Its geographical position made Holland a crossroads of European trade, and it possessed in the Indies one of the richest of all colonial empires. Yet Holland's progress toward industrialization was slower than that of neighboring states.

In 1813, the House of Orange was restored to power under King William I (1813–1840), an uncompromising absolutist who dominated the lethargic States-General. A tireless man of considerable ability and vision, William played an important role in the country's economic revival. In 1830, the Belgian revolt deprived him of half the population of his kingdom but left his authority over the rest unimpaired. Under his successors, William II (1840–1849) and William III (1849–1890), a Liberal party emerged to agitate for constitutional reform. In 1848, the king wisely yielded by granting a constitution which transformed the archaic States-General into a modern Parliament elected by the wealthiest citizens. Although the suffrage was extended in 1887 and 1896, it did not become universal until 1917. The constitution established the responsibility of ministers to the Parliament, but the last vestiges of royal power did not disappear until the reign of Wilhelmina (1890–1948).

For many decades, the major issue of Dutch politics was that of education. While the Liberals insisted upon a secular public school system, the Center (Catholic) and Conservative (Calvinist) parties finally succeeded in getting (1889) state support for confessional schools. The Center and Conservative parties also took an interest in the social question created by industrialization late in the century and were responsible for the passage of compulsory disability insurance and pensions for the elderly, widows, and orphans. Considerable progress was also made in slum clearance and in better housing for industrial workers.

On gaining their independence from the Dutch in 1830, the Belgians established a constitution modeled on the English system, with a monarchical figurehead and bicameral legislature to which the cabinet was responsible. As king they chose Leopold of Saxe-Coburg, a German prince of pronounced liberal views. Leopold I (1830–1865) adhered strictly to the constitutional lines. Of all continental parliamentary systems, that of Belgium corresponded most closely to that of Britain. The existence of only two or three parties made possible relatively stable cabinets which were in power long enough to give effective leadership. Although the constitution of 1831 restricted the vote to the highest taxpayers, a reform of 1894 extended it to all male citizens over twenty-four. Nevertheless, the law provided for plural voting, giving the wealthier and better educated citizens two or even three votes.

In Belgium, as in Holland, the issue of education was acute. The Liberal party, dominant in the years 1847–1884, insisted on secular public schools. The Catholic party, whose era of power lasted from 1884 until the World War, retained and even radically extended the public school system, but introduced religious instruction. Rapid industrialization, in which again

Belgian development paralleled that of Great Britain, produced a significant urban working class, which after 1885 gave its political allegiance to the Socialist pary at the cost of the Liberals. After 1890 several important social reforms were passed, regulating factories, legalizing trade unions, and providing for accident insurance and old-age pensions. Under Leopold II (1865–1909), an extensive and rich colony was acquired in the African Congo.

Scandinavia Like the Netherlands, Denmark was severely reduced in size during the nineteenth century. For siding with Napoleon she lost Norway in 1814, which went to Sweden. Yet she retained the duchies of Schleswig and Holstein as possessions of the Danish crown, despite the fact that they were inhabited mostly by Germans. An attempt in 1848 to incorporate them into the Danish state led to a war with Prussia which was indecisive. In 1864, the incorporation of Schleswig produced a conflict with the German Confederation that ended in defeat. The cession of the duchies meant the loss of some 200,000 Danes living in northern Schleswig.

Although Denmark escaped revolution in 1848, Frederick VII (1848–1863) promulgated a constitution as a concession to the growing liberal movement. Henceforth the crown shared legislative power with a bicameral legislature, whose lower chamber was elected by a restricted suffrage based on property. The question of ministerial responsibility produced a long quarrel between the crown and the liberals of the lower chamber during the reign of Christian IX (1863–1906). In 1866, the king achieved a revision of the constitution, which made the ministers responsible only to the upper chamber, part of whose members he appointed. Backed by the dominant Conservative party, he was able to defy the Liberal party, which was supported on this issue after 1880 by a growing Social Democratic party. Although the Liberals assumed power in 1901, it was not until 1914–1915 that a series of amendments formally broke the power of the upper chamber, establishing ministerial responsibility to the lower chamber and extending the suffrage to all men and most women above the age of twenty-five.

During the period of Conservative rule, Denmark acquired a very progressive system of social insurance. In 1891–1892, the Old-Age Pension and Health Insurance Acts were passed. The Danish economy was primarily agricultural, and in the 1890's the government made it possible for peasants to acquire land. By 1905, ninety-four percent of all farms were freeholds. Rural cooperatives flourished in Denmark and added to the economic welfare of the farmers.

Sweden's acquisition of Norway in 1814 was her compensation for surrendering Finland to Russia. From the start, however, the union of the two countries was uneasy. The Norwegians had to be conquered by Marshal Bernadotte, the former Napoleonic general who since 1810 had been the heir to the Swedish throne. The two peoples were incompatible from almost every standpoint. While Sweden was dominated by a landowning nobility, Norway was a democratic country of small farmers and fishermen who detested titles. Even Bernadotte felt it wise to accept the Norwegian constitution drafted by the rebels of 1814, which provided for a single chamber with final legislative power and elected indirectly by taxpayers. The government of Sweden, on the other hand, was nearly absolute. Bernadotte, who ruled as Charles XIV (1818–1844), was a tight-fisted autocrat who jealously guarded royal prerogatives over the Estates-General, a feudal body composed of four chambers representing the nobles, clergymen, burghers, and peasants. Although the Estates-General gave way in 1863 to a modern bicameral legislature, the nobility established their dominance in both houses, and the king retained an absolute veto. The upper house was chosen by the provincial assemblies and the lower chamber by a restricted suffrage based on property.

As the century progressed, the disparity between Norway and Sweden grew. While Norway fostered a commercial class with far-flung shipping interests, Sweden began to develop her rich mineral resources through rapid industrialization. Her social structure became complicated through the appearance of a capitalistic bourgeoisie and a factory proletariat. All efforts to integrate the two kingdoms failed and, in fact, the Norwegians objected increasingly to the king's control over their foreign affairs. When Oscar II (1872–1907) refused their demand for a separate consular service, the Norwegian Parliament voted in 1905 for independence; this decision was ratified by the public in a plebiscite. The Swedish government reluctantly agreed, and a Danish prince accepted the Norwegian crown as Haakon VII.

Further democratization followed in both countries. Norway had already adopted universal manhood suffrage in 1898, and in 1906 direct election was introduced; full female suffrage was achieved by 1913. The king became a mere figurehead in 1913 with the abolition of his power of suspensive veto. In Sweden, universal manhood suffrage was achieved in 1909 for the election of the lower house and the property qualification for election to the upper house was lowered. Later, female suffrage was granted and proportional representation applied to the election of both houses. With the accession of Gustavus V (1907–1950), the responsibility of the cabinet to the lower chamber was fully established. Although some social legislation was passed, a Socialist Party developed, and, in 1914, succeeded in capturing one-third of the seats in the lower chamber.

Switzerland In the family of nations, Switzerland is unique. At the beginning of the nineteenth century, it was a mere confederation of twenty-two cantons loosely uniting a population of diverse linguistic and religious character. Each canton was autonomous in domestic matters and even conducted in some degree its own foreign affairs. While fifteen cantons were German speaking, five were French and two Italian. Protestants predominated in twelve cantons, Catholics in ten. What bound the cantons together was their common Alpine geography, their common republican institutions, and their intense desire to maintain the country's independence.

During the European reaction after 1815, most cantons followed a conservative policy under considerable pressure from the great powers. But in the period 1828–1847, called by the Swiss the "era of regeneration," a liberal movement developed which caused most cantonal governments to grant rights such as universal manhood suffrage, equality before the law, and freedom of the press. In 1834, these liberal cantons accepted a program of religious reform which guaranteed freedom of worship and provided for secular education. In order to make these reforms general throughout the confederation, the liberals demanded a stronger central government. The conservative cantons resisted, forming a league (*Sonderbund*) for common defense. A brief civil war resulted (1847) in victory for the liberal cantons.

The new constitution that emerged from this conflict provided for a stronger federal union, some of whose features were modeled after those of the United States. Legislative power was vested in a bicameral legislature whose upper chamber represented the cantons and whose lower chamber was elected by universal manhood suffrage. The two chambers chose the executive body, or Federal Council, of seven coequal members. The cantons retained control over such matters as education, religion, police, and public health; but the central government assumed power over foreign policy, customs, currency, military affairs, and the postal and telegraph systems. A constitutional revision of 1874 made public education a federal prerogative. Two significant amendments of 1874 and 1891 provided for popular referendum and initiative. These popular privileges—the right to initiate legislation by popular petition and the right to decide by popular vote on critical issues—are the hallmarks of Swiss democracy. Another is the militia system established in 1874, which requires every able-bodied citizen to undergo military training for a certain number of days each year. The quality of its training, its popular and defensive character, and its freedom from political involvement made the Swiss militia a model for other democratic countries.

During the century, Switzerland experienced an impressive economic growth and diversification. The rigors of tending sheep and cattle on the steep slopes and of cultivating the narrow valleys bred a nation of thrifty people. Tourists from all Europe came in increasing numbers to enjoy the spectacular scenery, enriching the innkeepers and stimulating the economy in general. Despite sparse natural resources, the Swiss turned to manufacturing with spectacular success. Swiss clocks and watches, textiles and leather products, cheese and milk chocolate became known throughout Europe and the rest of the world for their excellent quality.

Spain In contrast to the smaller states of northern Europe, Spain and Portugal experienced great difficulty in establishing stable liberal systems of government. Early in the nineteenth century, Spain had a new middle-class elite which succeeded in instituting the most advanced suffrage law on the continent. Taking advantage of the weakness of the monarchy, they introduced indirect universal male suffrage in the Cadiz consitution of 1812. Yet the Spanish liberals were unable to consolidate their gains, owing to the backwardness of the economy, the low rate of literacy, and conflicts among the liberals themselves. The intellectual culture and political ideas of modern Spain were derived from the more advanced countries of north-western Europe, but its economy and society more nearly resembled the backward regions of the eastern Mediterranean or eastern Europe. This duality led to grave contradictions between advanced political forms and the actual conduct of governmental affairs.

The constitution was abolished by Ferdinand VII (1814–1833) in 1823. Upon his death, the succession to the throne was disputed by moderate liberals, supporting the claims of his infant daughter Isabel II (1833–1868), and traditionalist absolutists, supporting the claims of his younger brother, Don Carlos. Civil war raged from 1833 to 1840, resulting in victory for the liberals over the "Carlists." They established a new constitution of mixed powers with a restricted suffrage. During the reign of Queen Isabel, rival factions continued to struggle for power; there were repeated uprisings and coups. Because of their narrow base of support, Isabeline liberals had to rely increasingly upon the army to maintain their power. In 1868, a joint military-civilian revolt deposed Isabel and turned out the faction associated with her rule. A constituent assembly (Cortes) was elected to draft a new, more democratic constitution and to found a new dynasty. After a lengthy search, which at one point helped to trigger war between France and Germany, the throne was accepted by a liberal Italian prince, Amadeo of Savoy (1871–1873). But King Amadeo was unable to overcome the persistent factionalism of Spanish politics. After he abdicated, Spanish radicals established a decentralized federal republic, which collapsed in chaos within a year.

The army then restored the Bourbon dynasty under Isabel's son, Alphonso XII (1875–1885), who promulgated a new constitution providing for a cabinet responsible to a bicameral Cortes whose lower chamber was elected by a limited suffrage. Two parties, Liberal and Conservative, alternated in power on the English pattern. For half a century, this restored Bourbon regime gave Spain political stability. After 1890, universal male suffrage was restored and a series of constitutional and social reforms were passed.

By the early twentieth century, Spanish stability was again threatened. A number of reformist and revolutionary groups arose, all of which were dissatisfied with the slow economic and social progress. They took as their model the advanced industrial countries of northern Europe; by contrast, Spain's agrarian economy appeared stagnant and backward. To make matters worse, Spain was defeated in war by the United States in 1898 and lost the remains of her historic overseas empire. Spanish society entered the twentieth century in a disillusioned and uncertain mood, increasingly at odds with itself.

Portugal The history of Portugal parallels that of Spain. While Peter IV (1826) accepted a moderate parliamentary regime similar to that of Great Britain, the throne was seized from his infant daughter Maria II (1826–1853) by her uncle, the absolutist Dom Miguel (the Don Carlos of Portugal). With British help, the constitutionalists defeated the "Miguelites" in 1834. Nevertheless, the rest of Maria's reign, like that of Isabella II, was marked by ministerial instability and frequent revolts. The regime's survival depended upon the support of the generals, for the peasant masses were indifferent to politics. As in Spain after 1875, two factions of constitutional monarchists, the "Regenerators" and "Progressives," alternated in power, dominating the Parliament by skillful management of elections. They were professional politicans interested primarily in their own power and enrichment, rather than in social reform or the public welfare.

Even after losing Brazil, Portugal possessed a very large colonial empire in Africa, India, and the Far East; but the expense of its administration and development was greater than its financial return. Burdened by heavy taxation, angered by official corruption and social injustice, the urban classes grew resitive. Republicanism, socialism, and anarchism spread. Carlos I (1889–1908) attempted to meet the crisis by resorting to absolutism, but he and the crown prince were assassinated in the streets of Lisbon. Two years later, Manuel II (1908–1910) was overthrown by a revolution which ended with the proclamation of a republic. From the outset, the Portuguese republic, modeled after that of France, was troubled by radical agitation, strikes and riots, royalist uprisings, and military coups which foreshadowed its ultimate destruction and the creation of a dictatorship in 1926.

FURTHER READING For general surveys of British and French history in this period see the notes for Chapter 3. On British constitutional development see K. B. Smellie, *A Hundred Years of English Government* (2nd ed., 1951); D. L. Keir, *Constitutional History of Modern Britain, 1485–1951* (5th ed., 1953); and C. S. Emden, *The People and the Constitution* (2nd ed., 1956). The works of Asa Briggs are useful: *Victorian People* (1954) and *The Making of Modern England, 1783–1867* (1959); G. K. Clark summed up the changing views on the third quarter of the century in * *The Making of Victorian England* (1962). Biographies of important figures are E. Longford, *Queen Victoria* (1965); H. C. Bell, *Lord Palmerston,* 2 vols. (1936); and W. D. Jones, *Lord Derby and Victorian Conservatism* (1956).

The best biography of Napoleon III is J. M. Thompson, *Louis Napoleon and the Second Empire* (1954). R. L. Williams has illuminated Napoleon's health and psychological problems in *The Mortal Napoleon III* (1971); earlier he described in fascinating detail his social environment in *The World of Napoleon III, 1815–1870* (1962). Two other studies are P. Guedalla, *The Second Empire* (1922); and A. Guerard, *Napoleon III. An Interpretation* (1943). Important aspects of the second empire have been treated in several monographs: T. Zeldin, *The Political System of Napoleon III* (1958); D. Pinkney, *Napoleon III and the Rebuilding of Paris* (1958); and L. M. Case, *French Opinion on War and Diplomacy during the Second Empire* (1954).

*Books available in paperback edition are marked with an asterisk.

Introductions to the history of the smaller states are those by A. J. Barnouw on Holland (1944); H. van der Linden on Belgium (1930); W. Oechsli on Switzerland (1922); Karen Larsen on Norway (1948); Ingvar Andersson on Sweden (1956); and H. Livermore on Portugal (1947). Good surveys of Spanish history in the nineteenth century are those of R. Carr (1966); H. L. Livermore (1948); and S. de Madariaga (1943, 1958). Important books dealing with special problems are S. G. Payne, *Politics and the Military in Modern Spain* (1967); and G. Brenan, *The Spanish Labyrinth* (1950).

8 The Age of Unification: Italy, Germany, and Austria

On the evening of January 14, 1858 the Emperor and Empress of France, on arriving at the Paris Opera to hear a performance of *William Tell*, were nearly assassinated by Felice Orsini and his band of Italian patriots. Three bombs ripped their carriage and spread death and injury through the crowded street. Although Louis and Eugénie escaped unharmed, the former was morally shaken by the event. It forcibly reminded him of his participation in the Italian revolution of 1831 and of his professed dedication to the principle of national self-determination. A few months later he entered into a secret agreement with Sardinia, the aim of which was the exclusion of Austria from Italy and the reorganization of the Italian peninsula along national lines.

This act inaugurated a period of national wars which, in the short space of eleven years, brought about a radical revision of the European map and a reconstruction of the balance of power. By 1870, both Italy and Germany had been unified; Austria had been reorganized into a Dual Monarchy; and France, which set the machine in motion, had been replaced by Germany as the leading power on the continent of Europe. Like the sorcerer's apprentice of Goethe's famous poem, Napoleon evoked demonic forces which he could not control. But he was less lucky than the apprentice, for he was eventually destroyed by them.

Italian and German unification was chiefly the work of two men of genius, Count Cavour and Otto von Bismarck, although the former owed much to Napoleon and Garibaldi and the latter to the Prussian army and its superb leadership. Both were favored by the international situation of their times. The Crimean war had dissolved long-standing European power relationships by alienating Austria and Russia. The war brought France and Britain together, but this entente did not endure. The British were averse to continental alliances that might entangle them in wars for the interests of other states, and after 1859 they grew suspicious of Napoleon III and

1215

Attempted Assassination of Napoleon III by Orsini and Gang. Before the nineteenth century political assassinations were comparatively rare in central and western Europe. Ideological movements and political involvement of the masses made statesmanship a hazardous occupation. (The Bettmann Archive.)

of his presumed intention to expand toward the Rhine. For the first time in many decades, the European political situation was fluid. To the skilled diplomatist, adept at political maneuver, it offered unique opportunities.

THE UNIFICATION OF ITALY

With the failure of the revolution of 1848–1849, the Italian peninsula sank back into the political torpor that had characterized the 1830's. Even at the height of the struggle, the Italian masses had remained unmoved. The poverty-stricken peasants preferred to attack their landlords rather than the Austrians; they were more concerned with the problem of subsistence than with the ideals of liberty and unity. Those patriots who rallied to the national cause belonged to the thinly developed stratum of the educated middle class: chiefly lawyers, doctors, students, and shopkeepers. After the collapse, their leaders fled abroad: Garibaldi to America, Mazzini to London, and Manin to Paris. Following his defeat at Novara (March 23, 1849), Charles Albert abdicated in favor of his son, Victor Emanuel II (1849–1878), and slipped away to Portugal, where he died four months later. Yet his efforts were not totally in vain, for he left behind a lasting monument in the *Statuto*.

The Establishment of Sardinian Leadership Granted by royal decree on March 4, 1848, the Sardinian *Statuto* was the first enduring modern constitution on the Italian peninsula. It was one of mixed powers. While the king was granted the executive power including the right to appoint cabinet ministers, conduct foreign policy, and command the armed forces, legislative power was shared by the king and a bicameral legislature, that is, a senate appointed by the monarch and a lower house elected by restricted suffrage.

Victor Emanuel II in 1878. He had the good fortune to find a minister of genius, to gain help from outside powers in uniting Italy, and to govern during a period of general prosperity. His image was inflated beyond recognition by official panegyrics. (The Mansell Collection.)

Victor Emanuel II was neither inspiring nor statesmanlike. While not lacking in shrewdness, he was poorly educated and more interested in horses, hunting, and women than in governing. This he normally left to others, with the consequence that the lower House gradually established its primacy over the cabinet as well as over the senate. Although at moments of great crisis, like that of 1859, the king briefly reverted to authoritarian rule, parliamentary government became customary. By 1860, the practice was well along; and, by 1876, it was conclusively established.

Count Camillo Benso di Cavour (1810–1861) did more than any other statesman to bring about parliamentary government. Born an aristocrat, Cavour began his career as an army officer, but was compelled to resign because of his liberal convictions. Turning to farming, he made a fortune from his family estates by applying the newest agricultural techniqes and later branched out into business and banking. Cavour was a "modernist," vitally concerned with economic and scientific progress, but with little interest in Italy's history or cultural achievements. Yet he was also a royalist who believed that monarchy was necessary for social and political stability, and an Italian patriot who longed for the establishment of a kingdom of Italy under the House of Savoy. A close student of constitutional government abroad, he was a gifted parliamentarian, persuasive as a speaker and adept at forming majorities out of diverse political groups. Politically he was a "realist," or as some would have it an "opportunist," more concerned with effective action than with the pursuit of abstract goals. His ideal was the "golden mean," the avoidance of extremes. As prime minister, his chief political backing came from a coalition of center groups, the *connubio*, formed in 1852. His liberalism did not prevent him from harrying republicans and suppressing the republican press.

Taking office as prime minister in November 1852, Cavour set out to prepare Sardinia for the role she was to play in the coming unification of Italy. Through public works (roads, railways, harbors) and the encouragement of business enterprise, he successfully promoted the economic growth of the country. Abandoning Charles Albert's slogan that "Italy must win her own salvation," he cultivated close relations with France and Britain. Over the initial opposition of the public, the chamber, and the other cabinet ministers, he brought about the alliance which committed 15,000 Sardinian troops to the war against Russia in the Crimea. As compensation for this aid he hoped to gain the neighboring duchy of Parma. While this was denied, he did succeed in obtaining for Sardinia a seat at the Congress of Paris in 1856. With the help of the English delegation, moreover, he managed to bring the Italian question before the Congress and hence before the forum of Europe.

Count Cavour in the 1850's. While intoxicating to Italian patriots, his unification of Italy under a unitary, middle-class monarchy has been criticized by historians because of the number and degree of the social problems it left unsolved. (Italian Cultural Institute.)

The War of 1859 At Paris, Cavour achieved a significant moral victory; but his aim was a military coalition against Austria, for he was convinced that the Austrians would never voluntarily relinquish their position in Italy. In January 1858 Orsini's bombs provided the final stimulus which made it possible. Five months later came Napoleon's offer of an alliance, and on July 20, Cavour met secretly with the Emperor at Plombières to learn the terms.

What Napoleon offered bore a close resemblance to the old scheme of Gioberti (see p. 1131). Once Austria had been driven from the peninsula, Italy was to be reorganized into four kingdoms under the presidency of the pope: a kingdom of Upper Italy (Sardinia, Lombardy, Venetia, Parma, Modena, and the Romagna) under the House of Savoy; a Kingdom of Central Italy (Tuscany and most of the Papal States) whose throne was to go to the Duchess of Parma; Rome and its surrounding territory to remain under the pope; and the unchanged kingdom of Naples. France was to receive, as compensation for her aid, the districts of Nice and Savoy, and the bargain was sealed with the betrothal of Princess Clotilde, Victor Emanuel's fifteen-year-old daughter, to Prince Jerome Bonaparte, the Emperor's thirty-seven-year-old cousin, whom she had never seen. The bargain was far from Cavour's liking, for he envisaged Italy as a unitary monarchy, rather than a confederation, but his primary aim was the ejection of Austria and without France this was impossible. He was aware, moreover, that wars create fluid situations in which many unintended things can happen.

Under the agreement, the provocation of the war was left to Sardinia, but Cavour's task was eased by the folly of the Austrians. On March 9, Piedmontese reserves were mobilized, and French troops began to assemble at Marseilles for embarkation. Instead of waiting for the enemy to put themselves in the wrong, Emperor Franz Joseph and Baron Buol, Austrian Foreign Minister, precipitated the war by an ultimatum to Sardinia demanding her demobilization. On April 29, the war began.

Austria's military commanders proved to be as inept as her diplomats. By delaying the assault, they lost the chance to defeat the Sardinian army before the French arrived. In June, French and Sardinian forces invaded Lombardy forcing the Habsburg army, in two great battles at Magenta and Solferino, back upon the fortresses of the Quadrilateral. Then, suddenly, to the dismay of the Italians, the fighting abruptly ended. Acting independently of Cavour, Napoleon negotiated an armistice with Emperor Franz Joseph at Villafranca on July 11. His motives were several. He was aware that his victories were more the consequence of good fortune than good generalship; he was distressed by the mounting casualties and the sight of mangled bodies on the battlefield; though in retreat, the Austrians were still undefeated; Italian revolutionaries, encouraged by Cavour, were speedily violating the terms of Plombières; and in the north, the Prussian army was mobilizing on the Rhine frontier with the apparent intention of supporting Austria. When he heard of Napoleon's betrayal, the high-strung Cavour flew into a towering rage and resigned.

The Birth of the Kingdom of Italy (1860) The terms of Villafranca were indeed a far cry from Napoleon's promise "to free Italy from the Alps to the Adriatic." While Sardinia obtained Lombardy, Austria kept Venetia and was to be included in an Italian confederation headed by the pope. The rulers of Austria's satellite duchies in central and northern Italy, who had been driven from their thrones on the outbreak of hostilities, were to be restored, though not by force. Yet force would have been necessary, for the revolutionary governments in Tuscany, Modena, and the Papal Romagna were bent on union with Piedmont and refused to surrender their powers.

On the other hand, Napoleon found he needed something more concrete than glory to present to the French people. Cavour, who returned to power on January 20, 1860, struck the obvious bargain, ceding Nice and Savoy to France, while gaining (after the formality of plebiscites) annexation of the duchies and the Romagna to Sardinia. Naturally, Cavour did not regard these acquisitions as the last. What he visualized was the gradual annexation of the rest of the Papal States and Naples, working from north to south. This plan, however, was soon frustrated by the fantastic achievements of Garibaldi.

Born in Nice of humble origins, Giuseppe Garibaldi (1807–1882) had served in the wars of Latin America, where he mastered the art of leading irregular forces. An Italian patriot and republican in sympathy, he was close to Mazzini and had commanded the troops of the ill-fated Roman republic of 1848. Yet he was no doctrinaire, and in 1860 accepted the leadership of the House of Savoy as the most practical solution to the problem of Italian unity. Learning of political unrest in Sicily, he formed in Genoa a force of one thousand men to attack the island and its decadent Neapolitan government. Landing at Marsala on May 11, 1860, he gathered recruits as he marched inland, defeating the Neapolitan army at Calatafimi and taking Palermo before the end of the month. By the end of July, he controlled the entire island of Sicily. On August 22, he crossed the straits to the mainland. The Neapolitan army and government disintegrated before him and on September 7 he entered Naples in triumph.

In the beginning, Cavour had opposed this seemingly mad-cap expedition of Garibaldi. He feared it would antagonize the European powers and he disliked the democratic, republican forces that stood behind the venture. In victory, the latter might easily insist upon a more radical constitution for Italy than Cavour desired. Hence it was essential for him to gain control of the southern revolution, which Garibaldi had launched with such astonishing success, lest it fall into the hands of the Mazzinians. In August, he attempted to forestall Garibaldi by staging an insurrection of moderates in Naples before the guerrilla leader could cross to the mainland, but the rebellion failed. When Garibaldi took Naples, Cavour incited insurrections in the Papal States and used this as a pretext for intervention. Sardinian troops marched southward through Umbria and the Marches and finally crossed the Neapolitan frontier.

Two Italian armies were now face to face, each with a different conception of the future. There was a threat of civil war, but Garibaldi chose to yield. He surrendered his command and retired with a bag of seed corn to his rocky farm on the island of Caprera to live as a simple, if celebrated, farmer. Although bitter at Cavour, he was no self-seeker and was too great a patriot to resist the Sardinians. In October and November, plebiscites were held in the Papal States and in the Neapolitan Kingdom which ratified their union with the north. On March 17, 1861, the kingdom of Italy was proclaimed under the House of Savoy and the Sardinian constitution of 1848. Less than three months later, Cavour, worn out by his arduous labors, died

Giuseppe Garibaldi During the Campaign for Unification. He is regarded by some as the ablest leader of volunteer troops in history. (The Bettmann Archive.)

at the age of fifty-one. It was an irreparable loss, for after him Italy did not produce another statesman of comparable stature.

The Completion of Italian Unification The establishment of the Italian Kingdom, with its capital at Florence, left the task of unification still unfinished. Venetia was still in Austrian hands and Rome and its environs remained under the pope, protected by an expeditionary force of French

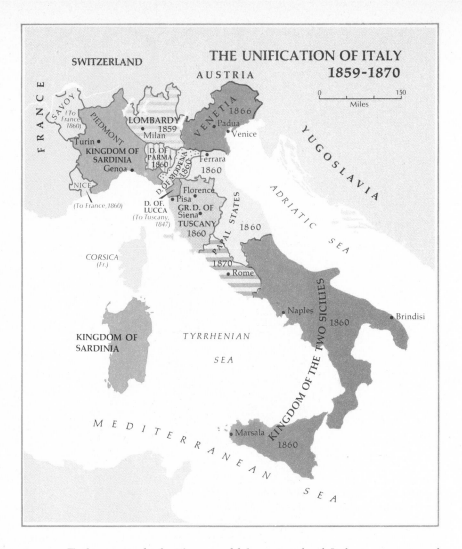

THE UNIFICATION OF ITALY
1859-1870

troops. To have attacked either would have involved Italy in an unequal struggle against a major European power. But in 1866, under circumstances that will be described in the next section, Italy formed an alliance with Prussia against Austria. In the war that followed, the Prussians were victorious and Italy gained Venetia. Four years later, the Prussian army marched again, this time against Napoleon, who was compelled to withdraw his troops from Rome. The Italian forces entered on their heels, and the embittered Pope Pius IX withdrew into the Vatican, where he remained by his own choice as a virtual prisoner, unreconciled to the stroke of fortune that had deprived him of temporal rule. The Italian capital was transferred from Florence to Rome.

Italy now had a single government; yet the problem of Italian unity remained. Centuries of disunion had created regional differences and fierce local loyalties which were to be overcome only with difficulty. There was as yet no common tongue comprehensible to all Italians, and even the word "Italy" was unfamiliar to many. Cavour had rejected the federal in favor of the unitary system of government, and this meant the imposition of Piedmontese laws and institutions upon the rest of Italy, which was resented. Most southerners felt as though they had been conquered by the north.

Equally serious were the economic and social cleavages which the unification failed to heal. Even in 1860, the *risorgimento* remained a middle-class movement in a largely peasant society. Garibaldi's thousand were students, independent artisans, and professional men. The support they received from the Sicilian peasantry was not inspired by patriotism, but by hatred of exploiting landlords and oppressive Neapolitan officials. Yet Garibaldi had no interest in social revolution and soon took the side of the landlords against the looting and rioting peasants. However they differed on political issues, the middle-class Italian nationalists who triumphed in 1860 thought alike on the social question. In the decades that followed little was done to alleviate the wretched poverty of the southern peasants or the harsh conditions of labor in Italy's infant industries.

<table>
<tr><td>THE UNIFICATION
OF GERMANY</td><td>**The Prussian Reaction** When they dissolved the Prussian Parliament on December 5, 1848, Frederick William IV and his reactionary ministers shrewdly granted a constitution which, although providing the appearance of constitutionalism, did not have its substance. While a bill of rights was included, the clauses were very elastic, and the guarantee of freedom of the press did not prevent a rigid censorship. The constitution spoke vaguely of ministerial "responsibility," but the executive power, including the right to conduct foreign affairs and command the armed forces, was retained by the king. Legislative power was shared by the king and a bicameral legislature. The House of Lords was appointed by the king and became the stronghold of the aristocracy. The Chamber of Deputies was chosen by an indirect suffrage which, while nominally universal, was actually very restrictive. The voters were ranked in three classes according to the taxes they paid, with the wealthiest electing the largest number of deputies and the poorest the least number. At election time, governmental pressure was exerted to bring in favored candidates. For nearly a decade, the system sufficed to produce a compliant majority.</td></tr>
</table>

The reactionary cabinet, headed by Otto von Manteuffel, was also shrewd enough to appreciate that the moving force behind the revolution had been the social distress of the peasants and artisans. In order to appease the former, the government liquidated what remained of the servile dues of manorialism, enabling about 640,000 farmers to become freeholders. Efforts were made to protect the artisans by reviving the guild system, which the liberals of 1848 had sought to destroy. But the reaction was also assisted by the deep discouragement of the liberal opposition after its defeat in 1848. Some radical leaders (like Carl Schurz) emigrated; others gravitated toward socialism; a few made their peace with conservatism. By the 1860's, only a small band of determined democrats remained and they were no longer revolutionary.

During the 1850's, the energies of the German middle class were absorbed in a rapid economic expansion, and within a few years Germany reached the front ranks of the industrial nations. Between 1850 and 1860, coal production in Germany grew from six to twelve million tons, while pig-iron production increased from 215,000 to 529,000 tons. A new entrepreneurial class appeared, as did a sizeable factory proletariat. It was a period of rapid population growth and urbanization. Agriculture also changed. The landlords of the great estates east of the Elbe led in the application of the new agricultural techniques. Higher production and improved transportation enabled them to export grains to distant markets. Many founded rural industries, such as breweries and sugar refineries. These changes required the application of modern business accounting and management. Big landowners tended to become agrarian capitalists.

Yet the political consequences of these economic and social changes were not great. If the broad expansion of the German middle class had occurred before 1848, the course of the revolution might have been otherwise. But it occurred at a time when German liberalism had lost its zeal. The new businessmen took no active part in national politics, except to vote for liberal candidates. The candidates themselves were drawn from the old political elite: largely civil servants and landowners. Most were "notables" possessing social prestige, but lacking independent status, "more concerned with political discussion than with political success." If the government had ignored their interests, the new entrepreneurial class might have been driven into active opposition, but the Prussian bureaucracy promoted the growth of heavy industry, and in 1861 adopted free trade in the interest of greater industrial and agricultural export. Hence the businessmen were content to leave the affairs of government in the hands of established authority. When, in the 1860's, Prussian liberalism again underwent a crucial test, the inadequacy of its social support was once more glaringly evident and its ultimate defeat as great as that in 1848.

The "New Era" In October 1857, the reactionary Frederick William IV suffered a stroke that incapacitated him until his death in 1861. His brother, Prince William of Prussia, supplanted him first as regent and finally as king with the title William I (1861–1888). It was common knowledge that the two royal brothers had long been in disagreement on political matters. During the 1850's, William had been sharply critical of the government's suppression of popular liberties. His first act was to dismiss the reactionary cabinet, replacing the fallen ministers with men of his own viewpoint. In the press, the new government was hopefully dubbed the "New Era." In November 1858, the electorate endorsed it by returning the former liberal opposition with an overwhelming majority.

William's disagreement with his brother was, however, one of policy rather than of basic philosophy. Both were divine-right monarchists and

EXPANSION OF PRUSSIA AND THE UNIFICATION OF GERMANY 1815-1871

0   200
Miles

Legend:
- Prussia, 1815-1866
- Annexed to Prussia, 1866
- Joined with Prussia, North German Confederation, 1867
- South German States in German Empire, 1871
- Alsace-Lorraine, Ceded by France to German Empire, 1871
- Austrian Dominions Excluded from German Confederation, 1866

believed that God had given them the right and duty to govern. William had not meant to arouse enthusiasm from liberals by his appointment of the new-era cabinet. "What have I done," he asked resentfully, "to merit praise from that crowd?" Before many months had passed he was at odds with the moderate conservatives of his cabinet and by 1861 he was deeply involved in a conflict with the Chamber of Deputies.

Reorganization of the Prussian Army   The issue that produced this dispute was the reorganization of the Prussian army. William came to power with the conviction that the Prussian army was inadequate for the task that would be expected of it in wartime. With his Minister of War, Albrecht von Roon, he determined to double the size of the army, to establish a three-year period of service for most conscripts, and to demote the popular militia (*Landwehr*) by relegating it to the rear in time of war. The European crisis of 1859 had convinced even liberals that reforms were necessary. But they suspected that the government's proposals were intended to heighten the authority of the monarchy and the aristocratic caste at the cost of the bourgeoisie. In this they were absolutely right, for Roon and William intended to use the three-year service period to inculcate habits of discipline which would make the conscripts in future years obedient subjects and staunch supporters of monarchical authority. They regarded the militia, whose officers were primarily bourgeois, as a "politically false institution," in contrast to the more disciplined regular army, whose officers were mostly noblemen.

In 1862, the liberal majority in the chamber finally refused to finance this reform. William sought and found a new Minister-President willing to govern in defiance of parliament. He was Bismarck.

Otto von Bismarck   Otto von Bismarck (1815–1898) is one of the most arresting personalities of the nineteenth century. Although his mother was a commoner, his father was a Junker aristocrat; and this was the only heritage that mattered to Bismarck. His dynamic will to power was tempered by a highly developed sense of responsibility grounded in a sincere religious faith. Yet the Christian doctrine of love and charity influenced him little, for he was cynical of human motives, was malevolent toward those who opposed him, and readily exploited men and moral forces to achieve his ends. While a staunch royalist and supporter of monarchical authority, he was never an absolutist, believing that some kind of legislature was necessary to check the vices and follies of kings, ministers, and bureaucrats. He was also a realist concerned with problems of power rather than principle, and in foreign affairs he maintained that the statesman's sole purpose was pursuit of the reasoned interest of the state.

For four years—from his appointment in September 1862 until the sudden capitulation of the opposition in 1866—Bismarck ruled Prussia without the cooperation of Parliament. To the anger of the deputies, he pointed out that the constitution contained a "gap": when crown and parliament disagreed, there was no higher authority to decide the issue; since the life of the state could not stand still, the crown had to govern as it saw fit. The liberals were impotent to bring down his dictatorial government. Their traditional reverence for authority, their distaste for revolution, their fears of the lower classes, and uncertainty over the degree of their popular support combined to prevent them from any positive action against the Bismarck cabinet.

Prince Bismarck in the 1870's. Those who met him never forgot the tall, powerful frame and piercing eyes. The effect was heightened by the military uniform that he constantly wore. He held a reserve officer's commission, awarded after only one year's training. (Radio Times Hulton Picture Library.)

The Victories over Denmark and Austria Fundamentally Bismarck was a Prussian patriot who, from his early years, believed in the necessity of Prussian expansion. It galled him that Prussia occupied a position secondary to Austria in German and European affairs. He came to power as Minister-President of Prussia in 1862 with the determination to demand that Vienna grant Prussia parity with Austria in Germany and recognize Prussia's right to expand in northern Germany. By establishing close relations with Russia and France, he believed, Berlin could isolate Austria and force her to yield. If that strategy should fail, he was willing to consider war. Yet Bismarck made his first major move in foreign policy in alliance with Austria rather than against it. The unwary Austrians cooperated with Prussia in making war on Denmark in order to rescue Schleswig-Holstein. While separate from Denmark, these duchies were possessions of the Danish crown. Most of Schleswig and all of Holstein were inhabited by Germans. In 1863, Copenhagen attempted to incorporate Schleswig into Denmark in violation of treaties signed earlier. As in 1848, the fate of the northern duchies appeared to be a crucial test of the vitality of German nationalism; and a wave of anger swept through Germany. In a brief campaign (December 1863–June 1864), the German armies forced the Danes back from their fortified line, the *Dannevirke*, took the fortifications of Düppel by storm, and compelled the out-numbered Danes to make peace. Prussia assumed control over Schleswig, Austria over Holstein.

Once the Danish war was over, Bismarck resumed his original course against Austria, which he succeeded in isolating. By offering to help suppress a Polish uprising in 1863 he reinforced the long-standing friendship between Prussia and Russia. In Paris, he obtained the promise of France's benevolent neutrality. Italy, on the other hand, agreed to go to war with Prussia against Austria.

On the night of June 15, 1866, the Prussian forces attacked. While the Italian army was decisively beaten by the Austrians at Custozza, the Prussian columns, guided by the strategy of Helmuth von Moltke penetrated Bohemia and shattered the main Austrian army at Königgrätz on July 3. To the astonishment of Europe, the war was suddenly over. The terms imposed by Bismarck cost the Habsburg monarchy Venetia—which was ceded to Italy—and her association with Germany—which dated back to the Middle Ages. Prussia annexed Schleswig-Holstein, Hanover, Hesse-Kassel, Nassau, and the free city of Frankfurt. These gains linked her eastern and western provinces and gave Berlin undisputed dominance over the North German Confederation organized in 1867 to include the states north of the Main River.

Bismarck's Use of Nationalism   The wars of 1864 and 1866 were accomplished by Bismarck with an almost surgical neatness. In both cases the diplomatic preparation was consummately skillful and succeeded in isolating the foe and staving off foreign intervention. Bismarck was not a nationalistic crusader, but a skilled practitioner of *raison d'état*. He left millions of Germans in Austria and the Russian Baltic out of the union and advised them that their future lay with the Habsburg monarchy and with Russia rather than with Germany. His aim was the strengthening of Prussia, not the unification of all German speaking peoples in Europe.

While he was not motivated in his actions by German nationalism, Bismarck did exploit it for his own political ends. Since 1858, he had believed that Prussia could find an important ally against Austria in the German national movement. Despite his conservative Junker origins and his Prussian bias, he grasped that in the nineteenth century wars of conquest had to be justified on moral grounds. Wars for purely dynastic ends were impracticable in the age of military conscription and popular movements. By mobilizing the nation in support of Prussian policy, furthermore, he hoped to consolidate his gains. Through the pressure of German nationalism he intended to force the German lesser states to abandon their particularistic attitudes and submit to the leadership of the Hohenzollern monarchy.

German nationalism was useful to Bismarck from yet another standpoint. In the emerging era of the masses, the doctrines of legitimacy and divine right were no longer adequate to justify authoritarian rule. If it was to endure in this new dynamic age, the aristocratic-monarchical system had to be rebuilt upon the foundation of national patriotism. By appropriating the cause of German national unity, Bismarck severely weakened the liberal opposition. Liberals had always believed that they alone could unify Germany. Suddenly they awoke in 1866 to the fact that a conservative government had accomplished what they had failed to achieve in 1848. As a consequence, most liberals cooperated with Bismarck in establishing the constitution of the new North German Confederation.

The Victory over France Once this policy of associating Prussia with German nationalism had been adopted, it was obvious that German unification could not halt at the river Main. Yet Bismarck was aware that any attempt to include the south would antagonize the French. Napoleon had encouraged the war of 1866 on the assumption that the conflict would give Paris the opportunity to establish its influence in southern Germany and even to expand toward the Rhine. Prussia's quick and overwhelming victory frustrated this ambition. But Bismarck also suffered disappointment where the south was concerned. During 1866–1870, he hoped to establish close ties with the southern states that would gradually lead to their union with the north. By early 1870, this program appeared to have failed. Most southerners were Catholics who feared the Protestant north and disliked the prospect of being "Prussianized." Southern resistance to the completion of German unification appeared to stiffen. This was the situation when Bismarck began (February 1870) actively to promote the candidature of Prince Leopold of Hohenzollern for the throne of Spain.

Leopold belonged to the southern, or Sigmaringen, branch of the Hohenzollerns. Hohenzollern family law required that he obtain the approval of King William before accepting the offered crown. Under Bismarck's urging, William reluctantly "approved." But before the Spanish *Cortes* could act, the news of Leopold's candidacy reached Paris (July 2, 1870). The reaction of the French public, press, and government was excited and bellicose. France seemed threatened by encirclement.

To Bismarck's distress, King William yielded to French pressure and consented to the withdrawal of Leopold's candidacy. The French appeared to have scored a great diplomatic triumph. However, Napoleon and Foreign Minister Gramont overreached themselves by demanding that William promise he would not permit a renewal of the candidacy at a later date. William refused in an interview with Count Benedetti, the French ambassador, at the summer resort of Bad Ems. The King's report of this episode was the famous "Ems Dispatch," whose publication by Bismarck at Berlin in an edited version made war inevitable.

It has not been proved that in 1870 Bismarck deliberately plotted to bring about war with France. Yet it is evident that he expected a major crisis over the candidacy and that the crisis would put new life into a decaying national movement. In the past, war, or the threat of war, with France

(1812–1815, 1840, 1859, and 1867) had always produced an upsurge of national feeling in Germany. Bismarck precipitated the crisis; it was the French who determined that it would end in war. By their excessive demands, Napoleon and Gramont confronted Bismarck with the necessity of choosing between diplomatic defeat and war. He chose the latter course.

At the outset, on both sides of the Rhine, the war was highly popular. Bismarck fought it as a national war, consciously whipping up German patriotic sentiment in order to bring the divided nation together. The southern states joined in the struggle, and the combined German armies poured into France in three great columns. In successive battles the French army, poorly prepared and badly led, was pressed back upon Sedan, where on September 3 it surrendered. Napoleon himself was one of the prisoners. Yet the war did not end. A revolution occurred in Paris, and the revolutionary government under the fiery Leon Gambetta proved extraordinarily successful in raising new armies in the south of France and organizing a guerrilla campaign in the German rear. Not until Paris had been besieged, bombarded, and starved into submission in late January 1871 did the French acknowledge defeat.

Excitement on the Paris Boulevards after the French Declaration of War. Frenchmen regarded the Hohenzollern candidature as an attempt to encircle France, while Germans treated France's objections as but another unjustified interference in the affairs of other nations.

Under the terms of the peace treaty, France was compelled to pay an indemnity of five billion francs. But the most grievous loss was the cession of the provinces of Alsace and Lorraine to Germany. While the inhabitants of Alsace and much of Lorraine spoke a German dialect, they considered themselves Frenchmen and most remained unreconciled to their fate until their return to France in 1918. Bismarck's purpose was strategic rather than national, for the Vosges mountains and the fortress of Metz were regarded as indispensable to the future defense of Germany. To most Germans, however, the arguments of the historian Treitschke were probably persuasive. The Alsacians and Lorrainers, he declared, were German and had to be saved, even against their own will, from the contamination of French culture.

The German Constitution   For Germany, the greatest gain of the war of 1870 was the completion of her unification. The impact of war and the joy of conquest dissolved the hard crust of southern particularism. In delicate negotiations, Bismarck succeeded in uniting the southern states with the north. On January 18, 1871, in a dramatic ceremony held in the Hall of Mirrors of the palace at Versailles, William I was proclaimed "German Kaiser."

The constitution Bismarck had devised for the North German Confederation became without essential change the constitution of united Germany. This document provided for a system of mixed powers that repeated for Germany, though in a more complicated pattern, the basic power arrangements of the Prussian constitution. As German Kaiser, the king of Prussia was granted supreme command over the armed forces and full control over foreign affairs, including the right to declare war and make peace. He had the authority to appoint the chancellor and all other national officials. National laws were enacted by a bicameral legislature composed of a *Bundesrat*, representing the state governments, and a *Reichstag*, elected by universal suffrage. Although the Parliament was given control over Reich revenues and expenditures, the size and financial support of the army was fixed for a period of years. While the Reich had a federal structure, two-thirds of united Germany was composed of the unitary state of Prussia. She possessed seventeen of the fifty-eight votes in the *Bundesrat*, and in practice this sufficed to dominate that body. It took only fourteen votes, moreover, to block constitutional amendments. Through its position in the *Bundesrat* the Prussian government (meaning the king and his cabinet) could effectively prevent any undesired legislation.

THE HABSBURG EMPIRE

The Austrian Reaction   At the age of eighteen, the Emperor Franz Joseph (1848–1916) was not well fitted for the task of governing the Habsburg Empire. To be sure, he was not unintelligent, possessing an excellent memory and ready comprehension. But he was completely lacking in imagination and approached the problems of government with the temperament of a minor burearucrat who relies upon rules and regulations to meet every situation and is more concerned with administrative details than with the formulation of policy. Spartan in his personal tastes, he was driven by an exalted sense of duty and fortified by a deep religious faith. He was a divine-right monarchist, highly conscious of the Habsburg heritage, which he had resolved to preserve. Sensing, perhaps that his crown belonged more to the past than to the future, he remained averse to all that was modern and new in this dynamic century. He was as opposed to the convenience

The Dual Monarchy of
AUSTRIA-HUNGARY
1867

of electricity, bathrooms, telephones, and finally motor cars as he was to constitutional experimentation. The ministers he preferred were like himself: meticulous, sober, hard working, and addicted to routine. Unlike his great rival, William I, he found it difficult to tolerate strong personalities. Yet the problem that confronted the Emperor and his ministers, that of holding together a multinational empire in an era of growing cultural nationalism, was extremely difficult, perhaps insuperable.

The ministers with whom Franz Joseph began his reign—Schwarzenberg, Bach, Bruck, and Stadion—sought to solve the problem by a policy of rigid centralization. Prince Schwarzenberg, the Prime Minister, was a cynical man of the world who firmly believed in the efficacy of force; and the other ministers were moderate liberals, who readily abandoned the revolution for careers under the authoritarian monarchy. After Schwarzenberg's death in 1852, Franz Joseph himself assumed the presidency of the cabinet, but the driving force in the government was the bourgeois lawyer Alexander Bach, the Minister of the Interior. During the 1850's, the Schwarzenberg-Bach regime ruled the country with an iron hand, operating through an all-powerful bureaucracy backed by the army and the Catholic

Church. Justice, education, taxation, administration, and local government were reorganized and made to conform to the unitary pattern, whose objective was the molding of a single instrument of power. Bohemia and Hungary, their revolutions suppressed, were subjected to the direct rule of Vienna. For Bohemia, this meant a reversion to her earlier status (since 1627) of an imperial province; for Hungary, it meant the suspension of ancient institutions and privileges of local self-government. A revolution from above had followed the revolution from below.

The Transition to Constitutionalism   Since 1789, failure in war has usually had severe internal consequences for European states. Autocratic governments, if they are not overthrown, are compelled at least to appease a public opinion outraged by vain sacrifices, financial chaos, and the incompetence of diplomats, generals, and military commissariats. This is what happened to the Habsburg monarchy as a result of her defeats in the Italian war of 1859 and the Prussian war of 1866.

Franz Joseph and his Wife Elizabeth Soon After Their Marriage in 1854. Elizabeth was often called the most beautiful woman ever to occupy a European throne. She was assassinated by an anarchist in 1898.

Franz Joseph was only too glad to accept the peace of Villafranca offered by Napoleon in 1859. He was already badly shaken by the news of popular unrest; by the disloyalty of his Hungarian and Italian troops; and by his own mistakes as commanding general, a role for which he had neither the talent nor the preparation. Returning to Vienna, he faced the new situation by abandoning the Bach system in favor of the constitutionalism he found so distasteful. In October 1860, an imperial "Diploma" established a central Parliament (*Reichsrat*), whose deputies were to be chosen by the provincial

Diets, which were to be revived. Hungary was to regain its status of 1847. Most Hungarians, however, remained unappeased, for they wanted the restoration of the autonomous powers granted by the monarchy in March 1848. But German liberals were also dissatisfied, for they feared that the federal character of the October Diploma would imperil the cohesion of the Empire.

Confronted with this resistance, Franz Joseph quickly reversed himself, permitting Anton von Schmerling, who had replaced Bach as Minister of Interior, to issue the February Patent (1861). Supposedly just a gloss on the October Diploma, the February Patent actually changed its entire character. Federalism was abandoned for centralism, the revived provincial Diets surrendering almost all legislative power to the *Reichsrat*. The latter became a bicameral Parliament whose House of Lords was appointive and whose House of Representatives was chosen by the provincial Diets. The Diets were chosen by an unequal suffrage based upon four *curiae* composed of large landlords, chambers of commerce, townsmen, and peasants. The large landlords and wealthy townsmen had the greater representation; and in Bohemia this worked to the advantage of the Germans and to the disadvantage of the Czechs, who were mostly rural.

The system was one of mixed powers, for the emperor retained control over the cabinet, had unrestricted authority over the armed forces and foreign affairs, and possessed an unlimited veto over legislation. There was no bill of rights and no guarantee of an independent judiciary. Old taxes could be raised without parliamentary approval and in an emergency the cabinet could rule by decree. One writer has described the new regime as the "Bach system with a constitutional overcoat."

The autocratic power of the emperor was heightened by the fact that the Hungarian Diet refused to send delegates to the *Reichsrat*, and the Polish and Czech delegates soon withdrew from that body when their demands for provincial autonomy were denied. Schmerling was left with a rump Parliament, in which the German liberals of the Austrian provinces (who favored centralization), the German landowners from Bohemia (who feared the Czechs), and the Ruthenians (who feared exploitation by the Poles) alone supported the new institutions. In essence, the Schmerling government was a government of the German minority over the Hungarian and Slav majority. The intransigence of the Diet in Budapest led to its dissolution and thereafter Hungary was again ruled by the imperial bureaucracy.

Schmerling believed that this system, if it was to endure, required the backing of the forty million Germans who lay beyond the Habsburg frontier. Hence, he hoped to bring about a reform of the German Confederation which would strengthen Austrian primacy in that body and by this means to buttress his rule over the Czechs and Hungarians. But Schmerling's attempts in 1862 and 1863 to establish a great German "empire of seventy millions" were defeated by Prussian obduracy, despite considerable support from the German lesser states. Following the second defeat, the Habsburg government lost its initiative in the German question to Bismarck. In 1863–1864 Franz

Joseph and his ministers foolishly permitted themselves to be drawn into the war against Denmark, from which Prussia alone stood to profit. Austrian foreign policy, boasted one of Bismarck's collaborators, was now being made in Berlin. Schmerling and his colleagues did not realize until the fall of 1865 that Austria was being deliberately exploited by Bismarck in the interest of Prussia.

Establishment of the Dual Monarchy   Prussia's victory over Austria at Königgrätz in July 1866 was undoubtedly one of the decisive battles in modern history. At one blow, it severed the centuries-old connection between Germany and the Habsburg monarchy. The new principle of the unified national state, promoted by Prussia, was triumphant over the ancient concept of universal empire, represented by the Habsburgs. In the past, the Holy Roman Empire and the German Confederation had linked the Germans with the peoples of central Europe. But now the connection was lost, to be reborn only in the Hitler era in the brutalized form of German conquest. Undoubtedly, the split of 1866 restricted the horizon of the Germans, speeding the decay of that cosmopolitan outlook that had predominated in the eighteenth century and the growth of that inverted national sentiment characteristic of Germany in the twentieth century. The unifications of Italy and Germany also stimulated the ambitions of the subject peoples of the Habsburg Empire to seek their cultural and political autonomy and hastened the day when central Europe would dissolve into nation-states.

Franz Joseph and many other Austrians surrendered the connection with Germany only with the greatest reluctance. For four years, there was still some hope in Vienna of its reconstruction. Indicative of this attitude was the appointment of Baron Friedrich von Beust as Foreign Minister in October 1866. For thirteen years Beust had been prime minister of Saxony, Austria's best ally in the war against Prussia. Throughout his career in Saxony, Beust had fought for the independence of the small states against encroachments by the great powers. He arrived in Vienna hoping to prevent Prussia's further expansion and perhaps even to rebuild the Austrian position in Germany.

Obviously such a policy required a settlement with Hungary. Without it the support of the Magyars could not be counted upon in any further difficulties in Germany. Even before the war of 1866, the possibility of Hungarian disloyalty had caused the emperor to open negotiations with the moderate faction in Budapest headed by Francis Deák. Deák had recommended a dualistic reorganization of the Empire in contrast to the unitary and federal schemes previously attempted. Interrupted by the war, these talks were now resumed. Although Deák nobly refused to exploit the defeat at Königgrätz by raising his demands, the negotiation was difficult. At the crucial moment, Beust lent his assistance and later persuaded Franz Joseph to accept the finished agreement, claiming all the credit for the settlement in his memoirs.

The "compromise of 1867" divided the Habsburg Empire into two great segments, Austria and Hungary, under a single monarch with a common army and common foreign policy. Henceforth, the Empire had two capitals, Vienna and Budapest, each with its own cabinet and bicameral legislature. Both cabinets were technically responsible in the political sense to their respective Parliaments; but in practice the Austrian cabinet, owing to the instability of the lower chamber, became the instrument of the crown. While the suffrage laws of the two halves differed, their effect was to enable the wealthier Germans in the west and the wealthier Hungarians in the east to dominate their respective chambers at the cost of the lower classes and other nationalities.

Toward the outside world the dual monarchy of Austria-Hungary, as it was now called, presented a united front by virtue of the fact that Franz Joseph, as Emperor of Austria and King of Hungary, commanded the common army and retained full control over foreign affairs. Three imperial ministers (for war, foreign affairs, and finance) assisted him in performing these functions. There was no imperial cabinet, although an informal crown council (composed of the monarch, the three imperial ministers, the two prime ministers, and others specially summoned) gave its advice on crucial decisions. Legislation for the monarchy as a whole, including the common budget, was passed by the "delegations," composed of sixty members from each parliament. The delegations met annually, alternating between the two capitals; they deliberated and voted separately. Constitutional changes were only possible by the concurrent action of both parliaments and were subject to monarchical approval.

Paradoxically, the Hungarian settlement, which Beust hoped would be the prelude to the restoration of Habsburg power in Germany, proved to be its greatest obstacle. The Magyars were quite aware that they owed their new autonomy to the severance of the Habsburg monarchy from Germany and that its reconnection would only strengthen the German population of the Empire to their own disadvantage. Geography, moreover, made the Hungarian government far more concerned with the Balkan region than with Germany. Napoleon entered the war of 1870 under the assumption that Austria-Hungary would come to his support. But neither the Austrian Germans nor the Hungarians had any interest in making war with France against Germany. France's defeat and the founding of the German Reich were followed by Beust's dismissal in November 1871. There was no longer any prospect that the Habsburg dynasty might resume its historic role in Germany.

FURTHER READING   For general works on Italian, German, and Habsburg history, which include the period of unification, see the notes to Chapters 3 and 4. The volumes by D. M. Smith are important: *Cavour and Garibaldi, 1860,* and *Italy, A Modern History* (1959); his *Garibaldi, A Great Life in Brief* (1956), is too brief. The best biography of Cavour is still W. R. Thayer, *The Life and Times of Cavour,*

2 vols. (1911); but see also A. J. Whyte, *The Early Life and Letters of Cavour, 1848–1861* (1930). Works on special topics are S. B. Clough, *The Economic History of Modern Italy* (1964); E. Hales, *Pio Nono: A Study in European Politics and Religion in the Nineteenth Century* (1954); and A. C. Jemolo, *Church and State in Italy, 1859–1950* (1960).

On German unification, see O. Pflanze, *Bismarck and the Development of Germany* (1963). E. Eyck, *Bismarck and the German Empire* (1950), is an abridgement of a three-volume biography in German. The social underpinnings of the political events of unification are studied in two books by T. Hamerow, *The Social Foundations of German Unification: Ideas and Institutions* (1969), and *Struggles and Accomplishments* (1972). Important monographs on diplomatic problems are L. Steefel, *The Schleswig-Holstein Question* (1832), and *Bismarck, The Hohenzollern Candidacy, and the Origins of the Franco-German War of 1870* (1962). The conflicting views of important historians are reprinted in O. Pflanze, ed., *The Unification of Germany, 1848–1871* (1968).

The nationalities problem of the Habsburg monarchy is analyzed in R. A. Kann, *The Multinational Empire*, 2 vols., (1950–1964). A standard biography is J. Redlich, *Emperor Francis Joseph of Austria* (1929). English language studies of other personalities are rare, but see A. Schwarzenberg, *Prince Felix zu Schwarzenberg* (1947). G. W. Clark, *Franz Joseph and Bismarck* (1934), is an important monograph on events leading to the war of 1866. Two very readable military histories are G. A. Craig, *The Battle of Königgrätz* (1964); and M. Howard, *The Franco-Prussian War* (1961).

PART XIV

The half-century before the First World War was a dynamic and creative age which produced the greatest prosperity known in human history up to that time. During this period the acquisition of wealth and power became such a dominant force in European life that an outstanding American historian, Carlton J. H. Hayes, has called the last decades of the nineteenth century "a generation of materialism."

During this period the liberal principles of the early nineteenth century achieved their maximum influence. The ideals of personal independence and individual initiative were never more prized than in the last decades of the nineteenth and the first decades of the twentieth century. Yet at the same time they were increasingly undermined by changing conditions of life and the shifting current of European intellectual development. There was a trend toward bigness in western society which made these ideals seem naive and unrealistic to many. The size of everything was expanding: population, governments, armies, empires, business concerns, profits, and social tensions. Uncontrolled competition did not meet the needs of big business striving to maximize profits, of workers seeking a decent living standard, of countries wanting to expand their industrial systems in a hurry. The principles of independence and individualism were jeopardized by the growth of centralized control and coordination. Laissez faire had never had much influence in central and eastern Europe, and in the west during the decades before the First World War there was also a movement toward economic protectionism. Government intervention to regulate social conditions increased even in Great Britain, the homeland of laissez faire. The pressure of growing social consciousness and concern for the working classes accentuated the trend year by year.

The new cultural trends also contradicted the creed of classical liberalism, for philosophies based on environmental determinism, on class and national struggle, denied the autonomy of the individual. New scientific discoveries about the force of the unconscious and of instinct were no more than efforts to gain a better understanding of man's nature, but they reinforced a growing cult of violent self-assertion. The liberal ideal of the rationality of man was discounted by "realists" and anti-intellectuals. Thinking was supposed to lie in feeling, in race, or class. There was no longer any need to discuss problems, for intellect was fallacious. Only the emotions and the feelings of the heart were deemed to be true.

In western and northern Europe, this period saw the achievement of political democracy. Britain, France, the Low Countries and the Scandinavian states completed the establishment of parliamentary governments based upon equal adult male suffrage. In these countries, democratic liberalism triumphed over moderate liberalism, the concept of full popular sovereignty over the rule of an upper-class elite. But in central Europe, constitutionalism remained a fiction which masked the continued power of traditional, semi-authoritarian regimes. Parliaments existed in Germany and Austria-Hungary, but they never attained control over the state. In Russia, there was not even a facade of constitutional government until 1906, and then the powers of the Russian assembly were almost completely emasculated within two years. In southern Europe, liberal idealists also suffered severe disappointments. Spain, Portugal, and Italy did not succeed in establishing genuinely democratic governments, and the same was true of almost all the new Balkan states that emerged following successive defeats of the Ottoman Empire.

FORD MADOX BROWN'S "THE LAST OF ENGLAND." (Birmingham Museum and Art Gallery.)

INDUSTRIALIZATION
AND SOCIOPOLITICAL
CHANGE, 1870-1914

LEGACY OF THE PAST

The rise of heavy industry is illustrated in this 1875 painting of "The Rolling Mill" by Adolph von Menzel. (Staatliche Museum zu Berlin.)

The era of the late nineteenth century left at least three major legacies to the institutions and attitudes of the contemporary world.

First, the institution of liberal democracy in politics and government was first effectively established in the advanced countries of northwestern Europe and the English-speaking world in this period. Liberal democracy went on to become a fundamental ideal throughout most of the western world in the twentieth century, and to some extent in parts of the "Third World" of Africa and Asia later on.

Second, full-scale industrialization for economic production was first achieved in the most advanced countries, such as Britain, Belgium, the United States and Germany, in this period. By the end of the nineteenth century it had become a major goal for the less developed parts of Europe. During the course of the twentieth century it has become a fundamental aspiration for most of the modernizing countries of the entire world.

The third, the era contributed new subjectivist and nonrational cultural forces (discussed in Chapter 2). The new emphasis on willpower, the use and emphasis of emotions, and the catering to the pleasure principle have successively become more influential during the twentieth century, even though these standards often become mutually contradictory. In part they helped to give rise to the twentieth-century radical mass movements, and have become powerful factors in molding the attitudes and problems of contemporary civilization.

MAJOR EVENTS, 1870-1918

1870—

       Third French Republic (1871–1940)
       Revolt of Paris Commune (1871)
       Kulturkampt in Germany (1870–1878)
       Economic Depression (1873–1879)
1875—   Constitutional laws passed under Third French Republic (1875)
       Russo-Turkish War (1876–1878)
       Rise of Tariff Protectionism (after 1879)

1880—

       Alexander II of Russia assassinated (1881)
       Economic Depression (1882–1886)
       British Parliament passes Third Electoral Reform Act (1884)

1890—   Bismarck dismissed as German Chancellor (1890)
       Industrialization in Russia (1890–1914)
       Economic Depression (1892–1896)
1895—

       Dreyfus Affair in France (1898–1906)
1900—   Economic Recession (1900–1901)

       Lenin forms Bolshevik Party (1903)

1905—   First Russian Revolution (1905)
       Separation of Church and State in France (1905)
       Constitutional crisis in Hungary (1905)
       Stolypin's "wager on the strong" begins in Russia (1906)
       Universal male suffrage in Austria (1907)
       Daily Telegraph affair in Germany (1908)

1 Economics and Society

By the last decades of the nineteenth century, the industrial revolution had spread across Europe to the east and south. It had passed Sweden, and was reaching Austria, Russia, and northern Spain and Italy. Only the larger western nations and Belgium were truly industrialized by 1914, but the effects of industrialization touched nearly everyone. As the economies continued to grow, industrial organizations grew ever larger, until by the end of the century, the anonymous mass organization of giant trusts and cartels had begun to reduce personal enterprise and dwarf the individual. Not only were the economy and the industrial structure becoming bigger and more complex, the same was true of society itself. The population had expanded enormously, and millions of people all over Europe were on the move, carrying European society and culture to five continents. The process started in Britain at the end of the eighteenth century was now being repeated throughout most of Europe, with the burgeoning of giant cities and the displacement of great numbers of people. New social problems, often similar in nature to those already seen in Britain, were emerging all over Europe. The peasantry gave way to the urban workers as the largest social class in the most advanced countries, and the workers frequently regarded themselves as deprived of an adequate return for their labor. They, in turn, sought organizations of their own to face the power of capital and the new industrial combines. This lead to increasing tension, more strikes, and sometimes to violence. The twentieth century thus dawned on a new world of industrial and technological marvels, but a world marred by social discord and strife.

THE EXPANDING INDUSTRIAL ECONOMY

During the second half of the nineteenth century, industrial development in the western world achieved a previously unimagined momentum. The most basic factor in industrial growth was the rise of the heavy-metals industry, for steel was needed for railroads, bridges, and many parts of the new high-speed machines that were being turned out in ever greater numbers. Ordinary cast iron was too brittle for most of these new needs, while wrought iron was too soft and pliable for many others. Steel was, conversely, in the highest demand, for only steel was able to withstand the stresses placed on metal in most of the new machines and transportation devices. Originally, the tempering process was so expensive that steel could not be purchased in large quantities. A major scientific break-through for this problem came in 1856, when the Englishman Sir Henry Bessemer developed a new process to make cheaper wrought iron, and thus lower the eventual cost of steel production. Bessemer invented a blast furnace which drove air through the molten metal to produce such extreme temperatures that pig iron could be purified much more quickly and cheaply. Important as this development was, it had certain limitations. If the "blow" were continued for too long, much of the iron might burn; the Bessemer system did not work properly with phosphoric ores—yet the largest deposits in western Europe, those in Lorraine, France, were phosphoric; and, finally, no way existed for controlling the amount of carbon that remained in the iron and determined the kind of steel produced.

Consequently, the search for new methods went on and in 1866, William Siemens, an Englishman of German origin, and Emile and Pierre Martin, brothers of French nationality, developed a new process—the open-hearth method—in which the molten iron was reduced in a shallow pan by playing hot air and gas on it. This method allowed the testing of the amount of carbon as one went along and the drawing off of the mix when it had the right proportions. Then, in 1878 two English chemists, Thomas and Gilchrist, discovered that if the furnace were lined with magnesium limestone, the limestone would absorb the phosphorus and the process could go on as though there were no phosphorus. These various technological improvements resulted in a lowering of the price of steel by one-half between 1856 and 1870 and thus made available a cheap material for building machines, rails, and boilers which would sustain the stresses and friction of high speeds and heavy loads. Eventually, different alloys were perfected to give special qualities to the finished products; petroleum products were made available to take the place of animal fats and vegetable oils in lubrication; and improvements were made in such important processing operations as rolling and slitting.[1]

This metal was so important to modern industry that steel production soon became a prime index of a nation's industrial strength. Britain produced about 250,000 tons of steel in 1870, but 8,500,000 tons in 1913. Germany produced only a little over half as much steel as Britain in 1870; but by 1913, her steel industry was turning out over 20 million tons a year. The real giant was, however, the United States, which in 1913 produced more steel than Britain, Germany, and France combined. The diffusion of new industrial techniques had thus helped to shift the balance in industrial leadership from Britain and France to Germany and the United States.

---

[1] Steel was poured into molds and allowed to cool enough to take shape so that it could be handled in solid blocks before running it into rolling or other mills. In the 1960's a process was developed whereby cooling was done so rapidly that the flow was continuous from furnace to rolling mill.

Steel was only one example of this, for, in the last decades of the nineteenth century, industrial technology was being radically changed by new inventions. Characteristic new industries were those based on chemistry and electricity, and in both fields Germany showed herself extremely proficient. Rapid expansion in chemistry produced a startling variety of synthetic products, ranging from new clothing fabrics to new metals such as aluminum, first discovered in 1827 and developed into a major industry by the beginning of the twentieth century. An even more important product of chemical research was rubber (1844), which added new dimensions to the world of machinery. By the turn of the century, the electrical industry was growing rapidly. Development of an effective electric motor, of electric lights, and of other uses for electrical power were bringing in an electrical revolution. Similarly, though the steam engine remained the basic source of mechanical power until the First World War, new kinds of motors—the internal combustion engine and its variants, such as the Diesel engine—were also being developed.

An International Economy The basic ideology of capitalist expansion had been economic liberalism, which stressed freedom from outside interference (laissez faire). This had meant individual enterprise and initiative on the domestic level and free trade on the international plane. The movement toward reduction of tariffs made impressive advances during the middle of the century, reaching a climax in the 1860's. Though only Britain among larger countries maintained a policy of absolutely free trade, other governments had made concessions to laissez faire, with the result that there were fewer barriers to international commerce than ever before in European history.

International commerce and finance were greatly facilitated by the stability of national currencies during the second half of the nineteenth and beginning of the twentieth centuries. The convertibility of different monetary systems, from the British pound to the Russian ruble, was achieved through the nearly universal adoption of the gold standard. It was expected that the currency of any civilized country would have a precise equivalent value in gold, and that it would be backed by sufficient gold deposits to guarantee its stability. The pressure to adopt the gold standard was strong, and every European government managed to achieve this end, though only with great exertion on the part of poorer lands.

International commerce expanded enormously not merely between the various nations of Europe, but even more between Europe and the rest of the world. Industrial Europe could not feed its mechanical system without raw materials from the primitive areas, nor could its prosperity continue to grow without an expanding market for its production. As a result, the commercial and financial network of the European economy spread beyond all national boundaries, carrying international division of labor to a degree that might have surprised even Adam Smith. An industrial nation like Britain sold machine-produced goods in almost every part of the world, but bought the greater share of its food from cheap foreign agricultural producers. Grain came from Russia, America, and Argentina, mutton from Australia, bacon and eggs from Denmark, oranges from Spain. Argentina, in turn, borrowed capital and technology from Britain, bought steel from Germany, special textiles from France, matches from Sweden. Business affairs became supranational to the extent that financiers in London and Paris did not hesitate to do business with their nation's enemies in time of war. During the Crimean War, for example, the Russian government floated new bond issues on the London stock market.

The Gap Between Industrial and Nonindustrial Countries Yet this vast web of international commerce and finance did not mean that economics was moving toward a level of international equality, for, economically speaking, there were two different worlds by the end of the nineteenth century. The basic split did not lie between capitalists and workers, nor between the original industrial nation, Britain, and a newer industrial country like Germany. Rather, it was the broadening gulf between the industrialized society of western Europe and North America on the one hand, and the nonindustrialized world of southern and eastern Europe, plus all the rest of the globe, on the other. The principal dividing line now lay between societies with universal education, streetcars, fully developed railway systems, organized sanitation and hospitals, a high consumption of steel—and those that still lived in a basically rural setting.

So much wealth was accumulated by west European capitalists that they had resources for massive investment in the nonindustrial areas (a process that is discussed in more detail in Part XV). As their capital holdings mounted, west European countries were able to import more goods from abroad than they actually paid for in their direct export trade. This was not because exports were declining, for European commerce continued to increase year by year and in 1900 it had reached more than 10 billion dollars. Rather, this was simply because the economic pre-eminence of the industrial countries enabled them to live off the wealth of the world and consume ever-increasing amounts of goods which they did not have to produce directly themselves. The outstanding example of a mature industrial nation consuming more than it currently sold or produced was Great Britain which, in the years just before 1914, was annually purchasing almost three-quarters of a billion dollars more goods than it sold. The difference was paid for by what were called "invisible exports," based on accumulated capital. These "invisible exports" were of several kinds. In addition to the large return from loans and money placed in foreign enterprise, the British merchant marine—by far the largest in the world—had a mammoth carrying trade that was extremely lucrative. Another item of importance was Britain's insurance system, again the best developed in the world, with the famous Lloyd's of London leading the way. Businessmen of five continents purchased British insurance, adding to the nation's income.

In this capitalist-dominated international economy, countries geared primarily to agriculture and the export of raw materials usually operated at a disadvantage. The new industrial goods were relatively scarce and difficult to produce, so that they drew a high price on the international market. Foodstuffs and raw materials became ever more abundant, so that the relative value of rural produce tended to decline. Nonindustrial regions were therefore caught in a continuing international "price scissors," which meant that they must export more to earn an equal or lesser amount.

Moreover, the latter part of the nineteenth century was a period of general deflation, since the amount of the circulating currency was limited to the available supply of gold supporting it. The world's gold supply did not keep pace with the expansion of production, which meant that less money was in circulation to deal with more goods. The price level consequently tended to fall, and the market value of food products and raw materials fell even more seriously. This was especially hard on the economy of nonindustrial regions, much of whose earnings often went to pay interest or principal on capital loans from European financiers.

The "Business Cycle" The international economy was entirely unable to escape that central process of modern capitalism, the "business cycle." During the first half of the nineteenth century, general business depressions were usually triggered by bad harvests. After 1857, agricultural factors tended to lose their importance. Disorders within the capitalist system were caused mainly by the natural rhythm of commerce and industry, and there were successive periods of slump and depression at the following times between the years 1855 and 1914:

1857–1859	1892–1896
1865–1868	1900–1901
1873–1879	1907–1908
1882–1886	1912–1913

During the nineteenth century, this process of overexpansion, followed by contraction and renewed expansion, was assumed to be the "natural law" of economics. It was emphasized that each successive upswing carried the economy to a greater peak than it had known before the last depression, so that constant progress was made from one cycle to another. This was true enough, but the problem was that there seemed no way to avoid the cycles, and by the end of the century they were becoming more frequent. It was no wonder that more and more people began to consider the advisability of some kind of government economic regulation to control the cycle.

The Rise of the Cartel The market for industrial production was now so large and complex, and the competition between firms in the same line of production so troublesome to each other, that it became highly desirable to work out some form of coordination between enterprises to avoid the disadvantages of competition and exercise some control over market conditions. There began an irreversible tendency for companies either to expand their own facilities to include as many aspects of their branch of industry as possible, or to combine their firms as larger organizations to meet common problems.

Such combinations consisted of two basic types, known as "horizontal" and "vertical." Vertical combinations were carried out by large concerns that wished to control either marketing outlets or necessary resources for production. In addition to owning blast furnaces, for example, the steel corporations purchased their own coal and iron mines, transportation facilities, fabricating plants, and machine works. In this way, they controlled all the successive stages in the manufacture of goods made out of steel.

Horizontal combinations of a different sort were made by firms that were in mutual competition. Various coal, steel, or chemical producers would make agreements with each other on prices, sales districts, amount of production within a given period, and so forth, in order to protect themselves from the risks of the open market. These combinations of firms were especially noticeable in new industries, such as oil and aluminum. They were most common in Germany, where they were known as "cartels." Large heavy-industry cartels like those of Krupp and the great chemical combine, I. G. Farben, dominated large segments of German economic life and were even encouraged by the government.

Supporters of combination said that such concentrations led to greater stability and increased efficiency. The multiplication of resources made it possible to streamline techniques and introduce assembly-line methods of mass production, while near-monopoly of output and control of the market helped to prevent extreme fluctuations. Yet all these developments were a painful contradiction of the ideas of economic liberalism, for they made it clear that enterprise was no longer in any real sense "free" or "individual." Competition and personal initiative, those cornerstones of laissez-faire ideology, were being eliminated by the advantages of superorganization.

Economic Stimulation by the Government According to the doctrines of classical liberalism, the state was supposedly irrelevant to economic progress so long as it kept the peace and had the decency otherwise not to interfere. Abstract theory notwithstanding, the realities of government and economics in the nineteenth century were considerably at variance with the liberal ideal. In fact, the character and success of every economic system have been to a considerable degree determined by the role of prevailing political institutions. By and large, the governments of most west European countries from 1860 to 1914 tried to avoid unnecessary interference and present the most favorable climate for industrialization. In practice, however, this did not always result in respect for the strict laissez faire preached by many liberals and businessmen. Promoting capitalism and industrialization frequently meant that the state must take the lead in encouraging capital formation, economic concentration, business security, or such fundamental items as railroad construction. In Germany, the state built many of the railroads itself; in Austria, France, Italy, and Spain governments fostered the loans necessary to get the railroads built. This was also the case in the capitalist paradise of the United States.

Spread of Protective Tariffs   Moreover, the international economy, at its height, was being partially arrested by the growth of national restrictions. After the triumphs of free trade during the 1850's and 1860's, an almost irresistible countertendency set in, and tariff levels began to mount on almost every side. A paradox of the last part of the nineteenth century was that, as the European economy became more international in scope and structure, many political and economic leaders became more nationalist in attitude, so that by the beginning of the twentieth century, policies of economic nationalism were gaining favor all over the continent. It was in part the very achievements of economic liberalism that encouraged this reaction in the direction of state regulation. The extent of industrialization, the costs of competition, market complexity, the disastrous results of depression or even of declining sales volume, brought loud cries for government protection.

Britain had been able to afford free trade and open competition because she originally held a great lead in industrial production over other nations. Latecomers, hoping to catch up with her, could not easily adopt the same policy. Nationalistic programs re-echoed the arguments of the German theorist Friedrich List, whose *National System of Political Economy* (1840) had long before pressed for state protection and encouragement of industry, contending that no nation could be strong, fully independent, or completely civilized if it remained primarily a producer of raw materials. These arguments were reinforced after the national unification drives of Germany and Italy. A further push was provided by the international depression of 1873, which was quite severe, driving prices and wages drastically downward. The food producers of industrial nations like France and Germany were especially eager for government protection from foreign agricultural competition, since railroads and shipping lines were now bringing American and Russian grain into the European market at very low prices. Industry quickly demanded the same security, and in 1879 the combined interests of German industry and large landlords forced a sizeable new protective tariff through the Reichstag. Other continental governments followed suit, so that from about 1880 the movement away from low tariffs and relatively free trade became general. The tariff increases of the 80's and 90's frequently led to ruinous tariff wars that went far beyond the necessary protection of infant industry. National protection thus became an economic way of life; industries learned to expect it and rely upon it. Not only was the state now playing an important role in preserving the market for domestic production, but it also helped find markets abroad through the general process of imperial expansion. (See Part XV)

SOCIAL CHANGE   The "population explosion" that causes such concern at the present time was already under way in Europe during the nineteenth century. An increase in the birth rate due to earlier marriages had helped to encourage the trend. In later decades, the birthrate in western and central Europe declined steadily, due to the practice of birth control and an increased emphasis on family comfort and security. Sanitary and medical improvements, however, caused the death rate to fall much faster. In primitive regions, the death rate per thousand has usually been forty per year, approximately equalling the birth rate; but in North America, Great Britain, and Scandinavia, the death rate had fallen to approximately nineteen by 1914 and was still on the decline. It was only slightly higher in Germany and other western countries. Therefore, by 1914 the life expectancy at birth of an inhabitant of western Europe or North America was nearly fifty years, or almost twice that of people in some parts of Asia or Africa. Equally important, the increase in food production due to sweeping agricultural changes, as well as the great growth in industrial output, made it possible for the western world to support a greatly expanded number of people. During the course of the nineteenth century, the population of Europe increased threefold.

Urbanization There was no room in the traditional structure of European rural life for this great population growth, especially since the proportion of people needed to produce food was decreasing all the time. Most of the surplus went into the cities, swelling the industrial labor force and turning western and central Europe into an urban society. By 1914, sixty percent of the population of Germany and the Low Countries, and two-thirds of the inhabitants of Great Britain, lived in cities of over 20,000 residents.

The new urban society lacked the cohesion or the personal ties common to the old rural order. Built upon industrialization, it reflected the impersonality of the factory. The corporation was an anonymous employer who lacked the personal identity of a landlord. Class status was increasingly determined by wealth rather than by family heritage. In the new hierarchy, the sense of social responsibility that had earlier governed the relationship between the upper and lower classes in rural districts was lost. Thus, there was little sense of tradition or mutual respect between classes in the cities and, when living standards for the workers failed to rise rapidly enough, it was not surprising that many of the latter supported socialist groups and other movements of rebellion.

Emigration The opportunities in the European city were paralleled and even surpassed by the potential of the new lands of the western hemisphere and the British empire. Heavy rural population density in Europe, temporary economic depressions, social catastrophes such as the Irish "potato famine" of the 1840's, the desire to escape authoritarian government or persecution—such as that suffered by the Jews in Russia—all stimulated emigration. During the apogee of European liberalism, there were scarcely any political barriers to emigration, and development of new transportation facilities, especially the introduction of the steamship, made rapid travel easier and cheaper than ever.

The result was that between 1840 and 1914, some fifty-five million Europeans emigrated to other continents. Possibly as many as twenty percent of them eventually returned to Europe, but the bulk remained to make new homes abroad and thus expand the number of Europeans inhabiting other parts of the world.

"Welcome to All." This cartoon from the 1880's depicts a beneficent Uncle Sam welcoming immigrants from Europe. The tide of outward emigration was motivated by hope for economic improvement, freedom from social and economic exploitation, and also the avoidance of military conscription.

Predominance of the Middle Classes   The second half of the nineteenth century was the golden age of the European middle classes. For five centuries, the urban middle classes had been slowly increasing in power, wealth, and importance until they had now become the predominant social group, at least in the western half of the continent. Having displaced the aristocracy as the dominant group in society, the upper stratum of the middle classes—sometimes known as the "high" or "grand bourgeoisie"—became the new upper class. The middle classes in general constituted a social stratum that constantly broadened in size. It ranged from the millionaire financier down to petty shopkeepers and even white-collar workers. The lower-middle class was far from affluent, but its members clung to the status of economic semi-independence which distinguished them from the hired hand. Greater opportunities for education increased the proportion of professional men in society, such as doctors, lawyers, teachers, and engineers.

It was the middle classes that had created the industrial system and thus revolutionized the conditions of human life. The middle-class style of life relentlessly destroyed the archaic forms, pretenses, and artificialities of aristocratic society, reorienting interest toward the principles of work and productivity. The middle-class system was founded on a sense of independence and private property. It was basically liberal and resisted efforts to curb personal freedom. The middle classes were largely conventional, and they insisted on respect for decorum and standards, setting the tone for what has since been called "Victorianism." Though customarily associated with Britain, these attitudes were characteristic of much of the society of western and central Europe.

Toward the Emancipation of Women   Another major result of middle-class liberalism was greater freedom for women. Three basic factors involved were increased education, the decline in the birthrate, and greater economic prosperity. Young women who had received formal education were less likely to be content with no other interest save housekeeping, while the decline in the birthrate freed more and more of them from the onerous task of bearing and rearing large flocks of children. For the first time in human history, women began to have opportunity for professional interests. Economic development provided them with hundreds of thousands of positions in shops, in clerical positions and in industry. An active movement to win voting rights for women was carried on by "suffragettes" in Britain, but before 1914 the only country to grant them electoral suffrage was Norway. The predominant feeling was still that women's place was in the home, and the emancipation of women politically and socially only reached a climax in western Europe after the First World War.

Suffragette Leader Emmeline Pankhurst Being Arrested by London Police, 1914. Mrs. Pankhurst was one of the most active leaders of the English women's suffrage movement on the eve of World War I, the classic forerunner of today's "Women's Lib." (Radio Times Hulton Picture Library.)

In Britain, members of the female suffrage movement grew very impatient of the long delay in being granted the vote. If nothing could be done by ordinary means, these "suffragettes" were willing to break the peace in order to make their demands heard. They chained themselves to public buildings, insulted the king at the theater, threw acid into mailboxes, and even smashed art objects in the British Museum. When arrested, they sometimes went on hunger strikes, to which the police responded by "forced feeding" through tubes jammed down the young women's throats. The female suffrage movement finally gained its objective in Britain after the First World War, but its radical tactics were one more example of the growing unrest which seized society in the years before 1914.

A major paradox of nineteenth-century European civilization was that the period of greatest material prosperity hitherto known to man was also the period of greatest discontent. Many members of the lower classes were dissatisfied, not because they lived more poorly than had previous generations, but because they were learning to hope for much more than their ancestors had even dreamt of. The very opportunities offered by a modern industrial environment became a source of active discontent when workers were unable to take advantage of them. Monotonous factory conditions largely destroyed the pride in individual creativity once felt by the old artisan class, and work was more and more regarded as mere drudgery whose only possible compensation could be greater pay. If wages were higher, so were prices in the cities. There was little or no job security, and cycles of depression temporarily reduced workers to misery. Housing was usually quite inadequate, and to many workers it seemed that only a small portion of their production was ever returned to them. Such new factors as the increase in literacy, the crowded conditions and personal contact of mass society, the agitation of socialists and labor organizers—all made it possible to rouse the hostility of the lower classes in a more conscious and concentrated manner than could have occurred in earlier generations. Workers were interested in security and higher living standards just as much as they were in political representation.

Nevertheless, despite their reasons for resentment, workers in western Europe did not at first eagerly follow socialist doctrine. Until the 1880's, the only countries in which a large, concentrated worker class had arisen were Britain and Belgium. The emerging urban working class at first remained largely illiterate, making it difficult to carry on agitation by means of printed matter. Perhaps most important of all was the fact that, despite continuing inequities, the third quarter of the nineteenth century brought increased income to most segments of the lower classes.

British Trade Unionism In Great Britain, the first country to industrialize, a kind of aristocracy of labor was formed by the numerous printers, mechanics, carpenters, and railwaymen. These skilled workmen could see little to be gained by a revolutionary death struggle for the sake of some vague utopia. Instead, in the 1850's and 1860's they set up "craft unions" to organize all the members of any particular skilled trade, stressing purely economic objectives and ignoring politics. They had a constructive effect on economic affairs, helping to increase wages, improve working conditions, and stabilize the relationship between capital and labor.

Living standards of the ordinary unskilled and semiskilled workers rose more slowly, and during the lean years of the 1870's and 1880's discontent among these social groups became pronounced. It reached a climax in the great London dock strike of 1889, which was the most effective labor stoppage of the century and which ended in a slight victory for the poorly treated dock hands. These years saw the advent of a second kind of union, the industrial union, which was not limited to members of a single craft,

London Match Seller, 1892. Not all the population of late Victorian England participated in the new industrial prosperity. In the large cities, particularly, there was a sizable population of the sick, unskilled, under-employed or criminal, and some still eked out an existence as street vendors. (Courtesy of the Trustees of the British Museum.)

On Strike by Hubert Von Herkomer. This painting depicts the bitterness, grim determination and worries about supporting their families that were common to many trade unionists who went out on strike. (Royal Academy of Arts.)

but organized all the workers in any given industry, regardless of their rank. During the next decades, large industrial unions were built up, so that by the beginning of the twentieth century approximately twenty percent of the total British labor force had been organized. This was a higher proportion than in any other country.

A native brand of nonrevolutionary socialism appeared in the Fabian Society, an organization of middle-class intellectuals founded in 1883. The Fabians strongly opposed violence and illegal activity, proposing instead to

educate the British public to a need for moderate, democratic socialism. Their immediate goals were small, gradual reforms, such as wage increases, improved working conditions, and public ownership of municipal utilities. Discounting the very idea of a radical class struggle, they participated in the organization of a democratic Labor Party for Britain in 1900.

The Rise of Marxist Socialism, 1860–1890   There was much less labor-union organization on the European continent than in Britain. Whereas such groups had been legalized in Britain as early as 1825, they were scarcely tolerated in any continental nation until the 1880's and in some cases did not gain full freedom until after the First World War. Consequently, the working-class movement in France, Germany, and other lands was in large part originated by socialist theorists and organized socialist political groups. Unlike trade-union leaders, who were interested in concrete, limited gains, the socialist intellectuals were theoretically bent on revolution.

The first effort to draw together all the European trade unionist, socialist, and anarchist groups was the International Working Men's Association formed in London in 1864. Within ten years, this "First International" broke up, harassed by police repression on the continent and wracked by bitter internal conflict between revolutionary socialists led by Karl Marx and the anarchists of Bakunin.

In the 1870's, the philosophy of Karl Marx emerged as the dominant doctrine of European socialism. Its success was due to several factors. Marxism was presented as the only form of "scientific" socialism, based on rigorous intellectual analysis, to form a carefully unified world view of rationalist materialism that was congenial to the temper of the age. The Marxists' stress on solid organization gave their groups a structural advantage over rivals. Finally, the Marxists wielded a two-edged sword: while holding aloft the banner of an eventual revolution in the future, they led workers in seeking immediate economic improvements in their existing situation. Between 1875 and 1883, separate socialist parties of Marxist ideology were founded in Germany, France, Belgium, and Spain, while a handful of Russian *émigrés* set up a Russian Marxist organization in Switzerland. Though Marx's followers had to combat other versions of socialism in both France and Germany for a decade or more, they soon outdistanced their rivals. In 1889, six years after Marx's death, the Marxist parties of various countries got together to form a new international organization, soon dubbed the Second International. Both anarchists and evolutionary trade unionists were by definition excluded, giving the Second International an ideological unity that its predecessor lacked. From its headquarters in Brussels, the Second International served as a coordinating center for international Marxism.

Though Marxism clearly predominated, it did not win a total monopoly of the working-class movements in Europe; there were exceptions both in the most advanced and also in the most backward nations. In Italy, for example, Marxist socialism was slow to win a following; and in Spain, it had only a small number of adherents. Many workers of these countries were still living in a preindustrial environment and lacked the education or the opportunity for political self-expression. In Spain, especially, they were easily won to the doctrines of utopian libertarianism and blind violence spread by the anarchist followers of Bakunin.

Anarchism Anarchism, or Bakuninism as it was sometimes called, had nothing to do with Marxist socialism, for it abhorred organization, discipline, and excessive intellectuality. Its proponents stressed complete liberty from government or central organization and formed mutually independent voluntary committees and syndicates. The anarchist trade unions in Spain thus ignored political and economic meliorism, concentrating instead on strikes and revolutionary plans to level all existing institutions. Being largely disorganized, the anarchists lost ground steadily to the Marxists in France and Italy, but the movement continued to grow in Spain. Since the anarchists lacked political cohesion, they could best express their cataclysmic ideals by the organization of small terrorist bands, which left a red mark on part of western society at the end of the nineteenth century. Victims included many heads of state, such as the Italian king (assassinated in 1900), the United States president (1901), and the French president (1904), as well as many lesser figures. The anarchist faith in direct action led to a temporary resurgence of the movement around 1900, which was labelled "Anarcho-syndicalism" and will be described later.

Orthodox Marxism and Revisionism, 1890–1914 The Marxist parties found themselves in a highly contradictory situation during the last decades before the First World War. Contrary to Marxist theory, the economic situation of the working class, at least in western Europe, improved considerably in the latter part of the nineteenth century. Meanwhile, to enlist grass-roots worker support, the Marxists (or Social Democrats, as they called themselves) had formed labor unions wherever possible, and their movements were becoming mass organizations. Without exception, the social democratic parties began to present candidates who were elected to the various parliaments of continental Europe. As socialists became involved in activity of this sort, their basic political emphasis began to change. Socialist deputies did not try to overthrow their parliaments, but to persuade them to pass more social reform measures for the benefit of the lower class. Consequently, improved conditions and the extension of universal suffrage made it possible for the socialists to gain much more influence than before, while, on the other hand, encouraging a decline in revolutionary spirit.

As living standards improved and workers forgot some of their complaints, it was natural that Marxist doctrine should undergo revision. The most noted critique was the book *Evolutionary Socialism*, published in 1899 by a German socialist deputy and intellectual, Eduard Bernstein (1850–1932). Bernstein argued that violent class struggle was no longer necessary, that the new economic and political conditions made it possible for the working

Mikhail Bakunin in 1869. When this photo was taken Bakunin was about to become Karl Marx's chief rival and enemy in the First International. Bakunin was the father and inspiration of violent revolutionary anarchism in the late nineteenth century, but his individualist, libertarian creed found many more followers in the more advanced western societies of Spain, Italy and France than in the anti-individualist society of his native Russia. (Radio Times Hulton Picture Library.)

class to achieve its aims through peaceful, evolutionary measures. He contended that universal suffrage and parliamentary pressure could bring about a classless society without resorting to revolution or a "dictatorship of the proletariat." Bernstein's thesis seemed merely to provide ideological clarification of what had already become the practice among most west European socialists but, nevertheless, he was officially condemned by the orthodox leaders of the German Social Democratic Party.

A more influential revisionist was the French socialist leader Jean Jaurès (1859–1914). Jaurès was fundamentally a humanist progressive and democratic republican for whom the dictatorship of the proletariat had little meaning. In order to retain some kind of ideological coherence, Jaurès insisted that he was a faithful Marxist and that Marxism was sufficiently elastic to be adapted to democratic, parliamentary conditions. Eloquent, idealistic, and inspiring, Jaurès was by far the most popular of French socialist leaders, and hoped to remake his party into the successful champion of evolutionary reform in France. He was, however, severely hampered by radical doctrinaires in France.

Jean Jaurès Addressing a French Socialist Rally in 1913. Jaurès was the most popular socialist leader in France. Though nominally Marxist, he championed a humanitarian and democratic socialism. Jaurès was a vehement pacifist, internationalist, and anti-militarist, and was assassinated by a right-wing nationalist in August 1914 as World War I began. (Roger Viollet.)

Orthodox Marxists, led by Karl Kautsky (1854–1938), the "Marxist pope" of the German party, waged a strong campaign against such ideological revisionism and officially condemned Bernstein's argument. Nonetheless, the daily activities of most socialist groups did not differ greatly from Bernstein's position. Though the Marxists refused to participate in parliamentary government, in most countries they also refrained from overt revolutionary activities. Most socialist trade unionists concentrated on moderate, practical economic reforms.

Syndicalism after 1900 Radicals in the working-class movements eventually became disgusted with what they called the "opportunism" of complacent

Assassination Attempt at the Wedding of Alfonso XIII of Spain, 1906. "Propaganda by the deed"—assassinations and terrorist bombings—was a frequent tool of European anarchists from 1890 to World War I, and was more common in Spain than in any other country. Several attempts were made to kill Alfonso XIII, and this bomb thrown at his wedding procession killed numerous innocent bystanders. Anarchists murdered three Spanish prime ministers between 1897 and 1921. (Gersheim Collection, University of Texas.)

socialist party bureaucrats and trade unionists. Some of the most active espoused a new form of revolutionary activity known as "syndicalism." "Syndicalism" is derived from the French word for trade-union (*syndicat*) and was based on the idea that the unions themselves could become the dominant institution in society. This was to be achieved through an enormous general strike that would cripple all other activity and enable the workers to impose their power on government and society. The most forceful philosopher of syndicalism was a retired French engineer, Georges Sorel (1847–1922), whose *Reflections on Violence*, published in 1908, insisted that middle-class society was lazy, corrupt, immoral, and in need of a rude awakening. He declared that the use of violence was good in itself, for it was supposed to revive a sense of purpose, encouraging selflessness and solidarity while forcing its practitioners to live seriously. Sorel declared that the workers could be kept in a mood of high moral dedication by inculcating the "myth" of the general strike, which would symbolize the beginning of an apocalyptic utopia.

Syndicalism exerted its greatest appeal between the years 1902 and 1912, and may have been encouraged by a temporary slowdown in the rate of economic improvement. In France, Spain, and Italy, where unions had theretofore been comparatively small and weak, syndicalism gained ground rapidly, for its simple, sensational doctrines rejected the need for painstaking professional organization. However, syndicalism soon brought disillusionment, for its fundamentally anarchist attitude made coordinated effort very difficult. Syndicalist strikes, if sometimes widespread, were sporadic, disorganized, and usually ineffectual. In key countries, where the trade unions were solidly organized, such as Britain, Germany and Austria, syndi-calism gained almost no support at all.

Despite the failure of revolutionary agitation and the ambiguous nature of the socialist parties, large sectors of the European working classes remained deeply dissatisfied in the years before the First World War. Even Britain experienced more strike actively than ever before, and outbursts in Italy and Russia in 1913-1914 had threatening overtones. The established governments remained solidly entrenched and few revolutionary leaders expected a grand cataclysm within the next decade, but the persistence of class conflict left the future uncertain.

FURTHER READING A very useful interpretation of demographic developments is A. M. Carr-Saunders, *World Population: Past Growth and Present Trends* (1936). For the new trends in late nineteenth-century economics, see Joseph A. Schumpeter, *Capitalism, Socialism, and Democracy* (3rd ed., 1950); Robert Liefmann, *International Cartels, Combines and Trusts* (1927); Jacob Riesser, *The German Great Banks* (1911); G. W. Edwards, *The Evolution of Finance Capitalism* (1938); Herbert Feis, *Europe, the World's Banker, 1870-1914* (1930); and Folke Dorving, *Land and Labor in Europe, 1900-1950* (1956). W. W. Rostow, ** Stages of Economic Growth* (1960), provides a stimulating interpretation of the process of industrial development.

The most useful general introductory studies of Marxism are George Lichtheim, ** Marxism, An Historical and Critical Study* (1961); and Bertram Wolfe, ** Marxism, 100 Years in the Life of a Doctrine* (1965). Lichtheim's ** A Short History of Socialism* (1970) provides a sympathetic but not uncritical synopsis of the socialist ideas and movements. Harry Laidler, ** History of Socialism* (1968), is a more detailed survey. See also G. D. H. Cole, *A History of Social Thought*, 3 vols. (1953ff.). The best general introduction to the Internationals is M. M. Drachkovitch, ed., ** The Revolutionary Internationals* (1966). Julius Braunthal deals more extensively with the First and Second Internationals in his *History of the International* (1967). The revision of Marxist orthodoxy is analyzed in Leopold Labedz, ed., ** Revisionism* (1962); and Peter Gay, ** The Dilemma of Democratic Socialism* (1952). There are several introductions to anarchism; perhaps the best is George Woodcock, ** Anarchism* (1962). M. P. Fogarty, *Christian Democracy in Western Europe* (1957), provides a survey of Catholic labor movements.

There is a plethora of works dealing with socialist and labor movements in individual countries. For Britain and France, see G. D. H. Cole, *A Short History of the British Working Class Movement* (1947); Val Lorwin, *The French Labor Movement* (1954); and Harvey Goldberg, *The Life of Jean Jaurès* (1962). On Germany and Italy, Carl Schorske, ** German Social Democracy, 1905-1917* (1955); Richard Hostetter, *The Italian Socialist Movement* (1958); and M. F. Neufeld, *The Italian Labor Movement . . . from 1800 to 1960* (1961).

---

*Books available in paperback edition are marked with an asterisk.

2 Cultural Fragmentation

By the end of the nineteenth century, the spiritual and cultural unity of Europe, in dissolution for nearly 200 years, had nearly disappeared. Intellectual skepticism, the attractions of the new materialism, and the pressures of urbanization and industrial life combined to decrease the influence of the Christian churches, which had provided the traditional spiritual and cultural guidance of the western world.

THE WANING INFLUENCE OF ORGANIZED CHRISTIANITY

Many new cultural trends of the nineteenth century were inimical to Christian belief. There was a tendency to think that science was the only way to true and certain knowledge, and attacks on the allegedly unscientific character of miracles and apparent contradictions in the Bible became stronger. Some went still further, affirming that anything that could not be verified by scientific experiment was not knowable or worth knowing. More and more educated people adopted the attitude called agnosticism, which maintained that it was impossible to answer the basic religious questions of life. Beyond the agnostics there were militant atheist societies, devoted to combating not merely Christianity but the very idea of God.

Growing indifference to religion was especially marked in the larger cities, where it was strongest among the extremes of the rich and the poor. Church organizations proved slow to meet the changing patterns of society in some countries, and failed to provide facilities for parish organization and spiritual guidance in the newer industrial communities.

The Protestant Churches The late nineteenth and early twentieth centuries were a period of overall decline for the Protestant churches, but the pattern was complicated. In general, there was a steady growth in church membership among most Protestant denominations in North America, while British and American Protestants developed a large overseas missions movement that began to build new Protestant churches in parts of Asia and Africa. In that sense worldwide Protestantism began to reach an all-time peak during the late nineteenth century.

Balanced against this, however, was the decline in church membership in the original homelands of Protestantism in northern and northwestern Europe. In Britain, church membership had seemed to be expanding among the lower classes during the early and middle decades of the nineteenth century, but in later years started to register a marked decline. The true religion of the new unified Germany was neither Lutheranism nor Catholicism but nationalism. To the loss in church members was added the growing secularization of culture and the dwindling influence of Christian belief among many nominal church members.

At the end of the century, there emerged a new movement in several churches; called the "Social Gospel," it strove to make religion "relevant" by directing its energies toward social reform. Some theologians tried to "modernize" Christian doctrine by smoothing out apparent inconsistencies and de-emphasizing miraculous phenomena that could not be explained scientifically. Modernism was strongest among Protestants, though some Catholic theologians were also influenced by this current. Orthodox Protestants sometimes reacted by stressing "fundamentalism," which insisted that the literal word of the Bible and traditional doctrines alone were the only religious truth.

Roman Catholicism   At first, Catholicism refused to make any concessions to philosophical modernism and political liberalism, which was usually associated with religious freethinking and anticlericalism. In 1864, Pope Pius IX's *Syllabus of Errors* condemned most modern social theories and institutions, such as labor unions and parliamentary democracy. Proclamation in 1870 of the infallibility of the pope when speaking *ex cathedra* on matters of faith and morals was designed to remove lingering doubts as to where final authority lay. In 1907, Pope Pius X (1903–1914) declared modernism in theology to be a heresy, thus assuring maintenance of all traditional Catholic dogma.

Catholicism became engaged in a long series of conflicts with the modern state, which was determined to eliminate special ecclesiastical privilege and jurisdiction. This strife was most serious in Italy, where the Catholic Church failed to come to terms with Italian unification and nationalism, and lost its sovereignty over the papal states (1860), including the city of Rome (1870), where the popes remained self-styled "prisoners" in the Vatican for the next half-century. Similar conflicts occurred in most other Catholic countries, and in united Germany the church had to face Bismarck's *Kulturkampf* (see Chapter 5). In the long run, some of these trials may have been a blessing in disguise for Catholicism. They reaffirmed the church's international character and encouraged concentration on its spiritual tasks.

Catholicism underwent considerable revitalization during the latter part of the nineteenth century, and was probably more vigorous in 1900 than in 1800. Though its public power and membership had declined in some countries, there was more dedication and zeal among many of the faithful. Altogether, more new religious orders were founded in the nineteenth century than in any other century of church history.

In 1893, an encyclical by Pope Leo XIII (1878–1903), *Rerum novarum* ("Concerning New Things"), marked a new approach to social problems. It criticized both capitalism and socialism, but stressed the importance of improving the conditions of the lower classes and indicated that Catholic organizations must assume more initiative.

From that point, Catholic social endeavors became more active, forming Catholic labor unions in every nominally Catholic country and in other ways paralleling some of the work of new Protestant groups, such as the Salvation Army, dedicated to serving the poor. Catholic "Social Christianity" or Christian Democracy eventually took form as a political movement in France, Spain, and Italy during the second quarter of the twentieth century and, paradoxical though it might have seemed in light of the pronouncements of Pius IX, helped to broaden the base of liberal democracy.

PROBLEMS OF THE NEW SCIENTIFIC THOUGHT

For many people, the decline in the influence of Christianity in the latter part of the century was no cause for alarm, but rather a logical consequence of the opening of a newer, better, era. The half-century preceding the First World War was probably the most optimistic period in the history of western civilization, carrying the rationalist faith of the Enlightenment to new heights. More than ever before, men believed that the physical forces of the world were under human control, that their environment was mutable, and that they had the power to create all manner of new wonders to make life more attractive. The basis of this optimism was faith in science, for science revealed the "laws" that governed the physical universe and made it possible to cope with the world in a rational, objective, and precise manner. The western world was being turned into the most healthy and comfortable society that anyone had dared imagine. Science seemed a thoroughly beneficent force, bringing only good to man and well able to replace the consolations offered by religion for the trials of human existence.

Such was the general view. Yet during this very period of optimism, there appeared new scientific theories and discoveries which did not entirely fit in with the simple progressivism of the earlier scientific world-view. This eventually provoked concern and reassessment in the thinking of those intelligent enough to perceive the incongruities.

Darwinism In the natural sciences, the most important concept of change and evolution was the one developed by Charles Darwin (1809–1882). Over many years, Darwin made careful observations of fossil remains in various parts of the world and studied the similarities between them and living forms. In two major books, *Origin of Species* (1859) and *The Descent of Man* (1871), he endeavored to describe how the various species had evolved from more primitive prototypes to their present structure. According to Darwin's theory, the evolution of species resulted from a series of very small changes continued over very long periods of time and aided by isolation of organisms from each other. In Darwin's theory, partially based on that of Thomas Malthus, the influence of natural environment was in no way so beneficent as in Newton's universe of harmony and order. It was, instead, an unrelenting source of challenge and danger, creating a "struggle for existence." It was this struggle for existence that, to Darwin, revealed how biological change took place.

Every species inherited a given set of characteristics for this life struggle. Many of these characteristics were, however, inadequate. The world contained many more organisms than could possibly survive. Any species unable to fight off its foes, feed itself, and so reproduce itself would die. Those that survived had certain characteristics enabling them to do so, and these qualities were transmitted to their descendants. This was known as the "survival of the fittest," as the result of "natural selection." This process of selection and change under the pressure of environment was ubiquitous, and supposedly functioned in human development about the same way as in the evolution of other animals.

Near the end of *Origin of Species*, Darwin summarized in this way the process he had postulated:

It is interesting to contemplate a tangled bank, clothed with many plants of many kinds, with birds singing on the bushes, with various insects flitting about, and with worms crawling through the damp earth, and to reflect that these elaborately constructed forms, so different from each other, and dependent upon each other in so complex a manner, have all been produced by laws acting around us. These laws, taken in the largest sense, being Growth with Reproduction; Inheritance which is almost implied by reproduction; Variability from the indirect and direct action of the conditions of life, and from use and disuse; A Ratio of Increase so high as to lead to a Struggle for Life, and as a consequence to Natural Selection, entailing Divergence of Character and the Extinction of less improved forms. Thus, from the war of nature, from famine and death, the most exalted object which we are capable of conceiving, namely, the production of the higher animals, directly follows. There is grandeur in this view of life, with its several powers, having been originally breathed by the Creator into a few forms or into one; and that, whilst this planet has gone cycling on according to the fixed law of gravity, from so simple a beginning forms most beautiful and most wonderful have been, and are being, evolved.

This quotation shows that, no matter how stark the view of nature and the struggle for existence was in Darwin's theory, Darwin himself regarded the process with satisfaction and even complacency, accepting a kind of inherent law and greater wisdom which guided the violence, waste, and death pervading all nature. To thousands of other people, however, the publication of Darwin's theories, coupled with the suggestion that the human race had itself evolved just like the animal species, was intensely disturbing. Many religious people were upset because Darwin's ideas seemed to place in doubt the concept of a single divine creation, of man made in the image of God. They feared that evolutionary theory would undermine morality and religious belief. The more extreme and intemperate religious leaders called Darwin's theory blasphemy and sacrilege, charging somewhat inaccurately that Darwin claimed men were descended from monkeys.

*"Am I a Man and a Brother"
from Punch, 1861.* This cartoon
from the famous English satirical journal poked fun at the
furor over Darwinist evolution
theory and its supposed implications for human anthropology. To thousands of others,
however, the Darwinian notion was no laughing matter,
and doctrinal duels over the
accuracy of the evolutionary
hypothesis and its possible
derivations or implications are
being fought down to this
day.

Staunch supporters of science rallied to the defense of Darwin's work,
though Darwin himself rarely participated in the resultant controversy,
which waxed greatest in his native country, England. He had never attempted
to explain the *causes* of evolution, or the origin of the first species, for he
could never expect to offer the slightest knowledge of such things. Rather,
Darwin's work was descriptive, and dealt more specifically with intermediate
stages of development. He and his closest associates eventually made it clear
that they did not in any way intend to apply the process of evolution to
human social or ethical standards, stating that the progress and felicity of
the human race could be achieved only to the degree that it fostered moral
and spiritual superiority instead of the survival of the merely physically fit.
With a certain ingenuous air, Darwin even affirmed that in the present state
of western civilization it was precisely those social virtues which stressed
productive cooperation that were most useful in survival.

Darwin's theory was by no means the mortal threat to Christianity that
some alarmists assumed it to be. The original Christian concept of the unity
of creation made it possible to comprehend certain similarities between the
development of the animal and the human worlds. These similarities had
long been accepted by theologians. Concerning the notion of evolution itself,
even orthodox Christians no longer felt compelled to believe that the six
days of creation in Genesis were six literal twenty-four hour periods. On
the other hand, neither evolution nor any other scientific hypothesis could
be used either to support or to refute religious faith. If religion was being
undermined, the basic cause was the structure and values of modern society.
The more perceptive religious leaders could adjust without great difficulty
to the verifiable aspects of Darwinian theory; they well knew that the needs
ministered to by religion would not be erased simply by further scientific
investigation.

Anthropology Another new science that produced potentially disturbing
implications toward the end of the century was anthropology. Cultural
anthropologists in increasing numbers studied the social organization,
practices, and values of different groups of people all over the world. The
conclusions they drew were originally designed to be of professional scientific interest, but after seeing comparisons of the habits and needs of the
South Sea Islander, the African native, and the American Indian, some
readers could scarcely resist the thought that there was no such thing as
an absolute norm of conduct. For example, the most influential anthropological study of the age, Sir James Frazer's *The Golden Bough* (1890), indicated
that the ritual and theology of Christianity had counterparts among primitive
religions, even those relying on witch-doctor chants. Standards of behavior
were all made to seem relative to environment and social need. What was
useful or moral in one culture or civilization might prove disastrous in
another. Some standards worked in one environment, while in a second,
only a different type could succeed. These writings encouraged a general
attitude of skepticism or relativism—there were no absolute verities.

Psychology Perhaps the new interpretation of human nature that was most thoroughly disturbing to existing opinion in both Christian and secular thought was that which evolved in the field of psychology. Study of psychology as a separate branch of natural science was pioneered in the 1870's, and its first significant results were achieved some years later by the Russian Ivan Pavlov (1849–1936). While investigating salivary reflexes in dogs, Pavlov observed that, instead of salivating only in response to food, as was normal, the animals in the experiment would begin to salivate as soon as they heard the approaching footsteps of their keeper, which they associated with subsequent feeding. Such learned reaction to an artificial stimulus was called a "conditioned response." Pavlov's famous experiments indicated that the behavior patterns of animals are strongly influenced by environmental conditions and sets of stimuli, and that, therefore, animals frequently react in a merely automatic fashion. Similar studies using human beings as subjects seemed to show that a great deal of human behavior is not so much the result of rational design as of automatic response to training (i.e., repeated stimuli). Some of Pavlov's followers carried this line of thinking to the point of insisting that conditioned habits might become so ingrained as to be hereditary. The tendency of these theories was toward a virtual denial of the autonomy of the individual personality.

Freudianism Of all the psychologists, by far the most profound in his influence was the Viennese physician Sigmund Freud (1856–1939), the father of psychoanalysis. Freud's outstanding contribution was to reveal the role of the unconscious in civilized man. By the "unconscious," Freud meant those thoughts and feelings of which an individual would not ordinarily be aware, but which nevertheless could markedly influence his behavior. Freud came upon this discovery in his efforts to treat patients afflicted with certain nervous disorders. Puzzled and challenged by the refractory nature of such cases, he eventually hit upon the technique of "free association" to get at the real cause of the malady. In "free association," Freud had the patient tell him whatever might come to mind, without holding anything back. Freud began to perceive the symbolic nature of symptoms such as paralysis of an arm, and related this to various conflicts, thoughts, or feelings that were being "repressed" by the patient and therefore not accessible to the latter's conscious reasoning power. Freud believed that repression occurred because certain thoughts or feelings came into conflict with the individual's moral standards; being unacceptable, they had to be put out of the person's conscious mind, but could not be eliminated from his unconscious. As a result, repressed feelings came to have drastic and frequently harmful effects. After several sessions of psychoanalysis, Freud might be able to discover the exact nature of the conflict troubling the patient. By encouraging the latter to face the problem squarely, Freud could help him to recover mental and emotional health.

That the repression of unconscious instincts was a common phenomenon was further established through Freud's study of dreams and of slips

Sigmund Freud. As the creator of modern psychoanalytic theory, Freud has had a major impact on twentieth-century culture. His hypothetical design of the structure of human personality remains the most coherent of such theories. Freud's influence ultimately became much greater in the United States than in his native Europe.

of speech. From all these investigations he inferred that the influence of the unconscious was characteristic not merely of nervous patients but of mankind in general. He gradually elaborated his ideas into the first comprehensive theory of personality, placing emphasis on the importance of early experience, the motivational aspects of erotic and aggressive drives, and above all, the enormous—though hitherto little suspected—influence of the unconscious.

Freud's pioneering methods gained increasing acceptance at the beginning of the twentieth century and have served as the foundation for modern psychological theories and treatment of emotional disorders. The discoveries of Freudian investigation were, however, taken by many to mean that men were governed by unconscious, irrational drives which it was very difficult to dominate, and that reason and intellect were not so much the basis of human nature as were these passions. Nonetheless, unlike some of their contemporaries, the Freudians were not antirationalists. They believed that a search for truth and understanding could solve the problems of most people. At the same time, their work revealed the psychological damage that might result from the rigid attitudes of a restrictive society which attempted to repress basic instincts. Those who read Freud's writings during the next generation used them to support the growing protest against "middle-class" attitudes and "Victorian" morality, so that indirectly Freud's work contributed to the loosening of moral attitudes soon to become very marked.

The New Physics At the beginning of the twentieth century, new theories were introduced in physics that were just as disruptive to established ideas as those propounded by psychology. Whereas Isaac Newton's universe had been simple, regular, and easy to understand, the vistas opened up by investigation of the subatomic world were incomprehensible to most people

Albert Einstein. Author of the "Theory of Relativity," Einstein ultimately became perhaps the most famous of all twentieth-century mathematicians and scientists. To many writers, his theory of physics has seemed to symbolize the uncertainties of the modern age. (Radio Times Hulton Picture Library.)

and seemed to make little sense in terms of ordinary human reality. In 1900, Max Planck introduced the "quantum theory," which held that energy flowed in sporadic waves and that, when one reached the smallest subdivisions of the physical world, there was no such thing as observable cause and effect. A principle of indeterminacy seemed to govern subatomic particles, just like the irrationalism or meaninglessness of which pessimistic philosophers spoke.

Some years later, Albert Einstein (1879–1955) produced mathematical formulae indicating that space and matter were not absolute factors but simply relative to each other, that space "curved" in time, that matter and energy were interchangeable. The concept of motion was supposed to be no longer valid in an absolute sense, for all measurement of position, like time itself, was relative. Einstein's formulae were termed the "theory of relativity," and in large measure displaced the old Newtonian physics, with its simple laws of gravitation, uniformity, and absolute motion. Newtonian physics, if technically inaccurate, had always been something of a philosophical consolation. Einstein's relativity brought bewilderment and a certain feeling of insecurity.

Max Weber and Sociology Many of these new intellectual problems found a focus in the writings of one of the most central figures of early twentieth century thought—Max Weber (1864–1920). The scion of an upper middle-class family in Berlin, Weber received a broad education in the social sciences. Over a span of twenty years, he grappled with the need to find some sort of methodological tool with which to study social and political forms. To explain the process of motivation and decision in society, Weber used the notion of "ideal types"—that is, an abstract model of certain basic kinds of personalities or reactions which tended to represent a common and important professional or social pattern at a given time and place. Examples of each of these "types" existed, and yet the type itself was an abstraction that necessarily left out some of the precise differences that existed among individual people. An example of an ideal type would by the typical seventeenth-century Puritan, who was supposed to represent the fundamental characteristics of his social group, or the "capitalist" in Karl Marx's thought, whose qualities were supposedly representative of a whole class. Weber tried to develop ideal types that were as precise and objective as possible, but they could not be more than pragmatic approximations. However, using a whole cluster of different constructs of this sort, one could study the process of social interaction, and the formation of values.

Weber's famous study is *The Protestant Ethic and the Spirit of Capitalism*, in which he studied the curious relationship between early Protestant theology, Protestant social ethics, and the tendency toward capitalism. Weber never said that Protestantism was responsible for capitalism, as some commentators mistakenly reported. Rather, he tried to show how one set of values in a given context over a period of several generations tended to effect a very different and unexpected kind of social development. In all his work,

Weber rejected any one-sided interpretation of social causation. He believed that theories of both materialistic and spiritual motivation might be equally valid, depending on the precise relationship between pertinent factors.

Weber tried to hold in tension the conflicting power of rational control and irrational instinct in human affairs. To the end, he affirmed the values of the modern Enlightenment, with their insistence on the primacy of human reason. Yet this very emphasis on rationalism and organization was producing what Weber considered to be the most important social phenomenon of the twentieth century—the proliferation of bureaucracy, the dominance of what was later called the "organization man." Weber feared that bureaucracy and super-organization would eventually engulf the entire human domain, if the process were not corrected. This would mean an end to individualism and even to human liberty as previously understood.

As an alternative to the evils of machine existence, Weber was fascinated by a basic human phenomenon that he labeled "charisma." This was defined as "an extraordinary quality" of social and political leaders, causing men to submit to their personal authority, even though this might be in contravention of the established system or bureaucratic structure. The great danger was that charisma was essentially irrational. It could easily be misused, throwing man back on the opposite horn of the rationalism-irrationalism dilemma. Weber tried to face up to this problem, and yet there was no simple answer. When asked at one point in his career exactly what his studies in paradox and complexity meant to him personally, Weber is said to have replied, "I want to see how much I can endure." He found no simple solution, only a renewed and more careful application of the rational life that had been the ideal of the earlier liberal age.

Social Darwinism During these latter decades of the nineteenth century, the number of new scientific inventions, and of new scientific theories, was expanding in all fields. Such was the prestige of science that there was a tendency for many ordinary people to want to accept some of these new ideas as norms for social and political life. And yet, the intense professional specialization demanded by industrial society did not make it easy for the ordinary layman to understand the precise implications, or lack of them, in learned scientific theories. Hence there occurred a growing tendency toward vulgarization of new ideas. In an age of science worship, the social theorists, political ideologues, and intellectual popularizers seized upon purely scientific concepts and tried to apply the principles of natural science to topics for which they were never intended. The worst distortions were made of the new findings and concepts produced in biology and anthropology.

Darwinian evolution, for example, was quickly converted into a *reductio ad absurdum* for laissez-faire liberalism. It was argued by many social theorists that Darwinism showed that unremitting competition was the law of life, just as capitalists had stressed in an earlier generation. These men reasoned that since science was the key to practical knowledge, the apparently scientific doctrine of evolution must be valid for every aspect of the life process, regardless of Darwin's own explicit demurral. The world was thus made an arena of constant conflict—of competition for survival among human ideas and institutions, as well as among animals. Since everything was continuously evolving, there was nothing that could be relied upon as permanent or inherently valid. All things were determined by this competition, and it was the test of success alone that mattered. "Nature red in tooth and claw" was paralleled in the human environment by ruthless destruction of weakness and incompetence, because evolutionary processes permitted only strength and efficiency to survive. Hence there arose the school of "Social Darwinism," which stood for the most unremitting competition in human society, especially in the economic system. The most representative of the Social Darwinists was the Englishman Herbert Spencer (1820–1903). In numerous works, Spencer insisted that the progress of the human race could be achieved only by free and unregulated competition. Though he did offer the pious hope that the higher stages of evolutionary progress would result in a spirit of altruism, this could only be enjoyed at some undetermined date in the future. Meanwhile, Spencer would have had the functions of government reduced to the absolute minimum in order not to interfere with individual competition. He even opposed compulsory sewage and sanitation measures by municipal authorities. As Spencer's colleagues said, the individual had the right to conduct his own fight with typhus unhampered by state regulations.

Some of these concepts were so absurd that the main vogue of Social Darwinism passed fairly rapidly. By 1890, it had been forced to retreat before the proponents of organization, regulation, and social reform. Statesmen and social leaders were coming more and more to believe that society had an interest not in promoting ruthless competition that might end in indiscriminate suffering, but in making the lives of individual people more comfortable and healthy through a modicum of security. Furthermore, even Darwinians began to worry that the course of evolution was not working out right, that material prosperity for many had still not guaranteed a safe future for humanity as a whole.

Racism   During its relatively brief life, Social Darwinism helped to encourage the most insidious new doctrine to appear in Europe during the second half of the nineteenth century—racism. Racism had even less foundation in science than did Social Darwinism, but its theorists tried to find logical justification in the work of physical anthropologists, who studied the various physical and cultural characteristics of the main races of the human species. From this point, a host of pseudoscientists employed the tools and findings of cultural anthropology to support pet prejudices. They claimed to adduce evidence that certain races were more "highly favored," blessed by "natural selection," to use a Darwinian term. It was generally assumed by this group that the white race was superior, and that certain nationalities within the white race, such as Germans or Anglo-Saxons, were superior to others. After a half-century of middle-brow worship of scientific achievements, it was not difficult for many ordinary people to accept the pseudoscientific doctrines of racism.

The rise of racist nationalism had especially serious meaning for the Jewish community of central and eastern Europe, checking the century-long trend toward Jewish emancipation. Everywhere save in Russia, Jews during recent generations had enjoyed the first opportunity in their modern history to become assimilated into the societies in which they lived. This had been in accordance with the basic tenets of liberalism, and, as young Jews were increasingly permitted the same opportunities as Gentiles, they left Judaism in large numbers, in a process precisely comparable to the de-Christianization of much of Europe. Racism, however, introduced a new kind of anti-Semitism at the end of the century. It encouraged a new raising of barriers and revival of persecution, not because of religious difference, but because Jews supposedly constituted a separate race. The spread of racial anti-Semitism in turn provoked the rise of a new secular Jewish nationalist movement, Zionism. An organized force by 1897, Zionism proposed the re-establishment of a national home for Jews in Palestine, from whence their forefathers had been expelled two millennia earlier. Even Zionists, however, could scarcely have foreseen the incredible extremes that anti-Semitic racism would reach in the twentieth century.

PHILOSOPHY AND THE ARTS

Pragmatism The new philosophical trends of the latter part of the nineteenth century strongly reflected the prestige and attitudes of science, yet at the same time reacted sharply against the vogue of scientism. On the one hand, there was a continuation of the positivist emphasis of the earlier generation. This was most explicit in the English-speaking world, and more precisely in the United States, where the philosophy of "pragmatism" was developed by the American thinkers Charles Peirce (1839–1914) and William James (1842–1910). Pragmatism insisted that values should be judged by their practical effect in human affairs. Truth, for the pragmatist, was what was valuable in his own life, whatever worked or achieved its ends. There was no unchanging principle of reality; reality was only what was real or meaningful for each individual. Things that worked might be "good" or "true" or "real." Practical utility was the final test.

Critics of pragmatism condemned this philosophy as amoral and relativistic, saying that it denied moral standards and glorified mere practical success. James defended pragmatism by saying that it did not propose license be granted to all individual whims, for any normal person would realize that he could not gain practical satisfaction from indulgence in socially harmful acts. He could maximize reward and minimize loss only by a sense of moderation. One might believe in the Christian religion, on the other hand, simply because it made one feel happier and more secure. Nonetheless, the criticism still remained that pragmatism offered only the most tenuous philosophical support for civilized standards, and could lend itself to vulgar worship of success or even of social exploitation.

Antirationalism Science could not hope to solve all the emotional, spiritual, and moral dilemmas of existence, and the scientific world-view came to seem more and more irrelevant to mortal thinkers composed of flesh and blood. The end of the century, therefore, saw an increasing revolt against materialism and positivism among the cultural elite, paralleled by an extraordinary rise in irrationalist, antiscientific attitudes. It was commonly felt that the emphasis on science and even on rational intellect was dehumanizing man, turning him into an insensitive machine. More and more writers began to hammer on the theme that men lived by their will power, their spirit, or their emotions, rather than by the dictates of cold, calculating intelligence. It was increasingly common to hear philosophers say that men acted as they did, not because their goals or motivations had any objective value, but simply because they wanted to.

The French philosopher Henri Bergson (1859–1941) emphasized that men were borne upon a wave of what he termed "creative evolution," a vital spirit that seized them from the depths of the emotional unconscious. In fact, Bergson insisted that scientific intellect could never grasp true reality, since the real world was in constant motion and the intellect could only analyze something that did not move. Because reality was constant change, the intellect was basically incapable of comprehending it. Reality could only be intuited—seized through artistic or emotional insight. It could not be "known."

Such ideas reinforced a growing attack on rationalism at the beginning of the twentieth century. The antirationalists, or irrationalists, of the years after 1900 believed that human life was being twisted and stunted by belief in reason alone. They hoped to point the way toward a broader, freer existence that would serve human needs and talents. In the process, however, the more extreme antirationalists seemed to deny ordinary functions of the intellect, to override the sanctions and standards of society. Such tendencies might have dangerous effects, as was seen a few years later in the rise of the Nazi and Fascist Parties, which so emphasized antirationalist impulses.

More moderate antirationalists did not, however, wish to circumscribe the function of reason, but merely to point out its limitations so that reason would be employed more adequately, as in the case of Freud. They had no desire to plunge humanity into a black night of superstition or intolerant passion, but rather to train and refine man's nonrational drives.

Nietzsche Perhaps the most symptomatic thinker of the age was the German philosopher Friedrich Nietzsche (1844–1900). The son of a Lutheran minister and a philologist by profession, Nietzsche suffered from ill health most of his life and had to discontinue his academic career at an early age. Though most of his adult years were spent in semiretirement, he produced a considerable volume of writing about cultural and social values. Nietzsche's style is frequently misleading; he seldom employed the technique of organized exposition, but used aphorisms, poetic expression, and highly condensed

Henri Bergson. Bergson was the most popular of all modern French philosophers, and in the early twentieth century was certainly the most influential. His concept of the *élan vital* or "vital force" propelling human affairs was opposed to materialism and to pragmatism. It influenced other sectors of life in France and Europe far beyond the philosophy classroom. (Radio Times Hulton Picture Library.)

"The Sick Nietzsche," Detail of a Portrait by H. Olde. Friedrich Nietzsche became the most famous of all late nineteenth-century European philosophers. His concepts of "the will to power" and "the Overman" were much more popular with artists, writers and certain kinds of radical young politicians than with professional students of philosophy. Nietzsche died young, apparently of syphilitic complications. (Radio Times Hulton Picture Library.)

statements which frequently obscured his true meaning. He was, above all, confused and depressed by the decay of the Christian framework of European civilization. "God is dead," wrote Nietzsche, "and we have killed Him." By this he meant that the religious beliefs and values that had nourished Europe for nearly two millennia seemed to have lost their meaning for current society. Like many of his contemporaries, Nietzsche was left seeking new values to fill the gap. He had nothing but the utmost scorn for the official values and hypocritical piety of the respectable middle classes of his day, insisting that their Christianity was a sham, the product of a slave morality that emphasized weakness, helpfulness, and lack of accomplishment. The Socialist movements he considered even worse, saying that they only wished to level Europe downward into a human herd. He felt that the result of the society of his day was to destroy all individuality and authenticity in human life, submerging human beings beneath bourgeois materialism and hypocrisy, proletarian mediocrity, or the mob spirit of anti-intellectual nationalism.

Nietzsche thought a solution could only be found in a sense of life which would altogether transcend ordinary mundane existence. A new kind of man was wanted, an "Overman," who would develop qualities far beyond the imagination of the average herd-man. The "Overman" would prize neither self-renunciation nor vulgar self-acquisition, the two polarities of contemporary society. He would instead value courage, honesty, self-control, self-expression, daring, creativity, a harmonious balance between mind and body, the fulfillment of his finest instincts, and intellectual excellence. Nietzsche did not see the "Overman" among any of his contemporaries, but believed that he would come into existence through the practice of a new self-honesty and a striving for excellence and endurance that would be quasi-religious in spirit. He thought that the only thing left after the demise of Christianity would be the creation of a new devotion to quality and harmony that was essentially pagan in character.

Nietzsche's most important works, such as the eloquent and fascinating *Thus Spake Zarathustra,* were virtually ignored during his lifetime, but after his death they gained an enormous vogue among the cultural elite of Europe. Few readers had an adequate idea of what Nietzsche really believed, but the vividness of his writings, together with the very provocative quality of his thought, created a great impression. Many so-called "Nietzscheans," however, cheapened the concept of the "Overman" into a crude notion of physical dominance. His idea of an elite was used to justify tyrannical dreams of racial superiority or military conquest. Thus the distortions of Nietzsche's style and the contradictions of his own philosophy made the influence of a perverted "Nietzscheanism" a further expression of the vulgarization of European life, against which his work was in fact a searing protest.

The Vogue of Naturalism in Literature The materialistic emphasis of industrial society had strong repercussions in literature. It encouraged new esthetic styles, since some writers attempted to imitate the scientific method, writing novels and short stories that were intended more in the nature of case studies than as products of literary fantasy. The mark of industrial society and Darwinian science was most directly reflected by the Naturalist novel of the 1880's and 1890's. The Naturalists wanted to go beyond the so-called realistic novel of the preceding generation and reach the very marrow of life, the mainsprings of existence that were too vulgar or shocking to have been discussed before. The French novelist Emile Zola (1840–1902), most significant of the Naturalists, wanted his novels to be so faithful to the physical details of human life that they might even have the force of

scientific law, constituting a sort of literary anthropology of French society. The scientific value of Zola's novels is doubtful, but he wrote with an unerring eye for the more brutal aspects of behavior. Most Naturalists lacked the pretensions of Zola, and the more commercial sector of this school dwindled into pornography. To writers like the Naturalists, the seamier side of human nature was most significant. The average human being was represented as the victim of forces over which he had little control. In an age in which many philosophers glorified the will, scores of novelists wrote about spineless, listless human beings who could not answer for their own lives.

Painting The decades prior to the First World War were a period of revolutionary change in music and painting, reflecting both the novelty and stimulus of the new technological society as well as its underlying confusion.

In painting, the first major break with the traditional canons of form and perspective was made by the French impressionists in the 1870's and after. Though impressionism has since become a standard mode of modern painting, its first appearance was greeted with the most extreme critical displeasure. Impressionism was not, however, inspired by the subjectivistic distortions common to some later painting, but was theoretically based on the most recent scientific discoveries in light and photography. These revealed that contrasting colors, when placed side by side, are, beyond a certain distance, fused by the eye into a single tone. Therefore instead of painting solid, continuous colors on canvas the impressionists broke up sections of light and color into very small parts. Viewed farther away, the small bits of color blended into a clear, harmonious "impression" of the object the painting was to represent. The most outstanding impressionist painter was Claude Monet (1840–1926), who devoted his long life to hundreds of studies in the tonalities of nature until his work seemed to dissolve into a personal vision of the inner composition of light and color itself.

By 1900, impressionism was becoming well accepted as an artistic technique and was in turn being superseded by new modes of painting. The major transitional figure was the French artist Paul Cézanne (1839–1906). Though he had on occasion been identified with the impressionists, Cézanne restored the use of line in his work, and employed contrasting color tones to create planes and a new sense of depth, modeling forms through brush-

Paul Cézanne's "The Large Bathers" (1898–1905). This is one of the major achievements of Cézanne, the most influential new French painter of the early twentieth century. He went beyond impressionism to re-emphasize the use of line and forms, creating a new sense of depth and perspective. (Philadelphia Museum of Art.)

strokes and broken patterns of color rather than reducing them to an impressionist pattern. In turn, the fifteen years before the First World War saw the beginning of a new style by French and Spanish artists called cubism. Cubism dissolved the form of conventional reality into cube-like shapes which expressed the artist's own perspective of the physical word but denied common-sense visual perception.

At the same time, young poets and painters in Italy and Russia started a new movement called "Futurism," which mirrored the mechanical universe of modern industry. Futurist paintings were largely devoid of human elements, revealing a world of mechanical frenzy, with gears meshing, and pistons moving at high speed, or industrial sites uninhabited by human beings. From this point it was but a short step for young Russian painters in 1910 to do away with all attempts to portray objects or reality at all. They produced paintings without any objective content, but merely full planes of color, lines and geometrical forms. Developed more consistently after 1912 by Wassily Kandinsky and others, this was the beginning of the "abstract" painting that was to become so popular a few decades later. It will be more fully discussed in Part XVI, Chapter 6.

The literary and art world of the late nineteenth and early twentieth centuries was complex and in a state of rapid change which did not follow any one trend or formula. It was extremely eclectic for, on the one hand, realism and materialism were dominant motifs; on the other, there was a strong tendency to escape from reality into esthetic fantasy, or "art for art's sake."

CLASS
DIFFERENCES
IN CULTURE

The Emergence of the "Intellectual" By the end of the century, the expansion of educational opportunity was producing a greater number of intellectually qualified people than ever before, and this gave rise to a new group in European society, known from its Russian counterpart as the "intelligentsia." For the first time in western history the intellectual class was sufficiently large to form an indistinct but nonetheless visible social group. The "intellectual" as a vocational type was now fairly common, the word first being used regularly in France during the 1890's. An intellectual might be anyone with a specialized education or literary training who spent time writing or working with intellectual or, at least, broadly cultural problems. He might merely be someone who read widely and reflected a great deal in private, but the "intellectual" now existed as a significant aspect of the European scene. The intellectuals were at the heart of the cultural and scientific developments previously surveyed.

The underlying malaise of European culture at the end of the century preoccupied many intellectuals. In contrast to those who sought to avoid it by esthetic escapism, some thinkers and writers hoped to solve the problem not by turning their backs on society but by participating in its most serious affairs. More and more, intellectuals felt a need to seek solutions for the great social issues of the day, to give moral and philosophical leadership to western society. Given the decline of religion, the intellectual was almost prepared to fill the role of a surrogate priest. Intellectuals formed the backbone of the Russian revolutionary movement; their influence in public affairs in France became apparent during the Dreyfus case.

Middle-Class Culture It should be kept in mind that naturalistic novels, pessimistic works of social protest, and the esoteric expression of the ivory tower cult were not the typical cultural fare of Europe at the end of the century. As opposed to the formal culture of the period, which was largely restricted to the intellectual elite, there existed a middle-class culture, much more conventional in form. This esthetic milieu lay somewhere between crude popular tastes and high-brow expression, and in fact established the dominant patterns of respectable art well into the twentieth century. It continued most of the ordinary art forms of the past, and was in turn religious, romantic, sentimental, and inspirational. Self-help tales and stories of moral development were common reading fare, for such literature suited the seriousness of the bourgeoisie.

Mass Culture At a certain point, however, middle-class tastes dwindled off into a new phenomenon—popular culture. The rise of such a thing as a literate popular culture was made possible by the achievements of industrial society, which, for the first time in human history, enabled a majority of the population to possess rudimentary ability to read and write. The emerging mass culture found its expression in sensationalist literature, in art without depth or subtlety, in music with simple rhythms or melodies intended to inspire humor, gaiety, or sentimentality. This booming market was fed by cheap paper novels, filled with lurid tales of violence and adventure, and by the appearance of a new kind of newspaper. Termed the "yellow press" in the English-speaking world, it specialized in highly sensationalistic, vulgarized accounts of trivia that would appeal to the semieducated. The coming of mass culture thus created a new problem concerning the utility and moral value of common entertainment and vulgarized reading matter printed in bulk. The optimistic insisted that crude forms of mass culture were a necessary phase of growth, since it could hardly be expected that the broad masses attain patrician appreciation of the arts within a single generation or two.

When speaking of European society as a whole, it is important to stress the limited effect of the intellectual changes of the late nineteenth and twentieth centuries. The conflict between the new ideas themselves, and their contradiction of old standards, led to increasing fragmentation of a culture that could no longer claim unity of values or standards. Yet at the beginning of the twentieth century, most of these ideas influenced the average European only indirectly or not at all. The attitudes of earlier generations still prevailed. Though the nineteenth-century social and cultural structure was increasingly pressed, it still retained its balance and its belief in order and progress. It was not until the great twentieth-century crises of war and depression that the sinister results of irrationalism, voluntarism, and the cruder forms of materialism showed their full effect.

FURTHER READING The best general account of the Christian churches in the nineteenth and twentieth centuries will be found in the four volumes of K. S. Latourette, * *Christianity in a Revolutionary Age* (1959–1961). Two briefer surveys in paperback are Alec Vidler, * *The Church in an Age of Revolution* (1961); and J. L. Altholz, * *Churches in the Nineteenth Century* (1967).

The best way to gain an understanding of intellectual and cultural history is to read the original works of the thinkers and writers of the period. Cheap paperbound editions of most leading writers of the late nineteenth century are available in any large college bookstore. For the social thinkers, the following selections are useful: The * *Viking Portable Nietzsche* (1954); Sigmund Freud's *A General Introduction to Psychoanalysis* (1949), his most complete exposition for the layman; Charles Darwin's *On the Origin of Species by Natural Selection* (1936); A. J. Nock's edition of Herbert Spencer's *Man versus the State* (1940); and H. H. Gerth and C. W. Mills' * *From Max Weber: Essays*

*Books available in paperback edition are marked with an asterisk.

in Sociology (1946), which also contains a cogent intellectual biography of Weber.

For lengthier surveys of European culture in these years, see the corresponding sections in George Mosse, *The Culture of Western Europe* (1961); C. J. H. Hayes, *A Generation of Materialism, 1871–1900* (1941); and, at greater length, the classic by J. T. Merz, *History of European Thought in the Nineteenth Century*, 4 vols. (1924). On the writing of history in this period, G. P. Gooch, *History and Historians in the Nineteenth Century* (1913), is a standard work. H. S. Hughes, *Consciousness and Society* (1958), treats the changes in social thought. Loren Eiseley, *Darwin's Century* (1958), and J. W. Burrow, *Evolution and Society* (1966), discuss the effects of Darwinism. See also Jacques Barzun, *Darwin, Marx, Wagner* (1941). C. S. Hall, *A Primer of Freudian Psychology* (1954), gives a simplified account of Freudianism. Ernest Jones, *The Life and Work of Sigmund Freud*, 3 vols. (1953), is the standard biography. On developments in physics, see Ernest Zimmer, *The Revolution in Physics* (1936); Leopold Infeld, *Albert Einstein* (1950); and E. N. da C. Andrade, *An Approach to Modern Physics* (1957). B. S. Meyers, *Modern Art in the Making* (1958), is an informative introduction to new tendencies in the arts.

3 Problems of Liberal Democracy in Britain, France, and Italy

In the latter part of the nineteenth century, parliamentary liberalism in western Europe moved steadily nearer direct political democracy. Key steps were the passage of the second British Reform Bill, in 1867, and establishment of the Third French Republic on the basis of universal male suffrage, in 1871. Nevertheless, the transformation of the restricted elitist liberalism of the early nineteenth century into political democracy encountered a number of serious problems.

The first had to do with the extension of the suffrage. Most of the countries of western and northern Europe moved toward universal male suffrage by degrees. Only France in 1871 and Spain in 1889 adopted this standard directly; even in Britain, successive reforms of the suffrage left a minority of the adult male population unenfranchised until 1918; and in no country except Norway were women allowed to vote at all.

The second problem had to do with the nature of representation and the quality of political leadership. In France and Italy, particularly, there was considerable criticism of the parliamentary system itself, on the grounds that political parties under the electoral system merely promoted cliques of pals and fostered corruption.

Rather more important was the question of the relationship of political democracy to social and economic democracy. By the end of the nineteenth century, there were growing demands all over western Europe that government processes become more active in promoting the material well-being and advancement of most of the population.

Finally, for the larger countries, there was the issue of the relationship between domestic problems and foreign ambitions and responsibilities. This led to conflict over imperialism, military expenditures and army service.

In Britain, France, and the smaller but advanced countries of northwestern Europe, these problems were largely resolved on the basis of greater freedom, democratic participation, and increased attention to economic problems. The weight of such pressures was most acute in more backward countries like Spain and Italy. Though considerable progress was made there as well, the more limited resources of less-educated societies and less-developed economies, together with the prestige demands of international competition, led to growing internal tension and cleavage.

GREAT BRITAIN

Gladstone and Disraeli Indicative of the new age in British politics was the fact that the two dominant British statesmen of the 1870's and 1880's, William Gladstone (1809–1898) and Benjamin Disraeli (1804–1881) were both of middle-class origin. Gladstone was the son of a wealthy Scottish merchant, while Disraeli's father was a scholar of inherited wealth and a Jewish background. As leader of the Liberal party, Gladstone was a deeply

"The Two Augurs." This English cartoon of 1873 satirizes the divergent styles and personalities of the two great competing English party leaders—the Conservative Disraeli, witty, pragmatic, and perhaps a bit cynical; and the Liberal Gladstone, stern, moralistic, and perhaps a bit self-righteous. Each in his way served English government well, setting an example of the competition and cooperation of both elements in a two-party system that was the admiration of most other countries. (Radio Times Hulton Picture Library.)

religious man who saw politics in moral terms. The Conservative Disraeli was more detached and skeptical. Gladstone looked upon his rival as unprincipled, whereas Disraeli considered his Liberal counterpart hypocritical. Both were great orators, Gladstone being famous for his mellifluous voice and noble gestures, Disraeli for his penetrating wit and telling phrases.

Extension of British Reformism As a result of the Reform Bill of 1867, both the Liberals and Conservatives were compelled to compete for popular votes and respond to the demand for further reform. Gladstone's first cabinet (1868–1874) was one of the most dynamic in British political history. Its Education Act established a system of public schools and provided for the subsidizing of indigent students, responding to the need for an educated modern electorate and labor force, and also recognizing the apparent lessons of the victories of the northern army in the American civil war and of the German army in the wars of 1866 and 1870, which seemed to demonstrate the superiority of troops educated in free public schools. Between 1870 and 1873, competitive examinations became the basis for entry into the civil service, the undemocratic practice of public voting was ended by introducing the secret ballot, and the judiciary was reorganized and unified. Finally a series of basic reforms in military practice were inaugurated. Army service was reduced from twelve to six years and a number of archaic practices, such as flogging, payment of "bounty money" for recruits, and the purchase of officers' commissions, were abolished.

The drive for reform, stimulated by the competition for votes, continued under Disraeli's second cabinet (1874–1880). In one remarkable year (1875) successive enactments legalized trade union picketing (Gladstone had earlier legalized the right to strike), provided for slum clearance and the construction of working-class housing, prohibited the adulteration of food and drugs, and established public sanitation on a national basis. The Education Act of 1876 made public education compulsory for all British children. These measures were indicative of what Disraeli called "Tory democracy," the concern of the Conservative party for the urban lower classes.

At that point, Liberals and Conservatives differed less over domestic issues than about foreign policy. In preparation for the election of 1880, Gladstone conducted his famous "Midlothian campaigns," the like of which Britain had never seen. This septuagenarian orator captivated great audiences with speech after speech denouncing, in an "ecstacy of moral indignation," the imperialistic foreign policy of the Disraeli cabinet. Though Gladstone had earlier resigned the leadership of his party, the Liberal victory in 1880 was a great personal triumph and brought him back to power. For the first time in the history of British politics, the voters had directly chosen their own prime minister.

The second Gladstone cabinet (1880–1885) inaugurated further reforms. The Corrupt Practices Act (1883), which prohibited bribery and undue influence in elections, was followed by the third Reform Act of 1884, which extended the suffrage to most rural laborers. An attempt by the House of

Lords to block this further widening of the suffrage led to popular agitation ("The Peers against the People!" "Mend them or end them!" were the cries) and failed to prevent its enactment into law.

The Struggle for Irish Home Rule   The record of constructive legislation in the years 1868–1885 demonstrated the effectiveness of the British parliamentary system and the vitality of its leadership. Against this achievement there has to be weighed one weakness: the failure to take the necessary steps to reconcile Ireland, where resentment against 300 years of control by Britain was mounting.

The Irish question had three aspects: religious, economic and political. The religious issue was settled in 1868, when Gladstone disestablished the Anglican church in Ireland, freeing the Catholic majority of the Irish from paying taxes to support a Protestant state church. The economic problem stemmed mainly from the fact that most Irishmen were landless peasants who rented the soil they tilled from great landlords, many of whom were of English descent. After the middle of the nineteenth century, there were major changes in Irish agriculture leading to the beginning of the breakup of large estates, a growth in the number of peasant owners, and improved conditions for renters. Nonetheless, these changes came too slowly for many Irish peasants, gripped as they were by a revolution of rising expectations. They demanded an end to all landlordism and the result was violence. Secret societies fluorished; evicting landlords and their agents were boycotted, terrorized, and even murdered. The British government responded with an increase in police and judicial power, and economic conditions in Ireland steadily improved in the last decades of the century.

In the long run, the most serious program was the political issue of home rule for Ireland. The old Irish parliament had been abolished in 1801, but the extension of the suffrage and introduction of the secret ballot led to the emergence of a highly vocal Irish Home Rule party. Its main leader, Charles Stewart Parnell (1846–1891), was a Protestant aristocrat of English descent who took up the Irish cause and, with his block of more than eighty Irish Home Rule deputies, proved one of the most skillful tacticians in British parliamentary history, bringing about the fall of Gladstone's cabinet in 1885 and that of Lord Salisbury (the Conservative leader since Disraeli's death in 1881) the following year.

Gladstone then accepted the principle of Irish autonomy and when he returned to power in January 1886 the "Grand Old Man" of British politics presented a Home Rule Bill to parliament. His own Liberal Party split over the issue, however, and the bill failed. In retrospect, this appears to have been the beginning of the decline of the Liberal party, which in only one subsequent election (1906) was ever again able to attain an absolute majority in the House of Commons. Parnell's own career was shattered in 1890 when it was revealed that for some years he had been living out of wedlock with the wife of a dissolute army officer who had abandoned her.

Nevertheless, the main part of the Liberal party had become dedicated

Pensketch of William Gladstone.
This sketch was made of
Gladstone in his old age,
when the Liberal lion was
leading his final climactic fight
for Irish Home Rule. It
capped a long career con-
stantly devoted to reasonable
reform. Gladstone's espousal
of the Irish cause demon-
strated the ability of English
Liberalism to remain true to
its principles and progressively extend their application
to the new needs of the time.
(Courtesy, Museum of Fine Arts,
Boston.)

to the achievement of Home Rule. In 1892, at the age of 83, Gladstone
formed his fourth cabinet; but his Home Rule Bill was defeated in the House
of Lords. The next Liberal government eventually introduced a third bill
which finally passed in the spring of 1914. By that time, the issue had become
complicated by a division among the Irish themselves. In contrast to the
agricultural south, Ulster in northern Ireland was an industrial region inhabited predominantly by Protestants. Rather than accept the rule of Catholic
Dublin, Ulsterites began to arm themselves, with the encouragement of
Conservative leaders and British army officers. The southerners too began
to drill a volunteer militia, and Ireland trembled on the brink of civil war.
The sudden outbreak of the First World War in Europe then produced a
greater crisis, which distracted attention, and home rule was postponed for
the duration of the conflict.

Home Rule Demonstration at Scarborough. The controversy over Irish Home Rule aroused more emotion than any other issue in British politics at the end of the century. This drawing depicts Unionist rioters breaking up a Liberal Home Rule demonstration at the town of Scarborough on July 4, 1892. (Courtesy of the Trustees of the British Museum.)

Economic Problems Britain's role as pioneer of the industrial revolution had earned it great wealth; but in later generations, the economy paid a price for its earlier primacy. Manufacturers were sometimes reluctant to retool to take advantage of newer technological improvements in the 1880's and 1890's. By the turn of the century, it was possible to say that some industries, especially coal mining, were suffering the maladies of old age. After other nations had begun to industrialize and erect barriers against British products, the export market became less certain. There were three serious depressions in British iron and steel between the late 1870's and early 1890's, shaking confidence and leading to new apprehension about foreign competition, especially from Germany and the United States.

Agriculture, in particular, was in serious difficulty. Britain's laissez faire permitted the entry of ton upon ton of American, Argentine, and Russian grain that undersold domestic crops. Between 1850 and 1860 grain prices fell fifty percent, while the wages of farm laborers were on the rise. Large areas of farmland were consequently withdrawn from cultivation and the nation grew accustomed to importing most of its food, though this might become a major problem in wartime.

These problems did not mean that the British economy was stagnant, for they led to improvements which increased the efficiency of British factories. Although Britain's position of primacy had been irrevocably lost, in 1914 it was a much more wealthy and progressive nation than in 1870. Between 1896 and 1913, British exports doubled in value. During the two years 1911–1912, thirty percent more capital was invested abroad than during the whole decade of the 1890's. Only in comparison with the growing industrial might of the United States and Germany was Britain falling behind.

Joseph Chamberlain. One of the dominant figures of British public life at the turn of the century, Chamberlain was leader of the "Liberal Unionists" who tried to combine Liberal party politics with imperial expansion and opposition to Irish Home Rule. This photo was taken in 1895 when Chamberlain was Colonial Secretary. His two sons followed in their father's footsteps, becoming major figures in British government after World War I. (Courtesy of the Trustees of the British Museum.)

The Rise of the Labour Party   Though Britain had become one of the two or three wealthiest countries in the world, this wealth was still poorly distributed and the lower twenty to thirty percent of the population lived in relative misery. The Liberal party continued to get the votes of labor, but it did little to cope with new social problems. Gladstone was strongly dedicated to laissez faire and the Irish question dominated his attention. While the Conservatives took some interest in the problems of the urban

David Lloyd George. Leader of the more radical sector of the Liberal party before World War I, Lloyd George came to prominence as the Chancellor of the Exchequer who promoted progressive taxation in 1909. He later became head of the Liberal party, prime minister during World War I, and one of the "Big Three" at the Versailles Peace Conference in 1919. (Courtesy of the Trustees of the British Museum.)

lower classes, their energies were often absorbed in foreign policy and the expansion of the empire.

Nonetheless, until about 1900 the leaders of Britain's organized labor saw little need to found a political party of their own. Trade unionism flourished better there than anywhere else in the world, and British workers were accustomed to improve their lot by collective bargaining rather than political action. Hence an effort to found an Independent Labour party (1893) on the principles of "Christian economics" did not prosper. It was not until the formation of a Labour Representation Committee in 1900 that the roots of the modern British Labour party began to take hold.

In the following year, the "Taff Vale decision" finally convinced trade unionists that they could not depend on the established political parties to defend their interests. After a strike in Wales, the Taff Vale Railway Company had brought suit against the railwaymen's union for recovery of the financial losses it had suffered. The British courts ruled for the company, threatening the entire future of trade unionism, for such a decision nullified the unions' most powerful weapon—their right to strike. Since the two Conservative cabinets that governed between 1895 and 1905 showed no interest in remedial legislation, the unions began successfully to push their own candidates in by-elections. In the next general election (1906), twenty-nine Labourites won seats in parliament. The Labour party had been born, beginning the ascent that enabled it, during the 1920's, to replace the Liberals as one of the two major parties in Britain.

The Reforms of the Liberal Government (1905–1914) Although its decline had begun, the Liberal party was still capable of significant social and political reforms. Under the cabinet of Sir Henry Campbell-Bannerman (1905–1908) an act of parliament nullified the effect of the Taff Vale decision, while other bills improved working conditions for sailors and suppressed "sweat shops." The most dynamic of the Liberal ministers was Chancellor of the Exchequer, David Lloyd George (1863–1945). Small of stature, red-haired, and blue-eyed, Lloyd George was a skillful, energetic politician with a streak of the demagogue. He had worked his way up from poverty and had a fundamental dislike of privilege. When the government faced major new military expenses in 1909, he introduced a sweeping tax reform in the annual budget bill. This increased income and inheritance taxes, imposed a new levy of twenty percent on the unearned increment of land value (collected whenever properties changed hands), and raised the excises on tobacco and spirits.

After passing the House of Commons, the budget bill was vetoed in the House of Lords, where Conservatives deemed it "socialistic." Since 1906, the peers had vetoed or crippled no less than seven bills dealing with such matters as educational and land reform. With the rejection of the budget, however, the House of Lords overreached itself; for since the seventeenth century, money bills had been the exclusive prerogative of Commons.

The Liberals seized the opportunity to remove this obstacle by introducing a Parliament Bill that ended the veto power of the upper chamber. This produced the greatest political crisis in Britain since 1832, and two successive elections were fought over the issue in 1910. Though reduced in number, the Liberals still controlled Commons with the help of the Irish Home Rulers. Finally, in 1911 the Lords were compelled to accept the Parliament Bill, for otherwise King George V (1910–1936) would have packed the chamber with new peers of Liberal viewpoint. Through this act, the

Turn out the Radicals who would sell your Birthright.

THE·RADICAL· GOVERNMENT TAKES ITS ORDERS FROM · ITS · IRISH MASTER

HOME RULE Agreement

IRISH AMERICAN DOLLARS

N·REDMOND IRELAND

VETO NO SECOND CHAMBER

BUDGET

VOTE FOR

☞ **FOSTER** ☜

And a STRONG SECOND CHAMBER TO PROTECT BRITISH RIGHTS.

House of Lords was formally denied the power to stop money bills and could only delay other legislation until it had passed the lower house in three successive sessions (that is, for two years).

The Liberals then passed the National Insurance Act of 1911, which helped protect workers from the effects of sickness, accidents, and unemployment. The plan was financed by contributions from the state, the employees, and employer. Other reforms regulated working conditions in mining and in other dangerous occupations and established unemployment bureaus for those out of work. The Liberal reforms of 1911–1913 thus began to translate political democracy into social terms, taking the first steps toward what would eventually emerge in the mid-twentieth century as the welfare state.

Great Britain in 1914 Though the Liberals themselves had begun to renounce laissez faire and espouse social reform, these changes did not come rapidly enough to retain the allegiance of many in the working classes. The years immediately before the First World War were marked by increasing social conflict. The old respect for authority and due process of parliamentary law appeared to be breaking down. There seemed to be widespread psychological revolt against the strictures of Victorian personal and social ethics. During 1910–1913 the trade unions, angered by the fact that prices were rising more than wages, launched a wave of big strikes. As we have seen, those at the other end of the social scale, the peers, were attempting partially to subvert the British constitution by vetoing a money bill. Venerable aristocrats and Irish terrorists alike seemed prepared to tolerate violence over the issue of Home Rule for Ireland. Another example of growing disrespect for traditional decorum was the disorders created by suffragettes demanding equal rights for women.

Although it could have been argued that by 1914 no other large country in the world had achieved so much political and social progress as Britain, this progress had engendered an atmosphere of rising expectations and a populace eager for ever more change. British society was thus facing severe internal tensions when the great storm broke on the continent.

THE THIRD REPUBLIC IN FRANCE Ever since the Revolution of 1789, France had been seeking a stable and effective system of government that would avoid the extremes of radical democratic republicanism and authoritarian monarchy. Its most successful compromise was the liberal authoritarian regime of Louis Napoleon, which had been destroyed by the Franco-Prussian War. When, early in 1871, Frenchmen elected by universal male suffrage a National Assembly to make peace with Germany and build a new government, its composition was predominantly conservative, reflecting the outlook of the peasantry and provincial middle classes who constituted the bulk of France's population. The new Assembly immediately found itself in conflict with Paris, where political sympathies were much more radical. Thus, the history of the new Third Republic began with the most bloody political and social conflict that Frenchmen had seen since the great Revolution.

The Paris Commune Parisians had resisted longer and suffered more from the war than had most other parts of France. Many lower-class Parisians were unemployed and seriously in debt, and they expected that the new government would inaugurate a more democratic social and political order. Because of the tension with Paris, the conservative new National Assembly held its deliberations at Versailles, thirty miles outside the capital. Conflict increased when the Assembly canceled the war-time moratorium on rents and debts in Paris and stopped payment of salaries to members of the National Guard. When government troops were sent to occupy the capital in March 1871, they were driven out by armed Parisians. An independent government, called the Commune of Paris, was proclaimed in the capital.

The Commune was not socialistic. Its radical leaders were inspired more by the Jacobin ideals of 1793 than by nineteenth-century proletarian revolutionism. The only economic reform undertaken, other than restoration of the moratorium on debts and rents, was an innocuous decree abolishing night work in bakeries.

Nonetheless, leaders of the National Assembly found themselves faced with an all-out civil rebellion and they were determined to crush it without mercy. Most middle-class Frenchmen associated the Commune with the violent proletarian "June Days" of 1848 and identified it with bloody anarchist or socialist revolution. In two weeks of brutal fighting, government troops forced their way into Paris. The Communards executed hostages they had taken, including the Archbishop of Paris; government forces in turn continued summary executions for days. Perhaps 15,000 were shot, nearly as many as had perished during the revolutionary terror of 1793–1794.

The legacy of the Commune was a harsh one. It had sent a shudder of horror down the spines of the middle classes, widening the differences between them and the workers and encouraging a spirit of stern hostility, not to be overcome for half a century, toward any kind of Leftist or working-class organization in France.

Consolidation of the Third Republic France as a whole was neither royalist nor republican, but politically moderate and suspicious of overly powerful government. The exact nature that its new political regime would take was not clear in 1871, but two-thirds of the deputies in the National Assembly were monarchists. On the other hand, there was a strong current of republicanism in the lower and lower-middle classes, and most republican leaders were much more moderate than had been the Communards. France's new head of government was Adolphe Thiers (1797–1877), a pragmatic politician who came to feel that a conservative and limited republic would be the best bridge for France's political division. Within two years, however, after public bond subscriptions had paid off the war indemnity to Germany in record time, monarchist leaders forced Thiers from office.

His successor was Marshall MacMahon (1808–1893), a leading, if incompetent, general of the Second Empire whose task was to prepare the restoration of the monarchy. During the next two years, this proved to be almost impossible because of the division between the two branches of the Bourbon dynasty. When it seemed that a compromise had been reached, the senior Bourbon pretender nonetheless refused even to accept France's patriotic symbol since the 1790's, the tricolor flag, and hopes for a restoration faded.

If there was to be no monarchy, France's government would have to be republican. A series of constitutional laws were drawn up in 1875 to establish a bicameral legislature composed of a Chamber of Deputies, elected by universal male suffrage, and a Senate, elected by indirect procedure. Ordinary government was to be conducted by a prime minister and his cabinet, but above them the president would wield strong powers of appointment. Monarchists tried to avoid the very mention of a "republic," and an amendment to insert the phrase "the President of the Republic" passed by a majority of only one vote.

Republican sentiment spread, due in large part to the divisions of the monarchists and the moderation of most republican spokesmen. In the 1875 elections, republicans won a majority in the Chamber of Deputies and continued to grow in power. Alarmed, President MacMahon forced the current republican prime minister to resign in 1877, but republicans insisted that the new regime must be a parliamentary government in which executive power should rest in the hands of a prime minister and cabinet responsible only to the Chamber of Deputies. New elections reaffirmed the republican majority and MacMahon himself was later forced to resign. The republicans had established that the executive power was based on the Chamber, avoiding concentration of authority. By 1878, they had won control of the Senate as well, and France was clearly living under its Third Republic.

Republicanism had triumphed because it was becoming a guarantee of stability. Most republican leaders of the 1880's were known as "Opportunists" who relied on compromise and moderation. They believed that the Republic represented the art of the possible, being based on the nation's middle-class social structure and devoted to the negative goal of preventing anyone from interfering with anyone else. Its democratic system gave voice to nearly every disparate faction, and life in the Chamber of Deputies became a series of bargains, deals, and compromises, blocking decisive action. This was satisfactory to most Frenchmen, who had learned to distrust strong central control. The republicans' lack of interest in social reform lost the support of most urban workers, but conversely their conciliatory approach began to win over part of the monarchist right.

Bourgeois republicans had only one major enemy—the Catholic church. The passion of their anticlericalism contrasted with the republicans' moderate approach to most other matters. They considered Catholicism the foe of democracy, enlightenment and modernity, an attitude summed up by the most popular republican leader, Léon Gambetta (1838–1882), in his famous declaration, "Clericalism—there is the enemy!" The Jesuits were expelled from France in 1880 and all teaching orders were forced to register with the state. New government schools were soon being built on all levels; and in 1882, elementary education, whether in public or private schools, was made compulsory. By the 1890's, however, anticlerical zeal seemed to fade and the church made a marked effort to conciliate the government.

Economic Growth By the 1880's, France entered a new period of modest prosperity based in large part on its productive peasant agriculture and the luxury goods—perfumes and art objects—for which it enjoyed an international reputation. In French business, however, the accent was on security and stability, and industrial production expanded more slowly than in Germany. Frenchmen often preferred to invest abroad and altogether exported one-third of their new capital.

A marked industrial upswing began around 1895. Technological improvements helped overcome the shortage of adequate ore for heavy industry that had hampered French factories since the pits of Alsace-Lorraine had been lost to Germany. Moreover, after 1892 the economy was shielded by an extremely high protective tariff.

By 1914, total industrial production was nearly three times as great as in 1870, take-home pay of workers had increased by fifty percent, and total national income approximately doubled. Thus France prospered under the Republic. The problem was that not all classes and sectors participated equally, and the productivity of the rural, small-town provinces of the south and west could not compete with the surge of the industrial northeast.

Political Discontent: The Dreyfus Affair In the late 1880's, signs of political unrest reappeared. Republican factionalism left the government weak, its continuity largely dependent on the professional state bureaucracy that administered affairs as cabinets came and went. Conservative interests were not fully reconciled, and it was difficult for French Catholics to be enthusiastic about the regime. The Republican government had built an impressive new empire for France in western Africa and southeast Asia, but the lack of an aggressive policy in Europe left patriotic activists restless and discontented. Desire for revenge against Germany was strong, and the formation of a new "League of Patriots" was directed against the government for having failed to take a strong initiative. In 1888, moralistic nationalists seeking action and unity found a hero in the handsome, red-haired, blond-bearded minister of war, General Boulanger (1837–1891), who was urged to take over the government. When his followers assembled to be led into action, his nerves snapped and he fled the country, committing suicide soon afterward. The prestige of parliamentary republicanism was further tarnished by a series of scandals in the 1890's, most of which had to do with the bribing of politicians.

The most serious scandal, which had nothing to do with financial peculation, was the "Dreyfus Affair," which broke in the late 1890's. Unlike previous exposes, however, it did not discredit the liberals but damaged the Right. In 1894, Captain Alfred Dreyfus, the only officer of Jewish background on the French general staff, had been subjected to a somewhat irregular trial on the charge of betraying military secrets to Germany, and sentenced to life imprisonment on Devil's Island. After a few years passed, several people besides Dreyfus' family became interested, and information was discovered indicating that the real author of the incriminating note to

Captain Alfred Dreyfus. This colorless and otherwise obscure French staff officer's arrest and conviction on trumped-up charges of espionage led to a major French political crisis at the turn of the century and a decisive victory for liberal democracy. (Radio Times Hulton Picture Library.)

the Germans was an aristocratic army major. It was difficult to obtain reconsideration of the case, because the army hierarchy regarded any questioning or interference as an attack upon its sacred honor and prestige, while the court system was slow and sometimes rather arbitrary.

By 1898, several of the nation's most distinguished political leaders and writers had taken a strong hand in the Dreyfus case and were determined to obtain justice for this solitary individual. Liberals of every shade and even some socialists rallied to the Dreyfus cause, insisting that French justice was meaningless if even one man could be convicted falsely. The anti-Dreyfus forces, on the other hand, numbered in their ranks all the foes of the Republic—royalists, ultra-nationalists, aristocrats, the Catholic hierarchy, army generals and anti-Semites. Lines were drawn between the two camps and there was rioting in the streets of Paris. A retrial was arranged, and it was found prudent to limit Dreyfus' sentence to ten years. The Dreyfusards demanded complete exoneration, which was finally won in 1906. The sharp antagonisms of the Dreyfus case re-emphasized the fundamental cleavage in French life, and once more strained the institutions of the Republic. After the liberals had finally won, they were determined to use victory to eliminate the power of the antirepublican forces.

The Reforms of the Radicals By the turn of the century, the key group in French politics was the Radical Socialist party. Despite their name, the Radicals were in fact neither radical nor socialist by twentieth-century standards, but stood for the "old radicalism" of the early nineteenth century—individualism, anticlericalism, and direct political democracy. They believed that republican institutions and an open society would not be secure unless the entrenched power of the army and the Catholic hierarchy was broken. After winning a strong majority in the elections of 1902, they proceeded to purge the army of high-ranking officers who had extreme royalist or antirepublican reputations.

After this came the final assault on the Catholic church. A series of laws were passed to evict most religious orders from the country; and in 1905 the Chamber abrogated the Concordat of 1801, officially separating church and state in France. The French Catholic Church was reduced to the status of a private religious organization, its resources seriously weakened.

These changes solidified the middle-class Republic to a greater degree than at any time since 1871. Under Radical leadership, it had succeeded in liquidating the problems of the past and removing the old political threat from the Right.

New Problems of the Twentieth Century   On the other hand, France had to face new twentieth-century problems of international competition and internal social conflict. Though the middle classes prospered, the government was hard pressed to find the funds to face the military challenge of an expansionist Germany. The living standards of workers did not rise as fast as industrial production, and social tensions became pronounced.

A new challenge began to arise on the other side of the political arena—the Left—for in 1905 the French socialist groups were finally united into one party. In the years that followed, the nation's economy was harassed by a series of widespread strikes, some of which were only ended after violence and the use of army troops. The Radicals, who remained largely in control of the government until 1914, did not hesitate to exercise a strong hand, for they considered coercive mass organization and proletarian revolt as subversive of Republican liberties as were monarchism or the Catholic church.

After 1905, however, the Radicals underwent the same fate as their republican predecessors of the 1880's, splitting up into a series of rival factions. Between 1911 and 1914, seven different governments were formed, and it was evident that the republican parliamentary system was better prepared to frustrate misuse of government authority than to build unified support for positive ministerial policy.

There had nevertheless been developed a greater underlying sense of national solidarity, at least in moments of international crisis, than had existed for four decades. Though many social and political critics were active on both Left and Right, a growing fear of Germany and the menace it posed had begun to spread through the country by 1905. Moderate Left and moderate Right could both participate in the rebirth of nationalist feeling, the *réveil national,* that was determined to meet the challenge and maintain

France's place in Europe. When disaster struck in 1914, working-class leaders and bankers alike closed ranks in an impressive display of national unity, preparing France for the bloodiest war in its history.

ITALY AFTER UNIFICATION: INTERNAL GROWTH AND POLITICAL CLEAVAGE

After achieving unification in 1860, Italy faced major problems of development and modernization that were as severe as those of any country in Europe. Basically, there were two Italies: the middle-class, progressive, and "European" north, which had provided the basis for unification, and the backward, illiterate, agrarian, and "Mediterranean" south. The mere fact of central government could not overcome the backwardness of the economy and the absence of education and technical preparation. After unification, even the rainfall declined in the south. The only answer for southern Italy seemed emigration. In certain years after 1900, the yearly totals for emigrants exceeded half a million.

Between 1860 and 1876, Italy was governed by the *Destra storica* (the "Historical Right"), the upper-middle class moderate liberals of northern Italy. They restricted the suffrage to a small elite but provided firm financial management of the new Italian state. For decades there remained a complete abyss between the anticlerical Italian government in Rome and the Papacy, which regarded the latter as a usurper. In 1876, the ruling oligarchy was broadened when a slightly more progressive group of liberals, known with some exaggeration as the "Left," came to power, but their rule resulted in few changes. As in Republican France, politics was dominated by bargain and compromise. In Italy, this became known as *trasformismo* ("transformism"), whereby potential rivals were bought off or brought into the system without major alterations.

Italian patriots became increasingly disgruntled because their underdeveloped country, though united, counted for little in foreign affairs. Under the nationalist liberal Francesco Crispi, who governed from 1887 to 1891 and from 1893 to 1896, an effort was made to promote colonial expansion in Africa; this resulted in a humiliating military disaster at Adowa in 1896.

Urbanization and industrialization had gotten under way, but at first their pace was slow, and social tensions increased. In 1890, the average per capita income in Great Britain was $155, in France it was $130, but in Italy it was only $40. In 1893, there were peasant revolts in Sicily, while anarchist cells and the newly formed Italian Socialist party were active in the north. Disorders in Milan and other northern cities during the spring of 1898 resulted in nearly 100 deaths. Two years later an anarchist assassinated King Umberto.

After the turn of the century, conditions began to improve markedly. Political leadership became more reformist and conciliatory, and the economy enjoyed the first modern industrial boom in Italian history. Production expanded rapidly, and Italian engineers were among the leaders in the development of the automobile.

The leader of the new orientation in politics was Giovanni Giolitti (1842–1928), who dominated public affairs from 1903 to 1914. Giolitti

Francesco Crispi, the "Strong Man" of Italian Liberalism in the 1890's. Staunch advocate of ultra-nationalism and Italian expansion in Africa, his career was shattered by the crushing defeat suffered by a small Italian army in Ethiopia in 1896. (Italian Cultural Institute.)

wanted to introduce genuine liberal democracy in Italy. He removed restrictions on labor unions and presented new laws for factory regulation and nationalization of railways. In this he won the cooperation of Italian Socialists, whose leaders were mostly moderate, practical men. After a few years, Giolitti was able to remark that "Karl Marx has been packed off to the attic." The Giolittian decade was a period of relative peace and prosperity, culminating in the introduction of universal male suffrage in 1913.

But Giolitti was adept at all the political bargainings of *trasformismo* and rejected grand ambitions and gestures. Hence, he drew increasing criticism from nationalists who wanted imperial expansion and radical reformers who said that the government was "impure." Critics of parliament went to great lengths to denounce what they deemed corruption and inefficiency.

The Socialists also grew restive, as more young workers, caught up in the tide of rising expectations, complained that their wages were not rising rapidly enough. A new wave of revolutionary Socialists, led by young extremists like Benito Mussolini (1883–1945), overthrew the moderate leadership in 1912 and inaugurated a radical course, culminating in the strikes and violence of the "Red Week" of June 1914.

The Italian system also came under fire from the radical Right, as a militant new nationalist movement demanded unity and expansion and preached the glory of battle. The poet Gabriele d'Annunzio (1863–1938), most influential leader of this trend, insisted that "Paradise lies in the shadow of the sword." When war broke out in 1914, one of his colleagues trumpeted:

A warm bath of blood was needed after so many damp, maternal tears. . . .
We are too many. The loss of thousands of carcasses embraced by death and different
only in the color of their clothing . . . would be a thousand times compensated for by
the removal from the world in a clear, noble, heroic manner of thousands of distasteful,
worthless, rascally, lazy, stupid, useless, bestial, disgusting, profiteering wretches. . . .
Let no one rhetorically point to mothers' tears. What good are mothers, after a certain
age, if not to cry?

On the eve of the First World War, Italy was subject to more diverse pressures than almost any other country in Europe. It suffered the problems of both backward and modernizing countries at the same time, and had to face challenges that found counterparts in such widely different countries as France and Russia. Dissatisfaction was becoming widespread. Militant minorities on both Left and Right were thirsting for direct action, and they were not long to be denied.

CONCLUSION By 1914, political democracy had largely become a reality in Britain, France, and Italy. All three had made great economic progress, though Italy, starting from much farther back, still had much ground to make up. A revolution of rising expectations was noticeable throughout Europe, as organized sectors of the lower classes demanded ever more rapid improvement in their conditions. Thus, all these countries experienced considerable difficulty in adjusting political democracy to the demands of social democracy. Criticism of the "old politics" was widespread, and there was growing apprehension over threats from abroad.

Despite sharp internal conflict, however, the three largest liberal democracies had achieved and maintained political stability. Their systems had showed the capacity to adjust to new needs, and when the test of world war came, all three were able to meet the challenge. Yet here too Italy lagged behind France and Britain. Though Italy's political system and society would survive the initial shock of the war, repercussions of violence and nationalism later undermined the liberal state and promoted the growth of fascism.

FURTHER READING The best survey of Britain in this period is R. C. K. Ensor, *England, 1870–1914* (1936). G. M. Young, * *Victorian England: Portrait of an Age* (1954), offers a rewarding portrait. For interpretation and readings dealing with the later years, see Herman Ausubel, * *The Late Victorians* (1955). The best biographies of the three leading politicians of the age are Philip Magnus, *Gladstone* (1954); Robert Blake, *Disraeli* (1967); and Thomas Jones, *Lloyd George* (1951). On the Liberals, see Colin Cross, *The Liberals in Power, 1905–1914* (1963); and George Dangerfield, * *The Strange Death of Liberal England, 1910–1914* (1935). See also Henry Pelling, *Popular Politics and Society in Late Victorian England*

(1968). L. J. McCaffrey, *The Irish Question, 1800–1922* (1968), is a balanced essay. Anne Freemantle, * *This Little Band of Prophets* (1960), treats the Fabian background of Labourism and S. Nowell-Smith, ed., *Edwardian England, 1901–1914* (1964), describes British life in the early twentieth century. For an economic survey, see William Ashworth, *An Economic History of England, 1870–1939* (1960).

The standard political narrative of the French Third Republic in English is D. W. Brogan, * *France under the Republic, 1870–1939* (1940). On such key issues as the Commune, the Church, and the Army, see E. S. Mason, *The Paris Commune* (1930); C. S. Philips, *The Church in France, 1789–1907* (1936), vol. II; and D. B. Ralston, *The Army of the Republic, 1871–1914* (1967). Douglas Johnson, *France and the Dreyfus Affair* (1967), is the best account of that topic. On the Socialists, see Aaron Noland, *Founding of the French Socialist Party* (1956); and on labor, Peter Stearns, *Revolutionary Syndicalism and French Labor* (1971). The Right is treated in René Rémond, *The Right Wing in France* (1966); and Michael Curtis, *Three Against the Third Republic* (1959). For the *réveil*, see Eugen Weber, *The Nationalist Revival in France, 1905–1914* (1959).

Three books are fundamental on Italian history in this period. For politics, C. Seton-Watson, *Italy from Liberalism to Fascism 1870–1925* (1967); for economics, S. B. Clough, *Economic History of Modern Italy* (1964); and on the Giolitti era and the coming of the war, John Thayer, *Italy and the Great War* (1964).

*Books available in paperback edition are marked with an asterisk.

4 Imperial Russia, 1856-1914

In the middle of the nineteenth century, Russia was closer to the primitive empire of Peter the Great than to contemporary western Europe. Russia's defeat in the Crimean War nevertheless came as a great shock. It humiliated the imperial government and indicated that ruthless autocracy resting on serfdom was unable to compete with the industrializing countries of the west. Twice before, after 1700 and 1807, military defeat had impelled the tsarist government toward reform. The disaster of 1855 led to the most sweeping change of all.

INTERNAL REFORM AND CONTINUED AUTOCRACY, 1860-1894

Alexander II and Emancipation of the Serfs By 1860, the population of the Russian empire passed seventy-four million, but of these approximately forty-seven million were enserfed peasants. Throughout the 1840's and 1850's, discontent among this vast submerged class had been rising. By the late 1850's, there were scores of serf rebellions each year in which the miserable and oppressed people of the countryside burned manor houses and sometimes murdered landlords before they were put down by military force. Russian society could no longer condone serfdom on moral grounds, and after 1855 it became increasingly clear that serfdom was economically and militarily inefficient as well.

Alexander II, who came to the throne in 1855, was a serious-minded autocrat concerned about the political and economic balance of his empire. He understood that serfdom was a social and economic evil that corroded Russian society, and wished his state to be as stable and effective as that of authoritarian Prussia, for example, which had found rejuvenation by freeing its serfs and reforming its administrative structure in 1807-1812. Accordingly, committees of noblemen and state bureaucrats were appointed to make proposals for the abolition of serfdom and in March 1861 the most extensive emancipation proclamation in human history was promulgated by the tsar. At one stroke, more than twenty million serfs were set free from bondage to landlords, and an equal or greater number of crown peasants were also freed from their obligations. They were given a sizable portion—about half—of the land under cultivation in Russia. In this way, the Russian emancipation was more paternal than the edict earlier in the century which had freed the Prussian serfs but had failed to provide them with land or economic security. In most districts, however, the peasants were given poorer, less fertile fields, while the richer sections remained in the hands of

Russian Peasants in the 1890's, Still Wearing Traditional Costume. Illustration from Tolstoy's Novel, Resurrection. *Until the 1930's the peasantry remained the largest social class in Russia, and in the late nineteenth century numbered nearly 80 percent of the total population. They had little to do with modern or westernized Russia, and long retained their traditional non-western styles of clothing and patterns of thought. Normally patient, submissive and longsuffering, they were nonetheless periodically capable of striking out with blind violence against those they considered oppressors.* (The New York Public Library.)

their former owners. Moreover, the peasants were not given land free of charge, but were forced to pay for it by installments over, a period of forty-nine years. These payments were to be used to amortize state bonds issued to indemnify the landowners.

Though the peasant was freed from personal servitude to his lord, he was not given freedom of personal movement, nor did he receive individual title to his land. Most Russian peasants lived in communal villages, and legal ownership of the new land was given to the village council, not to the individual peasants. Each peasant was theoretically placed under the control of his local council of village elders. He could not, for example, leave the village to work in the city without the latter's consent.

Thus the peasants were by no means satisfied with the terms of emancipation. They wanted a great deal more land and better soil than they actually received. Furthermore, they wanted it free of charge, without a crushing burden of debt. Financial credit and educational facilities were still denied to them. Consequently, agricultural techniques remained backward for decades, production continued to be low, and the living standard of the peasantry rose very little. Though the rural population continued to multiply with amazing rapidity, there was not enough industrial development in the cities to absorb the surplus. During bad years, the peasants were still near starvation.

Despite smoldering dissatisfaction, however, the post-emancipation peasant world was a great improvement on Nicholas' system. A small minority of the peasantry did prosper, for even within the village commune not everyone lived on the same level. Some peasants were much better off, held the richer fields, and employed their poorer neighbors as laborers. These more prosperous peasants, or *kulaks* (a word meaning "fists"), were able in turn to lease more land from landowners and thus expand the fields under their control. At first few of the peasantry could hope to attain *kulak* status, but for the next four decades the rural population tacitly acquiesced in the new organization of agrarian life.

Local Government, Judicial and Military Reforms The emancipation did not in any way ruin the nobles. They still retained the better sections of land and also received guaranteed income from indemnity bonds. Further reforms were soon introduced to provide provincial self-government, mainly in the interest of the upper classes. In 1864, an imperial statute established assemblies or *zemstva* which were chosen by two separate electoral groups, the landlords and peasants, and were designed to deal with local matters such as roads, bridges, sanitation, and education. In practice, these assemblies were dominated by the nobles, and the government, in turn, was careful to see that they never extended their power very far; but the *zemstva* were highly significant as the first experiment in self-government in the history of Russia. During the next few decades, they also were instrumental in improving health, educational, and transportation facilities in many parts of European Russia. In 1870, elective municipal councils were established for the larger cities of the empire. Suffrage was restricted to the wealthy, however, and the municipal councils had less scope for constructive action than the *zemstva*.

Only a few months after promulgation of the original *zemstva* decree, the Russian court system was drastically revised. The new statutes of 1864, partially modeled on the French legal system, established equality of subjects before the law and trial by jury for most major offenses, laying stress on due process of law and freedom of judges from political pressure. The tsar still reserved the right of special interference, and a variety of irregular courts, run by the army and the church, still retained their jurisdiction, but nonetheless, the result was the nearest thing to an honest, objective judicial system ever seen in Russia.

The last major reform was a broad reorganization of the Russian army. A modern general staff was established; brutal disciplinary practices were relaxed; the term of service was shortened; and, in 1874, universal conscription was declared for all social classes.

Despite many inadequacies, the great reforms were a decided improvement. Though they did not provide for constitutional government—which would at that time have been unworkable given the backwardness of Russian life—they did open the way for new forces in Russian society.

Growth of the Revolutionary Intelligentsia The "westernizing" trend among Russian intellectuals became more accentuated during the 1860's. Alexander II's reform era brought greater opportunities for education and travel, and the ranks of the intelligentsia, though still very small, steadily increased. The Russian *intelligenty* were not primarily "intellectuals," but simply those with a certain amount of education who took an active interest in public affairs or cultural activities. Most of the intelligentsia were comparatively young and remained intensely dissatisfied after the great reforms, which had begun a revolution of rising expectations for them.

For the radical wing of university youth, the entire Russian system was a tyrannical failure. They threw over all tradition and inherited standards, and made an idol of the writer and philosopher Nikolai Chernyshevsky (1828–1889), whose novel of revolutionism, *What Is to Be Done?*, became their political bible. Its hero, Rakhmetev, eschewed sentimentality and devoted himself to rigorous training, even going so far as to sleep on a bed of nails. All his thoughts and actions were devoted to the goal of revolution.

The idea of revolution became an obsession for the radical wing of the intelligentsia. They compared the most advanced standards and accomplishments of the West with the backwardness and authoritarianism of tsarist Russia, and concluded that the latter was so primitive and corrupt that it merited only total destruction. Their own ideas were made up of a paradoxical mixture of idealism and materialism. Revolutionary *intelligenty* made up of their own moral code, having no metaphysical or theological opinions other than a simple materialism. Believing in nothing but their own subjective norms of justice, they became *nigilisty* or "nihilists." Dimitri

Pisarev, one of their spokesmen, insisted that a pair of good boots was worth more than a painting by Leonardo, for the boots possessed practical value. Thus they liked to believe that their ideas were derived from objective reality alone. The conclusion drawn from their complete materialism was that the only proper goal of mankind was the establishment of a materialistic utopia, which could be achieved only by sweeping and total revolution. The principle of objective materialism was thus converted into subjective voluntarism. Martyrdom was considered the greatest of glories, whereas practical, tedious, workmanlike reforms were rejected as hopelessly inefficient.

Despite their rejection of religion and Russian tradition, in some ways the revolutionaries represented a modern form of Russian messianism. For centuries Russian culture had been nourished on expectations of the apocalypse, a mood of expansion, and a sense of a great historical mission to accomplish. This traditional Russian messianism, usually identified with Orthodox religiosity, was revived in a new form by the revolutionaries, eager to launch vast programs of utopian change.

Student revolutionaries helped to bring the main phase of the reform era to a close in 1866, when one of them made an unsuccessful attempt to assassinate Alexander for not having granted a democratic constitution. The ultra-conservative elements in the government then gained the upper hand, and state control and censorship were tightened; there were few significant changes in the Russian system after that.

The ideal of most of the revolutionaries was the "people," by which was meant the great mass of illiterate peasants. Middle- and upper-class members of the intelligentsia often felt guilty about the privileges they enjoyed, and the more radical came to insist that the peasantry was the only important social class. Since the peasants were dirty, miserable, and illiterate, they were held not to be so morally depraved as the upper classes. This trend of thinking developed into the doctrine of revolutionary populism, which believed that Russian society could only be redeemed by a great social upheaval that would establish agricultural socialism for the peasants, based on the communal system of the village *mir*.

In the 1870's, a new revolutionary association called "Land and Freedom" launched a campaign to "go to the people," trying to win the peasants for their vision of Russian populism. This effort was a complete failure. Illiterate peasants were not interested in populist socialism. They were loyal to the tsar and concentrated their animosity against landlords instead. Exhorted to rebel against tsarism, they turned on the revolutionaries and sometimes handed them over to the police, occasionally even murdering them outright.

Assassination of Alexander II Frustrated in efforts to spark a peasant revolution, the most violent populists organized a secret terrorist society, grandiosely named "The People's Will." Members were sworn to extort complete freedom from the autocracy by striking at the autocrat himself. In this they followed the example of the nihilistic young visionary Sergei

Nechaiev (1847–1882), who had been possessed with a demonic urge to destroy all existing institutions. In his "Catechism of the Revolutionary," he defined the latter as a "walking dead man," immune to all normal human emotions. Nechaiev emphasized that the end justified the means: whatever promoted the revolution, no matter how cruel or bloody, was moral. Even after imprisonment in a dank underground fortress where, chained to the prison wall, gangrene rotted his legs, he did not cease to plot and struggle. Nechaiev's example served to inspire "The People's Will." Between 1879 and 1881, at least seven plots were made to assassinate Alexander II.

Family of Alexander III. This photo portrait of the Russian imperial family, taken in the early 1880's, shows the strong-willed tsar, Alexander III, with his tsarina (a former Danish princess), their heir Nicholas standing beside her, and their four other children. (Radio Times Hulton Picture Library.)

By 1881, the tsar had decided that the loyalty of his subjects might be more easily secured by concession than by repression. Under the influence of new liberal ministers, a decree for an elected consultative council was drawn up in March. On the Sunday morning that this decree was signed, the tsar went out for his usual carriage ride, unaware that he was being stealthily stalked by "The People's Will." Two bombs were thrown against the imperial carriage, and the "Tsar Emancipator" bled to death at the palace within a few hours. The new decree for a consultative council was never promulgated.

Alexander III The slain autocrat was succeeded by his eldest son, who became Tsar Alexander III. The new tsar did not share his father's penchant for limited reform. After a few weeks, the consultative council was never even mentioned, but "The People's Will" was crushed by the secret police and its leading members put to death. Alexander III soon showed himself to be a very conscientious ruler with narrow, conservative ideas, many of which he derived from his former tutor, Konstantin Pobedonostsev (1827–1907), who became his most important counselor. Pobedonostsev was made Procurator of the Holy Synod, which controlled the Russian Church; and from this position he affirmed the principles that became the guiding philosophy of the reign of Alexander. Pobedonostsev was a man of intelligence and learning, and feared the moral influence of modern materialism and relativism. The key to rebellion and discontent, he believed, was the decline in religious fervor. Parliamentary government would ruin Russia, for it would create internal factions and separate the people from the tsar. With political and cultural freedom would come skepticism, agnosticism, and amorality. He felt that the only bulwark against this cataclysm was the principle of autocracy, supported by the spiritual resources of the Orthodox Church and the cultural unity that would be created by nationalism and forced Russification of the ethnic minorities in the empire. Thus, under Alexander III and his grey eminence, Pobedonostsev, the trend toward westernization in Russia was halted. The next thirteen years were a period of severe repression. Censorship was strict, all rebellious sentiment was sharply checked, and even the power of the *zemstva* was reduced.

IMPERIAL EXPANSION Despite the social and economic backwardness of Russia, the process of imperial expansion begun in the fifteenth century had scarcely abated for more than a single generation at a time. In the nineteenth century, it was reinforced by renewed competition with other powers and the impact of nationalism on members of the middle and upper classes.

Vigorous expansion in Central Asia and the Far East to some extent compensated imperial prestige for the defeat of 1856. Outlying lands of the Chinese empire were encroached upon. By 1860, the city of Vladivostok had been established on the Pacific Coast; a few years later, the Russians began to occupy the island of Sakhalin, north of Japan. During the 1860's and 1870's, their forces seized large sections of Central Asia, pressing the

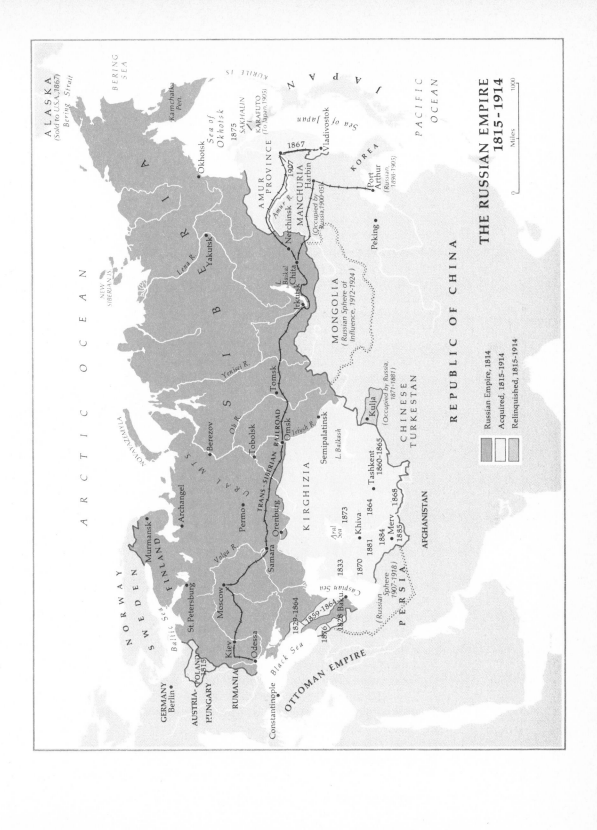

THE RUSSIAN EMPIRE 1815-1914

Miles
0   1000

Russian Empire, 1814
Acquired, 1815-1914
Relinquished, 1815-1914

ALASKA
(Sold to U.S.A.,1867)
Bering Strait

BERING SEA

KURILE IS.

KAMCHATKA Pen.

Sea of Okhotsk

SAKHALIN
1875

KARAFUTO
(To Japan,1905)

JAPAN

Okhotsk

Sea of Japan

Vladivostok

AMUR PROVINCE

1867

KOREA

Amur R.

1907

Nerchinsk

MANCHURIA

Harbin

Port Arthur
(Russian,
1898-1905)

1867

PACIFIC OCEAN

Occupied by Russia 1900-05

Peking

L. Baikal

Chita

Irkutsk

Yakutsk

Lena R.

E. S I B E R I A

MONGOLIA
(Russian Sphere of
Influence, 1912-1924)

REPUBLIC OF CHINA

Tomsk

Yenisei R.

S I B E R I A

Semipalatinsk

L. Balkash

Kulja
(Occupied by Russia,
1871-1881)

CHINESE
TURKESTAN

ARCTIC OCEAN

Berezov

Ob R.

Tobolsk

TRANS-SIBERIAN RAILROAD

Omsk

Irtysh R.

KIRGHIZIA

1873

Aral Sea

Tashkent
1864

Khiva
1881

1860-1865

Merv
1884

1868

1885

AFGHANISTAN

NEW SIBERIAN IS.

NOVAYA ZEMLYA

U R A L M T S.

Permo

Orenburg

Samara

Volga R.

1870

1833

PERSIA
(Russian
Sphere,
1907-1918)

Caspian Sea

Murmansk

Archangel

St.Petersburg

NORWAY

SWEDEN

FINLAND

Baltic Sea

Moscow

Kiev

Odessa

1829-1864

1859-1864

Baku
1828

1876

Black Sea

OTTOMAN EMPIRE

Constantinople

GERMANY
Berlin

AUSTRIA-HUNGARY

RUMANIA

POLAND
1815

frontiers of empire down to Persia and Afghanistan. Successful on the Asian continent, the Russian government nonetheless decided to avoid the complications of retaining its tenuous foothold across the Bering Straits on the far tip of North America. In 1867, all Russian rights in Alaska were sold to the United States for $7,200,000.

Russian interest was not drawn back to Europe until 1875, when a new outbreak occurred among Christian subjects of the Turkish empire in the Balkans. Russian nationalists adapted for their own purposes the doctrine of Pan-Slavism, which emphasized the ethnic and religious ties between the Russians and other Slavic peoples, especially the Orthodox Christians of the Balkans. They held that it was Russia's duty to lead and protect the smaller Slavic peoples, and this feeling was inflamed by the spectacle of Bulgarian Christians slaughtered by wanton Turkish troops. At the other end of Europe, British liberals were aroused by the same issue, and demanded "fair play" for the Bulgarians on the part of the Turkish government. This created an issue on which Russia could once more enter European power politics and score an advance in the Balkans. There were important strategic and economic issues involved in Russo-Turkish relations, as well, for the status of the Dardanelles was of vital significance to the grain export trade on which much of the Russian economy depended.

On the pretext of defending Christian subjects from further outrage, Russia declared war on Turkey in 1877. Despite a long stand by Turkish troops at the fortress of Plevna in Bulgaria, the Russians eventually drove them back to the very gates of Istanbul, and then prepared to liquidate the remains of the Turkish empire in Europe. Early in 1878, the Turks were forced to sign the treaty of San Stefano. By its terms sizable portions of frontier territory were transferred from Turkey to Russia. In addition, the boundaries of independent Serbia and Montenegro were enlarged, and a "Greater Bulgaria," comprising most of the southeastern corner of the Balkans, was established under Russian protection.

The Western Reaction At this point, the balance of power on the continent came into action to frustrate Russian ambitions. Neither Britain nor Austria was willing to see Russia establish itself as the dominant power in the Balkans in place of Turkey. The British, especially, feared the results of Russian expansion in the eastern Mediterranean, just as the long arms of this enormous empire were stretching down to the borders of British territory in south-central Asia. By the beginning of 1878, the British, recently aroused against the Turks, acted as if they were ready to go to war against Russia for having invaded Turkish territory. It was easy to whip up popular antagonism in London against the threat of Russian aggression. The rhyme of the music-hall balladeers expressed Britain's common feeling: "We don't want to fight, but, by jingo, if we do, we've got the men, we've got the ships, we've got the money, too." To avert war, the German chancellor, Bismarck, stepped in as a self-styled "honest broker." An international conference was quickly called to meet at Berlin and work out a compromise. Faced by a tacit coalition of the western powers, Russia had to give in. Autonomous

government for the Balkan peoples was ratified, with the exception of Albania, but Turkish territorial and political control was partially restored. Russia was allowed to keep only the province of Bessarabia on its southwestern border. The results of the Berlin conference were a grievous blow to Pan-Slavists and superexpansionists, but they did not entirely displease the tsarist diplomats, for the outcome did further Russian influence among the small Balkan peoples, as well as increase imperial territory in east-central Europe.

The diplomatic history of the next thirty-five years was marked by increasing competition between Russia and Austria for diplomatic influence in the Balkans. After being checked in an effort to control the Bulgarian government in 1887, Russian policy temporarily turned away from Europe in frustration. Until 1905, Russian energy was mainly concentrated on the expansion of the empire in the Far East. Russian economic interests moved into Manchuria, and loans were forced on the Chinese government to make the latter more subservient to tsarist influence. The imperial government thus obtained the right to extend the Trans-Siberian railway across Manchuria to Vladivostok. Here, however, the railway and forestry interests of Russia soon came into conflict with Japan, which was building a modern industrial and military system in the Far East. After 1895, Japan dominated Korea and, since her ambitions ran directly counter to Russian aims in southern Manchuria, a showdown seemed inevitable.

GOVERNMENT FINANCE AND INDUSTRIALIZATION

The tsarist government could never realize its goal of making Russia a true superpower, despite her vast territorial expansion, unless the empire developed a productive modern economy through industrialization. Russia had the manpower and raw materials but lacked capital and technology. Toward the end of the nineteenth century, the imperial government adopted a new policy of promoting rapid industrialization in order to make up the ground between Russia and modern western society. In view of Russian poverty and backwardness, the difference would be compensated for by squeezing money from the peasant agrarian economy through high taxation and massive exports of grain—practically the only commodity Russia could sell—to the west, while importing machinery and technical experts. Tax monies would then be funneled into industrial subsidies and investment, while foreign capital would also be encouraged to invest heavily in the potentially vast Russian market, protected by a steep defensive tariff. The Russian state thus developed the most elaborate program of government intervention and development of industry—most of which would be under private ownership—seen anywhere during the nineteenth century.

This policy began to reach its height under Count Sergei Witte (1849–1915), minister of finance from 1892 to 1903. During the 1890's, Russian railway mileage nearly doubled and coal production increased 300 percent. In less than twenty years, Russia moved from seventh to fourth place among world producers of pig iron. Approximately fifty percent of the empire's corporate investment came from abroad, but the government itself provided seventy percent of the capital behind the Russian rail network, as well as participating in new enterprises all over the empire.

Russia' rate of economic growth slowed after 1899, but accelerated once more in the years before the First World War. In 1914, the Russian economy was still far behind that of the West, but its rate of expansion was one of the highest in the world.

CULTURE AND SOCIETY

The Golden Age of Russian Literature Despite the general backwardness of Russian life, the empire enjoyed its cultural golden age during the reign of Alexander II, and the succeeding generation also produced many outstanding accomplishments. In no field was this more evident than in literature. A low level of literacy and a limited reading public did not prevent Russian writers from producing novels and short stories that won the admiration of the West and in many ways surpassed the work being done there. The nineteenth-century realistic novel reached its acme in the achievements of Leo Tolstoy (1828–1910) and Fyodor Dostoevsky (1821–1881), whose great books of the 1860's and 1870's found little or no parallel elsewhere. *War and Peace, Anna Karenina, Crime and Punishment, The Brothers Karamazov*—such novels displayed an insight into human nature, a profundity of moral and psychological observation, and a narrative skill that catapulted Russian literature into the front ranks. Tolstoy and Dostoevsky differed sharply from most of their western contemporaries insofar as they were both religious novelists, who wrote of the great moral and spiritual issues of modern civilization which were so often ignored by writers in the West. In his relentless probing of the human psyche, Dostoevsky became convinced that the major issue of the time was the loss of religious belief

among modern men, which resulted in the effort to achieve salvation through
a materialistic utopia constructed purely by human reason and human will.
Dostoevsky feared that this would conclude in a total tyranny beyond the
imagination's deepest fear. His writings thus took on prophetic significance
in the light of the later Russian development.

Russian Music In music, too, Russian composers such as Tchaikovsky
(1840–1898), Rimsky-Korsakov (1844–1908) and Moussorgsky (1835–1881)
produced work of the highest quality that was well received in the West.
The novels of Dostoevsky and the music of Moussorgsky might possess

a stark, febrile, even eery quality that was very different from the emotional pattern of the West, yet their esthetic and cultural value was undeniable. Though intensely Russian in the form of their expression, their richness and depth also made them the property of the whole world.

Emergence of Russian Science In science, individual Russians, such as the biologist Mendeleev (1834–1907) and the physiologist Pavlov (1849–1936), were also making outstanding achievements. Though Russian chemists and mathematicians received little help from the government's educational system, their personal accomplishments won them a reputation in the West. Science enjoyed great prestige among educated people of the younger generation, for it marked a sharp antithesis to the study of dead languages and religious ritual encouraged by the school system of an obscurantist autocracy. So long as the government's educational control showed suspicion of the natural sciences while stressing an insipid curriculum in the classical humanities, naive faith in science on the part of young rebels merely increased.

The Great Cultrual Gap in Russian Society The empire's brilliant intellectual elite had little or no contact with the bulk of the population, which was still submerged in misery and ignorance. In 1890, scarcely twenty percent of the Russian people could read and write. Yet this pattern was changing. The urban middle class was growing, and educational opportunities were gradually spreading. A middle stratum now existed that was becoming conscious of the empire's problems and of the price being paid for autocracy. A liberal middle-class opposition, anxious to achieve constitutional representation, was being formed for the first time in Russian history. It was the tragedy of Russia, however, that this middle-class liberalism did not begin to take shape until the turn of the century, when the old-style classical liberalism was already beset by demagogic radicalism even in the West.

The National Minorities By the end of the century, the sprawling empire, ethnically more heterogeneous than ever before, was composed of scores of different national groups. The Great Russians themselves made up only about half the population; in addition, there were the Ukrainians and White Russians, Baltic and Volga Germans, Poles, Finns, Lithuanians, Letts, Estonians, Rumanians, Armenians, Georgians, a great variety of different Turkish and Mongol peoples, and approximately five million Jews.

The most favored of the minority peoples were the Finns, who had enjoyed a separate constitutional government under the tsar ever since they had been incorporated into the empire in 1809. The most rebellious were the Poles, whose last great uprising occurred in 1863. It was suppressed with much bloodshed; and in the reprisals that followed, the power of the Polish aristocracy was seriously weakened. On the other hand, the conditions of the peasantry improved, and the latter part of the century witnessed the growth of Polish industry and the rise of a Polish middle class. This did not make the Poles any less nationalistic, but it encouraged a more practical attitude in dealing with the government. Meanwhile, active nationalist movements were developing among the Lithuanians and also among the thirty million Ukrainians who occupied the southern part of European Russia.

Under Alexander III, a rigorous campaign of Russification was waged against all the ethnic minorities which sought to eliminate diversities, to spread the influence of the Russian language and the Russian Orthodox Church, and to replace separate social and cultural customs with those of the Great Russians. This policy lasted until the end of the empire in 1917 and not a single nationality escaped its effects, for even the Finns saw many of their privileges stripped from them.

There was no attempt to Russify the Jews, however. Instead, they were sealed off from Russian society more rigorously than ever, denied educational opportunities, and restricted in cultural and commercial life. The Jews were made scapegoats for all manner of ills and had even been blamed for the assassination of Alexander II. The authorities tolerated and in certain instances encouraged bloody pogroms which cost the lives of hundreds and led to mass Jewish emigration from the empire after the 1880's.

POLITICAL
DEVELOPMENTS
1894–1914

When Nicholas II became tsar in 1894, he gave no indication of understanding any of the forces at work in the modern world. At first, he and his advisers proposed to maintain his father's system of repression and class exploitation unchanged. The new tsar was, however, hampered in this objective because, though not unintelligent, he was weak and indecisive. Possessing neither imagination nor concentrated energy, he was easily swayed by the Tsarina Alexandra. The empress was not noted for her intelligence, but she was determined and domineering. Superstitious in her devotion to the religion of the Orthodox Church, she insisted that it was God's will that nothing in Russian autocracy be changed, and always urged Nicholas to assert his personal authority. As she later wrote to him in one of her many letters: "Be more autocratic, my very own Sweetheart, show your mind. . . . Ah, my Love, when at least will you thump with your hand upon the table? . . . Oh, Lovey, you can trust me. I may not be clever enough—but I have a strong feeling, and that helps more than the brain often." The tsarina was an exceedingly zealous mother, determined that the powers of the throne would be handed on undiminished to the young tsarevich, born at the turn of the century. Since the Romanov heir suffered from incurable hemophilia (a tendency toward uncontrollable bleeding at the slightest lesion), this was a most hazardous goal.

Spread of Political Opposition   During the 1890's, the literate portion of the Russian population grew more restive, and opposition was becoming marked even among the liberal middle class and gentry of the *zemstva*. Many professional men—doctors, teachers, agronomists—had been hired by the

Nicholas, Alexandra, and their Children. A famous photograph of the ill-fated final generation of the tsarist dynasty: Tsar Nicholas II, the tsarina Alexandra, and their five children, eventually destined to be murdered by Communists in 1918. (Hoover Institution Archives.)

zemstva to improve conditions in the provinces, and these elements served as part of the base for a responsible new liberalism. They began to call for reforms and for a central assembly of all Russian *zemstva*.

During the years of harsh repression in the 1880's and 1890's, the spirit of populism had been kept alive by the spokesmen of the intelligentsia. Under Alexander III, the supporters of peasant socialism had been driven to refuge behind economic statistics and purely theoretical arguments, producing the phenomenon of "Legal Populism." The "Legal Populists" were philosophers and economists who argued that it would be disastrous for Russia to follow the same path of economic and social development that had occurred in the West. Instead, Russia should build on its strength, they said, concentrating its attention on the peasant economy. Superindustrialization and the formation of a great capitalist class were evils to be avoided. The "natural course" of Russian development would maintain a balance between light industry and agricultural production. Though the "Legal Populists'" most ambitious program called for a controlled development of heavy industry as well, they were successful in maintaining through the 1890's the old Russian revolutionary stress on peasant socialism. Their goal still was to avoid the economic dilemmas of the West.

The intellectual theorizing of "Legal Populism" gave way in 1901 to a new revolutionary organization similar to the "Land and Freedom" movement of the 1870's. The new group was called the Social Revolutionaries, or simply the SR's. Like their predecessors, the Social Revolutionaries made peasant socialism their goal and expected to establish full agrarian equality and cooperation as soon as the autocracy was destroyed. Idealizing the Russian peasant, they struggled to reduce all Russian institutions to his level. A principal weapon on which they relied in their battle with the autocracy was political terrorism. Special murder squads were formed inside the SR organization to assassinate policemen and cabinet ministers alike. After 1900, the number of political killings in Russia rose to startling proportions.

The Rise of Russian Marxism   The tsarist empire had never been very important to Karl Marx. Since Marxist socialism was predicated on class struggle inside an advanced industrial society, Marx had originally believed that Russia would be one of the last regions to undergo the revolution. At first, he had disdained the Russian populists as petit bourgeois reactionaries in disguise; he thought that at best they could be no more than a primitive eastern variant of the so-called "utopian" socialists. Only at the very end of his life did Marx's attitude begin to change. Reconsidering his own assumptions on the basis of material sent him by a handful of Russian admirers, Marx tentatively admitted the possibility of establishing workers' socialism in an underdeveloped country without having to go through the full cycle of western capitalist development. This is not to say that Marx ever approved of populism, for he considered the notion of mere peasant socialism hopelessly antiquated. It simply means that Marx did recognize, given the proper historical conditions, the possibility of leaping into the proletarian revolution before a fully western-style proletariat had been created.

The founder of Russian Marxism was Georgi Plekhanov (1857–1918), a man of aristocractic birth and a former populist who, in 1883, had broken with the "Land and Freedom" movement to establish, among a handful of friends in Swiss exile, the first Russian Marxist group. In the following decade Plekhanov had to construct Russian Marxism almost singlehanded. He believed in the classic Marxist canon, insisting that Russia would have to develop industrial capitalism in the same fashion as western Europe and could not rely upon backward peasant socialism. If anything, Plekhanov was more Marxist than Marx. He relied on abstract forces of historical development to create the eventual revolution, but he also tried to create a Marxist party that could lead and explain the process.

Much more than populism, Marxism became all the rage among radical Russian intellectuals in the 1890's, and dozens of clandestine circles sprang up in the larger cities. The reasons for this were more philosophical and emotional than they were economic or political. For one thing, the brief history of Russian populism had been plagued with defeat and frustration. Marxism was much more reassuring. Grounded on relentless determinism, "history decreed" the triumph of Marxism. It was supposedly scientific, and satisfied the longing of intellectuals for something that was hard-minded and "objective." Furthermore, under Marxist ideology, it was not necessary to oppose the development of capitalism in Russia, for this hastened the preconditions of revolution. If, however, the more intellectual or theoretical revolutionaries were attracted to Marxism, ordinary rebels and activists flocked to the SR's, whose policies were more direct and violent. The Social Revolutionaries were much the larger movement all the way down to 1917.

Lenin and the Origins of Bolshevism   The man who later took over the Russian Marxist movement and welded it into the most potent revolutionary force in the world was Vladimir Ilyich Ulyanov, known to history under his pseudonym of Lenin (1870–1924). The son of a distinguished school inspector who reached aristocratic rank, Lenin was filled with hatred of tsarism after an elder brother, whom he idolized, was executed following an abortive attempt against the tsar in 1887. This brought family disgrace and temporary ostracism, helping to turn the young Lenin toward revolutionism. He soon became a convinced Marxist, and after earning a law degree, engaged in revolutionary activity in St. Petersburg. That brought Siberian exile, which he endured for two years before escaping to the West in 1899. Abroad he quickly gained an influential position among Plekhanov and the older Marxists because of his intellectual ability and organizational drive.

Lenin had ideas of his own about how to bring about a Marxist revolution, and in some ways they were closer to the subjective voluntarism of earlier Russian revolutionaries like Nechaiev than to the orthodox western-style Marxism of Plekhanov. He believed that a Marxist party should be composed strictly of professional revolutionaries led by a tight centralized organization. Lenin tried to write this principle into the statutes of the Russian Social Democratic (Marxist) Party at its first general congress, held in exile at Brussels in 1903. His proposed wording of paragraph nine stressed that every member must engage in revolutionary activity under the organization's leadership. This clashed with the more liberal proposals by other leaders who wanted to attract a mass membership of workers and permit greater individual autonomy. In the ensuing controversy, some of the more moderate and democratic Marxists walked out of the congress, leaving Lenin with a temporary majority of twenty-two to twenty-one. He used this to establish the principle of the control of the Party's Central Committee over all the rest of the organization.

On the basis of this technical majority (*bolshinstvo*), Lenin labeled his supporters the Bolsheviks (Majorityites). The moderate, democratic elements, though in fact constituting a majority of the party, allowed themselves to be stuck with the name of Mensheviks (Minorityites). Lenin thus scored both a political and psychological victory, but the gulf between Bolsheviks and Mensheviks never closed, the Russian movement splitting into two different groups.

During the next fourteen years, Lenin kept his small faction organized and loyal to him through thick and thin. He was the very personification of revolutionary energy, often working seventy or eighty hours a week. Short, stocky, and prematurely bald, his face was highlighted by slanting gray Tatar eyes that settled on his opponents with a mocking and determined glance.

Unlike Mensheviks, Lenin believed that a socialist revolution could be carried out in Russia before capitalism and the proletariat were fully developed. He devised a strategy to use the mass of poor peasants in place of the still numerically feeble proletariat. The crucial factor for Lenin remained the party, since he did not believe that workers alone would ever develop the consciousness and unity needed for revolution. Mensheviks decried this as non-Marxist. They were quite willing to cooperate temporarily with middle-class liberals in a system of parliamentary democracy, whereas Lenin merely saw political liberty as the staging ground for socialist dictatorship. Though Bolsheviks and Mensheviks combined were fewer in number than the Social Revolutionaries, the Marxist groups were better organized and disciplined, so that their strength would be more effective in time of crisis.

Spread of Social and Political Discontent By the turn of the century, signs of unrest and dissatisfaction in Russia were multiplying. Middle-class liberals, pressing for constitutional monarchy, were harder to intimidate. The peasants, never fully satisfied by the reforms of the 1860's, were becoming more unruly. They were not interested in political forms, but demanded more land and freedom from onerous financial burdens. In addition, the numerically small urban workers, who scarcely amounted to ten percent of the total population, had begun to react against the harsh conditions in which they lived. During the mid-1890's, there had been a number of strikes in St. Petersburg. These encouraged factory legislation in 1897 that limited the working day to $11\frac{1}{2}$ hours. For the first time, revolutionary organizations began to draw popular support, at least in a few key centers and regions.

Unrest was intensified by the industrial and commercial depression of 1899–1903, which led to the first large-scale chain of strikes in Russian history. In response, several of the tsar's ministers insisted that the security of the empire could only be guaranteed through a forceful foreign policy that would quiet internal discontent and bring unity. When it became apparent that Russia would soon face war with Japan unless steps were taken to conciliate Japanese interests in Manchuria, advisers merely concluded that another successful war on the pattern of 1877 would unify the people behind the autocracy. Thus, in February 1904, no serious effort was made to avoid the Japanese attack on Russian installations in Manchuria that precipitated the Russo-Japanese War.

Before many weeks had passed, it became clear that the Russian empire was not equipped to fight a war in the Far East. Organization was wasteful and inefficient, the Trans-Siberian railway had not been completed, and supply was an overwhelming problem. As the months passed, this resulted in defeat, shortages, and universal frustration, so that the initial patriotic response of the people turned to intense resentment against the government.

The revolutionary organizations had opposed the war from the start, and the SR's stepped up their assassination campaign. Two of the tsar's ministers had been murdered in the past three years, and Plehve, chief executor of the government's repressive policy, was obliterated by a terrorist's bomb in July 1904. Six months later the Mensheviks organized a strike in St. Petersburg, and middle-class liberals made public demands for constitutional government.

The Revolution of 1905 Revolution was finally precipitated on a Sunday morning in January 1905, when tens of thousands of St. Petersburg workmen on strike tried to present their demands in a demonstration before the tsar's Winter Palace. The demonstrators were stopped by troops, who fired on them and killed several hundred people. The brutal treatment accorded the workers on this "Bloody Sunday," as it was called, helped to convince many in the lower classes that the tsar himself was ill-disposed toward his own people, that it was not merely the old aristocracy, but the very institution of tsardom, which oppressed them.

In the months that followed, strikes occurred with increasing frequency in most of the large cities, and there were peasant riots in a variety of provinces. The SR's continued to accelerate terrorist activities, killing several dozen government servants each week and blowing to bits the tsar's uncle, the Grand-Duke Sergei. By the beginning of June, it was clear that the Japanese war had been lost, and despair and frustration sowed rebellion within the army, while the crew of the battleship *Potiomkin* mutinied at Odessa. Summer weather helped spread revolution among the peasant millions, who created uproar in the countryside with the burning of manor houses and the murder of landlords. In July, a general Peasant Union was formed. Since most of the soldiers in the imperial army were expeasants, they began to refuse to obey orders. By October, a city "Soviet," or council, of workers' delegates had been formed in the capital and demanded the powers of self-government, while a general strike paralyzed economic activity.

"1905." A Communist propaganda poster of 1930 celebrating the 25th anniversary of the first Russian revolution, the abortive Revolution of 1905. (Hoover Institution Archives.)

Constitutional Concessions by the Autocracy There no longer seemed any hope of crushing the revolution by force. However, since there was little or no coordination behind it, imperial ministers hoped to divide the moderate liberals from the extreme revolutionaries by offering basic constitutional reform while avoiding sweeping revolutionary change. The government's "October Manifesto" promised full civil liberties and the election of a Russian parliament, the Duma, on a democratic basis. This seemed to approximate constitutional monarchy, though there was no mention of making the government responsible to the new Duma.

The "October Manifesto" shattered the front of the opposition. Most middle-class liberals were at least momentarily satisfied. The radical revolutionaries tried to carry on by themselves, but the high tide of popular feeling had passed and military discipline was being restored. During the months that followed, their resistance was crushed, save for continued acts of individual terrorism.

Middle-class liberals were in turn divided. One group, the Constitutional Democrats (or Cadets), pressed for further reforms and a responsible parliamentary government, while others were satisfied with the limited concessions already made. Before the first Duma met in 1906, the tsar further restricted its authority, depriving it of jurisdiction over fundamental laws. When the Cadets, who held a majority in the new Duma, protested vehemently, the Duma itself was soon dissolved.

After new elections were held, a second Duma met in 1907 with sixteen Marxists among its membership. These were soon arrested by the government, and suffrage for the next elections was rigged in favor of the upper classes. By the end of 1907, the Duma had become little more than an advisory assembly, and even the Cadets rarely protested.

The Russian people were once more relapsing into their accustomed apathy and submissiveness. Though the Social Revolutionary terrorist campaign continued through 1907, it accomplished nothing, while the Marxists, divided into two factions, were no more effective. Meanwhile extreme conservative elements—aristocracy, landlords, bureaucrats, army officers, and some from the middle classes—had formed a "Union of the Russian People" to support the government. Bands of fanatics and thugs known as the "Black Hundreds" were organized to divert popular feeling against the Jews and engaged in bloody pogroms in southwestern Russia.

Nevertheless, it was impossible to turn the clock all the way back. Despite the restrictions imposed, the Duma was an established fact, and the idea of political representation had finally broken through. Russia could never be quite the same again. Though the revolutionary groups had failed, they had gained invaluable experience which they would use once more in the future.

Stolypin's Agrarian Reform From 1906 to 1911, the dominant figure in the Russian government was the prime minister, Peter Stolypin (1863–1911). Authoritarian and nationalist, Stolypin would make no political concessions to the liberals. At the same time, however, he was a creative statesman who realized that autocratic government would not be able to survive unless basic structural reforms occurred in Russian life to reduce internal discontent.

Pyotr Stolypin. Prime minister from 1906 to 1911, Stolypin was the last strong man of tsarist Russia. His "wager on the strong" aimed at creating a large class of prosperous, independent peasant farmers as the backbone of social and political stability in Russia. (Hoover Institution Archives.)

Specifically, peasant agriculture, the empire's economic backbone, had to be put in a more healthy state if imperial society were ever to regain its balance. An efficient and independent class of peasant proprietors would provide political and social stability. Therefore new laws were made in 1906 enabling enterprising peasants to break the bonds of communal tenure that had been holding them for half a century or longer. Those peasants able to get ahead were to be allowed to hold land in their own name and hire others to work for them. Peasants unable to compete in a free economy could work as laborers or move to the city to provide a fluid labor force for industrial expansion. This was Stolypin's "wager on the strong," an attempt to form a class of independent, efficient, and satisfied peasants. During the next decade, it proved to be at least a qualified success. When the First World War began, Russian peasants were still heavily in debt, most of them did not have clear title to their land, and their living standard was extremely low, but seventy-five percent of the land was now in their hands, as high a percentage as existed in that paradise of the independent peasantry, France. The Stolypin reforms were the only significant change in Russian agriculture between the emancipation and the revolution of 1917. Their very success threatened the revolutionaries who found Stolypin the strongest bulwark of autocracy. Lenin, for example, considered him the only dangerous man in the government.

Yet Stolypin had many enemies inside as well as outside the government. During these years, the court circle and the upper level of the bureaucracy were wracked by intrigue and petty personal plots which corroded morale, sapped energy, and checked initiative. The extreme reactionaries among the tsar's advisers were jealous of Stolypin's influence, which they tried to curb by denouncing him as a cryptoliberal. Nicholas' own attitude toward his strong-willed premier was ambivalent at best, and Stolypin found himself more isolated within the government with each passing year. In 1911, he was assassinated by a Social Revolutionary terrorist who was also serving as double agent for the tsarist secret police.

Weakness of the Tsarist Regime in 1914 On the eve of World War I, the tsarist regime was still relying on the three institutions that had been its support for the past two centuries—the army, the bureaucracy, and the Orthodox Church. None of the three was very solid.

Russian Orthodoxy had always stressed ritual and formalism. Control of the church by the government had cost much of its spiritual vitality and spontaneity. Though large numbers of the peasantry still retained their faith and devotion, this piety was directed more toward the ritual than toward the inner spirit of Christianity. The bulk of the intelligentsia was militantly antireligious and atheistic. It is true that after 1905 some of the leading "Legal Marxist" thinkers, such as Pyotr Struve (1870–1944) and Nikolai Berdyaev (1874–1948) had returned to Christianity, but they were not representative of the younger generation. The real vitality of Russian religiosity lay not so much in the Orthodox church as in the "sects," the smaller schismatic or independent protestant groups, whose members were enthusiastic and in many cases increasing in number.

The most famous "religious" figure during those years was the holy man and charlatan, Rasputin (1872–1916). A Siberian peasant, Rasputin had developed extraordinary personal powers, in part based on the use of hypnosis. When presented at court, he made an overwhelming impression on the superstitious tsarina as a "friend" sent from God to save the life of the tsarevich, whose hemophilia he apparently could partially arrest through hypnosis or confident relaxation. Tsarina Alexandra would believe none of the reports about Rasputin's debauched orgies, and he gained enough influence to become an influence peddler in the government. Though Rasputin does not seem to have had any voice in high affairs of state, this weird personage was soon perceived by the government's critics as a symbol of all that was twisted and corrupt in the Russian system. By 1914, many believed that he actually ran the government.

The bureaucracy was in worse condition than the church. Bloated and muddling, it was sunk in a slough of intrigue and careerism. The bureaucracy was but a further obstacle to the kind of progressive leadership that alone could prevent revolt by removing the source of popular distress.

In the long run, the fate of autocracy was dependent on the armed forces. These had reached their nadir in 1905, and the process of rebuilding them was slow and expensive. The imperial army became the field of intrigue and status rivalry that inhibited rapid improvement. Progress was made between 1905 and 1914, but Russian military efficiency remained far below that of Germany or France. The economy, though expanding at a rapid pace, had not achieved the industrial potential to sustain a modern war machine.

Russia was struggling in the middle of a transition that Nicholas and his government had little understanding of and preferred to avoid. Establishment of the Duma inaugurated an era of broader and more representative politics, but any further change was resisted by the tsar. Tension increased in 1913, when a great strike in the Siberian gold fields touched off a new wave of walkouts in European Russia, and the future looked dark and uncertain.

The international scene was also foreboding, for Russia's Balkan diplomacy and the mechanics of the alliance system brought involvement in the international crises and war scares that culminated in the great conflagration of 1914. In the long run, frustration in war redoubled the feelings of frustration and rebellion at home. The government's hollow emphasis on militarism and prestige therefore not only contributed to the outbreak of the First World War, but eventually led to the collapse of the regime and the long-anticipated revolution in 1917.

FURTHER READING

The best general survey of this period is Hugh Seton-Watson, * *The Decline of Imperial Russia* (1952, 1968). The "Tsar Liberator" has been studied in W. E. Mosse, *Alexander II and the Modernization of Russia* (1958). T. H. von Laue, *Sergei Witte and the Industrialization of Russia* (1961), is excellent. There are two valuable symposia on the period of Nicholas II: T. G. Stavrou, ed., * *Russia*

*Books available in paperback edition are marked with an asterisk.

under the Last Tsar (1969); and George Katkov, et al., eds., *Russia Enters the Twentieth Century* (1971). Jacob Walkin, *The Rise of Democracy in Pre-Revolutionary Russia* (1962), presents a positive evaluation of Russian political development.

The two best works on the peasantry and the agrarian problem are W. S. Vucinich, ed., *The Peasant in Nineteenth-Century Russia* (1968); and G. T. Robinson, *Rural Russia under the Old Regime* (1932). On the Russian church, see J. S. Curtiss, *Church and State in Russia, 1900–1917* (1940). M. B. Petrovich, *The Emergence of Russian Pan-Slavism, 1856–1870* (1956), treats one form of Russian nationalism. Two different problems of the Russian empire have been studied in R. F. Leslie, *Reform and Insurrection in Russian Poland, 1856–1865* (1963); and Seymour Becker, *Russia's Protectorates in Central Asia, 1865–1924* (1965).

The classic account of intellectual life in nineteenth-century Russia is Thomas G. Masaryk, *The Spirit of Russia*, 2 vols. (rev. ed., 1955). The best literary histories are Dimitri Mirsky, * *A History of Russian Literature* (1949); and Marc Slonim, * *From Chekhov to the Revolution* (1953). For a study of key aspects of the two literary giants of the period, see George Steiner, * *Tolstoy or Dostoevsky* (1961); and Ellis Sandoz, *Political Apocalypse* (1971). The intelligentsia as a whole treated in Richard Pipes, ed., *The Russian Intelligentsia* (1961).

Middle-class progressivism has been studied in George Fisher, *Russian Liberalism* (1958). The best general account of populism is Franco Venturi's *Roots of Revolution* (1960). Insight into the origins of Bolshevism will be gained from B. D. Wolfe, * *Three Who Made a Revolution* (1948); Leopold Haimson, *The Russian Marxists and the Origins of Bolshevism* (1955); A. L. Wildman, *Russian Social Democracy, 1891–1903* (1967); and Donald Treadgold, *Lenin and his Rivals* (1956). The violent sectors of the revolutionaries are brilliantly depicted in Robert Payne, *The Terrorists* (1957).

5 Autocratic Monarchy in the Mass Age

In German nationalism, the Hohenzollern monarchy had found a new force with which to buttress monarchical authority and weld together the new state created by Bismarck. Yet there remained in German society cleavages that could not be entirely closed with the cement of national patriotism. For the Habsburg Empire, on the other hand, cultural nationalism was a disruptive rather than a synthetic force. The dual settlement of 1867 did not end the nationalities question, and the empire continued to be threatened by the growth of national sentiment among its subject peoples.

The region of the Balkans demonstrates the destructive, as well as the constructive, power inherent in the idea of nationalism. Until the emergence of Serbian, Greek, Bulgarian, and Rumanian nationalism, the rule of the Ottoman Empire, though woefully backward, inefficient, and corrupt, was not particularly oppressive. But when the national uprisings came in the nineteenth century, the rebels and the Turks turned upon each other with a ferocity born of religious and national hatred. One by one the Balkan peoples gained their independence from the Turks, but only after repeated crises which involved the whole of Europe.

GERMANY UNDER BISMARCK AND WILLIAM II

United Germany was a revolutionary creation of Prussian power politics. To be sure, its constitution was essentially conservative, for the vital powers of the state were left in the hands of the crown and the privileged position of the Junker nobility was preserved and even extended. Nevertheless, the expansion of Prussia cost the rulers of Hanover, Hesse-Kassel, and Nassau their thrones. Ultimately, it cost the three kings of Saxony, Bavaria, and Württemberg and more than a dozen other princes their sovereignty. Hence Bismarck's reconstruction of Germany dealt a severe blow to the principles of legitimacy and divine right.

Governments born of revolution are usually plagued by a sense of insecurity. What has been achieved by violence, until legitimized by time, is in danger of destruction by the same means. Hence it was only natural that Bismarck should have feared, during the 1870's, for the survival of the German Reich he had founded. Centuries of independence and dynastic rule had produced among most Germans local loyalties that could not be wiped out overnight, despite the growing strength of German patriotism. Southern Catholics were particularly alarmed over their inclusion in what appeared to be an essentially Protestant union. Many Hanoverians were bitter over their annexation to Prussia and sought to restore Hanoverian independence. Ethnic minorities in Posen (Poles) and in Schleswig (Danes) were even more

William I, King of Prussia and German Kaiser. William was very conscious of the Hohenzollern military tradition and of his authoritarian prerogatives. A person of modest talents, he chose men of great ability to serve him as ministers and generals and, despite conflicts, backed them in their tasks. (The Bettmann Archive.)

unhappy about their inclusion in a German nation-state. The inhabitants of Alsace and Lorraine were never reconciled to their separation from France.

Bismarck's great fear was that these internal foes of the Reich might combine with external ones. The emergence of a unified Germany was a severe shock to the other European powers. For centuries, Germany had been a convenient playground for the European game of power politics. Suddenly it had been transformed into the most important weight in the European balance of power. Military victories, brilliant diplomacy, size of population, and rapid industrialization made the Reich a force to be reckoned with. On many sleepless nights Bismarck was troubled by the apparition of a great coalition (France, Russia, Austria-Hungary) like that which had nearly ruined Frederick the Great in the Seven Years' War. In combination with the Reich's domestic enemies such a hostile alliance might bring about the dissolution of united Germany.

Political Parties After 1867, Bismarck sought to strengthen his new state by building up the central government at the cost of the state governments. In alliance with the liberals he pushed through the Reichstag a series of laws that reinforced national unity by giving Germany, for the first time, a common currency, a central bank of issue, common codes of law, a common judiciary, and standardized weights and measures. Many of these laws were sympathetic to the interests of industrial capitalism—particularly the commercial code of 1869, which was based on free enterprise, and the law of 1870, which ended most restrictions on incorporation. These statutes were beneficial to businessmen. They completed a long and gradual process by which the new entrepreneurial elite was integrated into the Prussian-German "establishment."

Bismarck drew his principal support during the first ten years of his chancellorship from the Free Conservative and National Liberal parties, both established in 1867. The free conservatives were composed of great nobles, generals, diplomats, high civil servants, and (later) great industrialists, while the national liberals represented the upper middle class (bankers, manufacturers, some high officials, and professional men). To the right of these parties stood the old Conservative Party, in which were many ultra-conservative noblemen who regarded Bismarck as something of a traitor. His adoption of the cause of German national unity and his violation of the principal of legitimacy was compared by them to "the fratricide of Cain, the betrayal of Judas, and the crucifixion of the Lord." On the left was the Progressive Party representing the lower middle class (shop keepers, artisans, small merchants, petty officials, and the like). The progressives clung steadfastly to liberal principles by refusing to accept the autocratic features of the German constitution. They were particularly distressed by the "iron budget," an arrangement whereby the Reichstag was only permitted to vote on military appropriations at intervals varying from three to seven years.

The emergence of two other political parties in the 1870's—the Center and Social Democratic parties—was indicative of continuing religious and social cleavages within the German population that national unity did not bridge. Founded in 1870, the Center was openly Catholic in composition and program. Its great strength lay in Bavaria and the Rhineland, among Catholics who felt that the exclusion of Austria had disrupted the religious balance in Germany to their disadvantage. By forming their own political party, they hoped to protect Catholic interests against the Protestant majority and the essentially Protestant regime in Berlin. Its religious character made the Center attractive to Catholics of all strata of German society and gave it a constant parliamentary strength that varied little from election to election.

By the end of the 1870's, it was also evident that mine and factory workers did not feel that Bismarck's Reich was sympathetic to their interests. In increasing numbers they began to vote for socialist candidates. The Social Democratic Party was founded at Gotha in 1875 through the fusion of two rival movements composed of the followers of Ferdinand Lassalle and Karl Marx. Much to Marx's disgust his followers, Wilhelm Liebknecht and August Bebel, accepted at Gotha a compromise program in which the state socialist views of Lassalle predominated. The new party was republican in program, and its rhetoric was often revolutionary, but not its deeds.

Bismarck regarded the Center and the Social Democratic parties as hostile to the Reich he had founded. Both had international connections that tended to take precedence over their loyalty to the German nation, the former as members of a universal church, the latter as participants in a world-wide socialist movement. Ultramontane Catholics seemed to threaten the territorial cohesion of the Reich, the socialists its social stability.

The *Kulturkampf* During the 1870's, Bismarck struck at the Center Party, which he denounced as a "mobilization against the state." He feared that German Catholics might join hands with the Catholic powers of Europe in a grand alliance against the new Germany. By putting pressure on the Catholic church, he hoped to force the Papacy to order the party to support his government. In this he had the enthusiastic help of the National Liberal and Progressive parties. The liberals rejoiced at the opportunity to separate church and state and to liquidate clerical influence in education. Liberals throughout Europe had been angered by Pius IX's Syllabus of Errors (1864), which condemned their doctrines as heresy. Along with many sincere Catholics, furthermore, they were outraged by the proclamation of the doctrine of papal infallibility in matters of faith and morals (1870). It was a Progressive politician, Rudolf Virchow, who declared that the attack upon the church that developed at this point was a "struggle for modern culture [*Kulturkampf*] against medieval obscurantism" and thereby gave the conflict its popular name.

During 1872–1876, a series of laws removed clerics from the public schools, made civil marriage obligatory, and attempted to place the clergy in general under the discipline of the state. Clergymen who refused to cooperate were imprisoned, including a bishop and two archbishops. Official support was given to a group of schismatics called the "Old Catholics," who rejected the doctrine of infallibility.

The action, however, was a failure. Instead of yielding, the Vatican severed diplomatic relations and prompted civil disobedience by declaring the laws null and void. Instead of dissolving, the Center party increased its parliamentary representation in the elections of 1874 from sixty-three to ninety-one seats. The Old Catholic movement found little response either among the clergy or laymen. Furthermore, the Catholic cause found support in Protestant Germany. Already angered by Bismarck's cooperation with the liberals, many conservatives feared that the Lutheran Church might be the next target of the anti-clericals.

Bismarck's Change of Front   After 1875, Bismarck decided to abandon his liberal course in domestic affairs. A period of feverish speculation had ended in a stock market crash in 1873 followed by a business depression. Liberals were blamed for the catastrophe and likewise Bismarck because of his association with them and his acceptance of their economic politics. As the depression deepened, manufacturers began to agitate more vigorously for the abandonment of free trade and adoption of protectionism. They wished to dominate the domestic market by shutting out foreign competition. Their agitation was soon reinforced by agrarian interests. Earlier, Prussian farmers had been free traders, for they enjoyed a lively export trade, particularly to Great Britain. Now the railway and steamship began to bring grains from North America and Eastern Europe for sale at prices that German estate owners could not match. Bismarck responded with the Tariff Act of 1879, which marked his departure from liberal economic policy by introducing protective tariffs on both manufactured and agrarian products. By responding to their mutual interests he consolidated an alliance between big business and big agriculture, which became the economic and social foundation of the imperial regime.

Bismarck could afford to bring his "liberal period" to an end because he no longer needed the help of the liberal parties for the task of consolidating the Reich. By the late 1870's, it was evident that the remaining Germany dynasties and states had no interest in regaining their independence from Berlin. Other developments abroad ended Bismarck's fears of a Catholic coalition directed against Germany in league with Germany's Catholics. In France, the republicans, who were vociferously anticlerical, won out in their struggle with Catholic monarchists; in 1879, Bismarck succeeded in binding Austria to Germany in the Dual Alliance. Hence it became possible for Bismarck to begin liquidating the *Kulturkampf*. The death of Pius IX and succession of Leo XIII in 1878 opened the way for negotiations with the Papacy. During the 1880's, the anticlerical legislation was gradually revoked.

The Antisocialist Laws   Despite his failure against the Center, Bismarck undertook after 1878 a similar campaign against the Social Democratic Party.

Continuing depression and a growing sense of alienation led more and more proletarians to express their discontent at the ballot box. By 1877, the party had succeeded in electing twelve deputies to the Reichstag; while the number elected was not large, the size of the socialist vote (483,000) was impressive. In 1878, two attempts upon the life of William I gave Bismarck, despite the fact that neither originated with socialists, the pretext he needed to force legislation through the Reichstag dissolving socialist organizations and banning the socialist press.

While wielding the whip, Bismarck held out the carrot. He sought to win German laborers to the monarchy through social reform. In 1883 and 1884, workers were insured against sickness and accidents, and, in 1889, against old age and disability. Germany now led the world in the field of social security. Yet neither whip nor carrot sufficed to defeat the socialist movement. Although more than 150 periodicals were suppressed and over 1,500 persons were arrested, the socialists succeeded in holding their party congresses in Switzerland and in printing their most important party journal abroad. In 1884, 24 socialists were elected to the Reichstag by 550,000 voters; in 1890 the number rose to 35 deputies and 1,427,000 voters.

Germany after Bismarck   After nearly three decades of power, Kaiser William I died in 1888 at the age of ninety and was succeeded by his son Frederick III. For many years, Frederick, whose wife was a daughter of Queen Victoria, had been at odds with his father and Bismarck on vital questions of policy. By the time he ascended the throne, however, it was too late for any fundamental changes, since he was already deathly ill with the throat cancer that killed him after ninety-nine days as kaiser. The young man of twenty-nine who followed him was unfit for the task of being the most

Kaiser William II and Officers Reviewing the Troops of a Crack Regiment. An inflated ego coupled with mediocre talents and unsteady nature made William poorly equipped for what was probably the most powerful single position in the world. (Culver Pictures, Inc.)

powerful ruler in the world. It is true that William II (1888–1918) was equipped with a good memory and quick comprehension, but he was lacking in patience, wisdom, and steadiness of purpose. As a public speaker, he had a dangerous proclivity for the striking and unguarded phrase which made newspaper headlines and irritated public opinion without achieving any political purpose.

Since William II's political views were conservative, Bismarck appeared to be firmly in power; yet on March 15, 1890, to the shock of the German public, he was suddenly dismissed. William had grown impatient with the elderly chancellor and was irritated by his dictatorial ways. But there were other, more concrete issues. Bismarck wished to renew and strengthen the antisocialist laws, while William preferred to attack the problem with further social reform. Unable to secure a lasting majority in the Reichstag, Bismarck was ready to consider a *coup d'état* and the abandonment of universal suffrage. But William wanted to be a popular king and had no wish to begin his reign with such an arbitrary act. Finally, he suspected the chancellor of bargaining with the Reichstag parties behind his back and resented Bismarck's insistence upon the rule that cabinet ministers could approach the kaiser only through himself.

William intended to establish his own personal rule. Yet he was incapable of this, shifting like a weathercock with every turn in the wind. Nor could he find another chancellor of Bismarck's stature to take the helm. His first choice was General Leo von Caprivi (1890–1894), an able man of progressive temperament who withdrew the antisocialist laws, reduced military service from three to two years, introduced in Prussia a progressive income tax, and lowered tariff duties. The latter measure earned him the hostility of the agrarians, especially the Junkers, who got him dismissed. Next the kaiser turned to Prince Chlodwig von Hohenlohe-Schillingsfürst (1894–1900), an octogenarian incapable of pursuing an active policy. His next choice, Bernhard von Bülow (1900–1909), appeared, on the surface, to have something of Bismarck's talent. A professional diplomat, he was adept at political maneuver, was an eloquent speaker, and knew how to win people. Yet Bülow was lacking in depth. He was a master at improvisation rather than policy, and his main objective in domestic affairs was to avoid crises. Finally, William resorted to a routine bureaucrat, Theobald von Bethmann-Hollweg (1909–1916), a man of administrative ability, but of no imagination and ill equipped to handle the great crisis that struck in 1914.

Economic Growth and Political Lethargy During the period from 1870 to 1914, the economic growth experienced by Germany made her the leading producer of manufactured goods in Europe. By 1914, she produced more than twice as much steel as Britain and nearly four times as much as France. She had also surpassed Britain in pig-iron output, although by a narrower margin, while Britain still held a small lead in coal mining. This great achievement came from the stimulation provided by unification, the availability of rich mineral resources, and an industrious and rapidly growing population (from 41,000,000 in 1870 to 67,000,000 in 1914). By 1914, sixty percent of Germany's population lived and worked in urban areas.

The fantastic rise of German industry and the growth of the middle class did not strengthen German liberalism. By 1900, both liberal parties had declined in voting strength and could usually command less than twenty-five percent of the seats in the Reichstag. Hence, neither had any vital interest in pushing for parliamentary government. Since 1883, moreover, the National Liberals had dedicated themselves largely to the interests of the entrepreneurial class. Although dominated by conservatives, the government was responsive to the needs of capitalism. Businessmen were favored by cartel laws, protective tariffs, the tax policy of the state, and the avoidance of further social legislation.

The seats in the Reichstag lost by the liberals were taken by the Social Democrats. Bismarck's persecution had only served to make the party popular among the urban lower classes. Between 1887 and 1903, its share of the total votes cast rose from 10.1 percent to 31.7 percent. In 1912, the socialists captured 110 of 397 seats in the Reichstag to become the strongest single party. Yet even they did not represent a vital force for the change of the status quo. While nominally Marxist, most socialist leaders had given up the idea of immediate revolution. They feared to jeopardize their positions by hazardous actions against the government and they were influenced by the argument that the working class might gain its ends through political agitation and trade union action. Their followers, moreover, were never revolutionary. Like the liberal bourgeoisie, the German working class was deeply influenced by the German traditions of civil discipline and obedience.

Nevertheless, the Social Democratic Party would certainly have collaborated with Progressives in any serious effort to bring about parliamentary

Berlin in the Late Nineteenth Century. (Below) *Villas of the Rich in the Kemperplatz.* (Right) *Tenements of the Working Class in the Slums.* Through the industrial revolution Berlin became a great railway, manufacturing, and financial center and the nation's largest city. The extremes of wealth and poverty also made it the center of the most successful socialist movement in Europe. (Ullstein Bilderdienst.)

government in Germany. Without the participation of the Center, however, such a coalition could not have succeeded. Despite what it had suffered in the 1870's from an authoritarian regime, the Center did not support such an objective. Its conservative leadership preferred to cooperate with the Conservative and Free Conservative parties in support of the government.

Situations did arise before 1914 which could have enabled a determined opposition to push through parliamentary government. The most significant occurred in 1908 when the blundering kaiser made a flagrant error in public relations. In an interview with a journalist of the London *Daily Telegraph* he made inaccurate and offensive assertions which antagonized every major European power and Japan as well. He also angered the German public by the statement that he had provided the British with a war plan for the suppression of the rebellious Boers in South Africa, whose cause had been highly popular in Germany. In the storm of public protest that followed, not a single important voice was raised, not even by the Conservatives, in the kaiser's defense. The opportunity had come to alter the Bismarckian system, but there was no serious desire to undertake it. The storm blew over.

In the winter of 1913–1914, on the eve of the First World War, there was a second incident of similar potentiality. In the Alsacian garrison city of Zabern, clashes occured between arrogant officers and angry civilians which led to public demonstrations of protest. The colonel in command replied by arresting the demonstrators. Throughout Germany there was indignation at this high-handed and illegal exercise of military authority over civilians. Yet the Chancellor and Minister of War, backed by the kaiser, defended the colonel's actions. Although the Reichstag voted (293 to 55) to censure the Chancellor, Bethmann did not resign and the incident passed without result. Once again, it had been demonstrated that there was no serious wish on the part of the majority parties and the public to change the system.

AUSTRIA-HUNGARY UNDER FRANZ JOSEPH

The dual monarchy of Austria-Hungary was a unique experiment in the history of modern statecraft. Critics called it "one body with two souls" and questioned whether the empire would be able to speak with a single voice in European affairs. Some feared, and others hoped, that the settlement would be "the beginning of the end of the monarchy." In the minds of many cultural nationalists the empire, even in its reorganized form, was an anachronism, whose dissolution was the prerequisite of progress in central Europe. Yet in the twentieth century, when the destructive character of the national idea has become so glaringly evident, some look back upon The Empire with nostalgia, regarding it as a useful institution whose liquidation in 1918 was an act of folly. It bound the peoples of central Europe together and with greater wisdom might have provided them with the basis for harmonious coexistence.

Unfortunately, Kaiser Franz Joseph and the Magyar gentry looked upon the Compromise of 1867 as the final, conclusive settlement of the Habsburg problem. In essence, it was an agreement between the Germans and Magyars for the joint domination, each in their respective spheres, of the other peoples of the Empire. "You look after your barbarians," Chancellor Beust is said to have remarked to the Hungarians, "and we will look after ours." In Hungary, this meant Magyar rule over Croats, Serbs, Rumanians, Slovaks, and Ruthenians; in Austria it meant German rule over Czechs, Poles, Ruthenians, Slovenes, and Italians. As their economic and cultural level rose, the subject peoples naturally became restive under this arrangement. Only a federal reorganization of the empire would have created a sense of justice that might have enabled the monarchy to survive.

Hungary Under the Compromise of 1867 Hungary was controlled by the Magyar gentry through an electoral process which discriminated against the Magyar peasants and urban population and against all other nationalities. As revised in 1874, the law stipulated educational and financial qualifications which permitted only six percent of the population to vote. Although the Magyars constituted only 44.4 percent of the whole, gerrymandered electoral districts kept the non-Magyars from equal representation. By such means, Magyar deputies controlled ninety-five percent of the seats in the chamber.

Not all Magyars were satisfied with what had been gained in 1867. Radical followers of Louis Kossuth still agitated for complete independence and a republican government. Another faction, led by Colomon Tisza, desired to preserve the monarchy but to abandon the common ministers and common army, reducing the union to the person of the monarch alone. Yet the parliamentary majority was held by the followers of Francis Deák and Count Julius Andrássy, who had been instrumental in negotiating the dual arrangement and were loyal to it. With Deák's retirement from politics and Andrássy's departure for Vienna to become Foreign Minister (1871), the party, popularly known as the "Deákists," lost its best leaders and began to disintegrate. In the end, the parliamentary system was saved in Hungary by Tisza's decision finally to accept the Compromise of 1867, merging his party with the Deákists to form the Liberal party. Until 1905, this combined party, which was far from liberal on such subjects as suffrage reform and the treatment of national minorities, usually dominated the parliament and cabinet. This dominance, like that of the Deákists earlier, was maintained at election time by tricking, corrupting, and intimidating the voters.

Although a Nationalities Act of 1868 promised to the subject peoples a high degree of cultural autonomy, the Magyars soon began to violate its word and spirit by an aggressive attempt to "Magyarize" the entire country. Magyar became the exclusive language of the civil service, which was largely the monopoly of the gentry class. By 1900, ninety-five percent of all state officials, ninety-two percent of all county officials and, ninety percent of the judiciary were Magyar. The subject peoples were not permitted their own school systems, and those the Slovaks established for themselves were dissolved in 1874. In 1883, Magyar was made compulsory for all schools and in 1907 teachers were made liable to dismissal if their pupils failed to master the language. By controlling education the Magyars controlled the professions. For example, eighty-nine percent of all medical men were Magyar by 1900. Eight out of ten newspapers were printed in the Magyar tongue, and the rest were largely German. The railway system was constructed to serve best the Magyar areas or to orient the subject peoples toward Budapest rather than toward their own national centers.

The most active resistance to Magyar assimilation came from Croatia. Like the Magyars themselves, the Croats were a "historic people" with a long political tradition. In the revolution of 1848 they had vigorously supported the crown against Kossuth's republic. Hence they felt betrayed in 1867 by the crown's abandonment of their interests to the Magyars. Although the settlement granted to the Croatian Diet provincial autonomy and the right to send forty delegates to the Hungarian Diet in Budapest, Croatia was actually governed after 1867 by a Magyar governor and Magyar officials who were totally without sympathy for Croat needs and aspirations. In 1912, the Croat constitution was suspended and an openly dictatorial regime was introduced. Yet this ruthless policy only served to make the Croats determined to seek, in harmony with the Serbs and Slovenes, a south Slav kingdom co-equal with Austria and Hungary.

Austria Under the Compromise of 1867 Although they constituted only 35.6 percent of the entire population of Austria, the Germans controlled the House of Representatives, the lower chamber of the central Parliament (Reichsrat). This was because of the "electoral geometry" system which divided the voters into socioeconomic groups, or curiae, and which favored the wealthier citizens, who were mostly German, and the urban areas, where the German tongue predominated. Thus, the Germans had a much higher representation than their numbers warranted. German supremacy was also aided by the fact that for a number of years the Czech deputies refused to take their seats in the House.

For nearly a decade after 1867, Emperor Franz Joseph was usually content to allow the German liberals who controlled the House of Representatives to choose the Cabinet. They were moderates whose liberalism did not include universal suffrage, fair treatment to minorities, or determined resistance to imperial authority. What interested them was constitutionalism, civic rights, laissez faire, centralism, and anticlericalism. Their legislative achievements were chiefly in these directions. Civil marriage was legalized and secular courts were given jurisdiction over marital trials. The schools were removed from clerical control and efforts made to place all Christian faiths upon an equal plane under the law. Finally, the Concordat of 1855 with the Vatican was formally abrogated. Military reforms introduced universal conscription, abolished corporal punishment, and modernized tactics and equipment. Trial by jury was introduced in press cases, the penal code humanized, and restrictions against Jews abolished.

Unlike the Magyars, the German liberals made no effort to assimilate the subject nations of Austria. Nevertheless, German rule was bitterly

Kaiser Franz Joseph in 1910. His was one of the longest reigns in European history—from the revolution of 1848 to World War I. While earnest and industrious to the end, he and his ministers wrestled with internal problems that were perhaps insuperable. (Brown Brothers.)

resented by the Slavic majority, particularly by the Czechs, who were the most economically and culturally advanced. The Czechs hoped to emulate the Magyars by attaining autonomy for the lands of the ancient crown of St. Václav (Bohemia, Moravia, and Silesia) and subjecting the German population of this region to their own leadership. In 1871, Franz Joseph, fearing violence in Bohemia, appointed Count Charles Hohenwart as Austrian prime minister with the charge to find a basis for settlement. Of course, the Germans were outraged, but so were the Magyars, who feared a similar grant to Croatia. Franz Joseph lacked the necessary resolution to proceed over this opposition to a federal solution of the Habsburg problem. Hohenwart was dismissed, and the German liberals were restored to power.

The economic policy of the liberal government after 1867 favored the development of business enterprise. It was a time of rapid economic growth made possible by the completion of the railway network. But it was also a period of wild speculation in which everyone, from the wealthiest entrepreneur down to the scullery maid, bought securities in the hope of quick gain. In the year 1869 alone the government chartered more than a thousand companies, many of them fraudulent. Stock prices on the Vienna Exchange shot upward, fed by stories of fantastic profits and the announcement of large, sometimes fictitious, dividends. In 1873, came the inevitable reckoning. The whole over-burdened structure came crashing down and the Austrian economy did not fully recover for a decade.

Because they represented the entrepreneurial class, the German liberals were held accountable for the crash of 1873. But they also lost favor with Franz Joseph by criticizing his foreign policy. At the Congress of Berlin in 1878, Foreign Minister Andrássy had obtained for the empire a protectorate over the former Turkish provinces of Bosnia and Herzegovina inhabited chiefly by Serbs and Croats. The German liberals were averse to increasing the Slavic population of the empire, but Franz Joseph resented their interference in matters of foreign policy. He responded to their attacks by dismissing the liberal cabinet, demonstrating once again that the emperor was the final authority in Austria and that parliamentary government was a mere sham.

Taaffe's Iron Ring Count Edward Taaffe became Prime Minister in 1879 with the declaration that he was an imperial—not a party—minister. His tactic was to rule above the conflicting nations, playing them off against each other. In Parliament, he replaced the German liberal majority with a coalition of forces, popularly called "Taaffe's Iron Ring," which was composed of Slavs, Poles, Czechs, clericals, and conservative Germans. He brought the Czechs back to the Reichsrat by granting the use of the Czech as well as the German language in the Bohemian "outer service," that is, by those officials in personal contact with the public. This created careers for the Czech middle class, since most German officials did not know Czech. Furthermore, a new suffrage law in Bohemia placed the provincial diet under Czech control, and a Czech university was established in Prague. For their cooperation, the Poles were allowed to dominate and assimilate the Ruthenians, and the Slovenes were granted the same privilege over other nationalities in the province of Carniola.

Taaffe was a man of great political gifts and his tactic of keeping "all the nationalities in a balanced state of mild dissatisfaction" was so successful that he retained his office until 1893. For a time national antagonisms appeared to decline; yet radical movements were in the making which presaged a new era of hate and violence. Czechs and Germans of the younger generation were dissatisfied with the compromises their elders had accepted under Taaffe. At Linz in 1882, a program was drafted which called upon the Austrian Germans, backed by the German Reich, to re-establish their

Workers in a Bohemian Coal Mine in the Late Nineteenth Century. The Austrian half of the Dual Monarchy made progress in industrialization in the nineteenth century, although its coal and iron resources were inferior to those of Germany and England. (The Bettmann Archive.)

hegemony over the Slavs and Magyars. One of the drafters was Georg von Schönerer, who later founded a pan-German movement demanding the union of all German-speaking peoples and preaching a doctrine of German racial supremacy. Deprived of their traditional leadership in the empire, some Austrian Germans began to seek in racial concepts the moral basis for its reestablishment.

In Bohemia, meanwhile, the Young Czech movement began, composed of radicals who demanded an autonomous Bohemia under exclusive Czech control. In the elections of 1891, the Young Czechs routed the moderates. Like Bismarck in 1866, Taaffe now determined to undercut the middle-class nationalists by appealing to the masses through the introduction of universal suffrage. But this proposal destroyed him, for the interest groups that composed his Iron Ring feared the lower classes and the subject nationalities whom they exploited. In the face of this opposition, Franz Joseph sacrificed his ablest minister in 1893.

The Collapse of Constitutionalism in Austria   Taaffe's fall was followed by a turbulent period in Austrian politics, during which national antagonisms steadily grew. Franz Joseph turned to the parliamentary factions for his successive cabinets, but those factions were mere interest groups representing the various nations and were without any comprehension of the needs of the empire as a whole. Cabinets fell over such issues as whether the Slovenian or German language was to be used in the grammar school of the Slovenian town of Cilli or whether the Czech language was to be permitted in the "inner" as well as the "outer service" of the Bohemian civil service. Peaceful debate in the Reichsrat gave way to shouting, whistling, banging desks, trumpet blasts, flying inkpots, and finally fist fights. In the Bohemian Diet, similar scenes occurred; and in the streets of Prague, fighting

Ethnic Conflicts in Austria Caricatured as a Card Game (1897). Prime Minister Kasimir Badeni (standing) dissolves the Reichsrat by dealing out parliamentary mandates to leaders of the ethnic factions. "Next time we will play without Jews," he says in the underlying caption. The joke was that the Jews were the only ethnic group not clamoring for special rights. (Bildarchiv d. Ost. Nationalbibliothek.)

broke out between Czechs and Germans. In the Tyrol, there was friction between Italians and Germans, and in Dalmatia between Slovenes and Italians. Only in Moravia (Czech and German) and Bukovina (Ruthenians and Rumanians) were workable compromises achieved between the rival peoples.

After 1900, Franz Joseph met this situation by dispensing with parliamentary ministers altogether. Henceforth the Austrian cabinets were filled with professional civil servants responsible only to the emperor. They legislated by decree, using an article of the constitution that provided for "emergency ordinances." Even the yearly budget was made law by this route. Theoretically the decrees could be abrogated by the parliamentary majority, but there was no majority. The Reichsrat lost its legislative function and monarchical absolutism returned to Austria.

New Political Parties The 1890's saw the development, nevertheless, of two political movements which promised to be imperial rather than national in scope. One was the Christian Social party led by Karl Lueger, perhaps the most skilled politician in Habsburg history. His program was a strange mixture of Catholicism, democracy, socialism, and antisemitism. The Christian Social party appealed, in other words, to both progressives and racial bigots, but not to any particular national group. Its chief strength lay with the lower classes in Vienna, where Lueger was five times elected mayor before Franz Joseph would confirm him in the post (1897). As mayor, Lueger was responsible for a program of municipal socialism unique for that age. It included public ownership of utilities, certain public services such as orphanages and funeral homes, and public works (parks, squares, boulevards) which added to the beauty of one of the world's finest cities.

The second political movement was the Social Democratic party founded in 1888 by Viktor Adler. One of the signers of the Linz program of 1881, Adler became a convert to Marxism as a result of his experiences serving the Viennese poor as a physician. The growth of industrialism in Austria had created the proletarian base for a socialist movement. Within a few years, more than fifty socialist journals had come into existence, the most influential being Adler's own *Arbeiter Zeitung*. The immediate goals of the Social Democrats were universal suffrage, social welfare legislation, and the secularization of public education. Like the German socialists, the Austrian party was revolutionary only in theory. Its program called for the retention of the monarchy and the reorganization of the empire on federal lines.

The success of two major political parties in appealing to the masses rather than to nationalities prompted Franz Joseph to adopt universal and equal suffrage for Austria in 1907. Perhaps, it was reasoned, the future of the monarchy lay in alliance with the lower classes against the quarreling middle-class nationalists. But suffrage reform did not provide the solution. While the Christian Socialists and Social Democrats scored significant victories in the election that followed, the chamber was still divided into some thirty political fragments. Three successive prime ministers failed to find a secure parliamentary majority. When war came in 1914, the Reichsrat was suspended.

Collapse of Constitutionalism in Hungary These events had their parallel in Hungary. After thirty years in power, the Hungarian Liberal party met increasing opposition from a separatist minority, which demanded that

Magyar be made the language of command for the Hungarian army contingents. This was tantamount to a demand for a separate Hungarian army, which in turn would have meant the destruction of the dual settlement. In 1905, the separatists won control of the chamber. But Franz Joseph was adamant where military matters were concerned. He appointed a loyal general as prime minister, suspended the constitution, and turned out the Parliament with bayonets (January 1906).

The emperor's ultimate weapon, however, was the threat of universal and secret suffrage. The mere announcement of his intent to introduce electoral reform struck terror in the hearts of the Magyar gentry. It meant the end of their exploitation of the Magyar peasantry and the subject peoples. They quickly capitulated on the army issue, and Franz Joseph rewarded them by abandoning suffrage reform. In 1910, the Liberal party, reorganized as the Party of National Work, regained control of the chamber amid turbulent scenes; one prime minister was injured in the chamber by flying objects and another fought several saber duels against his critics. Both Dualism and Magyar domination had been saved—but not for long.

TURKEY AND THE BALKAN STATES

Decline of the Ottoman Empire   Earlier it has been shown how the process of internal decay, national revolt, and foreign intervention compelled the Ottoman Empire to grant autonomy to Serbia and Montenegro (1829), independence to Greece (1829), and near independence to the Danubian Principalities of Rumania (1856). In July 1875, a new series of revolts and interventions began with a rebellion of the Slavs in Bosnia and Herzegovina, followed a year later by an uprising of Bulgarians. The rebels found support in Serbia and Montenegro who declared war against Turkey. But the Turks soon defeated the Serbs and Montenegrins and put down the Bulgarians. National and religious fanaticism combined to give the struggle a shocking brutality on both sides.

The whole of Europe was aroused by these events. But the Russians were particularly affected, for the rebel peoples were all Slavic. As shown in the previous chapter, Pan-Slavism and self-interest led Russia in 1877 to declare war on Turkey. By January 1878 the tsarist forces, after overcoming the valiant resistance of the Turks at Plevna, were within reach of Constantinople, and the creation of a large Bulgarian state extending from the Danube River to the Aegean Sea and the Albanian mountains, precipitated a major European crisis. At the Congress of Berlin (1878), Russia was compelled to accept a greatly reduced Bulgaria divided into two segments: Bulgaria proper to be fully autonomous, and Eastern Rumelia to be semi-autonomous. In addition, Serbia, Montenegro, and Rumania became independent states; Britain received the island of Cyprus, Austria the right to administer Bosnia and Herzegovina, and France the right to occupy Tunis.

Still, the process of disintegration continued. In 1882, British troops occupied Egypt, still nominally part of the Ottoman Empire, and established a British protectorate. Three years later the Bulgarians of Eastern Rumelia expelled their Turkish governor and joined with Bulgaria proper in a single

THE NATIONALITIES OF THE BALKANS 1878

Vienna

Danube R.

Budapest

H U N G A R Y

BUKOVINA

Dniester R.

BESSARABIA

Jassy

Pruth R.

Kishinev

MOLDAVIA

TRANSYLVANIA

Kronstadt

Galatz

Drave R.

Save R.

Morava R.

WALLACHIA

R U M A N I A

DOBRUJA

Constantsa

Belgrade

BOSNIA

Sarajevo

DALMATIA

HERZE-GOVINA

NOVIPAZAR

MONTE-NEGRO

Cattaro

SERBIA

Nish

Danube R.

Bucharest

BLACK SEA

Varna

B U L G A R I A

Sofia (EASTERN RUMELIA)

Burgas

Philippopolis

ADRIATIC SEA

ALBANIA

Skoplje

T U R K E Y

Adrianople

Constantinople

ITALY

Monastir

MACEDONIA

Salonika

Brusa

Dardanelles

ASIA MINOR

Smyrna

IONIAN SEA

IONIAN ISLANDS

Larissa

G R E E C E

Patras

Athens

AEGEAN SEA

RHODES

CRETE

Rumanians
Bulgarians
Croats and Serbs
Albanians
Greeks
Turks

0   300
Miles

MEDITERRANEAN SEA

state. In 1894 the Armenians rebelled, but were brutally slaughtered and suppressed. Greece attacked Turkey in 1896 in support of a rebellion on the island of Crete. Although the Turks triumphed, they were halted by the European powers, who forced the sultan to make Crete autonomous.

Turkey's weakness arose from the fact that it was still a primitive land with a sparse population depending upon a backward agriculture. The government was still absolute, headed by a Sultan who was at the same time a Moslem religious leader. Although Sultan Abdul Hamid II (1876–1909) began his rule by promulgating a constitution, it was soon suspended and remained a dead letter. Later in his reign, economic change came to Turkey. By 1908, there were 4,400 miles of railway track, three-quarters of which were in Asiatic Turkey. Constantinople became a crossroad for railway traffic between Europe and the Persian gulf. Economic change and the struggle against Balkan nationalists produced among the Turks themselves a national resurgence accompanied by revolutionary unrest. It will be seen how this movement culminated in a revolution in 1908, which overthrew Abdul Hamid and began the construction of modern Turkey.

Greece The Bavarian prince who ascended the throne of Greece as Otto I (1832–1862) never succeeded in understanding the country he had chosen to rule. He and his Bavarian advisers insisted on imposing a centralized and bureaucratized government upon a people whose whole tradition was democratic and opposed to central authority. Even under the Turks they had enjoyed a high degree of local self-government. The result was an insurrection in 1843 which forced Otto to desist. But thereafter he established an elaborate constitution and parliamentary government, which made little sense in a country of peasants and fishermen with a thinly developed merchant class. The king's foreign policy was also unsuccessful. In 1854, during the Russian attack on Turkey which launched the Crimean War, he attempted to detach Greek-inhabited Thessaly, Epirus, and Macedonia from the Ottoman Empire. But the western powers opposed him and occupied the port of Piraeus in order to halt the Greek action. In 1862, fresh insurrections forced Otto to flee the country.

King George I (1863–1913), a Danish prince, was more successful. He had the good fortune to arrive in Athens with a British commitment to surrender to Greece the Ionian Islands, a British protectorate since 1815. One of his first acts was to revise the constitution, introducing universal male suffrage and a unicameral legislature. Since the deputies were salaried, this was one of the most democratic constitutions of the age. But the government was marked by extreme ministerial instability, some corruption, and financial crises arising from excessive armaments, public works, and social reforms.

In 1881, the demand for Greek unity made some progress when, as a result of the earlier Congress of Berlin, Turkey surrendered most of Thessaly and a third of Epirus. But the Greeks of Macedonia were still under Ottoman rule. During the Bulgarian disturbances of 1885–1886 the Greeks were restrained from attacking Turkey by the great powers, but ten years later, at the time of the Cretan uprising, they finally went to war. As we have seen, the Greeks were saved only by the intervention of the powers. Another consequence was financial insolvency, which led in 1898 to the creation of an international commission to manage Greek finances. Yet the crisis did produce a talented leader in Eleutherios Venizelos, who after 1910 became prime minister and brought about the governmental and military reforms that enabled Greece to meet the crisis of the Balkan wars in 1912–1913.

Serbia Although it was the first of the Balkan states to gain autonomy from the Ottoman Empire, Serbia was not legally independent until 1878. A country of impoverished and illiterate peasants, it lacked the foundation for a progressive government. Serbian politics, furthermore, were dominated for generations by a feud between the Karageorge family, which had begun the revolt against the Turks, and the Obrenovich family, which had brought it to a successful conclusion. The struggle between these rival dynasties and their partisans was marked by repeated coups, the promulgation and abrogation of constitutions, insurrection, and assassination, and foreign intervention.

The unification of Italy convinced many Serb nationalists that Serbia must become the Piedmont of the Balkans, uniting all southern Slavs under her rule. But the wars fought to this end by Prince Milan Obrenovich (1868–1889) against Turkey in 1876 and Bulgaria in 1885 only demonstrated the weakness of Serbia. Serbia was saved in the former case by Russian intervention and in the latter by Austrian intervention. Angered by Russia's desertion of Serbia for Bulgaria in 1878, Prince Milan placed his country under Austrian protection in a secret alliance of 1881; and, with Habsburg approval, assumed the title of king in 1882. Yet this policy was increasingly unpopular with those Serb nationalists who lusted for Bosnia, Herzegovina, and Croatia.

Milan's successor, Alexander I (1889–1903) heightened public discontent by his authoritarian actions, his marriage to an ambitious woman of unsavory reputation, and the favors he bestowed upon relatives. In 1903 the pro-Russian faction triumphed when Alexander, his wife, and fifty supporters and relatives were brutally murdered in Belgrade. Peter I (1903–1921) of the Karageorge dynasty ascended the throne. He was an able monarch who dedicated himself to internal reconstruction, but his son, Prince Alexander, was heavily involved with the secret societies that were conspiring against Austria-Hungary, one of which, the Black Hand, succeeded in murdering the Habsburg Archduke Franz Ferdinand at Sarajevo in 1914.

Rumania Repeated Russian interventions had established the autonomy of the Danubian principalities of Moldavia and Wallachia under a Russian protectorate. But the Crimean War removed them from the Russian sphere and the great powers agreed that they were to have separate governments loosely joined by a central commission possessing some legislative power.

The Rumanians, however, took matters into their own hands by electing a common ruler in 1859, Colonel Alexander Cuza. In 1862, the two states were fused under the title Rumania. Cuza soon ran into difficulties with the feudal landlords by sponsoring a land reform for the benefit of the peasants. In 1866, he was kidnapped, forced to abdicate, and replaced by Prince Charles of Hohenzollern-Sigmaringen, a relative of King William I of Prussia.

As Carol I (1866–1914), this prince was blessed with a long reign. One of his first acts was to promulgate a constitution on the Belgian model with

Coronation of King Ferdinand I of Rumania in 1914. Liberation of Balkan peoples from Turkish rule led to the creation of several new dynasties. With pomp and circumstance they hoped to impress the masses and stabilize social and political conditions. (The Bettmann Archive.)

a bicameral legislature, a politically responsible cabinet, and a three-class suffrage system like the Prussian. During the following decades, Rumania prospered economically. The introduction of farm machinery and construction of railways made possible the export of cereal crops from the Rumanian plains to the rest of Europe. But Rumania also possessed important mineral resources, particularly oil and coal, which were developed with the aid of foreign capital. By 1914, her economy was the most advanced of all Balkan countries. But her largest social class, the peasants, did not share equally in this growing prosperity; and 1907 saw a peasant uprising, the suppression of which required 140,000 troops. A virulent, sometimes violent, antisemitism was one of the by-products of this struggle, for wealthy landlords sought to deflect the hatred of the peasants against the town-dwelling Jews, many of whom were successful traders and money lenders.

Like the Greeks and Serbs, the Rumanians also had their national irredenta. Millions of Rumanians lived in Hungarian Transylvania, Austrian Bukovina, and Russian Bessarabia. Yet her geographical location and size compelled Rumania to lean upon either Russia or Austria-Hungary for support in international affairs. In 1877, under some duress, Carol joined the Russians in the attack on Turkey and succeeded at the Congress of Berlin in establishing the full independence of his country. This enabled him in 1881 to assume the title of king. Yet his German origin and fear of Russia inclined him toward the West and in 1883 he signed a secret treaty aligning Rumania with Germany and Austria-Hungary.

Bulgaria The divided Bulgaria that emerged from the Congress of Berlin was a disappointment both to Bulgarian nationalists and to the Russian government. But what followed was even more disappointing to St. Petersburg. Since the Congress had excluded members of the Russian ruling family from the Bulgarian throne, the tsar chose a German relative, Alexander of Battenberg, who had served as a volunteer in the war against the Turks and whose father had once been a Russian officer. Yet this favorite nephew, once he was installed in Sofia, began to act like a Bulgarian ruler rather than a Russian satrap. The Russians were furious when the Bulgarian government cooperated with Austrian rather than Russian financial interests in the construction of a trans-Balkan railroad. In 1883, furthermore, Prince Alexander dismissed the Russian officials who held posts in the Bulgarian government. Yet these actions were highly popular with the Bulgarian public. In 1885, the Prince, by uniting the two Bulgarian states and trouncing the Serbs on the battlefield, appeared to consolidate his position. Yet his days in power were already numbered.

The Bulgarian constitution of 1879 provided for ministerial responsibility to a parliament elected by universal and secret suffrage. But the political life of the country was extremely factious, and was made more so by Russian and Austrian intrigues. In 1886, a dissident group of army officers broke into the palace and, waving their pistols in Alexander's face, forced him to scribble out his abdication, after which he was expelled from the country. He returned later, but only to abdicate in a more formal way, preferring, he said, to leave "by the light of day, instead of being dragged like a malefactor through the streets in the dead of the night. . . ."

The new government was also much too nationalistic to bend to the Russian will. To the annoyance of Tsar Alexander III it chose another German prince, Ferdinand of Saxe-Coburg, as ruler. Although he went unrecognized by the European powers, Ferdinand I of Bulgaria (1887–1918) was clever and lucky enough to maintain himself, surviving endless intrigues and plots. In this, he was assisted by an able minister, Stefan Stambolov, who had been instrumental in Ferdinand's election and now became the virtual dictator of Bulgaria. The son of an inn keeper, Stambolov was vitally interested in railway construction, industrialization, and commercial growth. In the end, his authoritarian ways produced a host of enemies, who forced his resignation in 1894 and assassinated him in the next year.

Stambolov's departure led to reconciliation with Russia, enabling Ferdinand to gain the recognition of the European powers. In 1908, he broke the remaining legal bond to Turkey, proclaiming Bulgarian independence and assuming the title, Tsar. Like the other Balkan peoples, the Bulgarians had territorial claims based upon cultural affinity. After 1886, their chief ambition was to annex the Bulgarian population of Macedonia, which was still under Ottoman rule. Stambolov had sought to achieve this through peaceful negotiation with Turkey. After him, the agitation for violent action increased, and nationalist societies on Bulgarian soil plotted and repeatedly attempted revolution in Macedonia. Later, it will be shown how Bulgaria and the other Balkan states, eager for national unity and territorial growth, combined against Turkey in 1912 and, after defeating her, fought each other over the division of the spoils. By 1914, the Balkan region was a tinder box of national hatreds which only wanted a spark to set all Europe ablaze.

FURTHER READING

For a list of general works on German and Austrian history see the notes to Part XIII, Chapter 4. W. H. Dawson, *The German Empire, 1867–1914*, 2 vols. (1926–1936), is somewhat dated. W. H. Simon, ed., *Germany in the Age of Bismarck* (1968), contains a long essay by the editor and important documents. A classic study on domestic politics is A. Rosenberg, * *Imperial Germany* (1964). The era of the 1890's is described by J. C. G. Röhl, *Germany Without Bismarck* (1968). Important studies of individual figures are N. Rich, *Friedrich von Holstein*, 2 vols. (1965); G. O. Kent, *Arnim and Bismarck* (1968); K. Epstein, *Erzberger and the Dilemma of German Democracy* (1959); L. Cecil, *Albert Ballin, Business and Politics in Imperial Germany, 1888–1918* (1967); and A. Dorpalen, *Heinrich von Treitschke* (1957).

*Books available in paperback edition are marked with an asterisk.

Good general histories on Austria are A. J. May, *The Habsburg Monarchy, 1867–1914* (1951); and E. Crankshaw, * *The Fall of the House of Habsburg* (1963). The older work by E. Glaise von Horstenau, *The Collapse of the Austro-Hungarian Empire* (1930), still has merit. On the nationalities problem in the empire see R. Kann, *The Multinational Empire,* 2 vols (1950). For the subject nations, see C. A. Macartney, *Hungary* (1963); S. H. Thomson, *Czechoslovakia in European History* (2nd ed., 1953); and the works of R. W. Seton-Watson, *Radical Problems in Hungary* (1908), *History of the Czechs and Slovaks* (1943), and *The South Slav Question and the Habsburg Monarchy* (1911).

On Turkey and the Balkans, see L. Stavrianos, *The Balkans since 1453* (1958); and F. Schevill and W. Gewehr, *The History of the Balkan Peninsula* (2nd ed., 1933). W. L. Langer, *European Alliances and Alignments* (2nd ed., 1950), contains much domestic as well as diplomatic history. Works on individual Balkan countries have been written by E. S. Forster on Greece (2nd ed., 1946); R. W. Seton-Watson on Rumania (1934), T. W. Riker on Rumania (1931); C. E. Black on Bulgaria (1943), and B. Lewis on Turkey (1961, 1969).

PART XV

The late nineteenth century was the grand age of European domination over most of the rest of the world. European technology and organization created power, and European states used their material superiority to carve out political and economic empires over the greater part of Africa and Asia.

Expansion was an integral part of European history in this period, but its effects were even more fundamental in the other continents. Here the protagonists of modern Europe encountered many millions of people who had created unique civilizations of their own, had made indispensable contributions to human development in earlier times, and in some cases were proud bearers of historical and cultural traditions that antedated those of Europe. Hence the modern world cannot be understood without studying the modern evolution of Asia and Africa in their increasingly close interaction with modern Europe.

Asia is a western concept. It is an elastic idea expanded and contracted through many centuries and now holding world-wide acceptance. It has no intrinsic worth, nor has it been precisely defined. It has been an arbitrary label for that part of the great land mass in the eastern hemisphere which is neither Europe nor Africa. Yet, in terms of marginality, size, and populations, Europe has been a peninsular projection of Asia as much as have either India or China. Differences in race, language, religion, and history between the subcontinents of India and China have been as extreme as have been their separate differentness from Europe. Indeed, communication between these major projections of Asia have been so poor in past centuries that Asia could never have been viewed as a single cultural unity or entity to the degree that such was ever approached in Europe.

Viewed in this light, therefore, it is wiser to completely separate stories of those two great centers of civilization—the Indic and the Sinitic—with their surrounding culture basins in South Asia and East Asia respectively. Between these two vast circles of civilization lies a great cultural "fault" which, very much like that great geological fault that runs down the many spines of Burma, Thailand, Laos, and Malaysia plunging into the Seas to emerge in the islands of the Indonesian Archipelago, has produced an overlapping and rubbing together of these two great cultural traditions and of the peoples representing them. Thus, because Southeast Asia has been a larger frontier zone for the meeting of Indic and Sinitic energies, it has tended to lie in the side-waters of history, without a clear, single identity of its own.

Africa also is a western concept which, like that of Asia and Europe, had its origins in the civilization that was cradled within the Mediterranean Basin. Each concept was stretched from its original rather modest meaning as encompassing a region adjacent to the Mediterranean and as bearing a Roman (Latin) designation (e.g., Africa, Asia, and Europa). Later, distinctions were made between the littoral regions of Africa Minor, Asia Minor, and Europa Minor, and the much more vast hinterlands. In the case of Africa, the concept grew from a compass of what is now North Africa until it encompassed all of the lands south of the Sahara and the Savannah. Much of this intellectual process was founded upon European ignorance and reflects a growing awareness of what by the nineteenth century was called the "Dark Continent."

GOLD PENDANT-MASK FROM THE IVORY COAST. (Courtesy of The Museum of Primitive Art, New York.)

ASIA AND AFRICA
IN THE AGE OF
EUROPEAN EXPANSION

LEGACY OF THE PAST

The emergence of Asia and Africa in modern history coincides with the expansion of major maritime empires from Europe. The legacies of this process, this expansion of power and influence from the West into Africa and Asia—whether viewed as mercantile, missionary, or military in character; or whether seen as a much more complex and comprehensive movement embracing all of these characteristics and much more—can be seen in the patterns of global trade and world markets which were developed; in the formation of modern political

The Procession of Five Nations. This Japanese woodcut shows five foreign nations identified by their flags—the United States, Britain, France, Russia, and the Netherlands—taking part in a ceremony in Toyko. (Courtesy of the Trustees of the British Museum.)

structures, especially of nation-states; and in the cultural transformation, whether in gradual steps or by rapid strides, by which ancient nonwestern societies were integrated and revolutionized. But most important of all, these changes were but simple manifestations of an even wider, more profound process by which the whole world and all its people began to draw together into a larger, single world society, or, at least, into a vast system of increasingly interdependent peoples.

MAJOR EVENTS IN ASIA, 1500-1900

1500—

Arrival of Vasco da Gama at Calicut (1498)

Capture of Malacca by Portuguese (1511)
First Battle of Panipat—Mughal victory (1526)

1550—

Accession of Akbar to Mughal throne (1556)
Francis Xavier in Japan (1549)
Portuguese settlement in Macao (1543–1557)
Japanese invasion of Korea (1592–1598)

1600—

Charter of English East India Company (1600); Dutch Company (1602)
Matteo Ricci in Peking (1601)
Commencement of rule by Tokugawa Shogunate in Japan (1603)
Closure of Japan to foreigners (1638)
Founding of Madras (1639)
Dutch capture of Malacca (1641)
Establishment of Ch'ing (Manchu) Dynasty (1644)

1650—

Sacking of Surat by Marathas under Shivaji (1664)
Reign of K'ang Hsi (1661–1722)
Opening of Canton and other Chinese ports to trade (1685)
Treaty of Nerchinsk (1689)
Bombay (1668) and Calcutta (1690) founded by British
Fall of Bijapur and Golconda to Mughals (1686–1687)

1700—

Death of Mughal Emperor, Aurangzeb (1707)
Reign of Ch'ien Lung (1736–1796)
Sack of Delhi by Nadir Shah of Persia (1739)
First Dutch-Japanese dictionary published (1745)

1750—

Carnatic Wars in India (1744–1761)
Overseas trade limited to Canton (1757)
Battles of Plassey (1757)
Defeat of Marathas at Panipat (1761)
Fall of Pondicherry (1761)
Grant of Bengal Diwani (1765)

1780—

Pitt's India Act (1784)
Acquisition of Penang by English East India Company (1786)
Defeat of Burmese by Thai at Ayuthia (1787)
Lord Macartney's embassy to Peking (1793)
Capture of Dutch Malacca (1795)
Fall of Mysore and death of Tipu Sultan (1799)

1800—

Conquest of Java by East India Company of Britain (1811)
Restoration of Java and Indies to the Dutch (1816)
Final defeat of Marathas (1818)
Founding of Singapore by Sir Stamford Raffles (1819)

1820—

Anglo-Dutch Treaty exchanging possessions in Malaya and Sumatra (1824)
Burmese attack on Indian Empire (1826)

1840–
    First Indo-Afghan War (1839–1842)
    First Anglo-Chinese or "Opium" War (1839–1842)
    Treaty of Nanking (1842)
    Founding of Hong Kong (1842)
    James Brooke established Raja in Sarawak, Brunei, and Borneo (1842–1848)
1850–
    Taiping Rebellion in China (1851–1865)
    Visit of Commodore Perry to Japan (1853–1854)
    Second Indo-Burmese War (1856)
    Second Anglo-Chinese War (1856–1860)
    The Great Rebellion or Mutiny of India (1857)
    Queen's Proclamation as Empress of India (1858)
    Russian frontier on Amur River established (1858)
1860– Treaties of Peking (1860); Vladivostok founded (1860)
    Conquest of Indo-China by France (1862–1882)
    Meiji Restoration; End of Tokugawa Shogunate in Japan (1868)
    Sino-American Treaty (admitting Chinese to U.S.) (1868)
    Opening of the Suez Canal (1869)
1870– Telegraph to Singapore (1870)
    First treaty between Britain and a Malay state—Pangkor Engagement (1873–
        1874)
    First Chinese ambassador to Britain (1877)
    Korea made an independent kingdom after conquest by Japan (1876)
    Satsuma Rebellion (1877)
1880–
    Sinkiang ceded to Russia (1881)
    Japanese position over Ryukyus recognised by China (1881)
    U.S.–Korean Treaty (1882)
    Ilbert Bill controversy in India (1883)
    Sino-Japanese clash in Korea (1884)
    Local self-government acts in India (1884)
    Founding of the Indian National Congress (1885)
    Final annexation of upper Burma to Indian Empire (1885–1886)
    Japanese constitution proclaimed (1889)
1890– Construction of Trans-Siberian railway begun (1890)
    Second Indian Councils Act (1892)
    Sino-Japanese War (1894–1895)
    Treaty for the Federated Malay States (1895–1896)
    Philippine revolt against Spain (1896)
    Philippines ceded to United States by Spain (1898)
    Open Door Policy proclaimed by United States (1899)
    Boxer Uprising in China (1899–1901)

MAJOR EVENTS IN AFRICA, 1799-1900

1800–   Fulani jihad in Nigeria (1799–1801)
            Napoleon leaves Egypt (1801)
            Mohammed Ali becomes governor of Egypt (1805)
            Mungo Park explores Niger (1805)
            Sierra Leone made British crown colony (1807)
            Britain abolishes slave trade (1807)

1810–

            France abolishes slave trade (1815)
            Rise of Shaka (1818–1828)

1820–   Conquest of Sudan by Egypt (1820–1828)
            Liberia established (1822)
            Caillé reaches Timbuktu (1827)

1830–   France takes Algiers (1830)
            Richard Lander explores Niger (1830–1834)
            Great Trek of Boers (1835–1837)

1840–   Seyyid Said in Zanzibar (1840)
            French defeat resistance in Algeria (1847)
            Liberia becomes republic (1847)

1850–

            Livingstone discovers Victoria Falls (1853–1856)
            Faidherbe governor of Senegal (1854–1865)
            Burton and Speke at Victoria Nyanza (1858–1859)

1860–

            British take Lagos (1861)
            Discovery of diamonds in South Africa (1867)
            Opening of Suez Canal (1869)

1870–

            Zanzibar slave mart closes (1873)
            De Brazza explores lower Congo (1875)
            Leopold II begins activity in Congo (1876)
            George Goldie in Nigeria (1879)

1880–   Stanley explorations (1879–1884)

            France occupies Tunisia (1881)
            Britain occupies Egypt (1882)
            Germans in Togo and Cameroun (1884)
            Berlin Conference (1884–1885)
            Mahdi defeats Gordon (1885)
            Gold discovered in South Africa (1886)
            Rhodes opens up Rhodesia (1889–1891)

1890–

            Fall of Timbuktu (1892)
            Guinea and Ivory Coast to French (1893)
            Conquest of Madagascar (1894)
            Italy defeated at Battle of Adowa, Ethiopia (1896)
            Reconquest of Sudan and Fashoda incident (1896–1898)
            French defeat Samori (1898)

1 European Imperialism, 1871-1914

One of the most striking expressions of the dynamic energy and power of Europe in the latter decades of the nineteenth century was its attempt to dominate most of the nonwestern world. During the years 1875–1900, almost all of Africa and a large portion of the Far East were staked out and annexed by the leading European states. This expansion was all the more extraordinary because the great colonial empires of the early modern age—those of Britain, France, Spain, and Portugal—had lost their finest possessions before or during the Napoleonic wars, the most important colonies breaking away from the mother countries to become independent nations. The only large trans-oceanic empires in existence during the half-century after 1815 were those of Britain and Holland. Even in Great Britain there was considerable protest against colonialism by the so-called "Little Englanders" who insisted that the government abandon notions of further territorial expansion overseas. The Russian empire alone had never ceased its policy of territorial annexation, but the gigantic tsarist domain was a direct geographic extension of the Russian homeland across the Eurasian continent, rather than an overseas empire.

The new imperialism of the late nineteenth century was closely related to the industrialization of Europe and to the reorganization of the state system in the 1860's. France had acquired a number of far-flung possessions during the Second Empire; (see pp. 1293–95) and by the 1880's, all the major powers vied in the contest of expansion. The fever of colonialism was so extreme that, save for the barrier of the Monroe Doctrine and the British Navy, it might even have led to the re-introduction of European imperialism in Latin America. Empire-building, regardless of the expense or danger involved, had now become the goal of any European government that wanted to keep up with the times. By the 1890's, this feeling had spread across the oceans to Japan and the United States, where it helped to create the bellicose mood of the Sino-Japanese, Spanish-American and Russo-Japanese Wars during the years 1894–1905.

Political Motivations for Imperial Expansion   The reasons behind this almost demonic drive for imperial control were complex, but the most important general motivation was political. After 1870 international affairs were in an increasingly anxious condition, for the anarchy of the independent state-system was mounting steadily and it was now clear that only might could prevail and make itself respected. There was no security in law or moral principle, but only in the naked fact of power. Colonies gave prestige, and offered potential increase in military and economic strength. This was one way of getting or staying ahead in the power race.

By the mid-nineteenth century, Great Britain had obtained complete control over the sub-continent of India, as well as a position of commercial hegemony in China and much of western and southern Africa. Although it had not originally been the goal of the British government to annex more territory in Africa and southern Asia, this was eventually done in order to secure Britain's vast naval and commercial routes from the encroachments of other powers. In turn, a rival government like that of France felt impelled to establish large colonial protectorates to increase its international power and offset the gains of Britain. Latecomers like Germany and Italy then endeavored to catch up with both Britain and France. In this fashion, the apprehension, ambition, and emulation of the major powers interacted to create a rising spiral of conquest and annexation.

The decisions for imperial expansion were in the great majority of cases made solely on the personal and professional calculations of the government officials involved. Contrary to what has sometimes been asserted, the governments of the major imperial powers were rarely urged on by public pressure during the heyday of expansion (1880–1900). After colonies and protectorates had been acquired, they were a great source of national pride for the peoples of the imperial powers, and the threat of war involved in imperial competition often aroused displays of patriotic bellicosity, but there were few organized public groups demanding a forward policy before 1900.

Rarely, however, was imperialism unpopular among the citizenry of the great powers. By the turn of the century, after territorial expansion had nearly reached its limit, the supposed glories of imperialism had made a considerable impact on the public mind. This was especially the case in Germany, whose late entry into the race frustrated its chance for major acquisitions. Military leaders were frequently attracted to colonial expansion, because this provided an opportunity to win combat laurels in time of peace in Europe. The popular press did its best to encourage these feelings by detailed accounts, both glamorous and gory, of colonial wars with the natives. Even hard-bitten trade-union chiefs in Germany, England and France could not entirely resist the emotional lure. There is no indication that the bulk of the lower classes in imperialist countries regarded the expense and energy invested in such enterprise as a capitalist fraud. The argument was becoming accepted that without international dominion no west European state could survive as a great power. Patriotic feeling prompted most people to cheer their nation's flag and army onward.

The Religious-Humanitarian Motivation A sense of moral responsibility for benighted peoples—in Britain often termed the "White Man's Burden"—also helped to motivate imperialism, at least among more idealistic individuals. Missionaries played an important role in this, and it was a missionary, David Livingstone, whose "discovery" by the explorer Stanley in 1871 first publicized the colonial regions in the popular press. Desire to convert the heathen and spread the gospel had been a basic factor in European expansion from the very beginning. The Bible societies and new missionary groups of the late eighteenth and nineteenth centuries revived this feeling. Above all, the anti-slavery movement, supported by Christians and humanitarians, was a powerful force in involving such countries as Britain and France in the unsettled portions of Africa. This was one of the activities of Livingstone, and found its counterpart in other groups, especially the French Catholic missions. Later on, however, the efforts of missionaries were sometimes used by a country like Germany as a fraudulent excuse for extending "protection" and annexing territory.

Economic Imperialism As the international division of labor grew, Europe relied increasingly on distant lands to provide certain necessary items of consumption as well as exotic luxury articles. Material for even such basic commodities as soap, candles, cables, and shirts came from overseas. There was thus a great incentive for European investment to move directly into raw-material-producing areas, taking over and transforming the native economy. Large surpluses of capital were being accumulated by the bankers and factory owners of western society, and they often found that a higher rate of profit might be obtained in less advanced lands. British and French bankers, for example, loaned money to Near Eastern potentates, bought the bond issues of distant governments, and even went on to form companies of their own to build railroads, start mines, or begin street car and municipal utility systems in other countries. Special plantations and processing plants were built, so as to enable colonies in Africa and south Asia to serve European needs directly. Investment of capital in backward areas soon became a multi-million-dollar business, in which all the industrial nations participated to some extent, for the opportunities were too favorable to pass up. By 1914 the foreign investments of Great Britain totaled twenty billion dollars, those of France reached nine billion, and those of Germany amounted to six billion. These funds represented one-fourth the total wealth of Great Britain and one-sixth that of France.

The result was a kind of economic imperialism whereby European finance dominated or strongly influenced the economic activity of much of the rest of the world. Such economic imperialism should not, however, be confused with colonial expansion. The two phenomena frequently did not coincide geographically; most of the capital British, French, and German investors sent abroad was not specifically invested within their nations' respective empires. Businessmen were not interested in the deserts of

Bultfontein Diamond Mine in South Africa, 1888. Gold and diamonds became the main attraction for further British economic and colonial penetration in South Africa in the 1880's and 90's, and were an indirect cause of the Boer War of 1899–1902. This photo shows some of the external apparatus involved in diamond mining. (Radio Times Hulton Picture Library.)

southwest Africa or in barren Pacific islands, even though the latter might be under their government's domination. Instead, independent countries like Turkey, Egypt, Mexico, Argentina, or even Russia offered much more attractive economic possibilities.

The exaggerated notion that such economic motives were the main cause of colonial expansion was first suggested by the British economist J. A. Hobson (1858–1940) in 1902, then repeated with a different twist in 1916 by the Russian Communist leader, Lenin. The latter's essay, "Imperialism, the Highest Stage of Capitalism," claimed that capitalism led to imperialism because, as the capitalist system concentrated wealth in ever-fewer hands, it exhausted the possibility of investment at home and was compelled to invest abroad. Whereas Hobson maintained that the elevation of working-class incomes would cure imperialism by increasing domestic consumption and thus open new areas of investment within the home country, Lenin argued that capitalists would never be persuaded to take this course and that the only cure for imperialism was the destruction of capitalism.

Hobson himself later admitted that the importance of economic motivation in colonial expansion had been exaggerated, and eschewed the critique offered by Lenin. There are at least two primary reasons why the Leninist thesis is incorrect: First, the grand era of colonial expansion in no way coincided with a period of impoverishment for the European working classes, but instead paralleled a fairly steady rise in their living standards.

Capitalists invested abroad not because they had milked Europe dry, but simply because even more money could be made elsewhere. Second, as previously mentioned, economic imperialism *per se* and political domination or colonization are two different things. The former is financial and indirect; the latter is military and political in character, resulting in direct control.

Where economic factors were influential in colonial expansion, they were but one aspect of a problem in which political or military concerns were equally significant. It is true, for example, that the raising of tariff barriers in Europe provided incentive for overseas territorial expansion, but this was because nationalists began to wonder if their country would be able to produce enough all by itself in case of war. Many imperialists stressed the notion that a large colonial empire would provide the mother country with the economic strength needed for self-sufficiency. Furthermore, much of the territory acquired, especially in Africa, was mere wasteland, uninhabited or uninhabitable. Such colonies cost money to administer, but offered little immediate reward. Their price could be justified only on the basis of national pride and the competition for power with other states.

COLONIAL EMPIRES AT THE TURN OF THE CENTURY

By the end of the nineteenth century, there were six significant overseas empires: those of Great Britain, France, Holland, Portugal, Germany, and Italy. The story of their expansion into Africa and Asia is told in Chapters 2 through 5. The nature of these empires varied a good deal, and the pattern of government employed by the imperial powers also differed from one state to another. In order to understand the differences, it will be helpful to survey the empires separately, as they existed about the year 1900.

The British Empire By far the largest, wealthiest, and most important of empires was that of Great Britain, which spanned the whole world and included territory on every continent, with a total population of approximately 600 million, or nearly one-quarter of the human race. There were enormous differences in development among parts of the empire. At the head stood the self-governing dominions—Canada; Australia; New Zealand; and, after 1909, South Africa. The majority of the population in all these lands, save South Africa, was white, mainly Anglo-Saxon. English emigrants to these areas who brought the skills and training of their countrymen at home, and so were given the right of self-government, beginning with Canada in 1867.

The keystone of Britain's Afro-Asian empire was the subcontinent of India. Not all of it was under direct British rule, but a single British administration coordinated Indian affairs on the highest level. Economic relations were highly developed and quite profitable to Britain. This was not so much the case with some of the extensive British domains in Africa. Considerable diversity existed there. Several of the more developed lands, beginning with Egypt, were held as "protectorates," and left to some extent under the subordinate government of their own leaders. Other colonies were taken

Cecil Rhodes in Camp. Governor of the British Cape Colony in South Africa, founder of Rhodesia, and unequaled promoter of British imperial expansion in Africa, Rhodes was one of the outstanding individual catalysts of late nineteenth-century colonialism. (National Archives of Rhodesia.)

over and controlled directly by British administration; and in a few regions, such as Kenya, English farmers began to move in as settlers.

In the Far East and West Indies, Britain held many islands and vantage points for either commercial or strategic use. Among these were such valued possessions as Malaya and Hong Kong in the Far East, and lesser holdings such as Jamaica in the West Indies. Throughout this vast empire a relatively small cadre of well-trained, devoted colonial administrators were on duty to bring British standards of government and justice to a broad sector of the people with whom they dealt. Despite the size and complexity of the empire, the British colonial system was on the whole the fairest and most efficient in the world.

The French Empire France's Third Republic ruled the second largest colonial empire, centered mainly in the great bulge of western Africa. There were three main sectors of French holdings: the Arab lands of northwest Africa, the desert and tropical regions of French West and Northwest Africa, and the Far Eastern territory of French Indo-China. Algeria was elevated to the status of an integral part of France, Indo-China was controlled on the indirect protectorate principle, and some of the African colonies were also governed indirectly through native potentates.

In theory, French colonial policy was directed toward the goal of "assimilation," which meant raising the native population to the level of French citizens through education and association. In practice, comparatively little was done to achieve this aim, and "assimilation" never went beyond a small native elite. Indo-China became quite profitable for some French investors, but aside from Algeria, few French colonial areas were suitable for European immigration. The entire empire absorbed only about thirteen percent of

France's exports. French tropical Africa, in particular, remained a great undeveloped region superintended by a small colonial staff.

The Smaller Empires Holland added very little to its empire in the nineteenth century, but concentrated on developing its old possessions, primarily the island archipelago of the Dutch East Indies. Colonial administration was reorganized and tightened, operating on an authoritarian and paternalistic principle. The main concern was to return handsome profits from the Indonesian economy. In the long run, the Dutch had less influence on Indonesian society than had the French or British on many of the colonial peoples whom they governed.

In the fifteenth century, Portugal had been the first European overseas colonial power. In the nineteenth century, Portuguese colonialism concentrated on extending control inland from her traditional coastal territories in southwest and southeast Africa, to form the two large colonies of Angola and Mozambique. In addition, the Portuguese still held small pieces of territory in south and southeast Asia. Portuguese policy may in some respects have been slightly less racist than that of other powers, but it was strongly authoritarian and paternalistic. Portugal long lacked the resources to develop its own territories, whose expenses were normally more than the profit derived from them.

The new Italian and German empires had in common the fact that both were of little concrete value. The strips of desert and jungle picked up around the coast of Africa by these two newly unified states were more of an economic burden than asset, in this regard resembling the African possessions of most other powers. The *raison d'être* of the German and Italian empires was prestige, though a few trading companies did make a profit from them. German colonial administration was direct and efficient, that of the Italians more indirect and less effective.

IMPERIALIST WARS AND GROWING FRUSTRATION, 1895–1905

The heyday of expansion was the last third of the nineteenth century, in which most of Africa and much remaining territory in Asia was divided up. By the 1890's, comparatively little territory remained, the competition was keener, and there was growing resistance from nonwestern society. The weaker and smaller powers of southwestern Europe—Spain, Italy, and Portugal—suffered humiliating frustrations and reverses. One of the major powers—Russia—lost a war in Asia, while a second—Britain—became bogged down for several years in a struggle in South Africa. Germany, which had mostly lost out in the territorial scramble, grew increasingly dissatisfied with its lack of imperial status, but found no opportunity by which to remedy it.

Portuguese expansionists hoped to unite Angola and Mozambique by means of a solid belt of Portuguese-controlled territory that would stretch all the way across the southern part of Africa. This was peremptorily vetoed by the British government in its "Ultimatum" of 1891. The dashing of Portuguese ambitions by the dominant power in southern Africa provoked in-

Japanese Artillerists Loading Siege Guns at the Siege of Port Arthur, Manchuria, 1905. The Russians were not prepared for the technological prowess displayed by the Japanese in handling modern weapons and military organization. Defeat in Manchuria was a stunning blow that led to political and social revolution in Russia. (Radio Times Hulton Picture Library.)

tense resentment within Portugal and led to a revolt against the government.

Five years later, Italy's attempt to move into Ethiopia was thwarted by a complete and humiliating defeat by the native Ethiopian forces at Adowa (1896). This brought down the strongest Italian government of the decade and quashed all expansionist efforts by Italy for the next fifteen years.

By that time, all that remained of the once vast Spanish empire were Cuba and Puerto Rico in the Caribbean, the Philippines and a few small island chains in the Pacific, and a few scattered possessions on the coast of Morocco. Cuba enjoyed a productive plantation economy but was the victim of gross misgovernment. Many of its inhabitants were eager for independence. The last great Cuban revolt began in 1895 and took the form of deadly, drawn-out guerrilla fighting. The Spanish army could dominate all the main areas of the island but was unable to crush resistance in the back country. Within three years, it lost 50,000 men, mainly to disease.

The issue was finally decided by the intervention of the United States in 1898. The American attack on Spain was in part the result of newspaper propaganda and the pressure of interests, but it reflected even more the restless energy of a dynamic country eager to make its influence felt in the world. The Americans were also motivated by a genuine desire to help the struggling Cubans attain their freedom. The American forces enjoyed overwhelming technological superiority, and it was all over within a few months.

Under the peace terms, Spain was forced to relinquish Cuba, Puerto Rico, and the Philippines. For the first time in more than four centuries, Spain had no empire. This required a bitter readjustment for the nation, and Spanish political sensibility did not fully recover from the psychological effects for half a century. Within seven years, from 1891 to 1898, all three of the smaller powers of southwestern Europe had met humiliating defeat or frustration overseas.

That the great powers might not necessarily be spared the fate of smaller states became clear within the next seven years. Between 1899 and 1902, the British government strained all its resources to win a contest for dominion in South Africa over the small population of Dutch Boer colonists. Russia suffered even more grievously from its war with Japan in 1904–1905, undergoing revolution at home and complete defeat at the hands of an oriental power in Manchuria. It was a bitter and crushing end to tsarist ambition in the Far East.

The Emergence of Nonwestern Nationalist Movements Soon after 1900, European imperialist expansion began to come to a virtual standstill. Not only was there little territory left to seize, but any further advance was likely to be fraught with grave conflict between the imperial powers themselves, for the major powers were becoming firmly established in rival alliances.

Conversely, nonwestern peoples were more active and rebellious than in earlier decades. Throughout Asia, there was a rising tide of discontent. Japan's victory over Russia gave hope to young rebels in such lands as Persia, China, India, the East Indies, and even Turkey.

Japanese Warships Opening Fire against Russian Positions at Port Arthur, Manchuria, 1904. This Japanese drawing shows heavy ships of the new modern Japanese navy shelling Russian shore positions. Japan's stunning naval victories over Russia in 1904–05 established her naval power in the western Pacific for 40 years, until finally defeated by the United States in 1945. (Radio Times Hulton Picture Library.)

Boer Defense Line outside Mafeking, 1900. The Boer War was one of the earliest prototypes of a twentieth-century "people's war" against colonial domination. Boer troops were composed of a citizens' militia such as these volunteers defending a Boer line outside Mafeking against the British advance. The effectiveness of popular resistance, together with the severe loss to the civilian population, both foreshadowed the character of anti-colonialist people's wars in a later generation. (Radio Times Hulton Picture Library.)

The nonwestern revolutionary movement of most immediate concern developed in the decadent Ottoman empire, which was falling apart under the pressure of Balkan nationalism and the power of more modern states. Young Turkish army officers had grown increasingly restive under the corrupt, backward, despotic rule of Abdul Hamid II (1876–1909). The most rebellious formed a secret society which called itself the "Young Turks," dedicated to a modernizing revolution in the Ottoman Empire. Their opportunity finally arrived in 1908, when they revolted and took over the weak Turkish government. The immediate effect of the "Young Turk" coup was to increase the empire's weakness and confusion, since the new regime lacked solid support and was unable to cope with foreign enemies. Nonetheless, the "Young Turk" movement marked a reversal of the trend of nineteenth-century Turkish history, for it was aimed at the modernization of Turkey and the reorganization of the empire. Not until after fifteen years of warfare with the Balkan states would Turkish revolutionaries be able to commence serious reform, and in that interval all the remnants of the Ottoman empire would be lost. Nevertheless, Turkey had begun to look ahead.

This was merely the most prominent of many expressions of nationalist rebellion and desire for sweeping reform or revolution among nonwestern peoples early in the twentieth century. Such stirrings were also present in Latin America, where a revolution wracked Mexico during the decade after 1910. The Manchu dynasty was overthrown by a native Chinese revolution in 1911. These nationalist revolts expressed not merely disgust with benighted and corrupt leadership at home, but were a radical rejection of European claims to superiority. From this time forward, the demands of colonial peoples swelled in intensity. Before revolts in Asia and Africa could achieve success, however, the European powers had to be seriously weakened by their own internal conflict. The sharp increase in hostile feeling between the European powers during the early twentieth century ultimately served among other things to reduce the power of Europe overseas.

FURTHER READING   The two classic critiques of modern European imperialism are J. A. Hobson, *Imperialism: a Study* (1902, 1948); and Lenin, *Imperialism, the Highest Stage of Capitalism* (1916, 1939). P. T. Moon, *Imperialism and World Politics* (1926), is a standard survey; and J. A. Schumpeter, *Imperialism and Social Classes* (1956), analyzes the social motivations.

English doctrines of imperialism are studies in A. P. Thornton, *The Imperial Idea and Its Enemies* (1959). On French and German imperialism, see Henri Brunschwig, *French Colonialism, 1871–1914* (1966); and M. E. Townsend, *The Rise and Fall of Germany's Colonial Empire, 1884–1918* (1930). B. H. Sumner, *Tsarism and Imperialism in the Far East and Middle East, 1880–1914* (1942), deals with Russian expansionism in Asia.

2 Integration of South Asia: The Indian Empire

Called a subcontinent, India[1] in fact possesses characteristics that normally define a continent. A peninsular projection from the great landmass of Eurasia as significant as either Europe or China, India is completely enclosed by the mountain ranges of the Kirthars and Sulaimans on the west, the Himalayas (and Karakorums) to the north, and Arakan Yoma on the east. The great northern mountain range stretches 1,500 miles from the Indus Gorge near the Hindu Kush to the Brahmaputra Gorge. Behind these mountains respectively are very dry deserts, high plateaus, or impenetrable rain forests. On both sides of the subcontinent, mountain chains run down to the sea—the Arabian Sea on the west and the Bay of Bengal on the east—which are in turn extensions of the Indian Ocean. Together, the mountains and seas separate the Indian subcontinent from other parts of Asia.

The historical importance of this geography can be found in the relative isolation and separate development of Indian civilization. A few mountain passes in the northwest, such as the famous Khyber and Bolan, have served as the main routes of entry into India both for large masses of migrating peoples and for invading armies. Other entrances, whether smaller passes or seaports, have until modern times been more important as commercial and cultural entrepots than as conduits for migration or conquest. When rulers on the northern plains of India have been strong, they have been able to hold the main mountain passes and to prevent invaders from entering India. Selucid Greeks and Bactrians were held back by the Mauryas (ca. 322–185 B.C.) and by the Sungas (185–180 B.C.). Similarly, the Turkish sultans of Delhi (1206–1290) held back Mongol hordes. When powers on the uplands of Afghanistan and Persia were strong—while they themselves have broken into the north—they have further helped to shield the subcontinent from invasions from Central Asia. Many warrior peoples have managed to invade India, however—the Aryans, Sythians, Greeks, Kushans, Parthians, Huns, and Turks. In 323 B.C. the forces of Alexander the Great subdued the

[1]Note: the geographical concept, not the present republic.

Punjab and marched down the Indus. Over seventeen hundred years later, in 1399, the horsemen of Tamerlane brought death and destruction to Delhi and North India. Yet, for all that, the whole subcontinent has never been overrun by a world power.

In demographic and cultural terms, the subcontinent contains over 2,000 separate communities, most of which neither intermarry nor interdine. These peoples speak at least sixteen major languages and hundreds of minor tongues and dialects. By processes of cultural history too complex to be detailed here, but related to conquest and migration over thousands of years, the civilization of India can be clearly divided between Aryan heartland of north India and Dravidian culture in south India. Not just Hindi (and Urdu), but all the main Indian languages from Gujarat to Bengal, are descended from the Aryan language, Sanskrit. (With Persian script and more Arabic words, Urdu is closely intertwined with Hindi.) Tamil lies at the heart of Dravidian culture in the south. While their oldest literature cannot rival the age of ancient Sanskrit, Dravidian peoples had reached an advanced level of civilization in India long before the coming of the Aryans (ca. 1700 B.C.); moreover, they seem to have been in commercial contact with ancient Mesopotamia and Egypt. (The Indus Valley civilization is thought to have been Dravidian.) Whatever the case, Aryans dominated the north, and Dravidians of the south seem to have remained relatively free of Sanskritic culture until after the reign of Ashoka Maurya (273–232 B.C.). It was Ashoka who sent missions to carry the doctrines of Gautama Buddha (567–487 B.C.) to far countries, most notably to Sri Lanka (Ceylon).

In short, migrations and conquests have brought many new peoples into north India. Often barbaric, culturally less sophisticated, but often possessing more advanced military skills, such peoples have, nonetheless, added enrichment and variety to Indian civilization. Among these, two movements stemmed from equally strong civilizations: the Hellenistic world of the Greeks (and Romans) and the Islamic world of the Arabs, Persians, and Turks (as early as 714 A.D., but mostly after 1000 A.D.). Commercial traffic at the time of the Greeks and during Muslim invasions, moving through seaports and mountain passes, was accompanied by movements of new, stimulating cultural influences. As many powerful ideas were carried out of India as into it by this means. Buddhist institutions, originating in India, could not survive resurgent Hindu competition and the later destructive forces of Islam. Nevertheless, Buddhist institutions not only spread to Tibet, Sri Lanka, and other countries of Southeast Asia, but also served to regenerate the already ancient civilizations of China and Japan. Commerce, conquest, and colonization from India into Southeast Asia was such that, in the West, the area later was referred to as "Greater India." Islam also moved eastward in this manner. Well before the Arab conquest of Sind (in 714) and long before the first Turkish raids, Arab merchants carried Islamic ideas to India. Many of our earliest views of India are records left by traders and travellers—Greeks, Arabs, and Chinese. Thus, the very geography of the subcontinent has served to limit kinds of contact and to preserve semi-

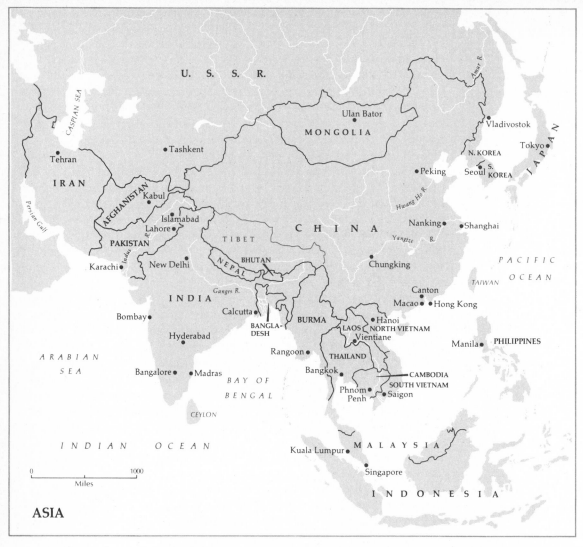

ASIA

isolation. Although there was sufficient cultural exchange between major civilizations to permit new outside influences to revitalize institutions within India, geography alone prevented India from ever being completely overrun (as happened to Europe, China, and Persia, whether by Sythians, Huns, or Mongols).

THE TRADITION OF FRAGMENTATION

India has never been one people either socially or culturally. Many separate societies and distinct communities were formed by the slow working of time, tradition, and ceaseless friction among increasing numbers of groups, whether ethnic or religious, dominant or subject (or slave). Some groups intermingled to form still other distinct communities. But most remained within tight social compartments, some remaining seemingly unchanged from prehistoric times. This "honeycombing" process over so many thousands of years has made India a fascinating ground for anthropological and archeological study. Evidence sifted out of archaeological diggings—from inscriptions on coins, metal plates, and stones, and from comparative analysis of texts and traditions, written and oral—serves to throw new light on this historic fragmentation. From such evidence, we can conclude that, by and large, the segmentation of social structures tended to prevent the formation of large-scale aggregations of political systems. Until modern times, therefore, large empires have been the exception rather than the rule in India.

Social Classes and Castes   Even before the classical age of the Mauryas, it seems clear that the many peoples in different parts of India were already divided into sharply defined social classes (*varnas*) and into countless castes (*jatis*).[2] Castes, hereditary communities separated by pollution rituals, did not permit their members to intermarry or to interdine with members of other castes. Separated from each other by the sacred and secret nature of their hereditary skills and by the separate customs, rituals, and values that accompanied their communal and occupational distinctions, castes gained an inner strength and tenacity which enabled them to survive for century after century. Family life within castes, especially those in upper classes, was bound by such strong ties that many ancient families have survived down to our day. According to Sanskritic tradition, society was divided into four proper classes or "colors" (*varna*), with all left-over peoples falling into a "fifth" or "colorless" category of outcastes and "untouchables." The highest *varna* was the Brahman. Brahmanical castes were responsible for priestly and scholarly functions. Brahmans preserved the sacred and learned traditions of Sanskritic civilization. Their civilization was founded more upon sacred rituals than upon commercial enterprise or political organization. Brahmans, like Latin priests of medieval Europe, possessed a universality in communication and style. They, more than any other class, gave cultural unity to the Indian subcontinent. No other class, not even warriors and merchants, had such a wide degree of mobility or travelled so far in their pilgrimages to sacred shrines. The warrior class (*Kshatriya*) and the merchant class (*Vaishiya*), although among the "twice-born" and hence elite communities, were more local and regional in their orientations and activities. *Shudras*, originally considered laboring, working people, counted for much less and were much more limited in what they could do. Lowest of all, however, were the *panchamas* ("fifths") or untouchables, whose function was to do the most menial forms of work. Peoples who had been conquered, enslaved, or who were from backward tribes fell into this lowest category.

THE EMERGENCE
OF EMPIRE

In the agrarian economy that was so central a feature of traditional life in India (at least into the late nineteenth century and even into the mid-

---

[2] *Arya* means "noble" as distinct from *dasya* or "servile." This distinction arose after Aryans became dominant in North India or *Aryavartha*, well before 1500 B.C.

twentieth century, in some parts), the village was the basic unit of government and politics. Products of all industry (agricultural or otherwise) were extracted from the primary producers (ànd their menial, landless laborers) by those who possessed the political and military strength to do so. Methods of extraction varied according to the strength and skill of the political, usually warrior, groups who did the extracting. Such extraction was usually limited, however, by the need to assure continued cultivation and production. Such was the design of political theory, as exemplified in such treatises as the famous *Arthasastra* (usually attributed to the astute Kautilya, the minister of Chandragupta Maurya), that claims of power would be, in our terms, practically "totalitarian." Such also was the strength of local resistance because of the social fragmentation, already mentioned, that royal authority of any sort or size was constantly undermined and "corrupted" by local influences. At times there could be so many tiny barriers to production and commerce erected by local forces that little more than subsistence production in villages could survive. A tendency toward political disintegration remained a persistent tradition in India.

Not until after the Punjab became a satrapy of the Persian empire and after the conquests of Alexander did the ideal of empire grow in India. Only twice, therefore, did imperial systems of significance develop; and then, under the Mauryas (322 to ca. 185 B.C.) and the Guptas (   ), this was confined largely to North India. Commencing again with the first incursions of the Turks in 1000 A.D. and culminating with the imperial expansion of the Mughals, from 1526 when Babar first led his small army onto the plains of Hindustan until the sacking of Delhi by Nadir Shah of Persia in 1739, the ideals and institutions of an all-encompassing imperial system gained strength. Attempts to bring all of India under one rule were often and repeatedly interrupted. Throughout the centuries, larger political structures that did develop failed to achieve enough stability to last more than a few generations. Despite their cultural brilliance, neither the Hindu nor Muslim dynastic systems perfected rules of succession that could ensure political stability and a smooth transfer of power from one generation to another. Thus, after the death of the last Great Mughal, Aurangzeb, in 1707, India began to witness yet another breakdown of political structures, accompanied by frequent episodes of chaos, rapine, and war. In many courts, life became degraded and social morality sank to depths. People ceased to be heirs of their own cultures and, indeed, some became strangers to their own traditions. In parts of the north, for example, illiterate Brahmans took to banditry and war.

THE COMING OF THE EUROPEANS

It was during the turbulence of the mid-eighteenth century that Europeans emerged as new forces to be reckoned with in the politics of south Asia. Contrary to most western texts, this emergence was not due to the overwhelming power and superiority of the West. Such an explanation is far too simple. What happened was neither sudden nor accidental, but the culmination of events beginning 250 years earlier.

In 1498, nearly thirty years before Babar brought the Mughals to power, a Portuguese fleet under Vasco da Gama rounded the Cape of Good Hope and reached Calicut. Armed with new technology that was beginning to revolutionize maritime shipping and navigation (size of ships, better sails, fire-power, instruments, maps and charts), it was possible for western Europeans to transform oceans from great barriers into grand highways. This new shipping made possible far less expensive handling of large cargos as well as more mobile and efficient use of military power. This, just as Arabs and Turks had been able to use the wide open spaces of deserts and steppes and dominate caravan traffic by establishing supply posts at strategic stages along the main routes, so European convoys and fleets were able to dominate ocean trade by capturing strategic outposts and building forts and stations along the coasts of every continent. Older trade routes and centers of power in the Middle East were by-passed. Fleets sent from Egypt by worried Arabs (aided by Venetians), anxious to save their precious spice trade, were soon destroyed. Indeed, within twenty years, the Portuguese could claim over-lordship in the Indian Ocean.

By 1600, Dutch and English fleets (having destroyed the Spanish Armada twenty two years earlier) appeared in eastern waters. These new forces—especially the English—did not belong directly to any crown nor were they intent upon conquest. They were far more interested in commercial profits and dividends for company stockholders back in London or Amsterdam. During the seventeenth century, however, the Dutch were far more powerful than the English. The Dutch company was actually an extension of the new Dutch state. The Dutch government depended far more heavily upon overseas holdings for its strength and prosperity in Europe. The English company, privately owned by London merchants, could count on no such support. As a result, weaker English forces could not hope to stand up to the Dutch in direct confrontations. After the Massacre of Amboyna in 1623, the best spice trade came under Dutch control. The English, while clinging desperately to less important footholds in the Spice islands (in Java and Sumatra), fell back on the mainland in India. Initially, English attempts to establish trading posts along the Coromandel Coast were decidedly "next-best" choices to survive Dutch competition from positions of weakness.

The Merchant Company The very weakness and precariousness of the English Company as a private venture, however, proved to be the basis of its greatest political strength. Without sufficient funds or guns to force its way, as the Dutch (and later, even the French) were wont to do, merchants of the English Company trading in the East relied upon the trader's best assets—namely, good bargains and good credit. Using soft words, caution, and skills of persuasion and bargaining, relatively weak English traders turned to other trading communities which felt threatened or which needed help and had something to offer. Local partnerships were formed with members of local merchant communities for the sake of mutually profitable enterprise. Very badly paid English merchants, trading privately on the side, were soon prospering handsomely (even when the Company itself often went nearly bankrupt).

How did it happen that such an apparently weak Company grew to such strength that, within a century and a half, it would have the temerity to challenge the authority of the Mughals? It all began with the "country trade." A cargo-carrying enterprise, the country trade's survival and success, depended upon carrying more goods more cheaply and selling such service for less than anyone else. It required undercutting competitors by managing ever-larger cargos at ever-smaller overhead costs. The main commodity in demand along the coasts of Africa and Asia was cloth, especially cotton fabrics. The Coromandel Coast had been famous for its fine weaving ever since Roman times. "Chintz," "calico," "muslin," and plain cloth of many kinds and colors were continually in demand. Hindu merchants made contracts for cloth manufacturing by cotton growing, thread spinning, fabric weaving, and dyeing communities in villages along the coasts of India. Previously, such manufactures had been carried in Arab *dows,* and later, in ships of the Portuguese. English merchants entered this trade. English ships carried cloth to different ports offering to sell it in exchange for local commodities—gold and silver, precious stones, procelains, ivory, lumber, chemicals, spices, and other products. These commodities in turn provided the merchants with the means to repeat the process: covering the "investment," advances for cotton production. In short, the English entered into the carrying trade that had been going on for thousands of years, but with one big difference: they did it more efficiently and less expensively, and thereby drove out competition. This country trade yielded such margins of profit that not only the English, but their Hindu, Armenian, and Portuguese (Portuguese communities, scattered along the coasts, became simply another trading community in need of profitable partnerships), and other partners, became wealthy. Indeed, English merchants in India were able to provide handsome dividends for company stockholders in London as well as for themselves. While most died in the East (poor or only modestly well off), some returned to England with huge fortunes. (One name, Elihu Yale, for example, made enough to endow a college in the American colonies. Another, Thomas Pitt, laid the foundations of a renowned political family.) Low-cost cotton shipped in bulk to Europe not only brought great strength to the Company but changed habits of dress in the West. Cotton came within the means of many more ordinary people, where previously only the high and mighty could afford linen. In the face of ever rising demands of cotton cloth, larger and larger *East Indiamen,* as cargo carrying ships of the Company were called, had to be built. Maritime and naval technology had to keep pace, growing to meet rising demands. It is small wonder that the French soon felt obliged to enter into so attractive a market and to compete for a share of this rich India trade.

The City-State Company In order to establish and maintain such profitable business, trading posts or "factories" as they were called at the time in India were required. Fortified places were needed, free from interference of local officials and from dangers of attack. Such troubles had constantly bothered European and Hindu merchants in such ports as Surat, Masulipatam, and Hugli. A chance for remedy finally came in 1639. In that year, the Raja of Chandragiri, badly in need of money so as to shore up his precarious throne (which disappeared soon after), "rented" out a small strip of the Coromandel Coast to the English East India Company. Five miles long by one mile deep, this strip contained several villages. By this act, the Raja made the Company into a petty "prince" (*zamindar* and/or *raja*) within his own domain. Thereby the Company became responsible not only for paying revenue (tribute, or *peshcash*) but also for the government of all persons under its authority. The new fortified outpost in this territory was called Fort St. George; but the town which quickly grew up around the open "free port" and which rapidly attracted a sizeable population by its prosperity was called Madras. A second city-state grew up at Bombay. Bombay was an island in the Konkan Coast which, in 1661, was given to King Charles II by Portugal as part of the dowry of Catherine of Braganza and which, thought to be worthless, was rented to the East India Company for the nominal sum of £100 a year. When Surat, the great entrepôt of Gujarat, was sacked by the Maratha forces of Sivaji a few years later (1667 and 1670), many merchants fled to Bombay, knowing that they would receive protection and be free to trade without harassment. A third important city-state of the Company was Calcutta. In 1693, after much trouble with Mughal officers of Bengal and after harassment and hostilities, by which its merchants had been obliged to flee into the swampy Sundarbans, the Company finally built its own station. Around Fort Willion, a city rapidly grew up which soon rivalled and then surpassed all the other cities of India for population and prosperity. In time, the Emperor Aurangzeb

The English Fort at Bombay from a Dutch Print of 1672. Bombay, an island on the west coast of India, was acquired by the Portuguese in 1534. It was ceded to Charles II of England as part of the dowry of Catherine of Braganza in 1661. It was then turned over to the East India Company by the British Crown in 1668, for an annual rent of £10. From such humble beginnings Bombay has grown into the greatest metropolitan center of India.

't Engelfe Fort in Bombaja

himself came to terms with this new settlement, known as Calcutta. He confirmed the Company in its position, granting it official recognition and status as a Mughal entity. Henceforth as a *zamindar* (land-holder) endowed with full authority and vested with ceremonial authority of the empire by virtue of a *firman* and *sanad* (treaty and deed of title), with control over a territory of twenty-four parganas, the Company-state of Calcutta became a local prince in its own right. Thereafter, by the political traditions of the country, it was free to dabble in local politics. Indeed, further examination would show that most of the great nobles of realm, even kings and emperors, had begun their political careers as *zamindars.* At the very least, it made sense for Hindu and English merchants to enter the "political game" so as to avert harm and to court respect, friends, allies, and other rewards.

The Military Company But politics in India was ultimately, especially in the eighteenth century, an art for warriors. In the words of Benoy Kumar Sarkar, "A swordless state [was] a contradiction of terms"—and in India every village or petty principality was either a state or an aspiring state. In the growing turbulences of succession to the Mughal throne, province after province broke away from imperial control—starting with Hyderabad and Carnatic (1724), Bengal and Bihar (1742), and others thereafter. Kingdoms crumbled and vanished (in Mysore, Tanjore, and Central India). Squadrons of Maratha riders, under the direction of the Peshwa of Poona and four other military houses (Holkar of Nagpur, Bhoslé of Indore, Scindia of Gwalior, and Gaekwar of Baroda) ravaged the subcontinent far and wide, to the very gates of Calcutta and Madras. Persian and Afghan invaders crossed the Punjab frequently after 1738–1739 and were no longer checked by imperial armies. By the mid-eighteenth century India was being disturbed by increasing chaos and general political instability. (Meanwhile, around the world, England and France continued to be locked in what was to be a century-long struggle for global mastery. What had begun in the campaigns of Marlborough and ended only after Trafalgar and Waterloo.)

For the Company, especially beginning in 1744, a series of challenges to its survival occurred. These, in turn, when successfully faced and surmounted, became occasions for growth and profound change. A process was set in motion by which the Company was transformed from an enterprise in which commercial interests were uppermost to one in which political logic prevailed. The long-standing amalgam of English and Hindu mercantile interests, which had given the Company such strength in country trade and in the governing of its city-states and which had provided access to pools of local skill and talent, was now widened and strengthened. As more and more ambitious and enterprising people poured into the bustling entrepôts of Madras, Bombay, and Calcutta, local Hindu leaders and local Company servants worked together to provide such social consensus and "public" harmony as was necessary for common interests in government. Country relatives and people from other important local communities were employed for keeping accounts, managing traffic, preserving peace, and countless other

Raja Sarabhoji of Tanjore (Ruled 1798–1832) Riding in a Procession and Followed by His Son Shivaji (Ruled 1832–1853). Preceded by elephants and musicians, followed by attendants with royal parasol, flywhisk, and fans, and accompanied by contingents of both cavalry and infantry, Sarabhoji is depicted by a Hindu artist in all the pomp and dignity of his role within the Indian Empire. The emperor, tutored by the great European missionary, Dr. E. F. Swartz, wrote English verse, drew in the European style, and avidly studied natural history and architecture. (India Office Library and Records, Foreign and Commonwealth Office.)

bureaucratic necessities. But these local Hindu communities provided more than imaginative leadership and administrative talent. They also provided armed forces. The manpower and the money necessary to make the Company a military power in India was provided by the peoples of India themselves.

Early Company records, village accounts, and various narratives (European, Hindu, and Mughal) give us a clear picture of how men from warrior castes were hired as *peons* or *pawns* (foot-warriors for police or military purposes); how they marched with pomp in town parades; how the chief law officer (for example, Pedda Nayak in Madras) was a Hindu (of Naidu caste); how such forces helped to defend the city against both Maratha and Mughal armies; and how such armed servants of the Company got special pay and privileges. Later, as needs changed and as military technology in Europe began to surpass that of India, more and more local fighting men were recruited. Drilled and disciplined under European officers, equipped with the latest weapons (bayonets, muskets, and field artillery), dressed in uniforms and paid monthly salaries and pensions (both new customs in India) and trained in maneuvers and tactics, soldiers in these new regiments developed feelings of solidarity and pride. Like other professional mercenaries of that era, whether infantry or artillery, these soldiers were known in India as *sepoys* and, as such, were distinct from *sawars* or "riders." In terms of status, by earlier tradition, *sawars* were esteemed highly, and *sepoys* were despised. Victory in battle, however, was to harden the *esprit de corps* of these new troops. Before the century was out sepoys of the Company would not only make a modern army of hardened veterans, but the largest standing army in the world.

Procession of Akbar II, Emperor (Ruled 1806–1837). Nothing signified the authority and legitimacy of the Indian Empire as much as the spectacle of its potentates appearing together in ceremonies such as this. The fusion of the Company Raj and the Mughal Masnad was thus demonstrated by such ceremonials, in which high officials of these elite communities mingled. Here, the Emperor and his sons, the British Resident and his countrymen, both high functionaries and civil servants parade together in all the oriental splendor of a royal event. (India Office Library and Records, Foreign and Commonwealth Office.)

Money was needed to pay for the increasingly expensive modern military establishments, but Company directors and stockholders in London were interested in healthy annual dividends and took a very dim view of military expenditures (or adventures, for that matter). It was the French Governor of Pondicherry, Joseph Dupliex, who solved this problem. (Founded in 1664, with its main stations at Pondicherry and Chandranagar, French competition against the English became severe by 1720.) In 1745, during the War of the Austrian Succession (known as the First Carnatic War in India), Dupliex's forces captured Madras. The Nawab of Arcot, to whom both English and French companies were subject, commanded the French to withdraw and sent a force of some 15,000 horsemen to enforce his decision. A puny force of about 500 sepoys with French officers defeated the Nawab's mounted army. At a blow, the reputation (and prestige) of European (sepoy) arms was born. Soon another prince at enmity with the Nawab of Arcot was asking Dupliex whether he could rent, if not buy, a small French-trained-and-led sepoy army. Glad to pay almost anything for the use of this new instrument and eager to fulfill his own ambitions for overlordship in the region, this prince agreed to a scheme whereby sepoy forces would be rented in return for regular payments in silver. For Dupliex, such a scheme had many advantages. Expenses for maintaining a sepoy army strong enough to defend French interests and possessions could be covered without any charge on the French company's treasury. Experience in the field, so essential for keeping a sepoy army in high efficiency and morale, could be achieved. Indeed, with handsome prizes and booty going to all concerned in each campaign, personal rewards could be especially high.

Finally, instead of actually receiving hard silver, which the local "contractor" prince found difficult to have in sufficient supply, revenue-collecting authority (and indeed, therewith, all government authority) over large tracts of territory containing hundreds of villages could be turned over to Dupliex. Thus, the task of collecting taxes to pay for their own upkeep would fall upon the sepoy officers and men themselves.

The system was ingenious. Silver for paying sepoys came from land revenue. Services of sepoys were sold to the highest bidder. Princes of India, competing against each other for political power, would compete against each other to provide the money and the means for the raising of larger and larger sepoy armies. In effect, Mughal princes vied with each other to see who would buy the very Trojan horses which, once inside their palaces, would be their undoing. From ancient times, land revenue had been and continued to be the source of political power. Thus, in effect, rulers of India actually encouraged and nourished the growth of European power to the extent that, as the numbers and strength of these new forces loomed larger within their palaces, they themselves ceased to be necessary (except perhaps for purposes of ceremony and legitimation) and could eventually be dispensed with altogether.

Yet, in the end, it was the British who ultimately won, outplaying the

Mahadaji Sindhia (Ruled 1782–1794) Entertaining a British Naval Officer and a Young British Military Officer (probably a light cavalryman). The occasion is a nautch (party where professional dancers entertained guests) at the emperor's house in Delhi. (India Office Library and Records, Foreign and Commonwealth Office.)

French at their own game. The French had been so successful that, with apparently incredible speed, they soon held sway over much of South India. Having gained ascendency in both Arcot and Hyderabad; and, by playing one prince against another, aiming to erect a great empire in India; and striving, therewith, to drive the British from India, they over-reached themselves. British fleets, supreme on the high seas by the middle of the eighteenth century, were able to cut off vital support from France and to provide timely help to beleaguered English forces in India. Also, many local merchants, soldiers, and princes in India, bitterly alienated by the high-handed and over-reaching ambitions of the French, became only too glad to discover what might be an alternative source of European-trained "sepoys-for-sale." The English Company was fortunate in its local servants, both European and Indian. One of these, having started his career as a writer, was Robert Clive. Another, a Tamil soldier who became a Company general, was Yusuf Khan. Each was only too glad for a chance to join a sepoy force (whatever the motive). Each soon proved to be daring and resourceful in the field, rapidly rising to positions of command. After much campaigning, the French and their princely allies were decisively beaten, both in the Carnatic and in Bengal. A battle outside the little village of Plassey (near Calcutta) in 1757, is often seen as the turning point. Actually, two more important events occurred in 1761: the French surrendered Pondicherry, thereby all but renouncing hopes of empire in India; and the Marathas, suffering a dreadful defeat at Panipat (near Delhi) where over a hundred thousand were slain, lost their bid for empire. Thus, the way opened for the English East India Company, with care and skill, to become the imperial successor to the Mughals. As early as 1765, Clive was able to persuade the emperor to appoint the Company as his chief financial minister (*diwan*) for the huge province of Bengal. Company Raj—indeed, the Indian Empire itself—can be considered to have begun at that time.

The Company Raj   Perhaps the single most notable achievement of the English East India Company was the political unification of the Indian subcontinent. Many other powers had tried and failed. Only the Company, however, succeeded in putting together a completely all-Indian political system—the first true Indian Empire. In fact, Company officials were the first to use the words "India" and "Indian" when speaking about the whole subcontinent and its peoples. Instead of Bengalis, Madrasis, or Gujaratis, Company people became the first "Indians." It is even true to say that Company scholars "discovered" India's culture for the world. Sir William Jones, late in the eighteenth century, translated Sanskrit and Persian classics. He became India's first Orientalist. Company servants also became aware of the great marvels of India's ancient civilization. Most important of all, the Company built a huge political system, encompassing not only the whole subcontinent but spreading its influence throughout the Indian Ocean basin. This system was divided into two parts: one of direct rule in what became known as "British India" and the other of indirect rule through what was called "Princely India." The Company's legitimate authority, therefore, included spheres both of sovereignty and of suzerainty. The whole country, but especially that which was directly ruled, was tied together with uniform systems of laws and courts and procedures; moreover, it was eventually linked together by a gigantic network of "grand trunk" roads, railways, postal services, and telegraphs. By the mid-nineteenth century, cheap communication and travel brought peoples together as never before, and they began to think of themselves as "Indians."

Among those who contributed to this process of Indianization, perhaps no one was more important than Warren Hastings. Not since the reign of the Emperor Akbar had a man of such capacity and strength ruled in India. A Company servant who arrived in Calcutta as a boy and became well versed

Bodyguard of Maharajah Ranjit Singh (c. 1838–1839). (India Office Library and Records, Foreign and Commonwealth Office.)

in the local culture, being fluent in both Bengali and Persian, Hastings developed into an astute political observer and a master of statescraft. Eventually rising to become the Company's first Governor-General (1772–1786), he gained respect and support from Bengali leaders by establishing peace and security and curbing wanton oppression (of both local petty tyrants and grasping Company servants). With great patience and skill, he established durable diplomatic relations among the princes of India, great and small; convincing them that he did not wish to expand the Company's dominions, he constructed a balanced system of alliances. In this way, he not only achieved a temporary political equilibrium within the subcontinent, he also brought great prestige to the Company. By his efforts, the Company became the leading power in India. In many ways, even to the use of gold script on Persian state documents, his was the style of a Mughal emperor. He never forgot that the legitimacy of the Company's authority came from the Mughals.

But to Englishmen sitting in London, Hastings was considered to be too "Indian." Company directors disapproved of costly adventures which increased power and territory without adding to trade and profits. Dividends, not dominion, was their aim. Parliamentary members frowned upon "oriental despotism" and "corruption." Determined to end corrupt practices among servants of the Company, to separate the Company's functions of governing from its functions of trading, and to establish better principles for governing in India without interfering with local customs and traditions, Parliament decided to assume supervisory control over the highest political affairs of the Company. To implement this decision, Parliament sent out Lord Cornwallis, the general who had surrendered to the American colonists at Yorktown. Cornwallis carried out three fundamental reforms: (1) Separation of powers—separation of the executive, judicial, and revenue branches of government, clearly dividing functions of sword, scales, and purse—was built into institutional structures; and, as a corollary, Rule of Law received special emphasis. (The judicial system, with firm regulations and procedures, was greatly strengthened.) (2) An imperial civil service of highly qualified, well-paid, "covenanted" officers was established. Later known as the Indian Civil Service (I.C.S.) and called the "steel frame" of administration, it became respected for its high standards of dedication and performance. Today it is known as the I.A.S. or Indian Administrative Service. (3) The Permanent Settlement of Bengal (1793) established the positions of the highest classes of that province. This was a system of agreements with local landed gentry which fixed them in their positions as local lords of society and guaranteed to them their possessions, privileges, and powers in perpetuity. By such means, the Company made sure of its constitution and insured its ability to govern with the collaboration and consent of local leadership.

Another British ruler of great ability was Lord Wellesley (1798–1805). As Governor General, he believed that, as much as possible, the British should rule over all of India and took steps to make the Company paramount. Knowing that Napoleon was in Egypt nursing grand designs for the conquest of India, Wellesley was ambitious and frankly aggressive in his plans to forestall French expansion. The Company's army, having recently defeated the Marathas, stood at over 300,000 strong. The device used by Wellesley to assure Company preeminence in India had a long tradition within the subcontinent; and, indeed, it had been regularly used by the Mughals. Under a system of Subsidiary Alliances, Wellesley gave an immediate choice to every prince, whether great or small: agree to a permanent alliance of subordination to the Company or face the prospect of possible forcible dethronement, if not immediately, then on some future unspecified occasion. In short, decide between permanent protection or permanent insecurity and possible abolition. Henceforth, so long as a prince left all foreign affairs to the British (that is, all acts of diplomacy, treaty, or war with any power outside a prince's own domains); so long as a prince permitted a British Resident (an agent-cum-ambassador-cum-administrator) to stay at his court as a sort of watch dog to see that treaty terms were honored; so long as a prince allowed a contingent of the Company army to be stationed permanently near his court—for his "protection"; and so long as a prince proved himself to be competent enough to control his own state and its people: as long as such conditions were met, a prince need have little to fear and might continue to rule over his domains in perpetuity. In other words, what Wellesley gave to the princes of India was very much like what Cornwallis had given to the *zamindars* in Bengal. Permanent Subsidiary Alliances were for Princely India what the Permanent Settlement was for Bengal.

Quite obviously not all the great and powerful princes of India felt that they should be treated as subordinate. Nor was Wellesley successful in persuading all of them, by either diplomacy or war. After some remarkable victories (won by his brother, Arthur Wellesley, later Duke of Wellington), some defeats were suffered and he was recalled. But the logic of Wellesley's system was carried on, almost by its own momentum. More wars were fought and, by 1818, most of the remaining princes had submitted to Subsidiary Alliances. Thereafter, the Company was the paramount power of India, some rule being directly under its Indian officers and much being ruled indirectly, through its Indian allies, the rajas and maharajahs. This indeed was an Indian Empire.

THE GREAT REBELLION

The extent of local, native participation within the machinery of the Indian Empire is only now being more fully recognized and described in historical scholarship. Yet, since English adventurers first grew rich "shaking the pagoda tree," down to the time when the last British officials took ship for Britain in 1947, many tens of thousands of Indians actively engaged themselves in the day-to-day machinery of imperial administration. For every eighteenth-century Nabob whose quickly made fortune enabled him to buy a "rotten borough" or seat in Parliament, there was an equally wealthy native Dubash who retired to build himself a palace or to endow a Hindu temple in Madras, Calcutta, or Bombay. One officer could exclaim (in 1853):

It is perhaps the wonder of the world, this Indian empire. Whilst the native soldiery give their heart's blood on the battle field and dying bless the power over them, that same devotion to a strange race sitting in the seats of the rulers is equally shown by the priesthood [Brahmans].

And in 1846, when thousands in Madras signed a memorial to Parliament, Hindu leaders could declare:

Wherever the British standard has been victorious in India, down to the last perilous engagements on the banks of the Sutledge . . . there Hindu blood has freely flowed to secure East India Company's dominion over our native land.

More than coercion was required to establish and maintain such an enormous and complicated political system. Its sustaining strength derived from a foundation of collaboration by hundreds of thousands of local officers and soldiers, all servants of the Company, and the silent consensus or passive support of millions of villagers.

But newer generations of young Britons coming out to India, especially after 1818, tended increasingly not to learn nor to understand from whence the Raj acquired its essential strength. Earlier Englishmen had been scrupulous to avoid giving offense to local sensibilities and had been careful not to violate indigenous rituals and traditions. Newer arrivals were not so careful. Moreover, after 1813, when Christian missionaries were permitted to enter India, some who roamed about the countryside preaching and trying to convert Hindu and Muslim villagers were far from courteous. During the 1820's and 1830's, European and Hindu reformers joined together in agitating against inhuman customs—against *sati* (widow burning), female infanticide, child marriage, human sacrifice, and ritual murder-and-robbery (*thagi*). In the north, especially where British rule was very recent, such attempts at reform were seen as offenses against traditional customs (*mamul*) and against religious duty (*dharma*). What was worse, many villagers began to fear that rumors that they might be forcibly converted to Christianity might be true. As a slow fuse of discontent began to burn, most government officials seem to have been heedless or altogether unaware of the growing dangers. When the Great Rebellion (or Mutiny) came, they were altogether unprepared.

Mutiny had long been a tradition in India. In the absence of other forms of political expression or of collective bargaining, boycotts or strikes (*hartals*) and mutinies by mercenary soldiers were not uncommon. Expressions of discontent, violent insurrections, and explosive incidents had occurred almost every year for three decades. Morale in the Bengal Army, especially among sepoys stationed near Delhi, had been low for many years. Discipline was lax; unfair pay, promotion, and grievances had long needed redress. Racial arrogance and snobbishness as manifested by new recruits from Britain was especially offensive. Insolent young men, green with inexperience, would ask whitebearded sepoy officers with the scars and medals of a

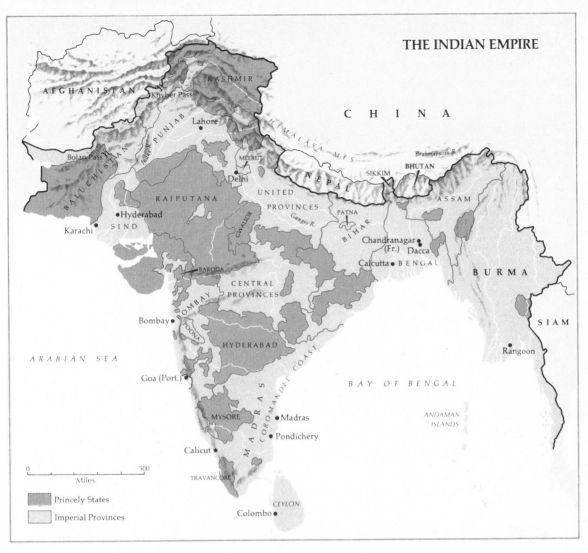

THE INDIAN EMPIRE

half century behind them to polish their boots. Finally, in 1857, rumors spread through the army that new cartridges being issued with the new Enfield rifle were greased with a mixture of cows' and pigs' fat and that the cartridges had to be torn open with one's teeth before being inserted into the rifle. Forbidden by their religious dietary laws to eat beef or pork, the sepoys viewed this as a deliberate attempt of Christian rulers to pollute Hindus and defile Muslims. That the new cartridge was actually the result of thoughtlessness in the Ordnance Department and that, when the mistake was discovered, the new issue was hastily withdrawn made little difference. Before corrections could be made, the great explosion that had been smoldering for years (and, indeed, forcast by Sir Henry Lawrence over a decade earlier) came.

"The Post Runner" by Kapur-Singh, an Amritsar Artist (1866). A *dak*-runner or postman who carried mail (*tappal*) from post-to-post (*dak*-to-*dak*) was the vital communication link of the Indian Empire. He ran about six miles in an hour and then passed his satchel on to the next man and so on, in a relay network that covered the whole subcontinent. In its day, the postal system of India was the most efficient, inexpensive, and reliable in the world. And in many ways it still is. Letters now reach across India in one day, and runners are still used to reach remote places. (India Office Library and Records, Foreign and Commonwealth Office.)

The first outbreak occurred at Meerut in May 1857. Sepoy regiments mutinied and killed their officers. As the conflagration spread to other cantonments up and down the Gangetic Plain, some of the civil population also rose against the Company. Some of the rebels marched on Delhi, putting European residents to the sword, taking control of the Red Fort (*Lal Qila*), and pledging allegiance to the aging Mughal Emperor. In the recently annexed Kingdom of Oudh, most of the countryside joined the rebels in concerted attacks upon the British Residence which, although beseiged, was fiercely defended and managed to hold on until help arrived. Eventually and significantly, however, although European troops were rushed out from Britain, it was the regiments of loyal sepoys from Bengal, Bombay, and Madras that played the vital part in restoring the authority of the Government of India. The Red Fort of Delhi was recaptured and other strategic centers were secured. Campaigns of sporadic fighting and punitive expeditions continued into 1858, long after the issue had been decided.

Like the American Civil War, the Great Mutiny marks a watershed in the history of India. Many lives were lost; atrocities were committed on both sides, followed by bitterness and distrust. Things were never quite the same afterward. Optimism was replaced by pessimism. Warmly cordial, if sometimes corrupt or casual, relationships so characteristic of the "Good Old Days of John Company" were replaced by a more cold, correct, and stiff relationship under the Victorian Crown. Both the Mughal throne and Company rule were abolished, the aged emperor dying as a prisoner in exile and the older civil servants retiring to pensions in Britain. In a new age of competitive examinations and bureaucratic centralization, Indians became "colonial" subjects of Queen Victoria.

FURTHER READING   A good introduction to the Indian subcontinent is found in P. Spear's * *India, Pakistan and the West* (1967). First published in 1949, this classic work is now in its fourth edition. Indeed, among general histories also, the works of Spear command the field. Most convenient and readable is his * *A History of India: Vol. 2* (1965). Equally attractive is the latest edition of his *India: A Modern History* (1961, 1972). His edition of V. A. Smith's classic *Oxford History of India* (1958), is comprehensive, detailed, and up-dated; moreover, the final portion has recently been separately published under the title, *Oxford History of Modern India; 1740–47* (1965). Two other standard general works should be consulted, as required: W. T. De Bary, * *Sources of Indian Tradition* (1958), especially Volume II of the paperback edition, which is the single most useful sourcebook and reader on all of India's civilization; and H. H. Dodwell, et al., *The Cambridge History of India* (1929, 1932) Vol. V and VI, which is a standard comprehensive view by the best British scholars of the time.

Three works on the Islamic legacy are especially useful: S. Ikram and A. Embree, *Muslim Civilization of India* (1958), is clear, graceful, and highly readable; Ikram and Spear, *The Cultural Heritage of Pakistan* (1956), is more subtle and penetrating; and P. Hardy, * *The Muslims of British India* (1972), is a work of sensitivity and breadth by one of the foremost authorities in the field.

On the British impact and the Indian Empire, a number of classic works give important and variant perspectives: The oldest of these, recently reprinted, is A. Lyall, *The Rise and Expansion of the British Dominion in India* (1894; 1968); P. Griffiths, *The British Impact on India* (1957, 1965), is excellent in its balance and artistry; L. S. S. O'Malley, ed., *Modern India and the West* (1941), is a collection of superb essays with a strong cultural emphasis; P. (Mason) Woodruff, * *The Rulers of India: The Founders* (1954), is perhaps the best work on the contributions of various Britishers, throughout several centuries, from a strongly British perspective; Edward Thompson and G. T. Garratt, *The Rise and Fulfilment of British Rule in India* (1934), is perhaps one of the best pro-Congress (Nationalist) works, disclaimers notwithstanding; and finally, H. Tinker's exceedingly useful * *South Asia: A Short History* (1966), gives especially fresh, insightful, and penetrating analysis, by a leading political scientist.

*Books available in paperback edition are marked with an asterisk.

3 Subjugation of Southeast Asia: Under European Rule

To the east of India and south of China lies a vast physical, historical, and cultural region. This region, because of its location and physical character, has retained a free-flowing looseness of structure and a remarkably persistent diversity. Three sets of contrasting features are central to an understanding of this diversity: geographic divisions between mainlands and islands; topographical and climatic contrasts between hill ridges and alluvial valleys or coastal plains; and a long history of cultural influences from both India and China, those from India having generally been older, wider, and deeper. As a term, Southeast Asia has come to include the countries of Vietnam, Laos, and Cambodia (known collectively as Indo-China); the Philippines and Indonesia; Malaya; Borneo; Thailand; and Burma.

Great barriers of some sort—mountains or seas—generally prevent too easy a flow of influences from one major high-culture basin into another. Within Southeast Asia, moreover, a series of minor barriers, running roughly north to south, have this same effect. In the far north, sharp and deep mountain-valley folds are pinched together closely. Moving southward, these folds widen, soften, and open out into lower hills and wider valleys until they reach broad plains and deltas at the mouths of the great rivers. (These features are specified by name below.) The chains of hill ridges then plunge beneath the sea and emerge still further south and east as the spines of island chains. There are thousands of islands—Indonesia alone has over 3,000 of them covering over 3,000 miles of ocean and the Philippines has more than 7,000 islands (many tiny and uninhabited) reaching far out into the Pacific Ocean. There is also a great amount of emptiness in Southeast Asia, large open spaces, either of seas and straits or of uninhabited (often uninhabitable) jungles and hills. Over the centuries this area has received wave over wave of migration from the north and west. The result is a region whose physical fragmentation and diversity is equalled by a cultural fragmentation and diversity seen nowhere else in the world.

The comparatively sparse population density over the region as a whole is worthy of emphasis. There are vast tracts of thick jungle, with small settlements and only occasional larger concentrations of population. There are also thousands of mainland pockets and island coves of habitation, some with primitive peoples still living in the Stone Age. Population density today is found either in the river deltas and valleys of the mainland or on the coastal plains where more intensive agrarian life has been possible. It is in such places that centers of civilization and political power prospered in the past. The largest, such as the plains of Java and Sumatra or the valleys of the Irrawaddy, Salween, Chaopraya, Menam, and Mekong rivers, gave rise to historic realms such as Srivijaya (in Sumatra) and Mataram (in Java), and kingdoms in what are now the countries of Burma, Thailand, Cambodia, and Vietnam (Cochin in the Mekong River Delta and Tonkin in the Red River Delta).

In many ways the Malay Peninsula, while actually connected to the mainland by a narrow and mountainous isthmus, is more truly part of island Southeast Asia. Culturally and historically, moreover, this isthmus has shared more with the archipelago of Indonesia than with mainland Thailand. Together the isthmus and Straits of Malacca have served as a sort of cultural divide between Thai and other mainland cultural pressures from the north and Malay-Indonesian cultural pressures in the south. In global terms, these same narrow straits have played a decisive, even strategic role in the east-west flows of commercial and cultural exchange.

One feature common to all of Southeast Asia is that nowhere, except for rare remains of bone, stone, or clay, are there clear traces of the earliest societies or of original agrarian settlements. No cities, no art objects, no written materials, no fragments of thought or philosophy, have survived to tell us of the quality of earliest human relationships. Most of the peoples of Southeast Asia can be seen as descended from successive waves of migrants from the north. In a process of downward filtration extending over thousands of years progressively more advanced and more organized societies (Malays, Chams, Mons, Thais, Burmans, Vietnamese, to cite some examples) have moved south from Central Asia or from South China. Some of these, the Malays in particular, have then moved from mainland to island Southeast Asia, and then to the open seas of the Pacific. Most of the cultural influences, however, came, broadly speaking, in three successive waves from the West—first from Hindu and Buddhist India, then from Islamic India and Arabia, and finally from Europe.

INDIANIZED
KINGDOMS

While trade from India began in prehistoric times, evidences of quickening commercial contact date from early in the Christian era. Records left by merchants, pilgrims, and officials (Greek and Chinese) reveal a process of Indianization at work. Hindu and Buddhist concepts of life, style, religion and royalty became dominant. In Sumatra, the Hinayana Buddhist kingdom of Srivijaya held sway for six centuries. In Java, where the Javanese-Hindu kingdom of Mataram flourished, sophisticated culture and power reached a zenith with the rise of Madjapahit (1293–1520). Similar kingdoms developed on the mainland: first the Funan, then the Champa, and later the Khmer kingdom, whose magnificent capital of Angkor has now gained such world renown for its profusion of richly ornate temples. The cities of Angkor in Cambodia (ca. 850–1431) and of Pagan in Burma (1044–1287) are considered to represent the classical period of history on the "Indo-Chinese" mainland. It was a period in which Theravada (Hinayana) Buddhism emerged as the supreme "high culture."[1] The decline of these cities was followed by the rise of the Thai (Siamese) center of Ayuthia (1350); and, thereafter, by centuries of Burmo-Thai rivalry. New challenges followed—from Islam, and from Europe.

Angkor Wat Ruins in Cambodia.
(Embassy of the Khmer Republic.)

Yet for all that, Indianization, developing under the influence of Brahman and Buddhist priests, produced essentially court cultures. Hindu and Buddhist influences provided values, rituals, or legitimization, and artistic forms for the ruling classes in each area. Influences upon rural villages were, if anything, extremely superficial—more to be likened to a glossy, thick lacquer upon dark and tough jungle wood. Court and countryside gave

[1]Only of Vietnam can it be said that the prevailing outside influence of premodern times was more Chinese than Indian. This is evidenced, for example, by its coming under the sway of the Mahayana ("Greater Vehicle") form of Buddhism, which came from China. Hinayana (or the "Smaller Vehicle," an earlier school of Buddhist thought) came via Sri Lanka (Ceylon).

complementary support to each other: intensive agriculture could not provide court revenues without a minimum provision of political security so as to ensure such agriculture. But, beyond such minimal ties, villages were like autonomous, self-governing little republics.

ISLAMIC IMPACT

The advent of Islam, especially as a political force in the thirteenth century, is considered by many scholars to be the turning point after which Southeast Asia emerges into the full light of history. There is little certainty about earlier events, although there are many theories surrounding the coming of Islam before the thirteenth century. (That successive waves of Muslim expansion occurred—first into the Arabian Sea, then onto the coasts of India, and finally on to Southeast Asia, the Philippines and China—and that Muslim traders found in Canton as early as the eighth century came by sea and that Mongol invasions and hegemony might have had a serious effect upon trade patterns in Southeast Asia: such views may be mentioned but they add little to our historical knowledge of the area.) Whatever the case, we know that Arab and Indian sailors and merchants and missionaries (Buddhist, Hindu, Islamic, even Jewish and Christian) had been increasing for centuries and that the Muslims became much stronger during the fourteenth century.

It is noteworthy that the founding of Malacca seems to coincide with the conversion of its ruler to Islam. This seaport, gaining its commercial and strategic importance from its location, where the Straits of Malacca come between Malaya and Sumatra, soon gained unrivaled political, economic, and cultural ascendency. Like medieval Venice or like modern Singapore (Malacca's successor, which is today one of the world's busiest seaports, handling over 60,000 ships each year), Malacca was a city-state. It depended exclusively upon seaborne supplies, even for its food. In 1403, its sultan was sufficiently fearful of threats from Thai princes and mindful of Chinese power to open diplomatic relations with China. Periodically thereafter, tribute was sent to Peking and paternal promises of support were returned. The extension of Chinese suzerainty and trade into the area, at least temporarily, apparently served to balance local powers. But the real domain of Malacca, beyond its footholds on both sides of the Straits, was its hold on overseas traffic. Every kind of goods came through its warehouses—food (rice, vegetables, fruit, and fish), spices (pepper, nutmeg, cinnamon), camphor, gold and tin, teak, ebony, rosewood and sandalwood from the surrounding area; textiles and gems from India; drugs (opium, coffee), wool, horses, glass, and strong metal products (tools, weapons) from further west; and silks, satins, brocades, damasks, porcelains and pearls, silver and gold from China.

What came to island Southeast Asia with this second great wave of influences from the West was an identification with another new, aggressive world culture. In Islam all men could enjoy equal claims to the mercy of Allah and equal opportunities for worldly success. Submission to the faith of Muhammad required only five relatively simple duties—praying five times a day, fasting, giving alms to the less fortunate, going on pilgrimage (*hajj*) to Mecca at least once, and reciting the creed from the common sacred text (the *Quran*) in Arabic, preferably at the weekly gathering place (*masjid*) of the faithful. Significantly, Arabic script began to replace the older Sanskritic scripts in island Southeast Asia during the fourteenth century.

Since Muslim strength was derived mainly from control of sea lanes, the spread of Islam to larger inland populations was very gradual. Consequently, while most people of Indonesia and Malaysia today express at least some allegience to Islam, older ceremonies, styles, and beliefs have persisted and these become stronger and more apparent the further one moves inland. Whether it was because Buddhist traditions in mainland countries such as Burma and Thailand were strong enough to effectively resist the new faith or because these countries were away from the main lines of sea trade—which seems more likely—the fact remains that, on the mainland, only the Chams (of Champa and/or Cambodia), peoples of similar language and culture to the Malay-Indonesians, paid much attention to Islam.

Thus, within a century, the lands and islands along the spice and silk sea route from Macau to Malacca (including Java, Borneo, and the southern Philippines) and from there through the Mediterranean to Morocco, where Muslims had been dominant since the seventh century, was largely in the hands of Muslims. Just as Arabs had earlier taken Islam from oasis to oasis and from one cosmopolitan-urban center to another, so also Islam, having come to Southeast Asia was carried from one seaport to another. There, however, it arrived as merchandise filtered through the gauze of Indian culture, completing a process begun several centuries earlier.

EUROPEAN INFLUENCE   But Muslim political dominance did not last long. Indeed, within just one century of Malacca's rise, Muslim power at sea was lost to the Europeans, who as early as 1297, had learned from Marco Polo of these richer trading possibilities. In 1487, after generations of probing down the west coast of Africa, the Portuguese rounded the Cape of Good Hope. A decade later Vasco da Gama reached Calicut and returned with a rich cargo of spices. By 1512, Portugal had an Asian maritime empire stretching from Mozambique and Muscat to Malacca and, later (1543), to Macau. Such was the wealth brought back by some adventurers that thousands sailed away eastward each year. Few returned to enjoy their rewards, however; many died of disease, disaster, and incessant war. Many others simply settled down, married local women, and never returned to their distant homeland. Indeed, in drainage of manpower alone, the cost of empire was a high one. Enviously observing rich returns, men of other nations soon set sail. Spanish ships crossed the Pacific to the Philippines; Dutch and English ships ventured into eastern waters.

By 1600, the balance of European power had shifted northward. Dutch and English fleets, previously depending on Lisbon for spices, took over from the Portuguese. Since, initially at least, the Dutch were stronger, it was they who next established a great seaborne empire. Founded on the Spice Islands (Java and the Moluccas), this was to last three centuries. Moreover, after it was restored to them by the British (in 1816), Dutch colonial control of the Indonesian archipelago remained until 1942.

Among Europeans—except for Spanish power in the Philippines (of relatively marginal significance in the area as a whole)—only the Dutch established influence over much of island Southeast Asia. From their center at Batavia (now Djakarta), and with help from local princes at odds with the Portuguese (or Spanish), Dutch squadrons maintained their superiority at sea. But on land Dutch control advanced very slowly. By the time Malacca fell to them in 1641, it was a port already declining in importance. A new southerly route across the Indian Ocean went directly from Madagascar and Mauritius to Java. To the north, on the mainland of Southeast Asia, there was little allure for Europeans. Western weapons, creeping into princely armies, may have made the incessant wars more gory; and foreign mercenaries, Portuguese in Burma and Dutch in Siam, sometimes fought each other. Ancient patterns of agrarian culture and political conflict continued— Burmese fought Thai; Thai fought Cambodian; and, as the state of Champa disappeared from the Mekong Delta, rivalry between Annam and Tonkin disturbed the land of Vietnam (Indo-China). All things considered, commercial incentives were too small to attract European interest.

Thus, during nearly three hundred years of relative equilibrium in mainland Southeast Asia, little European influence penetrated inland. Few changes came into the lives of ordinary people. Like other foreign intruders before them, whether Indian or Chinese, Europeans settled only in trading stations along the coasts, where they found an already thriving commercial system. By seizing certain strategic positions they turned the existing commerce to their own advantage, and benefited from a system that had been in operation for centuries. The local peoples, did not receive these intrusions with undue alarm. The newcomers seemed not so different from those before them. Never numerous and never apparently superior, except for bigger guns and ships and for better understanding of far oceans, Europeans inspired little awe. Barely visible, Europeans dominated major shipping lanes and long-distance trade; but most territory, even in the islands, remained beyond their grasp.

Actually, in Southeast Asia, "colonialism," as it is now so fashionably called and so often badly defined, did not commence until a century ago, over three centuries after Europeans arrived. This new and more drastic form of domination was partially a product of the Industrial Revolution. European expansion in the late nineteenth century, therefore, came with explosive force and brought profound changes. These changes occurred first in Europe and happened there much more quickly than elsewhere in the world. The first people to exploit new technologies, Europeans enjoyed a temporary head-start on the rest of the world, and for a single century, they enjoyed a decisive advantage. Energies released by rapid industrialization were truly phenomenal. In a relatively short time, when seen in light of all history,

Stone Head of Sivá, Cambodia, Twelfth Century. (Courtesy, Museum of Fine Arts, Boston.)

European countries "scrambled" to acquire domains—to fill the "empty" spaces shown on their maps. In Southeast Asia itself, most of this new expansion took place after 1870—that is, after steamships replaced older, smaller sailing ships and after the opening of regular steamship lines, telegraphs, and the Suez Canal in 1869. As industries of Europe required more and more raw materials and as rising prosperity brought demands for new commodities, ever-larger ships carried bulk goods westward (tin, tungsten, teak, rubber, oil, cotton and jute, as well as spices, tea, coffee, tobacco, and sugar) and returned to newly expanding markets with cargos of manufactured goods. And, in all the new trends, the British led the way.

EUROPEAN EXPANSION AND DOMINANCE

Britain As Britain emerged victorious from the clouds of the Napoleonic War in Europe (1814) and as it became paramount over India (1818), the whole globe seemed to lie at her feet. Certainly English writ ran throughout the whole basin of the Indian Ocean, from the Persian Gulf to Cape Town and eastwards, from Ceylon to Java and on to the edges of Canton. Although Britain returned the Indies (Indonesia) to Holland in 1816 (a gracious gesture which she was not obliged to make), British power seemed nevertheless inadvertently and inexorably to move ever outwards from the Indian Empire. Having given up Java under protest, Sir Stamford Raffles (an agent of the East India Company) purchased an island in the Malacca Straits and founded Singapore in 1819. The strategic position of the Straits, the sea passage between India and China, again became important. But the dominant position in maritime commerce achieved by this rapidly growing city in the following years was due as much to its jealously guarded status as an "open port," free of customs taxes and controls, as to its location. (Such indeed has been its continued growth that it is now the fourth busiest seaport in the world.)

In Burma, too, the British exhibited a presence—directly from the Indian Empire. Having previously suffered serious defeat in an attempt to sack the Thai capital of Ayuthia (1787) and having for years spurned British efforts to establish more orderly relationships, especially so as to fix and stabilize their common frontier with India, the Burmese made a series of disastrous mistakes. They failed to investigate or to appreciate the growing strength and resources of the Government of India. Isolated by barriers of complacency and ritual, the rulers of Burma did not realize the dangers of what they were doing nor the consequences they could suffer. The King of Burma moved forces into Assam in 1817 and, by attempting to invade Bengal in 1826, brought upon himself the full weight of India's armies. Burmese forces suffered crushing defeat; and over the next sixty years, they were defeated twice again. Step by step, Burmese kings were obliged to cede Lower Burma and then other provinces to the British. Before they fully appreciated the scale of their miscalculations or the realities of India's power, all of Burma had been absorbed into the Indian Empire. Thereafter, hundreds of officials, thousands of soldiers and merchants, and eventually millions of farmers and laborers swarmed into Burma from India. Indians moved into the great empty spaces of the Irrawaddy Delta to exploit the rich, largely untapped, resources of the country.

Meanwhile, Indo-British power had continued to expand, moving further into the states of Malaya and Borneo, and on to Hong Kong and Shanghai. Officially however, while this expansion depended upon strength inherent to the Indian Empire, it was separated from direct control by that empire. Under direct authority of the British Crown and the supervision of the Colonial Office in London, British interests beyond Burma were explicit and direct, that of Indian Empire was less obvious. While many Indians migrated to these new colonies, few were incorporated directly into local governments as bureaucrats, policemen, or soldiers. By the 1890's, British power in Malaya had been spread through a system of "indirect rule" by which existing Muslim sultanates were incorporated into a federal structure of government, under British authority.

France French efforts to acquire a foothold in Southeast Asia came much later and were more unashamedly aggressive. Missionaries from France had worked in Indo-China since the late seventeenth century; but not until the mid-nineteenth century, when missionaries were persecuted and executed, did France herself become involved in eastern activity. After demands for the safety of French nationals and for diplomatic stations were refused, armies of France marched in. The process of French conquest took twenty years, from 1862 to 1882. First the coastal portion of Cochin China (South Vietnam) was subdued. Five years later the rest was taken. At the same time, Thai rulers were forced to give up claims to Cambodia. Hanoi, capitol of Tonkin (North Vietnam), fell to France in 1882. A brief war with China was necessary to force recognition of French claims. Thereafter, a further claim over Laos as a protectorate completed the French empire in Asia.

Europeans as Colonials The French empire differed in form from that of other European dominion in Asia. Both the Dutch and British possessions were products of slow, gradual, practical, and usually careful construction over many generations. Their accretion involved centuries of local experience and they tended to expand behind a screen of local support and involvement in local politics. To a greater degree, both older powers tended to act more scrupulously in observing local forms of legitimization for their growing authority. Also, especially unlike the British, the French did not draw upon vast reservoirs of Asian manpower to do the actual work of conquering and administering Asian dominions. Very few Britons actually ruled. Rather, their rule over vast populations in Asia was accomplished by the agency of many tens of thousands of skilled indigenous bureaucrats and soldiers. In contrast, throngs of Frenchmen came out to the colonies in Southeast Asia: not only high civil servants and administrators, but minor functionaries such as policemen or postal clerks. During the late nineteenth century, moreover, the Dutch in Indonesia tended to follow the French example more than the British. Unlike the British, therefore, Frenchmen and Dutchmen formed larger ethnic communities within the plural societies of Southeast Asia. Such differences, both in style and in numbers of rulers, led to significantly different consequences. The Dutch and French tried to hold their empires with military force; but in no instance did the British fight against people they ruled in order to remain in Asia. In the end such differences left different legacies, whether of continued profitable cooperation or of bitterness and hostility. Reasonable political stability and economic prosperity in Malaysia and Singapore contrasted strongly with the strife and scarcity endemic in Indonesia and Indo-China.

Elsewhere in Southeast Asia also, western nations took advantage of their temporarily superior strength to conduct things to their own advantage. In the case of the rulers of Thailand, the British employed measures similar to those they had used against other principalities on the periphery of the Indian Empire. A semi-suzerain relationship was insisted upon. Such relations existed with the local ruler in Zanzibar, with the Sheikdoms of Eastern Arabia and the Persian Gulf, with Afghanistan, with Nepal, and with Tibet. Observing the results of Burmese pugnacity, Thai rulers grudgingly acquiesced in the British veiled protectorate. But when French power was asserted from the east, Thai rulers not only turned the British presence to their own advantage, but, by playing the British and French against each other, managed to retain a precarious independence.

The Philippines, on the other hand, had an entirely different history. Spanish rule, comparable to and contemporary with the Portuguese, stretched back nearly four centuries, during which a relatively quiet process of hispanization had transformed upper stratas of Filipino society. This in turn had led in the late nineteenth century to Filipino nationalism and a rebellion against Spanish rule very comparable to revolutions that had liberated Latin America half a century earlier. Unfortunately for the Filipinos, however, the Spanish-American War intervened. Having already lost its power to govern and quite willing to give up claims to an increasingly unprofitable dominion, Spain ceded the Philippines to the United States. The United States, filled with a new sense of its Manifest Destiny to bring the blessings of its "way of life" to less privileged, "backward" peoples, had to fight costly battles before her authority could be established. The assertion of American power, initially at least, resembled that of the French, in that it was imposed suddenly and radically, without benefit of those gradual processes by which the British or Dutch had become known and had gained some measure of local support and thus had developed some means to cushion if not resist cultural shocks.

ASIAN
IMMIGRATION AND
COLONIZATION

For centuries settlers had moved from the crowded and poverty filled coasts of South India and South China to the ports of Southeast Asia. This immigration increased greatly during the nineteenth century. For such settlers, the open spaces of Southeast Asia were a frontier where a man might at least lead a more comfortable and promising life. If lucky, he might someday return home as a rich man. Some did so; but many remained permanently.

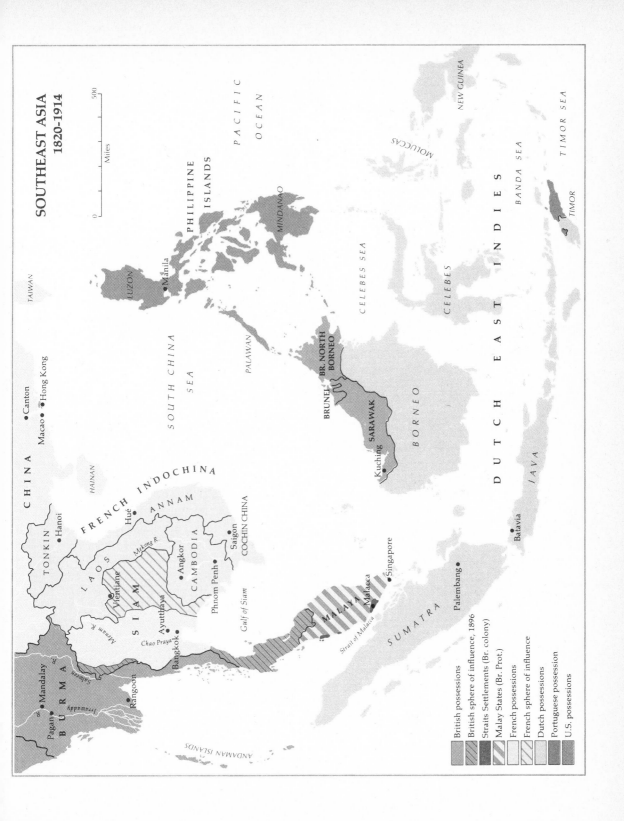

SOUTHEAST ASIA
1820-1914

Miles
0   500

CHINA
Canton
Macao   Hong Kong

TAIWAN

HAINAN

FRENCH INDOCHINA

TONKIN
Hanoi

ANNAM
Hué

LAOS

Mekong R.

Vientiane

SIAM

Ayutthaya

Chao Praya   Bangkok

Menam R.

BURMA
Mandalay
Pagan
Rangoon
Salween R.
Irrawaddy
Sittang

ANDAMAN ISLANDS

Angkor

CAMBODIA

Phnom Penh

Gulf of Siam

COCHIN CHINA
Saigon

SOUTH CHINA
SEA

PHILIPPINE
ISLANDS

LUZON
Manila

MINDANAO

PALAWAN

PACIFIC

OCEAN

BR. NORTH
BORNEO

BRUNEI

SARAWAK

Kuching

BORNEO

CELEBES SEA

CELEBES

MOLUCCAS

NEW GUINEA

BANDA SEA

TIMOR SEA

DUTCH EAST INDIES

TIMOR

MALAYA

Malacca
Strait of Malacca

Singapore

SUMATRA

Palembang

JAVA

Batavia

British possessions
British sphere of influence, 1896
Straits Settlements (Br. colony)
Malay States (Br. Prot.)
French possessions
French sphere of influence
Dutch possessions
Portuguese possession
U.S. possessions

Yet these immigrants tenaciously retained their attachments to India and to China, and clung to their old customs and styles. By their distinctiveness, they added diversity; by their energy and hard work, they contributed to economic development; but by their success and prosperity, they also provoked envy and enmity within societies where they formed minorities.

European colonial rule enabled great expansion of agriculture, commerce, and industry in Southeast Asia during the nineteenth century. Instead of small shipments of spices and other precious goods (silver, gems, silks, porcelains, and so on), ever-larger bulk cargoes became cheaper to move and hence in greater demand. Between 1880 and 1890, in the great river deltas of mainland Southeast Asia, rice production, no longer merely for subsistence needs, rapidly grew into a major export to world markets. These deltas, previously covered with thick jungles and thinly settled, now attracted masses of settlers who came not only from northern plains but from overcrowded parts of India and China. Jungles were cleared; drainage and irrigation and road systems were built. Millions of acres of new land came under cultivation in the years before World War I, and by World War II, millions of tons of rice—3.5 from Burma, 2 from Thailand, and 1.5 from Indo-China—were shipped annually to famine-prone parts of India and China as well as to Japan. As surplus crops were sold, new money economies came into existence. These were subject to hitherto never-experienced market ills: fluctuating price, predatory moneylending, mortgage, forclosure, landless labor and growing unemployment, alien merchant and landlord classes. The resulting impermanence and shallow rooting of capital, tenure, and labor tended to break down old social structures and to undermine indigenous traditions. Social cement weakened dangerously. Bankers, merchants, landlords, or migrant laborers, whose sole aim was to "get rich quick" and return to their homelands, had little stake in the future of the area in which they stopped, and made little contribution to its betterment or long-term development. Not surprisingly, crimes of violence increased rapidly.

What happened in Burma was in reality a process of Indian colonization and colonialism, more than it was British. The expanding economy—based on rice, teak, silver, and oil export—as it developed in this conquered province, brought great increases of prosperity to ever-larger numbers of Burmans and Indians alike. All went reasonably well within the "plural society" as long as overseas markets boomed. For example, by 1930, rice acreage had risen to 10 million; rice exports, to 3 million tons; and annual labor migration from India, to 777,000. But economic depressions, first appearing in the early 1900's, and culminating in the world crisis of the 1930's, shattered the delicately balanced social harmony. This brought increasing landlessness, lawlessness, and social conflict; until eventually, under the impact of Japanese invasion in World War II, the whole system collapsed. In the wake of violent racial tensions, most of the domiciled Indian minority of about 1.5 million (some 10 percent of a population that also included other sizeable non-Burman minorities such as Shans and Karens) were driven out of the country—first, after riots in 1931; then more massively and ruthlessly in

Rice Culture in Southeast Asia.
(John Dominis, Time-Life Picture
Agency.)

1941; and finally in repressive actions of new nationalist rulers, after Burma gained its independence in 1948.

During the 1870's to 1890's, as British influence in Malaya spread, another booming colonial economy developed. Labor-intensive production of such exports as rubber and tin brought hordes of workers from China and India. Despite its being dependent upon world market conditions, subject to fluctuations of demand, Malaya rapidly became one of the most prosperous countries in Asia, and enjoyed an enviable standard of living. But the outsider Chinese, Indians, and Europeans, whose energies had brought about these economic changes, were the greatest gainers. Ordinary Malay villagers, whose life-style was more relaxed and less aggressively competitive, saw themselves falling farther and farther behind in comparison to the affluence of newcomers. The result was not simply the growth of a plural society but growing social tension and alienation between ethnic elements of that society.

With the exception of Burma, where Indian merchants played the same role as economic middlemen that Chinese played everywhere else, no country in Southeast Asia escaped the powerful intrusion of energetic, gifted, and sometimes aggressive communities of Chinese, whose colonization (and indirect "sub-colonialism") had great significance. For whatever reasons, in Thailand, Thai and Chinese intermarried freely. By World War II an estimated one-tenth of over three million of Thailand's people were of Chinese origin. In Malaya, where intermarriage was not common, more than a third of the population was Chinese. Over eighty-five percent of Singapore's population was Chinese. About two million Chinese settled in Indonesia, and another million, in Indo-China (including Cambodia). By the time the second World War broke out, there were about twelve million Chinese in the whole of Southeast Asia. More importantly, Chinese occupied dominant positions in retail banking and commerce. So significant was their economic role, quite out of proportion to their numbers, that they froze out indigenous populations. Many towns and cities of Southeast Asia became substantially Chinese in character.

Not surprisingly, in each country, their dominant economic position eventually provoked the hostility of rising local nationalist movements, most of whose leadership was drawn from bureaucratic and government positions. This functional reinforcement of ethnic separation within rising "middle classes," and between merchants and bureaucrats, tended to increase suspicion and tension during the twentieth century, especially after each country gained its independence. Riots and repression occurred with increasing frequency. Thailand—and Malaya, after fighting Chinese-led Communist insurgents during the 1950's—took steps to limit Chinese immigration, influence, and economic activity. Burma, fearful of Chinese expansion, retreated into xenophobic isolation. Singapore seceded and declared herself a free city-state (1960). Indonesia, faced with one crisis after another, turned against all foreigners, and especially the Chinese, whom it blamed for upheavals. In 1965, an attempted communist takeover led to a wholesale massacre of the Chinese population. In Indo-China and the Philippines also, Chinese communities must defend themselves in the face of nationalist accusations.

NATIONALISM AND INDEPENDENCE

Peoples in Southeast Asia learned new techniques and ideas from their European rulers. Ultimately, as elsewhere, what the Europeans taught could be used to engineer their withdrawal. In later stages of their dominance, Europeans justified their rule by appeals to virtues intrinsic in their national genius or in western civilization. Claiming to bring light to peoples in darkness, at the same time, they often failed to admit the feelings of guilt which the wealth and power they had gained aroused within them. In short, Europeans taught peoples in Asia to rediscover and appreciate their own "national" glories; to remind Europeans of their own guilt feelings by showing inconsistencies between European ideals and European actions; and to acquire and apply modern science and technology in such a way as to send European rulers back across the seas from whence they had come.

The intrusion of western culture was reinforced by all of the institutional apparatus of schools, colleges, printing presses, newspapers, and hospitals. This brought about a revolutionary transformation among members of the more wealthy and privileged classes of each local society. A cultural synthesis occurred between local traditions and alien ideas and techniques. The extent of this process could be measured by rapidly increasing newspaper circulation, book sales, demands for admission to modern schools, and employment in modern professions. At the same time, the intrusion brought about a profound confrontation between western and eastern traditions. The consequence was another synthetic process, now called "neo-traditionalization," whereby Asian societies rediscovered the best elements in their own heritage and then, using western ideas and tools, recast these into more modern and appealing forms. In this regard, the impact of Christian missionaries had been especially profound, not so much for their contributions to modern education and health services as for their calls for "conversion" to new and lofty ideals, principles, and styles of life. At the same time, therefore, by appealing to such new symbols and, in effect, by asking for personal and social commitment to newly forged ideals, new generations of leadership were borrowing a phenomenon of western tradition which they had had ample opportunity to observe—namely, "conversion." They began demanding "conversion" by promising social transformation and reform in the name of new doctrines and ideologies. Having caught the western virus of nationalism, they developed new, hybrid forms of nationalism (and other ideologies with labels having "ism" suffixed to them, such as Marxism, and socialism). Christianity came to be regarded by some as just another tool of western domination and as a form of social separation and division by which minorities—often ethnic or tribal groups that had been dominated, threatened, underprivileged, or simply isolated—had been alienated from dominant majorities in a population. Thus, instead of bringing social peace and universal brotherhood, Christian culture in Southeast Asia was seen by some as reinforcement for old enmities or as incitement toward fissiparous tendencies.

FURTHER READING Among the general histories, D. G. E. Hall, *A History of Southeast Asia* (1964), has become the classic and is by far the most detailed and important single work. J. F. Cady, *Southeast Asia: Its Historical Development* (1964), is thoughtful and sensitive. A more cursory review is B. Harrison, *Southeast Asia: A Short History* (1963). Another excellent pair of later surveys are: N. Tarling, * *A Concise History of Southeast Asia* (1966); and J. Bastin and H. J. Benda, * *A History of Modern Southeast Asia* (1968). Both of these have useful bibliographic notes and reading lists; but by far the most thorough and detailed lists of readings are to be found in D. J. Steinberg, *In Search of Southeast Asia: A Modern History* (1971). This final work is far the most exciting single collection of recent essays, and is strongly to be recommended for anyone wishing to probe more deeply into the dilemmas of the region.

Among works on specific countries, the following surveys may be suggested: J. F. Cady, *A History of Burma* (1958), is the best, although one can also consult works by G. E. Harvey and A. P. Phayre. R. O. Winstedt, *The Malays: A Cultural History* (1953), and L. A. Mills, *British Malaya, 1824–1867* (1928), are the solid, standard works. C. E. Wurtzburg, *Raffles of the Eastern Seas* (1954), is a trove of lore about this adventurer, even if a bit heavy on detail. E. S. de Klerck, *History of the Netherlands East Indies* (1938), may be consulted; but perhaps the most influential works have been J. S. Furnival, *Colonial Policy and Practice* (1956), and *Netherlands India: A Study of Plural Economy* (1944), seminal works on the theory of "plural societies." J. D. Legge, *Indonesia* (1964), is an excellent paperback survey. Works by C. Geertz, *The Religion of Java* (1960), and *The Development of the Javanese Economy, A Socio-Cultural Approach* (1956), make important contributions to our understanding of Javanese life. J. Buttinger, *The Smaller Dragon, a Political History of Vietnam* (1958), gives us a readable account, in volume one, of developments up to 1900. M. F. Herz, *A Short History of Cambodia* (1958); and M. S. Viravong, *History of Laos* (1964), are among the few English works on the subject. More conveniently accessible, therefore, is J. F. Cady, * *Thailand, Burma, Laos, and Cambodia* (1964), which serves to provide both a short survey and a useful list of further readings. For Thailand (Siam), W. A. R. Wood, *A History of Siam to A.D. 1781 with Supplement* (1926), is standard and W. Vella, *The Impact of the West on the Government of Siam* (1955), and *Siam Under Rama III* (1957), are substantial contributions. O. D. Corpus, * *The Philippines* (1965), is a useful short survey. But for more critical depth, J. Phelan, *The Hispanisation of the Philippines* (1959) is superb. S. Arasaratnam, * *Ceylon* (1964) is also an excellent survey, with a good introduction and helpful readings, by a leading scholar.

Finally, V. Purcell, *The Chinese in Malaya* (1967); and K. S. Sandhu, *Indians in Malaya, 1786–1957* (1969); together with works by C. S. Wong on Chinese festivals and S. Arasaratnam on Indian festivals, provide a glimpse at strong minorities and problems of labor migration in just one country, a story which is retold for every part of Southeast Asia in V. Thompson and R. Adolff, *Minority Problems in Southeast Asia* (1955).

*Books available in paperback edition are marked with an asterisk.

4 The Awakening of East Asia

One of the world's oldest civilizations began in the valley of the Yellow River (perhaps as early as 3500 B.C.). Waxing and waning many times over thousands of years, it set standards of enlightenment and gave the world some of its important ideas in art and philosophy, in science and technology. Coincidentally, however, with the age of European renaissance, East Asia went into one of its periods of decline and stagnation. Heavy stylization and imitation replaced creativity and imagination; and much of the capacity for self-criticism waned. But more than this: believing (as it always had believed) itself to be the very center of the cultural world—the essence of civility and virtue surrounded by an outside world of crude barbarians—this civilization lost touch with some important hard realities. Allowing itself to be by-passed by events in the modern "outside" world, it was caught asleep and defenseless. About one fourth of the world's people, in China and Japan, were seriously affected by this process.

CHINA: THE HUMILIATION BY BARBARIANS

Revolution is a complete change in the whole way of life of a people—be that people a small family or a populous civilization and be that change only temporary, or profoundly permanent and continuous. Degrees of the size, scope, speed, and success or completeness of a revolution must be measured before its historical significance can be determined. Arbitrary as this definition of revolution is, it serves as a useful yardstick by which to measure the revolution that has taken place in China.

Change did not come to China quickly nor simply, certainly not to all the people at once but to small groups of people who gradually managed to get others to change. This profound process began slowly and painfully in 1839. Its pace was abruptly quickened by the National Revolution of 1911 and again by the Communist Revolution of 1949. The true dimensions of revolution in China cannot be fully comprehended without examining the whole process of change which occurred. Indeed, cultural and social ingredients of revolution which precede, prepare, and accompany more dramatic and sudden political changes with which the concept "revolution" is usually associated are essential parts of a whole and, as such, must be understood. Only then can one appreciate how China has been (and is being) transformed from an archaic, slumbering empire into an alert and growing world power.

The Dragon Asleep (to 1793) In 1644, the Ming dynasty, which had ruled China for 276 years, was overthrown. An alien warrior people, the Manchus, sat on the Dragon Throne. The new emperors, calling themselves the Ch'ing dynasty (1644–1911), soon enshrined Confucian traditions and allowed them, already in a state of advanced rigidity, to become elevated to extremes of obscurantism and high policy. By the end of the seventeenth century, the Manchu rulers controlled all of China and had brought peace to the region. From the interior (now northeast China), these people of the land had experience only in inland warfare—they ignored the bustle of Europeans on the high seas and along the coastlines. This is the China with which

Pilgrim Flask with Dragon Motif from the Ming Dynasty. (Victoria and Albert Museum, London.)

Europeans became familiar. Of this China Napoleon is reported to have said, "China is asleep. Do not wake her!"

But in what sense was China asleep? Its civilization had reached its high level a millenium earlier. Since then there had been very little important change. In that sense, China was static, seemingly unaware of important changes occurring in the universe. China was a world apart, seeing herself as the cosmic, global epicenter—"The Middle Kingdom"[1]—hence rightly holding aloof from all inferior peoples. China could acknowledge no equal, none from whom it could learn. Its elite class consisted of a scholar-gentry of *mandarin* officials and teachers. This elite was fully capable of providing leadership and introducing changes in the system. But, with few exceptions, until the late nineteenth century they did not wish to alter the shape of the rigid Confucian ideas that had molded their outlook. The very excellence of that system of knowledge, which had given them their status and security and income, blinded them. They did not dare to question verities or risk loss of certainties in exchange for what could not be visualized. With no wars to fight; a prosperous, peaceful, and well-ordered "rule by good example," in accordance with Confucian principles; a blissful (and fateful) ignorance of outside activity; and a conviction of their own superiority, the Ch'ing Emperors saw no cause for change (for which read "modernization"). Only when the survival of China herself was in jeopardy did her leaders consider the alternatives.

However, continual rebellions against the dynastic government saw to it that Ch'ing emperors were aware of danger to themselves and to the realm. A rising in Shantung in 1774 provoked by the greed of palace favorites, another rising of Muslims in Kansu seven years later, followed by a revolt in Formosa (now Taiwan), and further incidents set a pattern of increasing unrest. But such danger as was expected was seen as coming from the land, never from the sea; and special Manchu garrisons (called "banners") were kept at strategic locations. Only in Ming times, when war junks of great size and power had patrolled the Indian Ocean, had China produced strong naval power. (Pirates had been viewed as little more than a barbarian nuisance, and never as a serious threat.)

Any sustained contacts worthy of notice between China and the West began in the seventeenth century. Jesuits such as Adam Schall von Bell and Matteo Ricci conveyed thousands of volumes of European learning to China, several hundreds of which were translated, especially works in mathematics and science. But only a very small number of Chinese scholars came to understand and appreciate the significance of these works. Most, simply looked incredulously at the strange creatures from far away and then cosigned them to ranks among the "barbarians." This fundamental attitude predominated until the middle of the nineteenth century, and even later.

In 1793, China seemed to be at the zenith of its power. The Emperor Ch'ien Lung ruled over vast territories beyond China proper—Manchuria,

[1]China = *Chung* (central) *kuo* (kingdom).

Mongolia, Sinkiang, and Tibet. Annam, Burma, Nepal, Korea, and the Ryuku Islands were submissive, respectfully "kowtowing" and sending tribute. As aforetimes, the empire was governed by an elaborate civil service of scholar-administrators who worked through a structure of ministries—Ceremonies, Civil Affairs, Revenue, Works, Punishments, and War. Keen competition for all but the highest, Manchu-dominated positions was conducted through examinations which were open to all (except actors and common soldiers). Under this system, at least on paper, anyone with talent could enter the competition and could rise by merit. Ch'ien Lung's brilliant reign of sixty years was drawing to its close without dangers beneath the surface being very evident. Yet, by the nineteenth century, more and more official positions were being sold to the highest bidder and corruption was growing. Lord McCartney, sent as an envoy by the British Crown in 1793, was not deceived:

Thirteenth-Century Chinese Kuan Yin. The bodhisattva was revered as an incarnation of compassion. (William Rockhill Nelson Gallery of Art, Atkins Museum of Fine Arts, Kansas City, Mo.)

The Empire of China is an old, crazy, first-rate man-of-war, which a fortunate succession of able and vigilent officers has contrived to keep afloat for these nine hundred and fifty years past—but whenever an insufficient man happens to have command upon deck, adieu to the discipline and safety of the ship.

For his part, the emperor sent a politely condescending reply back to George III, in which he suggested future obedience and rejected Britain's request for a regular embassy, saying "We need nothing from you."

The Dragon Teased, 1793–1839 What happened to China suddenly in the nineteenth century can be compared to what happened to India gradually over centuries. Unaccustomed to danger from the sea and accustomed to treating foreign traders with extreme condescension, as barbarians unworthy of notice and having nothing worthwhile to sell, China was not prepared for the impacts it received. For centuries foreign merchants had been confined to a small waterfront area in Canton (Whampoa) and even then, only for certain months each year after which they were obliged to retire to Macao. A government-sanctioned monopoly of Chinese merchants, called the *cohong*, was the agency with which foreign merchants had to deal. All *cohong* actions were tightly regulated by imperial officers. Tariffs and duties were collected from barbarian traders ("foreign devils"), not for any interest in the goods which they brought but simply for the revenue due for the mere privilege of being there.

England had the greatest interest in this trade. Since the seventeenth century, its East India Company had come to Canton. Silk, lacquer, porcelain, but especially tea brought handsome profits in Europe. Company officials, comfortable with the wealth, culture, and dignity attendant on an almost exclusive monopoly, knew how to deal with China and were more than content to leave things as they were. They did not mind that, as "foreign devils," all of their letters, even those from their British sovereign, would not be accepted by imperial officials and that, even when handed to Chinese merchants, they had to be marked "petition." For their part, Chinese merchants, while they were able to make huge profits for themselves, had to make large annual presents to imperial officials in order to belong to the *cohong;* moreover, beyond such high and irregular exactions and fees (called *"squeeze"*) clandestinely demanded from the *Hoppo* (or Imperial Commissioner), their very lives stood surety for the conduct and behavior of "foreign devils." The price of the privilege for belonging to the *cohong* could be frightening.

Three parallel processes in particular may be seen as having combined to precipitate crisis, conflict, and change in China. First was the rise of competition and "free trading" interest among the Europeans, especially among the British. The end of the Napoleonic Wars heralded an age when free merchants, driven by the momentum of the industrial revolution, wanted to break all restrictions and barriers to their activities—particularly the exclusive control of the English East India Company over Asian markets.

The Factory of the East India Company in Canton, 1826. (Victoria and Albert Museum, London.)

After the company's monopoly ended in 1813, more and more merchants gathered in eastern ports.

Second was the rise of opium traffic. China had long known of this drug and its use for medicinal purposes. The opium grown in India (and Turkey) brought high prices in Canton. But China, by imperial edict (1796), had forbidden importing such "foreign mud." Nevertheless, the demand for this "mud" was such that, between 1800 and 1839, illegal opium cargos to China had grown from just a few hundred chests (of 120 pounds each) to over 40 thousand. Most of this cargo came in British ships from India, where its cultivation brought wealth to growers and revenues to government. The trade was not carried on by the East India Company itself, however, nor even (openly) by its servants, for whom the whole China trade was a much more valuable matter than merely smuggling opium. Rather, as prospects for quick profits mounted, the opium trade was carried on mainly by free agents—mostly British, American, Chinese, and Arab.

Thirdly, perhaps most fundamental and perhaps what finally precipitated armed conflict, was a growing impasse over concepts of law, both domestic and international. According to the law of China, for example, the maxim of "a life for a life" was cardinal, regardless of questions over innocence or guilt; and keeping that law was a community responsibility. Americans and other freebooting adventurers, used to frontier law and to looking after themselves as individuals, could accept such mishaps as might befall one of their fellows. Not so the British. Servants of the Company, wise and experienced in dealings with China, tried to control their "free" brethren and to prevent incidents; but when British free merchants did get into trouble with China they expected the Company and, after 1833, the British Crown to protect them. In matters of international law, China was equally adamant, refusing to deal with any state on equal terms, or as other than a vassal domain; and refusing to lift the restrictions and limits set on foreign trade and foreign traders. As one merchant put it, "China is as difficult to enter as Heaven." A famous letter addressed to Queen Victoria in 1839 by the New Chinese Commissioner, who had been sent from Peking to "Go, investigate, and act!" so as to abolish illicit opium traffic and who had little idea of the military power of Britain, threatened to invade her island and pound her people to bits if she couldn't stop the traffic. As he explained,

Articles coming from the outside of China can only be used as toys. We can take them or get along without them. Since they are not needed by China, what difficulty would there be if we closed the frontier and stopped the trade.

Such thinking, free merchants of Britain found intolerable.

The Dragon in Chains, 1839-1911 Crisis came in 1839. A few British warships and troops proved that Chinese fortifications could be penetrated almost at will. The world learned that all was not well in China. A devastating paralysis of self-assurance immobilized China's leadership. Conditions in China for the next 110 years (1839-1949) resembled those of earlier periods of turbulence during transition from one dynasty to another as, once more, barbarians broke into China, this time from the sea.

In 1842, the Dragon Throne was humiliated by the Treaty of Nanking and obliged to conform to alien norms and practices in diplomacy and commerce. Four ports were opened to world traffic. Foreigners were to judge themselves according to their own laws. Hong Kong was ceded to the British. "Extraterritoriality," so long a feature in India, gained new global credence. Again in 1858-1860, China was humbled by force of arms. The emperor fled from Peking and soon died. Supposedly to "set an example," his exquisite summer palace was burned. It was an example of barbarism never to be forgotten. Aliens sliced enclaves from the stricken body of China all along her coasts and into the interior. Of these "Treaty Ports," each governed by one or more foreign powers mainly to facilitate trade, the most famous and certainly the largest was Shanghai. Meanwhile, remote dependencies of the empire—Tibet, Mongolia, Korea, Taiwan, and Tonkin—broke (or were taken) away altogether. Authorities in China could no longer pretend to hold barbarian forces in check. They had to give away even more privileges and to pay indemnities. The Confucian gentry, who refused to admit to any equal, much less any superior culture, did as they had done in other dark ages. They retreated into themselves, their families, and their private worlds. Only when Japanese armies brought further defeat (1893-1895), and when the failure of the Boxer uprisings (1900-1901) brought further degradation, did the most stubbornly conservative and recalcitrant begin to see that really drastic changes were needed. By that time, however, the empire had become so weakened that a scramble to divide China among the world powers seemed likely to occur. This was averted by a timely intervention of the United States. America urged an "open door policy" by which "the independence and territorial integrity" of China would be preserved while not prejudicing foreign "spheres of influence."

The internal rebellions that had been erupting for years became more serious and endemic. The worst of these was the Taiping Rebellion (1850–1864), which shook the empire to its foundations and showed that perhaps the "Mandate of Heaven" was missing in Manchu Peking.[2] As in other days of dark turmoil, searches for a new mandate became more frantic; and the deep cultural trauma that accompanied such turmoil became ever more profound. As each of these upheavals took place, other groups of reformers, some-far-sighted and energetic, joined in the struggle to break the cultural chains of the past and to hasten change. Some, Yuan Shih Kai, for example, did this by joining the government and trying to restore and rebuild it along modern lines from within; some, such as Sun Yat Sen, by actively opposing imperial government and trying to replace it with something else; and some by first acquiring western education and then working as reformers within various walks of society. In all these avenues of change, active help from abroad facilitated reform, coming either from small groups of idealistic and dedicated individuals from the West (teachers, doctors, bureaucrats, engineers, soldiers, missionaries, etc.) or more passively from efforts by western powers who were alarmed at China's growing anarchy and unrest.

After the Taiping Rebellion, the impetus toward changes of every kind was greatly accelerated. The rebellion was begun by a village school teacher whose efforts to pass the imperial examinations had been repeatedly frustrated by the corruption of officials. Having read and half-absorbed some Christian literature and being much attracted to ideals of brotherhood, he founded a movement to establish a utopian society, a millenial kingdom, with himself as its head. Search for a new celestial mandate certainly motivated many of the Taipings. Others, less scrupulous adventurers, joined the movement for plunder, and by their excesses contributed to its undoing. Before the rebellion was ended, perhaps as many as ten million people had been killed. It was finally crushed by western-supplied and -trained imperial forces under able and dedicated commanders. These were assisted by the "Ever Victorious Army" organized and led by Charles Gordon, a British officer who had been enlisted in the service of the emperor.

Still, the question of the Mandate of Heaven hung unresolved. Though the dynasty had been saved, it had been saved by Chinese, not Manchu forces—proof that the Manchus were no longer in control. From this time onward, modern arsenals, training, and discipline were acquired by various

[2] The kings of the Chou dynasty (1100–256 B.C.), who had built the Great Wall, called themselves the "Son of Heaven," centered their ceremonial activity around their ancestor, "Heaven," and justified their conquests on the grounds that they had received the "Mandate of Heaven."

China's First Railroad, from a Shanghai Picture Magazine of 1885 or Later. (Columbia University.)

regional armies. These became a threat to the Throne—the forerunners of the armies of independent warlords whose rivalries later tore China asunder and doomed the National Republic. During the last decades of the nineteenth century, under the guidance of another Englishman (Sir Robert Hart), the Imperial Maritime Customs was established, bringing with it an efficient system of modern government to postal, telegraph and road services.

Years of foreign intrusion, oppression, and humiliation served to goad and provoke some elements of the archaic and rigid Confucian elite into an awareness that something was desperately wrong and that extreme measures were needed to save China from further degradation and misery. The presence of foreign enclaves all along the coasts, like so many blood-sucking parasites on the skin of Leviathan, served as continual irritants to remind China that strong actions might be necessary to restore itself to full health and vigor.

Stirrings of Renewal and Revolution   But the most profound changes came from the intrusions of new forms of education. China could not hope to escape the impact of Occidental culture with its scientific technology and its revolutionary movements. The building up of armaments, industries, and communications, without deeper changes in the cultural and social order, would not suffice. While old leaders tenaciously clung to the views that there was nothing to be learned from barbarians, mission and private schools steadily provided new knowledge to alert and venturesome students. These slowly brought about an effective transformation of the intellectual climate. New leaders arose who, with their new ideologies, began earnestly to work for complete revolution. They organized study groups and schools. They enlisted the aid of old secret societies and won the support of soldiers, whole battalions of them. Others worked in exile, teaching and writing and organizing. After 1905, when imperial examinations based on Confucian classics were suddenly abolished, the tap-roots by which scholar-officialdom had renewed itself for millenia were cut off. Thereafter, the young and the ambitious began to flood institutions of western learning. Loosed from the rigidities of Confucian tradition, but still closely tied to family loyalties, generations emerged filled with radical ideals and revolutionary commitments.

The old Empress Dowager Tz'u Tse breathed her last in 1908. Within hours, her son, the emperor, also died. She had ruled since 1861, sending an able general to put down the Taiping Rebellion, quashing the attempt of her son and his advisors to overhaul the government (1898), and instigating the abortive Boxer Uprising against "foreign devils." As Japan and Russia fought over which power would rule which part of the empire, and as tides of revolution began to engulf the Ch'ing dynasty itself, the death of this powerful figure, three years after imperial decrees had initiated sweeping changes, apparently removed one of the last obstacles to revolution. Three years later, on the Double Tenth (October 10) of 1911, soldiers in the tri-cities of Wuchang-Hankow-Hanyang mutinied. As news of their uprising quickly spread, province after province broke into revolt and went over to republican control. With surprisingly little bloodshed—some Manchu garrisons were slaughtered—revolution swept over most of China. But the long process of discovering a new "Mandate" had only begun, not to end until 1949.

JAPAN: THE
TRANSFORMATION
BY BORROWING

In a remarkable measure, the culture of Japan has reflected an extreme historical paradox. On one hand, none can mistake its derivation from and affinity to Chinese civilization. In a sense, Japan can even be considered a part, or at least an offshoot of that "Greater China" or "East Asia," the development of which has been so continuously autonomous and uniquely distinct from other great traditions of world history. China reached its classical high culture and imperial grandeur at least a millenium before Japan took misty shape. Japan drew many of her ideals of perfection and patterns from older models in Han (202 B.C.–220 A.D.) and Tang (618–906) China.

On the other hand, just as the British Isles always retained and valued their uniqueness and pugnacious independence, if not periodic isolation, from alien continental currents, so also the islands that make up Japan have done much the same, only in greater degree. Britain was conquered and ruled by the Romans, Vikings and Normans. Japan was never so conquered. Both were occasionally threatened by great armadas whether from the Spanish or from the Mongols and saved by great sea storms. As a consequence, attitudes of extremely protective isolation and xenophobia alternated with ravenously acquisitive emulation of alien styles and ways. As in Britain, the remarkably strong, persistent, and conservative society of Japan, sharply

Travelers Cool Off at the Ryōgoku Bridge. Woodblock print by Masanobu, *c.* 1740. (Honolulu Academy of Arts.)

broken along hereditary class lines, retained a capacity to absorb shocks and adapt to changes without loss of its essential character. Perhaps because earlier forms had never been completely overwhelmed and destroyed and perhaps because each change was superimposed upon layers of substratum from earlier sociopolitical traditions that still retained vitality, Japan seems to have been remarkably well prepared for rapid, revolutionary transformation. (What happened in Japan clearly demonstrates what could have been accomplished in China by an effective, far-seeing and more flexible imperial government.)

Meiji "Restoration," 1868–1912   What is often known as the "feudal" or Tokugawa period (1600–1868) in Japan entered its twilight with the arrival of an American naval squadron under Commodore Perry in 1853 and again in 1854. An essentially military regime, in which vassal warriors (*samurai*) combined with their noble lords (*daimyo*) under the weakening rule of the hereditary Tokugawa *shogun* or commander-in-chief of the emperor, was

Commodore Matthew C. Perry.
Perry's negotiation of the
Kanaga War Treaty of 1854
opened the first Japanese
ports to American merchant
ships as provision stations and
provided for the first American consul to Japan. A commercial treaty was negotiated
in 1858. (Sketch by a Japanese
artist.)

profoundly shocked and embarrassed. Faced by obviously superior military power and with tactfully polite and diplomatic requests for a trade treaty, it could only acquiesce as gracefully as possible. The next request, made by a joint flotilla of British, French, Dutch, and American warships in 1865, not long after European victories in Peking, was less polite and more demanding. The public humiliation of having treaties forced upon them from ships anchored in Osaka harbor was too much for *samurai* pride.

In 1868, led by western *daimyo,* anxious and dissatisfied forces united to overthrow the shogun, and for the first time in over a thousand years actual control of the government was again truly in the hands of the emperor. The sixteen-year-old Emperor Meiji (and his court) was brought from his ancient capitol at Kyota to the castle in Edo, from where the shogun governments had ruled for more than 250 years. As a symbol of the Restoration and of the deeper renewal that it signified, Edo was renamed Tokyo. What the radical young *samurai* leaders of this palace revolution really strove for was not so much the return of the emperor to active power as the legitimizing seal of his approval and authority upon sweeping programs of reform through which the whole nation would be profoundly changed and Japan emerge as a power in the world. They wanted to make sure that never again would Japan suffer such danger and humiliation.

Once the Tokugawa regime had been replaced, each successive reign brought fresh leadership and quickened the pace of change. Unlike what happened in China, however, this process was deliberately hastened and carefully guided and controlled by the state—with military classes at first playing a larger role and merchant classes then growing progressively more important as modern industrialization gained momentum. Experts were brought from abroad to help with the construction of factories, foundries, shipyards, armaments, and textile mills. They came to teach modern methods of production in such basic industries as energy, coal mining, and steel rolling; to build networks of roads, railways, postal and telegraph services; and to establish the latest improvements in administrative, banking, and revenue systems. At a very early stage, the importance of deeper, more fundamental reforms in educational, social, and political institutions was realized. Many old and rigid barriers of class were also abolished, and the *samurai* relinquished their special privileges. A constitution, granted by the emperor, provided for a cabinet of ministers who would jointly govern the realm only so long as they held the confidence of an elective Diet. A nationwide system of schools was developed so as to give each child at least a primary education. Generations of students and young leaders were sent abroad to study in every field so as to acquire and bring back all special kinds of knowledge and skill.

Such was the amazing speed of Japanese progress that, by the end of the Meiji reign in 1912, the world was startled to discover that a new sun had risen to world power in the East. This was dramatically demonstrated in two wars. In 1895, China's might was broken in a dispute over Korea; and in 1905, Russia's eastern fleet was sunk. Such victories, together with

An American Merchant and his Daughter in Tokyo. Colored Japanese woodblock print from the second half of the nineteenth century. (Copyright British Museum.)

the rapid appearance of Japanese products in world markets, brought a new awareness and self-respect to peoples in Asia. However, rapid development in Japan should not be confused with its becoming a "westernized" country. One cannot overlook the deeper bedrock of social and moral tradition from which such rapid changes could come. The behavior code inherited from the Tokugawa shogunates continued to prevail. Loyalty was the paramount virtue. Duty, within a hierarchy of superior/inferior relationships, came first; and the interests of a superior (father, ruler, nation) must be served. Guidance and command came not from the gods but from superiors. Somewhat paradoxically, the supposed divinity of the emperor and his throne served to enshrine this obligation of man to man. Universal and absolute obedience to authority proved to be a powerful dictum.

FURTHER READING E. O. Reischauer and J. K. Fairbank, *East Asia: The Great Tradition* (1960); and, with Craig, *East Asia: The Modern Transformation* (1965), are the monumental classics in the field. As invaluable sourcebooks of readings are the companion volumes edited by W. T. de Bary, *Sources of Chinese Tradition* and *Sources of Japanese Tradition* (1960, and later paperback editions). Two other standard texts, which have come out in several editions, are

P. H. Clyde, *The Far East* (1948, 1952, 1958, 3rd edition), and K. S. Latourette, *A Short History of the Far East* (1946, 1964, 4th edition). G. R. Quale, * *Eastern Civilization* (1966), is yet another such general survey. But perhaps one of the more fresh and readable accounts is that by G. Stokes and J. Stokes, *The Extreme East: A Modern History* (1964).

China Also highly readable and interesting is L. C. Goodrich, * *A Short History of the Chinese People* (1963). H. McAleavy, * *The Modern History of China* (1967), is detailed and well written. A shorter survey is Latourette, * *China* (1964). Another Spectrum paperback, edited by A. Feuerwerker, * *Modern China* (1964), contains some fine essays. That by M. C. Wright, "Modern China in Transition, 1900–1950," is especially noteworthy. C. P. Fitzgerald, *China: A Short Cultural History* (1961 3rd edition), is a survey of cultural achievements. Early contacts are described in G. F. Hudson, *Europe and China: A Survey of Their Relations from the Earliest Times to 1800* (1931). Three works on the opium war, giving different perspectives, are: A. Waley, *The Opium War through Chinese Eyes* (1958); M. Collis, *Foreign Mud* (1946); and E. Holt, *The Opium Wars in China* (1964). *The Taiping Rebellion* (1965), is only one of several solid works on this subject. M. C. Wright, *The Last Stand of Chinese Conservatism: The T'ung Chih Restoration, 1872–1874* (1957), is exceedingly useful. J. Bland and E. Backbone, *China under the Empress Dowager* (1910), is richly entertaining; and *The Boxer Uprising* (1963), by V. Purcell is a work of thorough research. The impact of alien ideas is found in the standard work by J. F. Fairbank and Ssu-yu Teng, * *China's Response to the West* (1954). J. Levenson, in his monumental, 3-volume * *Confucian China and Its Modern Fate* (1958–1965) follows the same theme.

Japan The great classic on Japan before its awakening in the nineteenth century is G. B. Sansom, *The Western World and Japan* (1950). Also very useful is his *Japan, A Short Cultural History* (1952 edition). D. M. Brown, *Nationalism in Japan: An Introductory Historical Analysis* (1955); R. A. Scalapino, *Democracy and the Party Movement in Prewar Japan* (1953); E. H. Norman's *Japan's Emergence As a Modern State* (1940); and G. C. Allen, *A Short Economic History of Modern Japan, 1867–1937* (1962 edition revised up to 1960), provide different perspectives on Meiji and Post-Meiji Japan. A convenient and well-written general work is W. G. Beasley, * *The Modern History of Japan* (1967). Also easily acquired are: A. E. Tiedman, *Modern Japan* (1955); M. W. Meyer, *Japan, A Concise History* (1966); H. Kublin, *Japan, Selected Readings* (1968); and D. C. Keane (ed.), *Modern Japanese Literature*.

*Books available in paperback edition are marked with an asterisk.

5 Africa in the Nineteenth Century

The image of Africa as the Dark Continent, devoid of culture and civilization, became popularized in nineteenth-century European society, but the truth was otherwise. North African states were proud bearers of classical Islamic culture and were part of the Mediterranean historical tradition, and in many parts of Tropical Africa, indigenous kingdoms, cities, and empires existed before the nineteenth century. Modern anthropologists and historians have shown that Black Africa was in the midst of state-building when the European drive to partition and occupy the continent took place under the New Imperialism. West Africa had the heritage of the great inland empires of Ghana, Mali, and Songhai and the coastal states of Ashanti, Dahomey, and Oyo; central Africa had the Kongo, Nyoro, and Ganda kingdoms; East Africa had the Swahili cities on the Indian Ocean and Christian kingdom of Ethiopia. In South Africa the great buildings of Zimbabwe are evidence of higher forms of polities.

Nok Head. The early Iron Age Nok culture flourished in northern Nigeria almost 2,000 years ago. (Copyright British Museum.)

There were a number of African peoples who did not live in centralized states or cities, and these politically fragmented rural folk, many of whom were less advanced socially, often attracted the attention of European writers and explorers. A myth of African backwardness was reinforced by pseudo-scientific theories popular in Europe which held that Negroid peoples were the least advanced of mankind. Europeans did not understand that many African peoples kept their historical experiences in the scrupulously preserved oral tradition, and erroneously concluded that many illiterate societies possessed no history. The net result was much misinformation about Africa and her peoples which allowed the Europeans to justify their eventual takeover of the continent.

Africa was not a political vacuum but an enormous continent, several times the size of Europe, which had its own political and cultural traditions. African society was different from Europe, however, and too often Europeans mistook differences for inferiorities. African family life furnishes a good example—polygamy was often the rule, a social institution well adapted for having many hands to work the land and herd animals. The important unit in society was the extended family, lineages, and clans, rather than the nuclear family which is characteristic of the West. African kingdoms had developed stable institutions of government such as kings, councils, ministers of state, bureaucracies, tax collectors, and armies. But Africa had not enjoyed the benefit of the scientific and industrial revolutions, and African technology remained at a lower level than Europe's, especially after 1800. Most Africans were living in the Iron Age (using iron weapons and agricultural tools) and were not all Stone Age people as some European observers mistakenly believed.

EUROPEAN OCCUPATION OF NORTH AFRICA

Egypt   European interest in North Africa was briefly rekindled when Napoleon occupied Egypt in 1798 with a retinue of scholars in his army. But the French were expulsed by British and Turkish forces in 1801. Following French-British skirmishes during the Napoleonic wars, Egypt was ruled by the Ottoman-appointed pasha, Mohammed Ali, who consolidated his power, broke free of the Ottoman empire in 1806, and became the commanding figure in Egypt until his death in 1849.

Both France and Britain sought to profit from the weakened status of Egypt after Mohammed Ali's death. Briefly, during the 1860's, Egypt's economy boomed because of the demand for cotton which a war-torn United States could not fulfill. Mohammed Ali's grandson Ismail came to the throne and continued construction of the Suez Canal, which the French diplomat Ferdinand de Lesseps had begun in 1859. Ismail ran up debts with European nations attempting to bring Egypt into the modern world with a navy, railroads, factories, and schools. His vision was great but his purse could not keep up the payments, and Egypt fell steadily into debt. The Suez Canal finally opened in 1869, but it brought little income to Egypt, and six years later Ismail was compelled to sell (to Britain) his shares in the international company that controlled the canal; even this did not stave off his creditors, and by 1879 he was bankrupt.

Ismail was deposed and a committee of European creditors took over financial direction of Egypt. Some army officers led a revolt in 1881 after being put on half-pay, took control, and threatened to repudiate Egypt's debts. Britain and France, the major creditors, decided to act in concert, but France faced an internal crisis and problems in Tunisia, so that in 1882 Britain alone invaded Egypt and set up a colonial occupation. This was to be one of the main factors causing the partition of all the African continent during the next several years, since other European powers now sought compensation for Britain's gain.

Algeria   France had long traded with the North African states directly opposite across the Mediterranean, and when in 1827 relations began to sour with the sovereign in Algiers over a French war debt from Napoleonic times, the French sent in a navy and army of occupation in 1830. Although this diversion was supposed to bolster the waning political fortunes of French King Charles X, he soon fell from power. But the French stayed on and

expanded their suzerainty into the interior. Opposition arose from the Muslim Abd al-Qadir and his followers, but France prevailed by 1848 and continued expanding into the interior, to make Algeria a possession larger than mainland France. The French and other Mediterranean European peoples settled into the rich Algerian farm lands to become winegrowers for an expanding European market. Increasingly the French thought of the western Mediterranean as a French lake and coveted other Muslim lands.

Tunisia France's interest in Tunisia had steadily grown after the occupation of Algeria, and Tunis increasingly looked to Britain for protection. By the 1850's, a wealthy trading community of French and Italian merchants joined with the growing Muslim bourgeoisie to ask for constitutional guarantees from the Tunisian rulers. Although the bey disregarded these reforms after a few years, they were an indication of the growing influence of European ideas. By the 1870's, British influence was replaced by the Italians, now unified and looking for areas of potential imperialistic activity. France therefore determined to act, and a dispute between the bey and a French company furnished the excuse for French forces to invade Tunsia in 1881. The bey turned over his finances and foreign affairs to the French, who now occupied the country, while he stayed on with nominal power. France thus took over Tunisia with few questions asked from Great Britain, which profited from the French diversion to occupy Egypt the next year.

Morocco Morocco, the westernmost Muslim country of North Africa, increasingly came under French influence from Algeria. Embroiled in a war with Spain in 1860, the traditional sultanate lost and was compelled to pay a large indemnity. This opened the door to European traders and forced the sultan to float a loan in London, based on customs receipts to be controlled by Europeans. Despite the efforts of Sultan Mawlai al-Hassan to unify warring groups in Morocco, and thus to stand strong against further European influence, and despite agreement among the major European nations in 1880 that the territorial integrity of Morocco should be maintained, French merchants and diplomats planned an eventual takeover of Morocco. This was accomplished in 1912, after the earlier Moroccan diplomatic crises of 1905 and 1911, when Imperial Germany rattled the saber in order to let France know that she disapproved of continuing annexation. In fact, Germany approved only on condition that France cede a part of her new equatorial African dominions.

Thus, by 1914, Morocco, Algeria, and Tunisia formed a solid block of territory under French control; Egypt was under British suzerainty; and the last of the "unclaimed" North African land—along the coast from Tripoli to the western border of Egypt (presently Libya)—passed to the renascent Italian state in 1912 as the prize for a late arrival to the scramble for colonies.

Bronze Plaque of Bini Warriors from Benin, Nigeria. Benin was the center of a brilliant African culture from fifteenth to the seventeenth century. (Copyright British Museum.)

THE RACE FOR EMPIRE IN TROPICAL AFRICA

European interest in Tropical Africa began after the mid-fifteenth century when Portugal's vessels first visited West African coastal kingdoms and settlements. Unlike the New World, where Europeans soon explored the interior regions, Africa's treasures, such as gold, ivory, and slaves were brought to the coast by African middlemen. For the next three centuries, most European traders stayed on the coast, reluctant to battle disease, hostile armies, jealous middlemen, and a debilitating climate.

The Portuguese were succeeded by the Dutch as the principal European power trading in African waters. Then, by the mid-seventeenth century, a rivalry broke out between Britain and France which was to last until the end of colonialism in Africa in the twentieth century. Originally these powers (especially Britain) participated in the lucrative slave trade to the New World, but after 1807, when the abolition movement got under way in Britain, the trade was slowly eradicated. On the coast of West Africa, France attempted an eighteenth-century white-settler colony in Senegal, which failed, but she continued her trading concessions; Britain set up Sierra Leone colony (1787) as a home for free slaves, which succeeded; and the United States followed suit by establishing adjacent Liberia as a similar type of colony in 1821. Private societies carried the burden of black colonization in the latter, and by 1848 Liberia became an independent republic.

France and Britain   The demise of the slave trade meant Europeans had to find other reasons for trading in Africa, and geographical societies from Britain and France sent out explorers in the first part of the nineteenth century to map the interior of the African continent. In their wake came missionaries to convert the African "heathen"; traders to circumvent the African middlemen; and, within a few years, military expeditions to protect the traders and other Europeans from African displeasure. Eventually, such crops as palm oil, peanuts, coffee, and cocoa were obtained from Africans instead of slaves.

By 1870, before the New Imperialism began in Europe, European involvement in Tropical Africa was already well under way. Britain and France still dominated trade but the appearance of several new European powers upset this delicate balance, and the net result within several decades was the partitioning and conquest of the entire continent. Since North and South America, Australia, and large parts of Asia had fallen under European dominion, it seemed natural that Africa should become Europe's last frontier.

Britain's position was pre-eminent because of her trading stations and zones of influence in West Africa (Sierra Leone, Gambia, Gold Coast, and the Nigerian coast), her naval and trading activities in Zanzibar and along the East African coast, and her supremacy over South Africa (seized from the Dutch during the Napoleonic wars). France was close behind with enclaves in Senegal, Ivory Coast, and Gabon in the west, and growing influence in Madagascar. It was apparent, however, that large stretches of Africa's coast were not spoken for, and the vast interior was not occupied at all. During the 1870's and 1880's, a kind of "manifest destiny" to possess

Africa swept over European imperialists; this aggressive impulse was rationalized as Britain's "white man's burden" and France's "civilizing mission."

Rivalry Among Other European Powers   The main cause of Africa's partition at European hands was the growing interest of other European powers such as King Leopold of Belgium; Germany; Italy; and a reawakened Portugal, who had managed to retain from her early holdings, Portuguese Guinea in West Africa and Angola and Mozambique in southern Africa. King Leopold who desired to be more than the sovereign of a small industrial state, was the first of these to entertain the idea of expanding into Africa. In 1876, he founded the International African Association, which sought to gain title to vast lands in the Congo River basin (the Belgian state itself was not officially involved until Leopold was forced to hand over the Congo in 1908). Leopold and an international consortium of businessmen ruled

"In the Rubber Coils." A serpent with head of King Leopold reflects the controversy over the Belgian king's exploitation of the Congo. (L. Sambourne in Punch, 1906.)

what became known as the Congo Independent State. Explorer-journalist Henry M. Stanley was instrumental in persuading Congolese chiefs to sign treaties which gave power and authority to Leopold; in many cases, they did not know what they were signing and assumed it was a gesture of friendship. Leopold's agents murdered some African leaders, and co-opted others.

German interest in Tropical Africa, dating back to early trading missions in West Africa from Brandenburg, was rekindled in the mid-nineteenth century by German missionaries and explorers. A small but determined minority of Germans became interested in colonies, and colonial societies were created to study and propagandize for annexing African lands. By the late 1870's, with Leopold's activity increasing, it was apparent that soon there would be little valuable coastal land left. Private citizens such as Carl Peters

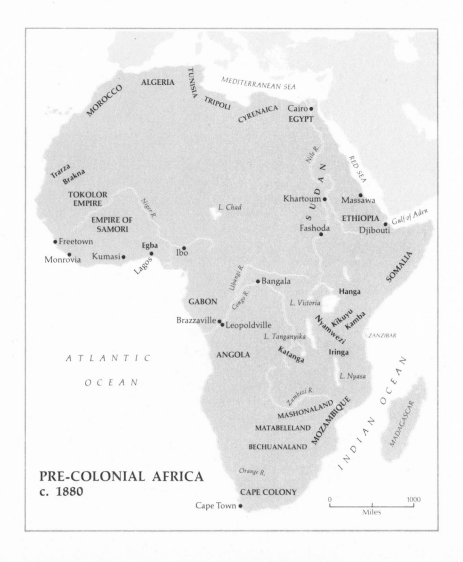

PRE-COLONIAL AFRICA
c. 1880

decided to act, to visit the lands in East Africa then under Arab influence and nominally ruled by the Sultan of Zanzibar, and to sign treaties with the chiefs putting the area later called Tanganyika under the protection of Germany. Opposed at first, Bismarck finally accepted such agreements; and in the space of a few years, German explorers also brought Togoland, Kamerun, and South-West Africa into the German zone of influence.

Hard on the heels of Portugal, Spain was the second European nation to reach Tropical Africa in the 1450's. But she did not stay; nor did she return, except to the small west-coast trading colonies of Ifni, Rio De Oro, and what is now Equatorial Guinea in the nineteenth century, and to Spanish Morocco and the Canary Islands in 1912. Content to expend her energies on exploration and acquisition in the New World, Spain was absent from the scramble for empire in Africa. She nevertheless supplied a footnote to the history of that continent. In the early 16th century, the first cargo of African slaves (America bound) left the west coast of Africa in a Spanish ship.

Besides the fact that new powers were entering the Franco-British preserve of Tropical Africa, there were rivalries in North Africa which added fuel to the fire. The British had taken over Egypt in 1882, much to the consternation of the French. Thus, when French explorer Savorgnan de Brazza explored the area north of the Congo River, France put a claim to it seeking compensation for the British action in Egypt—and to forestall the newcomer Leopold. Britain reacted to the German thrust into the neighboring Kamerun by putting forth renewed claims to the Nigerian coastline.

Partition Clearly a race for empire was in the making and Bismarck decided to call a conference of the great powers in Berlin during 1884–1885 to set down ground rules for European activity. He feared an unlimited projection of European rivalries into Africa would undo the balance of power he had so carefully nurtured in Europe. Leopold benefitted from the congress; he had previously gained recognition of his domain from the United States and now other powers followed, but on condition that his Congo Independent State allow international free trade. The powers agreed on paper that if one country's agents occupied a coastal area, and gave notice, this would constitute effective occupation. In actual practice, force of arms was usually the deciding factor. The scramble for Africa was legalized, Africa was to be partitioned and conquered. No African representatives attended Berlin. Never in the world's history was a collective decision made at one time to occupy an entire continent with so little deference to the inhabitants. And few voices of protest were heard in Europe.

Conquest With technical superiority assured by machine guns, cannon, and steam boats to bring supplies, the Europeans set off to divide and rule. Africa's fragmentation in languages (more than any other continent), cultures, states, and ethnic groups contributed to European military and diplomatic successes between 1885 and 1900, but only after bitter resistance. Relatively few Europeans ever took the field against Africans; they relied

*African, Captured in a Net,
Ready to Be Sold as a Slave.*
(Musée de l'homme, Paris.)

heavily upon trained African mercenaries. The conquest, which was generally over by 1900 (although it continued in some areas until 1914, and in Morocco, Ethiopia, and Libya after that), is best understood by looking at main geographical areas.

In West Africa, the footholds held by France in Senegal and along the upper Niger were expanded overland across the western and central Sudan, following a plan conceived of by General Louis Faidherbe, former governor of Senegal, who was France's architect of empire. The French military, already in action before the Berlin congress, sought greater laurels in a series of campaigns (often without approval from Paris) to master the Niger River valley and to extend the tricolor from the Atlantic to Lake Chad. The city of Timbuktu, symbol of Africa's impenetrableness, fell in 1892. By linking up with Lake Chad, France laid claim to a solid band of territory adjoining Algeria, and containing the British in their enclave of Nigeria. On the coast, France took over French Guinea, expanded in Ivory Coast, and completed the conquest of Dahomey, once a proud African state. This agglomeration of colonies was called French West Africa and gave France claim to Africa's biggest colonial unit. But it was an area of sparse population compared to the smaller British areas. Great Britain had extended inland from the Gold Coast and finally checked the powerful Ashanti state; Northern Nigeria was penetrated and the work of George Goldie, head of the Royal Niger Company, converted it into a protectorate which was eventually joined with the coastal holdings. The modern map of West Africa was drawn and imposed boundaries paid no heed to the fact that African states and ethnic groups were now divided.

King Behanzin of Dahomey. Here the ruler of a kingdom in French West Africa sits for a portrait before his deportation in 1894. (Musée de l'homme, Paris.)

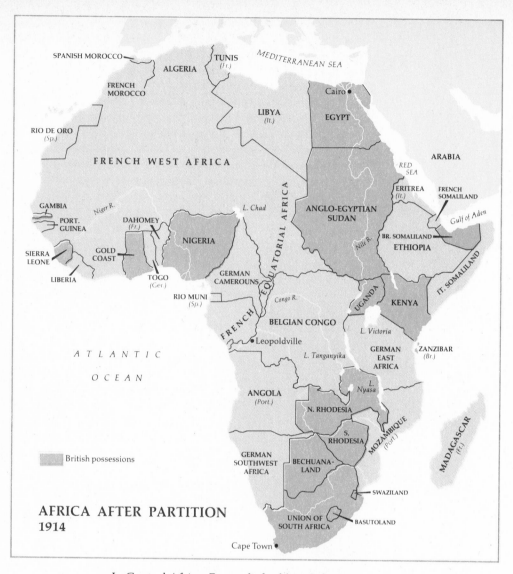

AFRICA AFTER PARTITION 1914

SPANISH MOROCCO

FRENCH MOROCCO

RIO DE ORO (Sp.)

ALGERIA

TUNIS (Fr.)

MEDITERRANEAN SEA

LIBYA (It.)

EGYPT

Cairo

FRENCH WEST AFRICA

ARABIA

RED SEA

ERITREA (It.)

FRENCH SOMALILAND

ANGLO-EGYPTIAN SUDAN

Gulf of Aden

BR. SOMALILAND

ETHIOPIA

IT. SOMALILAND

GAMBIA

PORT. GUINEA

SIERRA LEONE

LIBERIA

Niger R.

DAHOMEY (Fr.)

GOLD COAST

TOGO (Ger.)

L. Chad

NIGERIA

GERMAN CAMEROUNS

RIO MUNI (Sp.)

FRENCH EQUATORIAL AFRICA

Congo R.

BELGIAN CONGO

Leopoldville

UGANDA

KENYA

L. Victoria

ATLANTIC OCEAN

L. Tanganyika

GERMAN EAST AFRICA

ZANZIBAR (Br.)

ANGOLA (Port.)

L. Nyasa

N. RHODESIA

S. RHODESIA

MOZAMBIQUE (Port.)

MADAGASCAR (Fr.)

GERMAN SOUTHWEST AFRICA

BECHUANA-LAND

SWAZILAND

UNION OF SOUTH AFRICA

BASUTOLAND

Cape Town

British possessions

Nile R.

In Central Africa, France linked her Gabon possessions with the middle Congo and the central Sudanic lands to form French Equatorial Africa. Leopold rounded out the borders of the Congo Independent State after conflicts with East African Arabs; the Portugese, who claimed the mouth of the Congo; and the British, who sought lands adjacent to Northern Rhodesia.

In Northeastern Africa, the British moved down from occupied Egypt to conquer native forces under a spiritual leader who proclaimed himself the Mahadi (messiah). They gained control of the eastern Sudan in time to face a small column of Frenchmen advancing from the west in an attempt to link their western territories with the Red Sea. The outcome between

Kitchener and Marchand at Fashoda, where for a while the French and Egyptian flags waved side-by-side, was never in doubt; but the confrontation created consternation in Europe. The French finally backed down and the British became masters of the eastern Sudan.

Italy entered the race for empire after having won small concessions on the Red Sea in 1882. By 1896 she attacked the forces of Menelik II, sovereign of Ethiopia (Abyssinia), and hoped to resurrect a Roman-like African empire. At the battle of Adowa, Italy was routed by a well-armed and prepared Ethiopian army, which administered one of the first defeats to a European army by a non-Western people. Ethiopia and the Republic of Liberia remained the only two countries not controlled by the European colonialists. Liberia, however, was controlled by an Americo-Liberian elite which excluded native Africans from political participation.

On the East African coast, British influence over the Sultan of Zanzibar dated from the antislave patrols. On the mainland, the government took over administration of Kenya (then British East Africa) from the Imperial British East African Company. Missionary activity in Uganda led to British dominion in the interlake area around Lake Victoria, where Africans following western religious ideologies (both Catholic and Protestant) clashed with other Africans favoring Islam; the Protestants won, and their allies, the British, soon took possession of Uganda and arranged for a railway to be built from the Kenya coast to open up the interior. Further south, British missionary influence, typified by the widely reported activity of the medical missionary, David Livingstone, helped open up Nyasaland (modern Malawi).

In Southern Africa, a renascent Portugal was frustrated in her designs to link Angola on the Atlantic with Mozambique on the Indian Ocean. British power carried in this area thanks to Cecil Rhodes, financier, imperialist, prime minister of Cape Colony, who in 1889 formed a colonization company to take over new lands that eventually became known as Southern and Northern Rhodesia (now Zambia). Rhodes had become wealthy in gold and diamonds discovered in Boer-dominated Southern Africa. The Boers were descendants of early (1652) Dutch settlers at the Cape of Good Hope. In order to escape British domination, they trekked to the interior during 1836–1846; and, between the Orange and Limpopo rivers, the Boers created the independent republics of Transvaal and Orange Free State. But the wealthy mines brought hordes of outsiders and the Boers felt their independence was threatened. Rhodes hoped to extend British influence to the Boer republics, take over the area to the north (Rhodesia) and find further minerals, and eventually build a Cape to Cairo railway. Rhodes fell from power when his attempt to take over the Boer republics failed (the Jameson raid). The ensuing turmoil finally led to the Boer War of 1899–1902, in which Britain sought to bring the Boers back into her southern dominions. The Boers received encouragement from imperial Germany, but their guerrilla efforts proved to be weak, and they surrendered to Britain in 1902. The contest between Boer and Briton overshadowed the fact that African Bantu-speaking settlers and indigenous Hottentots (Khoikhoi) were slowly pushed on to poorer land, disenfranchised from public life, and put into a large economic proletariat from which there seemed little escape. Indeed, the problems of the so-called "white settler colonies"—South Africa, Rhodesia, and to a lesser extent, Kenya, were different from the rest of Tropical Africa, where Europeans sought to control and exploit, but not to settle and take away the land.

EUROPEAN GOVERNMENT OF TROPICAL AFRICA

As the conquest ebbed, soldiers and explorers gave way to colonial bureaucrats and administrators. But for the British, service in Africa ranked behind India; and the French, Belgians, and Germans had trouble recruiting for overseas work in an inhospitable climate. Since colonies were to pay for themselves from import and export duties, head taxes, and hut taxes, it was cheaper to recruit locally and to train African soldiers, police, and civil servants. Vast areas were often ruled by a handful of Europeans backed by African functionaries. How was this possible? There was an ever-present threat of force, use of modern weapons, and punishment for any who opposed European orders. The Africans were divided by artificial boundaries—for example, the Wolof people were partly in Senegal (French) and partly in Gambia (British). The map of Africa that emerged by 1914 was based upon the final phases of the conquest, reflecting European power projections onto the continent.

Different styles of administration characterized European rule, and publicists and apologists for colonialism wrote many volumes lauding their respective systems. The British favored "indirect rule," popularized by Frederick Lugard in northern Nigeria, where local chiefs and emirs were kept in office and traditional administration persisted. A British resident took charge of collecting taxes and was the ultimate authority. This was inexpensive rule, and during the 1920's and 1930's the British sometimes tried to carry out indirect practices in places where the Africans did not have chiefs. The British then simply appointed their own chiefs (warrant chiefs), an unsuccessful practice in most cases, since the appointees lacked traditional legitimacy.

Wooden Equestrian Figure from Dogon Culture in Mali. (Courtesy of the Museum of Primitive Art, New York.)

The French favored "direct rule," preferring to eliminate traditional chiefs and install French administrators in key positions. Local rule was usually entrusted to Frenchmen, aided by Africans who were often French-appointed chiefs. Orders were given from Paris and transmitted to Dakar and Brazzaville, the two great colonial capitals, and carried out through an elaborate chain of command. In the earlier days of European contact, France favored assimilation as a colonial policy and had encouraged the assimilation of coastal urban peoples in her oldest colony, Senegal. But conquest brought hundreds of new ethnic groups viewed as unassimilable, and a new policy of association was adopted: new colonies were to be associated with the mother country, not assimilated. The old policy of assimilation lingered in urban areas and favored the growth of an African elite.

Auxiliaries were needed to man the empire, and both Britain and France allowed a select group of young Africans to receive elementary and high school education. But Belgium favored educating a greater number of the Congolese at a rudimentary level, creating basic literacy, but stopping short of developing elites. Theoretically, Portugal offered assimilation to Africans, but few qualified. In fact, the great mass of Africans under colonial rule were *sujets,* as the French called them, with few rights before the all-powerful colonial administration.

Economically, colonial governments undertook few development projects after World War II. European merchants and large international trading firms controlled the economy of Tropical Africa, which meant raw materials such as coffee, cocoa, palm oil, peanuts, cotton, copper, gold, etc. were sent to Europe in exchange for pots and pans, cheap cloth, bicycles and sewing machines, and spirits. Trade was oriented for transportation from each colony to the mother country, with little provision for any intercolony traffic that would benefit Africans. Railways were built to drain the interior to the coastal ports. The advent of cash crops and large-scale mining caused many Africans to come in contact with a market economy for the first time. But many Africans found these economic advances toward modernization diluted by heavy import-export duties and taxes, and by the obligation in French areas to do forced labor. Africans felt themselves governed by expatriate Europeans who cared little for their welfare, despite colonial rhetoric, and the lack of interest in the colonies by the majority of Europeans at home in Europe confirmed this. Colonial novels and occasional colonial expositions called attention to foreign lands controlled from Europe, and school children learned how the map of Africa was colored by empires, but the average citizen was indifferent to the fate of his country's overseas charges.

AFRICAN REACTIONS TO COLONIAL RULE

The African continent had been relatively inviolate before the mad scramble of the conquest. Coastal Africans were in European economic spheres of interest, but the great majority of Africans lived traditional lives. After the conquest was over by the eve of World War I, only Liberia in West Africa and Ethiopia in East Africa remained independent—the rest of the African peoples had lost their right of self-determination and lived under colonial flags. Resistance to the partition had come from such brilliant African commanders as king Samori Touré, who kept the French forces at bay for more than two decades in Guinea; Lat-Dior, who fell in battle rather than see his homeland split in two by the railway construction in Senegal; and countless others, while many African chiefs, signed accommodating treaties with the Europeans rather than bleed their country by force of arms. For the first several decades of the twentieth century, sporadic outbursts of popular discontent and threats of mass uprisings continued to indicate the African will to resist alien occupation.

The total impact of European rule was double-edged for common African folk. On the one hand, they benefitted from new roads and railways, cash-crop markets, a ready source of buyers for their raw materials, some schools, and greater contact with the technology of a modern world. On the other hand, their leaders were undermined or destroyed; their land was

Capture of King Samory by French Captain Gouraud in 1898. (Photo Marlinque-Viollet, Paris.)

occupied by uninvited aliens; their minerals and raw material resources were taken away for great profit—to the Europeans; and they were dominated culturally, religiously, and politically by a strange and unsympathetic culture. For Africans, the nineteenth century was a time of great troubles and humiliation; for the Europeans, it was the high point of empire.

FURTHER READING

A recent general survey of African history, which contains excellent chapters on Africa in the nineteenth century and its relations with Europe, is R. W. July, *A History of the African People* (1970). Also still useful is the fourth edition of Roland Oliver and John Fage, *A Short History of Africa* (1970). The student interested in an anthropological approach to African history should see G. P. Murdock, *Africa: Its People and Their Culture History* (1959), which has an index to all ethnic groups in Africa. A more popular introduction to Africa's past is Basil Davidson's *Africa: History of a Continent* (1966), with excellent color photos of African monuments.

There are many books on European exploration, such as R. I. Rotberg, *Africa and Its Explorers: Motives, Methods, and Impact* (1970); and Robin Hallett, *The Penetration of Africa up to 1815* (1965). Colorful specialized studies include A. H. M. Greene, *Barth's Travels in Nigeria* (1962); and J. Simmons, *Livingstone and Africa* (1955).

Nineteenth-century traditional African states are examined in Daryll Forde and Phyllis Kaberry, *West African Kingdoms in the 19th Century* (1967); M. G. Smith, *Government in Zazzau* (1961). Two Islamic states are covered in Yves Saint Martin, * *L'Empire toucouleur* (1970); and P. M. Holt, *The Mahdist State in the Sudan* (1958).

An excellent introduction to the partition of Africa is Raymond Betts, * *The Scramble for Africa* (1966); see also John Hargreaves, *Prelude to the Partition of West Africa* (1963); for West Africa; Henri Brunschwig, * *L'Avenement de l'Afrique noire* (1963); for Equatorial Africa; and Ronald Robinson and John Gallagher, * *Africa and the Victorians* (1961), for the British in Egypt and elsewhere. The latter should be supplemented with W. L. Langer's *The Diplomacy of Imperialism* (2nd ed., 1950), for a sound treatment of European diplomatic aims.

Biographies of Europeans in Africa provide a convenient way to study the partition. Roland Oliver's *Sir Harry Johnston and the Scramble for Africa* (1957); John Flint's *Sir George Goldie and the Making of Nigeria* (1960); and Margery Perham, *Lugard* (2 vols., 1956 and 1960) are representative studies for East and West Africa.

For early African reaction to European partition see T. O. Ranger, "African Reactions to the Imposition of Colonial Rule in East and Central Africa," in *Colonialism in Africa, 1870–1960*, L. H. Gann and P. Duignan, eds. (vol. 1, 1969); Wilfred Cartey and Martin Kilson, * *The Africa Reader: Colonial Africa* (1970), and Yves Person, *Samori* (1969–1970).

Two works on the nineteenth century by Nigerian scholars deserve special mention as early works by African scholars with an African point of view: K. O. Dike, *Trade and Politics in the Niger Delta* (1956); and J. F. Ade Ajayi, *Christian Missions in Nigeria, 1841–1891* (1965).

Basic to understanding North Africa is C. A. Julien, *Histoire de l'Afrique du Nord* (1931); for gaining an overview of Egypt, John Marlowe, *Anglo-Egyptian Relations, 1800–1953* (1954); for Ethiopia, A. M. Jones and E. Monroe, *The History of Ethiopia* (1960); and for South Africa, the two volumes of Monica Wilson and Leonard Thompson, *The Oxford History of South Africa* (1969–1970).

*Books available in paperback edition are marked with an asterisk.

PART XVI

The early twentieth century was a time of intense nationalism, which became the dominant political force of the period. The new nationalism differed greatly from idealistic nationalism in that it was shrill, aggressive, and frequently contemptuous of other national groups. Together with imperialism, the new nationalist spirit did much to increase the bellicosity and restlessness of the European powers.

There was increasing emphasis on the idea of violence. One manifestation of this was the rise of militarism as a semi-official creed in Europe. Another was the activity of anarchists, who stressed the legitimacy, indeed the desirability, of physical assault.

Yet despite the influence of militarists, violent nationalists, and revolutionaries, in 1914 there was still general confidence among many ordinary Europeans that they were on the threshold of an era that would bring to full blossom the principles of liberal enlightenment and prosperity. It was not until war had disrupted much of European society that antiliberal forces gained enough strength in certain countries to reverse the earlier trend toward increasing individual liberty.

The First World War was a vast historical catastrophe whose effects were felt around the globe. Despite the immense destruction, after the war ended in 1918 many hoped that a new era of peace, freedom, and prosperity would finally begin. In part, the failures that brought the Second World War were the consequences of the peace settlement that ended the First.

There were two men in 1919 with something new to say—Lenin and Wilson. Wilson won the propaganda battle of 1918–1919 because his concept of national self-determination expressed so forcefully the yearnings of the masses for popular government and national independence. His vision of a just peace could not, however, be realized, for European nationalism was much too exclusive to be compatible with the degree of international cooperation that Wilson envisaged.

The five years 1919–1923 were filled with local wars, economic depression, social unrest, and attempted revolutions. After 1923, Europe began temporarily to return to normal. The next five or six years were a time of optimism, in which there was widespread belief that the western world was once more on the way toward peace and prosperity. This brief period of well-being was noteworthy for a new spirit of reconciliation in international politics—the "spirit of Locarno." This mood was unable to survive the economic depression of 1930, and the loss of energy and confidence was so pronounced that the way was cleared for new fascist movements.

Fascism was compounded of many things: insecurity due to economic breakdown, loss of social and national purpose, fear of leftist revolution, frustration of nationalist ambitions, and persistence of the violent instincts encouraged by the First World War. The German version—nazism—was able to interweave the demonic qualities of Hitler with some of the people's most positive German characteristics, transforming German confusion of purpose into a violent concentration of energy.

By the late 1930's, Hitler decided that the opportunity had come for Germany to exploit European weakness and confusion. He never planned a six-year world war, but hoped to establish German domination of central and east-central Europe in a series of quick moves. The unexpected resistance of Great Britain to German aggression surprised and confused Hitler, who then ignored his original goal of keeping Russia and the western democracies isolated from each other. Thus, despite the incredible triumphs of Nazi arms in the years 1939–1941, Germany was once more unable to withstand the might of an international coalition. After six years of unparalleled destruction and genocide, the Third Reich collapsed in total defeat.

"THE GOLDEN FISH" BY CONSTANTIN BRANCUSI, 1924. (Courtesy, Museum of Fine Arts, Boston. William F. Warden Fund.)

THE ERA OF THE WORLD WARS, 1914-1945

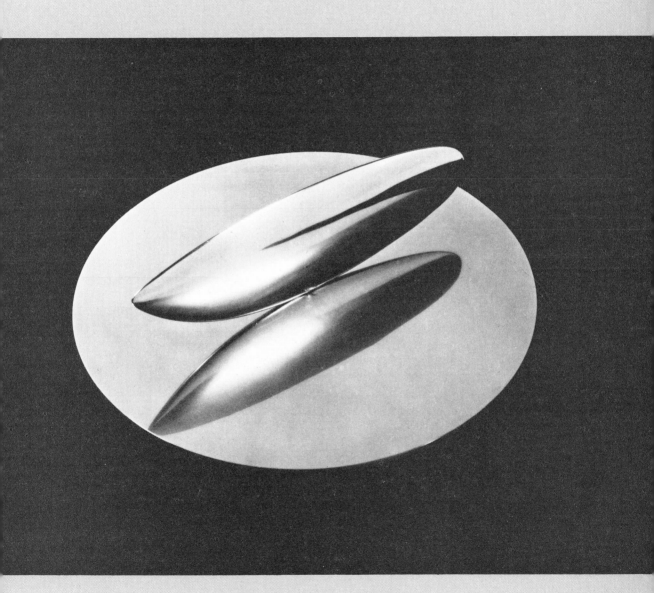

LEGACY OF THE PAST

The era of the early twentieth century that lasted from the first to the second World Wars has left several major legacies to the contemporary world, some positive and some negative.

In political forms and ideals, it has left three patterns. The first is that of the social democracy of the welfare state—the policy of trying to achieve minimal economic equality and security for the entire population to complement liberal political democracy. Such a program was first attempted by the advanced countries of northwestern Europe in the 1930's and has been espoused to some extent by all progressive countries in the contemporary world.

The second form is the kind of totalitarian state socialism now known as communism. Communism was first put into practice in Russia during this period as a means to expand the political, military, and industrial capacities of a backward country very rapidly. Since that time it has attracted the allegiance of a significant part of the contemporary world.

The third form is that of fascism and nazism, destroyed by military force in 1945 but still present as a specter of fear in the minds of our contemporaries. The term "fascist" has lost specific meaning, but stands vaguely as a reminder of human capacity to revert to the use of arbitrary force—whether the actual regime be Communist, right-wing nationalist, or of yet another form.

The extreme nationalism of the late nineteenth century has become possibly the most predominant single political passion of the twentieth century. It has spread far beyond the area of European conflicts where it was born, and in varying degrees a strong sense of nationalism has been inherited by nearly all the new countries and peoples of the contemporary world.

At the same time, the effort made to achieve an international rule of law through the League of Nations left an ideal in the minds of men, even though it originally ended in failure. In our own world, considerable effort is sometimes expended to realize the same goal through the United Nations.

MAJOR EVENTS, 1879-1945

1879–	Dual Alliance: Germany and Austria (1879)
	Rise of Tariff Protectionism (after 1879)
1880–	
	Economic Depression (1882–1886)
	Triple Alliance: Germany, Austria-Hungary, Italy (1882)
1885–	
	Germany and Russia sign Reinsurance Treaty (1887)
1890–	
	Franco-Russian Military Alliance signed (1894)
1895–	
1900–	Economic Recession (1900–1901)
	Entente Cordiale between Britain and France (1904)
1905–	
	Bosnian Crisis (1908)
1910–	
	Second Moroccan crisis (1911)
	Economic Recession (1912–1913)
	Balkan Wars (1912–1913)
	First World War (1914–1918)
1915–	
	United States enters the war (1917)
	Provisional Government in Russia (1917)
	Bolshevik Revolution in Russia (1917)
	Treaty of Brest-Litovsk (1918)
	Russian Civil War (1918–1920)
	Treaty of Versailles (1919)
	Foundation of Italian Fascist Party by Benito Mussolini (1919)
	Weimar Republic founded in Germany (1919)
	Comintern founded (1919)

1920–	First Assembly, League of Nations (1920)
	"Kapp Putsch" in Berlin (1920)
	Irish Free State (1921)
	N.E.P. begins in Soviet Union (1921)
	Mussolini's Fascist dictatorship in Italy (1922)
	Germany and Russia sign Rapallo Treaty (1922)
	German inflation (1923)
	"Beer Hall Putsch" in Munich (1923)
	French occupy Ruhr (1923)
	Primo de Rivera dictatorship in Spain (1923)
	Death of Lenin, rise of Stalin (1924)
	New Soviet Constitution (1924)
	Dawes Plan (1924)
1925–	Locarno Treaty (1925)
	Military dictatorship in Portugal (1926)
	Pilsudski coup in Poland (1926)
	General strike in Britain (1926)
	Pact of Paris (Kellogg-Briand Pact) (1928)
	Great Depression begins (1929)
	First Five-Year Plan, collectivization in Soviet Union (1929)
	Lateran Treaty (Mussolini and the Catholic Church) (1929)
1930–	
	Second Spanish Republic (1931)
	"National Government" in Britain (1931)
	British Imperial Statute of Westminster (1931)
	Hitler's Nazi regime in Germany (1933)
	Rightist but anti-Nazi dictatorship in Austria (1933)
	"Blood Purge" of Nazi radicals (1934)
	Second Five-Year Plan in Soviet Union (1934)
1935–	Germany begins official rearmament (1935)
	Italy conquers Ethiopia (1935–1936)
	Formation of "Popular Front" in France and Spain (1935)
	Government of India Act (1935)
	Egypt granted full sovereignty by Britain (1936)
	John Maynard Keynes, *The General Theory of Employment, Interest, and Money* (1936)
	Rhineland remilitarized (1936)
	Spanish Civil War (1936–39)
	Great Purges in Soviet Union (1936)
	German *Anschluss* with Austria (1938)
	Munich crisis: Germany occupies Sudetenland (1938)
	Great Purges end in Soviet Union (1939)
	Conquest of Poland (1939)
	Second World War (1939)
	Russian "Winter War" (1939–1940)
1940–	Germany invades France, Denmark, Norway, Holland, Belgium, and Luxemburg (1940)
	Battle of Britain (1940)
	Germany conquers Yugoslavia and Greece (1941)
	Germany invades Soviet Union (1941)
	Japanese attack brings U.S. into war (1941)
	Italy surrenders (1943)
1945–	Yalta Conference (1945)
	Germany and Japan surrender unconditionally (1945)

1 Background: Power Politics and the Coming of War

Between 1871 and 1914, the European powers greatly expanded their imperial power overseas, while experiencing the longest period of relative peace since 1789. Palace revolutions occurred in several small countries, but they did not affect the whole of Europe. There were a number of limited wars, but they did not involve the great powers against each other. Yet this record was abruptly terminated in 1914 by the most fearful conflict that the continent had yet seen, a war that involved all the great powers and ended in revolutions overthrowing the governments of three of them.

One of the reasons that the minor crises of this period did not for so long erupt into a general war was that much of the energy and attention of the powers was drawn away from Europe into imperial expansion overseas. Another was the restraining influence exercised by the guiding genius of Bismarck until 1890. The Prussian statesman desired peace once Germany had been united; but after his dismissal, Germany became a disturbing, rather than a stabilizing factor in European politics. Over the decades, the growth of nationalism and militarism, fed by chauvinists and demagogues, had an unsettling effect on the policies of European governments. Under these influences, the balance-of-power system, which required reasoned diplomacy (including careful assessment of the vital needs of others), could no longer perform its stabilizing function. It was no longer a safety net for daring aerialists, but a web in which all were caught and doomed to mutual destruction.

THE BEGINNING OF THE ALLIANCE SYSTEM   After the unification of Germany, Bismarck's diplomatic aims were primarily conservative, intended to retain what Germany had already gained. He regarded the balance of power as indispensable to that end. For two decades, he manipulated the balance from the position of fulcrum, shifting the German weight first one way and then another to preserve equilbrium. Bismarck was convinced that the French would never reconcile themselves to their defeat and the loss of Alsace-Lorraine in 1871. Hence Germany could only look to Austria-Hungary, Russia, and Britain as potential allies. But Britain and Russia could not ally, for their interests were in conflict from the Balkans to China. In view of this, there were only two possibilities open to Germany: she could combine with Austria-Hungary and Russia or with Austria-Hungary and Britain. The former combination was that upon which Bismarck usually depended, but at crucial moments, when it appeared on the point of rupture, he prepared to shift to the latter.

The most difficult aspect of an alliance of Germany, Austria-Hungary, and Russia was the conflicting interests of the latter two powers in the Balkans. After Russia's victory over Turkey in the Russo-Turkish War of 1877–1878, Britain and Austria-Hungary both protested Russia's creation of a large Bulgarian principality stretching nearly all the way across the Balkan peninsula. When Bismarck mediated as a self-styled "honest broker" at the international Congress of Berlin (June–July 1878), the Russians had to content themselves with a lesser Bulgaria divided into two principalities. Tsar Alexander II and his advisers felt that they had been deserted by Bismarck, but were not prepared to take the alternative of allying with republican France.

The Austro-German Dual Alliance Relying on Russia's estrangement from France, Bismarck negotiated the Dual Alliance with Austria-Hungary in October 1879. This firmly bound Germany and Austria-Hungary together in the event that either were attacked by Russia, and committed Austria-Hungary to benevolent neutrality should Germany be attacked by France. It became the first permanent alliance in the history of Europe (previous alliances had always been formed for specific objectives and then dissolved).

The Dual Alliance became the Triple Alliance when Italy joined it in 1882. The Italian government was motivated by anger over France's seizure of Tunisia, which the Italians coveted, and by the need of support from Catholic Austria against the papacy, which remained unreconciled to Italian unification.

Bismarck's purpose in negotiating the Dual Alliance was to warn Russia rather than to alienate it permanently. He elicited British support to help restrain Russian expansionism in the Balkans, but continued to try to cultivate a special relationship with the tsarist regime. Germany thus remained on better terms with Russia than did any other major power, and in 1887 this resulted in a secret "reinsurance treaty" between Berlin and St. Petersburg. Its terms guaranteed the benevolent neutrality of both powers toward each other in the event that either was attacked by a third. Since the Reinsurance Treaty and the Dual Alliance were both stated in defensive terms, they were technically not in conflict with each other. Bismarck had no intention of supporting Russia in the event of a war in the Balkans against

Austria-Hungary or Britain; his purpose was to make Russia dependent on German policy and thus unable to provoke a major conflict.

Germany's "New Course" and the Franco-Russian Entente Bismarck's delicate juggling act did not, however, survive his expulsion from the German government in 1890. The Germany of William II announced a "New Course," which aimed at a more active foreign policy and allowed the Reinsurance Treaty with Russia to lapse. This left Russia without any official ally. The only other large country on the continent in a similar predicament was France, which had been alone ever since 1871. The Germans calculated that the gulf between western republicanism and tsarist reaction precluded cooperation, but it soon became evident that Frenchmen and Russians did not feel this way. Their two governments signed a treaty of friendship in 1891.

It was true that France and Russia had few joint interests. Russia was concerned about the Balkans and the Far East; its government was the most authoritarian in Europe. France was interested in western Europe and north Africa; its political structure was the most democratic and representative on the continent. The two countries had but one thing in common: both needed an ally. France wanted security against Germany; Russia wanted potential help against Austria-Hungary or Britain. Therefore their agreement was expanded in 1894 into a full-fledged mutual defense alliance against attack by any member of the Triple Alliance. Within four years after Bismarck's dismissal, Germany had lost her pivotal position in European politics and the continent had divided into two rival alliances.

Congress of Berlin, 1878, by Anton Werner. This well-known painting portrays the leading participants at the most important diplomatic conference of the late nineteenth century. In the center foreground, Bismarck, the host, shakes the hand of the Russian foreign minister. To Bismarck's right is the Austro-Hungarian foreign minister, Andrassy, and farther to the latter's right, the great British prime minister, Disraeli. (Radio Times Hulton Picture Library.)

The emergence of the alliance system did not of itself, however, immediately threaten the peace of Europe. Germany still had no new ambitions in Europe, while the Franco-Russian entente was at first a somewhat uncertain association. No real teeth were put into it for more than a decade.

Meanwhile, the major activity of most of the great powers continued to be imperial expansion overseas.

THE ORIGINS OF THE FIRST WORLD WAR

The dominant political passion in Europe was not the class struggle predicted by Marx but rather the surging sense of nationalism, which overrode social divisions and provided group identity. National sentiment had grown steadily during the nineteenth century and reached new heights after 1900. As was shown earlier, nationalism and liberalism were, in the beginning, companion movements which reinforced each other. The freedom of peoples was considered the natural counterpart of the freedom of individuals; neither was thought secure without the attainment of the other. New developments in the middle of the nineteenth century, however, revealed that these objectives were not necessarily harmonious. In many cases, national self-determination could not be achieved without violence, which tends to breed a mood of intolerance that stifles freedom. The revolutions of 1848 demonstrated that the quest for national unity or independence could easily lead to the demand for domination over alien peoples. The careers of Louis Napoleon and Bismarck had shown that nationalism and authoritarianism were actually compatible, that the spirit of nationalism could be exploited to suppress popular liberties. After 1870, the growing struggle for power in European politics was accentuated by a strident, chauvinistic nationalism which insisted upon the greater rights of some peoples at the cost of the freedom, unity, or prosperity of others.

The Role of Nationalism Nationalism had become almost universal and existed in a number of different varieties. British nationalism, for example, was positive but restrained. Many Englishmen were so sure that they were better than other nations that they felt little need to indulge in blatant boasting and gratuitous abuse. Less secure nationalists from other countries had to use louder voices. This was especially the case in Germany, where nationalist feeling had expanded enormously since the 1860's. By 1900, it affected the working class just as much as the rest of the population. Germans were proud of their country and their accomplishments, which they felt did not receive due recognition abroad. Therefore, expansion and aggressive attitudes tended to be popular with the people; voluntary civilian participation was what made influential associations of such groups as the "Naval League" and the "Pan-German League." Italian nationalism was somewhat similar to that of Germany, save that it was less powerful and less pervasive. Rebellious Italian bourgeois wanted to overcome class struggle by driving Italy ahead to a position of world influence.

Small, disunited or defeated peoples experienced strong nationalist reactions against their situation, which they were willing to try to change by force. The nationalism of small national groups that had not yet won independence or were not fully unified was most obvious in the Balkans and in east-central Europe, where millions of people still lived in the multinational empires of Russia, Austria-Hungary, and Turkey. Agitators among such peoples as the Serbs hoped eventually to unite all Serbs in a greater Serbian kingdom, even if this necessitated destruction of the Habsburg empire. Nationalism of this sort was potentially very explosive since the small Balkan nations could usually rely upon Russia to support them. After Germany had become the protector of Austria, Balkan nationalism could easily drag the great powers into a general war.

Even in France, where modern European nationalism had originated, there was a new growth of nationalism after about 1905. This *réveil national,* or "national reawakening," was centered in Paris and based primarily on fear of Germany and the threat of war. It was not, however, limited to any one social class and it reflected a sense of solidarity that encouraged the government to more positive action against Germany. Such nationalist sentiment, reflected in some fashion by almost every country in Europe, magnified the effect of the diplomatic conflicts that mounted in intensity after the turn of the century.

Militarism and the Glorification of War   Nineteenth-century thought had glorified competition and struggle on all levels of life. Classical liberalism and Social Darwinism had both agreed that people prospered most when they competed against one another with all the energy at their command. This attitude, basically concerned with economics, had been paralleled on the diplomatic level after 1850 by the new emphasis on *Realpolitik.* Successful statesmen were to accomplish what was desirable for themselves and their governments irrespective of moral restraint or the cost to other people.

The most sinister development of all was the rise of militarism in Europe after 1870. In earlier decades, classical liberals had opposed large standing armies because they cost too much money and might be used for tyrannical purposes. However, the growth of nationalist feeling, the development of industrial society, and the increasing diplomatic anarchy all combined to create a new emphasis on military preparation. France, Russia, Germany, Italy, and Austria-Hungary all kept large standing armies, each based on universal conscription and numbering hundreds of thousands of men. The only exception was England, who relied on her navy. Size and expense rose constantly, with little prospect of the trend being reversed. This was especially the case after the turn of the century. During the decade 1900–1910, the average annual military appropriation increased for every major power. The greatest per capita burden for army expense was borne by the French and Germans, but the cost of the British navy threw the heaviest average burden of all on Great Britain. After 1910, the rate of increase was even more vertiginous. Many leading commanders believed in the inevitability of war, an attitude well expressed by a German general, von Bernhardi, who in 1908 published a book entitled *Germany and the Next War.* He prophesied a general European conflict and urged the Germans to be prepared, confident though he was that German might and spirit would triumph.

As the standing armies grew and as concern for security became more intense, military leaders exerted increasing influence over political decisions.

In most of the major countries, they had drawn up complex mobilization plans which they would not consider changing regardless of the political implications. German military planners were, for example, insistent that Belgium, France, and Russia would each have to be invaded in sequence should war occur. Military leaders possessed particular influence among the two Germanic governments, where, to cite another example, the determined and aggressive General Conrad von Hötzendorff, chief of the Austro-Hungarian General Staff, helped to impose a bold and dangerous policy toward Serbia.

Moreover, after the turn of the century Europeans seemed genuinely bored. They had had four generations of peace and prosperity, but many of them were now looking for some kind of new excitement. There was a fairly widespread feeling that a test of blood would somehow "reinvigorate" society. It was held by some that a good fight was needed every generation or so to keep the population in shape. In Italy, an erstwhile esthetic movement like that of the radical "Futurists," who were mostly poets and painters, found intense fascination in death and destruction. Like many members of the prewar generation, the "Futurists" were nihilists attracted by power and movement for the sheer exhilaration of the experience. War they reckoned to be the greatest joy of all, and praised "the beautiful ideas that are death-bringing." Such absurdities reflected the conscious feeling of only a small minority of Europeans, but the structure of international politics was so competitive that these elements sensed great opportunities for realizing their values on a grand scale.

Germany's "World Policy" Germany's position among the great powers in the age of imperialism was quite anomalous. Though it had the most productive economy and the strongest army in Europe, Germany lacked an empire of any significance. Even minor states such as Holland and Portugal had a brighter "place in the sun" of world imperialism than did mighty Germany, and this situation became intolerable to German statesmen and nationalists. In 1897, the German government therefore announced that a new era of "world policy" had begun, in which German interests would be systematically advanced all around the world and an effort would be made to lift Germany to the ranks of the major imperial powers. It was by no means surprising that German nationalists wished to have their country win the same position held by all other major European powers, but this was a sharp departure from the conservative "continental" policy of Bismarck. Moreover, the new German nationalist ambitions had few concrete goals, for nearly all prospective colonial territory had been occupied. Since practically the entire world had been divided into colonial spheres of influence among the other powers, Germany could not hope to win new status abroad without upsetting the existing balance.

"World policy" held serious implications for Germany's relations with the leading imperial power, Great Britain. German leaders determined to build a mighty navy that would rival the British fleet, and hundreds of

*"The Peace of Europe is Assured,"
Puck Cartoon, 1893.* A British
sketch satirizes the beginning
of the great rival alliances.
The German Kaiser William
II, after recently dropping the
Reinsurance Treaty with Rus-
sia, leads away his Austrian
and Italian allies of the Triple
Alliance. The Russian tsar,
Alexander III, in turn escorts
his new French ally. Note that
Germany and Russia are por-
trayed as the two superpowers.

thousands of civilians enthusiastically supported the new "Naval League."
After 1898, constantly increasing naval appropriations were voted every two
or three years by the Reichstag for, as one chancellor later put it, "the general
purposes of national greatness."

Whereas Germany was basically a continental power, the British were
an island people who lived on trade and had to protect the largest overseas
empire in the world. Their leaders believed that Britain must maintain a
"two-to-one" ratio of naval superiority, by which the British navy was to
be as strong as the next two largest fleets combined. The British, too, began
to vote increased appropriations bills. Introduction of a new type of super-
battleship, the "dreadnought," in 1906 made many of the previous vessels
obsolete, and the naval race waxed ever hotter and more expensive.

The Anglo-French Entente and the First Moroccan Crisis For half a
millennium, enmity in one form or another between France and Britain had
been a frequent factor in European affairs. After the dawn of the new
century, however, these two nations viewed with mutual apprehension a
third power—Germany. Moreover, the British government was quite apprehensive about imperial competition in Asia from the Russian empire, and
sought to reduce the scope of tensions and rivalries it faced overseas.
Following a series of discussions, the French and British governments arrived
at an *Entente Cordiale,* a "friendly understanding," on outstanding colonial

disputes in the spring of 1904. France formally acquiesced in Britain's position in Egypt and the Sudan, while Britain recognized France's primacy in Morocco. This was in no way a defensive alliance, but merely a pledge of friendship and mutual understanding.

Nonetheless, it was a blow to German policy, for it tended to bind the two leading colonial powers together in support of the colonial status quo, excluding German interests. The German government finally decided to take matters into its own hands and test the solidity of this Anglo-French entente. On March 31, 1905, Kaiser William II alighted from a German warship at Tangier and delivered a vigorous speech that emphasized the importance of maintaining Morocco's independence. The German government then demanded an international conference to decide the future of Morocco. Such a meeting eventually convened at Algeciras in southern Spain at the beginning of 1906, but all the other powers save Austria-Hungary and Morocco voted against Germany. Their support of the dominant pattern of great power colonialism turned the conference into a German defeat, and the attempt to breach the Anglo-French entente only made it firmer.

In the following year (1907), the French government helped to promote a colonial understanding between Britain and Russia. This agreement recognized Afghanistan as a British sphere of influence and divided Persia, the main bone of contention, into three zones—one under Russian influence, one under Britain, and the third neutral. Though this arrangement fully satisfied neither power and nearly collapsed several years later, henceforth there was talk of a "Triple Entente" of Britain, France, and Russia that might eventually emerge as a barrier to German policy.

The Dilemma of Austria-Hungary and the Bosnian Crisis German leaders protested that their country was being "encircled" by a hostile net of anti-German military and colonial agreements. The power most threatened, however, was Austria-Hungary, for the unspoken corollary of the new arrangements was that the other major powers (with the exception of Austria's ally, Germany) were abandonning the Balkans to Russia as a Russian sphere of influence. Russian imperialism, having been thwarted in Asia, sought to drive Turkey from the Balkans altogether and to replace both Turkey and Austria-Hungary as the dominant power in southeast Europe. To this end, Russian policy encouraged militant Balkan nationalism, one of whose goals was the dismemberment of the Austro-Hungarian empire.

Austria-Hungary, in turn, sought to strengthen its military and diplomatic position against Russian penetration and against Balkan nationalism. In September 1908, the Russian foreign minister therefore offered the Austrian government a deal. In return for Austria's acceptance of the opening of the Turkish straits to Russian warships, Russia offered to recognize Austria's official annexation of the Serbian-inhabited provinces of Bosnia and Herzegovina, which Austria had legally administered under international law since 1878.

Seeing a golden opportunity to check Serb expansionism and subversion of their own empire, the Austrian leaders suddenly seized the initiative. In October 1908, the Austrian government officially announced the incorporation of Bosnia-Herzegovina before Russia was ready to force the issue of opening the straits. The Austrian move led to a storm of indignation from other powers, who feared that it might upset the existing balance. Amid the resulting tension, the Russians feared to go through with their own plans.

Tiny Serbia was even more aggrieved and, expecting Russian support, began to prepare for war against Austria. Eventually, after Germany made it clear that she would support Austria if the latter were attacked by Russia, the tsarist government gave in and the annexation of Bosnia-Herzegovina was officially accepted. Both Russia and Serbia were humiliated, and vowed revenge.

The Second Moroccan Crisis Though the Bosnian affair had ended in victory for Germany and Austria, the kaiser and other German leaders felt increasingly frustrated. Their efforts to implement "world policy" had not won a greater "place in the sun" for Germany, but had elicited fear and hostility, and a closing of the ranks of other imperial powers against them. To make matters worse, there was no real coordination of leadership in the German government. The kaiser himself was too emotional and indecisive to lead, the civilian chancellors lacked authority and the General Staff was a law unto itself. For lack of a consistent policy, the German government adopted an uncertain course of menace and bluff to try to win greater imperial status.

In July 1911, the German gunboat *Panther* was sent to the Moroccan port of Agadir to "protect German interests." The ostensible reason for this move was that France had recently dispatched troops to occupy the interior of Morocco and was in the process of converting Morocco into a French protectorate. Since German interests in that region were already protected by a special treaty, Germany's real objective became clear when her foreign minister suggested that France compensate Germany by relinquishing the French Congo. This was diplomatic blackmail, but France was in no position to go to war, and a compromise was arranged whereby Germany agreed not to interfere in Morocco in return for the gift of a strip of jungle in the French Congo.

For the third time in six years, a crisis had ended without fighting. Nonetheless, Germany had been close to war with France just as she had earlier been on the brink of conflict with Russia. The naval race between Britain and Germany grew more intense, and the entire continent was crisscrossed with rivalry. In 1912, Britain and France concluded a secret naval agreement for joint deployment of their fleets in case of war. This arrangement, which did not become known to Germany, virtually assured Britain's participation on the side of France should a general war break out.

The Balkan Wars The immediate origins of the First World War lay in large measure in the struggle for control of the remnants of the Turkish

Empire in the Balkans. After 1908, Turkey was temporarily at her nadir. So frail a power as Italy was able to seize the Turkish-controlled region of Tripoli (or Libya) across the Mediterranean in North Africa in 1911.

What Italy had done with Tripoli, the small Balkan states planned to do with the remainder of the Ottoman Empire in Europe. With Russian encouragement, a "Balkan League" was formed by Serbia, Montenegro, Bulgaria, and Greece in the spring of 1912. The four governments declared war in October 1912, and in a brief, victorious campaign drove the Turkish forces all the way back to Istanbul.

This alarmed Austria-Hungary, which feared that an enlarged Serbia and Montenegro would spearhead the disintegration of the Habsburg empire. Despite Russian insistence, Austria's government was determined that Serbia not achieve an outlet on the Adriatic. An international conference was hurriedly called in London and arranged a compromise by creating an independent Albania on the Adriatic coast (blocking Serbia and satisfying Austria-Hungary) while awarding Serbia more land in the interior.

Hardly had peace been established when a second Balkan War broke out in the middle of 1913, after protracted disagreement among the Balkan states about how to divide the rest of the conquered territory. Bulgaria now fought her three former allies, who were joined by Rumania and their former enemy, Turkey. In the outcome, Bulgaria lost all her winnings, while the Turks managed to get back a small portion of their losses.

Both Russia and Austria-Hungary believed that the hour of decision in southeast Europe was near. Turkey had been almost eliminated and Russia's influence had notably increased, but Russia had also been forced to back down over Bosnia in 1908 and over Albania in 1913. Russia's ally France had been completely successful against Germany in Morocco, but had been forced to submit to a kind of diplomatic blackmail over minor African territory in 1911. Thus Russian militarists were not satisfied with the dominant positions of the French and Russian empires, but were eager for a showdown with Germany and Austria-Hungary in order to secure Russian dominance in southeast Europe. One Russian military journal stated in the spring of 1914, "We are preparing for a war in the west. . . . The whole nation must accustom itself to the idea that we arm ourselves for a war of annihilation against the Germans."

Conversely, Austrian leaders were more than ever convinced that South Slav nationalism, led by Serbia and backed by Russia, was a mortal threat to their empire. The feeling grew that a showdown must not be postponed whatever the risk. In 1909, Field General Helmuth von Moltke, Chief of the German General Staff (and nephew of the Prussian leader of 1870), had promised explicitly to back up a military initiative by Austria-Hungary. The German leaders felt that they could not afford to permit the weakening of their only ally, preferring anything to "encirclement" by rival powers. If war was likely or inevitable, German generals calculated that their forces were strong enough for victory.

While the Austro-German Alliance was being tightened, the French and Russian governments were promising each other not to back down at the next crisis. Great Britain, still the only major power without an official defensive alliance in Europe, was relinquishing much of its independence to draw nearer France. Lines were becoming drawn, and in informed circles uneasiness mounted. After visiting Europe in the spring of 1914, a keen American observer wrote, "The whole of Germany is charged with electricity. Everybody's nerves are tense. It only needs a spark to set the whole thing off." The German ambassador in Paris gloomily observed that "peace remains at the mercy of an accident."

FURTHER READING A provocative general view of European diplomacy throughout this period is given by A. J. P. Taylor, *The Struggle for Mastery in Europe, 1848–1918* (1954). The most detailed survey of late nineteenth-century diplomacy will be found in two general works by W. L. Langer, *European Alliances and Alignments, 1871–1890* (1931) and *The Diplomacy of Imperialism, 1890–1902*, 2 vols. (1935).

Perhaps the best brief re-examination of the causes of the war is L. C. F. Turner, * *Origins of the First World War* (1970). Three classic detailed accounts are S. B. Fay, *The Origins of the World War*, 2 vols. (1930), which tends to give Germany the benefit of the doubt; B. E. Schmitt, *The Coming of the War*, 2 vols. (1930), which is more favorable to the entente; and Luigi Albertini, *The Origins of the War of 1914*, 3 vols. (1952–1954), which is the most thorough and objective.

For specific treatment of German policy and interests, see G. A. Craig, *From Bismarck to Adenauer* (1958); R. J. S. Hoffman, *The Anglo-German Trade Rivalry, 1875–1914* (1933); E. L. Woodward, *Great Britain and the German Navy* (1935); and P. R. Anderson, *The Background of Anti-English Feeling in Germany, 1890–1902* (1939). The diplomatic struggle in the Balkans may be approached through Charles Jelavich, *Tsarist Russia and Balkan Nationalism* (1958); W. S. Vucinich, *Serbia Between East and West* (1954); and E. C. Helmreich, *The Diplomacy of the Balkan Wars, 1912–1913* (1938). On the rise of nationalism and militarism, see B. C. Shafer, *Faces of Nationalism* (1972), and Alfred Vagts, *A History of Militarism* (1959).

*Books available in paperback edition are marked with an asterisk.

2 The First World War

The only major power whose vital interests were seriously threatened by the European alliance system and the new diplomatic and military moves since 1905 was Austria-Hungary. The growth of Balkan nationalism, together with the increase of Russian influence directed against Austria, threatened the breakup of the Habsburg empire. For years, some Austrian leaders had urged that Vienna seize the initiative and stifle anti-Habsburg South-Slav agitation in Serbia before it was too late. The Austrian government had always resisted these pressures until the final crisis arose in 1914.

OUTBREAK OF WAR

On June 28, 1914, after completing an inspection of Bosnia, the heir to the Austro-Hungarian throne, Franz Ferdinand, and his wife were assassinated in the garrison town of Sarajevo. Their killer was an idealistic young school teacher who had been primed for this bloody work by a secret Serbian extremist organization called the "Black Hand." This act lit the fuse, for the Austrian leaders, who had been openly defied, now had an excuse to bring Serbia to its knees. Before acting, however, the Austrian foreign minister, Berchtold, and the chief of staff, General Conrad, had their government inquire of Berlin as to what Germany's attitude would be. The German government replied that Austria-Hungary must achieve a final solution of the Serbian question. Austria-Hungary was therefore given a "blank check" on which to draw German support in case Russia intervened.

Nearly a month passed before Austria-Hungary's official ultimatum was given to Serbia. Its terms required that Serbia submit to precise stipulations for the punishment of terrorists and the elimination of nationalist agitation, which amounted to a partial surrender of Serbian sovereignty. The Serbian government's complicity in the assassination was only indirect, and it hoped to build international support by accepting all Austrian demands save one which would have allowed Austrian officials to enter Serbia to supervise enforcement. The Austrian government demanded complete submission. When the time limit expired on July 28, it declared war on Serbia.

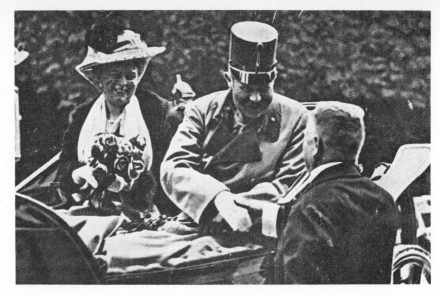

Archduke Franz Ferdinand and Wife Shortly before Their Assassination at Sarajevo, June 28, 1914. Austrio-Hungarian Archduke and heir Franz Ferdinand on the beginning of the inspection tour that led to his death and to the beginning of World War I. Austrian security officials showed extreme negligence on that day. (Radio Times Hulton Picture Library.)

In St. Petersburg, the tsar's military staff insisted that they must support Serbia without delay. Otherwise Russia would lose the position of influence it had recently regained in the Balkans and would be superseded by Austria. Even before Austria declared war on Serbia, the Russian army began to mobilize against both Austria and Germany at the same time, calculating that if war broke out, Russia would have to face both powers simultaneously. Yet, though the military leaders considered their mobilization tantamount to a declaration of war, the Russian government was reluctant to take official responsibility for opening hostilities.

Germany's Declaration of War on Russia and France The German kaiser and his civilian chancellor had apparently never thought that Austrian initiative would provoke a major war. Only belatedly did they try to restrain Austria; but by then, German policy had passed into the hands of the military. On July 30, Moltke, chief of the general staff, sent two telegrams to his Austrian counterpart, declaring, "A European war is the last chance of saving Austria-Hungary. Germany is ready to back Austria unreservedly." On July 31, the German government sent a note to St. Petersburg demanding that Russia cease mobilization. After much vacillation, the tsar permitted his army to continue its preparations. At the same time, Moltke was insisting in Berlin that "the unusually favorable situation should be used to strike . . . . France's military situation is nothing less than embarrassed . . . . Russia is anything but confident; moreover, the time of year is favorable." Since the Russian government continued to mass large forces on the German frontier, on August 1, Germany declared war on Russia.

All German military planning was based on the assumption that a two-front war would have to be fought against France and Russia. The

German generals believed that their main objective should be to knock France out as soon as possible, for the French army was of higher quality than the Russian and, besides, it would take the Russians much longer to get their massive military machine into full operation. As if in anticipation, the French president, Poincaré, had recently tightened the bonds of the Franco-Russian alliance, and France had secretly pledged to fight Germany and Austria-Hungary if Russia should become involved in a general conflict over the Balkans. The French army began to mobilize, and was met with a German declaration of war on August 3.

Great Britain's Declaration of War on Germany The German blueprint for the invasion of France, called the Schlieffen Plan, required concentration of the bulk of the German forces for a drive westward through Belgium. Thence, they would turn south, encircling Paris from the west and rolling up the main French units to the east. Germany therefore handed an ultimatum to Belgium demanding free passage for German troops in their attack on France. Though the Belgian government refused, German units crossed the Belgian border in the early hours of August 4. This violated the official treaty of Belgian neutrality, recognized as international law for the past seventy-five years, but contemptuously referred to in the Reichstag as a "scrap of paper."

The invasion of Belgium brought Britain into the conflict, for the British government believed that it could not stand by and see both France's position and the independence of the Channel shore threatened. Though there was no official defensive alliance between Britain and France, the two powers had a clear agreement for naval cooperation. Somewhat to the surprise of the German government, Britain declared war on Germany on August 4. The British foreign minister, Sir Edward Grey, noted with sad accuracy that "the lights are going out all over Europe."

The Question of Responsibility These complex events plunged Europe into the most disastrous conflict that it had ever known. Both sides made elaborate efforts to place the whole blame on the other, and when a peace treaty was finally signed in 1919, the entire guilt had officially to be borne by Germany. The next generation of historians wrote many volumes seeking to show who was really responsible, and some later began to suggest that in fact no one was actually to blame, but that the war had just happened. It would seem that neither extreme is fully accurate. Obviously no nation or single group of nations was either wholly to blame or entirely innocent, but it should be equally clear that some governments and certain officials bore more responsibility than others. Those most directly connected with the initiation of hostilities were the leaders of Austria and Serbia, for the latter permitted the assassination to take place and the former premeditatedly planned to use it as an excuse to crush Serbia, if only in a limited war. German and Russian militarists must bear heavy responsibility for turning this situation into a general conflict, for they insisted on mobilizing forces against each other before either had become directly involved in the action. Furthermore, the German leadership had intervened specifically to urge Austria forward in the hour of crisis. Though France bore less responsibility, the French government had strongly encouraged Russia to take a bellicose stand. Britain was the least involved, but even the British failed to use their full influence to limit the spread of the conflict. They felt that the pressure of their obligations and the general truculence of Germany forced them to participate in a war caused originally by the problems of the backward half of the continent.

In the years before the war, many ordinary people had never understood the implications of the steadily growing military machines or the dangers of successive crises and interlocking alliance systems. But to other Europeans—the politically conscious and more literate elements, the nationalists and activists on all levels—the outbreak of war was not at all unexpected. In fact, it had so long been anticipated that many heaved a sigh of relief. Widespread dissatisfaction with the values and leadership of modern nations existed even among the privileged groups in society, accompanied by fundamental boredom with bourgeois life. For many Europeans, the war thus came as a providential occurrence, a "lightning flash that would clear the air." There was a common feeling that battle would bring the solution to many of the major problems of the day. This attitude was shared both by Austria-Hungary's General Conrad and by members of the Serbian "Black Hand," by conservative German nationalists and by radical Russian revolutionaries. The four years of bloodshed that followed did eliminate many prewar problems, not by providing solutions for them, but by destroying governments and ruining the dominant social classes in central and eastern Europe.

Germany's Opening Offensive Against France The first phase of the German campaign went almost perfectly, for Belgian resistance was soon overcome and hundreds of thousands of German soldiers poured into northeastern France. Though the German General Staff was not actually aware of it, French preparations complemented their own scheme, for the French "Plan 17" called for an all-out offensive due east across the German border. This was completely stymied. German units were well supplied with machine guns and cut the gallant French infantry down in swathes. Within one month, the French had suffered 300,000 casualties, had failed to cross the German border, and were seemingly unable to stem the main German assault sweeping down from Belgium.

The German plan required that the principal striking force be extremely fast and powerful so as to outflank the bulk of the French army. The German troops, as it turned out, however, were not sufficiently numerous to sustain the momentum of their attack, especially after several divisions were transferred to the east. When the German drive neared Paris, it became badly snarled and almost ground to a halt. At that moment (September 6), the French threw their last reserves into a counter-attack. The Battle of the Marne, as this engagement was called, broke the German offensive and forced a retreat. During the autumn of 1914, both sides extended their lines to the Channel coast between Calais and Ostend. The fighting now settled down to desultory trench warfare along an enormous fortified line which soon extended from the Channel all the way across northeastern France to the Swiss border.

Stalemate in the East On the eastern front, Russia mobilized more quickly than had been anticipated and within the surprisingly brief period of seventeen days threw her forces into ill-prepared invasions of East Prussia and the Habsburg Empire. The appearance of sizable Russian forces on German soil caused consternation among the German leaders in the east, and brought their replacement by two new men, the previously retired General Paul von Hindenburg (1847–1935), and a brilliant staff general, Erich Ludendorff (1865–1937). The defense of East Prussia was greatly facilitated by the fact that the two invading Russian army corps failed to maintain contact with each other. It was thus possible to concentrate the German forces and destroy each Russian army separately. The organizers of victory, Hindenburg and Ludendorff, emerged as the first major German war heroes.

Far to the south, the Russian invasion of the northeast sector of the Habsburg Empire won a qualified success. Sheer force of numbers enabled the Russian troops to occupy all of Austrian Galicia before the Austro-Hungarian army was able to form a stable defense line. To make matters worse for Austria, the original campaign which sparked the war—the invasion of Serbia—was a total failure. Tough Serbian troops drove the Austro-Hungarian forces out of their country and back onto Austrian soil.

Prospects in the Winter of 1914–1915 When the chill of late autumn arrived, little was to be seen of the cheering crowds that had ecstatically welcomed the outbreak of war in Vienna, Paris, Berlin, and St. Petersburg. Both sides had been expecting a quick victory, for few people believed that the heavy strain of modern war could be borne by any participant for very long. Joy and expectation changed to grief and dismay as the casualty figures continued to mount. Within the first seventeen months, France alone was to have nearly two and one-half million casualties.

The western front had almost immediately become immobile. Hundreds of thousands of men on each side stared out into no-man's land from the shelter of rows of trenches or huddled in tiers of bunkers built deeply underground. Life in the trenches was full of misery, mud, and lice. Heavy concentrations of artillery all along the front exhausted the nerves and made a mole-like underground existence necessary for survival. When the big guns were not firing, sharpshooters took their deadly toll, and night in the advanced trenches was made tense by recurrent trench raids. The Germans introduced one of the grimmest features of all in the spring of 1915 when they began to use chlorine gas. While this did not change the military situation, it required all soldiers to be outfitted with gas masks and sent casualty lists even higher.

Aerial warfare also made its debut at the beginning of the conflict, and swift progress was made in the development of military warplanes. Through most of the war, they were used for reconnaissance, combat with other planes and limited ground attack. Though a series of German zeppelin raids on London in 1917 caused extensive property damage, loss of life and public panic, truly efficient bombing planes could not yet be made. Air power was not a decisive factor in the war, but it added considerably to the expense, terror, and casualty lists.

The Triple Entente, as the Anglo-Franco-Russian alliance was now called, had greater total economic resources than the Central Powers and, in the west, stood a slightly better chance of winning a war of attrition. Its weak link was the tsarist empire. Russian inefficiency was only partially offset by a great mass of manpower, and the weakness of Russia's political and economic system soon made it clear that a long war would place the empire in grave peril.

The Search for Allies As soon as the fighting fronts became temporarily stabilized, each side made strenuous efforts to win allies among the neutral powers. The Entente scored the first success soon after the outbreak of hostilities when the Japanese government declared war on Germany. Japan was, however, interested only in seizing German possessions in the Pacific; it contributed little or nothing to the progress of the war in Europe. The Central Powers gained a more significant ally when Turkey entered the war on their side in the autumn of 1914.

The main prize among the neutrals was Italy. Years earlier, the Italians had made it clear that the nominal Triple Alliance, binding them to Germany and Austria, had little significance. It was never more than a defensive agreement, and since Germany had struck first against France, the Italians were under no legal obligation. Furthermore, they had officially excluded from the original treaty any participation in war involving Britain. Italy had no interest at stake in the fighting and her most experienced leaders advised neutrality. Only a minority of the nation had any desire to become involved, but nationalist fanatics waged an intense propaganda campaign to whip up popular support for participation. Government leaders soon began to dicker with the two sides to see which would offer the higher price for Italian support. Here the advantage lay entirely with the Entente, since the territory coveted by the Italians lay within Austria. It was not difficult for the three Entente powers to promise compensation from their enemies' land, while the Austrian concessions were too small to be attractive. The secret Treaty of London, signed in April 1915, between Italy and the Entente allies, promised Italy all the Austrian Tyrol up to the Brenner Pass, plus Trieste, Albania, and further gains to be made at the expense of Turkey. Italy declared war against the Central Powers in May 1915. Her entry into the fighting thus had all the earmarks of a cynical bargain in *Realpolitik.* Italy was fighting not for vital interests but for a previously measured pound of flesh.

The Campaigns of 1915 With sizable Russian forces still occupying Austrian and German soil, the German High Command decided to devote most of the year 1915 to clearing the eastern front. The Russians were in poor condition to withstand an all-out offensive, for their stores of munitions had been largely exhausted during the four and one-half months' campaign of the previous year. Russian industrial capacity was entirely insufficient to provide enough artillery, or even enough rifles, to outfit the tsarist army. A general German-Austrian offensive began on May 1, and soon the entire Russian front was being rolled up in Poland and Galicia. The German forces proved infinitely superior in training, leadership, and equipment. By mid-September, all German-Austrian territory had been freed, most of Russian Poland had been occupied, and the Central Powers had advanced 200 miles. The Russians had lost 300,000 men in prisoners, and an even greater number in killed and wounded.

While their main effort was being carried out in the east, the Germans were forced to suspend offensive operations in France. This gave the French an opportunity to launch a major offensive of their own. In May 1915, after a gigantic artillery barrage, they began the largest effort thus far in the war to blast a way through the western front. There was no surprise in this kind of tactics, for any attack became obvious days in advance. The German fortifications were built so skillfully that most withstood bombardment, and after the cannon ceased, the machine gunners returned to their trenches to slaughter the attacking French infantry by the thousands. A succession of assaults was carried on from May through September, as waves of French troops advanced with suicidal courage, but it was all to no avail. Though France suffered over half a million new casualties, the front line had scarcely changed position.

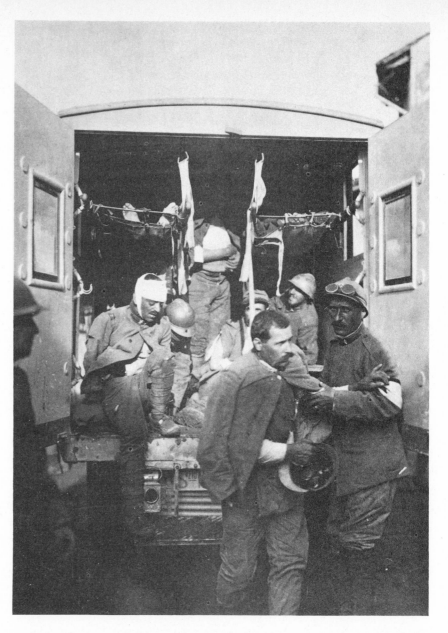

Italian Military Hospital Van in World War I. Italy's military experience in World War I, like that of all other participants, was both costly and frustrating. Her battlefront was stationary, casualties were high, and no spectacular victories were recorded, yet the Italians fought with tenacity and continued the struggle to victory. (Hoover Institution Archives.)

Defeats of the Entente in the Balkans The only new idea for breaking the stalemate with Germany in 1915 came from a handful of resourceful strategists whose spokesman was Winston Churchill (1874–1965), First Lord of the British Admiralty. They argued that continued slaughter on the western front was futile, and that the way to knock out the Central Powers was to strike through their weakest flank—the Turkish empire and the Balkans. A surprise attack on the Dardanelles would capture Istanbul, knock

Turkey out of the war, keep open the supply line to Russia, and prepare the way for invasion of Austria-Hungary. It was finally agreed to send a task force, but the allied commanders could never decide whether or not the operation was worth supporting in strength. The allied fleet steamed into the Dardanelles at the end of April and, despite heavy naval losses, put an invasion force ashore on the Gallipoli peninsula. Resistance at first was light, but the attackers were too few to press the assault. By the time they were reinforced, the Turkish defenders had increased their resistance considerably. Losses mounted as the British tried unsuccessfully to drive inland. Heat and sickness took a heavy toll during the summer months, while the Turkish forces grew stronger. At the end of the year, the allied forces had to be evacuated. The Dardanelles operation was well-conceived, but was executed with extraordinary clumsiness and ended in complete failure.

Meanwhile, the Central Powers had enticed Bulgaria to declare war against the Entente by promising large territorial gains at Serbia's expense. In the last months of 1915, an overwhelming force was assembled to knock out Serbia, which had previously resisted Austria's best efforts. German troops accomplished what their allies had not been able to do; and by the end of 1915, all Serbia had been conquered. The Central Powers now completely dominated the Balkans.

The Western Front in 1916: Verdun and the Somme With the southern and eastern fronts under control, the German command decided to concentrate on the western front in 1916. A massive attack was prepared against the fortress of Verdun, the center of the French defensive line in northeastern France. The assault began late in February after intensive bombardment. The Germans intended to maintain the pressure until either the allied line cracked or the already weakened French army bled to death in a war of attrition. For two months, desperate fighting raged; but the new French commander, General Pétain (1856–1951), had a certain genius for defensive tactics, using his resources with great skill, maintaining the spirit and vigor of his troops as much as possible. Week after week German artillery and infantry thundered to the assault; the French held their ground grimly and threw back their enemy in savage counter-attacks. There was a lull at the end of April, but the Germans resumed the offensive early in June. The French committed their last reserves, and their troops grimly repeated the cry "They shall not pass!" Though two French forts had fallen, the pressure was eased in July when the British launched a great offensive of their own farther north. The French line had held.

By mid-1916, the British had had time to train a mass army of volunteers and were able to carry their full weight of the fighting in the west. On July 1, in their first large-scale offensive of the war, hundreds of thousands of British troops charged over the top against German positions along the Somme River. Once more, however, underground fortifications proved able to withstand days of continuous cannonades. As at Verdun or in the attacks

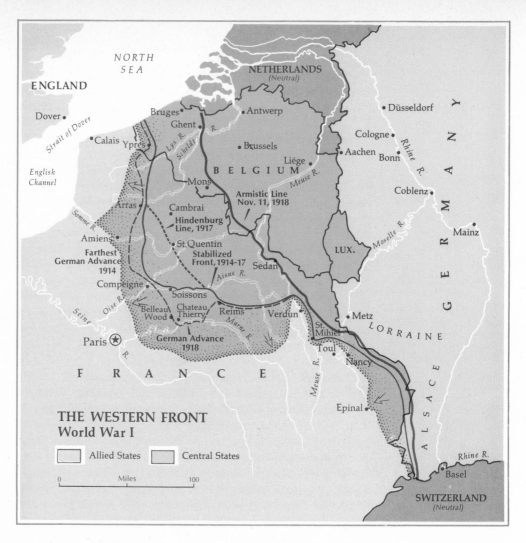

THE WESTERN FRONT
World War I

☐ Allied States   ☐ Central States

0 —— Miles —— 100

of the previous year, almost nothing was gained although massive assaults continued throughout the summer. In this war of attrition, losses had been about equal during 1916. The Germans had lost more at the Somme than the allies—650,000 to 614,000—but less than the French at Verdun—336,000 to 362,000.

After two years of war, there was little enthusiasm; discouragement and the beginning of despair were widespread. Fantastic casualty figures staggered the imagination. The technique of battle had led to a stalemate, with the defense clearly holding the upper hand over the offense on the western front.

The Brusilov Offensive on the Eastern Front On the eastern front, the Russians made one last effort in 1916. Plans for a new offensive were placed in the hands of the dapper, white-bearded little General Brusilov. Russia's

THE EASTERN FRONT
World War I

Allied States

Central States

0   Miles   300

original army of 1914 had already been destroyed. To replace it, energetic efforts were made to call up all the best physical specimens in the population to form a large new force capable of turning the tide of the war. By the time operations began, only the front-line units were fully equipped. Many soldiers in the second and third rows were expected to pick up the weapons of those who had fallen before them. Nonetheless, the "Brusilov Offensive" began in the summer of 1916. During the first days, it completely broke the line of the dispirited Austro-Hungarian troops and several hundred thousand prisoners were taken. The German portion of the line held firm, however, and soon the ill-equipped, ill-trained Russians were brought to a halt. The German counter-offensive regained all the Russians had previously won plus a good deal more. When the summer's fighting had come to an end, Russia had lost another million men and its army was nearly finished.

An accidental by-product of the "Brusilov Offensive" was the entrance of Rumania in the war on the allied side. The Entente powers were willing to promise the most cherished Rumanian ambition—annexation of Transylvania—and the initial success of the Russian offensive seemed to indicate that the tide was running in the Entente's favor. It took very little time to show that the Rumanian decision had been woefully premature. As the Germans hurled the Russians back in disorder, they easily overran Rumania and occupied Bucharest. This was, however, the only unqualified success of the Central Powers during 1916.

Wartime Government Changes By the end of 1916, discontent and suffering were widespread throughout Europe. The German population was undernourished and Austria-Hungary could be governed only by the broad use of martial law, while troops from the national minorities deserted en masse to the enemy. Italian civilians were grumbling and restive and in France the loss of life was weakening the nation's will. Russia was on the brink of collapse. Only England seemed able to continue with her resolution undiminished.

Among all the belligerent powers, stronger government control was developed to meet the demands of a war of attrition. This tendency went farthest in Germany, where by mid-1916 the army leadership had largely superseded the imperial government. The dominant voices in policy were those of Marshal Hindenburg, the new commander-in-chief of the armed forces, and General Ludendorff, chief of the general staff.

In England, Asquith's Liberal government had been broadened into a "national union" to include the Conservatives in 1915. Asquith was later succeeded as prime minister by the former radical David Lloyd George, who stressed all-out attention to the military effort under a vigorous, increasingly centralized government.

France had entered the war under the auspices of a "sacred union" of all patriotic elements, from the syndicalist left to the reactionary right. Growth of despair and defeatism in the spring of 1917 shattered the "sacred union," and leadership passed into the hands of the sternest republican of them all, the aged Georges Clemenceau (1841-1929), over seventy-five but possessed of an iron will to victory. Clemenceau preserved the supremacy of civil government over military leadership in France, but his form of civilian rule was nonetheless semi-dictatorial, aimed solely at shoring up French morale and keeping the country in the battle.

The Collapse of Tsardom and the Beginning of the Russian Revolution
The first casualty of the war among the major powers was Russia. The

empire of Nicholas II had fought hard but was not prepared for a long struggle. It lacked the industrial development for modern war; and, most of all, it lacked efficient, coordinated leadership. Each month gave further proof of the government's incompetence. An arbitrary bureaucratic clique ran the administrative and military system, while the court was dominated by obscurantist elements associated with the superstitious tsarina. As early as 1915, the economy showed serious signs of strain. Whereas Austria-Hungary, even weaker than Russia, could be supported by Germany, Russia's allies proved unable to break through the Dardanelles to her aid. In two and a half years, the Russian army lost at least two million dead and almost as many in prisoners.

The First Revolutionary Barricades Raised by a Mutinous Russian Army Petrograd (St. Petersburg) March 1917. The strains of war provoked dissolution of political and social morale on the Russian home front, leading to riots and mutiny in the capital that brought the collapse of the Russian government in March 1917. (Hoover Institution Archives.)

Though the people had at first rallied round the government with patriotic enthusiasm, they later experienced profound disillusionment. It seemed to many that the government had deserted them. After the bloody failure of the Brusilov offensive, desertions from the army increased greatly. Enormous suffering during the winter of 1916–1917 brought popular discontent to a climax. Russia's transportation system broke down and the larger cities were deprived of regular food shipments.

On March 3, 1917, lines of civilians in St. Petersburg who were waiting for rations spontaneously burst out in demonstrations against the government. Soon the streets were filled with rioters, and units of raw recruits, already succumbing to defeatism, mutinied and joined the demonstrators. The rebellion quickly spread to other cities. Front-line regiments were on the verge of desertion and the tsar found it impossible to control the situation. Leaders of the Duma urged abdication, and on March 12 they set up a provisional government. Four days later, the tsar abdicated the Russian throne.

The new Provisional Government was determined to carry on the military struggle in order to preserve Russia's honor and bring the downfall

Russian Troops Fleeing before a German Advance, 1917. In 1917 the Russian Army entered the stage of dissolution due to poor leadership and lack of equipment, which destroyed morale even more than defeat in battle and loss of manpower. It was the internal collapse of the Army that opened the gates of political revolution in Russia.

of German militarism. Yet the middle-class liberals of the Provisional Government represented only an enlightened minority of the Russian people. They lacked popular support, and the Provisional Government's refusal to lead Russia out of the war immediately led to widespread hostility. The popular demand for peace was skillfully exploited by Lenin's Bolshevik revolutionaries and was a major factor in enabling the Bolsheviks to seize power from the Provisional Government in November 1917. By that time, Russia had virtually ceased to participate in the military conflict.

The War at Sea When the war began, the major goal of both fleets was to strangle their enemy's supply lines. The British Royal Navy still held a lead of five to three over the German fleet in tonnage of warships in operation and, assisted by the French, quickly won control of the seas. It established a blockade of the German coast and bottled up the German fleet. German merchant shipping was driven from the ocean and any kind of cargo in neutral vessels that was deemed of value to the German war effort was confiscated. Germany's overseas colonies were isolated and later occupied.

The Germans were soon left with but one weapon that could reply to the British blockade—the submarine. Contrary to international principles, the submarine could not surface to identify and search merchant ships, for a surfaced submarine was an easy target. Moreover, its crew was too small to man a merchant vessel and bring it into port. The U-boats had therefore to strike swiftly and silently, often without identifying the nationality of the ship under fire, and took an increasing toll both of Entente and of neutral shipping.

Neutral nations, led by the American President Woodrow Wilson (1856–1924), had at first protested the character of Britain's blockade of Germany, but made much more vigorous complaints against submarine warfare. The torpedoing of the British liner *Lusitania* in May 1915 aroused a storm of resentment in the United States, for over 100 of the more than

1,000 victims were Americans. After several more such incidents, the German government promised Wilson that no more merchant ships would be sunk without warning. It nevertheless threatened to resume unrestricted submarine warfare at any time if the British did not moderate the terms of their blockade.

In contrast to submarine activity, Germany's surface warships had rarely ventured out of home port since the war began. On a few occasions, however, attempts were made to lure a small portion of the British high seas fleet into battle at uneven odds. The last such sally, at the end of May 1916, led to the only great naval encounter of the war. A detachment of cruisers was sent out as a decoy, followed by the German battleships. The ruse failed, and the Germans soon saw the main British high seas fleet steaming down upon them. Fighting raged intermittently for ten hours off the coast of Jutland before the Germans succeeded in making their escape. Though British losses were twice as heavy as those of the Germans in this battle of Jutland, the Royal Navy retained control of the North Sea. The Central Powers were still isolated from the outside world.

By the end of 1916, the German high command realized that the war of attrition was not working in its favor. Military losses had been severe, the British blockade was a grave handicap, and Germany's main ally, Austria-Hungary, was more a burden than a source of support. On the other hand, if Germany could turn the tables at sea and establish a submarine blockade of Britain, she could strangle the British economy and drive that country from the war. This would in turn isolate France on the western front and make her an easy victim.

The German government therefore decided to reverse the war of attrition at sea by resuming unrestricted submarine warfare against allied commerce at the beginning of 1917. It realized that this would probably mean the entry of the United States into the war on the side of the Entente. Since the latter was already extending massive economic support to Britain and France, German leaders calculated that the United States could hardly contribute more to the opposing side than it was doing already. The Americans had no standing army of any importance and German leaders calculated that they could not put a large number of troops in position on the western front for at least a year. By that time, if all went according to plan, Germany would have won the war.

Entry of the United States into the War   In the United States, sympathy for the Entente had been building up since the beginning of the conflict. Economic interest and moral indignation about the rights of neutrals and small nations, cleverly exploited by British propaganda, combined to favor France and Britain and to work against Germany. The German government contributed to this feeling by its own clumsiness and hostile attitude. The resumption of unrestricted submarine warfare brought anti-German feeling to a climax, for it meant the sinking of many American ships. Bowing to popular demands, the United States government entered the war against

1466 THE ERA OF THE WORLD WARS, 1914–1945

the Central Powers on April 6, 1917. President Woodrow Wilson saw this decision as a moral commitment to defend the rights of neutrals and small nations against the rule of force.

It was to be nearly fifteen months before American troops made their appearance at the fighting front in large numbers, but American industry quickly swung into war production. The United States Navy and merchant marine aided the British and French in keeping the Atlantic sea lanes open. The British were already learning to develop new defenses against the submarine, using mine barrages, depth charges, hydrophones, and the convoy system to increasingly better effect. Just as the U-boat offensive was taking its heaviest toll, the struggle began to even out. American shipping more than made good British losses, and the struggle of attrition once more began to go against the Central Powers.

The Western Front in 1917   The stalemate on the western front nonetheless persisted throughout 1917. The failure of another French offensive in March led to the breakdown of morale in a large part of the French army. Discouraged by heavy losses and poor leadership, and enraged by misleading government propaganda, entire divisions refused to obey orders. Though discipline was soon restored, the French army had reached the limit of its resources.

The brunt of the fighting on the western front fell upon the British, whose commanders continued to employ the same costly, futile methods used in 1915 and 1916. Huge artillery barrages followed by massed infantry assaults in Flanders during the summer of 1917 gained only a few hundred yards and cost the British forces half a million casualties. The German army remained on the defensive in the west, while seeking to force Russia to make peace in the east. It scored a notable victory in the south during October, when mixed Austro-German forces shattered the Italian front at Caporetto and drove their dispirited enemy far back into Italian territory.

War Weariness and Efforts for Peace   The first political groups among the belligerents to work for a direct, nonmilitary end to the war were certain segments of the Socialist parties in each country. At first, most Socialists had loyally supported the war effort of their particular country, but in the course of the conflict their idealistic patriotism became severely strained. One reason for this was the acquisitiveness of the war aims formulated by each belligerent: German officials spoke of annexing Poland and part of Belgium, France wanted Alsace-Lorraine and possibly even the dismemberment of Germany, Italy coveted Trieste and Dalmatia, and so on. All this ran counter to the rationalizations of patriotic Socialists, who came increasingly to believe that they had been tricked into supporting a sinister imperialist struggle.

Pacifist Socialist internationalists held general conferences in Switzerland in 1915 and 1916, demanding immediate peace "without annexations or indemnities," the withdrawal of Socialist representatives from belligerent

Military Chiefs of the Western Allies, France 1917. From left to right: Pétain (France); Haig (Britain); Foch (France); Pershing (United States). During the last phase of the war in 1918, Foch was made supreme allied commander on the western front.

governments, and resistance to all war appropriations. In April 1917, the internationalist left wing of the German Social Democrats broke with the majority of that group to form the Independent German Socialist party, in opposition to the war. At approximately the same time, Socialist ministers withdrew from the French government in a further expression of the war weariness that had begun to grip France. In Germany this feeling later spread from the Independent Socialists into the ranks of middle-class liberals. The latter passed a "Peace Resolution" in the Reichstag during July 1917, asking for a negotiated compromise to end the conflict.

Wilson's Fourteen Points   When the United States entered the war, President Wilson spoke of a "peace without victory," avoiding vengeful reprisals. In January 1918, he issued his famous "Fourteen Points," listing the goals to be achieved by a just peace. These included general aims such as disarmament and freedom of the seas, but also dealt with specific problems such as the need to restore the territorial integrity of Belgium, Serbia, and Rumania; return Alsace-Lorraine to France; and establish an independent Poland. Ultimately, Wilson believed that the only goal that could justify the carnage of the war would be the creation of a worldwide association of free democratic nations to avert future conflict. This aim was expressed in his final point, which first mentioned the plan that eventually took shape as the postwar League of Nations.

The Treaty of Brest-Litovsk   Efforts toward peace in western and central Europe were encouraged by the rise of bolshevism in Russia. After overthrowing the Provisional Government and establishing a Communist dictatorship, Lenin proposed an immediate end to the war through transformation of the struggle into a socialist revolution. Eagerly looking for signs of upheaval throughout the continent, he called upon soldiers everywhere to desert their trenches. To him, the conflict was a capitalist, imperialist struggle soon to end in a shattering social revolt that would overthrow all existing regimes. He believed that it was not necessary to continue the fight against German militarism because the German working class would soon be reduced to such misery by the war that it would rise up against its own government. Consequently, he prepared for a unilateral peace with Germany. Russia's western allies were thunderstruck: they protested that Lenin could not simply walk out of the war; but that was exactly what he intended to do.

   Germany's terms were hard, for the Baltic region, Russian Poland, and the Ukraine were detached from the Russian state. Faced with these draconian demands, some Bolshevik leaders would have preferred to continue the war, but Lenin insisted that the results of the negotiations would be only temporary. The outbreak of social revolution would soon wipe away all Germany's gains, but meanwhile the most urgent need was to consolidate the Communist regime in eastern Europe. Lenin had his way. On March 3, 1918, a Russo-German peace treaty was signed at the town of Brest-Litovsk, east of Warsaw. It provided for the detachment of the western third of European Russia, and was the most drastic blow suffered by Russian sovereignty since the Mongol invasion of the thirteenth century.

Lenin was confident that all this would quickly pass away. Like Woodrow Wilson, he wanted a general peace without national vengeance or annexations, but through different, competing means. Whereas the American president stood for the triumph of middle-class democratic order, Bolshevik agitators zealously propagated the ideal of international socialist revolution.

Germany's 1918 "Win-the-war" Offensive The German high command knew that 1918 was the year of decision, for by its end American power would be fully mobilized and time would work against Germany. Moderates within Germany were urging a negotiated peace that would end the war and still enable their country to preserve some of its gains. The high command, however, refused to consider a negotiated peace, for they and key government leaders felt that only a complete triumph would guarantee the future of the German regime. Socialists and liberals were gaining support with each passing month, and only a definitive military victory could assure the upper classes continued dominance within Germany.

General Ludendorff concluded that the German army must make one more major effort on the western front. In March 1918, after Germany's last reserves of first-class manpower had been trained and organized, he launched the first of a series of massive "win-the-war" offensives against the British sector of the front. German tacticians had developed a variation on the outmoded method of frontal assault. The new German tactic was to concentrate all the artillery preparation on one area, pulverizing it with a short barrage which would end before the enemy had time to call up sizeable reserves. Then swift columns of shock troops struck directly through the weakened sector, centering all their force on one part of the line, piercing it, then quickly fanning out to the rear to extend their gains, while a second assault of the same kind struck some other point. These quick, concentrated thrusts which took the enemy by surprise were much more effective than the previous tactic of continuous bombardment followed by mass attack on a broad front.

The offensive, which began on March 21, was directed against the British lines in Flanders. The attackers had numerical superiority and in less than a week pushed back the whole front over forty miles. In this crucial hour, a joint commander-in-chief, the French Marshal Foch (1851–1929), was chosen to coordinate both armies and eliminate French defeatism. The French and British finally stopped the German push just short of its major objective, but two more German offensives followed in April and May, and German troops fought their way to the Marne, less than forty miles from Paris.

The first three phases of the German offensive fell just short of decisive victory. The attacks were costly, however, and the German command had begun to run short of troops. Time worked against the Germans, for American soldiers were arriving in France in increasing numbers and first saw action on June 4.

A week later, the Germans resumed the offensive farther southeast, following it with the fifth and final phase of the offensive in July. This was advertised to the German people as the *Friedenssturm,* the "peace-attack," but Ludendorff lacked the strength to impose a decision. The initial German assault carried across the Marne, then soon bogged down.

On July 18, Marshal Foch launched a general counterattack. Rested and reorganized French and British forces, supported by nine fresh American divisions, maintained a staccato rhythm of assaults on different parts of the German lines. The Germans were thrown off balance, and lacked the reserves to plug gaps.

An American Platoon Advancing Against the Germans, France, 1918. The arrival of well-equipped American infantry in increasingly large numbers on the western front in the summer of 1918 was the final decisive factor in turning the tide of war against Germany. (National Archives.)

August 8 was, as Ludendorff himself later admitted, "the black day of the German army in the war." On that date, the British used a large fleet of their new armored tanks to breach the German defenses, and general retreat ensued. Every month, 250,000 American troops were arriving in France, and the military situation of Germany was becoming hopeless. By the middle of September, the imperial army had been driven back to the "Hindenburg Line," a heavily fortified position west of the prewar German frontier. Here, the Allied attack stalled momentarily, but constant pressure wore down the German forces more and more with each passing day.

Collapse of the Central Powers   The whole position of the Central Powers had begun to dissolve. After several years of struggle, British-led forces had won control of all the Turkish Near East. In the Balkans, the military energy of Bulgaria and Turkey had been nearly exhausted since the previous year. Greek liberals, with French and British aid, had seized control of the Greek government during 1917 and had brought their nation into the war against the Central Powers. In mid-September 1918, the French and British launched a highly successful Balkan offensive from Greek bases, knocking Bulgaria out of the war within a fortnight. Collapse of the Balkan front, together with ever-mounting pressure in the west, was forcing Germany to the wall, and Ludendorff suffered a brief nervous breakdown. After recovering, he decided that the German army could not go on and told the kaiser on October 3 that Germany must prepare to ask for peace. In order to create a more favorable attitude among the enemy, he had insisted that a new government be formed in Berlin which would reflect the nominal political majority in the Reichstag and would thus be based on democratic parliamentary principles. A liberal aristocrat, Prince Max of Baden, was asked to form the new government, which even included members of the moderate majority Socialists. There followed several reforms in political structure which promised to transform Germany into a liberal constitutional monarchy.

There were two main reasons for this insistence on civilian government and democratic forms by the German military. The first was that the army leaders knew that the war was lost, but hoped to escape having the blame for defeat placed on the military by shifting the burden of an armistice to a democratic civilian government. The second reason lay in the peace proposals of Woodrow Wilson, who stressed that the purpose of the war was to "make the world safe for democracy." He had pointed repeatedly to Germany's authoritarian monarchy as a basic cause of the war and had urged the Germans to install a democratic regime as a major step toward peace. Like Bismarck in 1871, Wilson insisted that peace must be signed with the representatives of all the people, not merely with a defeated militaristic aristocracy. What made this attractive was his insistence that between democratic countries there could be no vengeance, only a "peace without victory." German leaders therefore reasoned that, if their government could be made to look more democratic, it might expect easier terms from the western Allies.

In October, the Austrian front collapsed. The Italians reversed their disaster of twelve months earlier by striking out in their most successful offensive of the war. The Austro-Hungarian army was rapidly disintegrating, troops from the national minorities simply throwing down their guns and walking home. The whole Habsburg empire was in grave economic distress and there was starvation in the cities. Austria could not carry on the war, and on November 3, her government signed an armistice with the Allies.

That same day, a red flag went up over the big German naval base at Kiel. Sailors of the imperial fleet had mutinied. Councils of workers and soldiers were being formed in the larger cities, in a manner alarmingly similar to that of the Russian Soviets. Germany was on the brink of revolution, and the socialists threatened to wash their hands of the government

if the kaiser did not abdicate immediately. The radical Independent Socialists and worker extremists launched a general strike on November 9. On that day, William II abdicated, crossing the border to Holland. A republic was proclaimed within a few hours. Two days later, on November 11, 1918, German representatives signed an armistice with Allied commanders, ostensibly on the basis of Wilson's Fourteen Points. The great war was finally over.

Immediate Results of the War The war had taken the greatest military toll of life in European history. Both Germany and Russia lost at least two million men each, while France lost well over one million, and the British Empire 700,000. Nearly 500,000 Italian troops had been killed, and the Austro-Hungarian armies had lost over 800,000 men. The small kingdom of Serbia suffered disproportionately high losses. Furthermore, among all belligerents some twenty million men had been wounded, and many of them were permanently disabled.

The war had broken up three empires—Germany, Austria-Hungary, and Russia—bringing social revolution in its wake. During the first months of 1919, leftist uprisings sputtering throughout Germany, while Russia was engulfed by a great civil war between the Bolsheviks and their opponents. Fighting raged through the Baltic lands from Finland to the East Prussian border, and a brief Bolshevik dictatorship was established at Budapest in April 1919. Austria escaped serious turmoil only through the greater discipline of its Social Democratic party. Even in Italy, one of the victors, there was a strong movement for socialist revolution in 1919–1920.

The war had wrought profound changes in civilian life all over the continent. In France and Britain, as well as in Germany, individual freedom of choice had been swallowed up by the demands of war. Universal military service, coupled with war industry deferments, had determined every man's lot in life. Similar pressures affected women, for hundreds of thousands were taken out of the home for the first time in their lives and put into factories and workshops.

The years 1914–1918 saw introduction of the "planned economy," whereby industry and all other significant branches of production were to a greater or lesser degree coordinated by the government. Even profits and wages had come increasingly under the purview of the state. In place of the world economy of the prewar period, most belligerent nations had to strive for the utmost in economic self-sufficiency. Such needs sharply accentuated the earlier decline in liberal values, for the old system of individualism and private competition was found to be too slow and wasteful. Both workers and business leaders became accustomed to economic coordination by the state, and were not eager after the war to lose the security which it provided.

The war seriously weakened Europe's economic domination of the rest of the world. Stifled by blockade or absorbed in war production, European industry could not supply its prewar markets, and native economies in other continents were learning to fill many of their own needs. The enormous expense of the long conflict strained every nation's economic resources, piling up huge debts for the next generation. Much of the surplus accumulated by European finance during the nineteenth century was dissipated in the short space of four years. The United States had still been a debtor of Europe in 1914, but huge war purchases by France and Britain had made her the chief creditor nation in the world. Europeans now owed Americans approximately ten billion dollars. Economically and diplomatically, the margin of power in world affairs was passing to the United States for whatever use the latter cared to make of it.

The sense of order and stability in Europe, seriously threatened before 1914, had now been lost. The best elements of young manhood had been cut down on the battlefield, and those who survived often felt little enthusiasm about their good fortune. Some young people during the next two decades constituted a "lost generation," confused and made skeptical by the war, lacking in ideals and values, desperately seeking solace or a way out of their uncertainty. Many thousands of the veterans, who for four years had been taught to hate and to kill, could not disarm psychologically. They had to go on fighting, under new banners if necessary, but keeping alive the nihilistic flame of the war.

Political change and economic confusion proved equally hurtful to many older members of the middle classes. Pensioners and those living on fixed incomes could not survive in the postwar inflation that gripped many countries. The status and prestige of professional men and of the broader middle class was seriously threatened by these years of continuing crisis. People learned to live amid constant uncertainty that found expression in one extreme or the other. As a way out, force and willpower were often valued over intellectual analysis. The important thing was to provide a solution and to carry it out, to "decide," irrespective of consequences. This emphasis on "decisionism," contemptuous of caution or delay, helped to project the irrationalism of the war period on the following generation. The end of the war in 1918 was thus merely an armistice, or a truce, but not peace.

FURTHER READING Three general histories of the war may be recommended: B. H. Liddell Hart, * A History of the World War, 1914–1918 (1934); Cyril Falls, * The Great War (1959); and L. C. F. Turner, * The First World War (1967). In The Guns of August (1961), Barbara Tuchman provides a vivid narrative of the beginning of the conflict. Gerhard Ritter, The Schlieffen Plan (1958), studies German plans for the invasion of France. The best account of the Russian military is N. N. Golovin, The Russian Army in the Great War (1931). Ernst Junger's Storm of Steel (1929) reveals the attitude of some of the front-line elite of the German army.

On the war at sea, consult A. J. Marder, The Anatomy of British Sea Power (1940), and From the Dreadnought to Scapa Flow, 2 vols. (1965). The standard account of the submarine is R. H. Gibson and Maurice Pendergast, The German Submarine War, 1914–1918 (1931).

F. Fischer renders a harsh judgment of * Germany's Aims in the First World War (1967). British policy is studied in Paul Guinn, British Strategy and Politics, 1914–1918 (1965); and J. C. King, Generals and Politicians (1951), deals with that of France. The social effects of the conflict are treated in Arthur Marwick, * The Deluge: British Society and the First World War (1965); Albrecht Mendelssohn-Bartholdy, The War and German Society (1938); and David Mitrany, The Effect of the War in Southeastern Europe (1936). George Katkov presents a revisionist account of the tsarist collapse in Russia 1917: The February Revolution (1967). A. J. Mayer, Political Origins of the New Diplomacy, 1917–1918 (1959), analyzes the reorientation of diplomacy in the last year of the war. Two good accounts of the last phase of Austria-Hungary are Z. A. B. Zeman, The Break-up of the Habsburg Empire, 1914–1918 (1961); and A. J. May, The Passing of the Habsburg Monarchy, 1914–1918, 2 vols. (1966).

*Books available in paperback edition are marked with an asterisk.

3 The Peace Settlement and Problems of the 1920's

The peace conference that assembled at Paris in January 1919, was the largest gathering of diplomats to meet in Europe since the Congress of Vienna, more than a century earlier. There were delegates from most countries of the world, and nearly every eye was turned toward the American president Woodrow Wilson, who represented the moral conscience of the victorious coalition. From the beginning, Wilson had emphasized that the purpose of the war was to "make the world safe for democracy." To Wilson, this meant two things: the establishment of democratic nation-states throughout Europe and a system of collective security—the future League of Nations—to avoid another war. Wilson's political ideals were rooted in nineteenth-century liberalism. He believed in political liberty and national self-determination, the right of every ethnic group to enjoy unity and independence under democratic government.

The Fourteen Points had in part been designed to give hope to the oppressed nationalities of east-central Europe. They certainly had this effect, for by the beginning of 1919, nationalists throughout Europe were looking to the Paris Peace Conference and the Allied leadership to meet their ambitions. The problem was that many of these ambitions differed considerably from Wilsonian ideals. The American president did not fully appreciate the complexity of ethnic intermingling in east-central Europe. Intense nationalist rivalry as well as strong class division and rebellious land hunger on the part of the peasantry made any facile political solution impossible.

Moreover, Wilsonian ideals had to confront a diplomatic legacy antedating America's entry into the war. In 1915–1916, the Allies had signed a series of secret treaties to divide the eventual spoils of victory in central Europe. Italy had been promised Austrian territory across her northeastern border, Rumania was to receive Transylvania, Serbia was to get Bosnia, and so forth. Similarly, attractive offers had been made to the Poles by both the Allies and the Central Powers, while Czech nationalists worked fever-

Presidents Wilson and Poincaré Arrive at the Paris Peace Conference. President Woodrow Wilson momentarily became the dominant figure in the western world in 1918–1919. Leader of what had suddenly become the strongest country on earth, his idealist proposals for a just peace and the right to national self-determination won him popularity among millions in western and central Europe.

ishly for an independent Czechoslovak state. Wilson had never ratified or approved any of the secret treaties, and had by implication renounced them in his Fourteen Points, but at the same time his emphasis on democratic national self-determination encouraged some of the goals pledged by the secret treaties.

As the war drew to a close, all these peoples—Poles, Italians, Serbs, and Rumanians—were anxious to see that they received the territory that had apparently been promised them. By September 1918, Britain and the

United States had already decided to recognize Czech independence and, implicitly, the end of the Habsburg Empire. On December 1, 1918, the re-established Rumanian government took over Transylvania, and the Prince Regent of Serbia proclaimed the union of the three south Slav peoples under his dynasty, thus forming the kingdom of Yugoslavia. Even before the Peace Conference had fully assembled, the historic Habsburg Empire had vanished and central Europe was being reorganized into a series of smaller independent countries.

THE PEACE
SETTLEMENT

In January 1919, therefore, the Paris delegates were faced with two primary tasks: redrawing the boundaries of east-central Europe in accord with the new order and making an adequate peace settlement with Germany. On January 18, a plenary session was held among representatives of all nations that had declared war on the Central Powers. This was a bulky and unwieldy assembly, lacking any machinery for proceeding efficiently with the business at hand. It was clear that the Japanese delegation was more influential than that from Lebanon, and that Britain carried infinitely more weight than Portugal, yet adequate steps had not been taken to determine by what technique the conference would arrive at decisions. As Colonel House, Wilson's closest personal advisor, later wrote, "The great fault of the political leaders was their failure to draft a plan of procedure."

The "Big Three" In order to get on with the main business, the heads of the more important countries began almost immediately to meet in secret conferences. At first, this took shape as a Council of Ten, but it soon became clear that only the top western powers counted. More specifically, these were the "Big Three"—the United States, Great Britain, and France, sometimes joined by Italy. As it turned out, the major decisions of the Conference were reached by personal negotiation between the representatives of these countries, Wilson of the United States, David Lloyd George of Britain, Clemenceau of France, and Vittorio Orlando of Italy.

As was only to be expected, these leaders differed widely in their attitude and approach. The Europeans did not really share Wilson's concern for a completely impartial peace. Of the three prime ministers, the only one even partially amenable to Wilson's point of view was Lloyd George, and Lloyd George himself was committed to a somewhat more vengeful policy by his demagogical tactics in the British "Khaki Election" of December 1918, in which he promised the voters to "hang the Kaiser." He was, nevertheless, a supple and pragmatic politician who realized that Britain's basic need was not to annihilate Germany but to help achieve a settlement that would restore stability on the continent and promote a new balance of forces. As usual, Britain's main concern was her empire and her commerce, not the problems of central Europe. Lloyd George was relatively ignorant of the latter, and had difficulty, for example, locating Transylvania on the map.

Clemenceau was more difficult. The French leader was nearly seventy-eight years old, and worn by fatigue and cynicism. His position had the advantage of simplicity, for Clemenceau had extremely precise goals: maximum security for France against Germany and compensation for French war losses. Wilson's democratic idealism held no meaning for him, and the old French premier could see little sense in Wilson's Fourteen Points, observing, "After all, the good Lord only had ten." He and the American president had trouble bargaining with each other, despite the political talent of both, and it was usually up to Lloyd George to serve as middleman, sitting, as he put it, "between Jesus Christ [Wilson] and Napoleon Bonaparte [Clemenceau]."

The League of Nations Clemenceau and nearly everyone else at the Conference were willing to agree to Wilson's plan for a League of Nations which, after all, might be a useful step toward that national security sought by the French. However, the central issue and main stumbling block of the Conference was the claim France made against Germany. Here Clemenceau would concede very little. Wilson worked under a severe handicap in trying to reduce the French demands, for two reasons. First of all, as American chief executive he was far from home and had to return to Washington on official business only a month after the Conference opened, forcing him to hurry negotiations both before he left and after he returned. Second, it quickly became clear that majority opinion in the United States did not necessarily support his own interpretation of the issues. The Republican Party controlled the United States Congress after the 1918 elections and isolationist sentiment was strong. In order to placate it, Wilson was compelled to include a clause in the League of Nations charter recognizing the Monroe Doctrine, and to omit a provision for an international army to enforce the peace. This weakened his moral position at Paris by demonstrating that the United States intended to protect its own special interests even while asking others to surrender theirs for the common good.

French Demands Against Germany Clemenceau finally agreed to discard the French idea of detaching the Rhineland as a separate buffer state, but it was conceded that this part of western Germany would be kept under Allied military occupation for fifteen years, and that Britain and the United States would come to the aid of France were she ever again to be attacked by Germany. These two provisions were annexed to the forthcoming peace treaty. Wilson suffered a more serious defeat on the issue of war reparations to be paid by the defeated nations. His original stand had been that Germany should pay for the actual damage done by her armies, but that, contrary to the treatment Germany herself had meted to the vanquished in 1871, she should not be charged a large indemnity simply because she had lost. As Wilson feared, what France and several other nations wanted was a large indemnity which would pay for much of the war's total expence. The exact sum, though it was to be very large, could not yet be specified, nor was any precise reckoning made of the terms or period of payment, but on the question of reparations, Wilson had to give in all along the way.

The Frustration of Italy During the discussions, it was conceded that Italy, the fourth most important country at the Conference, would receive the South Tyrol and the Trentino and Trieste districts from the remnants of the Habsburg Empire. The two latter regions were inhabited by Italians, while the South Tyrol was deemed essential to Italy for strategic reasons. Italy's appetite increased with the eating, however, and her delegation also demanded the Yugoslav seaport of Fiume, which was largely Italian in population. Wilson was determined to prevent this, and neither Clemenceau nor Lloyd George had any interest in further argument with him merely for the sake of Italy. The Italian war effort had not been of much help to the Allies, and it was troublesome to find that Italy's maximum claims conflicted with those of Serbia (now part of Yugoslavia), another member of the victorious coalition.

Some of their demands unsatisfied, Orlando and his Italian colleagues withdrew in a petulant mood, finally walking out of the Conference altogether and returning to Rome. Wilson then made another gesture of democratic faith in appealing to the "Italian people" directly to renounce the selfish claims of their leaders. This move backfired, for almost everyone save the American president was out to grab as much as possible in 1919. When the original Conference ended in the month of June, it had been agreed, as mentioned earlier, that Italy would receive the Trentino and Trieste regions and the South Tyrol, even though that meant incorporating a quarter million Germans. Nothing was said, however, about giving Italy any of the coastal cities later included in Yugoslavia, and this merely added more fuel to the country's current political crisis.

The Treaty of Versailles At the end of June 1919, German delegates were invited to Paris to sign the treaty that had been prepared. Seven months earlier, when the armistice was arranged, the Germans had understood that they would have a chance to negotiate a just peace along the lines of the Fourteen Points. The delegates arriving at Paris were therefore astounded to learn that they were now being handed a prearranged document on a take-it-or-leave-it basis. The original head of the delegation resigned in disgust, and German patriots demanded that the treaty be refused, denouncing it as a *Diktat*.

Despite the cries of outraged national feeling, Germany was in no position to resume hostilities. Under the terms of the armistice, the German armed forces had been required to surrender warships, airplanes, and many of their guns as well as to evacuate the western bank of the Rhine. The Allied naval blockade was still in effect, and there was no way out for Germany. Her delegates signed the treaty on June 28, 1919, in the Hall of Mirrors at Versailles, the very spot where the organization of the German Empire had been announced in 1871.

Not all the terms of the Versailles Treaty came as a surprise, for Germany's gains in the east from Brest-Litovsk had already been wiped out by the armistice. Similarly, the return of Alsace-Lorraine to France had been

more or less understood. The cession of small strips of land to Belgium and the northern part of the province of Schleswig to Denmark, as well as the holding of plebiscites in Upper Silesia, were all in accord with the professed Wilsonian principle of national self-determination.

In addition, however, to the return of Alsace-Lorraine, the treaty awarded to France the use of the coal mines of the rich adjoining Saar basin for fifteen years. Together with the Silesian plebiscite, Poland received her promised "outlet to the sea" by being given the "Polish Corridor," a broad strip of land cut directly across western Prussia to the Baltic, separating East Prussia from the rest of Germany. The large German-inhabited port of Danzig was to be governed as a "free city" under the supervision of the League of Nations. Finally, Germany had to consent to a fifteen-year military occupation of the Rhineland, as well as to the demilitarization of a zone thirty miles wide on the east bank. These territorial provisions of the treaty came as a great shock.

The treaty provided that Germany be stripped of her colonies. Wilson insisted that these territories should not, however, merely be annexed by other powers, so a complex system of mandates under the League of Nations was to be arranged. The former German African colonies would be supervised by the League to make sure that the natives received full justice. The former German islands in the Pacific were to be administered by Japan, Australia, and New Zealand.

Determined to prevent the revival of German militarism, the Allies prohibited the construction of offensive weapons, such as airplanes and submarines, and limited the size of any future German army to 100,000 men. Similar restrictions were placed upon the German navy, and the German merchant fleet was forced to hand over the greater part of its tonnage. The nation had to agree to pay five billion dollars in reparations within two years; the final bill was as yet unspecified and would only be announced when the initial payments had been completed. In German eyes, the crowning piece of ignominy contained in the treaty was Article 231, the famous "war guilt" clause, by which Germany had to assume full responsibility for starting the war.

The Minor Treaties   After the treaty with Germany, subsequent treaties were separately made with each of the German allies in the war—Austria, Hungary, Bulgaria, and Turkey—which officially redrew the boundaries of central Europe and the Balkans. The peace settlements with Austria and Hungary were actually a great deal harsher than that made with Germany. Austria was reduced to no more than Vienna and the German-speaking western provinces of the former empire. It was too small to form a very successful independent state, but the treaty of Saint Germain forbade union with Germany, condemning Austria to isolation, restricting her military strength, and obligating her to pay a certain amount in reparations. Furthermore, it deprived Austria of three million German-speaking inhabitants of the former Habsburg provinces of Bohemia and Moravia, now incorporated into the new Slavic state of Czechoslovakia.

If anything, the treaty of Trianon signed with Hungary was even more exacting, for it stripped the former kingdom of Hungary of three-quarters of its territory and two-thirds of its population. Not only were the minority groups of previous years freed from Magyar rule, but one-third of the Hungarians themselves were now included in the neighboring states of Rumania, Yugoslavia, and Czechoslovakia. Hungarian patriots could never accept this, and throughout the following quarter-century they sought some means of revising the treaty or of restoring parts of their kingdom. Bulgaria, however, received more lenient treatment, for the Treaty of Neuilly deprived the latter of no more than a few border regions. Both Bulgaria and Hungary were required to pay a nominal sum in reparations as well as to limit severely the size of their armies.

A successful treaty with Turkey was not worked out until 1923. In 1919, the real ruler of Turkey was a nationalist general, Mustapha Kemal (1881–1938). He rejected the original Allied terms, which, in addition to taking away the Ottoman domain in the Near East (Palestine, Syria, Arabia, and Mesopotamia), would have given the southwestern coast of Asia Minor to Greece. A brief Greco-Turkish war ensued, during which the Greeks were driven back into the Aegean. The 1923 Treaty of Lausanne recognized Turkish sovereignty over all Anatolia as well as the immediate territory north and west of Istanbul. The former Ottoman territories of the Near East were held as League of Nations mandates by Britain and France. Though the empire had disappeared, postwar Turkey was now a compact national state, bent on westernization and modernization. A veritable revolution occurred peacefully in Turkey during the 1920's and 30's under the authoritarian but progressive hand of Mustapha Kemal, who came to be called Atatürk, "Father of the Turks."

Results of the Treaties   Any estimate of the fairness or the results of the peace settlement depends on the standards invoked. German criticisms, for example, have always been met with the reply that the Treaty of Versailles was relatively mild when compared with the precedent set by Germany herself in the winter of 1918. Its terms were not nearly so draconian as those German leaders had forced upon Russia at Brest-Litovsk. Germany was restricted, but certainly not crippled or placed under any insuperable handicap. For the first time, a serious attempt had been made to satisfy the cries

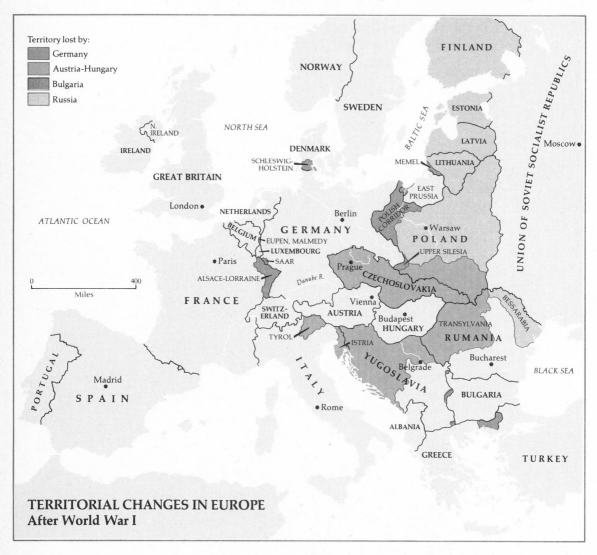

TERRITORIAL CHANGES IN EUROPE
After World War I

for independence of the smaller nations of east-central Europe. Here Wilson's ideals triumphed, although on other issues they were frustrated.

Admitting these obvious facts, there are still a number of criticisms that can fairly be made of the treaties. For example, the "war guilt" clause inflicted on Germany was unhistorical and meaningless, an unfortunate provocation of German resentment against the Allied nations. More fundamental was the fact that the treaties ignored basic economic problems. This was true both with regard to the Versailles Treaty and the treaties signed with the smaller countries. The German settlement, for instance, made no effort to determine exactly how the reparations eventually to be made could ever be collected satisfactorily, or even how the calculation of the bill itself could be adjusted to economic reality. With regard to the small countries, the treaty makers paid little attention to the fact that the new independent states of east-central Europe did not form natural economic units.

Furthermore, despite the great emphasis on national self-determination, the new boundaries in the east were not always drawn so as to avoid the problem of minorities. Here the conflict between idealism and self-interest often resulted in the triumph of the latter. The problem was much more complex than Wilson ever understood or admitted, for there were few clear-cut ethnic boundaries in east-central Europe. Border areas were ethnically mixed and there were numerous territorial enclaves of minority groups. No hard and fast rule could be applied, and the fairest solution would probably have been the establishment of several regional federations. Once the principle of the nation-state had won total acceptance, however, it had to be applied as best the diplomats could. The new sovereign nation-states usually included new ethnic minorities, often composed of part of a formerly

Austrian Socialist Militia Returning from a Skirmish with Rightist Militia, 1927. The end of the war did not bring true peace to central and eastern Europe. The new Austrian republic became increasingly torn by strife between left and right, and finally lapsed into dictatorship in 1933. (Austrian National Library.)

dominant national group. The principal advantages from this process were reaped by Serbia, Rumania, and the Poles and Czechs, who were either members of the victorious alliance (as in the case of the first two) or the strongest of the formerly oppressed peoples (as in the case of the latter). The major victims were the defeated nations, for the Germanic inhabitants of South Tyrol and of the Sudetenland, as well as millions of Hungarians, were arbitrarily incorporated as minorities in other countries.

Wilson was not fully satisfied with this arrangement. However, he intended that its negative effects be softened by the inauguration of a new era in European affairs, in which the cold-blooded balance-of-power system and naked self-interest would be replaced by the rule of international law. This change was to be effected by the League of Nations, which Wilson relied on to administer the treaty and make whatever adjustments might be necessary to remove inequities. He insisted that the United States must support the treaty and the League, and refused to make concessions to the spirit of American isolationism when the agreement was submitted for ratification by the Senate. Wilson's foes among his fellow countrymen were numerous; led by the Republican Senator Henry Cabot Lodge, they ruined all his hopes when the United States Senate rejected both the treaty and the League in 1920. The abrupt withdrawal of American diplomacy from Europe brought the League under the leadership of Britain and France, who had not been very eager for the organization in the first place.

As it turned out, the Treaty of Versailles could not be enforced, and this in itself was the most unsatisfactory consequence of the peace settlement. In this sense, the treaty was either too mild or too harsh. It has been suggested that the peacemakers ought either to have given Germany an extremely lenient peace, conciliating her and drawing her into a new European order, or else have punished her so severely that she could never regain her former position as the most dynamic country in Europe. The failure to do either the one or the other meant that when Germany eventually recovered her power, she would demand far-reaching changes in the order of Europe.

Problems of East-Central Europe Outwardly, the peace settlement marked the triumph of representative government throughout east-central Europe. Three autocratic empires had been dissolved, and each newly created government had a constitution and a nominally representative parliament. However, independence brought grave problems and the new states established in the east had great difficulty in achieving stable peacetime conditions. A major handicap was the fact that the region was overwhelmingly agricultural and its economy lagged far behind that of the west. The bulk of the population was peasant, social leadership having traditionally been exercised by the aristocracy. Only one country—Czechoslovakia—had undergone industrial development, contained a sizable middle class, and was able to sustain representative government.

To provide an economic basis for national independence, most countries of east-central Europe made efforts to carry out basic social reforms, of which by far the most important was distribution of land among the poverty-stricken peasantry. Land reform was no problem in Finland, Bulgaria, and Greece, for here the peasants already owned most of the land. But in other countries, most of the farmland had been held by the aristocracy; breakup of these holdings would destroy the basis of the old caste society. A definitive influence in tipping the scales in favor of nominal land reform was the nearness of the Soviet Union, whose new collectivist society lay all along the borders of these countries. The ruling class of east-central Europe hoped that land reform would eliminate the potential appeal of communism.

A substantial reform was carried out in the newly independent Baltic states of Estonia, Latvia, and Lithuania, and in the advanced democracy of Czechoslovakia, where over half the land was transferred in small units to new owners. Distribution in these countries was made less difficult by the fact that much of the land had been held by aristocratic Germans who had now lost political status. In Rumania and Yugoslavia, there was also an attempt to break up the big estates, but very little was accomplished in Poland and Hungary. The large holdings in these last two countries were the most sizable in Europe. Though a major land reform was promulgated in Poland in 1925, it was never adequately enforced. Even less was done in Hungary, where the brief dictatorship (1919) of the terrorist Communist Bela Kun had increased the anxiety and the stubbornness of the upper class.

Even when carried out, the land reforms often did little to aid the east European economy. The average holdings were too small to be farmed efficiently, and the peasants could not get the credit to buy machinery or attempt improved methods of cultivation. In the Balkans, twice as many peasants might produce only one-third as much grain on a given piece of land as in Holland or Denmark, and the governments were slow to take positive steps to improve their productivity. In Yugoslavia during the 1920's and 30's, only forty cents per capita per year was spent on agriculture. The population of east-central Europe was growing rapidly, even though there were already more people trying to live off the land than could be supported. Since industrialization was in its earliest stages, there was scant urban employment to relieve the pressure. Between 1920 and 1940, the living standards of much of the eastern peasantry declined and constant malnutrition was the rule for millions.

When some efforts were made to industrialize, as in Poland, Rumania, and Hungary, they were financed by squeezing the peasant sector of the population. Prices for manufactured goods went up, but the prices of agricultural produce were static or even declined. Most of the state revenue was collected by indirect taxation, which fell heaviest on the peasantry. Such taxes by the 1930's amounted to seventy-three percent of total receipts of Rumania, and were almost as high in Yugoslavia and Bulgaria. Given this basic social and economic imbalance, the outlook for most of east-central Europe was gloomy.

The dissatisfaction of the peasantry and the division between political factions caused the ruling groups to grow more uneasy with each passing year. It became harder and harder for the monarchs and government leaders to resist the temptation to restrict political liberty. In Poland, several dozen separate political parties made government almost impossible. Therefore, in 1926 Marshal Pilsudski (1867–1935), the hero of Polish resistance against Russia, set up a military dictatorship. King Alexander of Yugoslavia seized authoritarian control over the government of his hybrid kingdom in 1929, as did King Carol of Rumania in 1930 and King Boris of Bulgaria a few years later. By the early 1930's, the only country of east-central Europe that still maintained parliamentary government was progressive, partially industrialized Czechoslovakia.

The steady rise of authoritarianism in east-central Europe during the 1920's did not really solve any of the problems of the region, but merely preserved civil order and the traditional class structure. The erosion of representative government exacerbated one of the basic problems, that of national minorities. An authoritarian Poland discriminated against Jews and strongly repressed White Russians and Ukrainians. Dictatorial monarchy in Yugoslavia basically meant the rule of Serbia over the Croats and Slovenes. Rumania held down a large Hungarian minority; and so it went. A decade after the Versailles Treaty, nationalist discontent was as widespread as before the war.

It should be understood, however, that the new authoritarian regimes of east-central Europe were basically old-fashioned and relatively easygoing. They were not dynamic dictatorships of the new "fascist" variety that will be discussed in detail in Chapter 5. They were not "total" tyrannies and usually lacked a distinct ideology or any very clear economic organization. They were fundamentally conservative and disinterested in rapid social change. Their establishment completely reversed the seeming triumph of democracy in east-central Europe, which many people thought had been achieved at Versailles.

DIPLOMATIC
PROBLEMS
OF THE 1920's

The League of Nations When the League of Nations first assembled in Geneva in November 1920, there were forty-four official member nations from all parts of the globe. Conspicuously absent, however, were the countries defeated in the war—Germany, Austria, Hungary, Bulgaria, Turkey—and also the new revolutionary state, Soviet Russia. In time, membership expanded to include nearly all the sovereign countries of the world, and by 1926 all the central and east European states had joined save Turkey and the Soviet Union, who entered in 1932 and 1935, respectively. However, the new League was initially run by the western victors, Britain and France, since its original sponsor, the United States, had refused to join.

These two countries had opposite conceptions of the goal and function of the League. After the peace of Versailles had been signed, Britain tended once more to want to forget European problems and withdraw into her former "Splendid Isolation." Britain's basic interest was in her imperial affairs and her export trade. She rejected any interpretation of the League's function as that of enforcing international law in cases of serious dispute.

With the exception of the Labor government of 1924, British representatives did not want to give the League real power, but only to use it as an informal assembly where nations might discuss problems of mutual interest on which they would not be inclined to disagree.

French policy, on the other hand, was centered on continental problems. The main concern of the French government was to maintain complete national security against the German menace, which had been defeated but not eliminated. In 1919, the British and American leaders had promised that their countries would sign a treaty guaranteeing aid to France in the event of any future German attack, but American rejection of Wilson's policy had voided the pledge. Thus, after the treaty had been signed, France had no immediate guarantee of collective security other than the League. The French government consequently tried to do what it could to strengthen the League's power.

As organized, the League lacked effective machinery to keep the peace in case of military aggression against one of its members. There was no provision for automatic military or economic action to repel invasion, nor was any decision made in this connection binding upon all members. In 1923 and 1924, two new proposals were presented by French and British representatives, requiring international quarrels to be presented to the League's agencies and stipulating that all member nations must come to the aid of any state that was attacked. Neither was enacted into the League statutes, the principal opponent being the new British Conservative government, which soon reversed its predecessor's stand.

Before long, there was abundant evidence that, in matters involving the great powers, the League's authority was a dead letter. In the long run, the new organization contained no more than the bare bones of Wilson's project. Its effective work was largely limited to such matters as regulating international communications and controlling the drug traffic.

War Reparations Defeated, disarmed, and economically dislocated, Germany was nevertheless a source of acute concern to European diplomacy in the early 1920's. After Britain and the United States reneged on their pledge to guarantee France's borders against Germany, the French became more insistent on direct satisfaction of their demands against the defeated enemy. Concretely, this meant full and rapid payment of war reparations. The exact figure Germany was to pay had not been specified in the Versailles Treaty, and two full years were required before France and England were able to agree on a complete bill. When this was presented in 1921, the total of $35,000,000,000 was so staggering that the new German government rejected it. To change the Germans' minds, French troops occupied three cities in the Ruhr during the month of March, and Germany finally had to agree to pay the full amount.

The British, on the other hand, were rapidly losing interest in forcing Germany to pay heavy reparations. British leaders wondered if it was economically possible or even desirable that Germany make the payments.

They felt that a healthy, prosperous Germany was necessary for a progressive Europe, but suspected that French policy was based on the long-range goal of ruining Germany in order to restore French dominance.

Under a moderate liberal government, the German republic at first made an effort to keep up with the payments. However, postwar difficulties kept the volume of trade low, and Germany did not have the exchange balance to meet the schedule. The government debts of most central European countries were mounting rapidly in the early 1920's, for the conversion to a harmonious peacetime economy was difficult. Like that of Austria, Hungary, and even France, Germany's government tried to meet official obligations simply by printing more and more currency. This resulted in severe inflation of the mark, so that by the second half of 1922, Germany's financial position was becoming impossible. At an international conference in October, the German delegation became so concerned over the attitude of Britain and France that it sought diplomatic insurance by signing an agreement, known as the Treaty of Rapallo, for friendship and economic collaboration with the Soviet Union.

French Troops Occupy the German Ruhr, January 1923. Military occupation of the German industrial district of the Ruhr was the major overt effort made by France to secure full compliance with the letter of the peace settlement. (French Embassy Press & Information Division.)

The Rapallo Treaty shocked the other powers, and, after Germany failed for the third time to meet part of her reparations payments, the French replied forcefully in January 1923, when French and Belgian troops occupied the entire Ruhr in order to force Germany to pay. This vengeful act quickly backfired, for Britain condemned the move and there was strong disapproval from other countries. The patriotic reaction in Germany was extreme, and the Ruhr inhabitants adopted an attitude of passive resistance. Meanwhile, Germany temporarily fell into internal chaos, as the inflation reached astronomical proportions. The turning point came in September 1923 when Gustav Stresemann (1878–1929) formed a middle-of-the-road government and pledged resumption of reparations payments. After a few more months, the French government withdrew its forces and the situation gradually eased.

Hands Off the Ruhr! This subsequent German poster denouncing occupation of the Ruhr was a typical expression of German patriotic resentment. Moreover, France's use of black Senegalese troops as part of the occupation force greatly exacerbated German racist feeling. (International Institute of Social History, Amsterdam.)

The inflation in Germany was ended by recalling all the old, useless currency at the rate of one trillion old marks to one new "Renten mark."

The French Alliance System In 1924, it became clear that the occupation of the Ruhr had been a failure, and French leaders began to doubt the possibility of enforcing the letter of the Versailles Treaty by military means. They became less interested in forcing Germany to submit to various restrictions and obligations and more concerned about the goal of merely maintaining France's national security against any potential resurgence of German power. Though France's army was currently the strongest in the world, such superiority was relative to the weakness of Germany, and French leaders wanted to supplement it with independent alliances. To this end, military agreements were signed with Belgium (1920) and Czechoslovakia (1924), and a treaty of friendship and consultation was arranged with Poland in 1921. Czechoslovakia, Rumania, and Yugoslavia, the principal beneficiaries of the demise of the Habsburg Empire, signed a series of agreements among themselves, which formed a "Little Entente" between the three countries to oppose any possible Habsburg restoration in Austria or Hungary. France then associated herself with the Little Entente by treaties of friendship with Rumania (1926) and Yugoslavia (1927), thus hoping to turn the anti-Habsburg agreement into an instrument for maintaining the status quo throughout western and central Europe.

These Little Entente pacts had scant value, for France's erstwhile allies were not strong, with the possible exception of Czechoslovakia, and France was separated from them geographically. Furthermore, the French army was purely defensive-minded and never at any time during the 1920's and 1930's made preparation to use the kind of offensive tactics needed to implement an alliance with central European states. Thus the French alliance system for containing Germany was impressive only so long as it was not put to the test. It provided security only because Russia had temporarily been eliminated from Europe and because Germany was temporarily weak and disarmed.

Briand and the Spirit of Compromise By 1924, the series of postwar crises had passed, and there was a new feeling of calm and even a desire for cooperation. This mood was most strongly expressed by the British Labour government of Ramsay MacDonald and the current Radical government in France, both of which hoped to promote harmony in Europe. The lead was taken by MacDonald himself and the new French foreign minister, Aristide Briand (1862–1932). Briand and many other French liberals were opposed to further attempts to coerce Germany, and early in 1924 a new formula was devised to handle the reparations problem. This arrangement, called the Dawes Plan in honor of the American financier who headed the negotiating committee, reduced the annual German payment and arranged for a special loan to enable Germany to meet the first installment. For some years American and British banks poured far more money into Germany in the form of loans and investments than the Weimar Republic paid in reparations to the Allied powers.

The central international figure of the half-decade of optimism and good feeling that followed was Briand, who served as French foreign minister from 1925 to 1932. Briand firmly believed that lasting peace could be won only through free and equal understanding with Germany in accordance with the Covenant of the League of Nations. An ex-Socialist and a consummate political tactician, he was willing to work for practical compromise and met a man of like mind in Gustav Stresemann, who had become the architect of Germany's foreign policy. Stresemann believed that, for the time being, Germany could become prosperous and secure only through a policy of "fulfillment" of the peace treaty. This brought Stresemann strong criticism from German supernationalists, even though he always explained privately that he proposed fulfillment only in order to make Germany strong enough and respectable enough later to bring about a revision of the terms.

Locarno In October 1925, representatives of France, Britain, Germany, Italy, and Belgium met at the Swiss resort of Locarno, where they signed a series of agreements guaranteeing one another's frontiers. According to the main Locarno treaty, all five countries promised to respect and preserve the existing Franco-German and German-Belgian boundaries, and they also signed bilateral arbitration treaties to handle any future disputes. In 1926, Germany was officially restored to respectability by admission to the League of Nations. The Locarno treaties were basically a pledge by Germany to refrain from trying to win back Alsace-Lorraine. The friendly reconciliation of France and Germany inaugurated what was called for some years the "spirit of Locarno," an attitude of neighborliness and cooperation by the western powers which seemed to banish the very thought of war.

The Locarno spirit ignored, however, a number of unpleasant realities. Nothing at all had been said about Germany's eastern border and the problem of the Polish Corridor. Indeed, the most respectable German politicians privately agreed that something would eventually have to be done about getting back the lost territory in the east. Special arbitration treaties were signed with Czechoslovakia and Poland, but there was no mention of guaranteeing the existing frontiers.

The next general diplomatic agreement of the Locarno era, the 1928 Pact of Paris, was sufficiently general in theory to include everyone. Better known as the Kellogg-Briand Pact, this was a document prepared by the French and American foreign ministers in which all the western powers agreed never to go to war again. The goal sought was irreproachable, but the means employed were irrelevant, because the Pact carried no provision for enforcement and hence was virtually a dead letter.

The last great compromise effort to solve the reparations problem was made in 1929. A new agreement was made, called the Young Plan in honor of the American businessman who headed the committee. It fixed the total bill more precisely and at a lower level than under previous arrangements, limited German payments to fifty-nine years and removed the humiliating requirement of foreign supervision. The French then agreed to evacuate the Rhineland ahead of schedule, breaking another link in the so-called "shackles of Versailles." Surprisingly enough, the Young Plan aroused loud protest in Germany, for German nationalists were not satisfied with a mere easing of conditions—they wanted to be rid of reparations altogether.

Thus, though the second half of the 1920's was an interlude of relative stability and good feeling, it did not provide permanent solutions to any of the outstanding problems left by the peace settlement. It has frequently been suggested that the atmosphere of the Locarno era was made possible in part simply by the general economic prosperity Europe enjoyed during these years. This affluence was a limited and precarious one, however, and when the great social and economic crisis of depression struck, the European political structure was shaken to its very foundation.

THE ECONOMICS OF POSTWAR WESTERN EUROPE   The accumulated demand of the war years resulted in a sudden increase in buying after the fighting ended in western Europe. That was followed by temporary depression, however, and full recovery did not get underway until 1922. The next seven years witnessed rapid expansion of industrial production for most of the economically advanced countries.

Technological Change and Economic Growth   The 1920's were years of broad technological change, with emphasis on the "rationalization" of production. Techniques pioneered in America, such as the assembly line, standardization of supplies, and use of interchangeable parts, were widely introduced in Europe. New kinds of machinery, such as the rotary kiln for cement, continuous rolling mills, and electric furnaces for steel production, helped greatly to increase efficiency. Prewar chemical inventions were expanded and a new industry—plastics—began to emerge. The greatest technical innovations of all were in the field of transportation and communication. Radios were soon mass-produced, while automobiles and trucks were coming off the assembly lines in ever-increasing numbers. The airplane was now produced for commercial use, and for the first time, rapid travel between widely distant points was made possible. By 1929, the general European industrial index stood twenty-eight percent higher than in 1913.

One consequence of the trend toward rationalization was accentuation of the growth of cartels, especially in Germany. Another result was a fundamental change in the working force, for increasing mechanization produced greater emphasis on administration and research so that the number of actual production workers increased only slowly whereas clerical and secretarial employment of all kinds was multiplied several times over. Since proportionately fewer men were employed in actual physical labor, more and more workers preferred to consider themselves members of the lower "middle class." The general trend was therefore toward a lessened sense of class antagonism.

Economic Weaknesses   Yet this new industrial prosperity had definite limits. The whole agrarian sector of the economy was in large measure excluded. War losses had taken a disproportionate toll of the peasant population and, by the time full prosperity had been restored in the 1920's, international competition forced farm prices into a serious decline. West European farmers could not afford to take advantage of new machinery and had to go into debt simply to remain in business. The result was that agriculture by the later 1920's was on its way to becoming a virtually stagnant sector of the economy. Hundreds of thousands of rural people continued to move to the cities, so that by 1930 Europe was even more heavily urbanized than before.

A variety of factors frustrated the full growth of the European economy at the end of this decade. One of these was national barriers in the form of high tariffs. International cooperation and marketing were severely hampered by the congeries of large and small nation-states of Europe. National barriers also limited emigration of excess population, and new United States immigration laws of 1921 and 1924 sharply restricted further entrance of people from the poorer countries of southern and eastern Europe.

Another factor hampering the European economy was the shaky structure of much of European finance throughout this decade. The war had left a trail of massive inflation and weak government finance throughout central Europe and even in France. As previously explained, the German economy had been able to cope with reparations largely on the basis of sizable loans from the United States and could hardly sustain such a burden from its regular balance of foreign trade and payments.

The war had cost the west European export trade a significant share of its former world market. With non-European industrialization forging ahead, the west European economy had to run fast simply in order to stand still in relation to the rest of the world. Moreover, not all the organizational changes in European industry increased efficiency. The only effect of some of the new cartel empires was to increase the personal power and wealth of industrial magnates.

A final element of weakness in the economy of the 1920's was the fact that the lower classes did not participate fully in the general prosperity. Wages rose, but often not so fast as did productivity. This meant that the working-class movement made relatively few gains during the 1920's, save in special cases such as the Socialist administrations in Austria. The attitude of management had changed little as a result of the war, and there was scant concern to increase the benefits or purchasing power of employees.

The Great Depression   The United States served as cornerstone of the international economy of the 1920's, but its own industrialization had been even more rapid than that of Europe, and financial speculation was greatly overextended. The strain caused American stock values to crumble suddenly on Wall Street's "Black Thursday" of October 24, 1929. The result of this

financial collapse was a sudden contraction of American credit to Europe, and a steady decline in American trade.

The impact was felt to a greater or lesser extent by every European country. Central Europe was most seriously affected because of the great volume of short-term American loans to Germany and Austria. During 1930, the German credit system was driven to the wall and in May 1931, Austria's greatest financial institution, the *Kreditanstalt,* went bankrupt. These financial disasters resulted in serious shrinkage of international trade and, as exports declined, factories in the most heavily industrialized countries began to lay off more and more workers until their numbers climbed into the millions. It was thus the countries with the most modern and complex economies that were the hardest hit, but the less industrialized countries also felt the effects, for the slump in commerce made it impossible to market much of their agrarian exports. Not merely were the industrial nations threatened with social catastrophe, but the under-developed European countries saw all hopes of bettering themselves frustrated.

The "New Economics" of Keynes Businessmen could not cope with the crisis, for the technological revolution of the 1920's had not been accompanied by any revolution in business psychology. The basic response was retrenchment and deflation. The old emphasis of nineteenth-century liberal economics on sound financing, cutting back production, and waiting for things to level out was the only remedy that most employers could think of. The trouble was that this depression began to go into its fifth and sixth years without much prospect of levelling out. If the capitalist system was to survive, a fresh approach was needed for the solution of its problems. This was supplied by the so-called "new economics," of which the most influential theorist was the Englishman John Maynard Keynes (1883–1946). Keynes believed that the goal of economic activity was simply to achieve the maximum volume of production and employment. In his classic, *The General Theory of Employment, Interest, and Money* (1936), Keynes dismissed as futile the old laissez-faire notion that all unattended ills would balance out in the long run, writing that "in the long run, we are all dead." At the same time he derided Marxism as insufficient and irrelevant to the complex economic structure of the twentieth century. The crux of Keynes' study therefore concerned the way in which government could stimulate the national economy without resorting to socialism. Limited intervention in vital areas was the answer. Keynes believed in deficit spending to encourage production—"priming the pump," as it was called in the United States. His economic theory offered a rationale for government action to check depression without socializing the entire economy, and thus tried to encourage a new kind of solution, free from both conservative poverty and radical tyranny.

Something of this sort was already being attempted by the United States and the Scandinavian countries, but most of the free countries of western Europe failed to achieve any integrated program to cure the depression. A variety of different actions were taken which, by themselves, sometimes made matters worse. The general rise in tariff barriers, for example, meant that international trade was likely to remain at a permanently low level. Segments of the economy were given special subsidies in most countries, but this often encouraged dependence rather than recovery. Public works programs were only temporary stopgap measures. Though the original balance of the economy was restored in Germany and England by 1936, some countries were not so fortunate. Even in France and the United States, only mobilization for World War II was to put all the unemployed back to work. By that time, the whole diplomatic structure of the 1920's had collapsed, and an entire generation of European civilization seemed to have been wasted.

FURTHER READING

There is a balanced evaluation of the Versailles Conference in Paul Birdsall, *Versailles Twenty Years After* (1941). Harold Nicolson, *Peace-making, 1919* (1933), is a shorter, more personal account. One of the most trenchant early criticisms was that of J. M. Keynes, *The Economic Consequences of the Peace* (1920), which can be balanced by Etienne Mantoux, *The Carthaginian Peace—or the Economic Consequences of Mr. Keynes* (1952). The influence of revolution and counter-revolution on the peace settlement are studied from different viewpoints by J. M. Thompson, *Russia, Bolshevism, and the Versailles Peace* (1966); and A. J. Mayer, *Politics and Diplomacy of Peacemaking* (1967). See also Alma Luckau, *The German Delegation at the Peace Conference* (1941); René Albrecht-Carrié, *Italy at the Paris Peace Conference* (1938); T. A. Bailey, *Woodrow Wilson and the Lost Peace* (1944); and Stephen Bonsal, *Suitors and Suppliants: the Little Nations at Versailles* (1946).

F. L. Carsten, *Revolution in Central Europe, 1918–1919* (1972), gives a general account of the immediate postwar crisis in central Europe, and the dilemma of Germany is discussed in Klaus Epstein, *Matthias Erzberger and the Dilemma of German Democracy* (1959). Thomas G. Masaryk, *The Making of a State* (1927), is the classic account of the formation of Czechoslovakia. The best discussion of the problem of the German minority there, from the German viewpoint, is Wenzel Jaksch, *Europe's Road to Potsdam* (1963).

The best one-volume survey of east-central Europe in this period is Hugh Seton-Watson, * *Eastern Europe Between the Wars, 1918–1941* (1945); but see also C. A. Macartney and A. W. Palmer, *Independent Eastern Europe* (1962). Fundamental books on other east-European countries are Hans Roos, *A History of Modern Poland* (1965); H. L. Roberts, *Rumania* (1951); and C. J. Smith, *Finland and the Russian Revolution, 1917–1922* (1958). David Mitrany, * *Marx Against the Peasant* (1951), is a key study of the peasant problem.

The principal study of the League of Nations is F. P. Walters, *A History of the League of Nations*, 2 vols. (1952). The origins of the French alliance system are studied in P. S. Wandycz, *France and Her Eastern Allies, 1919–1925* (1962). J. K. Galbraith, * *The Great Crash, 1929* (1955), gives a readable account of the beginning of the depression. The best biography of Keynes is R. F. Harrod, *The Life of John Maynard Keynes* (1951).

*Books available in paperback edition are marked with an asterisk.

4 Communist Russia, 1917-1939

One of the most momentous consequences of the First World War was the establishment of the Communist dictatorship in Russia. For the next twenty years, Russia lived apart from the rest of Europe, absorbed in an enterprise fraught with incredible anguish and suffering—the development of a totalitarian Communist system of state control over all major aspects of life. By 1930, Communist Russia had set the pattern for twentieth-century dictatorships and had become the first successful totalitarian socialist state.

THE COMMUNIST REVOLUTION AND CIVIL WAR

Weakness of the Provisional Government In 1917, the tsarist regime was not overthrown by a revolutionary uprising but collapsed under the pressure of military defeat. The downfall of tsardom threw Russia into political and social chaos. After three years of world war, most Russian people sought peace and material well-being at almost any price, and had little interest in political leaders who would not cater to these demands.

The Provisional Government, formed in Petrograd by leaders of the former imperial Parliament, planned to establish constitutional democracy in Russia. It also stood for the respect of legal rights, due process of law, and the honoring of Russia's international commitment to remain in the war against the Central Powers. Its stress upon meeting all legal obligations ran directly counter to the desire of the lower classes for an immediate end to the war and for sweeping economic changes. During the spring and summer of 1917, the prestige and influence of the Provisional Government declined steadily.

The Soviets The demand of workers, soldiers, and peasants for drastic change was represented by the "Soviets" (Councils) that quickly sprang up in almost every city of Russia. Their organization was at least in part spontaneous, just as in the 1905 revolution, for representatives of the various factories, professions, and regiments began to meet together as soon as the tsarist regime had crumbled. The Soviet of Petrograd (as St. Petersburg was then called) assumed a major role and acted like a second government. It is important to note that, in the beginning, the Soviets were not merely a tool of the organized revolutionary parties, but reflected the radical feelings of a large segment of the lower classes. At first, the political group most closely connected with the Soviets was the Menshevik faction of Russian Marxists. The Mensheviks could not gain full leadership of the Soviets, however, because the Mensheviks were committed to cooperation with the Provisional Government and shared its respect for law. Contrary to Lenin's Bolsheviks, they did not believe that the time for socialist revolution would arrive until after a democratic parliamentary system had been fully installed in Russia.

Meeting of a Soviet of Soldiers' Deputies Petrograd, 1917. Organization of revolutionary soldiers' councils or soviets was a prominent feature of the first phase of the Russian revolution. After the Bolshevik coup, the soviets were brought under dictatorial central control.

Bolshevik Seizure of the Government Lenin's Bolshevik faction was able to take advantage of the political chaos in Russia and impose its own dictatorship because of several factors. It was the best-organized revolutionary group in Russia. Its leader proved an extraordinarily shrewd revolutionary demagogue who was able to exploit the desires of the lower classes in a ruthless and sweeping manner. None of his competitors in other parties was sufficiently unscrupulous to imitate these tactics.

Only a few months earlier, Lenin had been deeply pessimistic about the prospects of revolution in Russia in the near future, and the sudden collapse of the monarchy caught him by surprise. He saw that a great opportunity had arrived, yet he had no way of reaching Russia from exile in Switzerland across a war-torn continent. He was rescued from this predicament by a strange ally, the German high command, which was only too glad to promote revolution and chaos in Russia. Lenin and other *émigrés* were shipped back to Russia via Finland, crossing Germany in a "sealed train."

Lenin arrived at Petrograd in April 1917. At that time, the membership of the Bolshevik party was no more than 80,000. It had fewer supporters in the Soviets than did the Mensheviks and many fewer followers in the country at large than did the Social Revolutionaries. Being non-Marxist and stressing independent peasant communes, the Social Revolutionaries were still the largest of the radical organizations, for they appealed directly to the great bulk of Russia's population—the peasantry. The relative strength of Lenin's group was nevertheless greater than its size would indicate. In contrast to the Social Revolutionaries, or even to the Mensheviks, the Bolsheviks were trained, professional revolutionaries with tight organization and a leadership greatly superior in practical ability to that of their rivals.

Lenin decided on a bold plan to catapult his small group into control of Russia. He announced a three-point program calling for an end to the

May Day in Petrograd, 1917. This popular celebration by worker groups occurred in the square in front of St. Isaac's cathedral in Petrograd during the early libertarian phase of the revolution, before the Bolshevik takeover. After that all spontaneous demonstration was banned. (Hoover Institution Archives.)

imperialist war, expropriation of the larger landowners, and the transfer of all power to the Soviets. He undercut the Social Revolutionaries by outdoing them in application of their own doctrine: all land for the peasants. Moreover, the Bolsheviks won growing support in the Soviets by going far beyond the Mensheviks in their revolutionary demands.

At this stage, Lenin's most successful plea was his call for an end to the fighting, a demand which struck a responsive chord in almost every Russian heart. The Bolshevik leader called upon soldiers to throw down their arms and desert the fighting lines. Many of them were doing just that, and the Provisional Government, unable to improve conditions at home or carry on the war, lost support steadily. In May, a new cabinet was formed, representing all the left-wing groups except the Bolsheviks, who refused to participate. The strongman of the new government was Alexander Kerensky (1881–1970), a young Social Revolutionary leader who served as minister of war. The Provisional Government was still pledged to carry on the war in a spirit of solidarity with the western Allies, yet it promised a war without imperialist motives, a war without annexations and indemnities. In the summer of 1917, however, France, Britain, and Italy would not renounce war aims, and the Provisional Government could offer the Russian people no ideal making it worthwhile to carry on the struggle. A final effort to resume the offensive in southwest Russia ended in total collapse.

By July, the constant agitation had so excited the soldiers and workers of Petrograd that they could no longer be restrained. A demonstration grew into a street march against the government. This revolutionary flareup again

Participants in a Bolshevik Demonstration Scattering under Gunfire, 1917. In their campaign of mass revolutionary demagogy to undermine the Provisional Government, Bolshevik agitators organized large street demonstrations that often produced or provoked violence. (Radio Times Hulton Picture Library.)

took Lenin by surprise. The Bolsheviks were not yet prepared for a coup against the Provisional Government, and they tried to calm the marchers. The whole action was premature, for the government still had the strength to quell the rebellion, and the Bolshevik leaders had to go into hiding.

Kerensky became head of the Provisional Government, but despite its temporary success, the power of that body continued to decline. An effort by moderates in September to bring the government under military tutelage failed completely. Supposedly loyal troops, when moved to the Petrograd area, soon succumbed to revolutionary propaganda. Lacking any independent force on which to rely, Kerensky had to cooperate with the radical left once more. By October, the Provisional Government had become a hollow shell.

Recovering from their setback in July, the Bolsheviks gained a majority in the Petrograd Soviet, where Lenin's hyper-radical propaganda carried the day against Menshevik moderation. Leon Trotsky (1879–1940), the Marxist hero of the 1905 revolution, had moved over to Lenin's faction and, after being elected chairman of the Petrograd Soviet, became head of a "Revolutionary Military Committee," which organized the Bolshevik workers' militia (Red Guards) and revolutionary soldiers in preparation for a *coup d'état.*

In the early hours of November 7, 1917, the Bolshevik forces seized all the vantage points of Petrograd, and within hours had captured or put to flight every member of the Provisional Government. Lenin's party had won control of the Russian capital. It had happened so quickly and easily that the other political groups were at a loss to respond. The coup had been timed to coincide with the convening of the second All-Russian Congress of Soviets, representing the local councils all over the country. When the Congress of Soviets met on the afternoon of November 7, Lenin fulfilled his long-standing propaganda slogan of "All power to Soviets!" by nominally transferring the sovereignty of the Provisional Government to this body.

This ceremony was in fact sheer stage-play to serve appearances. What actually happened was that the Congress of Soviets was forced to accept a Council of Peoples' Commissars, composed of the top Bolshevik leaders, as head of the new government. Power had not passed to the Soviets, as Lenin tried to make it appear, but to a Bolshevik dictatorship dominated by himself.

Lenin immediately arranged that the Congress promulgate two far-reaching decrees—a peace decree, calling upon all belligerents to conclude an immediate peace, and a land decree, giving the peasants all the land not already in their hands. By these acts he cut through all the restraints that had bound the Provisional Government, and showed that the Soviet regime would carry out a thoroughly revolutionary policy. All the institutions of the tsarist era were dismantled, and the power of the Russian Orthodox Church was neutralized by separation of church and state, confiscation of church lands, and abolition of all civil prerogatives of the clergy.

Suppression of the Constituent Assembly   Ever since the fall of the tsar, Russia had been awaiting the election of a Constituent Assembly, which would have the people's mandate to build a new political regime. The Provisional Government had, however, postponed the balloting for several months, and when it finally occurred on November 25, constitutional rule had already been overthrown by the Bolsheviks. Even so, the election made it clear that Lenin's faction did not have the support of the bulk of the population. As representatives of the peasantry, the Social Revolutionaries received 21 million ballots—a clear majority of the popular vote. The Bolsheviks won only 9 million, while the liberals and Mensheviks, who had been swept aside in the revolutionary furor, received very little support at all.

At this point, Lenin's power had become too great to be thwarted merely by popular vote. In one of his customary political frauds, the Bolshevik leader announced that ballots cast for the Social Revolutionaries did not count, on the grounds that the latter no longer formed a single organized group. When the Constituent Assembly finally met in January 1918, it lasted only one session. On the evening of the first day, Bolshevik militia emptied the chamber, and the Constituent Assembly ended almost as soon as it had begun. The brief ten-month interlude of constitutional government in Russia was over.

Consolidation of Communist Power Conclusion of the Treaty of Brest-Litovsk early in 1918 ended the war with Germany and left the Bolshevik dictatorship free to consolidate its power inside Russia. The name of the party was soon changed officially to "Communist" in order to distinguish the Bolshevik form of dictatorial socialism from the social democracy of western Marxists. At first, the Communists held control of most urban regions of Russia through the city Soviets. Opposition was confused and unorganized, but quickly grew in volume throughout the former empire as the dictatorial character of Communist government became apparent. The majority group in the other radical movement, the Social Revolutionaries, had ranged itself against communism even before the November coup. After Brest-Litovsk, the minority or "Left" Social Revolutionaries, who had at first supported the Communists, also turned on them because of their apparent capitulation to German imperialism. Both branches of the peasant-oriented Social Revolutionaries now found that the revolution had been snatched away from their hands. They were not slow to reply with the same weapon used against tsardom—political terrorism.

To cope with this resistance, the Communist Government had already formed special organs of repression. At the end of 1917, the Council of People's Commissars created a special state security police, known from its initials as the Cheka (and later successively renamed and relabeled OGPU, NKVD, MVD, and KGB). The Cheka had its work cut out, for in 1918 Lenin himself was wounded and several of the principal chiefs of the secret police were assassinated by the counter-terrorists. By that time, the Communists had launched an official "Red Terror" to crush all political opposition in the territory under their control. Thousands of people were shot by the Cheka during the next few years. Meanwhile, all parties save the Communists were outlawed in Russia, and the 1918 Congress of Soviets completed its work with a new constitution which converted Russia into a one-party dictatorship.

The Civil War As the months of 1918 passed, organized opposition to communism began to emerge in every corner of Russia. The conservative groups and middle-class elements started to recover from the shock and defeatism of the previous year as they endeavored to combat the new despotism, located not in the former capital, St. Petersburg, but once more in Moscow, to which the Communists had moved to escape German guns. The anti-Communist forces were mostly led by officers of the former tsarist army, who grouped together motley elements of aristocrats, conservatives, bourgeois, peasants, Cossacks, and members of the national minorities. In the early months, these "White" forces were few in number and sorely in need of equipment; they were nearly driven from the field by the masses of "Red" militia.

The Whites, however, began to receive limited shipments of supplies from the western Allies, who were hostile to the Communist regime, in part because of its revolutionary character, but mainly because it had deserted the anti-German alliance. In the middle of 1918, France, Britain, and the United States hoped to encourage the revival of hostilities against Germany by a new and more liberal Russian regime. Eventually, all three countries, and Japan as well, sent small contingents of troops to coastal cities in support of the Whites. Furthermore, tens of thousands of former Czech soldiers in the Austro-Hungarian army, who had earlier either been captured by or deserted to the Russians, formed a Czech Legion that turned against the Communists and temporarily seized control of much of central Asia and eastern Russia. By the latter part of 1918, a number of different White armies had been formed, in Siberia, in the Ukraine, along the Volga, and in the Baltic region. With the Russian economy prostrate and the people resentful and confused, it was increasingly difficult for the Communist regime to hold its ground.

The situation was made even more complicated by rebellion of the many national minorities in the former empire. All four of the Baltic peoples—Finns, Estonians, Letts, and Lithuanians—quickly seized the opportunity to break away from Russia. Fifteen million Polish subjects of the former empire were now being included in a new independent Poland. The various peoples of the Caucasus region—Georgians, Armenians, and others—were likewise not eager to be forced under the yoke of a new centralized dictatorship. The most serious single problem, however, was that of the Ukraine. During the late nineteenth century, a handful of Ukrainian intellectuals had managed to build a nationalist movement of some proportions among the nearly thirty million Ukrainians who inhabited the southwestern part of the Russian empire. Since the Ukrainian dialect differed slightly from Russian, and since the region had enjoyed a brief period of autonomy under Cossack rule in the seventeenth century, it was argued that the Ukrainians constituted a separate people that deserved independent government. The sense of nationalism was fairly strong among members of the Ukrainian middle class and among some of the more prosperous Ukrainian peasantry. After the overthrow of the tsar, the Ukrainians had established a Rada, or assembly, to govern their district from Kiev. Their aim was to play off the Bolsheviks against the Whites and German occupation authorities to win independence for the Ukraine. After Brest-Litovsk, the Rada was driven from Kiev, however, and replaced by a German satellite government under the reactionary Cossack general, Skoropadsky. In November 1918, with the defeat of Germany in the west, Skoropadsky's government crumbled and the nationalist Rada, now under a forceful leader, Simon Petliura, began to revive. The kaleidoscopic succession of forces in the Ukraine made it impossible for the Communists to establish their authority firmly in the region.

Marshal Mannerheim of Finland. Marshal Gustav Mannerheim, a professional Finnish officer who had become a general in the old tsarist army, may be considered the father of independent twentieth-century Finland. His leadership ability and military genius were key factors in enabling Finland to escape Russian domination during the civil war.

By the beginning of 1919, White armies were converging on Bolshevik territory from three different directions—west, south, and east. Had the Whites possessed this strength one year earlier, communism would not have been able to survive. As it was, the Communist leaders had used the intervening months to good advantage. A mass Red Army was built up under the leadership of Leon Trotsky, the revolutionary hero of 1905 and coordinator of the 1917 *coup d'état*. After the discipline of the tsarist army had been destroyed, it was necessary to reimpose an even stricter regimentation on the new Red forces. Lack of trained military leadership was solved by enrolling thousands of former tsarist officers to staff the Red Army. The loyalty of these elements was in turn made certain through the practice of placing a Communist political commissar with each battalion. The commissar was in charge of morale and political conduct for his unit, checking the military leadership, rousing the disheartened, eliminating the potentially disloyal. Trotsky directed much of this military effort himself from the vantage point of an armored train that rolled back and forth from one section of the front to the other. His inspired skill in organization, the Communist advantage of having interior lines to defend (making it easier to transfer reserves), the effectiveness of Red propaganda, the revolutionary zeal of the Communist elite—all these began to give increasing strength to the Red Army. When the Whites were finally able to exert direct pressure against Petrograd and Moscow in early 1919, the Red Army had just enough strength to hold out.

The Communist Victory The power of the Whites was greatly diminished by the fact that their various forces were scattered from one end of Russia to the other. There was no political unity behind their efforts, for every variety of anti-Communist, from extreme reactionary to Social Revolutionary, was represented among them. Their economic resources were slight; and as 1919 wore on, the western governments did not care to provide them with enough arms to defeat the Bolsheviks. Once Germany had been beaten, France and Britain showed less and less concern about what kind of regime might rule Russia. Lacking unity, geographical concentration, and adequate supplies, the Whites began to falter and, in some sectors, to fall apart. Their propaganda appeal was much less than that of communism, for the Whites seemed to promise little more than some kind of return to the past. By the end of 1919, the Red Army was able to seize the initiative on every front.

During 1920, the White armies were defeated, each in turn. Much of the peasantry had been convinced by Lenin's demagogy that only a Bolshevik regime would assure them ownership of all the land. Furthermore, most of the White units were poorly disciplined and somewhat despotic in their treatment of the civilian population; in the popular mind, they become more and more identified with reaction and with foreign intervention. When a well-organized, progressive government was finally instituted by General Wrangel in the southern Ukraine in 1920, it was too late. Adequate supplies

The First Women's "Battalion of Death," Red Army, 1918. The extent of the Russian revolution may be gauged by the fact that only in Russia were women's combat battalions formed. They were very few in number and saw little action, but symbolized the total mobilization, reversal of traditional roles, and ferocity of the revolution. (Hoover Institution Archives.)

were not forthcoming from abroad, and Wrangel's forces were nearly isolated.

The fighting was not over yet, however. The temporary collapse of organized Russian power between 1918 and 1920 had made it possible for the western border regions to consolidate their long-sought independence. The Baltic peoples asked no more than to be left alone, but the new Polish state, organized in Warsaw, was much more ambitious. Its nationalist leader, Colonel Josef Pilsudski (1867–1935), wanted to reverse previous roles by establishing Polish control over much of southwestern Russia. Taking advantage of the prolongation of the civil war, a newly organized Polish army invaded the Ukraine in the spring of 1920. Fortunately for the Communists, the Poles would not cooperate with Wrangel, nor were they in turn well received by the Ukrainian nationalists. The steady increase in the size and efficiency of the Red Army soon made it possible to throw the Poles back in disarray. In a grand counter-offensive, the Communists advanced almost to the gates of Warsaw before being stopped—French supplies and a French military mission having helped to prepare the Polish defense. The Communist forces then turned back to rout the remainder of the White resistance and suppress the remnants of Ukrainian nationalism, but they were unable to recover the western fringe of the old empire. Conservatives in other lands somewhat prematurely hailed the Communist defeat before Warsaw as one of the "decisive battles of the world," because they thought it marked the end of Communist expansion westward.

War Communism Under the chaos of wartime conditions, Lenin and his associates had not been able to organize a truly socialist economic system. Instead, they had resorted to what was called War Communism, a hybrid program that nationalized basic urban industries containing more than five or ten employees, but did not pretend to organize the economic activity of the rest of the country. Military conscription and forced labor battalions had brought the whole urban population under Communist control, but the peasantry had been almost impossible to dominate. In order to obtain the foodstuffs necessary to keep the army and the factories operating, the regime of War Communism had had to resort to forced requisitions, collected from the peasants at bayonet point.

By 1920, Russia was a wreck. It has been estimated that only sixty-two percent of the country's farmland was being cultivated and that industrial production was only sixteen percent of the 1913 volume. The collapse of transportation and ordinary economic exchange shrunk the urban population, while large-scale famine in numerous districts had caused a slight population decline.

The peasantry still represented at least eighty percent of the Russian population, and they disliked War Communism or any other variety of Communist regimentation. They had preferred the Reds to the Whites largely because the Reds had promised them land, but Marxism was meaningless to the peasant masses, who were sick of all war and desired only to be left alone to farm their land. They hoarded their foodstuffs because the urban economy produced little to offer in exchange. Forced government requisition provoked increased resistance, and there were numerous minor peasant rebellions against the regime. Lenin had tried, in turn, to foment "class war" in the countryside by turning poor peasants against the wealthier peasants. This tactic achieved scant success. The people were in general so exhausted that the Communist state got nowhere by attempting to flog them into action. Moreover, the vast peasant masses so far outnumbered the depleted urban population that there seemed some question as to whether the government would control the peasantry or the 125,000,000 peasants would swallow the government. As a leading Communist writer lamented, "The immense peasant tide will end by engulfing everything. . . . The peasant will become master of Russia, since he represents numbers."

The government could not go on in this fashion, for even the revolutionary elite was restive. At the beginning of 1921, sailors of the Kronstadt naval base on the Baltic, once the shock troops of revolution, broke out in mutiny against the Communist regime which seemed to defraud their hopes of freedom and well-being. Lenin admitted to his fellow Communists, "We have failed to convince the broad masses." He therefore decided to allow the people a breathing space and attempted to win the support, or at least the acquiescense, of the peasantry.

The NEP In March 1921, at the time of the Kronstadt rebellion, Lenin announced a "New Economic Policy" for Russia. The NEP (as it was abbreviated) amounted to a partial restoration of capitalism. It was aimed at encouraging the revival of agriculture and of basic light industries for the consumer trade, so that the foundation of the economy could be reconstructed. Peasants were freed from forced requisition and class war, being asked to pay no more than a minimal tax in kind on their produce. Private enterprise on the local level was legalized, so that simple articles might be produced as quickly as possible.

The most radical sectors of the Communist party criticized the NEP as a surrender to capitalism. Lenin did not, however, have the slightest intention of permitting small-scale capitalist enterprise to continue indefinitely. The NEP was no more than a temporary measure to get the economy back on its feet, and would be abandoned as soon as that object had been obtained, in line with Lenin's old strategy of "two steps forward, one step back." At no time did the partial capitalism of the NEP cover the entire Russian economy, for the key sectors, such as heavy industry and transportation, were entirely controlled by the state. The socialism which dominated these "commanding heights" would be extended over the other sectors as soon as conditions permitted.

At the time, the NEP was referred to as the "peasant Brest-Litovsk," but economically it was more or less successful. The first year of the new policy coincided with the climax of a disastrous drought and famine in southeastern Russia during which three million people perished; but after that, conditions improved. Restoration of private enterprise for simple consumer goods provided a market for peasant produce, and within several years the economy became somewhat better balanced. Nonetheless, urban productivity did not expand so rapidly as agrarian output, so that the peasant was still caught in a "price scissors," whereby his goods drew proportionately less in exchange for industrial goods because of the latter's continued scarcity. Peasant economic resistance therefore never disappeared entirely, and this presented a serious problem for the future.

The Soviet Constitution of 1924 and the Nationalities Problem With the promulgation of a new constitution in December 1924, the organization of the Communist regime became well defined. What emerged was the product of conditions peculiar to Russia; Karl Marx had never left any blueprint for a Communist state and, once the Communists were in power, they had had to improvise.

An indirect system of voting, based on the Soviets, was maintained. Only workers were allowed the suffrage. Each local district elected its own Soviet, but the members of the local Soviet chose the members of the provincial Soviet. In turn, the latter selected the representatives who sat in the Soviet of each of the federal republics into which Russia was now nominally divided. This new federative system constituted the major innovation of the 1924 constitution.

One of the worst political problems under the old empire had been the bitter resentment of the subject nations against centralization and russification. In the early, hopeful phase of the revolution, Lenin had announced support for the national aspirations of all the peoples of the empire seeking freedom. It soon became apparent, however, that most of the smaller national

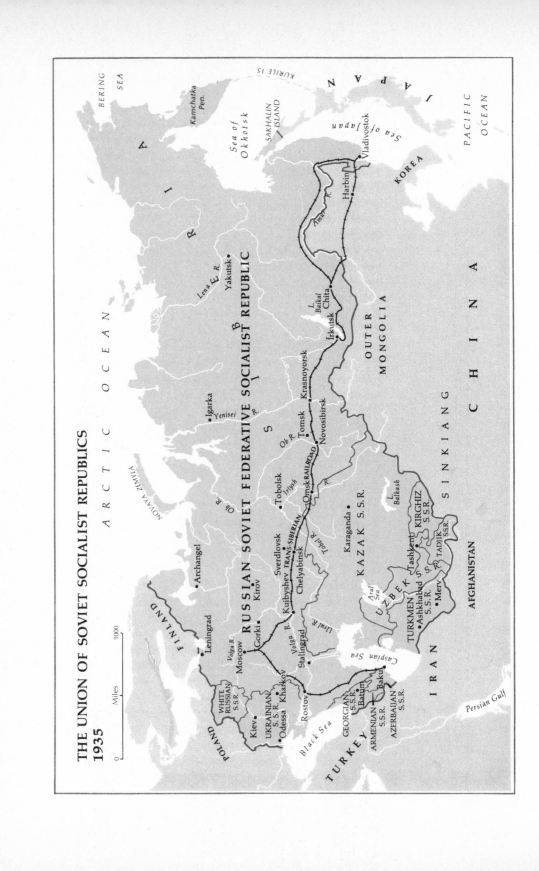

THE UNION OF SOVIET SOCIALIST REPUBLICS
1935

groups had scant desire to become Communist. The Communist regime could retain its control over them only by organizing a new-style empire of its own, first fully delineated in the 1924 constitution.

The new Communist empire was divided into several constituent Soviet Socialist Republics (SSR's), each nominally "independent." However, only the larger ethnic groups—the Great Russians, Ukrainians, White Russians, and Caucasian peoples, all of whom inhabited European Russia—were represented by the separate SSR's. Of these, by far the most extensive was the mammoth Russian Soviet Federated Socialist Republic (RSFSR), based on the Great Russian population which comprised half the inhabitants of the Soviet Union. The RSFSR also included all of Russian Asia. The less numerous, more primitive Asian peoples—such as the Tatars, Kirghiz, and Turkestani—were not allowed SSR's of their own, but were instead to be represented by seventeen "autonomous republics" and "autonomous regions" created inside the RSFSR. This system of member SSR's, and the autonomous regions within them, was intended to solve the nationalities problem, providing for centralized government and regional autonomy at the same time.

The third Russian constitution, that of 1936, made a further gesture toward federalism by establishing a bicameral Soviet Parliament, composed of a Soviet of Nationalities and an all-union Soviet, which, like the American House of Representatives, represented the entire population on a proportionate basis. This Soviet parliament then theoretically chose the members of the executive branch of the government, still known as the Council of People's Commissars.

The Role of the Communist Party All this apparatus was no more than a façade, for leadership rested not in the hands of the Soviets or the member SSR's, but in those of the Communist party. In theory, the Party was directed by a Central Committee of approximately seventy members, which was supposedly elected by the All-Party Congress that met every few years. In practice, however, the Central Committee was chosen and manipulated by its own executive arm, the Politburo (Political bureau), which was virtually self-perpetuating. The only check to the Politburo was the Party Secretariat, which served as the link between the Politburo and the Party organization at large. The Secretariat and the Politburo thus dominated the entire Party, down to the lowest level, from a rigidly centralized structure. The Party leadership pulled the strings in every sector of government, for Party members composed a large proportion of the delegates in every representative body, from district Soviets on up. No decision could be taken that was not in strict accordance with the Party line.

The Party membership numbered over half a million in 1924 and reached nearly three million by 1941. This was an enormous increase over the prerevolutionary membership of the Party, but still represented only a tiny fraction of the total Russian population, for Party members constituted a narrow elite in Soviet society. They were organized on the basis of local cells which were established in each institution and area of Russian life. No school, plant, or farm district was lacking a small nucleus of Party members. It was not easy to be a Party affiliate, for card-carrying Communists had to submit to rigid discipline and were to serve as examples to other Soviet citizens. They had to attend regular indoctrination sessions and study the Party line with great care. During the 1920's, over half the Party members were young people still in their twenties. The strain upon them, and the tendency toward mental depression, were very great. Of all Party members who died in the first three months of 1925, suicides accounted for nearly fifteen percent. As the interpreters of policy to the common people, they were the cement that was supposed to hold Soviet society together. Despite many doubts and hardships, they succeeded in filling this role. The expanded mass Party was still faithful to Lenin's original concept of a trained, disciplined, professional revolutionary group, now engaged in leading Soviet citizens to a gigantic reorganization of their homeland.

RUSSIA IN THE 1920's

The bloody years of civil war had a searing, traumatic effect on much of Russia's population. Though some of the rural sectors managed to live through the great upheaval with little change, the triumph of the Communist revolution inevitably brought with it a radical transformation that spread through the greater part of the social structure. In the urban centers, especially, the new revolutionary society kindled a great sense of liberation, at least during the early years. The keynote was modernism and progress, with a categorical downgrading of tradition and the old ways. The Communists not only wanted to destroy the influence of tsardom and capitalism, but they also wanted to change social values. This meant the rejection of religion, the liberation of women, expansion of education, and freedom of artistic expression.

Subjection of Religion   Though the Russian Orthodox Church had lost much of its vitality long before the revolution, many millions of Russians remained Christians and the influence of religion was potentially a major obstacle to a dictatorship based on atheistic materialism. During the revolution, the Orthodox Church was subjected to every form of persecution, and organizations such as the "League of the Godless" were formed to wipe out the very idea of religion. Full eradication of religious conviction was, however, a herculean task whose end was not in sight. Independence had never been part of the tradition of Russian Orthodoxy, and by the mid-1920's church leaders were willing to accept a position of subjection under the Communist system. Vigorous anti-religious propaganda, coupled with all manner of restrictions on religious activity, was maintained, but many church communities, Orthodox or otherwise, were still permitted a tenuous existence so long as they made no effort to combat communism.

Anti-religious Playing Card in the Soviet Union. This exemplifies one small aspect of the massive anti-religious campaign organized by the Soviet Union at its inception. It purports to show a Jew at prayer and is intended to blaspheme and de-sacramentalize religious images. (Roger Viollet.)

Social and Cultural Experimentation   Revolutionary communism promised a "workers' culture" to replace the old art forms, and liberation to the oppressed sex—women—as well as to exploited classes. Its subsequent "proletarian art" rejected most of the esthetic innovation of prerevolutionary Russian culture, and the Communist regime was in turn repudiated by most of Russia's leading writers and artists, many of whom emigrated. During the 1920's, however, there was still a limited degree of freedom of expression, and some new achievement was made in Russian literature. A few writers even published veiled critiques of the regime. Evgeni Zamiatin's novel *We* posed the problem of mass collectivism turning into something even worse than the old tyranny. Of the new Communist writers, the most gifted was the symbolist poet Vladimir Mayakovsky (1893–1930), whose sometimes crude but vivid and original imagery seemed to capture the spirit of the new generation.

A novel style of dramatic theater was introduced by the director Meyerhold, who experimented with radical stage settings. It was the motion picture, however, which came to the fore. The possibilities of the cinema as an instrument of propaganda were quickly grasped, yet some Soviet movies transcended mere indoctrination. While the noted Sergei Eisenstein (1898–1948) began his career with direct propaganda films, such as *Ten Days That Shook the World,* his eventual mastery of camera techniques and settings won him a reputation as one of the greatest directors of all time.

By the end of the 1920's, however, the libertarian exhilaration had faded from Russian society. The Soviet state demanded total conformity and eventually clamped strict controls over every aspect of literature and culture. In 1930, Mayakovsky, like several other Russian poets in recent years, committed suicide. Creativity virtually disappeared from Russian culture, not to reemerge until the 1950's.

During the first years of the regime, Communist enthusiasts vowed a drastic change in relations between the sexes and a new "revolutionary morality." Doctrines of free love, assisted by birth control, legal abortions, and easy facilities for the abandonment of children, won a wide following in the lax atmosphere of the larger towns, where the revolution had the most adherents. "Revolutionary morality" eventually threatened a breakdown of family life in the cities. Deaths of parents in the famine and civil war, together with mass abandonment, led to an enormous increase in the number of orphaned or uncared-for children, whose total reached several million and severely strained government facilities. After more than a decade, the regime adopted a neo-conservative policy, encouraging chastity and traditional marriage, reducing the availability of abortions, and making all parents legally responsible for their children.

The Power Struggle after Lenin's Death Lenin suffered a serious stroke in 1922 and died within less than two years. From the beginning, he had dominated the Communist movement, and it is quite possible that without him there could never have been a successful Bolshevist revolution. His rule had not been based on ironclad dictatorial control of the Party apparatus so much as upon overwhelming personal ascendancy over other Party leaders. He had not bullied the Party so much as he had cajoled and maneuvered it. As the creator and master strategist of communism, his personal dominance had been almost unquestioned.

Lenin had made no specific provision for a leader to follow him after his death. No single person held his unquestioned preeminence, and a great deal of friction and jealousy immediately appeared among his successors. The second most outstanding personality in the Party was Leon Trotsky, the commissar for war and organizer of victory in the struggle against the Whites. A brilliant ideologist with great literary gifts, Trotsky had a strong streak of visionary romanticism which lifted him to heights of inspired leadership in times of public crisis, but incapacitated him for the ordinary dirty work of practical politics. Until 1917, Trotsky had been a lone wolf, joining the Communists only shortly before the revolution.

There were other men who had acquired positions of great prestige in the Party. Grigory Zinoviev (1883–1936), a director of propaganda and secretary of the Communist International, was one of the best known. Zinoviev was, however, a vain and jealous man who lacked clear intellectual perception or practical political intelligence. Superior in capacity was Nikolai Bukharin (1888–1938), a favorite of Lenin who described him in one of his last documents as "the most brilliant young theoretician" in the Party. Bukharin was, however, primarily an intellectual, broad-minded and individualistic. He could easily be outmaneuvered in everyday political tactics.

Far overshadowed by these and other luminaries was the Party's organization man, a colorless Georgian revolutionary, Iosif Dzhugashvili, who had adopted the pseudonym of Stalin (derived from the Russian word for "steel"). Stalin had worked his way up to the Central Committee by 1912 as a specialist on the nationalities question, but he played a secondary role in the 1917 revolution. Lenin had chosen him for commissar of nationalities in the Bolshevik government of 1918 because of his experience with the ethnic minorities. During the civil war, more brilliant Party leaders had found him useful, for he was content to handle routine matters of organization and economic inspection, serving as commissar of the workers' and peasants' inspectorate. Since Stalin lacked outstanding intellectual gifts and showed no sign of ideological originality, he seemed a perfect choice for dull tasks. Looked down upon by more brilliant men, Stalin became secretary-general of the Party apparatus, immersing himself in practical problems of organization. He became acquainted with provincial leaders and their membership problems throughout the Soviet Union, and eventually controlled Party appointments on almost every level. In the process, he acquired thorough familiarity with the structure of power and the technique of manipulation in a totalitarian society. This was a secret the flashier Party leaders never learned.

Outwardly, Stalin usually seemed modest and unassuming. He never occupied the limelight at Party congresses, but listened quietly to other delegates and smoked his pipe. He even gained a reputation for moderation, since innate cautiousness led him to avoid extreme positions. It was not

Lenin and Stalin in 1922. The two leaders of the Soviet regime, shown about the time of Lenin's first stroke. Lenin was the creator of totalitarianism and mass terrorism in modern government. Stalin merely expanded and perfected the Leninist system, for there was no aspect of Stalinism not already clearly foreshadowed in the policies of Lenin before 1922. (Radio Times Hulton Picture Library.)

until the last months of his life that Lenin had suddenly taken notice of Stalin's ambition, as well as of the underlying harshness of his personality. After Stalin had dealt tyrannically with minor sections of the Party, Lenin wrote, "Comrade Stalin is too rude . . . and insulting to the other comrades. . . ." Lenin had evidently come to the conclusion that the advancement of Stalin was a mistake, that a replacement should be found as Party secretary. Before he could act, however, death had overtaken him.

By 1925, Trotsky was extremely critical of the direction being taken in the Soviet Union. He opposed continuation of the NEP, with its toleration of petty capitalism. Trotsky pressed for continuation of revolution abroad, for a "permanent revolution" that would go on without respite. He urged a program of forced industrialization under state planning inside the Soviet Union, to create the indispensable base for Communist society.

Other members of the Politburo were highly apprehensive lest this proud and brilliant commissar for war step into Lenin's shoes. They seemed oblivious of the fact that it was not the keen, eloquent Trotsky, but the bureaucratic intriguer Stalin who was actually gathering the reins of power. Stalin cleverly took advantage of this resentment against Trotsky to form an anti-Trotsky coalition with Zinoviev and others. Contemptuous of such petty maneuvering, Trotsky did not at first even bother to fight back. He did not try to use Lenin's own notes against Stalin, disdaining conflict with an unintellectual bureaucrat. As a result, Trotsky's power was progressively stripped away, and in 1925 he resigned his position as commissar for war. At no time did Trotsky attempt to lead a revolt against his enemies. To him, as to other Old Bolsheviks, the revolution was invested with a quasi-religious mystique. To fight against the power structure created by the revolution led one to eternal damnation. Trotsky accepted defeat almost like a contrite sinner.

Having virtually eliminated his most serious rival, Stalin felt free to drop his former allies. He next joined forces with Bukharin and the most moderate wing of the Party, which opposed forced industrialization and a sudden end to the NEP. This move turned the tables against Zinoviev and those who had first supported Stalin against Trotsky. Such tactics of divide and conquer worked splendidly, for all Stalin's potential rivals were blinded by either personal vanity, jealousy, or ideological abstractions. Zinoviev had encouraged Stalin to use the secret police as a weapon of totalitarian rule and to create a cult of Lenin which stressed the power and omniscience of the Party leader. Suddenly, the Cheka was being used against Zinoviev's followers as well as Trotskyites; when the former finally agreed that Trotsky had been right in demanding greater intra-Party "democracy," it was too late. Bukharin was equally tardy in realizing that he served as a dupe of Stalin, for he was interested mainly in theory and in going slow so as not to "distort" the revolution. Bukharin believed that Zinoviev and Trotsky were dangerous men, and he did nothing to prevent their expulsion from the Party in 1927. Zinoviev's spirit was completely broken; after confessing imaginary errors, he was readmitted to the Party, though stripped of all influence. Trotsky, more stubborn, was eventually banished to foreign exile.

Stalin next labored to break the power of Bukharin and the moderates who had supported him against Zinoviev and Trotsky. Having helped to crush the strongest opponents of the Party secretary, Bukharin was now isolated and defenseless. Too late, other Old Bolsheviks lamented that they had not made common cause with Trotsky. By 1929, Stalin was in full dictatorial control of the Party. All opposition, moderate or extremist, was ruthlessly eliminated. The destiny of the revolution now lay in the hands of a totalitarian engineer of ruthless skill in manipulating the tools of power.

International Communism   At the time of Brest-Litovsk, Lenin had been expecting social revolution to break out in the rest of Europe within a matter of months. The newly established Russian Communists called upon all other Socialist parties to join with them in launching a great wave of worldwide revolution. However, as has already been seen, west-European socialists had lost much of their revolutionary impetus by 1918. Only a minority of the Socialists in other countries responded to the call for immediate and violent rebellion. By 1919, the Social Democratic parties of western and central Europe had begun to split between the moderate, democratic majority and the violent minority which was bent on the dictatorship of the proletariat. Separate Communist parties were founded by radical dissidents in almost every country of Europe. Since most members of the Socialist International refused to align themselves with dictatorial Communism, Lenin decided to form a new Communist federation. This was set up in 1919 as the Third or Communist International, known in abbreviation as the Comintern.

Lenin's hopes for international revolution were soon dashed. The parliamentary democracies of western Europe, with the exception of Italy, survived the trials of the immediate postwar period. A Communist uprising in the industrial German Ruhr during the spring of 1919 was drowned in blood, and a year later the revolutionary Italian Socialists also lost their drive. The only momentary success came in Hungary, but it lasted no more than a few months. In mid-1919, a Hungarian Communist named Bela Kun rallied the revolutionary wing of Hungarian socialism and set up an insecure, Communist-style dictatorship in the Budapest region. Kun's "Red Terror" and his harsh dealing with the peasantry made the regime unpopular with most classes, and it was soon overthrown by a conservative-militarist reaction. The Comintern could not lay deep roots, and after 1920 revolutionary prospects in most of western and central Europe vanished. Outside the Soviet Union, it was the democratic Socialist parties, not the new Communist groups, that held the allegiance of most of the working class.

Soviet Foreign Policy The Soviet Union's policy of subversion had made her a pariah among nations, without allies, and the object of the enmity of all European governments. She was herself weak and exhausted, and was now threatened by a hostile world. It was impossible to continue the old policy of unalloyed revolutionary agitation. In 1922, the Soviet government tried to effect a transition back to more traditional methods of diplomacy. This effort was directed by Georgi Chicherin (1872–1936), who held the post of Soviet foreign commissar from 1918 to 1930. By clever negotiation and a certain amount of guile, he prevented international sanctions being imposed against Russia for her foreign debts. At the same time, Chicherin signed the Rapallo Pact with representatives of the German Republic, providing for mutually beneficial political and economic relations between the two powers. During the next two years, the foreign commissariat made constant efforts to improve Russia's international position, and by 1924 most of the major western nations had granted diplomatic recognition to the new regime.

All the while, however, the Comintern remained active. Revolution was still being fomented in Germany, Bulgaria, China, or wherever there existed an attractive opportunity. Little or no effort was made to coordinate the labors of the foreign office, on the one hand, and the revolutionary agitation of the Comintern, on the other. The inevitable result of this inharmonious duality of Soviet policy was that Comintern agitation sabotaged the more orthodox practices of the foreign office. Moreover, the passage of time did not bring any greater success to the Russian efforts at subversion abroad, and all immediate opportunities in China and east-central Europe soon went down the drain. Annoyed by Comintern meddling, Britain withdrew her diplomatic representation from Russia in 1927, by which time the latter was very nearly as isolated as in 1920. Ten years of Soviet foreign policy and agitation had been an almost complete failure.

The Soviet Union was now shut off from Europe by a *cordon sanitaire* of anti-Communist states all along her western borders. The Soviet economy was too weak to support foreign adventure or large-scale revolutionary activity. Even Party members were exhausted by the hard decade of 1917–1927. Consequently, the new leader, Stalin, who had little faith in spontaneous revolution, tended to downgrade the Comintern. He subordinated revolutionary agitation abroad to the diplomatic interests of the Russian government. The new goal of Soviet foreign policy was to win for Russia a reputation as a peace-loving and reasonable country. This approach was in large part negative, aimed at preserving the existing equilibrium; avoiding foreign threats; and maintaining harmonious, if distant, relations with the outside world. After 1927, the Soviet Union had begun to withdraw inward, absorbed in the gigantic social and economic transformation of Stalinism.

STALINISM

Stalin was in no way an original thinker, but he responded to obvious facts with clear-cut solutions. Faced with the frustration of Communist efforts abroad, he had developed the doctrine of "socialism in one country." This argument stressed that the revolution could best be served by constructing a powerful base for socialism in the Soviet Union alone, at least for the time being. Stalin insisted that the Soviet Fatherland could survive in isolation, provided that its own resources were fully developed. Such a goal was reassuring for most Communists and held patriotic appeal for the people as a whole. The new postrevolutionary generation of bureaucrats holding positions in the Stalinist apparatus was relieved to hear that it was not necessary to sacrifice everything for "permanent revolution" at the four corners of the earth.

The basic aim of the socialist revolution was supposed to be construction of a socialist economy, presumably with the emphasis on heavy industry. By 1927, however, state-owned heavy industry had scarcely regained the level of 1913, while the privately owned sector of the economy— agriculture and small manufactures—flourished. There were now approximately twenty-five million peasant farmers in Russia, almost all of whom owned land of their own. Russia in the 1920's had developed the most thoroughly petit-bourgeois rural structure of any large European country save France. Some Party members feared that socialism was being drowned beneath peasant capitalism, but Communist moderates insisted that socialist industrialization was impossible until the economic productivity and security of the great majority of Russians—the peasants—had been further increased.

Originally Stalin had pretended to agree, condemning the "super-industrializers," who wanted to bring a sudden end to the NEP. By 1927, he reversed himself completely. The logical corollary to "socialism in one country" was a massive industrialization campaign, regimenting the peasants and destroying every trace of the NEP. At that time, Russia did not have a truly socialist economy, but Stalin believed that anything was possible through force and willpower.

Industrialization   Early in 1928, the Stalinist leadership announced plans for the immediate industrialization of the whole Soviet economy. Given the state of Russian backwardness at that time, this was perhaps the most ambitious economic project ever conceived in human history. A gigantic blueprint of central planning was drawn up by the government planning commission (Gosplan) to coordinate and systematize what was intended to be the greatest industrial complex in the world. A Five-Year Plan, covering the period 1929–1933, was adopted early in 1929. Its objective was to increase total industrial output 250 percent, and heavy industry by some 330 percent. Agrarian production was scheduled to rise 150 percent, and peasant reluctance would be met by collectivizing 20 percent of the peasant farms.

This was a stunning proposal. No one had dreamed of attempting so vertiginous a rate of socialist industrialization, but Stalin now held such complete power that all opposition in the economy could be thoroughly eliminated. This presented no problem in the towns, where NEP shopkeepers and artisans were driven out of business or in some cases rounded up by the OGPU and taken away to do forced labor. The real problem, however, was the peasants.

Collectivization of Agriculture   Stalin and his planners were determined to bring the peasants under state control, for three reasons. First of all, if eighty percent of the population continued to enjoy economic independence in the countryside, a regimented industrial structure was impossible. The totalitarian system required domination of the entire population, which could be done only within a collective framework. Second, food production for the new industrial centers had to be guaranteed. Third, it was hoped that collective farming would be more efficient, thus diverting millions of peasants for factory work in the cities.

Therefore, in mid-1929, the campaign to regroup the peasants on collective farms was speeded up to include ultimately the entire rural population. Most peasants wanted only to be left alone, but all who actively resisted were categorized as *kulaks*, or dangerous peasant capitalists. Stalin declared, "We must smash the *kulaks*, eliminate them as a class. . . ." When peasants tried to defend themselves, OGPU squads and even the Red Army were called in. Some villages were surrounded by machine-gun detachments, and the inhabitants slaughtered. All this was a shattering moral experience for idealistic Communists, who saw the forces of the revolution being used to massacre peasants.

The brutal and remorseless collectivization drive imposed a tremendous strain on Russian society, but Stalin never reckoned in terms of human suffering. After a brief respite in 1930, collectivization was speeded up once more, and by 1932 approximately sixty percent of the peasantry had been organized under the new system.

The harsh years of the First Five-Year Plan had taken a tremendous toll, however. Ten million *kulaks* had been uprooted. Thousands had been shot, and many more had been driven off to starve or sent to do forced labor, but the majority were transplanted to the barren wastes of central Asia, where hundreds of thousands of them died from adverse conditions. Since only a small amount of private property could be taken into the collective farms, the peasants slaughtered hundreds of thousands of head of livestock. The total number of cattle in the Soviet Union declined by more than fifty percent. Rural production was temporarily disorganized; and in 1932–1933 there was another tremendous crop failure in southeastern Russia, bringing mass famine in its wake. Altogether, at least five million peasants perished during this half-decade.

Famine in South Russia. In this photo a man drags off the corpses of two members of his family for burial or cremation. Famine and epidemics in south Russia, produced by the havoc of civil war, took several million lives in 1921–1922. It was the first of the gigantic human disasters engineered by the Leninist-Stalinist regime, to be followed by the millions of deaths in the collectivization and famine of 1929–1933 and the great purges of 1936–1939 —the greatest series of peacetime catastrophes imposed by state policy in the history of any country during the twentieth century. (Roger Viollet.)

After winning such a gigantic struggle, Stalin made several concessions. First of all, the new collective farms, or *kolkhozes*, were not state farms, but were to be owned instead by the community of *kolkhoz* members. They worked the land under joint management and divided the profits among themselves. Moreover, each peasant family was permitted to keep some of its own tools, a few of its private cattle, and an individual garden plot on which it might raise special crops for personal profit. The *kolkhoz* was not fully satisfactory from the doctrinaire Communist viewpoint, but it was the most adequate compromise under Russian conditions. By the time the

Second World War began, ninety percent of the rural population was grouped on collective farms.

It was now relatively easy for the state to control the peasantry. Emphasis was laid on rural mechanization, and Russia soon had developed some of the largest tractor factories in the world. All the heavy equipment, however, was kept in centralized machine tractor stations, under the direct control of the state. The peasantry remained sullen and did not work with great enthusiasm. Food production rose very slowly but, from the government's point of view, the important thing was that all food production was now under state control, and there was no longer any problem about collecting whatever was available for the growing industrial population.

Progress of the Five-Year Plans Stalin emphasized that the only Communist state in the world would have to convert itself into a mighty arsenal, or run the risk of falling prey to the capitalist world. He said bluntly in 1931:

To slacken the pace means to lag behind, and those who lag behind are beaten. . . . We are fifty or a hundred years behind the advanced countries. We must make good this lag in ten years. Either we do it or they crush us.

A sense of frenzied pressure lay over the Soviet Union during the 1930's. The goals set were fantastically high, but this titanic effort succeeded in grasping the imagination of part of the population, especially among the Communist youth, and genuine enthusiasm attended some of the work. All manner of difficulties were encountered, since it was very hard for inexperienced directors and foremen to make a great, complex industrialization program function. After several years had passed, central planning became badly snarled. The main problem was one of supply and organization. Some factories received too much material, others not enough. There was an abundance of skilled labor in a few regions, but most went short. Transportation shortages made it difficult to keep supplies moving. World-wide depression froze revenue from foreign trade, and collectivization temporarily disoriented the rural economy. As a result of these manifold difficulties, scarcely half the goals of the First Five-Year Plan were met. Even that, however, was a great accomplishment and increased general industrial productivity by over 100 percent.

Norms for the Second Five-Year Plan, covering 1934–1938, were set considerably lower, aiming at an annual increase of thirteen to fourteen percent, and these goals were largely met. At the end of the decade 1928–1938, Soviet industry claimed to have achieved the following approximate increases:

Electricity	650 percent
Coal	400 percent
Steel	450 percent
Machine tools	1400 percent

Even though these figures were considerably inflated, it was an extraordinary achievement. Among modern nations, only traditionalist-capitalist Japan ever increased its basic industrial output so rapidly. The Soviet accomplishments seemed doubly impressive because they occurred during a decade of international economic depression. Throughout the whole process, however, the Soviet Union relied heavily on advanced equipment, designs, and engineering assistance from the capitalist West. Stalin himself later admitted that two-thirds of the large industrial enterprises in Russia during the 1930's were built with varying quantities of help in terms of equipment or engineers from private sources in the United States.

All this was done at great cost. The Soviet economy possessed little capital wealth, and it had to be created by forced saving. During the early 1930's, the Soviet Union may have suffered the greatest peacetime decline in actual living standards known to any modern country. To get the last ounce of energy out of underfed workers the regime relied on wage-slavery on the early nineteenth-century pattern, often using piece rates instead of fixed salaries. Pay was sharply differentiated according to individual status, skill, and output.

Very little effort was spent on producing consumer goods. Instead, heavy industry was stressed for state factories and the armed forces. The Second Five-Year Plan coincided with the rearmament of Germany, led by a Nazi regime theoretically dedicated to the destruction of communism. This only resulted in further Russian emphasis on heavy industry, and by the late 1930's Soviet military production probably exceeded that of Nazi Germany.

By 1938, as a result of this imbalance, Russia was producing more locomotives than any other country in the world, yet the techniques of the Soviet textile industry were backward, and the country was barely able to clothe itself. The average citizen lacked adequate housing, a varied diet, and many of the simple amenities of civilized life; but the Red Army had more iron and steel lavished on it than any other fighting force in the world.

The Great Purges   The Five-Year Plans strained every aspect of Soviet life. The strain also weighed on Stalin, for he was attempting to exercise one-man control of the first modern totalitarian state together with a massive economic transformation. Many Russians bitterly resented the hardships and absolute tyranny imposed on them. Even Stalin's wife began to object to the brutalities of the system. One evening, after Stalin had given her a tongue-lashing in public, she committed suicide. The "Man of Steel" was momentarily shaken by this act of despair, but none of his picked subordinates dared accept responsibility for replacing him. Each passing month brought greater tension, and the dictator's personal isolation constantly increased. The more Stalin looked around him—and the harder he drove the Russian people—the more suspicious he became even of the regime's privileged strata. There was increasing apprehension of Nazi Germany, and Stalin decided that before any crisis arose all alternative elites in the Soviet Union must be destroyed.

In December 1934, one of his chief deputies, Sergei Kirov, was murdered in the former capital, Leningrad (as St. Petersburg-Petrograd was now called). Though the killing actually seems to have been arranged by Stalin's police, it was used as proof of a massive conspiracy against the government. The NKVD began large-scale arrests, sending thousands of people to labor camps. A year later the purge began to broaden, affecting Party members at every level. By mid-1936 the NKVD was reaching into every sector of society: factory managers, engineers, surviving *kulaks*, former members of the middle class. The purge was most thorough, however, among Communist Party veterans. The "Old Bolsheviks," the pre-1917 members of the Party, would become the natural leaders of the Soviet Union if Stalin were ever replaced; therefore they were scythed down relentlessly. The more people deported or slaughtered by the NKVD, the greater became Stalin's paranoia. Between 1936 and 1938, several spectacular Moscow "show trials" were staged, in which Zinoviev, Bukharin, and dozens of other former leaders were placed on exhibition to recant publicly their "crimes" against the Soviet regime. The Old Bolsheviks completely lacked the will to resist the secret police. They had dedicated their lives to the project of revolution; iron will and brute force had now incarnated the revolution in one man whom they would not think of attacking in their last hour. They made their "confessions," as the secret police demanded, then filed back to await the executioner in the NKVD dungeons.

By the beginning of 1937, the purge was arousing extreme anxiety among the leadership cadres of the country. No one knew whose turn would come next. There was talk that the Red Army officers might rebel and overthrow Stalin. To forestall that danger, a massive purge was carried out in the officer corps during 1937–1938. Nearly eighty percent of all officers over the rank of captain were removed, and hundreds of them were shot. The head of the NKVD was himself liquidated. Later on, the director who had purged him was also shot, and so it went. The purge seemed destined to go on forever. By 1938, millions of people had been arrested and deported to the wastes of central Asia and Siberia, while thousands had been executed outright. The managerial class and Party members were caught in the grip of paralyzing fear, for there was no escape from the NKVD.

At the beginning of 1939, the great purges ended almost as suddenly as they had begun. Stalin had decided to let up, for he had shown that he was able to break the back of any potential opposition.

At the height of the purges, in 1936, Stalin had installed a new Soviet constitution, which he called the "freest in the world." Universal suffrage was introduced, and the rubber-stamp elections to the Soviet parliament were now made direct, because, as Stalin had put it, all the bourgeois elements in Soviet society had either been re-educated or liquidated.

After Stalin, the central authority in the land was the secret police, now headed by a fellow-Georgian whom Stalin trusted, Lavrenti Beria (1899–1953). The NKVD, later relabeled the MVD, administered an enormous concentration camp empire that stretched over large sections of the Soviet

Union. By 1939 there may have been as many as eight or ten million persons, male and female, doing forced labor in forests and on canals in Siberia, central Asia, and the Arctic Circle. The raw materials and public works produced by the NKVD camps formed a sizable sector of the Soviet economy, though its cost in terms of human lives and suffering was incalculable.

Soviet Society in 1939 Twelve years of Stalinism had wrought staggering changes. Russia was now becoming an urban society; twenty million peasants had moved to the cities in a little over a decade. Russia possessed the world's largest hydroelectric dam, the largest tractor factory, and some of the largest steel mills. Total industrial productivity was about to overtake that of Germany, making the Soviet Union the world's second greatest economic power.

The imprint of the *vozhd*—the leader—lay over all this. Stalin was deified, his pictures and statues on display everywhere. History was being rewritten to make his early career look more impressive. All of Russian life was being made "monolithic" according to the leader's directive. Initiative and nonconformity were shunned like the plague. After the purges, no writer, no engineer, dared express his own ideas or mannerisms.

Life in the great new industrial centers was gray and monotonous, with large families cramped into one- and two-room apartments. On the collective farms there was more room, but also a heavier malaise of distrust and resentment. Variety in Soviet life seemed nonexistent. There was not even comic relief, for everything about the new society was deadly serious.

However, the worst effects of this system were mitigated by the sense of participation in a common enterprise which the regime dinned into the people. The accent lay on work; only productivity was glamorized. Russians were not distracted by specious romanticization of conspicuous consumption, for such a thing did not exist. Everyone understood that he was living in a workers'society. A new category, the "hero of labor," emerged as the nominal ideal of Soviet life. All workers were urged to become "Stakhanovites," in emulation of a coal miner who had supposedly mined over one hundred tons of coal in a single day.

By 1939, a whole new postrevolutionary generation had grown up that knew nothing of pre-Communist institutions. The opportunities for professional development under the new system might be largely determined by the state, but they exceeded the opportunities offered by the preindustrial economy. Workers might be paid less than in the West, but there was no unemployment. Whereas there had been only 20,000 doctors in Russia before the revolution, there were now over 100,000. In 1914, only 112,000 Russian youths could attend universities. By 1939, there were 620,000 enrolled.

The Five-Year Plans created an entire new professional elite in Russia. Though the re-enserfed peasantry might show a sullen resentment against the regime, the new professional and industrial cadres were Stalin's creatures and evinced a definite loyalty. To that extent, Soviet social engineering had

Scissors Grinder, 1912, by Kasimir Malevich. The prerevolutionary Russian art world was one of the most fertile, radical, and innovative in Europe. Russian painters such as Malevich pioneered the new style of "abstract" painting, that eliminated ordinary form and recognizable content. (Yale University Art Gallery.)

achieved success. If the ordinary population was alienated, a new elite had been forged that would hold the totalitarian system together in its hour of deepest trial.

Atavism of the Leninist-Stalinist System   The Leninist-Stalinist system in Russia was revolutionary insofar as it had constructed the first modern state totalitarianism, using industrial technology to build a society and economy of government collectivism. Yet in Russia, only the scope of modern technology was truly new. In spirit and structure the Soviet regime had in many ways revolved back (the real meaning, after all, of revolution) to the old Russian system of complete state and collective tyranny that had grown out of the oriental despotism of the Mongols during the Middle Ages. Stalin's main hero was not Karl Marx but Ivan the Terrible. Russian Communism did not so much repudiate western-style capitalism—which had scarcely existed in Russia—as the short-lived effort between the 1860's and 1917 to liberalize Russia. In place of representative government and the emancipation of serfs, Leninism-Stalinism reverted to the old Russian pattern of total government power, state domination of the economy, and the re-enserfment of the peasantry through collectivization. Russia was thus once more divorced from the liberalism and individualism of the western world.

In its Leninist variant, Marxist ideology was used to justify collectivization and total control. The modern materialist utopia of world revolution replaced the traditional messianism of imperial Russia and its "Third Rome." The system was, however, much more Russian than Marxist. Liberal revolutionaries and those who took classic Marxism seriously had earlier argued that the forces of liberal progress and individualism must first be encouraged in Russia lest the revolution revert to the historical Russian system based on oriental despotism. But "Leninism," as distinct from western Marxism, stood precisely for the despotic eastern pattern of state organization. The success of Bolshevism was due in large part to the historical conditioning of the Russian people to submission and the use of what one Old Bolshevik called "boundless compulsion"—whether by the Mongols, Ivan the Terrible, or Stalin. Thus the Leninist-Stalinist system represented the old Russia more than the new Europe, the modernization of old despotic, serf-based Muscovy rather than a new liberating force. The novelty lay not in the dogma of Leninism—which was grossly contradictory and all debate about which was forbidden—but in the massive application of modern technology to the development of totalitarian government based on an economy of state capitalism. Under Stalin, the Soviet Union was on its way to becoming the second strongest power in the world.

FURTHER READING Two recent brief treatments of the revolution are the symposium edited by Richard Pipes, * *Revolutionary Russia* (1968); and R. V. Daniels' *Red October* (1967). W. H. Chamberlain, * *The Russian Revolution, 1917–1921*, 2 vols. (1935, 1954), is still a standard account; the best pro-Bolshevik treatment is E. H. Carr, *The Bolshevik Revolution, 1917–1923*, 3 vols. (1950–1953). O. H. Radkey, *The Election to the Russian Constituent Assembly of 1917* (1950), analyzes the only democratic elections in Russian history. The side that lost the Russian civil

*Books available in paperback edition are marked with an asterisk.

war has been studied by Richard Luckett, *The White Generals* (1971); and G. A. Brinkley, *The Volunteer Army and Allied Intervention in South Russia, 1917–1921* (1966).

The principal biographies of the top Bolshevik leaders are B. D. Wolfe, * *Three Who Made a Revolution* (1948, 1964); Louis Fischer, * *The Life of Lenin* (1962); Isaac Deutscher's three-volume study of Trotsky (1954–1963); E. E. Smith, *The Young Stalin* (1967); and H. M. Hyde, *Stalin* (1971). See also A. B. Ulam, *The Bolsheviks* (1965). The best history of the party is L. B. Schapiro, *The Communist Party of the Soviet Union* (1960, 1964). The formation of the Soviet imperial dictatorship has been examined by Richard Pipes, *The Formation of the Soviet Union* (1954, 1964), and L. B. Schapiro, *The Origin of the Communist Autocracy* (1955, 1965).

Two important introductions to the cultural background of totalitarianism are Hannah Arendt, * *The Origins of Totalitarianism* (1951, 1966); and Jacob Talmon, * *The Origins of Totalitarian Democracy* (1952, 1965). R. V. Daniels, *The Conscience of the Revolution* (1960), treats internal Communist opposition to full totalitarianism. The best account of the Stalinist purges is Robert Conquest, *The Great Terror* (1968). For the economic and psychological aspects, see S. Swianiewicz, *Forced Labour and Economic Development* (1965); and Arthur Koestler's fine novel, * *Darkness at Noon* (1941).

Pierre Sorlin, * *The Soviet People and Their Society* (1969), provides a general account of Russian social history since 1917. Official church-state relations are examined in J. S. Curtiss, *The Russian Church and the Soviet State, 1917–1950* (1953); and suppressed religiosity is the subject of W. C. Fletcher, *The Russian Orthodox Church Underground, 1917–1970* (1971). For general treatments of the economy and of agriculture, see Alec Nove, *An Economic History of the U.S.S.R.* (1972); and Lazar Volin, *A Century of Russian Agriculture* (1970). Anthony C. Sutton, *Western Technology and Soviet Economic Development, 1930 to 1945* (Stanford, 1971), deals with a key aspect of Russian growth. Gleb Struve, *Soviet Russian Literature, 1917–1950* (1951) is a general survey.

The best broad accounts of the spread of Communism outside Russia are Hugh Seton-Watson, * *From Lenin to Khrushchev* (1961); and Franz Borkenau, * *World Communism* (1962). On the abortive Communist revolution in Hungary, see R. L. Tökes, *Béla Kun and the Hungarian Soviet Republic* (1967). George Kennan, * *Soviet Foreign Policy, 1917–1941* (1960), is a good brief survey for this period.

5 The Rise of Fascism and Nazism

Fascism was the only completely new kind of political movement that emerged in the decade following the First World War. It was a response to the problems of national development and individual identity that appeared in the wake of military defeat, political frustration, class struggle, and economic depression. Fascist ideology, which varied considerably from one fascist party to another, was a combination of various ideas. These included ultra-nationalism, belief in the use of violence, government dictatorship under charismatic personal leadership, class unity in place of class struggle, state coordination (though not state ownership) of the economic system, and militaristic expansion. None of these ideas was new, but prior to the end of the First World War, such doctrines had not been combined to form a new ideology for radical political movements.

FASCISM IN ITALY

The Origin of Italian Fascism The prototype of European fascist movements was the Italian Fascist party, founded in 1919 by an ex-Socialist, Benito Mussolini. Born of a lower-class family in north-central Italy in 1883, Mussolini had a harsh upbringing. In his youth he attracted attention as a spokesman for the extremist, anti-nationalist wing of the Italian Socialist party. Mussolini changed tack abruptly after the First World War began, espousing ultranationalism and military service as the highest goals to which men could aspire. He founded a new paper to urge Italian participation in the war, enlisted in the army himself, and was slightly wounded in combat.

Following the end of the war, Italy was thrown into turmoil. In the new elections of 1919, the moderate prewar middle-class groups were overshadowed by the voting power of two new mass movements, the democratic Catholic "Popular party" and the Socialists, now the largest group in Italian politics. The Socialists, having never supported the war effort, could capitalize on all the frustration and disillusionment that plagued Italian society in 1919. Reconversion to a peaceful economy had upset Italy to an even greater extent than some other countries, and hundreds of thousands of returning soldiers could not find work. During the war, the government had made many extravagant promises to the citizenry in order to keep the population behind the military effort. The peasants, in particular, had been promised radical land reforms. To cap it all, the nation's diplomatic aspirations had been in part frustrated at the Paris Peace Conference, and the east coast of the Adriatic remained in Yugoslav hands. Most Italians felt cheated and betrayed. Young men from the lower class wanted social justice; nationalists demanded that Italy vindicate her place in the world and seize the major east Adriatic cities. By 1920, the supernationalist poet Gabriele d'Annunzio had put aside his versifying to lead a special expeditionary force of volunteers which temporarily occupied the Italian-inhabited city of Fiume on the Yugoslav coast.

Such widespread discontent provided the opportunity for Mussolini to make a new start in political life. Early in 1919, he organized a number of unemployed and disgruntled veterans into a group called *Fasci italiani di combattimento.* The term *fasci* in Italian refers to bundles, or bands, and the small group of ardent nationalists so banded together were called *fascisti,* or "fascists," designating members of a tightly knit group. A year or so later, Mussolini reorganized this formation as the "Italian National Fascist party." The Fascists were a motley formation and for long had no distinct ideology. At first, they seemed to be trying to combine nationalism with socialism, for, besides insisting on greater prestige and benefits for the nation abroad, Mussolini continued to stress radical social reform at home. In 1919, the headlines of his newspaper screamed, "Make the rich pay!"

Insofar as the Fascists had a coherent program, it emphasized the following ideas. (1) National unity: All Italians should join together and not turn against their fellow citizens in class war. Reform should take place on a national level, but not by class against class. (2) Preservation of national institutions: The Fascists seemed to want to preserve traditional Italian culture and much of the existing social framework against international socialist revolution. (3) National expansion: Italy should play a more active role abroad and spread her influence throughout the Mediterranean. (4) The primacy of the state: The most important institution of the nation was its government. Only through service to the state could one express true patriotism. This took precedence over all other loyalties. (5) The role of violence: Fascists insisted that violence, in the proper time and place, was morally desirable. Only creative violence could rejuvenate a nation. They talked of smashing all opposition by force.

This Fascist philosophy emerged only gradually during the early 1920's. As Mussolini freely admitted, it was a pragmatic doctrine, built up to meet changing circumstances. Fascism was particularly attractive to young men of the lower middle class, many of whom were too young to have participated in the war. They organized strong-arm bands of *squadristi* (nicknamed the "Black Shirts" for their Fascist uniforms), who attacked Socialists in pitched battles in the street.

During the first two years after the war, it was not the Fascists but the Socialists who had seemed to constitute the most menacing political movement in Italy. Yet the latter soon showed that they were not true revolutionaries. They lacked the audacity to try to overturn the government by force; when the political leaders and industrialists did not accede to their demands, the revolutionary tide began to ebb. Sensing the flow of the new current, Mussolini and the Fascists directed all their venom against the Socialists. They accused them of subversion and treason and attacked individual Socialists in the street or kidnapped them to force doses of castor oil down their throats. Many respectable citizens, not yet sure that the Socialist revolution had been defeated, applauded Fascist violence and brutality as the shield of respectable society. The large landowners of northern and central Italy began to subsidize Mussolini; the Fascists in turn forcibly broke up the syndicates of farm laborers, replacing them with special Fascist unions ready to cooperate with the landlords. The Fascists grew more aggressive with each passing week. They began to assault and close Socialist headquarters in major cities all over northern Italy and even seized control of municipal governments.

The liberal middle-class politicians who had directed Italian affairs during the past two generations had lost control of the country. By 1922, the Socialist menace was completely dead and economic conditions were improving; but Fascism was relentlessly on the march. With civil disorder raging in many cities, the Fascists put their basic program very simply: "We want to make ourselves masters of the State."

In October 1922, the Fascists announced that their followers were launching a "March on Rome," which would end only by placing Mussolini

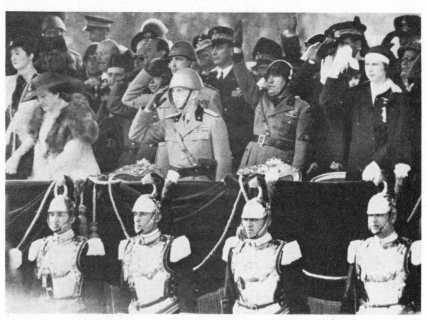

Mussolini as Warrior. Military parades and poses were very important to the public image of Italian fascism. Mussolini, who was essentially a politician not a warrior, increasingly preferred to present himself as the all-conquering warrior. Yet he never had complete power even at home; the head of state was the diminutive king, Victor Immanuel, who eventually helped to overthrow Mussolini in 1943. (Hoover Institution Archives.)

Mussolini as Father of the People. Fascism presented itself as a regime of social reform, development, and modernization; some aspects of these goals were accomplished, but only in part. Mussolini wanted to become known as the father of the Italian people, and here listens sympathetically to the woes of a peasant widow. (Hoover Institution Archives.)

in power. As thousands of Fascists converged on the capital by bus and train, the king, still constitutional head of state, wavered. He finally decided that the safest thing was to permit Mussolini to form a government and reestablish order and security. Moderate opinion hoped that the responsibility of government would turn the Fascists into middle-class conservatives. At the end of October 1922, Mussolini was named premier of Italy.

Development of the Fascist Regime   When Mussolini took office, only four of his fourteen cabinet ministers were Fascists, and the party had few representatives in Parliament. Despite such minority status, Mussolini threatened to have armed followers clear the assembly chamber unless he were given power to rule by decree for one year. This was quickly voted. Within seven weeks, Mussolini converted the Black Shirt gangs into an official Italian national militia, and political opposition was systematically repressed. Elections were held under special new regulations one year later, giving Mussolini a large majority of deputies in parliament. Save for the ultimate sovereignty of the king, Mussolini dominated the organs of political power.

   In June 1924, Giacomo Matteotti, a prominent deputy and critic of the regime, was murdered by hired assassins. This occasioned an uproar from the remainder of honest and responsible people in Italy, and the minority of anti-Fascist deputies walked out of parliament. Mussolini was temporarily shaken by this reaction, but his opponents could not remain united, let alone agree on what they might do. They waited, and failed to take action. After two more years, Mussolini was strong enough to crack down all the way. In 1926, all other political groups were officially forbidden. Italy was now a one-party dictatorship under the personal control of *il Duce* ("the Leader"), as Mussolini was called.

The Fascist government had been quick to conciliate the nation's economic leadership. Mussolini put an end to the income tax and plans for land reform, and also closed the commission that had investigated war profiteering. In 1925, an agreement was signed with the Federation of Italian Industrialists giving big business the right to regulate Italy's industrial economy under the authorization of the state.

In 1926, all economic activity was brought under the control of a series of syndicates (later corporations), one of which was set up for every branch of production. Each syndicate functioned as an arm of the government, though it was dominated by the association of employers or property owners in its field. These syndicates or corporations regulated disputes and economic problems, supposedly solving the class conflict by mutual representation under state supervision.

Mussolini also worked to gain the acceptance of the Catholic Church. Failure to accomplish this had been a principal weakness of the constitutional regime fascism had supplanted, for the great majority of Italians were still Catholic in religion. Though many Fascist leaders were extreme anticlericals, their Duce was an opportunist bent on the solidification of his regime. Consequently, Mussolini negotiated the Lateran Treaty with the papacy in 1929, temporarily solving most of the problems that had divided church and state in Italy for seventy years. The papacy was granted formal political independence and received full sovereignty over a small region around the Vatican, to be known as Vatican City. The Catholic Church was also given special influence over education, and the state agreed to recognize the regulations of canon law concerning marriage.

The formal political structure of the Fascist regime was not finally completed until 1938, when the Chamber of Deputies was replaced by a Chamber of Fasces and Corporations. The dictatorship had achieved what was termed a "Corporate State." In place of democratic political representation, the state was built around a single party and a series of economic corporations. One no longer voted for a political party, but was theoretically represented by a member of his economic profession. Under the Corporate State, independent trade unions could never appear. Though the government had the final word in economic problems, policy was in large measure controlled by the businessmen's representatives in the state corporations, so that Fascist corporativism became a veiled form of capitalist domination.

Labor disputes were rare in Fascist Italy. Affairs went along in a quiet, orderly, and at first moderately prosperous manner. All this made a favorable impression on foreign observers, who were apt to comment that Mussolini had "made the trains run on time." The regime long enjoyed favorable press reports abroad, and many western liberals had a sneaking admiration for the apparent success of Mussolini's system.

Domestically, it was completely stable, and the *Pax Fascista* went on to rule Italy for twenty-one years. A resurgence of underground political activity in 1931 was quickly suppressed. Had Mussolini been willing to rest on his laurels, he might have died of old age, still in power. But the Fascists also emphasized militarism and the use of violence. Mussolini liked to talk of mobilizing "eight million bayonets" to create a new Roman Empire. When new pressures and opportunities in foreign affairs arose after 1935, the Duce could not resist them. This brought eventual downfall, for it was only Italy's defeat in the Second World War, not spontaneous internal resistance, that finally overturned the Mussolini system.

NAZISM IN GERMANY

The loss of the First World War had a traumatic effect upon Germany, for it destroyed the nation's old political hierarchy and governmental institutions. The confusion and disorientation in Germany at the end of 1918 was so great that a promising opportunity was provided for the revolutionary working-class movements, which up to that time had been in a hopeless minority position. A new federation of radical socialists, named the "Spartacus League" in honor of the ancient Roman slave leader, worked to overthrow the remains of political authority and bring in a socialist system. Workers' councils held considerable power in some parts of Germany and, at the beginning of 1919, a general strike in Berlin came close to success; but gradually the revolutionary tide passed. This was because the crisis of 1918–1919 was not the conscious product of dissatisfaction with German society and government, but largely a sequel to national military defeat. Most of the German workers were not genuine revolutionaries, for they had begun to develop middle-class aspirations themselves. As the moderate elements labored to install a new republican system of government, the power of the extreme left wing dwindled.

Establishment of the Weimar Republic Elections for a constituent assembly were held in January 1919, returning a large majority for the middle-class liberals and the moderate wing of the Socialist Party. The deputies then convened in the old cultural center of Weimar to draw up a constitution that was one of the most progressive in the world. The government was established on the parliamentary system, with the chancellor and cabinet responsible to a Reichstag chosen by democratic suffrage. There was also an upper chamber representing the federal states. One unique feature of the Weimar Constitution, however, was Article 48, which enabled the president to exercise dictatorial powers in time of national emergency. This was understandable, since the first years of the Weimar Republic were a period of constant crisis.

The first regular government was formed under the leadership of the majority Socialists, who were headed by Friedrich Ebert (1871–1925) and Philipp Scheidemann. Its power was so insecure that Ebert had secretly to come to terms with the army high command. In return for the latter's support, the Socialist government promised not to undertake revolutionary reforms in the army. This agreement meant that, in contrast to all other German institutions, the army was able to maintain an unbroken tradition from Wilhelmian to Weimar Germany. The pact enabled the government to survive during the crucial period when it was being attacked by extreme left-wing revolutionaries. "Free Corps" units of ex-veterans with a taste for violence were formed to fight Spartacists and Communists both in German cities and in the Baltic region. Revolutionary leaders were summarily shot, and their armed militia broken up.

GERMANY
During the Weimar Republic

No sooner had the immediate danger from the left subsided than a new attempt was made against the regime from the right. In March 1920, Free Corps and monarchist conspirators temporarily seized control of Berlin in a coup called the "Kapp Putsch," after one of its chief organizers. The army refused either to support or to combat the Kapp rebels, whose revolt was broken by a general strike in Berlin. It had become clear that if Germany was not left-revolutionary, neither was it ardently republican. The nation's long background of political and military authoritarianism could not be shaken off so easily and, amid the continuing confusion of the early 1920's, the new Republic's future was not promising.

The great inflation and foreign intervention of 1922–1923 threw the country into chaos once more. Communists again broke out in rebellion, while rabid nationalists and separatist reactionaries planned the overthrow of the Republic. The government continued to print paper money to meet its obligations and the inflation reached fantastic proportions. It became necessary to carry a whole suitcase of bills to make a small purchase, and money lost all value. In the course of a year's time, the middle classes and all those living on fixed incomes were nearly ruined. Tens of thousands of people were driven to suicide or other desperate measures; crime and prostitution increased markedly.

During 1924, affairs slowly returned to normal. The Stresemann government had managed to restore confidence, and energetically repressed disorder. A large foreign loan enabled Germany to resume reparation payments without difficulty. During the next few years, vast amounts of credit poured into Germany, primarily from the United States. During the mid-1920's, Germany actually received from three to five times as much in foreign loans as she paid out in reparations. The influx of money also got German industry back into full production as export markets opened up once more. The years 1924–1928 were a time of prosperity, and political life temporarily stabilized around dead center.

Adolf Hitler During these years of relative prosperity, extremist nationalism was still active in Germany, and the role played by fascism in Italy was taken by a much more thorough-going movement called "National Socialism." Adolf Hitler, the National Socialist leader, was born in 1889, the son of an Austrian customs inspector on the Austro-German border. His early environment was unstable. Left an orphan in his teens, Hitler drifted to Vienna to study art. In the Habsburg capital, he lived the life of a bum, painting a few postcards and sleeping in flophouses. Young Hitler was consumed with bitterness and resentment. Feeding on crude doctrines of pan-Germanism, he developed a firm belief in the superiority of the Nordic or Germanic race over all other ethnic groups. He soon left Austria altogether and moved across the German border to Munich, where he greeted the declaration of war in 1914 with fervent thanksgiving. Hitler served four years in a Bavarian regiment, where he proved himself a good soldier and held the dangerous post of message carrier. He was twice wounded, once seriously, and was awarded the Iron Cross for bravery. Unlike most of his fellow soldiers, Hitler loved the war. It gave him a purpose and a sense of identification for the first time in his life.

Origin of the Nazi Party Discharged at the beginning of 1919, the ex-corporal drifted back to Munich, which had become a hotbed of political and social agitation. Hitler was soon impressed by a new anti-Semitic nationalist workers' movement, which he joined as Party Member No. 7. By 1920, he was devoting himself full-time to the tiny organization, which was renamed the National Socialist German Workers' Party, known simply

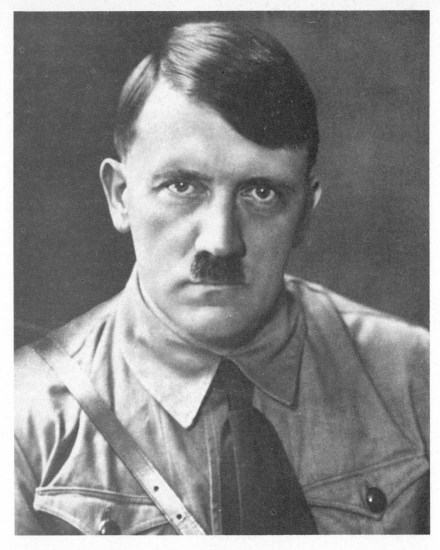

as the "Nazi" party from the pronunciation of the first two syllables in German. Within a year, Hitler's dynamic drive and demagogic oratory exerted a striking appeal, making him the *Fuehrer* (Leader) of the group. By the end of 1920, the Nazis had several thousand members and were expanding rapidly.

Initially, the party program rested on the twin poles of nationalism and socialism, trying to make the best of both appeals. The Nazis preached revenge for the humiliation of Versailles, proscription of the Jews, and radical economic changes, including confiscation of landed estates and nationalization of industry. They organized a street militia, the Storm Troopers, who wore brown shirts and paralleled the Black Shirt militia of Fascist Italy. During the early 1920's, however, the Nazis were but one of a number of competing hypernationalist movements in Germany ranging from the extremely conservative to the wildly radical.

The Nazis made their first bid for power in the crisis year of 1923, when French occupation of the Ruhr and runaway monetary inflation momentarily brought Germany to its knees. The Munich "Beer Hall Putsch" of November 1923, was an attempt to set up a rebel government in Bavaria; it received very little support and ended in abrupt failure. Hitler was arrested and sentenced to a few months in prison. As prosperity returned to Germany, political stability was regained and most of the population turned their backs on the radical movements, though Hitler continued to hold the support of a small hard core of fanatics.

During his brief stay in prison he wrote a long sketch of his life and political goals in *Mein Kampf* (My Struggle). He made no secret of the fact that he intended to subjugate German Jewry, but his main emphasis was on the restoration of German power in Europe, breaking the "shackles" of Versailles. He stated flatly that this would eventually take the form of a "push to the east," where overcrowded Germany might find "living room" on the plains of the Ukraine.

By the late 1920's, the Nazi party had learned to become more decorous and respectable. The emphasis on social revolution had declined, as Hitler moved closer to the conservative nationalism sponsored by German big business. Party propagandists played up patriotic sentiment and tried to arouse greater indignation about Germany's place in Europe. Yet the prospect for nazism was not very good by 1928 and party leaders could only hope for some kind of national or international crisis that would throw German society into turmoil once more.

Decline of the Weimar Republic During the years 1923–1930 Germany was ruled by a succession of coalition governments which managed to maintain outward political stability. There were six major parties, ranging from the Communists and Socialists to the right-wing nationalists. No group had the strength to govern by itself, and the politics of the Republic, influenced by a variety of special interests, were uninspiring. So long as economic affairs went well, few complained very much, but the Republic was incapable of eliciting enthusiasm. Lower-middle-class liberals generated little support for constructive reform, and the Socialists seemed to have run out of steam altogether. On the death of the Republic's first president, the moderate and patriotic Socialist Friedrich Ebert, the voters elected the aged Field Marshal von Hindenburg, who represented conservative nationalism, to replace him.

Originally, the Republic had been a strategem to enable Germany to escape the consequences of losing the war. Nationalist fanatics insisted that the Republic had been foisted on Germany by foreign enemies and internal subversives who had given the Fatherland a "stab in the back." This legend of political betrayal came to be accepted by millions of people. Since the Republic was always associated with defeat and humiliation, ultranationalists exhibited pitiless hatred toward the regime. Matthias Erzberger, who had

"Nosferatu." The theme of the demonic vampire with its superhuman and irresistible powers was prominent in German films during the 1920's. Some commentators on German culture believe that such movies helped to prepare the public mind for submission to an irrational, metapolitical force. (Museum of Modern Art Film Stills Archive.)

led the armistice commission, was assassinated by them in 1922, as was Walter Rathenau, the economic genius of the war years who served as one of the first Republican foreign ministers. Their murderers, like Hitler after the Beer Hall Putsch, were protected by some of the most respectable figures in society, for patriotic Germans felt that it was somehow no crime to slay men associated with the "shame of Versailles." It is possible to conjecture that, had there been a longer period of economic stability lasting into the 1930's, the Republic might have taken firmer hold in the hearts and minds of Germans. As it was, liberal democracy never became more than a strange, artificial system to millions of people, tolerable so long as things were going well, irrelevant when serious problems arose.

The German psyche had scarcely had time to recover from the trauma of the 1923 inflation when the great depression of 1930 struck. Of all European countries, Germany felt most heavily the effects of this debacle. Being even more dependent on the world economy than was Great Britain, she seemed at a loss to help herself. At one point, unemployment reached six million, and half the nation was suffering extreme need. The working class and the lower middle class became desperate. As the nation headed toward a social crisis that would make the 1923 catastrophe seem mild by comparison, the political prestige of the extremist movements rose enormously.

The parliamentary parties found it impossible to agree on government policy. The Socialists wanted to make large-scale compensation payments to the unemployed, but the conservatives refused to countenance "radical" measures. A new government was formed in 1930 under Heinrich Bruening of the Catholic Center party, but it was beset by fanatics of left and right and could not command a majority in the Reichstag. Chancellor Bruening therefore had to ask the president for the emergency powers specified in the constitution. These were granted by Hindenburg, and after July 1930, Germany was ruled by presidential decree, not parliamentary majorities.

The Rise of Nazism Amid this crisis of Republican authority, the Nazi party soon expanded into a mass movement. Membership rolls had grown but slowly during the prosperous years of the late 1920's, yet with the advent of mass unemployment, Hitler's following zoomed to phenomenal heights. Thousands of ex-Free Corps fighters joined the party, as did many hungry workers, but the bulk of the new members came from the lower middle class.

A major result of social trends during the Weimar period had been to impress middle-class values and the desire for middle-class respectability on the great bulk of the population, even including the industrial workers. Furthermore, in the reorganization of German business and industry that had taken place in the 1920's, the labor force had not even doubled, but the number of white-collar and clerical personnel expanded in some cases

Communist Militants Parade in Berlin, 1927. This photo serves as a reminder that National Socialism was not the only revolutionary movement in Weimar Germany. Middle-class fear of communism was one factor exploited by the Nazis in their rise to power. (Hoover Institution Archives.)

as much as six times. This newly found bourgeois status was threatened with obliteration by the depression; and once more, as in 1923, the lower middle class frantically looked for some way out. To many of them, it seemed more clear than ever that only a nationalist regeneration, emphasizing security, order, and hierarchy would be strong enough to protect them.

Hundreds of thousands of people found a political haven in the National Socialist party.

By 1930, Hitler's political cunning had increased considerably. Nazi propaganda had become carefully designed and fully pragmatic. It relied on calculated use of wholesale lies, for Hitler insisted that sweeping falsehoods, endlessly repeated, would make a powerful impression on the popular mind. The tone of Nazi propaganda was completely emotional. Logical argument was avoided, and something was offered for all groups save liberals, Jews, and leftists, who were denounced as "Traitors of the Fatherland." The Fuehrer showed himself a master demagogue in public speeches, casting an almost hypnotic spell over entranced audiences. He told Germans that there was nothing to worry about. No real problems existed that could not be solved by aggressive, unified nationalism. Germans were not called on to think or analyze their problems, but only to believe and obey. The Nazis unleashed a huge propaganda campaign for the elections of September 1930 and saw their parliamentary delegation leap from twelve to 107, making them the second largest political group in the country.

Street fights became daily occurrences, as Communist toughs and Nazi Storm Troopers brawled in public thoroughfares. The Brown Shirts did not limit their bullying to Communists, but assaulted democratic Socialists and middle-class liberals as well. Hitler saw victory in sight, and when Hindenburg's presidential term expired in 1932, decided to run the risk of competing with Germany's number one national hero in the latter's reelection campaign. Though Hitler lost, he rolled up so many votes in opposition to the now-senile Hindenburg that the election resulted in a moral victory for the Nazis.

Two months later, the Bruening government collapsed. Bruening was succeeded by a favorite of Hindenburg's, the reactionary aristocrat Franz von Papen. Clever and cynical, Papen believed that he could use the president's decree power to carry on a successful government and exploit the Nazis for his own ends. However, a new general election in July 1932, resulted in another Nazi avalanche. The latter won over two hundred seats, replacing the Socialists as the largest party in the country. Between them, Communists and Nazis held over half the seats in the Reichstag, making parliament unmanageable. Even with the dictatorial powers at his disposal, Papen did not know how to control the situation.

Since there was no way out, new elections were held in November 1932. The Nazis rallied for one more big effort, their third campaign within eight months. They had organized a fantastic number of mass meetings and torchlight parades, replete with forests of banners, flags, and emotional slogans, but their energy was waning. In the November elections, for the first time in years, the Nazis registered a loss. There was a distinct letdown in the party. Many Nazi leaders feared that the favorable moment had passed and such an opportunity would not arise again. In spite of this, Hitler remained iron-nerved and self-confident.

Despite the temporary Nazi setback, the government could count on even less voting support than before these elections, and Papen tried to convince Hindenburg that the only salvation of Germany lay in casting aside the constitution, dissolving the Reichstag, and ruling by decree. His plans were thwarted by the most influential voice in Hindenburg's circle, that of General Kurt von Schleicher (1882–1934), head of the political bureau of the German army. Schleicher persuaded the old president that Papen's proposals would prove dangerous, provoking civil war and foreign intervention. Hindenburg then insisted that it must be Schleicher who would lead the next government. The general accepted appointment as chancellor,

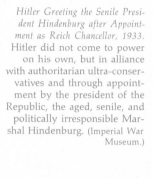

Hitler Greeting the Senile President Hindenburg after Appointment as Reich Chancellor, 1933. Hitler did not come to power on his own, but in alliance with authoritarian ultra-conservatives and through appointment by the president of the Republic, the aged, senile, and politically irresponsible Marshal Hindenburg. (Imperial War Museum.)

intending to institute sufficient reforms to pull Germany out of the crisis. Yet his government lasted less than two months, for it could not win popular support and was unable to achieve significant social reforms.

At this point, the oily Papen took his revenge on Schleicher, convincing Hindenburg that no chancellor could hope to govern unless he had a parliamentary majority. Papen then made a deal with Hitler whereby Hitler would become chancellor and Papan vice-chancellor. Many conservatives were demanding that Hindenburg appoint Hitler chancellor, and such a cabinet could count on a near-majority in the Reichstag. Certain that it would be he who would actually pull the strings, Papen got Hindenburg's approval of the new government. On January 30, 1933, Adolf Hitler, through legal constitutional procedure, became Chancellor of Germany.

The Nazi Dictatorship After becoming chancellor, Hitler wasted no time in establishing dictatorial control. New elections were called in order to provide his party with a parliamentary majority. Just before the voting, a mysterious fire broke out in the Reichstag cellar and gutted the building. The Nazis blamed it on the Communists and used it as an excuse to suspend constitutional liberties during the election. Nazis were placed in charge of the police, and Brown Shirts (or Storm Troopers) patrolled the streets, beating and bullying opponents, even dragging them off to private jails. Despite this intimidation, the Nazis failed to win a clear majority in the 1933 elections, receiving just under 44 percent of the popular vote.

This was, however, enough to allow the Nazis and their allies, the right-wing nationalists, to dominate the parliament. Hitler quickly moved to increase his margin by winning the acquiescence of Catholic deputies after a pledge not to infringe upon the prerogatives of German Catholicism. On March 23, 1933, he introduced an Enabling Act in the Reichstag, giving him power to rule for four years by decree. This measure was easily passed by the Nazi, conservative, and Catholic deputies who were supporting Hitler. Within seven weeks, the Nazi leader had raised himself from chancellor to virtual dictator with power to rule by decree, not limited even by the authority of the German president.

Both the Communist and Socialist parties were outlawed; soon afterward a new decree banned all political organizations save the Nazis, who became the official German political movement. The Catholic Center party, under the illusion that it had made a deal with Hitler, was eliminated along with the others. Free trade unions were soon broken up and replaced by a Nazi workers' front. In succession, all significant German institutions were coordinated under the Nazi "leadership principle," with all power proceeding from the Fuehrer downward.

Attitude of the German Army The only institution that could have stood up to the Nazi takeover was the German army. Since 1919, the army had been limited to a total enrollment of 100,000, although a moderate amount of secret rearmament had gone on throughout the Weimar period. The main similarity between the army of 1933 and the army of 1914 lay in its leadership, for the same aristocratic officer corps was in control. This small clique retained its class prejudice and its emphasis on a special place for the army hierarchy above society and beyond governmental interference. The army leaders hated Versailles and everything connected with German defeat. They were willing to accept a nationalist dictatorship that would restore German power, even though the aristocratic officers' clique was contemptuous of the rabble-rousing Hitler. More menacing to the army were the brawling, conscienceless hordes of Storm Troopers, who, under their leader, Ernst Roehm, had swelled to the total of three million. Though mostly an unarmed rabble, the Storm Troopers would have liked to swamp the small professional army altogether. Such a revolutionary inundation the military hierarchy feared most of all.

The "Blood Purge" Hitler was not interested in immediately revolutionizing Germany's society and economy, but in guaranteeing his power as dictator. By 1934 he had become aware of the danger of going too far and thus turning the entrenched power groups of German life, such as the army and the industrialists, against him. He was apprehensive about the radical Storm Trooper leadership in his party and decided to take it in hand. On June 30, 1934, a Blood Purge was carried out against the Nazi radicals and Brown Shirt leaders. Roehm and several dozen other top Storm Troopers were murdered, as were a number of politicians who had opposed Hitler, including General von Schleicher. In all, over one hundred people were killed, and Von Papen himself narrowly escaped death. The Storm Troopers faded into the background; the Nazi revolution had become more conservative. The army leaders and big businessmen felt reassured about the Fuehrer. When President Hindenburg died in mid-summer of 1934, Hitler combined the offices of chancellor and president, making his authority absolute.

A new Nazi elite, the black-uniformed SS (standing for "Protection Units") now took precedence. They served as a special security guard and the spearhead of the party, and were led by the modest-looking, bespectacled Heinrich Himmler, who had been a Bavarian chicken farmer. Himmler looked and sometimes acted like a petty file clerk, but he developed an extensive concentration-camp system which sealed off the regime's opponents.

Religious Persecution The Nazi propaganda chief, Josef Goebbels, claimed exultantly, "The Nazi victory was a propaganda victory." This was true to the extent that Hitler's triumph would not have been possible had not the clever and massive Nazi use of propaganda been able to sway the feelings of millions of ordinary Germans. Once in control of the state, the party propagandists constructed a vast machine of totalitarian indoctrination to reshape German thinking according to the party line. In this task, it was inevitable that Nazism attempt to erase the remaining influence of Christianity in Germany.

Nazism was a fully pagan movement; its moral standards were, in fact, more primitive than those of the pre-Christian Germanic tribes. However, during the first phase of his regime Hitler was careful not to antagonize Christian leaders too blatantly. He was aided in all his dealings with the churches by the fact that Christianity had already lost much of its popular influence.

Hitler followed somewhat divergent policies with respect to the Catholic and Protestant churches. As described earlier, he made a bargain for Catholic voting support in return for a pledge to respect Catholic rights. This agreement was ratified by an official concordat between the Reich and the papacy in the summer of 1933, in which the latter officially recognized the Nazi regime and regularized the legal relationship between them. It was soon clear that the condordat had little meaning. The German regime dominated education and indoctrination of German youth, who were enrolled en masse in Nazi juvenile organizations, while most Catholic schools were closed. Pope Pius XI protested with little effect.

The government later attempted to fuse all Protestant churches into a single Reich Church, with a Nazi-appointed head. Most pastors avoided open defiance, but a minority of Protestant ministers organized themselves as the Confessional Church in opposition to Nazi racism and any identification of Christianity with the Nazi regime. Eventually nearly one thousand leaders of the Confessional Church were sent to prison. In place of religious belief Nazi ideologists propounded a series of nationalistic myths, based on the supposed superiority of the Nordic race.

Anti-Semitism The reverse side of Nazi racism was its reliance on anti-Semitism, blaming all misfortunes on one small group, the Jews. Persecution of the Jews has a long history in Europe, dating back to the Middle Ages. It had declined during the nineteenth century, dwindling into milder forms of political and economic discrimination. Though Jews numbered less than one percent of the population of Germany, the Nazi line insisted that a vast Jewish plot constantly worked for the destruction of Nordic civilization; the Jews were responsible for Versailles, they had plotted the depression, and so on.

The emotions of millions of Germans were aroused by shrill anti-Semitic propaganda. For legal purposes, a Jew was defined as anyone with at least one Jewish grandparent, and once the Nazi regime had become firmly established, persecution was systematized. Jewish people were driven out of ordinary professional employment and forced to carry identity cards. After a German diplomat abroad was murdered in November 1938 in retaliation for this persecution, the incident was used as an excuse for a great pogrom throughout Germany, followed by mass arrests of much of the remaining Jewish population.

Economics of the Nazi State The Nazi regime had to bring Germany out of economic depression to make its power secure. The Papen and Schleicher governments, which preceded Hitler, had reduced taxes somewhat and embarked on a large-scale public works program, combined with direct relief to the poor. Hitler continued the policy of his predecessors, tightening controls and increasing expenditures on public works. By 1933, the downswing in productivity had already been halted; from that point, output began to go up again. To avoid inflation and pay for government expenditures, taxes in Germany remained high throughout the 1930's. Eighty percent of government expenditures were covered by taxation during the first five years of the regime, a much better record, for example, than that of the contemporary Roosevelt administration in the United States. The German economy was basically strong and efficient. What had been needed was a climate of stability and new stimuli to allow the natural productive forces to assert themselves.

German labor exercised few rights in this process, for the trade unions had been destroyed. They were replaced with a Nazi Labor Front, which propagated intense nationalism, a feeling of solidarity and sacrifice, and also arranged fringe benefits to take the workers' minds off other problems. Wages remained rather low, but at least everyone had a job and there was relative well-being.

Big business was enthusiastic over the initial results of Nazi rule, which reinforced the strong German tendency toward cartelization. An integrated system of economic controls was introduced in 1936, and domination of the big combines over smaller concerns was fostered by two successive Four-Year Plans to coordinate industrial expansion. This process of concentration was accelerated after the war broke out in 1939.

Business profits increased markedly, but so did taxes, and the government forced reinvestment of most profits in new industrial expansion. The German economy was not controlled by the cartels but by the Nazi state, which gave orders to the cartels. The trend was to place wealthy industrialists in the role of managers of a government-coordinated process.

Though bent on a war of conquest, Hitler was also a demagogue who wanted to provide plenty of consumer goods in order to retain popularity. By 1937, German industrial production was seventeen percent higher than in 1929, and part of the surplus was devoted to heavy consumer goods. Hitler pushed the construction of an *autobahn* network—the first system of modern superhighways in Europe. By 1938, domestic automobile production stood at twice the 1929 level. Car buying was encouraged by dropping excise taxes on automobiles and allowing new purchases as income-tax deductions. To put the auto in reach of the working class, plans were made to produce the low-cost *Volkswagen*—the "People's Car." Hitler's essentially utopian ideal was to provide the German people with both guns and butter under the domination of the Nazi state. "National Socialism" was intended thus to achieve what Communism promised but lacked the means to deliver.

THE SPREAD OF RIGHT-WING AUTHORITARIANISM

Imitations or variations of the fascist and nazi movements in other countries grew in numbers and prestige during the 1930's as the nominal solution to political and social confusion. Most of these movements had few direct connections with the Germans or Italians but were simply spontaneous

Nazi Party Rally in Nuremberg, 1934. The organization and symbolic impact of mass rallies was a major element of Nazi politics. The sense of mass support, overwhelming force, and total discipline and commitment was designed to intoxicate both participant and observer. (Imperial War Museum.)

efforts to find an authoritarian expression for radical nationalism in different lands. There were a half-dozen small fascist-style parties in France, and as many others in Belgium and Holland. The only places where such movements achieved any importance, however, were Hungary and Rumania, where virulent nationalism and dissatisfaction with the existing narrow conservative regimes helped to build mass support.

During the 1930's, new conservative authoritarian regimes were established in Portugal and Austria. These were not truly fascist governments, however, but conservative Catholic corporatist republics, introduced as the means to overcome severe internal dissension. In Portugal, the "Corporative Republic" of Dr. Antonio de Oliveira Salazar was officially installed in 1933, but it avoided association with fascism. The Portuguese system did not emphasize aggression or violence, and made little attempt at ideological indoctrination. Its style was quiet and conservative, shunning "all the heresies of the twentieth century."

Austrian politics in the late 1920's and early 1930's were nearly torn apart by a three-way struggle between the Catholic Christian Social party, the Socialists and the Austrian Nazis. In March 1933, the Christian Social chancellor, Engelbert Dollfuss (1892–1934), closed the parliament and began to rule by decree. The Christian Social party was then merged with right-wing militia groups to form a new movement, the Fatherland Front, on which to base the government. When Viennese Socialists rebelled in February 1934, the Austrian army subdued them, and all the Socialist organizations were broken up. Soon afterward, the government's other opponent, the Austrian Nazis, assassinated Dollfuss. He was succeeded by a Christian Social lawyer and professor, Karl Schuschnigg, who governed Austria until overthrown by Hitler in 1938. The shortlived Dollfuss-Schuschnigg regime, though authoritarian, was not a fascist state. Its aims were primarily defensive, trying to preserve the present structure of Austrian society and the country's independence, as the black shadow of German Nazism loomed ever larger over the border.

COMMUNISM, FASCISM, AND NAZISM COMPARED

At times there has been a tendency to lump communism, fascism, and nazism together as similar totalitarian evils, but it would be a mistake to overlook the fundamental differences in ideology and structure between them. At least in theory, Communists are "people of the book," grounded in an abstract intellectual interpretation of man and history written down in the mid-nineteenth century by Karl Marx. Communists consider themselves to be extremely rationalistic; they emphasize formal logic and chart elaborate written plans. They are total revolutionaries who leave few avenues of life unchanged. There is supposedly but one social basis for their ideology—the "working class," even though the direct benefit for the working classes may not be evident. Though communism lays overwhelming stress on modernization, it has never triumphed by its own power in any of the more advanced, modern western countries. It has been most successful in underdeveloped lands, and has had little appeal to the industrialized West.

Fascism and nazism, on the other hand, were avowedly anti-intellectual and rested on doctrines that formally emphasized the irrational elements in human nature. Though fascism eventually worked out something in the nature of a detailed set of doctrines, nazism never achieved a formally or intellectually codified ideology at all. Until 1948, European communism was largely kept under the centralized control of Moscow, but there have been as many different individual variations of fascism or national socialism as there have been separate fascistic parties. In theory, fascism and nazism were classless, resting on the concept of the whole nation. In practice, however, fascism and nazism appealed especially to the lower-middle strata. Whereas communism has tended to become a shortcut to partial modernization for backward countries, fascism and nazism have appealed most to partially modernized societies that already possessed a sizable middle class with a strong sense of nationalism.

Hitler and Mussolini Hitler and Mussolini have often been thought of as twin dictators, but there was considerable difference between the two men and their regimes. Until he fell under the influence of Hitler, Mussolini had tended to be pragmatic and often moderate. Though Italian fascism coined the concept of "totalitarianism," it allowed some nonfascist elements to enjoy partial liberty and never achieved a true totalitarian state. Similarly, there was for many years no racial doctrine in Italian fascist ideology. Mussolini himself had few fixed doctrines and increasingly accommodated himself to circumstances. Though he talked of a militaristic policy, he followed a more temperate course in practice and kept the peace for thirteen years, knowing that Italy could not gain from a major war.

Hitler was quite different. He carved out a series of weird, nihilistic goals near the beginning of his career and held to them unswervingly. Though he often showed a fine sense of tactics and timing, he was not so pragmatic and adjustable as Mussolini, but was bent on fixed, narrow ends. He was sexually perverted and his mind betrayed the marks of severe compulsive neurosis and emotional instability, conceiving irrational hatreds and enthusiasms of a thoroughly demonic nature which he was determined to see through to the end. Mussolini merely talked and strutted, but Hitler meant every bit of his bellicosity, and was willing to wage the most frightful war of all time. To resolve the "Jewish problem," he eventually slaughtered at least five million people. Italian fascism was comparatively restrained and conservative until the Nazi example spurred it to new activity; the radical and dynamic pace of Hitler hardly flagged from January 1933 to April 1945. In the process, anti-Semitism, concentration camps, and total war produced a febrile and sadistic nightmare without any parallel in the Italian experience.

FURTHER READING

Events surrounding the rise of fascism, nazism, and related movements are narrated in F. L. Carsten, *The Rise of Fascism* (1957). On Mussolini and the development of Italian fascism, see Sir Ivone Kirkpatrick, *Mussolini, a Study in Power* (1964); Angelo Rossi, *The Rise of Italian Fascism, 1918–1922* (1938); A. J. Gregor, *The Ideology of Fascism* (1969); E. R. Tannenbaum, *The Fascist Experience* (1972); and M. A. Ledeen, *Universal Fascism* (1972). C. F. Delzell, *Mussolini's Enemies* (1961), treats the Italian opposition to fascism.

The political history of the Weimar Republic is presented in Erich Eyck, *A History of the Weimar Republic* (1962). Salient aspects of its culture may be approached through Peter Gay, *Weimar Culture* (1968), and Siegfried Kracauer, * *From Caligari to Hitler* (1947); the latter is a fascinating psychological study of German movies. Key sectors of Weimar politics are treated in Hans Gatzke, *Stresemann and the Rearmament of Germany* (1954); and R. N. Hunt, *German Social Democracy, 1918–1933* (1964).

The best single volume on Nazi Germany is K. D. Bracher, *The German Dictatorship* (1970). The principal biography of Hitler is Alan Bullock, * *Hitler, a Study in Tyranny* (rev. ed., 1964). For the relationship between nazism and

*Books available in paperback edition are marked with an asterisk.

German society, see David Schoenbaum, * *Hitler's Social Revolution* (1966); and W. S. Allen, *The Nazi Seizure of Power: The Experience of a Single German Town, 1930–1935* (1965). E. N. Petersen, *The Limits of Hitler's Power* (1969), helps illuminate the nature of the Nazi system, and J. S. Conway, *The Nazi Persecution of the Churches, 1933–1945* (1968), deals with the suppression of religion. Two interesting cultural-psychological hypotheses about nazism are presented in P. F. Drucker, * *The End of Economic Man* (1969); and Erich Fromm, *Escape from Freedom* (1941). George Mosse, * *The Crisis of German Ideology* (1964), treats the cultural background.

There are several notable attempts at general treatment and synthetic interpretation of the various Fascist and Nazi-type movements. The most useful are Ernst Nolte, * *Three Faces of Fascism* (1966), and Eugen Weber, * *Varieties of Fascism* (1964); but two volumes edited by S. J. Woolf, * *European Fascism* (1968), and * *The Nature of Fascism* (1968), are also useful. For a broader dimension, see H. Rogger and E. Weber, eds., * *The European Right* (1966). Fascism in east-central Europe is the topic of N. M. Nagy-Talavera's excellent *The Green Shirts and the Others* (1970); and P. F. Sugar, ed., * *Native Fascism in the Successor States, 1918–1945* (1971).

On the Christian Social party and the corporative regime in Austria, see K. von Klemperer, *Ignaz Seipel* (1972); and Gordon Brook-Shepherd, *Dollfuss* (1961). The best biography of the Portuguese dictator is Hugh Kay, *Salazar and Modern Portugal* (1970).

6 Western Europe Between the Wars

The two decades between the World Wars were a troubled time for most parts of western Europe. A full five years were required to return to "normalcy." Only the period 1924–1930 could be considered stable, and during this time France had to deal with the inflation menace and Great Britain experienced the only general strike in its history. Save for two or three years in the late 1920's, Spain was in fairly constant turmoil from 1919 to 1939. The crisis decade of the 1930's created serious tension in almost every country of the West. Scandinavia alone seemed able to find a creative answer for the social problem, while France, hitherto the most stable large country on the continent, nearly foundered.

GREAT BRITAIN After the cheers of victory ended in 1918, the enormous cost of the First World War had to be faced by Britain's government and people. The proportion of war dead that Britain suffered was less than that of either France or Germany, but the ratio of slain officers—of the leadership cadres—was at least as high, due to the British insistence on personal example and volunteering. A large part of the young elite was dead. Economically, the war had cost forty billion dollars, one-third of Britain's shipping, over fifteen percent of its foreign investments, and many of its overseas markets.

Economic Problems Even before the war part of the British industrial plant was obsolescent, and since 1914 there had been scant opportunity for replacement and reinvestment. Some new industries such as electricity, chemicals, automobiles, airplanes, and steel were efficient and up to date; but older ones such as iron, coal, and textiles were falling further behind foreign competition each year. British preeminence in shipbuilding was diminishing. In some industries there were so many small firms with limited facilities that few reaped sufficient profit to afford the cost of full modernization. Though Britain stood second only to the United States in general economic strength in 1919, it was uncertain that she could maintain such a position, for the many export markets lost in the war would not be easily recovered. After a momentary postwar boom, British sales dropped rapidly; and by 1921 over two million workers were unemployed. The government inaugurated a mild protective tariff, beginning the reversal of Britain's traditional free-trade policy, and also sponsored a small program of subsidized housing. For the unemployed, whose number never dipped much below one million in the 1920's, the only solution attempted was relief payments. Later standardized as "the dole," this meager subsidy—about four dollars a week—became a regular feature of British life for the next twenty years.

The Fall of Lloyd George   The prime minister, David Lloyd George, was a Liberal leading a coalition government whose main support came from the Conservative party. After instituting an electoral reform that gave the vote to women over thirty, he led the coalition into the emotional "Khaki Election" of 1918, which was waged on a platform of ultrapatriotism and returned a Conservative majority. Though Lloyd George's opportunistic tactics had cost him the support of most of his own Liberal party, the Conservatives supported him as prime minister for four more years. He had led the nation to victory in the war and was still the most popular individual politician in Britain, "towering like a giant" over other leaders.

Lloyd George ultimately proved less successful in peace than in war. He tended to concentrate on foreign affairs, and was unable to cope with Britain's economic problems. Nor did the newly elected House of Commons show much understanding and initiative. A well-qualified observer aptly described the deputies as "a group of hard-faced men who looked as if they had done very well out of the war." Britain's new leaders from the remnants of the war generation were little interested in social reform or international cooperation; they stood mainly for the defense of established interests.

By 1922, persistent economic distress was weakening Lloyd George's government. Political circles were also dissatisfied over the handling of the Irish rebellion, and criticized the prime minister for encouraging the Greeks in their disastrous invasion of Turkey (1920–1921). Party factionalism returned, and the Conservatives wearied of following a Liberal premier. An all-Conservative cabinet was formed, winning a smashing victory in the 1922 elections. Lloyd George's followers were reduced to a tiny minority, and the active phase of the "Welsh Wizard's" political career abruptly ended.

Baldwin's Conservative Government   By the following year, the Conservatives had found a new leader in Stanley Baldwin (1867–1947). Baldwin lacked dramatic flair and had no understanding of economics; but he was patriotic, outwardly modest, and scrupulously honest. In electoral campaigns he emphasized, "I am not a clever man," and his sincere, stolid air inspired confidence among millions of voters. A consummate parliamentary tactician, he retained leadership of his party for fourteen years. During his first administration, he made one bold move, which was to attempt a full-scale protective tariff in order to bolster the domestic market and reduce unemployment. Support for free-trade was greater than the prime minister had calculated; it reunited the Liberal party. In a general election on this issue, Baldwin's government lost its majority and had to resign.

Though no party won a clear majority in the 1923 elections, a short-lived cabinet was formed by Ramsay MacDonald, the debonair, eloquent Labour leader, who won Liberal Party support for the first Labour government in British history at the beginning of 1924. Though gifted with both idealism and tactical skill, MacDonald found it hard to please both Liberals and Labourites, and was placed under heavy pressure by trade-union militants. After his government promised a commercial loan to Soviet Russia, the Conservatives brought it down and won a complete victory in new elections at the end of 1924.

Baldwin once more became prime minister, emphasizing security and stability above all else. Recovery had made scant headway in many of the nation's industries, but the new Conservative government presented no program to stimulate the stagnant areas. Instead, proceeding on the assumption that a sound Britain was based on a sound pound, it placed the pound back on the gold standard at its pre-1914 value, from which it had fallen during the war. This overvalued the pound in relation to foreign currencies, and made it all the more difficult for other countries to buy British goods.

The General Strike of 1926 The industry that felt the most pressure from declining sales and productivity was coal mining. The mine owners operated 1,400 separate companies, which lacked the will, resources, and imagination necessary for modernization. With the industry's productivity low and prices fairly high, exports could not be sustained under a more expensive pound unless costs were lowered. Rather than reorganize and attempt to increase efficiency, the mine owners decided to reduce wages and lengthen working hours. Since the general wage level was already meager, the Miners' Federation, backed by the Trades Union Congress, threatened to strike. In the spring of 1926, a royal commission issued a report that was generally favorable to the miners, suggesting fundamental reorganization of the coal industry. However, the report also recommended a temporary wage decrease until production had become more efficient. Neither side was willing to accept this plan. The miners' fundamental goal was nationalization, which they not inaccurately regarded as the only salvation for the numerous backward, small-sized companies that comprised the industry.

A partial walkout occurred at the beginning of May. The government broke off negotiations with the Trades Union Congress which then called for the only general strike in British history on May 3, 1926. Mining, transportation, and most branches of heavy industry, gas, and electricity were shut down; nearly twenty percent of the total labor force was involved.

Soup Line for the Poor in England. Large-scale unemployment and government relief services were permanent features of life in Britain between the wars. (Radio Times Hulton Picture Library.)

The government, however, was better prepared than the strikers, and enthusiastic volunteers kept all basic services in operation. Many incidents of petty property damage occurred, but no one was killed. At Plymouth, strikers and policemen whiled away their time playing football together. The unions lacked the funds to support a long walkout; and after nine days the Trades Union Congress accepted a weak compromise formula to call off the strike, though the miners resisted a full six months. The reorganization plan for the mining industry was put into operation and a Trades Disputes Act was passed, outlawing sympathy strikes. The results of the general strike left a legacy of bitterness that lasted twenty years. Nevertheless, its failure convinced most union leaders that significant reforms could not be achieved by direct action, and there were no social crises of this sort during the depression that began in 1929.

The Depression and the "National Government" Baldwin's government continued to hold power until the next regularly scheduled elections in 1929. It constructed a small amount of housing and converted the workers' dole and pension systems into an efficient national unit, but made no concerted effort to encourage prosperity. During 1927–1929 total British production remained sixteen percent under that of 1913, and exports continued to run ten percent below the prewar figure. Unemployment averaged at least twelve percent of the total labor force. The Labour party capitalized on general dissatisfaction to score a narrow plurality in the 1929 elections; and, with the help of the Liberals, Ramsay MacDonald formed his second government.

When the full effects of the world depression struck in the latter half of 1930, industries that had long been semi-stagnant declined further. By mid-1931 twenty-five percent of the working force was unemployed. The subsequent increase in dole payments threw the budget out of balance, resulting in loss of financial confidence and an international "flight from the pound." The Bank of England's gold reserve was nearly exhausted.

MacDonald's working majority was too small for him to attempt a radical Labourite solution to the dilemma, so he submitted to pressure to reduce the dole. This broke up the Labourite cabinet. To maintain political unity during the depression, MacDonald was asked to become head of a new National Government coalition in cooperation with the Conservatives. Most Labourites would not participate. That meant the eventual sacrifice of MacDonald's whole career, but he accepted nevertheless. Though it became necessary to go off the gold standard, the pound's value was stabilized after a loss of thirty percent, and the rate of the dole was lowered for the next six years.

The Conservatives dominated the National Government and British politics for the remainder of the decade. The once-powerful Liberal party had nearly disappeared from view, its more progressive members going over to Labour and many of its ordinary middle-class supporters voting Conservative. In the 1931 elections, middle-class people of all social gradations banded together to give the Conservatives a huge majority of 472 seats to only 84 for the entire opposition. MacDonald, having been expelled from the Labour party, served as prime minister with steadily diminishing effectiveness until his retirement in 1935. Baldwin then returned to lead the government for two years, but his health collapsed in 1937. He was succeeded by the strongest figure in his cabinet, Neville Chamberlain (1869–1940), son of Joseph Chamberlain and himself the former health minister and chancellor of the exchequer.

To combat the depression, the National Government did not attempt any integrated program of redevelopment. Instead, a lengthy series of patchwork measures was undertaken. The government adopted a strong system of protective tariffs and lowered the domestic interest rate. It helped to promote reorganization of the mining and textile industries and coordinated the electric power system. Extensive assistance was given to agriculture and a number of shipping subsidies were granted. The government also financed a considerable amount of home construction for the lower classes and continued the dole, sustaining domestic purchasing power.

Most commentators have castigated the National Government for not doing more to stimulate Britain's economy. As a matter of fact, the economy leveled out of the great depression in 1933–1935; and by 1937 industrial production was twenty percent higher than it had been in 1929. Industry concentrated on the domestic market, which expanded enormously. Real wages for those employed had been rising steadily since 1924; during these years most Englishmen were actually higher paid than ever before and spent more money on recreation than at any previous time. Compared with France or the United States, Britain climbed out of the 1930–1933 rut very quickly.

Such expansion was only relative, of course, for part of British industry remained stagnant and fourteen percent of the working force was still unemployed in the late 1930's. Worst of all, the National Government ignored the need for a psychological stimulus to raise the country's spirits. The dour, black-clad, unpopular Chamberlain was an efficient administrator and reformer, but he entirely lacked the public appeal of a Franklin Roosevelt—or an Adolf Hitler. Economically, the National Government's patchwork program was more successful than the American New Deal, but the upper-middle-class Conservative ministry never succeeded in imparting a sense of progress and participation to the English workingman.

REFORMS IN THE EMPIRE

The peace treaties of 1919–1923 provided for seizure of the German colonies and breakup of the Ottoman Empire. Under the League of Nations Mandate system, Palestine, Mesopotamia, and German East Africa went to Britain, while France received Syria, Lebanon, and the former German colonies of Togo and the Camerouns in Africa. However, events soon showed this extension of imperial power was more apparent than real.

Independence for Ireland   After the World War, Britain's empire was subject to more severe internal stress than at any time since the 1770's. This was partly due to the rising tide of native resentment in Asia, which increased during the 1920's and 1930's; but it was also due to keen desire for full independence by the only white population in the Empire that had not won such recognition—the Irish. This problem had a long history, stretching far back into the preceding century. Parliament had finally voted a Home Rule Bill for the island in 1914, only to suspend the measure for the duration of the war. When the fighting was over, Irish nationalists lost patience. They were now dominated by an extremist movement called "Sinn Fein" (Ourselves Alone), whose representatives, refusing to sit any longer in the House of Commons in London, set up a shadow parliament of their own in Dublin. Since the Irish would not cooperate in gradual implementation of Home Rule, the Lloyd George government launched full-scale repression of Sinn Fein, which led to extensive violence. The Irish Republican Army used murder, arson, and bombs in its fight against British authority. To counter the "IRA," an irregular police force was organized, called "Black and Tans" from the color of their uniforms. The Black and Tans were mostly former army officers and were not always scrupulous in the methods they employed. After several hundred people had been murdered in Ireland during 1920–1921, the British public began to feel revulsion at continued coercion, even though most of the killing was done by the IRA. At the end of 1921, Lloyd George signed an agreement with the Irish leaders, which gave most of Ireland self-governing dominion status under the title of "Irish Free State." The six northern counties, which were Protestant and partially industrialized, received a special position as autonomous "Northern Ireland," with both a Parliament of their own and representation in the British Parliament at London.

British Black-and-Tans Searching a Suspect during the Irish Troubles, c. 1920. The immediate postwar period was wracked with violence even in the British Isles. The struggle between British forces and the IRA (Irish Republican Army) was followed by an even more bloody civil war between moderates and extremists in the Irish Free State. (Radio Times Hulton Picture Library.)

As soon as this agreement had been signed, new civil war broke out in Ireland. The extremists refused to accept any association with Britain and, turning on the new Irish government, seized control of downtown Dublin. The Irish moderates who had signed the treaty were forced to be even rougher with their fellow countrymen than the British had been, and killed more supernationalists than had the Black and Tans. Yet though the new dominion government won this little civil war, the radical Eamon De Valera scored a complete victory in the Irish elections of 1932. After fifteen more years passed, southern Ireland declared itself a republic and left the British Commonwealth altogether.

The Statute of Westminster The framework for independence within the British Empire was established in the 1931 Statute of Westminster. This made clear that the laws and decisions of the properly constituted governments of the self-governing overseas dominions were fully sovereign. Canada, Australia, New Zealand, South Africa, and the Irish Free State were now bound to the mother country only by sentiment, commercial interrelation, and the symbol of the British monarchy. Should other portions of the Empire evolve into dominion status, they would enjoy the same independence. In this way, the British had accomplished something never done before in European history: the conversion of a centralized empire into a mutual association of free, or potentially free, peoples. Ties between Britain and all the independent dominions remained very close. During the depression, this relationship was tightened by a series of preferential tariffs, making the whole Empire a closed trading area for the benefit of its member peoples.

FRANCE   Few nations suffered more from the war than France. Nearly ten percent of its adult male population between eighteen and fifty had been killed, and total casualties approximated five million, including colonial troops. The northeastern region devastated by the fighting had been the most industrialized and productive portion of the country. Total industrial production in 1919 was only about sixty percent of the prewar level. In addition to destruction of machinery, railroads, and agricultural facilities, 800,000 buildings had been ruined. Despite such losses, French society came through the war with less change than that of any other large continental nation. The balanced structure of French property holding encouraged social order, and the national heritage of middle-class responsibility resulted in a considerable degree of political maturity. After 1918, the emphasis, as in England, was on conservative government and stability. The French, for the most part, simply wanted freedom to live their own lives.

Recovery from the War   The first postwar election led to a great victory for the right. The new Chamber of 1919 was nicknamed the "Horizon-Blue Chamber" because of the number of veterans who held seats. The government's main task was to foster rapid development of the war-damaged regions, and this was done with vigor. However, it cost a great deal of money

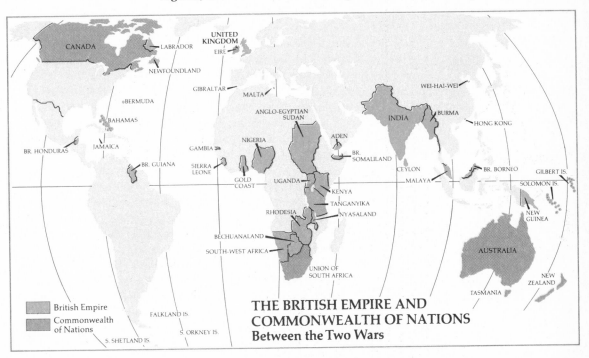

THE BRITISH EMPIRE AND
COMMONWEALTH OF NATIONS
Between the Two Wars

British Empire
Commonwealth of Nations

and the government's fiscal policy was highly unsound, relying on loans and indirect taxes. At the same time, the nation had to cope with the fluctuations of postwar trade and the expense of maintaining the strongest army in the world. All this encouraged a dangerous inflation.

Partly as a consequence, the "Left Alliance" won the elections of 1924 and for the next two years the liberal middle-class Radical party held office. The Radicals no longer stood for change and had little in the way of a program to offer. Their political orientation was ambivalent. Observers pointed out that the Radicals were like radishes, Red on the outside but White on the inside. Others said that though the Radicals' hearts were on the left, their pocketbooks were on the right. Regarding France's most pressing problems—rapidly mounting inflation and her war debts to the United States—the Radicals could not agree with their Socialist allies of the "Left Alliance," and resigned office in 1926.

By that time the franc had lost ninety percent of its prewar value, and France was in a state of financial panic. At the height of the crisis, a new right-center ministry was formed under Raymond Poincaré, the nationalistic wartime president who now assumed the more active role of prime minister. His firm, conservative leadership soon restored financial confidence. Savings were effected by reducing government expenses and plugging tax loopholes, thus making it possible to stem the flow of gold and securities abroad. The franc was eventually stabilized at a rate of five cents, though this was only twenty percent of its prewar value.

In the late 1920's the national economy enjoyed an Indian summer of surprising prosperity. The northeastern provinces had been rebuilt to a high level of industrial efficiency. The return of the iron and textile industries of Alsace-Lorraine had been a definite stimulus, so that France had become one of the world leaders in steel and textile exports. Perhaps equally important was the balance between industry and farming, which made the French economy nearly self-sufficient and helped cushion it against fluctuations in foreign trade. At the same time, there remained significant weaknesses in the economic structure. For one thing, French industry was still relatively narrow in scope, and individual factories were small compared with those of certain other countries. If industrialists should be faced with less favorable conditions than those of the 1920's, they would probably prefer security to further expansion and modernization. Moreover, the southern provinces were not keeping pace economically with those of the northeast, and there were still numerous semi-stagnant sectors retarding growth of the economy as a whole. Equally serious was the fact that workers' salaries had not advanced as fast as had productivity. Though the working-class movement had decreased both in size and militancy throughout the 1920's, ample evidence proved that this was not because the proletariat felt satisfied.

Poincaré retired in 1929, having enjoyed the longest continuous tenure in office of any premier in interwar France. No other leader was able to maintain unity so well as he, and little was accomplished during the three years of rightist government that followed. The Chamber of Deputies fell back once more on traditional pork-barreling and lobbying methods, ignoring or postponing treatment of serious issues. With the exception of a restrictied social insurance bill passed in 1930, it refused to do anything either to increase the government's resources or provide constructive social legislation for the nation at large.

The Depression France's relative economic self-sufficiency protected it from the full effects of the depression until 1932; after that, production spiraled downward with distressing rapidity and there was no relief in sight. A new lower-middle-class Radical government was organized, but it was soon overthrown only to be followed by a succession of short-lived ministries representing the center groups of the political spectrum.

As the economic crisis deepened, agitation by political extremists mounted. There were several petty riots in Paris, and rumors of Radical party collusion in a minor financial fraud (the "Stavisky Affair") provided more grist for the propaganda mills of Communist and right-wing authoritarians. Efforts to restore order in the Paris streets provoked a major incident when, on February 6, 1934, members of ultra-rightist and nationalist groups, together with the Paris mob, rioted before the government buildings. They threatened to storm the Chamber of Deputies and could only be quelled with gunfire. At least fifteen people were killed. After the most extensive bloodshed in Paris since the Commune of 1871, the government was forced to resign.

The moderate-conservative ministry that followed was no more effective than its predecessors, and several cabinets muddled their way through until it was time for the next elections. The strong man of the government during 1935 was Pierre Laval (1883–1945), successively foreign minister and prime minister. Laval had risen to the top through opportunism and had no faith in French democracy. As prime minister, he was relatively conservative; the only policy he offered to cope with the depression was relentless deflation. The more salaries were lowered and the tighter France held to the gold standard, the deeper the economy fell. Businessmen then cut back production even further, redoubling the effects of the slump.

The Popular Front The old pattern of French politics broke up under the strain. On the right, middle-class conservatives were beginning to renounce parliamentary government in favor of a variety of new fascist-type organizations. On the left, a "Popular Front" was formed in 1935 between Radicals, Socialists, and Communists. Communist cooperation was a new development, for during the 1920's, the Moscow-directed Communist parties, bent on a purely Communist revolution, had shunned collaboration with other groups. The advance of nazism and other fascist movements in the 1930's took the initiative away from Communist radicalism, throwing the Russian leadership on the defensive; hence it was in the interest of international communism to prop up nonfascist governments. This was the mission of the Popular Front. In France, concern to save the democratic

Léon Blum, Premier of France in 1936. Léon Blum, leader of the French Socialist party, became prime minister of the new Popular Front government in 1936. He represented the main attempt to achieve social and economic reform in France during the 1930's, but support dwindled and he did not long remain in power. (French Embassy Press and Information Division.)

republic from the authoritarian right coincided with a great need to solve unemployment and restore hope to the nation.

The Popular Front won an overwhelming victory in the 1936 elections, and the new prime minister was the eminently refined Socialist leader Léon Blum (1872–1950). His first task was to deal with a sit-down strike by one million industrial workers who demanded better conditions. Blum quickly negotiated a settlement that provided for a forty-hour week, a minimum wage, and paid vacations. The government went on to nationalize the Bank of France and a number of armament industries, and provide a marketing service for grain farmers.

This was the extent of Blum's reforms, for the coalition began to break down in less than a year. The Communists promoted their own interests, and hampered a more extensive program. The Radicals, fearing that Blum would take France too far left, started to desert the Popular Front. The workers demanded safeguards against inflation, while the rightists did all they could to block the government. Beset by this host of antagonists, Blum's cabinet collapsed in mid-1937 and the Popular Front, the only imaginative effort in France to cope with the depression, dissolved.

In 1938, the country was economically as stagnant as ever; politically, it was even more divided. Communism was rapidly gaining ground among the workers, while conservatives and nationalists were now saying "Better Hitler than Blum" in order to avoid any danger of revolution. Such a disunited and dispirited France was in no condition to meet the challenge of nazism.

SPAIN Spain had been neutral throughout the First World War and had profited greatly from the sale of raw materials, textiles, and metals to Britain and France during those four years. Yet, while the economy flourished, political and social problems increased. Prices rose more rapidly than wages, the political parties dissolved into quarreling factions, and the army officers threatened to rebel against the government if they did not receive higher rank and pay. The first general strike in Spanish history was attempted in 1917, and liberal politicians demanded a constituent assembly to draft a new constitution. After the war ended, the bottom dropped out of the international market, throwing many Spanish industries into serious depression. The most progressive region of the country, Catalonia, was the home of a local separatist movement and also the scene of four years of bloody labor disputes. Anarcho-syndicalists turned to violence, and the police replied in kind. The liberal constitutional system seemed helpless to maintain order.

The Primo de Rivera Dictatorship There was widespread consensus in Spain about the need for a change, but little agreement on the form this should take. For nearly a century, the ultimate power had been the army, but it proved woefully ineffective in 1921, when native insurgents in Morocco inflicted a great defeat and 9,000 Spanish troops were lost. The king, Alfonso XIII, who had meddled in political and military affairs, received much of the criticism that swept Spain after the Moroccan debacle. To save the monarchy, restore order, and try to encourage orderly development, General Miguel Primo de Rivera (1870–1930) established a military dictatorship in September 1923.

Though Primo de Rivera expressed admiration for Mussolini, this was not a fascist government. The Primo de Rivera regime was, instead, a military-based government without any precise political or ideological foundation. The dictator followed a highly personal, intuitive approach and claimed to be serving merely as caretaker until it was feasible to restore constitutional rule. In conjunction with the French, he finally put down the Moroccan rebellion in 1926–1927, while easily repressing disturbances inside Spain. For several years, the country enjoyed domestic peace and relative economic prosperity, and much of the population tacitly accepted the regime. However, when it later developed that Primo had no concrete plans for restoring parliamentary government, opposition increased. After the economy began to sag at the end of 1929, Primo's regime was doomed. Pressure from the king and fellow officers forced him to resign in January 1930.

The Spanish Republic Alfonso XIII hoped to make a gradual transition back to constitutional government, but even conservatives were losing sympathy for the crown, and the Spanish monarchy collapsed in the spring of 1931. A democratic Republic was proclaimed, and immediately fell under the control of moderate leftists. A new Republican constitution provided for civil liberty and social reform, but alienated the large Catholic population by separating church and state and denying the right of Catholic education

Rebel Moroccan Machine-Gunners, Tetuán, Spanish Morocco, 1924. The major colonial war of the 1920's was fought by Spain and France to establish firm control of their respective protectorates in Morocco. Abd el-Krim's Moroccan insurgents temporarily shook the power of European empire and to some extent presaged later national liberation movements, though finally defeated. (Radio Times Hulton Picture Library.)

for children. Government economic intervention in favor of trade unionists antagonized businessmen, and the concession of regional autonomy to Catalonia offended many Spanish patriots. A conservative coalition won the next elections in 1933.

The Socialist, Communist, and anarcho-syndicalist movements in Spain insisted that conservative rule would be the prelude to a fascist dictatorship. They launched a revolutionary insurrection in northern Spain in October 1934, that was put down by the army but left Spain divided into two bitterly opposed camps. All the leftist parties joined together in a Spanish "Popular Front" for the next elections in February 1936, which they won by a narrow margin. A cabinet of leftist moderates took office, but Socialists, Communists, and anarcho-syndicalists spoke of the new ministry as the prelude to violent leftist revolution. During the spring of 1936, the economy was plagued by the greatest wave of strikes in Spanish history. Militant conservatives, fascists, and activists within the army prepared for armed resistance. By mid-1936, Spain was on the verge of civil war.

THE SMALL COUNTRIES OF NORTH-CENTRAL EUROPE

Middle-class liberalism had failed to solve many of the problems raised by the depression in the larger countries of western and central Europe. Unwillingness to resort to state intervention or radical measures left the liberals unable to cope with the unparalleled economic problems of the time. Faced with the immobility of their governments, some citizens sought a solution by abandoning political liberalism in favor of authoritarian regimes capable of regimenting the economy.

This dilemma was never posed in Denmark, Norway, and Sweden, where pragmatic, evolutionary socialist parties wielded great influence. During the depression, they used the power of the state to subsidize sagging portions of the economy and to increase social insurance of almost every kind, thus placing an economic cushion under the lower and lower-middle classes. The government did not hesitate to set up businesses of its own for certain consumer items, and a substantial amount of home construction was also subsidized. Moreover, private cooperatives for both producers and consumers abounded, lowering prices and facilitating trade. As a consequence, there was less suffering due to the depression in Scandinavia than anywhere else in Europe. The cooperative attitude and democratic manner with which the new policies were carried out did not threaten any of the necessary rights of the individual but only increased true freedom. Switzerland, Holland, and Belgium were neither so forceful nor so successful in dealing with the depression, but the role of the government in economic life was increased in these countries also.

The postwar years witnessed the extension of democratic political privileges in most countries of north-central Europe. With the new Danish constitution of 1915 and amendments in both Holland and Belgium, universal suffrage had become established in five of the northern states. Belgium, the most industrialized of the small countries, removed another injustice when labor unions were legalized in 1921. The sixth of these countries, Switzerland, possessed the oldest representative government of them all, but was the only one that still excluded women from the vote.

Belgium, which suffered so greatly during the war, had made an energetic economic comeback during the 1920's. Its most serious political problem was due to ethnic division, not poverty. The Dutch-speaking Flemish inhabitants had developed a strong nationalist spirit of their own and demanded equal rights in culture, commerce, and government with the French-speaking Walloons, who had largely dominated the country. The problem was met by a series of laws passed after 1921, dividing the country into two separate administrative units on the basis of language, and extending this parity into the army and schools. The main political problem of neighboring Holland, on the other hand, did not concern domestic affairs but rather the rising tide of nationalist rebellion in its huge and wealthy colonial empire of the Dutch East Indies.

CULTURAL CHANGES BETWEEN THE WARS

New Forms of Artistic Expression The two foci of the art world in the 1920's were Paris and Berlin. The French capital quickly resumed its role as center of literature and the plastic arts, which it had held since the mid-nineteenth century. Young rebels continued to reject the world of "bourgeois" reality, and new movements such as "Dadaism" and "surrealism" enjoyed great vogue. "Dada" was supposedly taken from the name of a child's rocking horse. It had originated in 1917 as a protest against the war and, as a total rejection of contemporary society, it was anti-creative, anti-intellectual, and nihilistic. Practitioners of Dadaism insisted that the world made no sense, but that meaningful rebellion could be registered through untrammeled self-expression, with the most empty or absurd content—Dadaists made poems out of words clipped at random from newspapers; their paintings were often a melange of grotesque and inharmonious objects slapped together on canvas. The spirit of Dadaism was well expressed by the Spanish painter Salvador Dalí, who once read a poem to a gathering with his head encased in an ocean diver's helmet, from which no sound could emerge.

"Why Not Sneeze, Rose Sèlavy, 1921" by Marcel Duchamp.

Dadaism in turn led to surrealism, which strove for a "superreality" by discarding ordinary logic and sense perception to delve into the depths of the unconscious. Instead of careful, reflective work, some surrealist writers attempted what they called "automatic writing," letting their unconscious feelings flow into verbal expression as best they could, as though under hypnosis or in a dream. Surrealist painting attempted to reproduce the forms of subconscious feeling, often resulting in weird scenes and phantasmagoric shapes. In this way, surrealism was positive and doctrinaire, for it was specifically intended to reveal a new dimension of the human spirit.

A similar tendency in painting was found in the new school of "abstract" art, which eliminated most recognizable content to make of painting a composition of abstract forms and color tones. For the abstractionist, the mere arrangement of shapes and shades on canvas was the goal of painting. Though such work had been begun by Russian artists before 1914, the originator of this trend in the West was the Dutch painter Piet Mondrian, who developed a rigid, mathematical style of lines and geometric shapes.

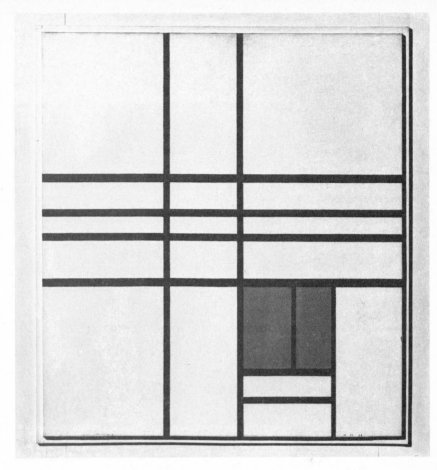

Composition by Piet Mondrian, 1936. Mondrian, a Dutch artist, developed one of the most severe and distinctive styles of abstract painting. Form is ignored, and the painting reduced to lines and planes of color. Abstractionism was a main contributor to what the Spanish philosopher Ortega y Gasset called the "dehumanization of art." (Philadelphia Museum of Art.)

The vogue of abstractionism gained greater currency during the fascist decade of the 1930's and the horrors of the Second World War, becoming, after 1945, the dominant style in western painting.

It was during the interwar period that the new architectural style known as "modern architecture" or the "international style" took form. The principal creators of modern architecture were the German Walter Gropius and the Frenchman Le Corbusier. Their goal was an honesty of design that employed structural steel and other new construction materials in a way clearly consistent with their function, avoiding all purposeless details and trim. Modern architecture eventually became more popular in the United States and Scandinavia than in most parts of continental Europe, though after 1950 it was the predominant new architectural style throughout the western world.

It was in Berlin, perhaps even more than in Paris and other cities, that the most varied and heterogeneous artistic life was carried on during the 1920's. There were definite reasons for this, since Germany was a well-educated nation whose social fabric had been torn more severely by the war and the inflation than that of any other western country. Sensitive young Germans were groping for a new creed or, at least, a new style. There was widespread feeling that restraint and inhibition were outmoded, that anything went and nothing was barred. The dominant esthetic movement in Germany was called "expressionism," continuing a prewar trend that

Audience Reaction at One of the Early German Movies, Berlin, 1919. The era of the 1920's constituted the first great age of the movies in popular western culture. Though these motion pictures were silent, the very novelty of such entertainment heightened its impact. (Hoover Institution Archives.)

stressed expression of any feeling, color, mood, shape, or desire simply to affirm the creative act, or perhaps, simply to affirm action in itself. Expressionists were almost always radical antitraditionalists. They looked toward a new, different, and more authentic society which they were never quite able to define. The leading prewar expressionist poet, George Trakl (1884–1914), had been killed at the beginning of the conflict, and other originators of the movement had also perished by 1918; but the expressionist vogue continued through the 1920's. Such painters as Ernst Ludwig Kirchner (1880–1938) helped to serve as a link between prewar and postwar expressionism. In many ways, this German art movement was similar to surrealism, save that it expressed deep and irrational emotions in more direct human form, rather than subordinating them to formal and dehumanized esthetic techniques.

The West European Novel Dadaism, surrealism, and expressionism had many exponents in literature as well as in the graphic arts, but the significant achievements in European fiction were more directly related to the refined, introspective novel of psychological realism that had flourished before the First World War. The most important single work of these years was the seven-volume novel *Remembrance of Things Past* (1913–1923) by the French writer Marcel Proust (1871–1922). It established the "stream of conscious-ness" technique, which dealt with the individual mind and personal feelings evoked by chance objects or internal analysis. Proust's language was so rich and precise, his sense of organization so careful, his mastery of mood so fine that his work was soon recognized as a masterpiece.

In Britain, a similar technique was used by Virginia Woolf (1882–1941), who eschewed external drama to concentrate on the inner feelings of sensi-tive and introspective subjects. This sort of psychological novel was, how-ever, too subtle, complex, and involved to appeal to any but a narrow circle of admirers.

The leading German novelist of the period, Thomas Mann (1875–1955), attempted a somewhat broader range of subject matter. He, too, was pri-marily concerned with individual values and the psychic process, but devel-oped a symbolist form that projected individual moral and psychological struggles in terms of the fate of a social class or an entire civilization. His masterpiece, *The Magic Mountain* (1924), was a symbolic novel interpreting the dilemma of European society on the eve of the First World War through the carefully analyzed perplexities of patients in a tuberculosis sanitarium.

The climax of the psychological novel came in the work of the Irish writer James Joyce (1882–1941). His long, verbally frank *Ulysses* (1922) was composed of internal monologues on a day's experience by three different characters. A later novel, *Finnegan's Wake* (1939), interwove drunken phan-tasy, dreams, and subconscious feelings in a brilliant, chaotic melange.

Social Criticism   It was not surprising that one of the most widely read books in the postwar years was *The Decline of the West*, first published in 1918 by an obscure German historian named Oswald Spengler (1880–1936). This work fitted the mood of many German intellectuals after defeat. Spengler looked at western civilization from a biological point of view and decided that it was in a state of decadence comparable to old age. The vital forces of the west were dying, such factors as faith and social discipline fast disappearing. On the one hand, western society was becoming more anarchic; on the other, weaker and less assertive. The ebullient confidence of an earlier day had vanished. In its place was left a timid, bureaucratic middle class, fearful of the future and unable even to govern its own society. For Spengler, the only thing that could save the West would be the appear-ance of vigorous and dynamic new leaders, who could take a flabby people in hand and establish a new sense of order and values, a new driving purpose. *The Decline of the West* did not hold up a mirror to western society as a whole so much as it did to France and central Europe, where political division and social confusion sapped the marrow of the population and made a successful settlement of the issues of the First World War almost impossi-ble.

The depression was a time of cultural change throughout Europe, for the great ambitions and sense of freedom of the artist in the 1920's had eventually dwindled into confusion of values. Many of the most purely "esthetic" painters and poets dropped their artistic notions and joined forces with the pseudo-religious new political ideologies, some becoming fascists and many more lining up with the Communist party. The totalitarian regimes of central and eastern Europe denounced the individualistic tendencies of modern western art as decadent and immoral. Both Nazis and Communists banned exhibitions of abstract painting and discouraged the production of esthetically refined or esoteric literature. All the dictatorial regimes emphasized a direct, massive, neoclassical style, which was particularly noticeable in the construction of their public buildings. They rewarded "positive," "constructive" achievement in the arts, such as the telling of simple, edifying tales or the use of grandiose poetic rhetoric. Stalinist Russia enforced a new doctrine of "socialist realism," which meant that literature was supposed to make a direct contribution to the triumph of socialism.

In the West, intellectuals were going through a crisis similar to that experienced by society as a whole. They felt that they had to take part in the great social and ideological struggles of the age, that they had to be engaged in the battle. The most vocal largely agreed that the present socio-economic order was insufficient, and many writers became outright Marxists, seeking a new social philosophy that could transcend both fascism and economic exploitation. Hundreds of them participated in the various Popular Fronts, for they wanted all men of good will to stand together to bring in a free, just, new order. The elaborate and often experimental literary style of the 1920's thus gave way to a new sobriety, a more common touch, which had direct impact.

Of all the new writers, the most effective was the proto-Communist French novelist, André Malraux. His gripping *Man's Fate* (1933) chronicled the frustration of the Communist movement in China during 1927 and spotlighted, as no other book of those years, the intense moral struggle behind the political issues of the day. Five years later, in *Man's Hope* (1938), he produced a similar, though less effective, narrative about life and death conflict in the Spanish Civil War.

Religion For European Christianity, the interwar decades were not a happy time. The Christian churches seemed to have little to say to hundreds of millions of people trapped by social and economic crisis. The Vatican signed concordats with Fascist Italy (1929) and Nazi Germany (1933), and many commentators interpreted Pope Pius XI's encyclical *Quadragesimo Anno* (1931), which recommended the formation of cooperative associations for workers and employers, as endorsement of the corporate state. However, the Catholic Church became inevitably involved in disputes with the totalitarian regimes as the 1930's wore on. In France, a number of Catholic writers such as Gabriel Marcel and Emmanuel Mounier tried to outline a new form of Christian social democracy that could overcome the apostasy of the lower classes and the spiritual and economic stagnation of the bourgeoisie.

The Protestant churches enjoyed no more success than Catholicism in withstanding the social aberrations of interwar Europe, for the same factors that had weakened Christian influence before 1914 were still operative (see

Part XIV, Chapter 2). The most significant new Protestant theologian during these years was the Swiss Calvinist Karl Barth. Conservative and neo-orthodox, Barth opposed "liberal" theology and insisted on a return to the original articles of Christian faith and Biblical precept, relying on the will and grace of God rather than human intellect or worldly assertiveness. Over a period of forty years, he was to produce a long series of theological works and Biblical commentaries. Barth's theology was not based upon a narrow exclusiveness, but included so many possibilities that a leading Catholic commentator has called it "the strongest development of Protestantism and the closest approximation to Catholicism." Though not primarily concerned with the social dimensions of religion, Barth indicated that the modern social crisis might lose much of its urgency if nominal Christians ever learned to exhibit simple faith in God's grace. He clearly recognized Nazism and fascism as basic perversions, and his work served as a strong encouragement to Christian anti-Nazi resistance in Germany.

FURTHER READING   The basic history of Great Britain between the wars is still C. L. Mowat, *Britain Between the Wars* (1955). Robert Graves and Alan Hodge, *The Long Weekend, 1918–1939* (1939), is an informal social history. Two biographies of key British leaders are G. M. Young, *Stanley Baldwin* (1952); and Keith Feiling, *The Life of Neville Chamberlain* (1946). C. F. Brand, *The British Labour Party* (1964), treats the growth of Labour; and A. J. Youngson, *Britain's Economic Growth, 1920–1966* (1967), charts economic change. F. S. Northedge, *The Troubled Giant: Britain Among the Great Powers* (1966), is perhaps the best treatment of interwar British diplomacy.

Three key works on the left and liberal sectors of French politics between the wars are Robert Wohl, *French Communism in the Making, 1914–1924* (1966); P. J. Larmour, *The French Radical Party in the 1930's* (1964); and Nathanael Greene, *Crisis and Decline: French Socialism in the Popular Front Era* (1968). The top biography is Joel Colton, *Léon Blum* (1966). On the collapse of Spanish liberalism, see Gabriel Jackson, * *The Spanish Republic and Civil War* (1965); and S. G. Payne, *Politics and the Military in Modern Spain* (1967), and * *The Spanish Revolution* (1970). Two useful introductions to Scandinavia are F. D. Scott, *The United States and Scandinavia* (1950); and J. H. Wuorinen, * *Scandinavia* (1965).

For general treatment of west European culture between the wars, many of the works cited for Part XIV, Chapter 2 are also useful here. On the new architecture, see Jurgen Joedicke, *A History of Modern Architecture* (1959). Richard Samuel and R. H. Thomas, *Expressionism in German Life, Literature and the Theater, 1910–1924* (1939), is helpful. Two direct approaches to Spengler and Barth are through H. S. Hughes, *Oswald Spengler* (1952), and Karl Barth's own * *Church Dogmatics* (1962).

*Books available in paperback edition are marked with an asterisk.

7 The Coming of the Second World War, 1933-1940

German nationalists had never accepted Germany's defeat in the First World War and had always insisted on altering the terms of the postwar settlement to Germany's advantage. After the Nazi regime came to power, Hitler exploited this feeling to the utmost and subjected it to a radical goal of German military domination. German expansionism was fueled not merely by a desire for revenge, but also by the sufferings of the depression—which made many Germans want a stronger, more secure role in Europe; by internal conflict before 1933—which made nationalists eager to cement unity by confrontation with other nations; and by the international disunity of the European state system, divided among a series of divergent powers that found it almost impossible to coordinate their interests and policies. Most of all, however, German expansionism was motivated by the ideology of nazism, the most extreme form of nationalism in history. Nazism was based on the twin concepts of race and space. It held that Germany needed more space to achieve economic security for an expanding population and that German racial superiority entitled it to seize the territory that Germans required. The combination of race plus space meant war.

Hitler seized the initiative in foreign affairs not long after rising to power in Germany, and for the next five years met surprisingly little resistance from Britain and France. There were a variety of reasons for the relative inaction of the western democracies. Not the least was a feeling of guilt, especially in Britain, about the terms of the Treaty of Versailles. Many public leaders persisted in thinking that Germany demanded no more than its rightful place among nations. Moreover, much of the natural elite of western Europe had died in the First World War; the dominant figures of the 1930's were old and irresolute. Most of all, memory of the ghastly losses in the last conflict encouraged an emphasis on peace at almost any price.

Adolf Hitler's goal was to achieve German dominance in Europe. This meant destruction of the Treaty of Versailles and the entire "system" connected with it; especially, this meant the assertion of German hegemony over eastern Europe, where the new states were smaller and weaker. The Fuehrer's outlook was thus basically continental and did not extend beyond the European mainland. Furthermore, it took Hitler several years, as we have seen, to consolidate his power in Germany. Despite his hysterical rantings on certain occasions, Hitler had considerable patience as well as strong nerve.

His immediate objective in 1933 was to end the armament restrictions imposed on Germany. In October 1933, after France refused to grant the equality of armed strength Hitler had requested, Germany withdrew from the League of Nations.

The emergence of a dynamic and aggressive dictator across the Rhine inevitably caused French leaders grave concern. Since Britain preferred to avoid involvement in continental affairs as much as possible, France's best hope for a counterweight against Germany was to strengthen her alliances with the small nations of the Little Entente—Czechoslovakia, Yugoslavia, and Rumania—in east-central Europe. The division and lack of resolution that characterized French politics in the 1930's made it hard, however, for the French to build an active policy. In practice, it proved very difficult to coordinate military and diplomatic plans with the smaller states east of Germany.

The only country besides Germany to change its policy radically after 1933 was the Soviet Union. Since coming to power, the nominal goal of the Communist regime had been to promote the revolutionary overthrow of other European governments. In the Nazi regime, however, Stalin saw a dire menace, and so tried to draw closer to the liberal western nations previously scorned by the Communists. Less than a year after Germany pulled out of the League of Nations, Russia joined that body and became the leading advocate of collective security, by which all member nations should join together to keep the peace. In 1935, the Communists espoused the doctrine of a Popular Front of all leftist and liberal political forces throughout Europe to hold the line against the advance of fascism.

Italy's Conquest of Ethiopia The first major military aggression by a European power after 1920 did not come from Germany, but from Italy. Mussolini's regime had not engaged in military aggression during its first twelve years. But Hitler's rise began to shift the power balance from stability toward aggressive action, while the protracted economic depression led Mussolini to seek new glory abroad to bolster his prestige and take the minds of Italians off their troubles.

The leadership of a second-rate power like Italy would not normally think of attacking another European power on its own, for fear of the complications involved. During the preceding generation, however, it had become standard practice to seize territory inhabited by nonwhites in Africa. Italian nationalism had failed in its first major African enterprise, when Italian forces were driven out of Ethiopia in 1896. By 1935 Ethiopia was the only region in Africa not governed or protected by a western power, and Mussolini decided to regain this erstwhile sphere of Italian influence and wipe out the humiliation of 1896. Since the direct interests of no European power were involved, the Italian government calculated that Ethiopia might be conquered with impunity.

The invasion began in October 1935. The Council of the League of Nations responded by formally branding Italy as an aggressor. It also voted an economic embargo on the shipment of certain kinds of materials to Italy, but excepted oil, without which the Italian armed forces could not have moved. Thus the partial embargo had scant effect, and the conquest of Ethiopia was completed by May 1936.

Italy's blatant success ended hope for the effectiveness of the League of Nations. Dictators could presumably ignore the League with impunity, and the star of authoritarianism was in the ascendence. Italy's triumph raised Mussolini to his peak of popularity. The sacrifices and repression imposed by dictatorship were gladly accepted so long as they led to imperial victory.

German Rearmament While Mussolini had been preparing his moves against Ethiopia, Adolf Hitler had, in March 1935, launched the rearmament of Germany. Military expenditures would not reach massive proportions until 1937, but the German intention to develop a major army was clear. The protest of the western powers was relatively mild, for none of them had ever managed to adopt a disarmament program, and it seemed unjust to deny to Germany the arms other nations refused to surrender.

Hitler won yet another triumph in 1935 when a plebiscite was held in the industrial Saar basin, which had been detached from Germany since 1919. Though most Saar inhabitants knew of the political tyranny that Nazi control would bring, ninety-five percent of them freely voted for incorporation into the Reich. The appeal of German nationalism and Hitler's dynamic new state seemed irresistible.

These successes encouraged Hitler to take advantage of the political uncertainty in France preceding the elections of 1936 to march German troops into the demilitarized Rhineland. The Versailles treaty had stipulated that Germany was not to rearm the entire left bank of the Rhine, but on March 7, 1936, German units were moved forward all the way to the French border. Once more, Hitler acted as if he were trying to exercise no more than the normal prerogative of any chief of state, occupying and arming the entire national frontier.

Hitler's move had been a pure gamble, for the French army was still much stronger than the German forces and could have thrown the latter out of the Rhineland with little trouble. Hitler had even given orders for immediate withdrawal if the French moved against them, but the latter could not make up their minds to do anything on their own, while the British government did not care to quarrel with Germany over the right to prepare border defenses. Joyous crowds greeted the German troops, and a major step in the revival of German power was completed without opposition. Rearmament of Germany's western frontier meant that in the future the French army would have to concentrate on this line, and would have great difficulty lending assistance to its allies in east-central Europe.

THE SPANISH
CIVIL WAR

Soon after the German reoccupation of the Rhineland and the Italian seizure of Ethiopia an explosive conflict broke out in Spain that threatened to involve all Europe. On July 17, 1936, portions of the Spanish army began a revolt against the leftist Republican government. The military coup was a failure, but the insurgents did win control of half the country. In the sector held by the Republic, a far-reaching social revolution began under the leadership of the anarcho-syndicalists and the Socialists. In much of this zone, churches were closed, municipal governments taken over by militia committees, businesses confiscated, and workers' cooperatives established. The conflict was characterized by fierce atrocities on both sides. The revolutionaries shot thousands of priests and "class enemies," while the army organized a "white terror" of its own.

Foreign Involvement The military rebels lacked the strength in the Spanish peninsula for a clear-cut victory. A few days after the revolt began, they sent representatives to Hitler and Mussolini asking for supplies and aircraft to help transport their main field army from Morocco to Spain. Both Hitler and Mussolini were at first reluctant to be involved, but each favored the defeat of the Spanish left and the establishment of a friendly right-wing government in Spain. By the end of July 1936, both Germany and Italy were sending small quantities of aircraft and munitions to the Nationalist rebels.

To put down the rebellion, the Republican regime had to purchase military equipment from abroad. Under international law, it had the right to buy arms from any other nation for suppression of an internal rebellion. The Popular Front government of France was at first willing to sell equipment to the Spanish left, but soon became alarmed at the prospect of being sucked into war with Germany over mutual participation in the Spanish conflict. The British were even less inclined to get involved, and therefore the two democratic governments decided on a formula of "nonintervention," whereby all nations would abstain from intervening in the civil war and would also curtail sales of military supplies. This presumably would confine the fighting to Spain itself and bring it to a speedy end.

Germany and Italy did all they could to delay any agreement on nonintervention, hoping in the meantime to provide enough aid to the rebels to enable them to win. On October 1, 1936, General Francisco Franco was named by his fellow officers as head of the new Nationalist state, and Franco's small forces converged on the Spanish capital.

At this point, another great power—the Soviet Union—decided to increase its own involvement. Through the Spanish Communist party, the Soviet government had been actively intervening in Spanish affairs for several years and had helped to precipitate the Civil War. During the first months of fighting, however, Stalin had sent only limited assistance to the Spanish left. When it seemed that Franco was about to win a military victory with fascist assistance, Russian aid was increased. Spanish leftist leaders were persuaded to ship most of the gold reserve of the Bank of Spain to Moscow, and sizable quantities of Russian material arrived in October 1936. These supplies, together with a Red Army military advisory mission and a Communist-recruited international volunteer force called the "International Brigades," were a major factor in halting Franco's advance at the very edge of Madrid.

The major role in organizing resistance on the Republican side was played by the Spanish Communist party, which swelled greatly in size. The fact that the leftist forces had to depend almost exclusively on Russian aid gave the Communists great influence, and they filled most of the command positions in the new Spanish "People's Army" that was organized by the Republicans in 1937. At the same time, the Communists were primarily responsible for moderating the social and economic revolution in the Republican zone. They helped to restore the authority of a reorganized Republican government, arguing that a facade of parliamentary democracy must be maintained in order to win support from the western powers.

Meanwhile, the French and British succeeded in getting all major powers to sign a nonintervention agreement. A permanent Nonintervention Committee was established at London to guarantee that the other governments would stay out of the Spanish conflict. Germany, Italy, and Russia participated with the greatest cynicism, none of the three having any intention of abiding by the agreement. All evidence that the totalitarian powers were violating the accord was ignored by Britain and France, who were determined to avoid the risk of an international war mushrooming out of the Spanish conflict.

Franco's Victory Throughout 1937 and 1938, Germany and Italy sent large amounts of materiel to Franco's forces, the Italians providing a field army that at one point amounted to 40,000 men. General Franco slowly organized a new National Syndicalist state in his sector of Spain, with a state party and a corporate economic organization somewhat similar to that of Fascist Italy. Franco was a careful, calculating pragmatist primarily interested in achieving absolute political unity under his personal control. The main spiritual and emotional support for his government came from the Spanish Catholic church, which in a pastoral letter of July 1, 1937, officially labeled the Nationalist effort a "sacred crusade," and in return regained all the privileges of which the Church had been deprived by the Republic.

By contrast, the leftist forces were weakened by severe internal division and waning military support. After mid-1937, Stalin reduced his military commitment in Spain for fear of becoming overextended. Communist influence in the wartime Republican government continued to increase all the while, provoking intense resentment among non-Communist groups. Lack of supplies and severe losses left the "People's Army" gravely weakened by the close of 1938. At the end of March 1939, Republican resistance collapsed.

Consequences of the Spanish Civil War The outcome of the Spanish Civil War was a signal victory for the fascist powers. It showed that Britain and France were reluctant to challenge the initiative of Hitler and Mussolini, and it established in Spain a dictatorship that was hostile to western democracy. Another result of the war was to draw Nazi Germany and Fascist Italy into close association. Until 1936, the two fascist dictators, Hitler and Mussolini, had looked askance at one another. Mussolini had been jealous of Hitler, had tried to thwart Nazi ambitions in Austria, and had opposed German rearmament in 1935. Germany was, however, the only state to show a friendly attitude to Italy during the Ethiopian affair, and only a few months

Hitler and Goering Review German Troops, 1938. By 1938 German rearmament had been in full swing for two years. Nonetheless, German forces were still weaker than those of France and Britain, or possibly the Soviet Union as well. (UPI.)

after that episode concluded, both Hitler and Mussolini found themselves intervening on the Nationalist side in the Spanish Civil War. It had been obvious from the beginning that Hitler and Mussolini had much in common, since both led militaristic, nationalist dictatorships. In power and dynamism, however, there was no comparison. Germany was becoming infinitely more potent, so that Hitler could carry out the program of expansion and conquest which for Mussolini largely remained in the field of rhetoric. In October 1936, Germany and Italy signed the "Axis Pact," or Anti-Comintern Pact, pledging the cooperation of both governments in resisting international Communism. This, in effect, created an informal diplomatic alliance, and after the end of 1936 it became more and more common to regard the two dictators as partners or allies. Such a status had been Mussolini's hope, but Hitler was the dominant figure from the beginning. The Italian Duce tied himself to the Fuehrer's chariot, which inexorably dragged him toward a fateful conflict.

AGGRESSION AND
APPEASEMENT

German Annexation of Austria The first step in Hitler's territorial expansion in central Europe was to unite the other independent German-speaking country, Austria, with the Third Reich. As explained in the previous chapter, since 1933 Austria had been controlled by a conservative Catholic dictatorship that feared and opposed Nazism. The murder of the Austrian dictator, Dollfuss, by Austrian Nazis in 1934 was a premature act that embarrassed Hitler. Thereafter he asserted that he had no intention of forcing Austria into union with Germany. What he had in mind was an increasing coordination of the two countries which would reduce Austria to the role of German satellite in preparation for its annexation. In 1936, the new Austrian dictator, Schuschnigg, had signed a treaty of friendship in which he promised to guide Austrian policy along lines acceptable to Germany. Schuschnigg, however, was desperately anxious to avoid falling into Hitler's snares, and began to arrest Austrian Nazis.

German Armed Forces Enter Vienna, March 1938. The Anschluss with Austria turned into a peaceful victory march for the German army. Though some of the new armored vehicles broke down on the road, they functioned well in view of the haste with which the operation was organized. This bloodless exercise offered useful experience for the invasion of Poland in the following year. (Federal Press Service, Vienna.)

In February 1938, while the Spanish Civil War was still raging, the Fuehrer called Schuschnigg to his residence in southern Germany and forced him to accept an Austrian Nazi as his minister of the interior, obtaining as well the release of all Nazis in Austrian prisons. Schuschnigg knew that only a desperate stroke could maintain his country's independence. The support of Mussolini could no longer be relied on, but Schuschnigg hoped to draw world attention to Austria's plight by a ringing affirmation from its people. He called for an immediate plebiscite of the Austrian population on his policy and the principle of Austrian independence. Hitler was furious, for if Schuschnigg's maneuver succeeded, it would be almost impossible to bring Austria into line. The Fuehrer therefore demanded postponement of the plebiscite. When Schuschnigg at first refused, the German army began to mass on the Austrian border. At this point it became clear that no one was interested in coming to the support of the Austrian dictatorship and that Hitler was indeed ready to invade Austria. Schuschnigg had no recourse save to resign; a Nazi was appointed in his stead, and the latter invited the German army to occupy Austria. Soon after, Hitler passed through his old home town of Linz and was later greeted by huge cheering throngs in Vienna. A rubber-stamp Nazi plebiscite within the next few weeks registered approximately ninety-nine percent of the population in favor of *Anschluss* (annexation) by Germany, and Austria was immediately absorbed into the Third Reich. Hitler had won another great victory without firing a shot.

The Sudeten Crisis Having won over six million Austrians to his Reich, Hitler's next target was the three million Germans—mostly farmers and shopkeepers—who lived in the mountains of western Czechoslovakia. This region, called the Sudetenland, comprised one of the most prosperous and vital parts of the country. Since its creation in 1919, Czechoslovakia had become the only progressive land in east-central Europe. The country was, however, ruled by the Czechs, who inhabited its center and governed both the Germans in the west and the Slovaks in the east. Though Slavic like the Czechs, the Slovaks were culturally and economically backward and

EXPANSION OF GERMANY
1936–August 1939

resented the dominance of their more advanced kinsmen. On the other hand, the German minority had been comparatively well treated, and at first had not shown active discontent against the Czech government. The Nazis did all they could to change this, organizing a strong nationalist movement among the Sudeten Germans which demanded complete autonomy from the Czechs.

As soon as the *Anschluss* had been completed, Hitler turned to the Czech question. The Nazis whipped up resentment in the Sudetenland while Germany applied pressure against the Czech government. Under the terms of the Little Entente, Czechoslovakia was a military ally of France, and should have been able to expect French aid in a showdown with Germany. French military leaders, however, were not anxious to help the Czechs, and pointed out all kinds of obstacles, chief of which was Germany's newly fortified western frontier. The British attitude was that an injustice had been done to the German element in Czechoslovakia and that the ideal of national self-determination expressed at Versailles could be vindicated only if the Sudeten Germans were given either complete autonomy or unification with Germany. Britain thus had little desire to support the Czech cause, whereas French conservatives were becoming more and more anxious to appease Hitler.

Throughout the spring and summer of 1938, the Nazis increased their propaganda offensive against Czechoslovakia. In May, the Czechs temporarily forced Hitler to back down by mobilizing their army on the German border. Hitler was not yet prepared for a military showdown, but his henchmen soon returned to the attack. As pressure mounted, he decided to run the risk of war by forcing the Sudeten agitation to a climax. Even though the German army had not completed rearmament, Hitler was confident that Britain and France would not support Czechoslovakia but would allow the Nazis to have their way.

The Munich Agreement By mid-September, the tension had increased to the breaking point. The British prime minister, Neville Chamberlain, went by plane to talk with Hitler in Bavaria. Chamberlain was determined to learn what Hitler's demands really were and to make the Czechs grant them. In conversation, Hitler was, as usual, very cagey. He made no concrete demands on the Czechs, only insisted that the problem must be solved immediately in accordance with the rights of the German people. This seemed to mean "self-determination," the right of Germany to annex the German-inhabited district of western Czechoslovakia. Chamberlain put heavy pressure on Beneš, the Czech president, to give in.

Beneš had already revealed the hollowness of Nazi agitation by calling in all the Sudeten leaders and demanding to hear their goals. When they had nothing more to ask than complete local autonomy, he granted that to them immediately. Beneš realized that Hitler had no concrete political demands, but planned to push the assault on Czechoslovakia as far as he could carry it. On September 21, he agreed to Chamberlain's terms for

cession of part of the Sudetenland, knowing this would only whet Hitler's appetite and reveal his insatiable ambition.

As soon as Beneš had agreed in principle to cession of part of the Sudetenland, Hitler demanded the whole district for Germany. It began to look like war and preliminary measures of mobilization were taken by the western governments. German generals were aghast, for they knew their own army was yet too weak to fight a general war. The Czech army was well trained and well equipped, numbering thirty-four divisions stationed behind admirable defensive terrain. Hitler, however, still thought he could bluff his adversaries into surrender.

In this assumption he was correct. The British recognized no responsibility to keep the Sudeten Germans inside Czechoslovakia, and were desperate to avoid a war. French leaders did acknowledge a moral obligation to the Czechs, and some of them believed that Hitler would have to be stopped soon, but France was too demoralized to make a stand alone. At the last minute, when it seemed that Hitler was about to give the order to seize the Sudetenland by force, the prudent and opportunistic Mussolini offered a way out. He proposed that the leaders of France, Britain, Italy, and Germany confer together to find the solution. Hitler, Mussolini, Chamberlain, and Daladier, the French premier, met in Munich on September 30. Chamberlain and Daladier gave way on almost every point: Germany could have the entire Sudetenland, whose occupation would begin immediately but proceed in several stages, and the final boundary would be determined by an international commission. Though Hitler did make concessions on the last two points, he got his major goal, the whole Sudetenland, without waiting.

Results of the Munich Agreement   On his return to London, Chamberlain told cheering crowds that he was bringing "peace in our time." The appeasement at Munich did not, however, preserve the peace; it merely delayed the war for one more year. Almost total surrender by France and Britain had increased Hitler's ambitions enormously, and he was annoyed that he had not proceeded to seize more. He did not think that France and Britain would ever fight unless attacked directly. "I have seen our adversaries at Munich," he said. "They are little worms."

The Munich settlement lasted only five months. At the end of February 1939, the Slovak population of the eastern half of what remained of Czechoslovakia was encouraged to rebel against the Czech government in Prague. Hitler had been posing as the friend and protector of the Slovaks; he could not afford to let the Czech government reassert its control effectively. Therefore he summoned the new Czech president, Hacha, to Berlin, and bullied him into accepting German "protection" for Czechoslovakia. Abandoned by everyone, the Czechs had given up any thought of resisting; on March 15, 1939, the German army occupied Prague. The Czech provinces of Bohemia and Moravia became a "protectorate" of the Reich, while in Slovakia a nominally "independent" government under authoritarian Catholic leadership was set up, functioning as a German satellite. Czechoslovakia had entirely disappeared.

The final dismemberment of Czechoslovakia sharply increased the concern of France and Britain, especially the latter. "Herr Hitler" had not kept his word, flagrantly breaking the Munich agreement which had been intended to preserve the inviolability of Czechoslovakia proper. Further, the occupation of Prague gave the lie to Hitler's pose of being no more than a German patriot working for the unification of all German-speaking people, for the bounds of the Reich now included millions of non-Germans.

Italian Occupation of Albania   The Munich experience had so lowered respect for the western powers that even calculating Mussolini indulged in new aggression. The Duce was greatly piqued at having been unable to participate in Hitler's triumphs, complaining, "Every time Hitler occupies a country he sends me a message." In order not to be left entirely in the shade by Hitler's occupation of Austria and Czechoslovakia, Mussolini's army occupied the tiny country of Albania on the opposite shore of the Adriatic in April 1939. Meanwhile, his Fascist propagandists were conducting a long-winded campaign, demanding the annexation of the "Italian" territories of Nice, Corsica, and Tunisia from France.

The Polish Crisis   After Munich, Hitler said, "I have no more territorial demands in Europe," but before a month had passed he was making new demands on Germany's eastern neighbor, Poland. The major German grievance against Poland since 1919 had been the existence of the "Polish Corridor," the strip of land that separated East Prussia from the rest of Germany. In spite of this, German-Polish relations had been quite amicable since Hitler's rise to power. In 1934, the two nations had signed a ten-year treaty of friendship and nonaggression, and Hitler had never displayed intense animus against Poles or seemed especially concerned about the Polish Corridor. In turn, the conservative and authoritarian government of Poland had allowed an old mutual defense treaty with France to lapse, hoping to remain on good terms with Germany. Their major enemy, as the Poles saw it, was the Soviet Union, which had nearly occupied Warsaw back in 1920. Further, the main ideological enemy of the Nazis was communism, and Hitler had sworn undying enmity to the Soviet Union. The Polish government therefore hoped to remain on good terms with Germany and play an independent role as the "sixth great power" in Europe.

All this began to change at the end of October 1938, when Ribbentrop, Hitler's foreign minister, demanded that the Poles grant Germany special transit rights through the Polish Corridor, as well as control of the great German-inhabited port city of Danzig. If this were arranged, the Germans said, Polish-German friendship might continue as before, and a joint policy might be pursued against the Soviet Union on the basis of the Anti-Comintern Pact. Poland, however, refused to make such concessions. The Polish leaders believed that they were in little danger from Germany, and that all they had to do was stand firm and Hitler would back down.

Conversely, the Fuehrer felt impelled to achieve a solution of the problem of the Corridor, for it was the principal territorial demand of German nationalists. Criticism of the separation of Danzig from Germany had been perhaps the most telling of all the territorial complaints made against the Versailles Treaty. Feeling inside Germany was much more intense over the Corridor than over the Sudeten question. A similar intensity was present among the Germanic population of the nominally Lithuanian port city of Memel. Memel had been part of Germany until 1919, but had been incorporated into the small nation of Lithuania, in spite of the fact that it was almost entirely populated by Germans. After Prague had been occupied on March 15, 1939, the citizens of Memel staged mass demonstrations demanding union with Germany. The Fuehrer called Lithuanian representatives to Berlin and forced the cession of Memel, at the northeastern tip of East Prussia, which became the latest addition to the Reich.

The Anglo-French-Polish Alliance and the Soviet Reaction The dissolution of Czechoslovakia and the annexation of Memel finally convinced the gravely disillusioned British leaders that Hitler could be held in check only by being shown that Britain and France would not tolerate German aggression eastward. French consent was won to an unconditional guarantee of the security of Poland from German attack. The Anglo-French-Polish alliance of March 1939 was an unprecedented move, marking the first time in Britain's history that the latter bound itself to the defense of an existing territorial frontier in eastern Europe. A similar guarantee was given to Rumania, and Britain began peacetime military conscription for the first time in its history. The British government had adopted a moral and political stand, but militarily the gesture meant little. Poland was out of reach of Britain's limited assistance, and was actually weaker than Czechoslovakia, for it was economically backward, its army was of poor quality, and its frontiers almost impossible to defend.

Meanwhile, Stalin watched the steady growth of German power with apprehension. He might have been willing to join the Anglo-French-Polish alliance if concessions had been made to him, but neither the Poles nor the British trusted the Soviet government. A military mission was finally dispatched to Moscow by the western powers in July 1939, but an agreement seemed unlikely. The major stumbling blocks were that Stalin wanted any anti-German alliance to guarantee all the territory along Russia's border from Finland to Rumania and make provision for Russian military cooperation in those countries. The Polish government feared Russian aggression almost as much as it did Nazi Germany, and such an arrangement was impossible.

THE BEGINNING OF WORLD WAR II

By midsummer 1939, Hitler was ready to move toward a showdown. His immediate goal was to reduce Poland to the status of a satellite state, deprived of Danzig and the Corridor, and otherwise dependent on Germany. He did not foresee a general European war during the next year because he believed that if he applied maximum pressure France and Britain would abandon Poland as they had abandoned Czechoslovakia. He therefore disregarded the pleas of some of his advisers to begin total military mobilization.

Hitler was nevertheless disturbed by Britain's firm stand. If negotiations between Russia and the western allies should result in agreement, Germany would be in a difficult situation. On the other hand, if Hitler could completely neutralize Russia, Britain and France would have to stand alone, making it more likely—according to Hitler's calculation—that they would give in. To accomplish this, Hitler undertook a radical reversal of alliances: the signing of a mutual defense treaty with Stalin that would partition eastern Europe between the two totalitarian powers.

The Nazi-Soviet Pact Deeply suspicious that he could ever obtain satisfaction from Britain and France, Stalin had already signaled his readiness to bargain with Hitler. After strong German encouragement, Ribbentrop was invited to come to Moscow, and on August 23, 1939, the most surprising diplomatic bargain of the century was made. Nazi Germany and Soviet Russia signed a nonaggression pact and agreed to consult each other on all major issues. A broad trade agreement accompanied the pact but, even more important, a secret protocol divided eastern Europe into German and Russian spheres of influence. Russia was to be allowed to dominate Finland, the Baltic states, and eastern Poland and Rumania. Stalin thus gained security against Germany and turned Hitler's wrath against Poland and the west.

Signing of the Nazi-Soviet Pact, August 1939. Under a portrait of Lenin, Ribbentrop (the German foreign minister), Molotov (the Russian foreign minister—seated), and Stalin sign the most cynical and vicious international agreement of the century. It divided eastern Europe between the two totalitarian powers and cleared the way for the start of war. (Hoover Institution Archives.)

Both signatories were satisfied, despite the breathtaking cynicism of such a deal between two dictatorships that had supposedly sworn undying enmity.

Hitler was sure that the west would grant him a free hand in Poland. On August 31, the Polish ambassador was given a list of final German demands. Hitler did not bother to wait for an answer. In the early hours of September 1, 1939, German planes struck military installations all over western Poland and armored columns crossed the border at widely separated points.

The Destruction of Poland The German tactic of *Blitzkrieg,* or "lightning war," was a radically new kind of fighting. Swarms of dive bombers attacked key centers, transportation hubs, and large cities, sowing panic and confusion among the enemy while the tanks of the armored Panzer divisions tore gaping holes in the enemy's lines and, heedless of flank attack, raced miles to the rear in deep penetrations, bypassing all main lines of defense and making it almost impossible for the enemy command to coordinate forces. The antiquated Polish army put up a brave but ineffective resistance and was torn to shreds within a fortnight.

Despite the impossibility of saving Poland, the western Allies honored their agreement. Britain and France declared war on September 3, two days after the German invasion had begun, and a general European war was underway. On September 17, when the Poles had been nearly crushed, Stalin ordered the Red army to occupy eastern Poland, which was done almost

Hitler Salutes the German Victory Parade in Warsaw, October 1939. The Polish campaign was quick and relatively bloodless, though German morale was initially not of the highest. But as soon as it was over, Hitler had to face a new war in the west that he would have preferred to avoid, at least at that time.

without resistance. By the end of September, Poland had been divided in two: Germany annexing the more populous and productive western portion, the Russians adding the eastern provinces to the Soviet empire. Like Czechoslovakia six months earlier, Poland had disappeared.

The "Phony War" in the West   The war on Germany's eastern border had thus been liquidated almost as soon as it began, but there now remained a decisive struggle with France and Britain in the west. For the time being, a general calm prevailed there. Most German forces had originally been marshaled in the east, in order to conquer Poland as swiftly as possible. On the other hand, Britain had no land army and the French were simply relying on a massive system of stationary defense barriers, the famous "Maginot Line," whose fortresses and emplacements they hoped would hold the Germans out.

In fact, almost no one went to war in 1939 with much optimism. There were no cheering crowds as in 1914; even in Germany, the appearance of an armored division in the streets of Berlin twelve months earlier had brought no sign of enthusiasm, only a glum foreboding. For seven months there was almost no activity on the western front, and as the winter of 1939–1940 dragged on, French soldiers began to call this a *drôle de guerre*, a "phony war." Few people in the West fully appreciated that this was merely to be the lull before a terrifying storm.

Aggression in the Baltic Region   While the uneasy stalemate on the Franco-German border lasted, Stalin meant to make the most of the free hand given him in eastern Europe by the Nazi-Soviet Pact. In 1939, Russia had suddenly been rehabilitated as one of the major powers in European affairs; her army was the second or third strongest in the world, and her leader was determined to push Russian authority as far as possible. After annexing eastern Poland in September 1939, the Soviet Union demanded that the three Baltic states sign mutual defense treaties permitting the establishment of Russian military bases within their borders. Under overwhelming Russian pressure, these treaties were signed in October, and Red Army units moved in immediately to set up bases.

One month later, the Soviet government requested the cession of several Baltic islands and certain strips of border territory by Finland, in order to complete Russia's defensive position in the eastern Baltic. Of all Russia's neighbors, the Finns were the most westernized and democratic. Sheltered by a harsh northern landscape and the partial fortifications of their "Mannerheim line," they were ready to resist all Russian pressure. Faced with this attitude, Stalin did not dally long, for he was determined to gain military domination of the east Baltic while the general situation favored him. At the end of November, the attack on Finland began. Though greatly outnumbered, the Finns were well prepared for war in the forests near the Arctic Circle. They fought with consummate courage, stopping the Russians with heavy losses all along the line. The entire world was soon cheering Finland in her heroic struggle with the massive Russian aggressor. Yet, though Sweden, Britain, France, and even the United States sent supplies, Finland was hopelessly outmatched. The brute strength of the Red Army slowly began to tell. As winter drew to a close, the Russians resumed the offensive, tearing a gaping hole in the Finnish line. Stalin then dictated a peace treaty, signed at the end of March 1940, that pushed the Russian border seventy miles westward.

Germany's Invasion of the Western Democracies Hitler had begun a two-front war in Europe without any real plan that would enable Germany to win a decisive encounter with France and Britain. The *Blitzkrieg* tactics that worked so well against weak forces on the Polish plains could not be easily employed against the well-fortified French frontier that was backed up by armored forces slightly superior in strength and firepower to those of Germany. The initial German plan merely called for a repetition of the opening phase of the First World War, advancing through Belgium to seize the channel ports and then facing a potential stalemate in northern France.

Throughout the autumn and early winter, Hitler had been half-hoping that the western democracies would be willing to call the whole thing off. Germany's main ambitions lay in the east, and after the conquest of Poland the Fuehrer had invited Britain and France to lay down their arms, but this they would not do. Britain, in particular, was determined to continue the struggle until Hitler gave up his ambitions and disgorged his conquests in eastern Europe.

Slowly, the British were resuming their blockade of the First World War, sealing off the North Sea to German shipping. To stop Scandinavian supplies

from flowing to Germany, Britain and France announced their intention of mining Norwegian territorial waters early in April 1940.

On April 10, the German forces beat them to the punch by overruning Denmark and carrying out amphibious landings in the major ports of Norway. The latter were so skillfully executed that much of Norway's power to resist was paralyzed. Despite considerable German losses, the invasion was soon a complete success.

In the meantime, German military leaders had belatedly devised a brilliant plan that would avoid another frontal war of attrition in northeastern France. On May 10, 1940, while lesser forces overran Holland and eastern Belgium, the main German armored units were concentrated behind one major spearhead which penetrated the Ardennes forest on the Franco-Belgian frontier. They shot through an undefended gap that the French had never supposed large armored forces could cross.

French leadership failed in the crisis. Allied units north and south of the invasion breakthrough were not coordinated, and French armored detachments were thrown into the fray piecemeal, then destroyed one by one. A strong concentration of Panzer (armored) divisions turned due west and drove through to the Channel, cutting off hundreds of thousands of French and British troops in Belgium and northern France. At the end of May, the British assembled every available craft and began a mass evacuation of Allied soldiers from the Channel port of Dunkirk. The operation was carried out with great skill and courage; by June 4 about 338,000 troops, two-thirds of them British, had been ferried across to safety in England.

The Fall of France The position of France had grown desperate. Mussolini declared war on June 10, while German divisions massed for the knockout

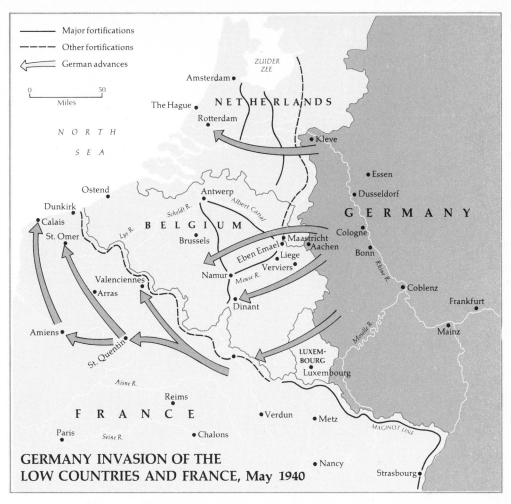

**GERMANY INVASION OF THE
LOW COUNTRIES AND FRANCE, May 1940**

Map legend:
— Major fortifications
--- Other fortifications
⇐ German advances

0   50
Miles

blow. Another great hole was torn in the French lines and Panzer units raced southward. Paris fell on June 14, and two days later the Chamber voted the premiership to the eighty-four-year-old Marshal Pétain, one-time hero of the battle of Verdun who was still a leading symbol for conservative nationalists. With the German army controlling over half of France, Pétain believed resistance was hopeless and arranged to surrender. The peace terms dictated by Hitler on June 22, 1940, divided the country in two. The northern and western provinces were occupied by the Germans, while the southeastern half of France was organized under a new authoritarian regime headed by Marshal Pétain and relegated to the status of a German satellite.

Pétain's government was known as the Vichy regime from the small resort town in central France that served as its capital. It had no constitution and no regular parliament, but was to be set up more or less on the pattern of a corporatist dictatorship. The best comparison was the equally conservative and Catholic governments of Spain and Portugal. Though old

Marshal Pétain's supporters talked of a "national revolution," there was no evidence of this. The traditional nationalist slogan of "liberty, equality, fraternity" was replaced by a new emblem, "God, family, fatherland." The Vichy regime was simply a ramshackle hodgepodge of special interests grouped behind a senile general, its main goal that of enabling what remained of France to live under Hitler's "New Order" as comfortably as possible.

The Battle of Britain   Britain was left alone to face Nazi Germany. The nation was now led by a bipartisan coalition headed by the independent Conservative Winston Churchill, for Neville Chamberlain, discredited by his prewar appeasement and tepid wartime leadership, had been replaced in May 1940. The new prime minister had served in the cabinet during the First World War and later as chancellor of the exchequer. For years he had warned of the danger posed by Hitler's ambition, and he had done more than any other man to prepare Britain to resist. In 1940, he was thus the logical choice to lead a national government in a struggle for survival. From the very beginning, he was more than equal to this task. Churchill rallied every available resource for resistance, and his eloquent voice and vigorous leadership inspired millions of Britons.

Hitler was baffled by this British determination. So far, all his enemies had collapsed. German forces dominated most of the European continent. Why should the British continue a hopeless struggle alone? Hitler announced that he was willing to grant them a generous peace without serious concessions on Britain's part; he would even guarantee the inviolability of the British Empire. Nevertheless, Britain continued to prepare to resist, as Churchill told the nation:

Upon this battle depends the survival of Christian civilization. Upon it depends our British life, and the long continuity of our institutions and our Empire. The whole fury and might of the enemy must very soon be turned on us. Hitler knows that he will have to break us in this island or lose the war. If we can stand up to him, all Europe may be free and the life of the world may move forward into broad, sunlit uplands. But if we fail, then the whole world, including the United States, including all that we have known and cared for, will sink into the abyss of a new Dark Age, made more sinister, and perhaps more protracted, by the lights of perverted science.

Let us therefore brace ourselves to our duties and so bear ourselves that, if the British Empire and its Commonwealth last for a thousand years, men will still say, "This was their finest hour."

Hitler would have preferred not to attack Britain, which he admired. To make war on Nordics was embarrassing, for it went against Nazi racial doctrine. However, since the British would not give in, Hitler approved a sketchy plan for the invasion of Britain, called Operation Sea Lion. Since proper equipment and training were lacking, German naval commanders insisted that a cross-Channel attack could not be successful unless Germany first obtained full control of the air.

In August 1940, there began three months of intensive aerial warfare over southern England and the Channel, which became known as the Battle of Britain. Though the Germans had about twice as many warplanes, the British equipment was good, the British pilots well-trained and courageous. Britain had developed a highly efficient system of air-raid warning and civil defense. Furthermore, her technicians were the first to perfect a new electronic device called radar for tracking airplanes, and by October the British had installed the first radar warning system. The *Luftwaffe's* bombing attacks caused heavy damage, but they were not enough to cripple Britain. Royal Air Force (RAF) fighters struck back with deadly effectiveness, and German losses in planes far exceeded those of the British. The Germans showed signs of indecisiveness, and kept changing their major targets. First they concentrated on ports and shipping, then switched to RAF bases, but failed to knock out either objective. In early September, the *Luftwaffe* began to rely exclusively on mass raids against London and the major southern cities. These were terrorist attacks, intended to frighten the civilian population into

1588 THE ERA OF THE WORLD WARS, 1914–1945

submission. Though the industrial town of Coventry was almost totally destroyed and parts of London were blasted into mounds of rubble and smoking ruins, the ferocity of the raids merely increased the British sense of solidarity and the common determination to resist.

By October, the weather had turned bad while German losses continued to rise, so it was finally decided to suspend Operation Sea Lion until spring. The RAF, backed by the spirited support of the entire nation, had given Nazi Germany its first military defeat. "Never in the field of human conflict," said Churchill, "have so many owed so much to so few."

FURTHER READING

A stimulating and controversial interpretation of the diplomacy of the 1930's is A. J. P. Taylor, *The Origins of the Second World War* (1961). Basic studies of the immediate origins of the war include L. B. Namier, *Diplomatic Prelude, 1938–1939* (1948), and *In the Nazi Era* (1952); and Elizabeth Wiskeman, *The Rome-Berlin Axis* (1949). For Italian policy, see Gaetano Salvemini, *Prelude to World War II* (1953); and on the Soviet Union, Max Beloff, *The Foreign Policy of the Soviet Union, 1929–1941*, 2 vols. (1947). For the *Anschluss* and the Munich crisis: Gordon Brooke-Shepherd, *Anschluss* (1963); J. W. Wheeler-Bennett, *Munich: Prologue to Tragedy* (1948); and Keith Eubank, *Munich* (1963).

Hugh Thomas, * *The Spanish Civil War* (1961, 1965), is a good one-volume study. On internal developments in the Franco zone during the Spanish Civil War, see S. G. Payne, * *Falange* (1961); and on the revolution in the Republican zone, see Burnett Bolloten, *The Grand Camouflage* (1961).

The Nazi-Soviet Pact and its breakdown are examined by G. L. Weinberg, *German-Soviet Relations, 1939–1941* (1954). For Finland, C. L. Lundin, *Finland in the Second World War* (1957). Heinz Guderian, * *Panzer Leader* (1952), is helpful on the development of *Blitzkrieg* tactics; on the campaigns in the west in 1940, see Telford Taylor, *March of Conquest* (1958). Alan S. Milward, *The German Economy at War* (1965), is the best study of German economic mobilization.

Walter Ansel, *Hitler Confronts England* (1960), treats Hitler's planning with regard to Britain in 1940–1941. On the Battle of Britain and the air war in the west, see Drew Middleton, *The Sky Suspended* (1960); Werner Baumbach, *The Life and Death of the Luftwaffe* (1960); and Adolf Galland, * *The First and the Last: The Rise and Fall of the German Fighter Forces* (1954).

*Books available in paperback edition are marked with an asterisk.

8 The Second World War, 1941-1945

By the end of 1940, much of the Nazi dream of dominating the continent had been realized. There were only two major powers outside German control: Britain and Russia. The British stood alone, their backs to the wall, while the Soviet Union was an ally and accomplice of Germany under the 1939 pact.

Despite the enormous German successes, Hitler was dissatisfied and uncertain. He was increasingly baffled by how to cope with Britain, which he preferred not to invade directly. The power he considered to be his main rival—though temporary ally—the Soviet Union, was stronger than ever before.

Throughout the second half of 1940, Hitler marked time, trying to decide on his next moves. So far, the war had been speedy and relatively economical. Fighting had been limited to the area near Germany's borders, and the conflict had not become a real world war, for only the European powers and the British Empire were involved. German military losses had been astoundingly light—only about 55,000 killed in the French and Polish campaigns combined. Very little strain had been placed on the German economy, and in the autumn of 1940 Hitler decided to cut back on war production and demobilize part of the army.

EXPANSION OF AXIS AGGRESSION
While Hitler remained indecisive, the initiative was seized by Mussolini. Envious of German conquests, the Italian dictator decided to attack Greece, which for decades had been involved in disputes with Italy over the sovereignty of outlying Greek islands. Italian troops crossed the Greco-Albanian border on October 28, 1940, but their invasion did not last long. The ineffective Italians were blocked in the border passes by poorly equipped Greek troops, who soon drove them into Albania once more. This defeat of the attempted Italian invasion of Greece was a humiliation for Mussolini, but it was also a complication for Hitler, since it left an unresolved Axis

front in southeastern Europe, just as in the northwest, at the time when Hitler's strategic thinking was being directed toward the east.

The Menace of Russian Power While Germany subjugated the liberal democracies of western Europe, the Russians had been strengthening their position in the east by widespread annexations of territory. In October 1940, Estonia, Latvia, and Lithuania had simply disappeared from the map, forcibly incorporated into the Soviet Union. At the same time, Stalin forced Rumania to cede the extensive northeastern border region of Bessarabia, once a part of the old tsarist empire. Russia's frontier had now been pushed another hundred miles or so west all along the line, and Hitler's apprehensions increased accordingly. By the end of 1940, the total industrial production of the Soviet Union was possibly greater than that of Germany. Russia's army was the largest in size and the third or fourth best in quality in the world. Her industrial and military machine was actually growing at a faster rate than Germany's.

Hitler had always emphasized that Germany could be strong and secure only after achieving the domination of eastern Europe and the destruction of the Bolshevik state. His 1939 agreement with Stalin had been a move to secure Germany's flank and win time. Now he began to worry about crushing the Soviet Union before it became too strong. Hitler encouraged the Russian government to consider the possibilities of expanding into the Middle East, but the Russians could not be lured away from Europe. Instead, Soviet representatives demanded an ironclad agreement on the division of eastern Europe between the two totalitarian partners. This Hitler would not concede; and in December, he gave German military planners the green light to prepare an attack on Russia for the spring of 1941.

This was a most grave decision that would greatly expand the scope of the war. With British resistance undiminished, Hitler was about to open hostilities with the immense Eurasian empire of Russia. German army leaders were reluctant, for they realized the limits of their strength. The Nazi regime had hesitated to curtail economic consumption inside Germany for fear of diminishing its prestige among the German people. Consequently both Britain and Russia had produced more of certain kinds of weapons during 1940 than had Germany. Hitler, however, had boundless faith in the German technique of lightning war. He thought that a quick campaign would suffice to eliminate the Red Army, and massive stocks of military goods would not be necessary.

The Role of Japan Though Hitler aspired vaguely to "world empire," in practice he thought almost exclusively in terms of Europe and neighboring areas. Nazi Germany did acquire one non-European ally, the militaristic state of imperial Japan, which aspired to hegemony in its parts of the world much as did Germany in Europe. In September 1940, the three Axis partners—Germany, Italy, and Japan—signed a Tripartite Pact pledging mutual aid in case any of them were "attacked by a power at present not involved

AXIS AND SOVIET EXPANSION, 1938-1941

International boundaries, 1938

German occupation, 1938-41
Italian occupation, 1939-41
Russian occupation, 1939-40
German annexation
German satellites
Other territorial changes

Murmansk

FINLAND

NORWAY
Oslo

Helsinki
Stockholm

Leningrad
Tallinn
ESTONIA

SWEDEN

BALTIC SEA

Moscow

NORTH
SEA

Riga   LATVIA

Smolensk

IRELAND

DENMARK   Copenhagen

LITHUANIA

MEMEL

GERMANY

U. S. S. R.

GREAT
BRITAIN

NETHERLANDS

Berlin

London

BELGIUM

GERMANY

Warsaw

Kiev

LUXEMBOURG

POLAND

Paris

Prague

SLOVAKIA

FRANCE

Vienna

1938

To
Hungary

1939

1940

Bordeaux

SWITZ-
ERLAND

AUSTRIA

Budapest

SLOVENIA

HUNGARY

RUMANIA

Sevastapol

Marseille

CROATIA

1941
To
Hungary

Bucharest

BLACK   SEA

SPAIN

ITALY

Belgrade

To Bulgaria
1940

YUGOSLAVIA

BULGARIA

CORSICA
(Fr.)

Rome

Sofia

Istanbul

SARDINIA

1941

To Bulgaria

ALBANIA

1941

Ankara

GREECE

TURKEY

Oran   Algiers

SICILY

Athens

Tunis

MEDITERRANEAN   SEA

CRETE

CYPRUS

ALGERIA
(Fr.)

TUNISIA
(Fr.)

0   400

Miles

Tripoli

Bengazi

LIBYA
(It.)

EGYPT (Br.)

in the European war or the Chinese-Japanese conflict." The target was the United States, which had begun to take a diplomatic stand in opposition to German and Japanese aggression.

In fact, however, Hitler was not interested either in neutralizing the United States or in involving Japan in his planned attack against the Soviet Union. He believed that the United States was already doing all it could to help Britain economically but was too weak militarily to affect the war in Europe before Germany would win it. All he expected of Japan was that its Asian expansion might well involve it in war with the United States and thus, by his mistaken calculations, leave him completely free to finish the war in Europe.

Nazi Domination of the Balkans   The German Fuehrer concentrated on consolidating Nazi power in the Balkans. After Rumania had been deprived of Bessarabia by Russia, Hitler decided to take the country under his protection. The Rumanians were forced to give up further territory to their southern and western neighbors, Hungary receiving western Transylvania and Bulgaria a smaller border strip. The Rumanian representative fell across the conference table in a dead faint when he heard the German decision; but his government, controlled by a reactionary, authoritarian monarchy, had no choice but to give in. Like Slovakia previously, Rumania, Hungary, and Bulgaria were lining up as German clients. Hitler was their only protection from the Soviet Union and, though he might make extensive demands on them, he would not disturb the conservative social order prevailing in most of this region.

The most recalcitrant Balkan country was Yugoslavia. This land was a composite creation of Serbs, Croats, and Slovenes, together with the regional variations (such as Dalmatia, Bosnia, and Montenegro) that existed within and between these groups. Croatians were Catholic and Serbs were Eastern Orthodox, save for the Muslim population of Bosnia. The Yugoslav state that had been created in 1919 did not represent the whole country equally, but was an authoritarian extension of the Serbian monarchy. The land had been torn by ethnic rivalry and bitterness for years, so that it was difficult for the weakened government to resist Hitler when he tried to force Yugoslavia to sign the Tripartite Pact in the late winter of 1941. On March 25, the government signed the pact, which already included Slovakia, Rumania, Hungary, and Bulgaria. Yugoslavia seemed to have been added to the list of Nazi satellites, but Serbian patriots were infuriated at the prospect of German domination. The very next day a group of nationalistic Serbian officers seized control of the government, deposing the regent and renouncing the Tripartite Pact.

It took only ten days to get the German Panzer divisions into position. On April 6, 1941, they attacked from the north and east, while wave after wave of dive bombers pulverized Belgrade, the Yugoslav capital. Within eleven days, the *Blitzkrieg* had destroyed the Yugoslav army. To save Mussolini's hapless forces in Albania, German tanks roared on across the Greek

Execution of Yugoslav Patriots, November 1942. During the German invasion Yugoslavia collapsed due to internal division. From 1941 to 1945 the occupied country was torn apart by a three-way conflict between Yugoslav communists, Croatian fascists, Serbian royalists and the German occupation force. At least a million people died.

border without stopping, all the way down to Athens. Before the end of the month, Greece had also signed an armistice. One of the swiftest, most devastating onslaughts of the war had made Hitler's control of the Balkans complete. The Fuehrer was now able to turn his attention due east.

The Invasion of Russia German leaders hoped to begin the attack on Russia by May 1941, but the Balkan diversion delayed their plans some six weeks. This assault was the greatest invasion ever attempted in the history of modern Europe, but the Fuehrer and other Nazi chiefs felt supremely self-confident. The German army would be assisted by an array of satellite forces from central and eastern Europe. In the north, Finland was willing to declare war on Russia to regain the land seized a year earlier. To the south, satellite Rumania agreed to support the attack in order to recover Bessarabia and occupy the southwestern Ukraine. Other military contingents could be expected from Italy, Hungary, and Slovakia. Save for the Finns, most of these forces had scant military potential, but Hitler brushed aside doubts and warnings. He insisted that the whole Soviet system was rotten and would collapse under pressure. The conquest of France had taken six weeks; since the Soviet Union was much larger, five months would be allowed.

At dawn on June 22, 1941, two and one-half million German troops crossed the Russian border behind powerful armored spearheads. The *Blitzkrieg* started with its usual overwhelming success. The *Luftwaffe,* in the air before sunrise, caught the Red Air Force by surprise and destroyed hundreds of Russian planes on the ground. Armored units drove deep into

Russia, surrounding and destroying sizable segments of the Red Army which had been massed along the border. Soviet leaders could hardly believe the magnitude of the disaster that threatened. By early August, the Germans had driven to Smolensk, 190 miles from Moscow.

At this point, the brunt of the attack veered southeast to seize the rich natural and industrial resources of the Ukraine. In September, Kiev, the Ukrainian capital, was occupied. Two great battles of encirclement alone had accounted for over one million Russian prisoners. On October 3, Hitler exulted, "The enemy is broken and will never rise again." The Fuehrer was so confident that as early as August he had ordered a cutback in German arms production.

During October, the German forces resumed the main drive on Moscow. It was getting very late in the year, however. Time and space were now working on the side of the Russians. They had retreated immense distances and suffered enormous losses, but the farther they withdrew, the more difficult it became for the Germans to supply their advance units, which were spread hundreds of miles deep across a two thousand-mile front. In mid-October the German columns forged ahead, due east toward Moscow, closing the distance to only about 100 miles. At the end of the month, however, the first signs of an abnormally early winter began to appear. Heavy rain and snow stopped the German tanks in their tracks, first turning the meager Russian road network into a quagmire, then freezing their motors. Had Russia possessed a good road system such as that of France, it might already have been defeated. The primitive conditions of the land were the Germans' main obstacle. One German column eventually reached the industrial suburbs of Moscow, but on December 3, the attack was brought to a halt by a combination of staunch Russian defense and a severe freeze accompanied by heavy snow. The German troops were not prepared for winter, while the Soviets enjoyed better clothing and supply. Three days after the German advance was stopped, new Russian divisions, transferred from Siberia, spearheaded a counterattack. Moscow had been saved; the great invasion of 1941 was over.

Nonetheless, the German assault had come very close to full success and the Soviet Union had already sustained huge losses. The best Russian farmland and the most important prewar industrial areas, together with nearly 75 million citizens, lay under German occupation. Nearly four million Russian soldiers had been captured, and hundreds of thousands of Red Army troops had died in combat.

These facts notwithstanding, the reserves of Russian strength and the resiliency of the Soviet system were much greater than most foreign observers had supposed. The Red Army counteroffensive was carried forward with new units from the great store of Russian manpower. Exhausted and ill-equipped German troops, freezing in the intense cold, were hurled back all along the line. German resources suddenly seemed inadequate to the task of dominating the 2,000-mile front. All estimates of military needs on the German side were found to be woefully insufficient. For example,

GERMAN INVASION OF RUSSIA, 1941-1944

International boundaries, 1939
Territory occupied by Russia, 1939-40
Axis occupation in Russia, 1941-44

NORWAY
SWEDEN
FINLAND
Helsinki
Leningrad
Farthest German advance
ESTONIA
Kalinin
DENMARK
LATVIA
Riga
Moscow
R U S S I A
LITHUANIA
GERMANY
Vilna
Smolensk
Berlin
Orel
Warsaw
Kursk
Volga R.
GERMANY
P O L A N D
German position, Spring 1944
Kharkov
German position, Aug. 1943
Don R.
Stalingrad
Kiev
Dnieper R.
SLOVAKIA
Dniester R.
Rostov
AUSTRIA
HUNGARY
Odessa
CASPIAN SEA
Grozny
RUMANIA
Sevastapol
ITALY
YUGOSLAVIA
Danube R.
B L A C K   S E A
BULGARIA
Istanbul
ALBANIA
T U R K E Y
GREECE
0   400
Miles

German forces fired fifty times as many howitzer shells in November and December, 1941, as were currently being produced by the poorly mobilized German armaments industry. Within the next three months, German military production increased twenty-five percent, but there was growing evidence that, in the long run, German industry would not be sufficient for the strain of war.

WAR IN THE PACIFIC AND UNITED STATES PARTICIPATION
At the very moment that German forces were retreating west of Moscow, the Japanese launched their carefully planned attack against the British and Americans in the Pacific, forcing the United States into war. For over a year, the United States had been granting sizable assistance to Great Britain, including a gift of fifty overage destroyers in September 1940. In mid-1941, President Roosevelt had left no doubt where his sympathies lay by meeting

with Churchill off the coast of Newfoundland to sign the Atlantic Charter, pledging both countries to work together to establish freedom and justice in the world. During the autumn of 1941, the United States navy had carried on a virtual undeclared war against German submarines in the North Atlantic. Hitler therefore considered America already in the war against Germany; after the Pearl Harbor attack on December 7, he spared further confusion by declaring war on the United States, and Mussolini immediately followed suit. In December 1941, the European conflict broadened into a general world war, the second of the century.

The Japanese armed forces quickly scored a series of astounding successes in southeast Asia, and having to fight a two-continent war on opposite sides of the world made the American and British military effort extremely complicated. Since Germany was by far the stronger and more dangerous foe, the United States government decided to concentrate against the Nazi empire, and to make the defeat of Japan secondary to the progress of battle in Europe. The American economy immediately began conversion to massive production of war materiel—the same determined process that had finally swayed the power balance in the First World War. At the end of 1941, few people in the world had a very clear idea of the huge volume of war production which the American system would attain during the next four years. Within a matter of months, the western Allies were able to assume the offensive against both Germany and Japan at the same time. In August 1942, began the long series of island campaigns fought by the Americans in the western Pacific. Some Japanese strongholds were conquered, others were bypassed, as the American counteroffensive slowly moved toward the home islands of Japan.

NAZI EUROPE **The New Order** The Nazi conquests of 1939–1941 temporarily established German domination over almost all of continental Europe, giving the German rulers their golden opportunity to create the unified "New Order" of purpose and discipline of which they talked. In the years 1940–1942, collaboration was not difficult to obtain. The reasons why many erstwhile respectable people worked with the Germans were various, but the principal factor was simply that for several years the world seemed to belong to the Nazis. Czechs and Frenchmen saw no point in opposing historical facts. Furthermore, as has been seen in an earlier chapter, fascism was a universal malady. The Nazis and Italian Fascists had their imitators in every European nation. After the German conquest, these elements rushed out to take their place at the head of the New Order in their particular countries. Most famous of the Nazi stooges was Vidkun Quisling, puppet ruler of Norway, whose very name became synonymous with "collaborator." The most bloodthirsty Nazi puppet was Ante Pavelich, leader of the Ustaši, the Croatian fascist party. His militia murdered all the Jews of Croatia and went on to slaughter several hundred thousand Serbians before his power faded in 1944.

The administrative structure of this short-lived Nazi empire was a rickety patchwork, pieced together as new areas were conquered. Much of the territory on the borders of Germany was incorporated directly into the

German Gunners Rejoice after Knocking Out a Russian Tank on the Eastern Front. During the first three years of the war German tank and gun crews were the most skilled in the world, even though their equipment was sometimes not the very best. After 1942 they were ground down by superior enemy numbers and firepower. (Hoover Institution Archives.)

Reich. Other regions were set aside for future German "colonization" and were ruled by German governors. Still other territories, such as Vichy France and Norway, were at first indirectly controlled through puppet dictators. Finally, at the farthest extremities of the Nazi domain, in occupied France, Belgium, parts of Russia and the Balkans, military government was the rule. In a separate category were the satellite states of eastern Europe, which were rarely interfered with until the latter stages of the war.

The main thing the Nazis wanted from this conglomeration of territories was booty. However, eastern Europe was too poor and German administration too confused under the Nazis to enable them to obtain very much from that half of the continent. The only exceptions were Czechoslovakia and Rumania. Otherwise, for supplementary industrial and food supplies, the Germans had to turn to France and the Low Countries. France alone provided forty-five percent of all the wealth extracted from occupied Europe. Special taxes, charges for occupation costs, and arbitrary commercial arrangements with the conquered regions were not enough, however, to bolster the German economy against the heavy pressures of total war. A severe manpower shortage appeared, for Germany lacked the human resources to garrison three thousand miles of fighting lines, hold down a conquered continent, and continue to increase war production. Millions of new workers, skilled and unskilled, were needed, and they could only be found among the captive populations. At first, hundreds of thousands of volunteers were won by recruitment, but as demands soared, the Germans resorted to forced labor drafts. By the end of the war, several million foreign workers were being held in Germany as slave labor.

Shipment to Germany for enforced labor was, however, mild compared with the treatment meted out to certain special categories of people under

(Right) *Corpses Stacked at the Buchenwald Nazi Concentration Camp.* (Below) *Survivors at Buchenwald Photographed by their Liberators.* Nazi extermination camps were the most unique and gruesome aspect of the Hitler empire. Though fewer people were exterminated in them than died in the labor camps of Stalinist Russia, their sole purpose was mass liquidation. Few Germans actually knew of their existence before 1945. (Hoover Institution Archives and Margaret Bourke-White, Courtesy of LIFE Magazine © 1943, Time, Inc.)

the New Order. From 1941 to 1943, three to four million or more Russian prisoners of war were cooped into great encampments and allowed to starve to death. The most implacable fate was assigned to Jews and Gypsies— lowest of all peoples on the New Order's racial scale, below even Russian sub-men. The logical culmination of the Nazis' fiendish anti-Semitism was reached at the beginning of 1942, when Hitler and his SS henchmen conceived a "Final Solution" of the Jewish question. A series of huge extermination camps, with scientific mass gas chambers and crematoria, were built in Germany and Poland. By the spring of 1945, at least five million Jews—the great majority of Europe's Jewish population—had been liquidated in the greatest campaign of genocide in human history. Such horrors later shocked the human imagination, and during the war they could scarcely be believed either by friend or foe. The facts were real enough, however, and afterward it was Hans Frank, the Nazi governor of Poland, who cried, "A thousand years will pass and the guilt of Germany will not be erased!"

The Resistance   Even though the full extent of Nazi murder and exploitation could not be seen by the average inhabitant of the occupied territories, day-to-day experiences of life under the New Order were enough to make him learn to hate Nazi imperialism. As the months passed, fewer and fewer people were willing to collaborate with Germany. By 1943, the majority of the conquered peoples were in a state of passive resistance, and some groups had already gone far beyond that.

In the occupied areas of the Soviet Union, however, there was at first surprisingly little armed resistance. Ukrainian peasants, for example, welcomed German troops as liberators from Communist oppression and collectivization. Only slowly did they learn to fight against the Germans after seeing that the latter brought not freedom and justice, but whips and chains. By 1942, the Soviet government had organized large-scale guerrilla activity behind the German lines. Russian influence in the resistance throughout Europe was furthered by the importance of the Communist party in combatting German occupation in France, Italy, and Yugoslavia.

The supreme head of the French resistance was General Charles de Gaulle (1890–1970), leader of the Free French National Committee in exile. De Gaulle had refused to recognize the French surrender or Pétain's satellite Vichy government. Instead he went into exile in Britain together with the French troops evacuated at Dunkirk. De Gaulle was extremely proud, even mystical, and supremely confident in his mission. He was very touchy about French honor, which he almost exclusively identified with his movement, and managed to keep alive a spirit of hope through France's darkest months. At first, his Free French National Committee was a movement without followers, for most Frenchmen were too dispirited to resist and the bulk of the nation fell into passive collaboration. After the Allied counteroffensive in the Mediterranean during the latter half of 1942, portions of the French overseas empire, which had never come under German domination, recognized de Gaulle's authority. By that time, Vichy was becoming increasingly discredited and the underground in France started to show signs of life. During 1943, de Gaulle was acknowledged as commander in chief by almost all the French resistance forces.

The most vigorous, effective resistance occurred neither in Russia nor in the west, but in Poland and Yugoslavia, where guerrilla bands were formed during the first year of occupation. The Yugoslav resistance was polarized between two violently antagonistic groups. The first was conservative, led by Colonel Draja Mihailovich. Mihailovich was a sincere, active patriot, but he was intensely Serbian and royalist. He made no appeal to

Croats and Slovenes, who were later won over by the rival resistance movement, headed by the Croatian Communist leader, Tito (born 1892). The latter held control of the Yugoslav Communist party even before the war began; after the German invasion of Russia he built up a well-knit resistance movement that stressed social reform and Yugoslav equality more than it did communism. Tito's "Partisans" proved an effective anti-German guerrilla force, while Mihailovich began to withdraw from the fight. He saved his forces for dealing with the Partisans and Croatians rather than fighting the Germans, hoping to avoid German reprisals against the Serbs. Tito had no such scruples, striking against Mihailovich and the Germans alike, heedless of the cost to the Yugoslav people. Impressed by the activity of Tito's movement, both the western Allies gave their support in 1943 to his group instead of that of Mihailovich.

The German Home Front The German people had never been enthusiastic about the war, but so long as things were going well, they had few complaints. Nazi totalitarianism had such an iron grip on the nation that doubt or resistance was strangled almost before it appeared. During the first two years of fighting, Germany had achieved such astounding successes that her people could scarcely question the genius of their Fuehrer.

Through 1941, the war had been easy on Germany. Its government refrained from demanding all-out sacrifice, and domestic consumption remained well above the depression level. The stalemate in Russia and the hard winter of 1941–1942 came as something of a shock, but Goebbels' propaganda machine minimized the seriousness of the situation, dwelling only on the "monster successes" of the previous summer. This did not, however, hide the facts of economic life. At the beginning of 1942, the German army lacked equipment for another full-scale offensive. Because of faulty allocation of manpower, the German coal mines were producing less than in 1940, and railroads, which had to bear the brunt of transportation, had been seriously neglected.

In January 1942, the government initiated a national emergency program, mobilizing economic resources for war. The following month, Albert Speer, the Fuehrer's personal architect, became Minister of Armaments in charge of war production. This was one of Hitler's most fortunate appointments, for Speer proved to be a genius in the organization of industrial productivity. Even Speer, however, could not do everything he wanted with the German economy. Nazi bureaucrats were extremely jealous of each other and had set up a bewildering maze of "fronts," organizations, bureaus, sections, and departments with overlapping jurisdiction. It never was possible to reduce this welter of confusion to any rational plan, and Hitler himself would have resisted granting complete control over the economy to any one man. Down to the very end, administrative inefficiency diminished the German war potential.

Only in 1943 did Nazi leaders fully realize the seriousness of their situation. Despite intensive Allied bombing, war production rose remarkably, and by mid-1944 stood at two and one-half times the rate of 1941.

In June 1944, when the western Allies opened the second front in France, Germany had more arms at its disposal than ever before; but by that time the strength of the opposing coalition had expanded to such overwhelming proportions that the Nazi cause was becoming hopeless.

After the end of 1942, Hitler's charismatic personal appearances became very rare. It was as though he could scarcely bear to face the German people. The public voice of the government was assumed almost entirely by Goebbels, who offered Germans every assurance of victory, and anesthetized their mental and emotional faculties with a steady barrage of propaganda. Besieged by Goebbels' rhetoric, sharply controlled on every side by the Gestapo, overworked, ever more heavily bombed from the air, the German people remained submissive and obedient. Though some were besieged by doubt, the masses followed the government to the bitter end.

THE WANING OF AXIS POWER

The Campaigns in Russia in 1942–1943 During 1942 and 1943, it was apparent that the major war in Europe was being fought in Russia. The bulk of the German army was engaged there, while on the other side of the lines the Soviet command was mobilizing nearly twenty million men (and several million women) for the struggle. The front reeled back and forth across distances of thousands of miles, and hundreds of Russian cities, not to mention innumerable villages, were razed in the process. Casualties had quickly mounted into the millions, tearing the fiber from both the opposing armies that had originally clashed in 1941. In physical terms, this was the most titanic struggle in history.

When the weather warmed in the spring of 1942, the Germans occupied a line considerably short of their deepest penetration the previous autumn. Though they had finally stopped the Red Army's counteroffensive, they no longer had the strength to resume the attack all along the front. Notwithstanding, Hitler hoped to score another breakthrough in a more reduced sector that would suffice to knock Russia out of the war. Some such plan was, in fact, Germany's only hope for a real military victory. Concentrating all his striking power in the south, Hitler's object was to advance to the Caspian Sea, and to seize the rich oil and coal resources of the Caucasus and the Don-Volga basin.

The offensive that began in July got off to a superb start. By late August, advance units had reached the Volga and were nearing the Caspian Sea in the south. The Red Army was temporarily in even more desperate straits than it had been in the previous autumn, for the last trained reserves were almost used up. With so much of the Russian population under German occupation, it was for the time being hard to bring to bear the customary Russian superiority in manpower. Morale in some units was low; mutiny broke out in several Soviet divisions. It had now become a race with time to see if the new Russian cadres could be trained, equipped, and thrown into battle before the Germans crossed the Volga.

A temporary delay in the enemy advance gave the Red Army time to create a major defensive stronghold at the big industrial city of Stalingrad

Russian Civilians Being Evacuated from the Siege of Leningrad, 1941–1944. The long German siege of Leningrad was one of the great epics of World War II. Though many were evacuated, several hundred thousand inhabitants died of privation, yet the city held fast.

on the bend of the Volga. Stalingrad lay in the very center of the German path, and Stalin ordered its defenders to resist to the last. After the Germans fought their way into the middle of the city, the defense stiffened. For two months hundreds of thousands of men grappled in a death struggle which blasted Stalingrad to bits.

By November, the new divisions of the Red Army were ready. They had already begun a gigantic pincers movement which finally encircled the German forces at the end of the month. Though all efforts to break the vise failed, Hitler refused to permit his beleaguered troops to withdraw. Sub-zero temperatures, heavy Russian attacks, and lack of supplies reduced the Axis forces to misery and starvation. To the very end, their Fuehrer hoped that a breakthrough by relief forces or a change in fortune would save them, but on February 3, 1943, after two-thirds of the German soldiers had been put out of action, the remnant surrendered. The Axis commanders lost 250,000 men killed or captured in their first great disaster. At Stalingrad, the war began to turn against Hitler.

From this triumph the Red Army drove on in a new winter offensive that wiped out all the German gains of 1942. Hitler's forces were now fighting in the Mediterranean as well as in the east, and it was impossible to replace the losses of the past year. When they tried to resume the offensive in the eastern Ukraine during the summer of 1943, they were stopped after very limited progress. The Red Army once more passed over to the assault, and began an interrupted but prolonged advance that finally carried Russian troops to Berlin and Vienna by the spring of 1945.

The Battle of the North Atlantic When the war began, the German navy was the fourth largest in the world. Though German surface ships were largely bottled up by the British during the first year of fighting, it was once again the German submarine fleet that constituted the most serious threat. Allied shipping losses rose during 1941 and the first part of 1942 until they temporarily exceeded the current rate of production. In the last months of 1942 the Anglo-American fleet began to gain control of the situation, and new shipyard programs exceeded the tonnage sunk. Thereafter, perfected convoy and patrol systems steadily reduced the U-boat menace, destroying such large numbers of submarines with such a low percentage of shipping losses that by the end of 1943 the German naval commander, Admiral Doenitz, despaired, "We have lost the battle of the North Atlantic."

The sea lanes were used by the two western Allies to deliver vast quantities of equipment to battle areas all over the world. Not the least of these supply priorities was American aid to Russia. During the next three years, the United States delivered billions of dollars of goods to the Soviet Union, including food, airplanes, and no less than 400,000 trucks, at the cost of many American lives. However, it was the Russians who were bearing the brunt of most of the actual combat, and they clamored for the Allies to open a "second front" against Germany in western Europe.

The War in North Africa Italy's entry into the conflict had proved to be almost unrelieved disaster for the Axis forces. Though approximately 500,000 Italian troops were moved into the Italian territories in north and northeast Africa, these units were almost completely destroyed by much smaller British forces within about nine months. By the beginning of 1941, Italian prisoners were being counted not by the head but by the acre. Mussolini's African empire had collapsed.

In a minor effort to rally Mussolini's forces, Hitler decided to send a small elite German unit, the Afrika Korps, across the Mediterranean in the spring of 1941. Its commander, Field Marshal Erwin Rommel (1891–1944), quickly became a living legend for the success and audacity of his leadership. His mastery of armored warfare found few equals in any theater of operations. He drove the British out of Italian Libya and back to the Egyptian border. Temporarily forced to retreat by a major British offensive at the close of 1941, Rommel later launched a new lightning assault in the spring of 1942 that pushed the British back across the Egyptian border again. At that point, Hitler refused further reinforcements, leaving the Afrika Korps greatly overextended, undermanned, and exhausted. Its fate was sealed on November 8, 1942, when a large Anglo-American expeditionary force landed in French Northwest Africa. Two weeks earlier, the British Eighth Army, under Lt. Gen. Bernard L. Montgomery, had launched a frontal attack on the German positions from Egypt. Assaulted from two directions, Rommel's dwindling forces had to retreat all the way back to Tunisia.

The new Allied landings, carried out in Algeria and Morocco by predominantly American forces, were under the command of the American general Dwight D. Eisenhower. A complicated political deal was then made which swung the French forces in Northwest Africa over to the side of the Allies, and Hitler belatedly began to pour men and materiel into Tunisia to hold an Axis foothold in North Africa. It was too late. Cornered in the northeast tip of Tunisia, the last German and Italian troops in Africa surrendered in May 1943. Approximately 200,000 more prisoners had been taken by the Allies. The Axis had lost more men in Libya and Tunisia than at Stalingrad, and Italy no longer had the will to go on.

Italy Withdraws from the War   After clearing North Africa of the Axis, the Allied army moved quickly to the invasion of Italy in order to knock Hitler's weak ally completely out of the war. Landings were successfully made in Sicily on July 10, 1943, and the outnumbered Germans were soon pushed off the island, the Italian defense having collapsed.

The loss of Sicily and the imminent invasion of the Italian peninsula brought Mussolini's downfall. On July 25, his own government rebelled against him and he was placed under arrest. Six weeks later, at the beginning of September, the British made the first landing on the Italian mainland. Soon afterward, the Italian authorities announced an armistice between their troops and the Allied forces, quickly formalized by unconditional surrender.

Hitler had no illusions about the faithfulness of the Italians. No sooner were the words of capitulation spoken than the sizable German forces in the peninsula moved into action, rounding up the Italian soldiers and seizing all key positions. Before Allied troops could make their way very far northward, they were met by an effective new German defense line. Italy was now out of the war, but most of the country was held by German forces, and mountainous terrain made the Allied advance difficult. It was not until the spring of 1944 that the Germans were forced back into central Italy.

The Anglo-American Aerial Offensive Against Germany   Initially, the German assault against Europe had placed great emphasis on air power, but the British and Americans were determined to turn the same tactic against the Germans. In both western democracies, aeronautical designers perfected huge four-engine bombers, capable of wreaking much more destruction than the smaller two-motored German craft employed during the Battle of Britain. Precision bomb sights and gigantic projectiles, called "blockbusters," helped to complete an awesome array of aerial potential which mounted steadily throughout 1942 and 1943. Thousands of heavy bombers stationed in Britain and North Africa carried out around-the-clock operations against German industrial and military targets. It was almost impossible to drop thousands of tons of bombs from great altitudes and have them all land precisely on the military target area. Thus it has been estimated that three out of every four bombs did not reach their planned target, but fell on adjacent regions. In the summer of 1943, 8,000 tons of bombs were dropped on Hamburg in six days, razing much of the city and bringing death to tens of thousands of civilians. On one occasion 1,800 tons of bombs were released over Berlin within a mere twenty-four minutes, blowing up four square miles of houses. Cologne was bombed 119 times and quite literally obliterated.

The *Luftwaffe* entirely lacked the strength to stop the raids, though it did take a heavy toll of the attacking planes. German technicians tried to reply by developing pilotless robot bombs (the V-1 and V-2) which caused significant destruction in Britain during 1944 but were not effective enough to weigh in the balance of the war. By that time, the Allied raids were beginning to make a dent in German industry, though it was not until the very end of the war that output was actually crippled by the bombardment. The principal effect was on the German cities, sections of which simply disappeared. Some 600,000 German civilians were killed, and the will to resist was eventually weakened.

The Liberation of Western Europe   The scope of German aggression had resulted in a somewhat incongruous anti-Nazi alliance between the two major western democracies and Soviet Russia. Neither the Anglo-Americans nor the Communists had actively sought such a union, but once under assault by Germany each was happy to have the other in the war on its own side. Since the fields of battle in the east and west were so far apart, there had been very little military cooperation between the Russians and the western powers, save for American shipments of materiel. After the tide of battle was reversed in the Allies' favor, the time had come to concert plans for the end of the war and the peace to follow.

Stalin, Roosevelt, and Churchill at Teheran, 1943. The Allied "Big Three" shown at their first wartime conference in neutral Persia, 1943. (Imperial War Museum.)

Consequently a meeting was arranged between Roosevelt, Churchill, and Stalin at the neutral Persian capital of Teheran at the end of November 1943. A main objective of the conference was to establish cordial relations between the three Allied leaders, so ideological differences were never raised.

ALLIED ADVANCES IN EUROPE AND AFRICA, 1942-1945

International boundaries, 1939

Allied powers

Axis domination

Major advances of the Allies

Major advances of the Russians

NORWAY

Oslo

SWEDEN

Stockholm

DENMARK • Copenhagen

FINLAND

Helsinki

Leningrad

ESTONIA

LATVIA

Riga

LITHU-
ANIA

Moscow

1944

1944

NORTH
SEA

BALTIC SEA

IRELAND

GREAT
BRITAIN

London •

NETHERLANDS

BELGIUM

ATLANTIC

OCEAN

1944

• Paris LUX.

FRANCE

GERMANY

GERMANY

1945

Berlin •

1945

• Warsaw

Kiev •

U.S.S.R.

1944

Dnieper R.

1945

1945

• Prague

POLAND

1945

SLOVAKIA

Dniester R.

1944

Rhine R.

1945

Danube R.

1945

• Budapest

RUMANIA

1944

SWITZ-
ERLAND

HUNGARY

1944

• Bucharest

Sevastapol •

1942

PORTUGAL

• Madrid

SPAIN

1944

CORSICA

1945

Rome •

ITALY

YUGOSLAVIA

• Belgrade

1944

BLACK
SEA

Sofia •

BULGARIA

Istanbul
•

SARDINIA

1944

ALBANIA

TURKEY

1943

GREECE

MOROCCO

SP.
MOROCCO

1942

Oran

1942

Algiers

SICILY

Tunis •
1943

TUNISIA

1943

1944

• Athens

CRETE

• Casablanca

M E D I T E R R A N E A N   S E A

M O R O C C O

A L G E R I A

Tripoli •

Bengazi •

1942

Alexandria •

El Alamein •

E G Y P T

L I B Y A

0   400

Miles

It was agreed that the western powers would soon open a major "second front" by means of a cross-Channel operation onto the French coast. Churchill, however, was still haunted by memories of the static slaughter on the western front in the First World War and was also keenly aware of the dangers of expanded Russian power in east-central Europe, which lay in the path of the advancing Soviet armies. As an alternative or a supplement to the cross-Channel invasion, he suggested an Anglo-American assault through the Balkans that would turn the flank of the retreating Germans and roll up all of central Europe from the south. Militarily, however, this would be a hazardous undertaking and, furthermore, Roosevelt wished to allay the suspicions of Stalin who had no desire to see Anglo-American forces in the Balkans. A firm decision was thus made to deal the *coup de grâce* to Germany with a grand Anglo-American assault across France, to begin in the spring of 1944.

On June 6, 1944, a sudden break in the weather over the English Channel made possible the successful launching of the greatest amphibious assault in history. Anglo-American landings quickly put ashore 100,000 troops across a sixty-mile beach area on the coast of Normandy. Having completely lost contol of the air, the German forces were impotent to turn back the invasion. For six weeks, a stubborn defense checked the Allied advance, but Eisenhower's forces built up overwhelming strength. On July 25, American armored units began a wide breakout around the German flank, then turned due east for Paris. By the end of August, nearly all France had been liberated as new Allied landings were made on the southern coast almost without opposition.

Meanwhile, the Anglo-American advance had been moving rapidly in Italy. On June 4, just two days before the landing in France, Rome had been liberated, and the Germans were retreating to the north. A free new parliamentary regime was already being established to begin the difficult work of building postwar democracy in Italy, and it appeared as though the entire peninsula would soon be free of German forces. In France, the Allied offensive was only brought to a halt when it neared the German border. Supply problems made it necessary to stabilize the main western front there for the winter of 1944–1945.

Collapse of the German Eastern Front About two weeks after the western Allies landed on the beaches of Normandy, German defenses in the east began to crumble before the Red Army's great summer offensive of 1944. During the summer, three German satellites—Finland, Rumania, and Bulgaria—were torn out of the Axis camp, and the Russian advance was halted only at the East Prussian frontier. In the north, the Finnish forces were thrown all the way back, and Finland itself was threatened with invasion. The Finns had joined the German assault on Russia only to regain the territory taken by the Soviet Union in 1940. Since mid-1943 they had been seeking an honorable way out of the war. Now they had no choice but to make peace on Soviet terms, which were about the same as those of 1940, save that a heavy reparations bill was attached.

On August 1, with Red Army units only a few miles away on the opposite shore of the Vistula, the Polish underground broke out in full-scale rebellion in the streets of Warsaw. The Poles had organized and half-armed thousands of men, but they could not throw off the Germans by themselves and were counting on the continued advance of the Russians to complete the city's liberation. The Red Army, however, did not budge. The fighting went on in the Polish capital for two months, and the historic city was blown up block by block. When it was over, at least 200,000 young Poles, the hope of the nation's future, had been slaughtered. From the Russian point of view, it was just as well to have as high a percentage as possible of the potential non-Communist leadership of Poland killed off by the Germans before the latter were driven out. The way would then be clearer for the recently established "Polish Committee of National Liberation," composed of Communist stooges, which the Soviets intended to impose as the government of postwar Poland.

During that fatal month of August 1944, the main energy of the Red Army was exerted in the south, where it had pierced the Carpathians and was advancing into Rumania. The Rumanian government, like that of Finland, was desperately looking for a way out of the war. On August 23, Rumania abruptly withdrew from the fighting and then her soldiers were ordered to join with the Russians against their German ex-allies. Huge Russian forces bore down on Bulgaria, the only Nazi satellite that had never declared war on the Soviet Union. Faced with a sudden declaration of war from Stalin, the Bulgarians accepted Russian terms and joined in the fight against Germany. The loss of Rumania and Bulgaria made it impossible for the Germans to hold Greece, which had to be evacuated. In turn, the Germans were being forced out of Yugoslavia, where Tito's Communist-led Partisans already held control of large parts of the country. The Red Army swept through western Rumania and the southern half of Yugoslavia, then turned north to invade Hungary. Here, the Germans built a defense line that held fast for a few months, as the autumn of 1944 turned into winter.

German Opposition to Hitler By mid-1944, it was clear to all intelligent Germans that the Reich was losing the war. The political opposition in Germany had been insignificant and, indeed, thoroughly squelched during the high years of Nazi triumph up to 1942, but military defeat encouraged bold action. Though the opposition remained microscopic in size, it included people from the most diverse elements. A number of plans had already been made to assassinate Hitler. For several years, a group of army officers had been conspiring against the Fuehrer, and had even planted in his private airplane a time bomb that had failed to explode. By early 1944, civilian and military conspirators were drawing closer together. After the invasion of France and the Russian summer offensive, they dared not wait any longer. The German resistance worked out the details of a far-reaching plot to kill Hitler and set up a new non-Nazi government that could bring peace. On July 20, they planted another time bomb, this time at Hitler's eastern headquarters (the "Wolf's Lair," as the Fuehrer himself called it) deep in

General Charles de Gaulle Returns in Triumph at the Liberation of Paris, August 26, 1944. De Gaulle's leadership of the Free French required a long and difficult struggle during the dark years of German occupation. Only in 1943 did the French rally to the resistance in large numbers, but by the time Paris was liberated de Gaulle had become the savior of France and for the time being its undisputed leader. (Imperial War Museum.)

the East Prussian forest. Its explosion killed several men standing beside Hitler, but the Fuehrer himself escaped in almost miraculous fashion. He immediately exacted fearsome reprisals and the best men of the German opposition were slain in the executions that followed. Hitler's tyranny over the Germans became more complete than ever.

Hitler's Last Counteroffensive   The Fuehrer still hoped somehow to win the war and talked of secret weapons and surprise moves that would turn the tide at the last moment. More realistically, he decided on a final reckless counteroffensive to throw back the Allies in the west and buy more time for Germany. The Nazi leaders still gambled on producing a rift between the western Allies and the Soviets, for it was upon a breakup of the anti-German grand alliance that Hitler staked his last chance for victory.

All of Germany's reserves were thrown into an attack on the western front on December 16, 1944. It began in the Ardennes forest of eastern Belgium, where the Germans had first broken through in 1940. Harsh winter weather enabled the attackers to achieve tactical surprise, and within a week the Anglo-American forces had been pushed back nearly fifty miles, creating a large bulge in their line. However, as the weather cleared and reinforcements were brought up, the tide turned and after a full month's fighting, all the ground lost by the Allies had been regained. Though this Battle of the Bulge failed to achieve the German objectives, it delayed the Allied breakthrough across the Rhine. Meanwhile, the German command called up old men and fifteen-year-old boys for the last bitter resistance.

Russian Troops Raise their Flag over the Ruined Reichstag after the Fall of Berlin, April 1945. Perhaps better than any other picture, this photo of the hammer-and-sickle flying over the Reichstag in a ruined Berlin symbolizes the total defeat of Nazi Germany.

The End In January 1945, the Red Army opened its victory offensive in central Poland. Warsaw was finally wrested from German hands as the Russians pushed across the eastern border of the Reich and occupied a large section of East Prussia. The weary, outnumbered, and inadequately armed German defenders could do little to stop the advance, which only halted when it neared Berlin.

In March 1945, the western Allies began the drive that soon carried into the heart of Germany. One bridge over the Rhine at Remagen was captured intact, and at the beginning of April, divisions of French, British, and American troops were pouring into west and central Germany. Many of Hitler's soldiers had virtually ceased to resist in the west. Allied forces advanced a total of 57 miles on April 11 to a point only 50 miles from Berlin. The Russian forces on the other side of the city were in the throes of reorganization, and the western armies might have been able to take both Berlin and Prague while the Russians regrouped. However, it was still the American policy to play as conservative a role as possible in central Europe and thus avoid aggravating the Communists. While the western forces waited, the Russians once more began to move ahead.

Further resistance was futile but the Fuehrer, immured in his concrete underground command bunker in the center of Berlin, ordered his people to fight on to the last. Hitler had by this time completely lost contact with reality. He decided that the Germans were not worthy of him, and said privately that if his nation did not possess the strength to win, the future then logically belonged to the "stronger people" of the east—the Russians. Absorbed in a fantasy of glorious destruction, he insisted that defeat must be preceded by a great devastating *Götterdämmerung*—a "twilight of the gods"—in which Germany would consume itself and as much of the European continent as possible in its death throes.

On April 13, the day after the death of President Roosevelt, Vienna was taken by the Red Army. Three days later, the final Russian assault on Berlin began. The Reich's capital, like almost all other large German cities, was a heap of rubble. Its defense lasted but two weeks. On April 30, Adolf Hitler shot himself, screaming curses and vengeance at the Jews in his last testament. Organized German resistance had collapsed. On May 7, German military leaders signed the terms of unconditional surrender at Eisenhower's headquarters in northeastern France. Three months later the United States Air Force dropped two of the recently developed atomic bombs on the home islands of Japan, and the Japanese government also surrendered. The Second World War was over.

FURTHER READING

Two of the best general histories of the conflict are Peter Cavalcoressi and Guy Wint, *Total War* (1972); and B. H. Liddell Hart, *History of the Second World War* (1970). The major accounts of the Russo-German war are Albert Seaton, *The Russo-German War 1941–1945* (1971); and Alan Clarke, *Barbarossa* (1965). The German side of the struggle is told in B. H. Liddell Hart, *The German Generals Talk* (1948); and Erich von Manstein, *Lost Victories* (1958).

The key study of the most important collaborationist regime is R. O. Paxton, *Vichy France* (1972). For German occupation in the east, see Alexander Dallin, *German Rule in Russia, 1941–1945* (1957); and George Fisher, *Soviet Opposition to Stalin* (1952). David Irving, *The Destruction of Dresden* (1963), describes the mass annihilation of German civilians from the air. The German resistance is portrayed by Hans Rothfels, *The German Opposition to Hitler* (1948).

On the naval war, see S. W. Roskill, *White Ensign: The British Navy at War, 1939–1945* (1960); and Friedrich Ruge, *Der Seekrieg: The German Navy's Story, 1939–1945* (1957).

The most eloquent account of wartime diplomacy and grand strategy is W. S. Churchill, *The Second World War*, 6 vols. (1948–1953). The problems of wartime relations with the Soviet Union are examined in Herbert Feis, *Churchill, Roosevelt, Stalin: The War They Waged and the Peace They Sought* (1957).

*Books available in paperback edition are marked with an asterisk.

PART XVII

Since the dawn of the twentieth century, when the dominance of Europeans over Africans and Asians, with the exception of the Japanese, seemed so assured, much has happened to reverse the tide of European expansion. Weakened and distracted by two world wars and a great depression, the process begun by the Portuguese over four hundred years earlier—the increasing subjection of non-European peoples to European rule—was not only halted but turned back upon itself. The very instruments by which western civilization had gained its superiority in scientific, technical, commercial, military, political and cultural strength were appropriated by the peoples of Africa and Asia and used to return European rulers to their homelands.

But simultaneously, two other components of western expansion continued unabated. First, the exceedingly energetic self-transformation—the pace of change—in the West continued to accelerate. And while European political power in Asia and Africa was in the process of steady diminution from 1900 onward, its rapidly increasing cultural power became more attractive, contagious, and intrusive—however deeply alien it continued to be to the rituals and styles of Muslims, Hindus, Buddhists, Confucianists, and other cultures in Asia. In fact, with the mutual interfusions of western and eastern cultures and of primitive and sophisticated styles (western culture even drew to itself and began to absorb all other cultures) even this acceleration seems to have turned on itself. Thus, in effect, what began to emerge after 1950 was a truly world-wide culture.

Second, the process of expansion, accelerated by European impacts, continued within all the countries of Asia and Africa. As a result, in every land, whether in India, Manchuria, or Nigeria, the advance of agricultural development and then industrial development has threatened the cultures, if not the very existences, of more primitive peoples. Chinese migrants began to flood into Manchuria and cast their eyes upon the great open spaces of Siberia. Nomadic tribes recoiled or were absorbed. Russians did the same in Central Asia and Siberia. Similarly, jungles in Southeast Asia were steadily hacked down so as to permit cultivation while jungle people in Assam, Burma, Borneo, Thailand, Laos, and Indo-China were pushed into ever smaller spaces and tighter conditions. Some primitive peoples disappeared altogether; others are disappearing.

The turning point in the abandonment of rule over Asian and African countries by Europeans was the Second World War and British withdrawal from India. Once India had been abandoned, no European power could retain local strength in Asia and Africa—at least not for very long. Indian independence turned the corner, soon followed by Burma and Ceylon. The Chinese Revolution of 1949 and the Japanese Miracle completed the major shifts of power and of alignment in Asia. The final withdrawal of Portuguese rule in Africa (Angola, Guinea, and Mozambique) would seem to bring this era towards its close. The question of the future of regimes in Rhodesia and South Africa remain.

ABSTRACTION IN INK AND BROWN BY KOSHIRO ONCHI. (Courtesy, Museum of Fine Arts, Boston.)

ASIA AND AFRICA IN THE TWENTIETH CENTURY

LEGACY OF THE PAST

The history of Africa and Asia in the twentieth century is part of the story of the contraction of Europe. The dismantling of the great maritime empires after 1947, the rise of new, independent states, and the increasing strength of such great powers of Asia as China, Japan, and India—such developments are themselves legacies of the two World Wars and of those processes of cultural and technological borrowing by which non-western societies were able to turn modern tools against the already weakened and war-devastated countries of Europe. In short, emergence of new power in Asia and Africa was itself a legacy of European decline.

MAJOR EVENTS IN ASIA, 1900-1974

1900-   Boxer Uprising in China (1899–1901)
Tz'u Hsi's edict promising reforms (1901)
Russo-Japanese War (1904–1905)
Abolition of Ancient Examination System in China (1905)
Partition of Bengal (1905; revoked 1909)
Budi Utoma founded in Dutch Indies (1906)
Founding of Muslim League in India (1906)
Young Men's Buddhist Association (1908)
Death of Kuang Hsu and Tz'u Hsi (1908)
Federal Council of Malay States (1909)
Indian Councils Act or "Morley-Minto Reforms" (1909)
Annexation of Korea by Japan (1909–1910)

1910-   National revolution in China, republic proclaimed (1911)
Royal Durbar in Delhi; new imperial capital announced (1911)
Sarejat Islam (1911)
Kuo Min Tang organized by Sun Yat Sen (1912)
Sun Yat Sen Withdraws from Presidency of China (1912)
Muhammadiyah founded in Jogjakarta (1912)
First Congress in Surabaya (1913)
Japan enters war against Germany (1914)
Twenty-One demands to China given by Japan (1915)
Indies Social-Democratic Association (1914)

1915-   Yuan Shiah K'ai attempts to found New Imperial Dynasty (1916)
Congress and Muslim League make "Lucknow Pact" on a constitutional
    plan for India (1916)
Japanese forces at Vladivostok, against Russian Revolution (1918)
Ceylon National Congress (1919)
Government of India Act or "Montagu-Chelmsford Reforms" (1919)
Jalianwala Bagh or "Amritsar Massacre" (1919)

1920-   "December Boycott" in Burma (1920)
Satyagraha Campaign for Swaraj led by Gandhi (1920–1921); Khilafat
    Movement in India supported by Congress.
PKI or Indies Communist Party formed (1920)
Communist Party of China founded (1920)
"Dyarchy" extended to Burma (1921)
Washington Conference and Treaties (1921–1922)
Japanese withdrawal from Shantung (1922)
Kuo Min Tang—Communist "United Front" (1923–1927)
Great Earthquake in Japan (1923)

1925-   Beginning of Northern Expedition under Chiang K'ai-shek (1926)
Nahdatul Ulama founded in Dutch Indies (1926)
PKI revolt in Dutch Indies suppressed (1926)
Rising by Communists crushed (1927)
Breakup of United Front in China (1927)
Simon Commission for India's Constitutional Reform (1927)
Vietnamese Nationalist Party (VNQDD) founded (1927)
Indonesian National Party founded by Sukarno (1927)
Establishment of National Republic of China at Peking (1928)
The "Crash" of World Markets (1929)—Great Depression began.

1930–	Simon Report on Indian Constitution (1930)
	Founding of Indochina Communist Party by Ho Chi Minh (1930, renamed Viet Minh, 1939)
	Japanese Conquest of Manchuria (1931)
	Saya San Rebellion in Burma (1931)
	Bloodless Revolution in Thailand (1932)
	London Round Table Conferences on India and Burma (1932)
1935–	Government of India Act of 1935; full provincial self-government
	Long March of Chinese Communists under Mao Tse Tung (1934–1935)
	Capture and release of Chiang K'ai-shek in Sian Mutiny (1936)
	Final takeover of Japan by militarists (1936)
	Outbreak of war between China and Japan (1937)
	Provincial elections in India, Indian ministries (1937)
	Ba-Maw Cabinet in Burma (1937)
	Congress Ministries resign in protest of India's entry into War (1939)
1940–	
	Burmese Nationalists jailed or driven underground (1941)
	Pearl Harbour (1941)
	Lahore Resolution (1940) in favor of a separate Pakistan
	Conquest of Burma, and all Southeast Asia, by Japan (1942)
	Cripps Mission to India and "Quit India" Rebellion (1942)
	Ba-Maw "Independent" Burma recognized by Japan (1943)
	Great famine of Bengal (1943)
1945–	Atom Bombs dropped on Hiroshima and Nagasaki (1945)
	Surrender of Japan and American Occupation (1945)
	Release of Congress Leaders from Jail in India (1945)
	Outbreak of Full Civil War in China (1945)
	War against Dutch in Indonesia (1946–1948)
	Viet Minh War against France (1946–1954)
	British Cabinet Mission to India (1946)
	Day of Direct Action, Calcutta Riots (1946)
	Independence granted to the Philippines (1946)
	Massacre of Aung San and his cabinet by terrorists (Burma, 1947)
	Independence and Partition of India and Pakistan (1947)
	Federation of Malaya agreement; outbreak of Communist "Emergency" (1948)
	Independence of Burma and Ceylon (1948)
	First Indo-Pakistan War (1948–1949) over Kashmir
	Indonesian Independence (1949)
	Chinese Malay Association (1949)
	Final victory of Communists in China (1949)
1950–	"The Terror," People's Tribunals, in China (1950–1952)
	Outbreak of Korean War (1950)
	End of Occupation and Treaty of Peace with Japan (1951)
	Geneva Accords and French withdrawal from Indochina (1954)
1955–	Bandung Conference (1955)
	"Hundred Flowers" episode in China (1957)
	Independence of Malaya (1957)
	"Great Leap Forward" Campaign in China (1958–1959)
	Flight of Dalai Lama to India (1959)
1960–	Sino-Soviet split (1960)
	Fall of Diem regime in South Vietnam (1963)
	Formation of federation of Malaysia (1963)
	Indonesian confrontation with Malaysia (1963)
	Sino-Indian War (1963)
	China's first explosion of nuclear bomb (1964)
	Gulf of Tonkin Resolution (1964)

MAJOR EVENTS IN ASIA, 1900-1974 CONT.

1965–	Indo-Pakistan War (1965)
	Abortive Communist coup against army in Indonesia (1965)
	Great Cultural Revolution in China (1966)
	Repression of Red Guards (1968)
	Secession of Singapore from Malaysia (1968)
1970–	American bombing of Cambodia and north Vietnam (1970)
	Cambodian coup and Civil War (1970)
	Withdrawal of America from Vietnam War (1970–1972)
	Bangladesh purge and Secession (1971)
	Indo-Pakistan War (1971)
	President Nixon visit to Peking (1972)

MAJOR EVENTS IN AFRICA, 1900-1974

1900– Boer War (1899–1902)
       British conquest of northern Nigeria (1900–1903)
       Congo passes from Leopold II to Belgium (1908)

1910–
       Morocco becomes French protectorate (1912)
       Blaise Diagne elected in Senegal (1914)
       Conquest of German colonies (1914–1915)
       African troops in World War I (1914–1918)
       Pan-African Congress, Paris (1919)

1920– National Congress of British West Africa (1920)
       Legislative Council established, Nigeria (1921)
       Egypt gains self-rule (1922)
       Frederick Lugard's *Dual Mandate* (1922)
       Aba, Nigeria, riots (1929)

1930–
       Neo-Destour party founded, Tunisia (1934)
       Ethiopia conquered by Italy (1936)
       Popular Front in France (1936)
       Nigerian Youth Movement (1930's)

1940–
       Liberation of Ethiopia (1941)
       Brazzaville Conference (1944)
       NCNC party in Nigeria (1944)
       RDA party founded in Bamako (1946)
       New constitution for Nigeria (1947)
       Nkrumah arrives in Ghana (1948)

1950–
       Mau Mau uprisings, Kenya (1952)
       Federation of Rhodesia and Nyasaland (1953)
       Algerian War begins (1954)
       Independence for Sudan (1955)
       Morocco and Tunisia freed (1956)
       Ghana first black colony freed (1957)
       Guinea gains independence (1958)

1960– Nigeria and most French colonies freed (1960)
       Civil war in Congo after independence (1960–1961)
       South Africa becomes republic (1961)
       Algeria and Tanganyika independent (1962)
       Federation of Rhodesia and Nyasaland dissolved (1964)
       Nkrumah overthrown (1966)
       Biafran war in Nigeria (1969)

1970–
       Amin in power in Uganda (1971)
       Breakup of Portuguese African Empire (1974)

1 Breakup of Empire: The Emergence of India and Pakistan

British rule fundamentally altered civic and cultural attitudes among the more prominent leadership groups in South Asia. Along with the concept of India as a single unified entity, the British contributed contagious new notions, new concepts about humanity and attitudes toward society, that helped to transform, modernize, and even revolutionize ways of thinking and of living for many in India. Truly revolutionary, were the ideas of the possibility of unlimited human progress and of "rights" for all men ("right" was especially alien)—that each person should have dignity and equality before the law and that by enacting reforms it should be possible to increase liberty for individuals. Many in Britain (Burke, Bentham, Mill, Bentinck, Macaulay) believed that British rule in India was a trust and that such rule should not last indefinitely. Eventual "self-government" in an open and secular society was seen as a desirable ideal, a duty to engage man's finest efforts. Sir Charles Trevelyan went so far as to envision a steady, peaceful development by which India would rise as a free nation and Britain would exchange a faithful subject for a staunch ally.

THE CULTURAL AWAKENING The influence of modern, westernized forms and methods of education in India can hardly be exaggerated. In 1835, Lord Macaulay who had gone to India to reform the legal codes, wrote: "We must at present do our best to form a class who may be interpreters between us and the millions whom we govern; a class of persons, Indian in blood and colour, but English in taste, in opinions, in morals, and in intellect." Thereafter, but especially after 1854 when a system of grants-in-aid for public education came into operation, admission to the new schools and university colleges was open and "without prejudice of caste, color, or creed." Emphasis was placed upon both literary and scientific subjects. English became the language of instruction and of discourse at all higher levels of public life, not only in the universities but also in the government offices, the courts, the professions, and the press.

New classes of well-off and influential people emerged. In previous centuries, merchant partners and other kinds of go-betweens had served as brokers between the rulers and the ruled. But as the power of Muslim and Hindu princes declined, prestige went to these new, English-speaking leaders who came from the bustling metropolitan centers of Calcutta, Bombay, and Madras. Most of them were Hindus. Some, such as the famous Tagore family, had gained their original wealth from large landholdings; but many others had arisen from government service where their educated sons found positions in such newly expanding branches as public works, postal and telegraph offices, railways, or irrigation. As demands for qualified professional men outside government grew and as professions became more lucrative, this pace of change accelerated. More and more village people learned that "the Government" allowed itself to be sued and that decisions might be appealed to the highest courts. Fees which English-speaking lawyers could charge kept pace with rising demands of legal services. More teachers and professors were needed to instruct the young so that they in turn could join the rapidly increasing numbers of officials, lawyers, doctors, engineers, teachers, and journalists. Thus, instead of an old fragmented society in which each tiny elite was isolated from the others by its own sacred and secret skills and rituals, an integrating, open and secular society began to emerge. Where there were many languages, one over-arching language drew the subcontinent together. Nourished by rapid and cheap communication in which comprehensive postal and railway systems carried letters, newspapers, and persons quickly to the remote corners, groups all over India came to realize their common bonds as leaders and representatives of their own people. Gradually these new leaders began to think of themselves as belonging to a nation and to keep in touch on common, "national" problems. Journalists and writers stirred up a rising "public" opinion on controversial questions. English pride in English history and English achievement prompted a search for identity with things Indian. As early as the 1830's associations of Indians began to form and to petition Parliament for reforms and for a greater voice in India's destiny. In the minds of more and more people, what had become the Indian Empire could also be united into a great nation.

THE WIDENING POLITICAL CONSCIOUSNESS AND EARLY MOVEMENTS

Initially, comparatively few of the former Muslim rulers worked with the British or had anything to do with them. Some searched for causes of Muslim decline and tried to reform or to purify the community of Islam; but most simply sank into despair, mourning the loss of their supremacy and sighing for the past days of Mughal authority. The Hindus faced the British in a very different way. They eagerly and energetically adapted themselves to the conditions of the new regime and became the main beneficiaries of it.

One of the most remarkable of these open-minded Hindus was Raja Ram Mohan Roy (1772–1833). A scholarly Bengali of high caste, whose family combined Sanskrit lore with Persian learning as Mughal bureaucrats, he had taught himself English; joined the Company's service; and, after becoming one of the wealthy landed gentry, retired so as to devote his full energy to humanitarian causes. Ram Mohan Roy wished to combine what was best from both worlds, Indian and western. He fought against superstitions, idolatry, polytheism, caste inequalities, and such inhuman customs as widow-burning and child marriage. He held debates with Christian missionaries claiming that they had distorted the teaching of Jesus, even learning Greek in order to speak with more authority. Seeking to combine the best elements of all religions, in 1828 he founded a monotheistic new faith and named it the Brahmo Samaj.

In subsequent decades, other movements followed. Some tended to be less intellectual, trying to revitalize and defend Hindu traditions by appealing to puritanical and devotional conventions. The Prarthana Samaj or Prayer Society was one such attempt. The Arya Samaj, founded in 1875 by Dayananda Saraswati, was another. It condemned "post-Vedic corruptions" and called all Hindus to the original, pure and simple ways of the Vedas. Without acknowledging influence from the West, the Arya Samaj nonetheless preached for conversion and followers, something quite untraditional. Still other movements were secular, cultural, or professional—such as the Bengal Landowners or the Madras Native Association. But, after the Mutiny, when many British rulers turned away from liberal attitudes, new classes of educated Indians with liberal and progressive ideals expressed disillusion and resentment.

The Indian National Congress The first step toward "a greater voice" followed the Great Mutiny (1857). In 1861, with the Indian Councils Act, the British sought Indian opinion by appointing Indians to newly organized legislative councils designed to advise the viceroy and the provincial governors. Certainly this was only "half a loaf" inasmuch as the "appointed" councilors could "represent" but a small minority—and those the educated elite. In the context of its day, however, it was a huge advance.

Matters came to a head in the 1880's in a controversy over the Ilbert Bill, a law which would have permitted Indian judges to preside over cases in which defendents were European. (By then, one of the most prominent and highly salaried officials, soon to become a Justice of the Madras High Court, was a Brahman.) So loudly did protests of residents in the private European community sound against this bill that Parliament forced the Government of India to back away from the measure. This obvious loss of nerve by the British rulers outraged Indian public opinion, and Indians suddenly realized that they had better organize if they were going to fight successfully against unfair social and political discrimination. Concerned members of local civic associations, both Indian and European, called for an All-India meeting. (Due to the developed network of railroads, All-India conferences had recently become possible and were becoming more common.) In 1885, delegates met in Bombay and organized the Indian National Congress. United in expressing its loyalty to the Empire, the Congress nevertheless did not hesitate to express its views candidly nor did it shrink from formally requesting greater participation in the decisions of government by Indians, and stating the goal of achieving eventual but complete self-government through gradual processes of political reform and cooperation with the British Raj. They called for a *representative* government and a legislature with "a considerable portion of *elected* members."

But did the Indian National Congress truly represent all Indians, regardless of social or creedal background? This was to become the central question and it was to bedevil if not actually retard political integration of the subcontinent during the next half century. Indeed, the claims were to have fateful consequences. Members of the Indian National Congress felt that it did represent all people in the country; moreover, since there was no other body which made such a claim, there also was no way to disprove it. But the fact remains that, out of its first seventy members, only two were Muslims. Nor did Muslims ever become numerous in its membership. For years they had been slipping further and further behind in influence and importance. Few had taken to modern education or acquired positions in public or professional life within the new India. Muslims had become increasingly sensitive and defensive about their weakness. Former rulers in India, their pride was still great; but their future seemed to promise them only perpetual inferiority if not thraldom in a modern India dominated by Hindus.

The Separation of Muslim Identity No one saw this more clearly than Sir Sayyid Ahmad Khan (1817–1898). He became for Muslims what Raja Ram Mohan Roy had been to Bengali Hindus—the symbol of renaissance. He had served the Company as a judge, and then returned from a trip to Europe in 1869 convinced that if Muslims were ever going to catch up and assume their rightful role in a modern India they must study the sciences and arts of the West. He accordingly founded a college at Aligarh in 1875. The Muslims continued to have trouble, however, in reconciling their Islamic heritage with western thought. Many who acquired modern education lost some of their Islamic fervor or forfeited the moral respect of their communities. On the other hand, those without modern education, while they could retain their hold upon the emotions of the faithful, tended to be less successful in leading Muslims to strength within an increasingly secular India. Of one thing they were all quite sure. They did not wish to be part of a Hindu India. Sayyad refused to join the Indian National Congress. He saw clearly that the more democratic government became, the more it would be in the hands of Hindus. A Hindu majority might someday even oppress the Muslim minority (even if Muslims made up over a quarter of the population). Many other Muslims tended to agree with Sayyad.

The All-India Muslim League The pace picked up rapidly after 1900. In Bengal and Bombay especially, young Hindu extremists resorted to terror tactics. In 1905, the Viceroy, Lord Curzon, decided to partition the mammoth province of Bengal. While Bengal was too big to be run effectively, this proposal did offer further attractions. It promised to give Muslims a ruling voice in a new East Bengal where they would hold a clear majority. It was also a way of cutting some ground from beneath the "nationalist" Hindus, the activists in particular. The Viceroy's action provoked a violent explosion. Accusing the British of deliberate divide-and-rule motives, many Hindus protested. B. G. Tilak, a Brahman who was militantly orthodox, advocated expelling the British from India, violently if necessary. Calling for immediate *swaraj* (self-rule), he declared that India should not have further social and political reforms until it was free of the British. (Of course Muslims had reason to question how much reform was wanted by an orthodox Brahman.) Tilak openly approved mass protest and terrorist activities. This led to his imprisonment. But even more moderate Congress leaders, such as G. K. Gokhale, were disturbed. A statement was put out strongly favoring responsible self-government for India as a dominion, like Canada, within the British Empire. The clamor was so strong that, once again, as in the Ilbert Bill controversy, the British rulers lost their nerve and called off the plan to partition Bengal. But this only provoked a counter-storm from Muslims, who felt themselves betrayed by the revocation. Intent on saving their community, Muslims founded the All-India Muslim League in 1906. As in the case of the Ilbert Bill, respect for British motives and authority suffered serious damage.

The Constitutional Reforms Obviously, in the face of such mounting pressures, political reforms were expedient and necessary. By the Morley-Minto Act of 1909, Parliament expanded the measure of representative government in British India from local to provincial and to central legislative councils. Elected Indians could have greater voice in these councils, but they could not have a majority of votes. In addition, seats in the councils would be "reserved" for representatives from various interest groups and communities. Dismayed at this special recognition of rights for "separate electorates" and claiming again to represent Indians of all faiths and communities, the Congress protested against what it saw as further evidence of divide-and-rule tactics. Caught between Congress claims and League demands, the British were unable to find solutions satisfactory to all parties. Their failures brought lack of confidence and increasing distrust. Processes of political integration, begun over a century and a half earlier, faltered.

World War I brought further profound changes and necessitated further constitutional reform. Indian contributions to the war effort, in soldiers, supplies, and finances, were of such importance that a grateful Britain could not ignore the question; moreover, in the terrible losses of lives and of treasure that it suffered, a greatly weakened Britain could not easily dictate the solution. During the war, India became an economic power, ranking eighth in industry and fourth in textiles. By 1916, nationalist demands began to rise. The Home Rule League, led by Annie Besant the English theosophist, insisted that India should have total self-government after the war. Indeed, for once the Congress and Muslim League made a joint resolution to the same effect. As a result, in 1919 the Montagu-Chelmsford Reforms (the Government of India Act) introduced a new concept, that of dyarchy—

double government. The number of Indian representatives sitting in legislative councils was increased to solid majorities, thus providing a first taste of responsible government. Henceforth, in the provinces, Legislative Assemblies would have Cabinet Government with control over most matters. Only on questions of finance and internal security, and then primarily at the All-India level, would powers of decision be reserved to the British executive. As before, "reserved seats" were to be filled by persons representing "separate electorates" from each community according to their proportional numbers within the decennial census.

ESCALATIONS OF CIVIL RESISTANCE AND COMMUNAL STRIFE

But before the new reforms could come into force, they were by-passed by the force of events. The British government, feeling threatened by the increasing nationalist propaganda and activity, enacted the Rowlatt sedition acts, which permitted "preventive detention" and criminal trials without juries. Such repressive methods might not have been questioned a century earlier, in an age known for its "oriental despotism." But procedures of "due process" for ensuring justice were by now too well-known to be set aside so lightly. A storm of protests broke across the country, and the voices of less-educated Indians heretofore unaffected by the issues of nationalism were to be heard among the protestors. Ex-soldiers, unable to adjust to civilian life, had turned to lawlessness. And communal riots and terrorism within the Punjab added further social tension. A frightened Punjab government overreacted to the growing unrest.

Gandhi Into the center of this storm stepped a figure whose role in nationalist activities was to be pivotal during the next thirty years. The organizer of large-scale demonstrations was Mohandas Karimchand Gandhi (1868–1948). Returned from South Africa, where for twenty-two years (1893–1915) he had gained fame by leading struggles against injustice, Gandhi had just the skills needed to mobilize massive civil resistence. More than that, he had developed a truly remarkable weapon for fighting the British. Called *satyagraha* or "truth-force," it was a method of fighting rulers through "nonviolent" noncooperation and thus putting intolerable pressure upon human conscience and feelings of guilt. (As a form of moral blackmail it was to be especially effective when used against the British.)

Gandhi called for an All-India *hartal* (strike or boycott). All shops were to close and all work to cease. An unruly mob at Amritsar, in the Punjab, killed some Europeans. Later, a huge crowd defied a curfew by meeting in a public garden in order to hold a nationalist rally. When General Dyer, the local army commander, ordered his troops to fire into the crowd, people were unable to escape because the garden was enclosed by a wall. At least 379 persons were killed. The Amritsar Massacre (or "Jallianwalla Bagh"), as it became known, profoundly shocked the Indian public. And, when the British Government refused to censure this terrible incident, Gandhi, declaring British rule "satanic," called for an all-out campaign of complete civil disobedience to drive the "devils" out.

The problem was that Gandhi could not control all of the protestors or make sure that all demonstrators were peaceful. Every campaign of nonviolence ended up with violence. Alarmed by the fire and killing in 1921, Gandhi called off his campaign and willingly went to prison. Emerging from prison in 1924, his power and popularity were such that, in the world press, he became a heroic symbol, larger than life. By his ability to reach the minds and hearts of simple village folk in India, he won a greater personal following than any man had ever done before. By his piety, his philosophy of non-violence (*ahimsa*), and his ascetic simplicity, he appealed to the loftiest of Hindu ideals. But by every symbol with which he captured the imaginations of Hindus, he frightened and offended Muslims.

Conferences and a New Constitution Riots between Muslims and Hindus increased in frequency and savagery. As the Congress gained in power and as Muslims felt threatened by Hindu domination, bloody clashes between peoples in India became more common. Deeds of violence were not checked by ideals of nonviolence.

Finally, in 1927, in the face of deteriorating and intolerable conditions, Parliament appointed the Simon Commission. The Commission's task was to find a solution to the impasse, how to govern India and please everyone. But again the British made a mistake. Not one of the seven Commission members was Indian. The Congress countered by calling a special All-India Conference of its own. This called for immediate and full self-government of India as a dominion within the British Commonwealth; but it also advocated the abolition of separate electorates. Some extremists, like Jawaharlal Nehru, wanted an independent India to withdraw from the Commonwealth completely. But once again, for the Muslim League and for Muhammad Ali Jinnah, who had emerged as its strongest leader, Congress proposals looked ever more dangerous.

Again Britain tried to satisfy the various competing nationalist demands, promising eventual dominion status and trying to restore confidence in the future of a united India. But since the demands of the Congress had not been met, Gandhi launched another large-scale campaign of civil disobedience. Defying an ancient pre-British law which reserved the right of making and selling salt to the state (king), he organized a grand march of 170 miles to the sea where, with newspapermen and photographers ready to record the event, he ostentatiously made some salt from sea water. His arrest was followed by widespread disturbances and further arrests. In the West, salt taxes were remembered as forms of medieval oppression suffered by the poor. Gandhi won wide sympathy, and public opinion put pressure upon the British Government. At Simon's recommendation, Round Table Conferences in which all interested groups could meet in a setting of equality were called. All went well until, in 1932, Muslim and Untouchable leaders flatly refused to consider the abolition of separate electorates. Insisting that all people must be seen simply as Indians without any creed, caste, or color distinctions, Gandhi refused to see how some groups could feel threatened.

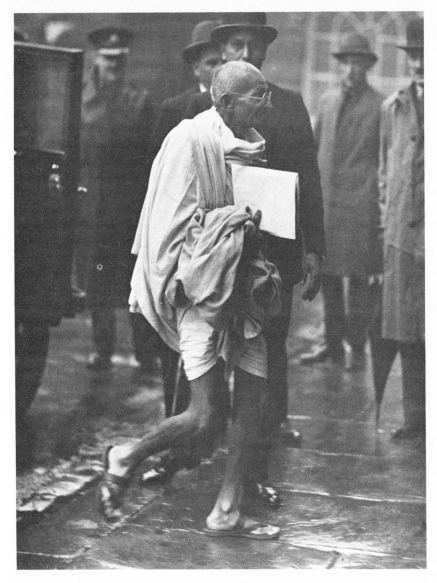

Mohandas Gandhi in London, September 1931. Gandhi is seen attending the second conference on Indian independence. Another sixteen years were to pass before British rule in India came to an end. (Kemsley Picture Service, London.)

At the same time he called the 60 million Untouchables a new name. Henceforth they would be *Harijans* or "Children of God" and must be seen as Hindus. He began fasting to get his way and was at death's door when Dr. Ambedkar, the leader of Untouchable organizations, surrendered. Unwilling to face the social stigma and shame of having caused Gandhi's death, he declared that Untouchables would no longer insist upon separately reserved seats in the legislature. Gandhi had won; but the cost would be greater than could be realized. The Congress was henceforth committed to the abolition of untouchability. Having survived through millenia, the tradition of segregation of castes and of outcastes from caste Hindus, as symbolized by separate status and privilege, was implicitly being disavowed. But to Muslims, who had looked upon Untouchables as being at least neutral non-Hindus if not also potential allies (and converts), Gandhi's action of absorbing Untouchables into Hinduism was seen as confirming their worst fears.

Eventually, after long and heated discussions, proposals emerged which became the basis of the Government of India Act of 1935. The Act, the essentials of which were later to be incorporated into the present Constitution of the Republic of India, provided that each of the then eleven provinces of British India would have its own elected legislature and a cabinet fully responsible to members of the legislature. Provision was also made for an All-India federation of provinces and princely states. Unfortunately, this proviso was voluntary and was never pursued with proper vigor. Governors still had certain veto power but use of this power was not foreseen as being likely to occur. This Act was the last constructive contribution to the unity of India made by the British.

THE PARTITION OF INDIA

The real break of the Muslim League away from the ideal of a Union of India began in 1937. Elections of that year gave the Congress control over eight provinces. In three of these, however, it had less than a majority. It could have responded to Muslim hopes and fears by inviting some League members to join it in forming coalition governments, especially in provinces where there were large Muslim minorities. In refusing to be generous and to share power, the Congress was indeed doing exactly what it had been accusing the British of doing for decades. As a consequence, Muhammad Ali Jinnah was forced to make a very difficult decision. No matter which way he went, this could have grave repercussions. If he urged Muslims to join the Congress, he would be admitting what had been vehemently denied for thirty years—that the Congress alone stood for all Indians. If he did not do so, his logic would demand the building of a separate state for Muslims. Younger, more extreme Muslims had for years been clamoring for a separate and free Islamic nation. The new state would be called Pakistan—"Land of the Pure." As fears grew and threats multiplied for the Muslim population, Jinnah felt obliged to listen. In 1940, his decision to aim for a national Muslim state to be created by partition of India into two separate nations was adopted at a Muslim League meeting in Lahore.

World War II hastened the final deadlock. Late in 1939, in disapproval of India's entry into the war, all of the Congress governments resigned. The British, with their backs to the wall and fighting for their very survival, refused to give up power but promised to hand over power completely at the end of the war. Again, as in its dealings with the Muslim League in 1937, the Congress was less than generous. Sniffing possible total victory, it refused to settle for anything short of an immediate and complete withdrawal of the British from India. In 1942, as war with Japan broke out and the British situation looked even more desparate, a gigantic "Quit India" campaign to drive out the British was launched by Gandhi. But, although violence and disruption were widespread for a few days, general public sympathy for the British was strong and they had little trouble putting the Congress leaders in jail. There they remained until the end of the war. Moreover, by withdrawing from responsible government and from freedom to act openly, the Congress forfeited much of its initiative and gave great opportunities to its opponents. The Muslim League celebrated a day of thanksgiving for deliverance from Congress rule and then set to work. Taking advantage of its freedom, it mobilized massive support from Muslims throughout India, collecting money and arms and preparing for an inevitable showdown. The League was prepared to fight, if necessary, to gain its objective of a separate Muslim state.

Immediately after the war, political struggles began in earnest. Again the Congress made a mistake. During the election campaign of 1946, it wasted time denouncing the British whereas, instead, it should have sensed where real dangers lay and spent time courting Muslim support. This failure soon became apparent in the election results which showed that, while the Congress had carried all caste-Hindu seats, it had only taken sixteen out of five hundred Muslim seats. Responsible Congress leaders, such as Gandhi and Nehru, simply failed to realize how genuinely threatened the Muslims felt and how weak and exhausted the British had become. Even so, when Nehru still remained adamant and uncompromising, Jinnah called all Muslims to a day of "Direct Action." All over India violence erupted, and in Calcutta nearly five thousand lives were lost in three days. Riots spread and

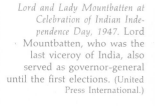

Lord and Lady Mountbatten at Celebration of Indian Independence Day, 1947. Lord Mountbatten, who was the last viceroy of India, also served as governor-general until the first elections. (United Press International.)

another twelve thousand died. Dreams of a united India vanished in the smoke of a rapidly growing holocaust. No longer prepared to pay what it would cost to maintain order and unity, the British Government announced its departure from India by the end of 1947. Within a matter of weeks, voting of partition took place in each province; boundary commissions were hastily set up in Punjab and Bengal where Muslim majority regions would go to Pakistan; and Parliament passed the India Independence Act. At midnight on August 14–15, 1947, authority was formally transferred to India and Pakistan. Never in history had rule over an empire been given up in this fashion.

But perhaps never in history was their such a terrible holocaust of civil violence as what followed. Horrible massacres in Punjab and Bengal were far worse than anything imaginable. At least eleven million people fled— Hindus and Sikhs to India and Muslims to Pakistan. How many lives were lost will never be known; but estimates vary between one and four million. The scars of bitterness and hate resulting from this great tragedy were to remain. For Gandhi, the partition and its aftermath of killing represented an ultimate failure. He went to Calcutta and declared that he would fast to death if the killing did not stop. In Delhi he fasted again. Then in January of 1948, as he was emerging from a prayer meeting, a young Hindu fanatic who deeply resented what Gandhi wished for Untouchables ran forward and shot him to death. Such was the shock of his death that it brought the killing to a halt.

How long the Partition will last remains an open question. Technically still at war, with periods of truce having broken into hostility in 1949, 1965, and 1971, India and Pakistan have yet to resolve their differences. Pakistan has yet to establish a viable constitution, connecting its rulers with its people; moreover, the loss of its eastern province of Bangladesh—which declared its independence in 1971—has not brightened her future prospects. Within India, on the other hand, processes of integration have continued. India has emerged as an important power, one which must be counted in the councils of world affairs. The strength of India today is far greater than was that of the Indian Empire during the 1840's when its western territorial boundaries were roughly drawn where they are today. India remains the dominant power in South Asia and only time can tell whether all the people of the subcontinent will someday once again come within the shadow of one authority.

SOUTH ASIA
SINCE 1950
In the period of over a quarter century since the countries of South Asia became independent of British rule, India has clearly emerged as the paramount power. While the traumas of the Partition and of its aftermath have been exceedingly costly to the subcontinent—in terms of horrendous military expenditures which the peoples of India and Pakistan have had to pay (probably double what such costs might have been for a single, Indian Union); in terms of slower economic development for India and especially for Bangladesh (East Bengal, formerly East Pakistan); in terms of dangerously slow political development for Pakistan; and, finally, in terms of a much

lower prestige and diplomatic role in global affairs—the importance of political stability in the area and the crucial bearing of such stability upon a larger international equilibrium and world peace require a closer look at recent history. The very facts, that three wars have been fought between India and Pakistan (peace has never been established nor truce formally ended) and that, in all these years, Pakistan has never established a viable constitutional relationship between the rulers and the ruled (an initial decade of chaos and corruption, followed by more than a decade of martial and dictatorial rule under Ayub Khan and Yahyah Khan, has then led to "leftist" rule by yet another strongman, Mohammed Ali Bhutto) have tended to exacerbate other problems in the area and to involve the other great powers of the world in the internal affairs of the subcontinent. This alone serves to contrast the development of South Asia from that of East Asia.

Internal Politics For seventeen years after independence, India was the "Realm of Nehru." In a land where cult of personality was traditional and where advancing age commended veneration, Nehru was lifted into the abode of the gods. He became a living legend and the fount of inspiration and hope. As successor to Gandhi, he was the *Ma-Bap,* the "mother-father" of the nation. With his knee-length coat (*sherwani*), his white "Gandhi" cap, and his silver-knob cane, he was more like the Grand Mughal holding court than like the leader of a parliamentary democracy. At a word or glance, officials and politicians would jump and wheels would turn. But when he went away from New Delhi, or even when he was out of sight, centers of power would relax and administrative actions would slow down.

Yet power in India was not simply autocratic. Political divinity did more than simply hold audiences. It took advice from notables. By the 1960's Nehru was the senior figure in Indian politics (and among world statesmen). He had held power longer than any other. Few at the beginning had doubted his brilliance, his dedication, or his idealism; but many had doubted his staying power and his ability to impose a strong will upon the Congress Party and upon the administration. He had managed to win leadership of the left wing of the Congress away from Subhas Chandra Bose without losing his popularity or strength among senior leaders of the right wing. Employing the ancient skills of a Brahman, he had applied tradition to the enormous tasks of cementing national unity. Vigorously secular in his outlook, he had been India's high priest of secularism.

Once in power, Nehru dealt first with his own party. Many creeds and interests of all kinds had found shelter under the umbrella of the Congress Party in the name of nationalism and independence. Nehru worked to smother Hindu reactionary fanatics, but without extinguishing Hindu values. Yet, he could not prevent emergence of the Jan Sangh Party as a force in North India, with its revived threat of Hindu extremism. His avowed "socialist pattern for society" also provoked the founding in 1959 of another right wing party, the Swatantra (Independent) Party, by the old veteran of the South, C. Rajagonalachari. Yet, on the left, the dashing and popular idealist, Jaya Prakash Narayan, left the Congress because it was not socialist enough. So did Acharya Kripalani. The Praja Socialists and other socialists hoped to become a regular opposition party; but they never were able to convince enough people that their socialism was better than that of Nehru. No one could overcome Nehru's mystique. After the death of the anti-communist Patel, the fall of Tandon, and the departure of Kripalani, no Congressman openly dared to oppose him. Nehru's hold on the country was so complete that, apart from the Communists who remained his only serious contenders, his greatest opposition came covertly from within his own party.

As a result, for many years Nehru's personal views were the national views of India. At every turn his ideas reflected Indian policy. Even so, they reflected a complex personality, a man who was a westerner by taste, education, and temperament, and yet a man whose ardent nationalistic beliefs amounted to a fanatic religion. Nehru held strong democratic convictions. His socialistic principles, learned from English Fabians, would not permit him to surrender individual freedom and dignity for Marxist mass compulsion. He saw India's development as a huge experiment. He wished for a national rebirth through liberal rather than autocratic or totalitarian means. This rebirth was not to be religious. It was not to be Hindu. It was to be secular.

With Nehru's death in 1964, a new age in Indian politics dawned. Unlike Gandhi, Nehru could not stand having equals. Consequently, he left an empty void. No strong leadership was trained and ready to take his place in the Congress Party. His successor, Prime Minister Lal Bahadur Shastri, was a courageous man. He succeeded in preventing the feuding factions within the party from fighting openly. But after his sudden death from a heart attack in January 1966, decay within the party gained speed. Indira Gandhi, Nehru's daughter, became the next Prime Minister. But behind the scenes was the powerful Moraji Desai, a puritanical Hindu who would have led both party and nation to the right. The elections of 1967 dealt blows to Congress power. Control in almost half of India's seventeen states fell to such parties as the Communists, the reactionary Jan Sangh, the Swatantra, and other locally strong parties, such as the D.M.K.[1] in Madras. As a result, state governments have become more powerful and the "Center's" power to make changes has often been weakened. Mrs. Gandhi's tactic has been to purge the party, driving its "old Guard" into opposition and rebellion, and then, turning left, to form electoral alliances with the moderate Communist parties.

Foreign Policies In external affairs also, Nehru was for years the sole author and director of Indian policies. Until the Hungarian and Suez crises of 1956, there was little criticism of his role. Few at home knew as much as he and few vested interests were concerned. Nehru wished to play a conspicuous

---

[1] *Dravida, Munetra, Kazagham.*

part in the world and he succeeded. He wanted recognition of India as an equal among the Great Powers. But, despite his quest for Indian self-respect and self-confidence, most Indians were ignorant about world affairs. Nehru was strongly "anti-colonialist." He was prejudiced against the western powers. The bones of ruined Western empires still littered Asia in 1947. This explains his harsh view of British actions over Suez in 1956. It explains his mildness toward Russian butchery in Hungary that same year. It explains his constant suspicion of the United States. And it also explains his blindness to the imperial ambitions of Red China.

Beneath all, however, India's foreign policies stood on a bedrock of solid realism. This realism was often covered by an airy idealism which deepened in color the further a problem went away from the frontiers of the subcontinent. On the world stage, Nehru sounded like a good, moralistic internationalist. He spoke about self-determination, cooperation, and conciliation for all peoples. But on or near India's frontiers, he was usually canny and hard-headed. He did not scruple to act with vigor in crushing any "dangerous" local self-determination or anything else which might harm India.

Irredentism. Belief in "redeeming" or regaining "lost" territory from foreign rule has remained. From the beginning, India has jealously tried to maintain, if not to expand, its territorial position in the subcontinent and to defend itself against forces outside its strategic frontiers. The toughness of Indian policy has lessened the farther it moved in concentric circles away from these frontiers. In dealings with such territories as Hyderabad, Kashmir, Nagaland, and Goa, India resorted unflinchingly to naked force. Attitudes toward Nepal, Bhutan, and Sikkim have been almost as firm.

Against no country, however, has India been more adamant and militant than against Pakistan. Relations between Pakistan and India can be compared with those that existed between the North and the South after the Civil War in the United States. The animosities between a man and woman after a long and painful marriage has ended in divorce could hardly compare to such enmity. The Partition of 1947 brought panic, bloodshed, and suffering for many millions. Perhaps twelve million persons fled for their lives. Perhaps one to three million died in communal massacres. Bitterness has deepened with the years. It seethes beneath the surface. It erupted into violence in 1965, and again in 1971.

At the outset, three causes fed this dangerous bitterness—partition payments, water control, and Kashmir. Water control and Kashmir were explosively dangerous—one, economic and the other, emotional.

Reparations for refugee property was an intricate problem. But lack of water in Punjab could provoke Pakistanis to war. India controlled all the headwaters of canals that irrigated the wheat fields of Pakistani Punjab; and her wish to divert these waters for great schemes in Indian Rajasthan was like a dagger at Pakistan's throat. Once or twice, India closed off water to Pakistan for two or three weeks; and this, Pakistan will never forget.

The Water Treaty signed by Nehru on September 19, 1960, tended to calm this conflict. By its terms, India kept the waters of three rivers (Sutlej, Beas, and Ravi) and Pakistan got waters from three rivers (Indus, Jhelum, and Chenam). The World Bank sponsored a scheme which fed Pakistani canals out of its three rivers. This cost a billion dollars. (Of this, about $177,000,000 was given by the U.S., $70,000,000 loaned by the U.S., and $58,000,000 given by the U.K.)

But Kashmir as a bone of contention involved the prestige of both sides. When, at Partition, the Hindu ruler of mostly Muslim Kashmir was unable to decide whether to go with India or Pakistan, the "acquisition" of Kashmir became a point of honor for Hindu and Moslem alike. India based its stand on legitimacy; Pakistan, on self-determination. India claimed Kashmir because in a desperate moment, the Hindu Maharaja signed over his power. India had stamped the Nizam of Hyderabad into the dust, on the grounds of self-determination, when he refused to sign away his power in 1950. Yet India never agreed to self-determination (by election) in Kashmir. For India, Kashmir has been the crowning symbol of its claim to being a secular state. Yet, for Pakistan also, Kashmir has been the crowning symbol of its claim to being an Islamic state. Most of the people of Kashmir have been Muslims. If they had been given half a chance, therefore, Kashmiris would probably have sought to merge Kashmir with Pakistan. Nehru himself had come from a Kashmiri Brahman family which long ago had moved into Hindustan. He cherished the dream that Muslims would willingly join in a secular Indian state. For supporters of an Islamic state, however, Nehru's dream was frightening. Islamic power could not succeed without also, at the same time, causing India to become a Hindu state. Such was the dilemma until the Islamic State itself was shattered by the Bangladesh Secession and the Indo-Pakistan War of December 1971.

Nonalignment. This policy was meant to be more than negative, more than escape from reality, or more than mere neutrality. As Nehru spoke of it, this was meant to be a positive doctrine, one based on national self-interest. It served as the Indian version of the Monroe Doctrine. Its underlying assumptions were: (1) that another world war would be nuclear; (2) that such a war would bring disaster to all; and (3) that India would not escape damage if not destruction. Nehru's tactics, therefore, were twofold.

His first approach was that of *positive isolation.* The Monroe Doctrine sought to preclude the spread of Old World rivalries to the New. It preferred a negative isolation, a withdrawal from international politics and responsibility. India's policy, on the other hand, aimed to free as much of the world as possible from the suicidal virus of war frenzy. It tried to quarantine this virus to the smallest space, preferably to America and Russia alone. But it also wished to encourage the rest of the world to take constructive, war-preventive activities. India's attempts to lead nations toward nonalignment were based on the notion that the more such nations there were the less likely war would become.

Unfortunately, India's efforts to isolate the great power blocs and to

Jawaharlal Nehru and Indira Gandhi in New Delhi. (United Press International.)

free other nations from danger often caused an estrangement with the United States. Ironically, while both India and America strove for peace, their tactics were diametrically opposed. Attempts by America to confine the cancer of Communist imperialism by aligning all non-Communist countries into defensive walls antagonized Nehru. Tense relations ensued. Both SEATO and the Baghdad Pact violated the Nehru Doctrine. They were held to be against India's interests. When Pakistan joined the American system of alliances and when air bases were built in Pakistan, India was shocked. Suspicion of Islam and of the West grew. The phalanx of "nonaligned" states in Asia and Africa was broken by American actions. Chilling winds of Cold War blew too close to India's doorstep. Even after China attacked India and Pakistan responded to America's help to India by becoming allied with China, India's policy did not really change.

Nehru's second policy was that of *positive conciliation,* that is, cultivation of good relations with both sides in the Cold War so as to produce a slow thaw. To Washington, however, this looked like a way to play off both sides in order to get as much as possible from each free. Moreover, this policy did not look impartial as much as dishonest and hostile. When India stayed within the British Commonwealth after throwing away the Crown, her action looked like veiled opportunism. Nehru's first visit to the United States in 1949 was a failure. His visit to Moscow, after Stalin's death, went so well that soon Bulganin and Khrushchev came to Delhi. In 1949, Red China was immediately recognized. Nationalist China was spurned as representing a new form of American imperialism. Visits to and from Red China followed. Washington felt constantly irritated by Nehru's "pious meddling."

India's leadership of "anti-colonialist" causes reached a climax with the Bandung Conference of Afro-Asian States in 1955. Nehru's doctrine of nonalignment was given an Indian name: the *Pancha Shila* or "five principles" of coexistence and nonaggression advocated mutual recognition of the equality of countries and insisted that peaceful coexistence should be the foundation for all international relations.

India's efforts to bring conciliation between the two great power blocks reached their zenith in 1956. Nehru felt he was the mediator between the Communist and the anti-Communist worlds. (He even allotted the building of three new steel plants equally to America, Britain, and Russia.) But then the earthquakes came. Calamities in Suez and Hungary brought the world to the brink of disaster. Nehru's blatantly uneven playing down of the slaughter of people in Hungary and his flirting with Red China gravely weakened his prestige and the strength of his doctrine. After the Chinese Incursion of 1962, his doctrine was swallowed in silence. The way in which countries surrounding India gloated did not help—*Pancha Shila* died.

The decade after Nehru's death, during most of which India's position in the world was under the astute management of his daughter, India continued its hurculean struggles to escape from the toils of its own economic predicament while, at the same time, trying to maintain and to strengthen its place as "paramount" power in the Indian Ocean. Since, in this latter object, little sympathy has come from Washington, India has felt itself obliged to turn more and more toward Soviet Russia for aid and support. Both countries have had reason to fear the motives of Red China.

Matters came to a head in 1971 when East Bengal broke away from Pakistan and then suffered incredible brutality and slaughter. At least a million people died and ten million fled to India for refuge. The fortitude and restraint with which India handled this terrible burden, providing food and medicine, so that neither epidemic nor famine struck down the hapless refugees, became a saga of voluntary humanitarian action. Finally, a few months later, war broke out. The efficiency with which the Indian Army moved was in marked contrast to its ventures with China almost ten years earlier. In the end, Bangladesh became a "client state" of India; India became more dependent upon the Soviet Union, and the gulf between India and America, as well as between India and China, grew wider than ever.

THE ECONOMY OF INDIA SINCE 1950

The paradox of the economic life in India is that, while many hover on the brink of extinction, others have never had it so good.

Poverty and Population For more than 240 million people, life has become fuller and richer than ever before. Most of these have been working people, who put in many hours at the factory, shop, office, and farm. Some, such as movie tycoons and ex-princes, have had it very easy. For another two-fifths of the people, conditions have been getting steadily poorer and more hopeless. Faced with the prospect of slowly skidding down the slopes of misery and want, in desperation such people often accept hazardous work and harsh conditions as coolies and near slaves—the exploitable. A final fifth of India's people, perhaps 120 million, have never known one full meal. For such, each day has always been a pitiful struggle to survive. Peoples of India may not have become poorer than they were in the days of the Mughals; but in comparison to the West, with its rapidly growing means for producing wealth, they have steadily fallen further behind. Even in comparison with India's own better classes (the top two-fifths), most Indians are becoming poorer. This means that the spread and variety in standards of Indian life are fantastic—much beyond the comprehension of people elsewhere. By contrast, the "poverty line" in the United States has been such that almost all its people would have been seen as prosperous in India. A mere whisper of new building or road construction brings running lines of hundreds of coolies—men, women, and children with baskets of dirt on their heads and a dole of boiled grain in their hearts. The labor of two men can be worth less than that of one bullock. A cycle-riksha *wallah* (fellow) pumps until his heart bursts, just for a few coppers a fare. How many died of heart attacks pumping the same vehicle before him? (In contrast, the American wonders how many cars he might afford during his lifetime.) In city streets many sleep under the sky with nothing to keep off the dew. Monsoon rains bring shivering, malaria, tuberculosis, and death. The average wage in India is less than $60 a year. Slight changes in prices can mean starvation. When rains fail, famine brings death to millions. For those who have known nothing else, pain and misery are a way of life.

For hundreds of years, numbers of people probably remained roughly constant, perhaps at about 100 million. Birth rates were high. So were death rates—from famine, disease, and war. War all but vanished after 1800. By 1872, the subcontinent held 206 million people. Modern medicine and famine relief affected the death rate dramatically, especially infant mortality. By 1971, population estimates reached 720 million (580 for India; 65 for Pakistan, 75 for Bangladesh). The death rate, still high, with average life expectancy still under 40 years, was so much lower than it had been that ten million people more have been added each year.

Under present conditions, too many people struggle for existence. Even though in India more food has been produced than ever before, the level of production necessary to sustain and satisfy life has never been as swift as the increase in population. Like Alice in Wonderland, food production in India has had to run faster and faster just for per capita consumption to stay where it was. Population increase has eaten up all extra food production.

Population Control and Social Welfare The drastic decline in the death rate has brought such spectacular increases in numbers of people, so many more mouths to feed, that this increase alone has more than cancelled all efforts to improve living conditions. If only population growth would stop, it has been argued, many of the increases in productivity could have brought benefits to people.

Since 1950, the Government of India has recognized the need to control population growth and has officially sponsored "family planning" programs. It has tried to educate people, to convince them that they should limit the number of children in each family. It has sought to discover new ways to limit the birth rate, to reduce it from 40 per 1,000 to 25 per 1,000. By 1965, more than 12,000 family planning centers had been established and were functioning. Since then, the campaign has been intensified. Village leaders had been recruited to support the program. People had been given basic information. It was hoped that, with mass production and distribution of "the Lippe's Loop" and "the pill," the birth rate could be cut just as effectively as the death rate. There were more grounds for believing that, unless this were successful, mass starvation for tens of millions of people would ultimately cause a disaster such as had never been seen. The countless deaths from starvation that occurred in Bihar during 1966 and 1967 were a stark reminder of what could happen.

But to persuade people to have fewer children could be no final solution. The old saying that "the rich get richer while the poor get children" was not without support. Poor people had to have children to help them in satisfying their basic economic needs and to provide security for them in their old age. For the poor, children have taken the place of health and life insurance, to say nothing of a host of welfare services which have been provided for needy people in the West. Until the stranglehold of caste prejudice could be broken down sufficiently and until true "public" with a sense of conscience and of compassion could develop, most of the poor and the most needy had to rely mainly upon their own devices. To be old, sick, poor, and without children was seen as being bereft of almost all help. When hard times come, such persons would be the first to die.

Through community development programs and Village Councils (*Panchayats*), attempts have been made to improve roads, schools, homes; to build health clinics, model farms, small scale (or cottage) industries; and to introduce recreation facilities, competitions, and clubs. The Government of India, however, has spent more money and shown more concern than state and local governments. It has worked to prevent epidemics, adulteration of processed foods, mass starvation from famine, and to improve sanitary conditions in villages and towns. Even so, water supplies in most cities are still not very safe for drinking and sanitation has remained exceedingly poor. The surface has hardly been scratched in many of the most serious problems.

Conditions among India's Untouchables and other so-called "depressed classes" and "scheduled castes" have received special attention; but again, this has been more from the Union and State levels than from the more immediate localities in which they lived. They have been given special representation in government, special employment by quotas to openings in administrative and military services, and special educational and economic opportunities. Nearly a million have been awarded special scholarships.

About 50,000 have been given the means with which to attend college.

India probably has over 300 million cows or more to say nothing of countless other animals. Some, like the famous Ongole bulls, are truly magnificent creatures. Most, however, are so famished and weak that they are a natural calamity. Useless cows and bulls, too weak to give milk or pull a plough, must compete with people for limited amounts of the same food. Yet, to Hindus cows have been sacred, not to be destroyed even to save the country. Cow-slaughter is prohibited by law. How a poor farmer could get along without his bullocks, even weak ones, which plough his fields, draw his water, pull his cart to market, and even provide his fuel, has yet to be determined.

Prehistoric Steattite Seal from the Indus Valley. The importance of the bull symbol in Indian culture dates from the earliest history of the subcontinent. This seal was found at excavations in the Harappa region of Pakistan, where the large, well-planned city of Mohengo-Daro flourished c. 3000–2000 B.C. (Archaeological Survey of India.)

Agriculture Almost four out of five persons in India live by growing crops. In spite the growth of such important market crops as tea, tobacco, cotton, and sugar, four-fifths of what is grown is food for domestic consumption. Cultivating land has been India's main industry. It should and could provide enough food. The Gangetic plain alone, one of the great alluvial areas of the world, should have sufficed.

But crop land in India is as crowded as land in the most industrialized parts of Japan, Western Europe, or the United States. With nowhere else to go and nothing else to do, more and more people have been forced to make a living off the land. Average holdings have shrunk and fragmented. A holding of five acres could often be broken into as many as twenty tiny plots, which then had to be divided equally among heirs who, in turn, were obliged to do the same among their children. The land itself has become so worn out from centuries of over use without adequate fertilization that crops are pathetically meagre, and even these are often ruined by drought, floods, and pests.

Generally, until very recently, crop yields in India were so low that Japanese farmers got at least three times more food from the same amount of land, as did the English and Danish. Crude methods were much to blame. Much the same light wooden plough was used as was used thousands of years ago, hardly scratching the ground. Up until very recently, fertilizer was rarely used. Even the cowdung, which might have been used to enrich the soil, must be burned as fuel to cook the family meal, since other fuels were too expensive. Seed was broadcast by hand; and, only in the 1960's were the newer strains of high-yield seed successful. Much of each harvest has been lost on old-fashioned threshing floors, in storage pits dug in the ground, and in transit to market. Rodents alone may have eaten up as much as half of each crop. (In short, despite great potential, India has not been able to make itself self-sufficient in food. Its meagre foreign exchange has had to be spent abroad for purchasing grain. The United States alone has loaned India grain worth over $3 billion.)

To make matters worse, at least half of all rural people have struggled under heavy land-rents and debts. For centuries land had been held by countless layers of landholders, landlords, hereditary tax collectors and the like, below whom were more layers of tenants, subtenants, even sub-subtenants. And below these, masses of landless laborers were ready to do any work just for a bit of food. Landlords at the top demanded one-half, even two-thirds, of each crop. In-between lords below them often demanded an equal amount out of that half or third which remained, the process being repeated at each step down the landholding ladder. This meant that each lower level had a much smaller share of the scraps of left-overs. Yet, such was the value of landholding status that some persons preferred to subsist in idle poverty, living off tiny scraps of rent squeezed painfully from the sweat and toil of some starving landless laborer. To do away with such thraldom, more land reform laws were passed in India during the past twenty years than anywhere else in the world. Yet these laws did not really change the essentials of power, the profound unfairness of the system, nor the old traditions. Even the Bhoodan or "Land Gift" movement of Gandhi's disciple, Vinoba Bhave, failed to achieve more than to arouse a spirit of giving and sharing.

Debt led to perpetual thraldom; while the moneylender also ran real risks. Often the simple villager who wanted money for some uneconomical ditch, or buying a pair of bullocks, could get a cheap loan from the Government or from the village Cooperative. If he wanted to marry off his daughter, perform a religious ceremony, or indulge some unproductive extravagance,

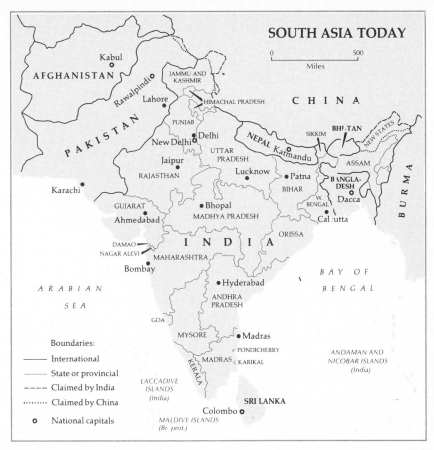

SOUTH ASIA TODAY

he had to borrow secretly at 100 or 200 percent compounded interest. If he did not wish to lose standing or even caste, among his fellows, such things had to be done. A man could borrow more than he made in ten years. Moreover, the lower his caste and social status the poorer he was considered as a credit risk. Once caught in such a debt, unpaid interest could grow so fast that he remained caught forever. His great-great grandchildren, yet unborn, were thus condemned to working for the moneylender. In many villages, the moneylender and the landlord were the same person.

The chains that have shackled India's great agricultural potential have yet to be broken. Fresh attempts to reform land holding and abolish debt bondage have been made. Better methods of farming and better seeds have been introduced. Cheap chemical fertilizers have come into use. Years have passed, however, and needs are still unmet. Cheaper fuel, which might release animal manure for enriching soil instead of for cooking, looks as distant as ever—due to a world energy crisis which has hit India more cruelly than any other country.

In the past, India was a leading country in the science of irrigation. Indeed, engineers came from India to California a century ago to help that state build its great irrigation schemes. Before 1947, India had 50 million acres under irrigation—more than any other country in the world. Great new works, huge dams and canal networks, have been constructed. These have assured regular water for crops, flood control, and hydroelectric power. Among the 77 major projects and countless minor ones, the most spectacular, the Bhakra-Nangal of Punjab, with one of the highest dams in existence (740 feet), and with 652 miles of canals, this scheme has provided water for up to six million acres, carrying water 425 miles into the Rajasthan Desert and providing over 2 million kilowatts of electricity. Already, over 84 million acres have been irrigated and plans for increases to 98 million have been made. With more abundant and constant water, so as to enable double- or triple-cropping, Indian agriculture can solve the problems of production. But the problems of distribution have yet to be solved.

Industry With the largest known deposits of high-grade iron ore; with almost limitless amounts of low-grade coal; with tremendous reserves of bauxite (for aluminum); with much of the world's manganese (for steel making); with most of the free world's mica (for electrical equipment); and with ample amounts of nuclear materials such as thorium, India is capable of great industrial power. The problem is not nature's bounty but man's use of that bounty.

Lack of development in oil and the production of electricity has obstructed growth. Discovery of important oil reserves in Assam and Gujarat assures potential, but, India has far to go before it fully exploits its own oil resources. Electricity production has been difficult. All of India's electrical power would not supply the needs of metropolitan London or New York City. Almost half of this has been produced by water power—which has had to depend upon monsoon rains. All large cities, most towns, and even some villages have electric lighting. But without much more steady and cheaper electrical power, industrial growth has been arrested. Large thermal and nuclear-thermal plants, the hope for the future, also depend on availability of fuels.

India's fame for fine craftsmanship is very old. Until the nineteenth century, more than a third of India's workers were engaged in producing handmade goods—peoples who are still skilled in weaving fine fabrics, in making rich carpets, in spinning fine gold and silver threads and laces, and in turning out soft, brightly colored and beautifully embroidered wool Kashmir shawls and radiantly lovely silk saris from Kanchipuram and Benares. Delicately wrought jewelry, silverware, brassware, and carving in rosewood, walnut, teak, and ivory have been equally noteworthy. In producing leather goods, India has ranked second in the world.

India has retained its historical leadership in the making of cloth. Hundreds of thousands of hand-weavers still make fine silk, cotton, and wool fabrics. But, as elsewhere, the industrial revolution to machine-made goods began with cotton textiles. During the American Civil War, modern mills grew up around Bombay. These textiles have become the largest single industry, employing almost a million workers and making cloth one of India's leading exports.

Heavy industry, requiring iron and steel began at the turn of the century. The privately owned Tata plants have grown until they are among the world's largest. With British, Russian, and West German help, three government-owned mills have also begun production. Growth has continued until the country now makes more than ten million tons of steel, over five times what it produced in 1948. (U.S. production = 100 million; Chinese = 20 million tons.)

Thus, India has certainly become an industrial nation. Since World War II, great expansion has occurred. Cotton and jute mills; coal mines; paper mills; fertilizer and chemical plants; sugar and oil refineries, locomotive works; railway coach shops; shipyards; bus, truck, and automobile plants—in all, India has over 11,000 factories. Producing such varied items as telephone equipment, wire and cable, electronic devices, refrigerators, air conditioners, fans, radios, ball bearings, light bulbs, razor blades, synthetic fabrics, antibiotics, tires, watches, pens, and many kinds of machines and machine tools; making her own guns ammunition, even planes, tanks, ships, and more than

Hand Labor in India. Workers sew sacks in jute mill near Calcutta. (Photo copyright by J. Allan Cash, London.)

1.5 million bicycles each year, some for sale in Africa and Southeast Asia—India's industrial capacity has shown enormous potential.

Yet industrial growth has continued to be much too slow. Most of India's raw materials, still exported, continue to feed the industries of other nations. Many manufactured items must still be imported. Power shortages and breakdowns often stop production. Lack of spare parts for imported machines causes needless delays. Failures in quality control hamper sales and threaten confidence. Although money is needed for rapid industrial development, the government's policies have discouraged investments. India's ability to buy from abroad has also been severely strained. With only about eight million industrial workers, such workers have become an elite. But employment of twice that number is necessary to relieve the strain of population pressure in rural areas.

Commerce Exchange is essential for an increase in prosperity, sufficient exchange not simply to purchase goods but to enable someone to buy—in ever wider spheres of exchange and at ever-faster speeds.

No other country in continental Asia or Africa has enjoyed a better system for surface travel. Important cities and towns are linked by no less than 35,000 miles of railways, almost 400,000 miles of roads, over a quarter hard-surfaced, and coast-to-coast airline connections. Most services are government owned and operated. Even though 1,000 miles of travel cost a third-class traveller less than six dollars and although half the passengers tend to ride "ticketless," railways have earned profits. Yet, nine out of ten people continue to use oxcarts, or bicycles, or *tongas* (horse carts).

Exchange of ideas and information has long been facilitated, within and between large cities, by telephones, by telegraph which reaches every corner of the land, and by postal service. Cities and towns have enjoyed English and Indian language newspapers, government-controlled radio broadcasts, and motion pictures. Even villages have radios and movies. (India's movie industry alone has become the second largest in the world, the largest in footage—for movies often lasting 4 to 5 hours.)

India has traded abroad since ancient times. Such trade now has come to over $4 billion each year, mostly with Britain and the United States. No country has sold so much tea as India; bringing twenty percent of her foreign exchange. Exports in indigo, tobacco, coffee, sugar, cotton, jute, hides, and lac have become important. Imports of necessary industrial goods and luxuries however, have for years brought a balance of trade deficit against India averaging over $0.75 billion annually. India has needed close to $1 billion each year in aid from foreign countries to make up the difference.

Too many barriers to exchange have continued to exist. Language, custom, and prejudice have played a part; but obstructions to the movement of money, goods, and services have been fully as serious. Driving across the country, trucks must stop at barriers to pay a customs duty (*octroi*) on the value of goods which they carry. Each such barrier makes the goods more expensive at their destination. Centuries ago there were so many toll stations that prices might go up by 100 percent every 200 miles. The power to tax commerce has tended to destroy it, especially when motives have been predatory. Too often this has been the case in India.

The slowness of exchange, and long delays, have stifled, if not killed, enterprise. Endless red tape, papers, and arguments impede the wheels of economic life, while suspicion and lack of faith have served to retard economic development in India. Growth and prosperity are not attainable without confidence and good credit.

The issue of India's economic future continues to hang in doubt. Disaster still lies in the shadows nearby. Prodigious efforts have been made to reverse many trends, but the great questions of timing and speed remain. Can the basic needs of India's people be satisfied quickly enough? Can the speed of all enterprises—agricultural, industrial, and commercial—more than match the rapidly increasing numbers of people? Most of all, can people develop enough confidence in each other, enough respect and faith, to make such speed possible?

Economic Development India has tried to complete goals set in a series of five-year plans; each plan was aimed at an increase in production. From 1951 to 1956, India tried to raise more food. From 1956 to 1961, heavy industry was stressed. Much money was spent on steel mills, big dams, power stations, and factories. From 1961 to 1966, while keeping up with all earlier projects, special attention was given to improving and expanding education at all levels—with emphasis upon schools and training of teachers. Since 1966, national concern has once more been focused on the ever-chronic food problems, agriculture, and irrigation.

India itself has not had the money it needed for the things it wished to do. Even though national income has risen from $16 billion in 1948 to over $40 billion in 1972 and even though personal income has risen from $45 to $56 a year during the same period, taxes have not brought the government what it has needed. Nor have the profits of private enterprise been enough to pay for ambitious (though necessary) plans. The *Budget* of India—the amount of money the Union Government can spend in any one year—has been very limited, hardly coming to more than $4 billion, not enough to meet the expenses for the state of California.

This shortage of money in India has been aggravated by the fact that, like many countries (including the U.S.), half of each year's budget has gone for military and defense needs. Worse still, instead of defending the subcontinent, most of the military forces of both India and Pakistan have faced each other. As a result, India did not have the strength to meet the Chinese invasion in 1964, when her frontiers were severely penetrated both in Kashmir (Ladakh) and in the North East Frontier Agency (NEFA). The war between India and Pakistan in 1965 was even more costly, in lives, equipment, and money. (An estimated ten thousand men were killed on each side.) The 1971 war was costlier still. Some in India thought that the government—the *public sector* as it has been called—should do all or at least

most of the work of developing the country. Some have even advocated *dictatorship* or more extreme forms of *socialism* and *state control*. It is argued that, if the government could force people to do what needs doing, plans would be carried out more quickly. Others have argued that there is no sense in *dictating* or *forcing*, that using a stick is not enough; people can effectively resist and undermine what they do not like or want. People must feel that there is some reason, some regard, if not for themselves at least for their children. This argument advocates greater freedom of choice for people themselves—for the *private sector*—and stresses the importance of private incentives and of private initiative, imagination, and enterprise, because people can do what they really want to do. The heavy hand of government restriction and regulation should be relaxed, so that business people can borrow money more freely from abroad (at lower interest rates), and thus speed up the buying and selling and moving of goods and money. The proponents of this argument see no point in the government's getting billions in aid and gifts from foreign governments. They have felt that governments do not know how to spend money wisely or efficiently. Since governments do not have to worry about making a profit to stay in business and since governments depend upon taxes, they do not need to be so careful—government spending, they say, has brought waste, if not corruption. Finally, they contend that it is quite inconsistent to have free elections but no free economy. The dilemmas remain unresolved.

FURTHER READING All general works referred to in connection with Part XV, Chapter 2, apply equally here.

On the rise of nationalist movements in the Indian Empire, a number of important works have recently emerged: J. Masselos, *Nationalism on the Indian Subcontinent* (1972), is among the best and most recent of these; A. Seal, *The Emergence of Indian Nationalism* (1968), is brilliant, provocative, but occasionally shallow in conceptual precision and research data; especially as applied to the south; D. M. Brown, * *Nationalist Movement: Indian Political Thought from Ranade to Bhave* (1966), has been a standard reader for twenty years; J. R. McLane (ed.), * *The Political Awakening in India* (1970), is an excellent collection of readings, with a fine introductory essay. The most thoroughly researched of any work yet done on the period between 1880–1905, is S. R. Mehrotra's *The Emergence of the Indian National Congress* (1971). On the opposite side, relating to Muslim nationalism, in addition to works by Ikram and Hardy (cited in Part XV, Chapter 2, consult K. B. Sayeed, *Pakistan: The Formative Phase, 1857–1948* (1968). For fresh and insightful analysis of problems, see A. T. Embree, * *India's Search for National Identity* (1972); and Hugh Tinker, * *India and Pakistan: A Political Analysis* (1962).

Events leading to the partition are covered by a wealth of literature. Among the more helpful of these is H. Tinker's little essay, * *Experiment with Freedom: India and Pakistan, 1947*. The classic work is V. P. Memon, *The Transfer of Power in India* (1957). A recent collection of valuable essays is found in C. H. Philips and D. M. Wainwright *The Partition of India* (1970), written by survivors who occupied important positions during that fateful episode. One of the best over-all surveys of the twentieth century is B. N. Pandey, * *The Break-Up of British India* (1969).

M. K. Gandhi's * *The Story of My Experiments with Truth* is an autobiography, a must for anyone seeking to understand the mind of this remarkable figure. B. R. Nanda, *Mahatma Gandhi* (1958), is well written, by a scholarly partisan. One of the classic works on Gandhian thought is the excellent study by J. Bondurant, * *Conquest of Violence: The Gandhian Philosophy of Conflict* (1955, 1965). Probably the best single work on India's first prime minister is M. Brecher, * *Nehru: A Political Biography* (1959); but Nehru's own classic * *The Discovery of India* (1966) is also essential reading for any student of Indian nationalism and of Nehru.

*Books available in paperback edition are marked with an asterisk.

2 Loss of Empires in Southeast Asia: Conflicts and New States

The final fifty years of European rule in Southeast Asia were remarkable for their comparative tranquillity. The more-or-less contained wars of previous centuries were replaced by rivalry in the global arena, where the major nations of Europe strove against each other. More massive and eventually more destructive, it was global conflict that ultimately broke the chains of European dominance in Southeast Asia.

WORLD WARS AND AFTERMATH The First World War (1914–1918) left a weakened western Europe. Not readily apparent at the time, nor easy to measure, this weakening was especially true of the British and French, two of the nations most concerned with their position in Southeast Asia. "National" will in the hearts of British and French peoples drained away in the blood, smoke, and fire of European trenches, and with it went the drive necessary to imperialism.[1]

Japan Takes Over When, in 1940, France and Holland fell and Britain was obliged to fight for her survival, Japan stood ready to implement her own schemes of conquest. First, she moved her armies into Indo-China, and then forced terms upon Thailand. After Japan's navy destroyed the American fleet at Pearl Harbor (December 7, 1941), her forces were able to conquer virtually all of Southeast Asia with surprising ease and speed. Hong Kong, the Philippines, Malaya, Singapore, Rangoon, Upper Burma, Java, and Sumatra fell in rapid succession. By May of 1942, the whole area lay under Japanese rule.

But what was destroyed was not simply European military power. Of

[1]In simple, arbitrary terms, nationalism and imperialism can be defined as concepts describing almost identical sociopolitical phenomena—namely, ideological manifestations calling forth the same kinds of faith and loyalty, the same fervor and fiery zeal of true believers. Springing from the same virus, so to speak, nationalism and imperialism can both be considered as stages of the same ideological disease. It is in this sense that these concepts are used here. For further reference, see Ernst Haas, *Nationalism and Imperialism* (New York: 1956).

far greater significance than their military defeats was the destruction of the political prestige of European rule. Without such prestige, the very authority by which the Western rulers had held the loyalties of local peoples and by which they had inspired respect and cooperation from local leaders rapidly vanished. This ability to command loyalty was so shattered that, except in Malaya (and, even there, only painfully), not even the total defeat of Japan could repair the damage.

In short, while devastation and war among foreign powers raged over their heads, local leaders could do little more than watch their former masters humbled. For them, the seemingly impossible and unbelievable, had happened. And, while Japanese soldiers quickly turned populations against themselves—perpetrating massacres, stripping territories for loot, and failing to provide for such minimal needs as public health and famine relief, insomuch that organized resistance groups sprang up—the antipathy they aroused was not accompanied by a desire to restore European power. By failing to preserve and to protect the societies within their dominions from the Japanese, Europeans lost their claims to loyalty. The Divine Mandate, the appearance of invincibility, they had so long enjoyed was gone, and the authority of European rulers could never again be the same. To be sure, the old rulers returned, albeit behind armies not their own—for either Indians or Americans or Australians or Chinese did much of the fighting. But the days of European rule were numbered.

Independence It is ironic that those who had done most of the fighting in Southeast Asia—the Indo-British forces under Lord Mountbatten and the Americans under General MacArthur—were the most eager to relinquish power and turn governments over to indigenous rulers. Honoring commitments made before the war to transfer power and grant complete independence, the Philippines (1946), Burma (1948), and Sri Lanka (Ceylon, 1948) were soon wholly free of foreign rule.

Burma's new rulers, during their first quarter century since independence, have been unable to restore internal strength and stability enough to look at the outside world with much confidence. Destroyed first by ravages of world war and then by incessant civil wars and disruptions; deprived of the huge laboring and managerial classes they had violently expelled; and divided by deep schisms of internal distrust and rebellion, both racial and ideological, Burma and her economy has yet to recover from the rapid changes of her modern history. As a result, the country has gone into isolation; indeed, into a kind of international hibernation.

Leaders in Malaya and Singapore, on the other hand, struggling with problems of federation, and for a time against Communist insurgency which was being encouraged and financed by foreign powers, were only too glad of British help. They remained so for another decade, after which they made rapid strides in taking control of their own countries.

A twelve-year guerrilla war was fought in Malaya. Its resolution was attributable to effective leadership, both British and Malayan, and to the

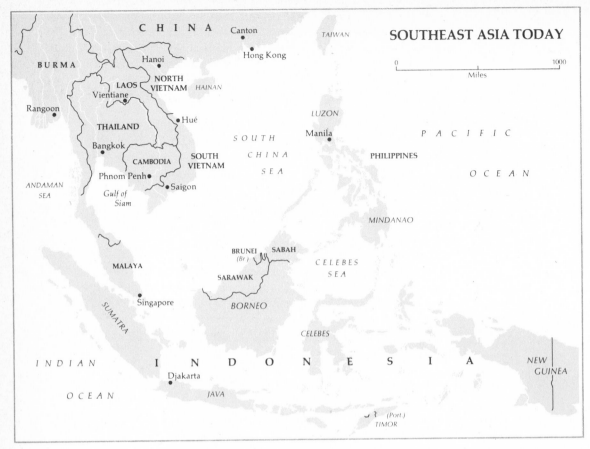

SOUTHEAST ASIA TODAY

fact that it was never successfully converted into a struggle for liberation from alien "colonialist" rulers. The Communist-led insurrection failed to win wide support because it was so largely Chinese—Malay and Indian leaders saw no advantage from substituting one form of subjugation for another. Much of the money and manpower for the resistance to Communist terror came from outraged people in Malaya. Using a mixed force of battle-hardened professional soldiers—Malay, Gurkha, Australian, and British—and working carefully to hold the sympathy of the country people, the British gained an early initiative which they never lost. After resettling half a million Chinese in "new villages" that could be easily protected from intimidation, and thus effectively cutting off sources of food and help from the terrorists, government forces steadily drove the insurgents further and further into isolation and defeat. But most importantly, positive political actions gave substance to assurances of full independence for Malaya, more rapidly probably than originally envisioned. As a consequence, those who witnessed the raising of the new national flag in honor of *Merdeka* (independence) in 1957 were not revolutionaries, but the very leaders who helped bring rebellion to an end.

Three years later the "emergency" was over. It had cost the lives of 2,473 civilians, 1,865 soldiers, 6,711 Communists, and some $5 billion to the British and Malayan governments. In 1963, a voluntary merger brought together the eleven states of Malaya, the city-state of Singapore, and the two Borneo states of Sabah and Sarawak, into the Federation of Malaysia. Because of racial tensions, however, the predominantly Chinese Singapore separated itself again and since 1968 has continued to thrive as the "free port," the "Hong Kong" or "Venice" of Southeast Asia.

For Dutch and French colonial rulers, on the other hand, the situation was very different. Both were surrounded by substantial European minorities, for whom abandonment of rule meant loss of employment, not just for high officials whose positions and prospects in Europe were quite secure, but for hundreds of thousands of lower level, less secure persons for whose families such loss, they feared, would be catastrophic. Dutch and French rule, with many vested interests in the colonies, enjoyed stronger support in the politics of Holland and France. Nationalist sentiments and cultural pride in these countries included not only a sound appreciation of economic benefits, which might be lost, but aspirations for "imperial grandeur." Such feelings had long since subsided among many leaders of Britain and America. Thus the end of colonial rule was stoutly resisted by many ordinary Dutchmen and Frenchmen whose strong feelings could not be ignored except by the more courageous leaders in Europe.

Unfortunately for all concerned, Dutch and French colonial rulers encountered equal if not stronger resistance in a new generation of nationalist leaders. Toughened and strengthened by hard experience and organizational work during the war, the nationalists were ready to make extreme demands. Moreover, since very little effort had been made to transfer responsibility for government operations to nationalist leaders before the war, neither side could draw upon a common experience in progressive, constructive compromise leading to constitutional reforms. Consequently, neither side could feel genuine confidence drawn from past cooperative efforts. Little middle ground was left, therefore, for constructive compromises so necessary for gradual, peaceful transition. The result, predictably, was a clash of wills, a polarization of opposition, and a resort to armed force on both sides, with severe repression by the colonial regime and bitter rebellion and revolutionary insurgency by the nationalists. The consequences, for common people both in Indonesia and in Indo-China, were to be disastrous.

INDONESIA   In the face of determined and well-organized resistance by nationalist forces in Indonesia and of mounting pressures of world opinion, the Dutch were not able to hold power for long in Indonesia. Without the military support of their wartime allies, especially the presence of Indo-British armies, they had neither the manpower, the resources, nor the will to carry on the struggle for very long. The Netherlands was a small country. Far from being self-sufficient, it depended upon the industriousness, enterprise, and commercial

Family at Work in Indonesia. Members of Indonesian family unite to produce crude rubber sheets of congealed latex. (Keystone Press Agency, London.)

vitality of its people. Without sufficient acquiescence, consensus, and active support from the peoples of Indonesia, the Dutch could not hope to continue their rule. They certainly could not hope to rule by force alone. Under the impetus of growing nationalism and increasing political consciousness and participation ("politicization" as this process is now sometimes called), sufficient or minimal support had eroded more and more.

On the other side, exactly such measures of political support for nationalist leaders had not only been steadily growing for over twenty years but had been greatly accelerated by the War. Having tasted some measure of power and independence during the Japanese occupation, whether as collaborators or as resistance fighters, nationalists had also gained experience. Most of all, their followers were able to appeal effectively to the sentiments and aspirations of ever wider circles of people, from students and traditional religious leaders to members of the old aristocracy and, most of all, to village leaders. Finally, under the charismatic leadership of Sukarno, the movement to get rid of Dutch rule was galvanized and raised to a pitch which could not be denied. In the face of such opposition the more realistic Dutch leaders, with support if not urging from liberal, moderate, and commercial interests, soon decided to end hostilities and to give in to nationalist demands. In their own economic interests, especially if any long-range trading benefits could be preserved, the Dutch saw that they had little choice.

Indonesian Independence Indonesia achieved its full independence in December 1949. With its enormous natural resources and potential for economic development, both in agriculture (food, fibers, etc.), minerals (oil, aluminum) and industry, the country was expected to grow in strength, prosperity, and international standing. Unfortunately, this was not to be the case, at least during most of the next twenty years. Despite its democratic idealism and its early attempts to establish representative institutions, the domestic peace and political stability of the new nation was increasingly disturbed by bitter factional strife and party power struggles. Among the many contending forces, traditionalist Islamic groups, the Communists, and the army were especially strong. The Indonesian army, well led, organized, and equipped, enjoyed high prestige because of its war against the Dutch. The army was jealous of its strength and determined that, come what may, what it considered to be national interests would not be subverted by any group, domestic or foreign. The Communist Party of Indonesia, with a history going back to the 1920's, gradually grew in strength and membership until, except for the army (by the 1960's) it was the most powerful single party in the country; moreover, by its continual agitating and building of para-military organizations, it posed a severe threat to all other political parties.

For many years, only President Sukarno was able to balance these forces and to preserve a semblance of national unity. An engineer whose dynamic career in nationalist politics had brought him to a place of leadership before the Second World War but whose skills as a demogogue and orator were greater than his skills as an administrator, Sukarno kept himself so busy playing off one party against another and arousing fears of foreign aggression and "neo-colonialist" exploitation (ever an effective way for insecure governments and dictators to draw support). Extravagant displays of internationalistic fervor and rhetoric, such as the Bandung Conference in 1955, were staged in the name of "peaceful coexistence" and *panchashila* (the "five principles of peace") on behalf of the "Non-aligned Third World."

Meanwhile, government neglect and inefficiency and corruption contributed to a general deterioration of the economy that was disastrous. Currency inflation became so pernicious that, for many, money simply ceased to have value. Those who could not live by subsistence agriculture or by exploiting their positions within governing structures suffered the most. The resulting insecurity further contributed to a spiraling process of political instability which not even Indonesia's four-year campaign of "confrontation" against Malaysia (1962–1966) could hide. The Communist Party, taking full advantage of this situation, drew President Sukarno ever more tightly into its own web. Few doubt that its plans for taking over the country by armed force was well advanced. Only the army stood in its way. In 1965, after spiriting Sukarno to a place of "safety," a coup against the army was attempted. Several generals were assassinated and a general Communist rising ordered. But the conspiracy misfired. General Suharto and strategically important units of the army, quickly recovering the initiative, carried out a ruthless campaign to exterminate the Communists, both root and branch, so that they would never again be able to threaten or take over the state. Before the crisis was over in 1966, hundreds of thousands (some say millions) are estimated to have been killed. Sukarno, his prestige and power broken, was allowed to live quietly with his disgrace until he died (1970).

President Sukarno's "Ticker-tape" Welcome in Peking. President Sukarno of Indonesia, left, and Chairman Mao Tse-tung drive in a rose-petal-covered car through the streets of the Chinese capital. (Camera Press, London.)

The new government, under President Suharto, has devoted itself to rebuilding the shattered economy and to the task of restoring stability. But despite remarkable achievements in economic rehabilitation and much foreign assistance, the general prosperity and the more equitable distribution of wealth that were promised in nationalist and revolutionary appeals remain as far as ever from the experience of most common people.

INDO-CHINA The history of Indo-China, especially of Vietnam, contains much more violence and tragedy than that of Indonesia. Most of Indonesia's troubles have been internal, due to the inability of its own society to overcome difficulties. Most of Indo-China's troubles, or at least a substantial proportion have been caused by external forces. Unlike the Dutch, the French were not as realistic—perhaps less hardheaded in terms of profitable business and more hardhearted in terms of national pride. Their resources, both human and economic, were drained in trying to put down a Communist-led nationalist movement; moreover, both the Vietnamese resistance and the French repression were supported and reinforced by major outside powers—China and the U.S.S.R. on one side and the United States (with Western allies) on the other side. Claims to leadership within the nationalist movements in Vietnam were more divided than in Indonesia. Whereas the flamboyant Sukarno could capture the hearts and imaginations of almost all politically conscious Indonesians (not even his opponents would disavow him publically, nor until 1966 would they act except in his name), there was no such unanimity of support for Ho Chi Minh.

Ho had received his advanced education in Paris. After careful training, he had gained further discipline and acquired years of experience as an agent of international communism. Yet, despite his many years of work outside Vietnam, he was also a dedicated nationalist determined to rid Vietnam of French rule. His opponents in Vietnam, also nationalists by their own lights, could accuse him of putting his international communism above his national patriotism, of being a foreign agent. (Such quarrels could be exploited by the French, for their own purposes.) Still, anti-Communist nationalists in Vietnam never gained as much strength as Ho Chi Minh; too many factions struggled for power, often putting personal interests above patriotism. Moreover, during the Second World War, America had given arms to Ho and, indeed, had allied itself with him in a common struggle against Japanese forces in Vietnam. This had been done because of his effectiveness as a nationalist leader.

At the end of eight years of fighting against the French, it was the forces of Ho Chi Minh which finally prevailed. The French alienated and lost local support; and the Viet Minh, tightly disciplined and directed by Ho and his lieutenants, established an intricate and efficent network of support. Using fear and terror more effectively than the French, these masters of the newest techniques of guerrilla warfare cut off French supplies and drove them into defensive positions which they then proceeded to make indefensible. Sup-

Ho Chi Minh in Younger Days. Educated in the West, Ho went on to become one of the dominant Third World leaders in Southeast Asia. (Wide World.)

plied with overwhelming artillery (and ammunition) by the Soviet Union, Ho's forces pounded French defenses. French resistance collapsed at Dien Bien Phu, not just because a French army was surrounded, beseiged, and beaten into surrender but because, at last, a French public was no longer prepared to pay so high a price for its pride. France withdrew from Vietnam in 1954.

Vietnam Yet, strangely, the lessons of French experience in Vietnam seem to have eluded American leaders. The Geneva Accords of 1954 called for a partition of Vietnam. North Vietnam, with its center at Hanoi and the Red River Delta (the former Kingdom of Tonkin), came under the rule of the Peoples' Republic of Vietnam as directed by Ho Chi Minh. South Vietnam, with its center at Saigon in the Mekong Delta (the former Cochin China), came under the Republic of South Vietnam as ruled by President Diem. Such was the mutual distrust that the plebicite, stipulated in the Accords, was never held in the South. North Vietnam refused to recognize the legitimacy of the regime in South Vietnam and sent guerrillas, infiltrators, and party organizers into the South. There they began a carefully orchestrated and patient campaign of subversion, terror, and gradual conquest to bring all of South Vietnam under their rule. The North's agents in the South organized the NLF (National Liberation Front) or "Viet Cong," which claimed that it represented the legitimate interests and aspirations of most people in South Vietnam. As an expression of international communism, this enterprise was supported by China and the Soviet Union.

The American Government watched these developments with alarm. John Foster Dulles, the American Secretary of State, saw his country as the champion of beleaguered and defenseless peoples who were falling prey to the menace of a gigantic, international movement of communist forces which were being directed and supported by Moscow. America was engaged in the Cold War, a world-wide struggle between freedom and slavery, between good and evil. As streams of refugees fleeing from North Vietnam mounted into the hundreds of thousands (some estimates ran into the millions), American sympathy and generosity expressed itself in many ways. But for American help, the Diem regime may not have survived. Yet, with much less dependence upon America, it might have become more self-reliant and strong.

What *might* have happened is arguable (and perhaps pointless). Nevertheless, as matters *did* turn out, increasing corruption and dissension and turbulence developed after John Kennedy became President. Buddhist groups, extremely disturbed by the growing strength of Roman Catholics in South Vietnam—Diem's family was Catholic and many refugees were Catholic—agitated against the Diem regime. Monks burning themselves to death in gestures of anguish were viewed on television by the American public. Moral outrage against Diem became world-wide. Students in Saigon led a revolt. Diem was toppled and murdered. As political stability deteriorated, the army of South Vietnam stepped into power. While the scale of

Central Market Area in Saigon, 1970. Despite the war in the surrounding countryside, the rhythm of city life continued unabated in one of Southeast Asia's largest and busiest capitals. (United Press International.)

Viet Cong terrorism increased to the point of becoming an all-out civil war in the countryside, one general after another failed to put together an effective government. Finally General Nguyen Thieu, with American support, began to assemble a more effective regime. Slowly and inexorably, step by step, American power became more deeply involved in the struggle for control of South Vietnam.

How this came about and what motives prompted each step in this "escalation" are questions which are still far from clear. Under successive American administrations, particularly under Presidents Kennedy and Johnson and with a sharp turn after the Gulf of Tonkin Resolution (1964), the American public found itself engaged in the carnage of a distant war which had been raging for over thirty (now forty) years and in which the numbers of dead and suffering people seemed interminable. But, like the French, Americans paid a price for their involvement which was far more profound and difficult to measure than they could anticipate. Beyond the untold billions of dollars spent; the millions of young men who were shuttled in and out of South Vietnam as "short-tour" soldiers for one year (half-trained and far from professional); the forces numbering over five-hundred-thousand men who were kept in South Vietnam; the more than fifty-thousand who were killed in the war (not counting the maimed):—is the fact that the war was brought back to the United States, with resulting deep and bitter divisions to American society. Civil war in Asia was transmuted into civil strife and turbulence in America. Experience in one country exposed fissures that already lay beneath the surface in the other. These general observations, unconnected by the hosts of details already well known to this generation, show us how much events in a shrinking world touch all men and, therewith, change distant peoples. In Vietnam, in Indo-China, the bitter struggles continue.

FURTHER READING Among general works, H. Tinker, *Ballot Box and Bayonet: Peoples and Government in Emergent Asian Countries* (1964), serves as a probing introduction. For fuller studies of national movements, see R. Emerson, * *From Empire to Nation: The Rise to Self-Assertion of Asian and African Peoples* (1960); C. Geertz (ed.), *Old Societies and New States: The Quest for Modernity in Asia and Africa* (1963); R. O. Tilman, * *Man, State and Society in Contemporary Southeast Asia* (1969), an excellent collection of essays; and the monumental volume edited by G. McT. Kahin, *Governments and Politics of Southeast Asia* (1964).

The above works, when combined with readings already suggested for Part XIV, Chapter 3, provide a starting point for further studies in Southeast Asian history. From this, one can branch off into works on various countries. For example, H. Tinker's *The Union of Burma: A Study of the First Years of Independence* (1959), is based largely upon contemporary conversations and interviews. On Vietnam, a second volume by Buttinger is but one of a host of studies: B. B. Fall, *The Two Vietnams* (1963); P. J. Honey, *North Vietnam Today* (1962), and *Communism in North Vietnam* (1963). Really first class studies of various elements of traditional Vietnamese culture, however, are almost non-existent in English. V. Thompson, *Thailand, The New Siam* (1941), provides a classic study of that country; and more recently R. Emerson and J. Baston have published works on Malaysia.

*Books available in paperbound edition are marked with an asterisk.

3 China and Japan in the Twentieth Century

China's attempts to regain her dignity, integrity, and power were beset with difficulties. Her efforts to catch up with the West were continuously frustrated by violent internal convulsions and, after 1930, by invasion from Japan.

The first great national leader to emerge from the national revolution of 1911 was Sun Yat Sen. A village youth, who had learned English in Hawaii and studied medicine in Hong Kong, Sun had devoted his life to overthrowing the Manchus, and to restoring a strong China. After years of revolutionary activity, mostly in exile and filled with discouragements and dangerous escapes, his name had become known over the world as a symbol of a changing China. He was in the United States when the revolt against the Manchus occurred. Two months later he was elected the first Provisional President of the Republic of China. Shortly afterwards, in a pitiful edict blaming the Ch'ing for the sorrows of China, the child emperor abdicated the Dragon Throne and delivered up its authority. Sun himself soon resigned and recommended Yuan Shih-k'ai, the military commander whose withdrawal of loyalty to Peking had been crucial, as President.

Weak Regimes and Warlords, 1912–1928 All started smoothly enough. A new government and national reconstruction was promised. A new party, the Kuomintang (KMT) later also called the Nationalist Party, was organized. A National Assembly was elected in which the KMT was predominant. But no sooner had Yuan Shih-k'ai become established than he promptly ordered Sun Yat Sen and the revolutionary leader Huang Hsing arrested as "rebels" and the Assembly dissolved. He tried to abolish the new constitution and to put himself upon the Dragon Throne. His dynastic dream died unborn, however, and he died in disgrace three years later.

The years of confusion that followed are sometimes referred to as the Age of Warlords. Military governors became local dictators. Peking, even though it remained the focus of hopes and of diplomacy, ceased to count as more than just another provincial center. Sun Yat Sen, long used to life

Sun Yat Sen and Wife, c. 1910. Often referred to as the "Father of the Revolution," Sun emerged as a symbol of a changing China. (Powers Collection, Hoover Institution Archives.)

in exile, and by now married to one of the brilliant Soong sisters, continued his efforts from Japan. After Yuan Shih-k'ai's death, he returned to Shanghai and then to Canton. His new Provisional Government, however, could make little progress against warlords. Without swords, he was almost helpless. As the days darkened all pretense of revolution seemed to vanish, at least on the surface.

Yet, just when all seemed lost, help came from Soviet Russia. After the Russian Revolution of 1917, Lenin received a cable of congratulation from Sun Yat Sen. In 1920, an agent of the new Comintern was sent to China to organize study groups into disciplined cells. One year later, some fifty revolutionaries from twelve cells met in Shanghai to found the Communist Party of China. Among its first members were Mao Tse-tung and Chou En-lai. At the Second Party Congress the following year, about a hundred members—mostly students, teachers, and writers—came together. While this was going on, an alliance between Moscow and Canton was arranged. A pledge of Soviet money and advisors to help the KMT was made to Sun Yat Sen. Chinese cadets were promised special training in Moscow. So that all Chinese Communists would join the KMT, it was agreed that communism and Soviet principles were neither suitable nor could they be imposed upon China. For his part, Sun Yat Sen entered into this arrangement because, while many other powers were interested in China's reconstruction, none gave active financial and military assistance. He found it necessary to take risks. While he was somewhat vaguely sympathetic to Marxist ideals, he felt that the dangers of Soviet power could be handled. For their part, with their dreams of world-wide revolution, Soviet leaders saw China as a good place to begin bringing their dreams to fulfillment. Moreover, since the Chinese Communist Party, a mere handful of intellectuals without grassroots support, was seen as too fledgling to carry out such aims on its own, Moscow hoped to speed up Communist expansion by working through the KMT.

The United Front, 1923–1927   To see that all went according to its wishes, Moscow next sent to China one of its veteran agents, Michael Borodin. Upon arriving in Canton (October 1923), Borodin's chief concern was to bring the Chinese Communists into the KMT. Since they would not give up CPC membership, he persuaded Sun to allow them to hold dual membership so long as they would agree to "work for the Chinese Revolution." Communist membership within the KMT soon came to ten percent of the total. Borodin also strove to so reorganize the KMT that it could control masses of people and eventually be able to dominate China. A far cry from the original party, the new KMT appealed beyond the old elites of society and enlisted common people from all walks, such as workers, peasants, petty shopkeepers, ordinary soldiers, and lower services. Within two years, membership exceeded 100,000. While not really a mass party in terms of China's population, it was at least more massive than anything previously organized. More important, the new KMT was totalitarian in form and function, most closely resembling the party of Lenin.

Finally, Borodin appropriated Sun Yat Sen's ideology. As far back as 1905, Sun had borrowed words from Lincoln's Gettysburg Address. Words about government "of the people, by the people, and for the people" had served as the basis for his "Three principles of the People" (*San Min Chu-i*). Seizing upon this idea, Borodin urged Sun to give a lecture series on these principles, concentrating upon nationalism, socialism, and democracy and using the plain speech of common people rather than the classical idiom. These efforts were extremely successful, causing great excitement and reaching more minds than ever before. His prestige enhanced, the "Father of the Revolution" as he was now designated, journeyed to Peking in hopes of getting the powerful warlords of the north to accede to national interests by stepping aside. But at this crucial moment (March 12, 1925), before he could accomplish his purpose, the cancer from which he had been suffering brought Sun Yat Sen's life to an end. His deathbed Will and Testament, soon enshrined as national ritual, emphasized the cause of National Revolution and of raising China to a place of independence and equality among nations, arousing all peoples of the world so as to attain this end. Thereafter, his words were memorized and recited at public events as a national pledge of allegiance.

Sun's death was quickly followed by an intricately complicated series of simultaneous conflicts—personal struggles for succession; factional struggles for party control; intensified struggles for national unification by conquering the north; and struggles against foreign threats, especially from Japan.

Ultimately it was Chiang Kai-shek, carefully groomed by Sun to take his place, who emerged as the new national leader. A trusted friend of Sun's, who had taken part in the 1911 revolution and who had been sent to Moscow to learn Soviet skills and tactics, Chiang had returned to take charge of the new KMT Military Academy at Whampoa and to become commander-in-chief of the new model army then being paid and equipped by Russia. This had been no ordinary army; for from the very outset its soldiers had been schooled by Chou En-lai in the totalitarian tactics of organizing the masses for class struggle, propaganda, and guerrilla warfare.

Chiang Kai-shek did not share Sun's zeal for the Communists and Soviet Russia. Personal experience had convinced him of their dangers. He saw that the Communists had been trying to use the KMT as their Trojan Horse, aiming to transform it into their instrument. The tempo of mass support mounted, built up by hero worship of Sun's memory, flag-waving marches, and slogan chanting demonstrations; and involving more and more people in modern politics—by 1926, the clamor to conquer Peking and to expel all foreign powers from China could not be ignored. On June 21, amid great celebrations, Chiang began the Northern Expedition. Within eight months half of China was under Nationalist Party rule and the remaining warlords faced defeat. But once again they were saved by events.

The Communists would not accept a national victory which they could not control. Using their battalions within the National Army, they began taking control of the whole movement at Nanchang. Destroying all who would not submit or who were untrustworthy, they set up a counter-government at Hankow. Chiang sensed his danger and, as commander-in-chief, immediately summoned a meeting for the announced purpose of saving the Communist/Nationalist "United Front." When the Communist forces failed to respond, he struck with great speed. Hankow was captured. Dissident battalions and party members were either killed or scattered. Communist cells in the south were smashed and attempts to revive them failed. Borodin and Madame Sun Yat Sen fled to Moscow and other Communist leaders escaped.

Elusive Nationalist Ascendancy, 1928–1937 The Nationalist armies were quickly reorganized and soon resumed the Northern Expedition. By June of 1928, Peking had been captured. All eighteen provinces of China proper and three provinces of Manchuria were soon united under the Nationalist flag. Elaborate ceremonies formally inaugurated the Second Republic of China, a second "corporate dynasty," with Nanking as its capital and Chiang Kai-shek as its President. Sun Yat Sen's dream of a Nationalist Revolution was declared fulfilled and his body was brought from the Azure Cloud

Monastery in Peking to Nanking to be enshrined in a great marble tomb near the Ming Tombs on Purple Mountain.

Yet despite all the pomp and pageantry, all the international acclaim, and all the hopes, the Mandate of Heaven still remained undecided. Actual control was far from achieved. Dissident parties, from Communists to warlords, continued to plot and quarrel and rebel. The two most serious threats came from foreign invaders and from domestic revolutionaries, the Japanese and the Communists. Both had lethal power. By coming simultaneously, the ultimate prevailing of the latter was assured.

Bases of Red Strength in the Peasantry The Chinese Red Army was born in the 1927 mutiny against Chiang at Nanchang. Led by Chu Teh, a Berlin-trained career soldier of remarkable skill, the retreating remnants of this uprising suffered defeat after defeat. These forces eventually joined Mao Tse-tung in his mountain refuge at Jiuchin in Kiangsi. Mao, whose genius for organizing his supporters was unmatched, saw the importance of harnessing the latent power of agrarian workers to his cause. Mao became the brains of the Chu-Mao team, which ultimately prevailed within the party, challenged Nationalist hegemony, and created Communist China. Chiang's determination to extirpate the Communists was frustrated by his having first to cope with the warlords. While he was so engaged, the Chu-Mao

Mao Tse-tung (left) with Chu Teh, 1938. Mao appears during his army days with the commander-in-chief of the Chinese Red Army. (Earl Leaf for Rapho-Guillumette Pictures.)

forces were able to take full advantage of three years' respite so as to consolidate and expand their power in the countryside. The very conditions that had facilitated local warlordism and frustrated nationalism enabled the formation of armed local soviets in the countryside.

China was overwhelmingly (eighty percent) an agricultural country. Its chief revenues and manpower had always come from peasant workers. Since the mid-nineteenth century, tax burdens had steadily increased as Peking tried to buy advanced armaments, purchase modern facilities, and pay foreign loans. Burdens of money lending and increasing landless tenancy had become devastating. Demands of cash crops had undermined self-sufficiency of villages. And modern manufacturing had ruined cottage industries. No patriotic Chinese leader, therefore, could ignore the plight of the peasant masses. Many piecemeal measures for reform had been tried. Few leaders, whether warlords or bankers or intellectuals, had escaped some sense of guilt about this plight. But it was precisely here that the KMT had early fallen into the trap that was to prove fatal. (Most early Communist leaders were no less blind.) Much early KMT support came from urban merchants and landed interests. Fear that land reforms, once they gained momentum, might turn against vested interests within the KMT had led to a dilatory lack of constructive action. As a result, a crucial decade (1927–1937) was wasted and chances of KMT support from agrarian workers was lost. Thereafter, as the holocaust of Japanese invasion drove the Nationalists from their urban-mercantile strongholds along the coasts and into increasing dependence upon the rural economy of the interior and, thus, upon support from its ultra-conservative landlords, their fate was sealed.

Mao meanwhile had moved Communists quickly away from their classical Marxist origins. Instead of distrusting the peasants, within only a few years he was showing how to organize agrarian unrest. Some feel that it was a KMT realization that aroused peasants would join the Communists that provoked the breakup of the CCP-KMT United Front of 1927. Whatever the case, victorious Nationalist armies certainly drove the Communists back into the countryside and into the arms of agrarian workers where, after years of experimenting with how to mobilize peasant forces, they devised radical ways not only for keeping land-loving peasants well fed but also happy enough to join their revolution. Only the Communists offered the social changes which alone would free the peasants so as to enable them to take full advantage of the best new methods of agriculture.

Yet, in the heyday of Nationalist strength, when revolutionary changes in rebuilding China were certainly begun, Red forces were no match for Chiang's modern and disciplined army of two million men. Finally, threatened with complete annihilation, in October 1934, the Communists began the retreat that was to become the now famous Long March. This epic achievement, in which it is said they covered 8,000 miles as they marched, by way of southwest China, far to the northwest wilderness near the border of Inner Mongolia, took more than a year. Bitter fighting followed them all the way; yet, although they lost four out of every five of the some 130,000 persons who began the journey, the Communist army avoided total destruction and established a new headquarters at Yenan.

Dangers of Invasion by Japan For a decade, anger and alarm at Japan's encroachments of China had kept mounting. Having already acquired Taiwan and special port privileges in 1895; annexed Korea in 1909; and made outrageous demands during World War I, when most powers were preoccupied in Europe, Japan had already all but taken away China's independence. Its integrity and power restored by the Washington Conference of 1922, China had then been left alone until, after the renewed civil wars of 1927, Nationalist ascendency over a united China had seemed inevitable. This, Japan had not been willing to allow. Serious trouble had begun again in 1931–1933, when Japan conquered Manchuria, then beseiged Shanghai, and then, in 1935, tried to seize much of northern China. So easily had Japan made these gains that its appetite had only been whetted. All the while, with humiliation following humiliation and with more and more people clamouring for all-out war, Chiang sternly bided his time and suppressed each dangerous or provocative incident. He knew that, as infuriated as they were, Chinese forces would nonetheless be mercilessly slaughtered, and that only a united and regenerated China could deal with Japan. He was confident that, given time, China could prevail. Thus, in desperate hopes of buying time, he endured almost unendurable pressures—taunts of cowardice, of appeasement, and of indulging his hatred of the Communists at national expense.

But what finally tipped the scales and perhaps led directly to World War II in Asia and to the Communist victory in 1949 was another mutiny in 1936. Whether or not it was inspired by Communist cunning, a tacit truce was made between some local Nationalist soldiers at Sian and their Red foes. Confident that he could personally awe the troops into obedience, Chiang fell into a trap and was captured. He would perhaps have been put to death had not the Communists intervened. His value as a symbol for the necessary struggle against Japan was appreciated. An agreement was apparently forced upon him—namely: he was to cease from civil war and tolerate all "patriotic" movements in a common struggle against the coming foreign aggression. Held at Sian at the peril of his life, Chiang was thus forced to renounce further efforts to exterminate the Communists and instead to join them in leading a campaign against Japan. As hysterical cries of relief at Chiang's safe release swept the land, what Mao Tse-tung well knew and Chiang most dreaded—an all-out war with Japan before China was ready to wage such a war—became almost inevitable. Both knew that the ensuing misery and chaos in China would bring about enormous changes, with great possible advantages for the Communists. All that was needed was the pretext for war. And this the Japanese found on the Double Seventh (July 7th) of 1937 at the Marco Polo Bridge near Peking.

In another respect also, the attack on China came at a crucial time. Republican China was at its highest point of success. Both economically and politically, the country was making rapid strides—in roads, railways, airlines, mass communications, finance, industry, and armaments. Successes in international diplomacy were bringing enhanced national recognition and prestige. In short, the longer Japan waited, the more difficult and expensive would be the task of trying to dominate China.

The War and Its Aftermath, 1937–1945 Within two years, the war machine of Japan controlled not only all of North China, the coasts, main cities, and railways, but even the key inland city of Hankow. Japanese occupation, while never complete, lasted eight years. Chinese people resisted in every possible way. To escape alien rule, masses of them—their government, their schools and universities, their libraries and laboratories, and even their factories and machinery—moved westwards hundreds of miles, as far as Chunking, Chengtu, and Kunming. In this way, for the first time, such interior provinces as Yunnan and Szechwan became industrialized, more populous, and socially transformed. Meanwhile, as bombs kept raining upon the hapless people, America and Britain tried to send assistance, mainly by volunteer air squadrons ("The Flying Tigers") and by shipping supplies, first by the Burma Road which countless coolies cut over the jungle mountains and then, after Burma itself fell, by flying aircargoes over "the Hump."

As Mao Tse-tung had anticipated, it was the Nationalist forces that suffered most heavily from the war with Japan. Their troops were the ones defeated in large-scale battles. Their government could be blamed for failing to protect people from barbarian depredations. Their compromises with the arch-conservative and corrupting elements in society, argued as unavoidable necessities for the sake of preserving China, slowly and silently stripped them of their popular mandate. This bleeding of popular confidence gave Communists just the chance they needed. Inch by inch, striking out of Yenan with small units, light arms, and guerrilla tactics, and applying lessons learned by countless experiments in setting up local soviets—in which basic agrarian reforms and revolutionary doctrines were welded into tough, new sociopolitical structures—Communists steadily built up strength and prepared for the ultimate showdown. Indeed, quietly they even organized common people of whole areas inside Japanese-held territories. Except on the surface, therefore, the new United Front was seldom more than fiction. Mao Tse-tung was later to boast that, during the War, seventy percent of his forces were directed against the Kuomintang, twenty percent to controlling his own territories, and only ten percent in forays against the Japanese. More and more, as the West prevailed against Japan, the Nationalist-Communist struggle for China mounted in bitter and deadly intensity.

Red Dragon Resurgent, 1945–1949 As the conflict widened and engulfed China, the war-ravaged economy collapsed. Production and trade stopped. Paper money became worthless. The Soviet Union, having conquered Manchuria and North Korea just before the Japanese surrender, turned huge amounts of arms stripped from 750,000 Japanese troops over to the Chinese

Red Army (and also took industrial, mining, and railway equipment back to Siberia for its own use). Thus equipped as never before, the Red Army was ready for the conquest of China. On the other side, American forces tried to help. But while the United States could give food enough to save millions of lives, it could do little to remedy deeper ills. General George C. Marshall was sent to bring the contending leaders together and to negotiate reconciliation in a national coalition. While he did manage a temporary cease-fire, he found that implacable differences could not be resolved. Most Americans, especially high officials, never really understood the depth of unrest and animosity in China.

Revolution in China. Chinese nationalists are rounded up by Communist forces. (George M. Lacks, Time-Life Picture Agency.)

Resentments in China over the country's ills and against foreign meddling were very strong. Neither of the two major political movements, while they shared deep hostilities about China's plight, showed any real interest in compromise. Concepts of "civil liberty" and "loyal opposition" were alien to China's tradition, even beyond comprehension. Traditionally, interests of the group had ever remained paramount over those of the individual. Despite all earlier polite talk about "liberties," the thought that each individual ought to be protected in at least some tiny corner of his life, where his privacy could never be touched by the state no matter how urgent the "public interest," had never been seriously considered by any important party. China's tradition had never admitted "counting of heads" to be the best way, much less a good way, to reach wise decisions. It might be acceptable to secure popular assent or to be assured of silent consensus ("Mandate"), but to ask people what should be done was unimaginable. There might be all kinds of intricate mechanisms to assure political control and continuity—checks, compromises, consultations, tribunals, and investigations—but never a majority decision. In sum, during all its years of revolutionary turmoil after 1911, China never experienced a truly republican government. All its "democratic" facades turned into fiascos. All through the years, no matter who sought to exercise power and to achieve paramount authority, whether Nationalist or Communist, the basic idea was to establish a completely monolithic rule on behalf of the people through an elite corps of select, highly trained, well indoctrinated, nonhereditary, and thoroughly authoritarian officials whose task it was to harness every aspect of life and energy to that gigantic leviathan, the Dragon of China.

When seen in this light, the victory of Communists in China emerges as simply another turn in the succession of dynastic cycles, albeit now of

A Toast to the Manchurian Truce. Mao Tse-tung and Chiang K'ai-shek share the same table in this photograph taken in 1945. (Jack Wilkes, Time-Life Picture Agency.)

"corporate" or "party" rather than of family dynasties, in the "revolving" and evolving of imperial tradition. As China emerged after the war, few questioned that it was ready to take its place among the great powers of the world. Chiang himself had already seen to that, making sure that no more limitations on sovereignty would exist. He had enjoyed the acclaim of the Allied Powers, Britain and America (1943), had been welcomed at the founding of the United Nations (1945), had signed a thirty-year friendship treaty with the Soviet Union, and had secured the return of Manchuria and Taiwan. Nevertheless, by relentless demonstration on the battlefields of civil war—by following examples set even before the Han took power from the Chin two hundred years before Christ—the Communists succeeded the Nationalists. Mao Tse-tung emerged as the leader of this New China and his Communist regime brought the revolution, first heralded by British warships in 1839, to completion. The Mandate of Heaven was reestablished in 1949.

Red Dragon Rampant: Tradition Restored   Lost in the details about desperate struggles of arms and ideas between 1911 and 1949 is the fact that, when all is said, these struggles over government were of comparative insignificance to most of China's peoples. Four out of every five persons in the huge ocean of humanity which makes China were agrarian workers. Tiny tinctures of new ideas, ideals, technologies, and styles of life trickled onto the surface of this ocean. The impact of the West, the transient consequences of the Taiping and other rebellions, the struggles for survival of the old regime and its Confucian supporters, the flounderings of early reform movements and republican forces, the rise and fall of the Kuomintang, and the final emergence of the Communists as the corporate successors of all previous dynasties—all these processes revolved around a more fundamental breakdown in the old agrarian system. The low and the poor in countless agricultural villages became more and more fed-up with their superiors, most of whom lived in towns and protected themselves from the unwashed by force of arms and cultural separatism. Had there not been an accelerating increase in the distance between ruling classes and those they ruled, such as had signalled the decline and failure of each previous dynasty, violent revolutionary changes might not have occurred.

Not until its autarchical tradition was fully restored, albeit with an unprecedented totalitarian monolithicity, could China again achieve economic autarky. Modern industrial machines began to arrive during the 1840's; but not until after 1895 did they really begin to gain importance. Later, when World War I cut off European manufactures, a chance to supply deficiencies came to local industries, especially to new textile mills. But internal instability and competing Japanese industry tended continually to stunt industrial growth. Even the great modern cities, such as Shanghai, failed to develop into their potential as industrial centers, continuing, rather, mainly as entrepots for mercantile and financial interest and for international trade. Neither did railways play any significant role, certainly not before the twentieth century, when large-scale construction began. Even then, China was without benefit of coherent policy. Furious competition and intrigue between the rival European interests providing most of the investment capital played no small part in perpetuating economic havoc. Thus, amidst financial and managerial and military turbulences it is no small wonder that railroad development and operations were sporadic.

Truly massive and sustained progress in the industrialization of China, therefore, had to await the advent of internal stability and peace. This seemed to come with the emergence of the Kuomintag and the Second Republic in 1928–1929. But with the attacks by Japan and further insurgency and rebellion within, followed by World War II and the civil war thereafter, such conditions continuously eluded the country. Thus, only after tranquility, stability, and control had been imposed after 1949 did the Industrial Revolution really reach more than just the fringes of China.

THE CHINESE "REVOLUTION"

The character of East Asia has dramatically changed since 1950. Both China and Japan have become world powers. Indeed, no accounting of global forces can be made without weighing them in the balance. Both Korea and Taiwan, symbols of political contention though they are, have themselves emerged as prosperous and powerful smaller countries. Yet, inescapably, the focus of world attention has been increasingly drawn to the almost miraculous metamorphosis of the emerging giants. From the perspective of her own power—whether natural or of human resources—China once again sees herself as the "Center of the Universe." Once again she is the Celestial Kingdom, clouded in secrecy, wrapped in silence, and answerable to no ordinary mortals—especially alien barbarians. Such indeed has been the magnitude of China's internal transformation during the past quarter century that, in its policies and postures, China behaves less and less like a "Paper Tiger" and ever more like the Iron Dragon of old—the epicenter of all things.

In all of their slogans, the rulers of Red China have urged haste and made frantic efforts to catch up with the power of other major countries so as to make their own country strong and secure. Such slogans have called for sacrifices; and indeed the costs and sacrifices for the people of China have been enormous.

Whatever gains had been made by Nationalist China, especially between 1928 and 1937, were wiped out by twelve years of war, first the war with Japan and then the civil war. By 1949, whole towns and factories; roads, railways, and communication lines; and great works of irrigation and flood control had been destroyed. Indeed, virtually all of China's economic and commercial life above the level of subsistence agriculture had collapsed.

Thus, as the Communist regime commenced its rule, drastic measures were required. Urgent rebuilding, reconstructing, and repairing of the economy came first—canals, dams, roads, rails, and much more. Such efforts were combined, however, with draconian efforts to drive out all political opposition. This was felt to require complete destruction of the old social structure before a proper rebuilding of a revolutionary society could be accomplished. As with the emergence of every other great new dynasty in China's history, all hostile ("corrupt," "alien," "capitalist," "imperialist") elements had to be swept out and all remaining elements reorganized before the realm could be put into proper order. Before such a tremendous transformation could take place, virtually the entire population of over 700 million had to be forced into frenzied activity. People had to be mobilized and galvanized into a gigantic monolithic structure having such dynamic force that the whole world would pause to wonder at the accomplishment. By whatever name it can be called and whatever its style, a totalitarian dictatorship "of the people" was established. It was directed by the Communist Party of China and by the forced sanctions of the Red Army of China, both instruments under the watchful eye of Chairman Mao Tse-tung.

Indeed, farfetched as it may seem, all of China was mobilized into one huge army—an army directed by the army. The Chinese Army became the elite force for implementation, serving as a vast cadre of officers working at every level and in every sector of the economy, whether in agriculture, industry, finance, cultural indoctrination, or whatever. This *was* the politics of China. As Mao Tse-tung so often said: "Political power comes out of the barrel of a gun." China's people became her "gun" and the army its bullets. At every turn of events and in every issue that was joined, it was the army which decided the struggle. Founded upon a peasant discontent, which Mao saw as having the force of "raging winds and driving rain," it was the army that conquered China from the KMT. It was the army, in one form or another, that carried out the great social and political purges by which China was divested of its older vested interests, hostile elements, and extraneous traditions which were seen as holding the country back. It was the army that carried out the elaborate restructuring of the whole society and the rebuilding of the great social machines for economic production, both agricultural and industrial. It was the army that carried out all the furious measures by which China became, first self-sufficient, and then a strong world power.

Economic Recovery First, inflation was quelled, revenues were raised to meet most urgent needs, and the whole fiscal structure was overhauled so as to provide a single centralized control over all resources. Money, credit, commodities, prices, and eventually all that moved (including people) came under state control. A device by which confidence in real units of economic value was restored, for purposes of exchange, was the use of fixed "baskets" of commodities rather than money prices as terms of reference. (Because of inflation, money had become all but useless and worthless.) Thus, measured units of grain, cloth, or coal replaced coins and currencies as units of value in relation to each other. In this way, by depending heavily upon what was in fact an elaborate system of bartering, a working balance between supplies of goods and services and demands for same was gained. Units of goods served as units for wages, for capital accumulation, for agricultural and industrial production, and for commercial exchange. Within one year inflation was under control.

The "Reign of Terror" Next, it was necessary to take control of all agricultural surpluses. All land was claimed by the state and taken away from its previous holders (landlords or "owners"). This task involved perhaps one of the most drastic and profoundly disturbing "civil" processes of deliberate execution (or executive action) in history—nothing less than war by a government on its people. Work teams began this process by moving from village to village, and area to area, explaining the need for "land reform" and then organizing landless laborers into effective political forces. These then provoked "class struggle" by calling meetings in which all accumulated bitterness and grievance were vented against the landed gentry, "despots and landlords," and all groups in positions of privilege or wealth. All real or imagined enemies of the regime, "counter-revolutionaries," and "running dogs of capitalists and imperialists" were rounded up in huge kangaroo courts in each locality. At such mass spectacles, where each local community or peasant association had formed and committed itself to establishing an entirely new world order and to searching out and destroying all "hidden enemies of the people," untold thousands were brought to trial, made to confess their guilt, beg repentence, and plead for mercy. In emotional scenes of mass consensus, sentences of death or of expiation were carried out on the spot. How many persons died during this "Reign of Terror" may perhaps never be accurately known. Estimates based upon published Chinese sources indicate that, over a four-year period reaching its frenzied zenith from June 1950 to June 1951, between 18 and 24 million persons were killed. How many more were sent away to do penance or to change their views in labor camps can hardly be guessed. While all this was going on, by the same forms of "peasant consensus," people were classified into categories of allegiance or hostility to the revolution and all lands and properties were redistributed, at first "equally" among the landless peasantry and then later "collectivized" and brought under government management. In this fashion, remnants of the landed gentry were wiped out and replaced by the local party apparatus and machinery. This "new democracy" of dictatorship by consensus ultimately moved toward the collectivization of the entire agrarian system into one vast, totalitarian monolith. In other words, the entire agricultural population was "enslaved" as never before—personal liberty was abolished and all were bound to toil for party taskmasters—so as to provide the machinery of state with means to pay for its equally radical, rapidly forced industrialization. "Equalization of tenure," in short, meant equal subjection of all men as workers for the new order, slaves to the monolithic structure. Yet, by such drastic means, "hunger" and "poverty" also seem to have been wiped out.

In order to ensure that not only the bodies but also the loyalties of all people would become subject to state control, the family of old China was systematically destroyed and restructured. This was done by completely changing the status of women and children. Reverence for parents and ancestors was attacked. Filial piety and fraternal fidelity were debunked. Children were encouraged to spy upon their parents and were rewarded for reporting and denouncing them. Wives and husbands were also inspired to inform against each other. By a new marriage law in 1950, women were removed from dependence upon men, insomuch that marriage, divorce, and belongings become strictly an individual, private matter. Only unitary families were encouraged; and even these, of indefinite duration. Thus, in perhaps one of the most revolutionary of all its measures, the state smashed the iron-hard bonds of loyalty and custom by which the extended family had survived all external assaults throughout the centuries. In any conflict of interests and loyalties between the family and the state, the Communist regime made sure that the state would prevail.

Production Meanwhile, under the shadow of such stark terror, cities and factories and roads were rebuilt by hordes of hand laborers. Businesses both large and small were taken over after further public trials which almost completely destroyed the small class of private entrepreneurs that had grown up in Shanghai, Tientsin, Canton, and other cities. Despite such extirpations, however, by 1953 reports from Peking showed that production had reached and even surpassed the prewar peak of 1937. Indeed, however backward Chinese industry had been when compared with the West, there is no denying the giant strides made during the 1950's, in both extraction of raw materials and the production of energy and manufacture of finished goods. One indicator of this success, which greatly elevated China's confidence and pride, came with the actual surpassing of the annual coal production of Great Britain in 1958. Within its first decade, China rose from ninth to third place, behind only the U.S.S.R. and the U.S.A., among the world's coal

Worker in Chinese Steel Factory. The steel industry helped lead the way during the production boom of China's first decade.

producing countries. Its growth statistics for iron, steel, and electrical power were equally dramatic. Despite being boycotted by most western countries, therefore, China proved herself capable of surmounting difficulties and of proving wrong those who doubted her capacity to build a strong industrial base. In fact, by hurriedly building up major industries and by continuing to do so even after the withdrawal of Soviet financial, material, and technical assistance in 1960, the leaders of China could show that, despite setbacks and delays, the growth of China's industrial might could no longer be questioned. The 1964 explosion of her own atomic bomb and the development of such ultimate nuclear weapons since that date has dispelled any lingering doubts as to whether China counts among the exclusive group of great world powers.

Revitalizing the Revolution   The constant danger or major difficulty of the Communist regime was the possibility of a decaying laxity within the Party and a consequent weakening of the Party's hold upon the population. Party members made up only about two percent of the population. Elite status and special privileges put them in a separate class, above the toiling masses. Such being the case, entry into the status of Party membership was extremely difficult. Rites of passage were perhaps crudely comparable to the examination systems of earlier regimes. Solemn ceremonies, rituals, and oaths of loyalty to the regime and its orthodoxy were mandatory. Each prospective member had to swear that he belonged entirely to the Party, submit completely to its dictates, and wholly deny himself to the point of being ready, without hesitation, to sacrifice his own happiness if not his very life for the Party.

Within the Party, an elite cadre served as the backbone of the Party. Comparable in role to that of noncommissioned officers in any army, these agents or officials were called the *kan-pu*. Carefully selected and continuously retrained, they controlled the Party cells. Their task was to know everything about every Party member, and to keep complete and detailed personnel records. In effect, this new elite class took the place formerly occupied by the traditional scholar-gentry. Above the *kan-pu* was a vast and elaborate Party superstructure. This hierarchical pyramid had the triennial meeting of the National Party Congress as its base, the semi-annual meetings of the Central Committee of some fifty to one-hundred members as its intermediate stratum, and almost daily meetings of the Politburo (Central Political Bureau of seventeen members) and constant administration of the Central Secretariat (of nine members) as its top. But even this top level had a concentrated executive, the Standing Committee consisting of the Party Chairman and four ranked vice-chairmen. Thus, a line of obedience ran from Party membership to the *kan-pu*, to the National Congress, to the Central Committee, to the Politburo and Secretariat, to the Standing Committee, and, ultimately, to one man who, ever since 1949, has been Mao Tsetung—the structure of the "peoples' democracy," both in theory and in practice, was actually dictatorship from above. The Chairman controlled the

Combining Manual and Intellectual Efforts in China. Children from a Peking school were sent out to work at a commune near the capital. During a break in the work they listen to a lecture on fertilizer. (Henri Cartier-Bresson, Magnum.)

Standing Committee; the Standing Committee controlled the Politburo; the Politburo controlled the Central Committee; the Central Committee dominated the National Congress; and the National Congress in turn directed the provincial and local units of the Party down to each *kan-pu* and his subordinates.

Perhaps one of the most radical contributions of Red China to the methodology of revolution and of totalitarian control was the refinement of a coercive system for manipulating human emotions, whether in individuals, in groups, or in great masses of people. Called "brainwashing" in Chinese slang, a science of empirical procedures was developed which made possible directed changes in patterns of motivation, thought and behavior. This was done by total control of the environment and information surrounding a person; by calculated intermixing of stimuli producing either high aspirations or terrors; by successively inducing and intensifying feelings of guilt and shame. Thus, irregular prolonging of deprivation, insecurity, tension, fatigue, and incessant indoctrination could shatter inner identity in human beings. And these pressures could be manipulated in such a way that only submission to authority would promise escape, any sense of release, or any peace of mind to the person or group of persons to whom the techniques were applied. Developed out of methods used in Yenan to "Leninize" party members; applied to American prisoners during the Korean War so that they "confessed" incredible things, such as germ warfare; and further developed by Liu Shao-ch'i by experimentation with "thought mobilization" which "washed" Marxist-Leninist-Maoist concepts into the minds of thousands of students and intellectuals, by the late 1950's this methodology was ready for application in large-scale, "mass line" campaigns. Indeed, through successive mass movements, Mao Tse-tung eventually used this technique for his "continuous revolution," even using it against the Party itself.

"Mass" organizing of the people was always the main task of the Chinese Communist Party, with mass meetings, rallies, campaigns, and movements as the most visible expression of its efforts. Merely to maintain the status quo, namely, to keep itself in power by administering and ruling the populace, was seen not only as insufficient, but even as dangerous. "Mass" organizations which could carry a continuous revolution to the country by trying to achieve some herculean goal or win some challenging struggle were essential to the health of the Party and of the regime. (Any person in the country could belong to a "mass" organization, without restrictions, dues, requirements, or tests of any kind. One such "mass" organization listed over 100 million members.) Such movements and campaigns served continuously to arouse the population in some great effort, to generate excitement (or alleviate deadly boredom), to expose failures, to "criticize" or punish secret enemies or shirkers, or to divert attention away from troublesome problems. A glance at three of these enormous movements serves to illustrate how the regime has dealt with what it saw to be internal difficulties or dangers.

The Hundred Flowers Movement was engineered to deal with a particularly worrisome and dangerous group that had remained effective after 1949—the *Chu-tzu*, or scholar-gentry, especially the modern scholars having various degrees of Western-style learning. The tradition of intellectuals having great influence on society was tremendous. Most of these scholars had been openly sympathetic to communist theory, which they tended to see as both scientific and idealistic. Some were party members; others had either written essays, poems, and novels in praise of revolution or against destructive traditions and harmful forces, such as the KMT. The new regime, while it needed the skills and supporting influence of intellectuals, was also distrustful of minds it could not control. To allow anyone to question its campaigns of "Hate America," "Love Soviets," or "Teach the Sayings of Mao" was unthinkable, high treason; and to allow some to "secretly worship" the United States, capitalism, or other "decadent" Western notions was to tolerate corruption, which was both contagious and deadly.

Consequently, Mao introduced a new "mass" movement in May 1956 seemingly designed to promote intellectual freedom. But the "Hundred Flowers" campaign was really aimed at bringing all intellectuals, all uncommitted and free-thinking individuals, especially critics, into complete subjection. Its conception came from a decree of the Chou Dynasty: "Let a hundred flowers bloom; let a hundred schools of thought contend." Free thought, free debate, free creativity, free criticism, and free expression in art, letters and science were publicly encouraged. At first, intellectuals were suspicious and cautious; fearful of being led into a trap, most kept still. Chairman Mao then tried another tactic. While encouraging free expression of criticism, he indicated that the regime would also argue in support of its own doctrines but also conceded that in a communist country certain limits to criticism were necessary. Slowly and then more boldly, criticisms began to emerge. Demands for more power, complaints against arrogance, conceit, and interference grew louder. Eventually, all pent-up emotions and frustrations felt during a decade of suffering were released. Some critics went so far as to say that the people really hated communism; that China's misery had increased under Red rule; that, if Party functionaries did not mend their extravagant and luxury-loving ways, they too would be overthrown and killed by the masses; and that even the ending of Communist rule would not be the end of China.

Such outpourings of hostility against the regime accomplished Mao's purpose. They showed how deep and widespread was the disaffection among the most influential elements of society. They also alarmed Party members enough to put them on full alert and to realize the necessity for reform within their ranks. Finally, they provoked a severe counter-attack by which the regime took steps to eradicate every glimmer of intellectual resistance. In June of 1956, mass protests and rallies denounced any who dared to call Communist rule into question or to suggest it was evil. Peasants, students, and workers joined in denouncing those scholars and thinkers who had dared to criticize the revolution. Soon all dissent was stifled and all dissonant voices fell silent. Humble cries of contrition were heard and those who had dared to criticize disappeared, never to be seen again. Thus, the "Hundred Flowers" campaign did what was intended. It flushed out latent ideological opposition and ruthlessly destroyed it, while, at the same time, it consolidated Party power as never before.

The Great Leap Forward was a campaign of exhortation to greater effort. Despite having a *"planned economy,"* which forced the entire country to conform to fixed rules so as to attain higher output, there were constant delays and disruptions. The First Five Year Plan, announced in 1953 as a crash program to reach ambitious production goals, was a success. But the costs were heavy. The Soviet Union, after sending some 30,000 technicians and building nearly 300 industrial plants, demanded prompt repayment on short-term loans, usually in the form of large amounts of food grains, raw materials, and manufactures; nor did it relent, even during the hard famine years of 1958–1962 when starving people fled to Hong Kong for refuge. Moreover, agricultural production continued to lag seriously. Despite claims to efficiency, in use of labor and in consolidation of farms, not enough was invested in agriculture. Nor can such factors alone serve to explain the failures of rapid growth in this sector.

The Second Five Year Plan had hardly begun in 1958 when Mao Tse-tung changed his mind. His decision, known as the "Great Leap Forward," was for everyone to work harder. Young people were to scour the countryside for more fuel, fertilizer, and raw materials. Old people were to mind the children so as to free women for work in fields and factories. Health was to be hazarded; leisure and sleep were to be cut. As in wartime, round-the-clock work was to continue.

The single most significant part of this mass movement was the setting up of People's Communes. The pilot commune was called "Sputnik." Soon communes sprang up all over China. Their object was to increase production dramatically; to mobilize and control peasants more closely, where collective farms had failed; to use labor resources more effectively; and, thereby, ultimately to pay for rapid industrial expansion through rapid increases in agricultural production. Some 740,000 collectives became 26,000 communes, each averaging about 5,000 families. All homes were to be destroyed; barracks were to be built for male and female workers and for old people who were to care for infants and small children; all were to eat in common dining halls; and spouses were to be with each other once every two weeks. Although, actually, very few models became that extreme, within a year the whole movement began to fade. Starvation diets; endless hours of work; demoralizing restrictions; and the very arrogance of the new taskmasters, the *kan-pu*, provoked such deep silent resistence that the whole barracks system became unmanageable. As a result, the whole campaign was undermined by silent clumsiness, delays, and frustration. Lands were badly cultivated and damage to crops, whether from human or from natural causes, was devastating. Fearful of punishment if demands to reach impossible goals were not realized, local officials gave falsified reports which, at each higher level, were further embellished. Unreal pictures of surplus production emerged. What happened in farming also happened in factories. Fabricating of output statistics caused such a scandal that the regime was forced to modify its policies.

Natural calamities such as droughts and floods were not uncommon in China's history. Nor was peasant resistance, low worker morale, or arrogance of oppressive officials. Practical limits to human endurance and practical importance of conventional wisdom and of old methods, especially when combined with the new, received official recognition. Familes were again permitted to grow their own food and live together. Working hours were shortened; ideological lectures and military drills were reduced; and incentives were increased. Overlord officials began to walk with more humility and to show more respect for age and experience. Chairman Mao himself spoke of compromise of the need for "walking on *two* legs." And thus, another cathartic campaign came to a close.

The Great Proletarian Cultural Revolution and the "Red Guard" was a movement aimed to shake-up, cleanse, and energize both the Party apparatus and the rising younger generation. Having dealt with the dangers of hidden hostility among intellectuals and having pushed his continuous revolution to over-extension and floundering by trying to drive people too hard, Chairman Mao set in motion yet another mass movement in the mid-1960's. Again, his scheme was extremely clever, setting two potentially dangerous forces into collision and thus cancelling any possible threats from either. The old scholar-official class and the modern student-intellectual class had been broken and eradicated. But the longer the Party was in power

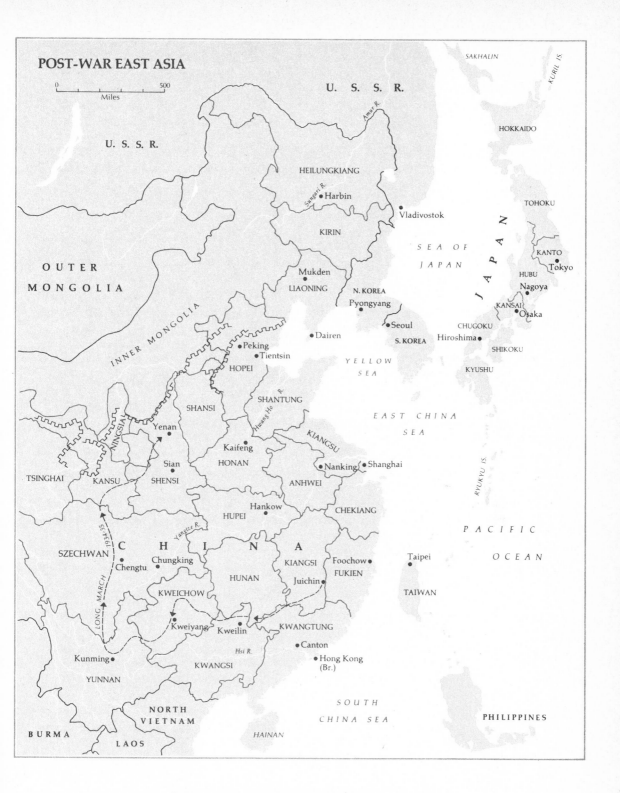

POST-WAR EAST ASIA

0 ——— 500
Miles

U. S. S. R.

U.S.S.R.

SAKHALIN

KURIL IS.

HOKKAIDO

HEILUNGKIANG

Sungari R.
● Harbin

● Vladivostok

TOHOKU

KIRIN

SEA OF JAPAN

JAPAN

KANTO
● Tokyo

OUTER MONGOLIA

● Mukden
LIAONING

N. KOREA
● Pyongyang

HUBU
● Nagoya
KANSAI
● Osaka

INNER MONGOLIA

● Dairen

● Seoul
S. KOREA

CHUGOKU
Hiroshima ●

KYUSHU

SHIKOKU

● Peking
● Tientsin
HOPEI

YELLOW SEA

SHANTUNG

TSINGHAI

SHANSI

Huang Ho R.

● Yenan

KIANGSU

EAST CHINA SEA

NINGSIA

● Sian
SHENSI

● Kaifeng
HONAN

● Nanking ● Shanghai

KANSU

ANHWEI

RYUKYU IS.

SZECHWAN

● Chengtu

C H I N A

HUPEI

● Hankow

Yangtze R.

CHEKIANG

PACIFIC OCEAN

● Chungking

KIANGSI
HUNAN

● Foochow
FUKIEN

● Taipei

LONG MARCH 1934-35

KWEICHOW

● Juichin

TAIWAN

● Kweiyang
● Kweilin

KWANGTUNG

● Kunming
YUNNAN

Hsi R.
KWANGSI

● Canton

● Hong Kong (Br.)

BURMA

NORTH VIETNAM

LAOS

HAINAN

SOUTH CHINA SEA

PHILIPPINES

1681   CHINA AND JAPAN IN THE TWENTIETH CENTURY

and the older and more comfortably settled were its members in their seats of power, the more complacent and difficult to manage became the entrenched bureaucracy of the new elite. Originally pliable and strictly subservient to central dictates, members of this elite began to quarrel and struggle over petty or personal objectives and to criticize Mao's methods and national goals. Regional and factional conflict not only threatened efficiency, but it also held seeds of much more serious national disruption, with potential dangers even for Mao himself. Some means had to be found to bring the entire apparatus to heel. What better catharsis could be found than to organize a mass movement of revolution against the Party itself? Nothing less than a thorough shakeup followed by its complete subservience to central control would suffice.

Another potential danger to aging leadership could come from an energetic younger generation of better trained, ambitious, and aspiring activists. Young people who had never known the "long march" of the thirties, the "war" of the forties, or the "terror" of the fifties could become disenchanted and frustrated. Unless their idealistic energies were harnessed and directed, they could become difficult. Well-fed, well-clothed, and well-indoctrinated with Marxist-Leninist-Maoist ideology, the revolutionary zeal of youth could be mobilized and put to use. By taking steps to have his sayings "canonized" as the "sacred writ" of the revolution, distributed in little red books, and memorized, Mao captured the imaginations of the young and set millions upon millions of them in motion. Calling them "Red Guards" and assigning them the task of "Protectors of the Revolution," Mao then turned them against the whole Party apparatus. With fearful fury they attacked all signs of arrogance, backsliding, complacency, dampening effort, or wavering loyalty to Mao within the Party. (Liu Shao-ch'i, Mao's second in command, was declared a traitor, hounded out of office and made to disappear in disgrace.) The forces let loose upon China by Mao were enormous. Indeed, for a time it seemed as if the whole country would dissolve in civil convulsions, so vehement and violent were the assaults upon established privilege and power within the Party.

Many have argued over the merits of the Red Guard movement. Some say that Mao's campaign backfired, got out of hand, and almost destroyed the state. However arguable this may be, in the end, a much chastened Party organization was only too glad to be rescued from the excesses of the "Red Guards" by the Red Army. Military campaigns had to be fought and in some cases months of effort were required. The Army had to put down not only the Red Guards; it also had to crush autonomous Party power in some provinces where local organizations had defeated the Red Guards and shown a capacity to throw off Peking rule. China emerged from another period of contrived inner turbulence in the sixties with both Party and youth cleansed of corrupting or disruptive tendencies. More than that, the Red Army was itself revitalized and "tempered" by the ordeal. Even the Army had to undergo cleansing. Lin Piao, the General who had been the number-two leader and the designated heir to Mao, fell into disgrace and was declared a traitor. His mysterious death in a plane crash in 1971 serves as a reminder that further revolutionary changes in political institutions may yet disrupt China before she secures a method of transferring leadership from Mao to his successors.

Revolution and World Power China, as she sees it, has regained her place as the center of man's civilization; and has returned to her traditional ethnocentric posture toward the world. Self-sufficiency and nonexpansion beyond what are perceived as historic or natural frontiers appear to underlie China's foreign policy since 1950. This underlying theme is not altered by other, varying motifs; indeed it brings coherence even to phases of international adventure which often seem inexplicable.

The compulsion to restore complete unity to historic Chinese boundaries and to secure all frontiers, as the best way to prevent civil war and foreign interference, serves to explain China's expansion into central Asia. The incorporation of Tibetans, Turks, Mongols, and other non-Han peoples within one vast realm of over 700 million people; attempts to sway (if not control) the direction of events in Korea and Vietnam; determination to recover Taiwan from "occupation" by "puppets of American imperialism"; and further extension of its shadowy influence and interests in Southeast Asia (Burma, Thailand, Malaysia, Singapore, Indonesia, and so on), if not also in Japan, should all be seen with these terms of reference in mind.

A militant, crusading rhetoric toward the outside world, with strident railings against the enemies of mankind in the "imperialist camp" and cries to follow Chinese models for "liberating" exploited peoples (and thus bring them into the "socialist camp") does not alter the deeper logic of China's policies. A belligerent face was shown to American-led anti-Communist policies of containment, especially between 1950 and 1954. The presence of an American fleet in the Taiwan Strait and confrontations over the off-shore island of Quemoy epitomized a continuing state of war. This was followed by a softer, diplomatic approach to Asian countries, epitomized by the Condung Conference of African and Asian states in 1955, when the five principles (*pancha-sheela*) of "peaceful coexistence" were enunciated, with negotiation and persuasion replacing armed hostility. After 1957, hostility again increased. An American build-up of the military power of Nationalists in Taiwan led, after increasing provocations, to the second Quemoy crisis in 1958. Tibet, which had been conquered in 1950, was subjected to harsh Sinicization under a process of "socialist revolution." This provoked a rising at Lhasa in 1959, during which the Dalai Lama fled to India. As harsh repression of Tibetans increased, Sino-Indian relations deteriorated. At issue was the exact demarcation of their Himalayan borderland, especially the strategic Aksai-Chin with its vital supply route between Sinkiang and Tibet. Brief hostilities finally erupted in October of 1963, rashly provoked by Nehru and ending in a crushing defeat for unprepared Indian forces by the Chinese.

Sino-Soviet Split and Sino-American Rapprochment Very different historical traditions, sociopolitical perceptions, and needs eventually brought about a cooling of relations between China and Russia. Each had grounds of suspicion, supported by memories of ancient hostility. Southern Russia, including Moscow, had been conquered and ruled by the Golden Horde. Turkestan, Mongolia, and Manchuria had felt the weight of Tsarist encroachments. Great population pressures in China prompted its leaders to look hungrily at the vast empty lands of Siberia, especially at Outer Mongolia which had been under China's sway. At the same time, apprehensions and fears, whether of "eastern peril" for Russians or of "northern peril" for Chinese, could easily be rekindled. Such collaboration as did exist between fraternal "socialist" followers of Lenin was chiefly between leaders and in the form of aid paid for by China. All that was needed to disrupt the alliance was for leaders to find some pretext. Since the alliance was founded upon ideology, ideological disagreement also served as its breaking-point. Differences in doctrine and emphasis produced friction: Soviet debunking of Stalin in 1956 severed Marxist-Leninist solidarity, so that Peking could become an autonomous center of doctrinal legitimacy. Krushchev criticized the Great Leap, by which Mao boasted that China would bypass Russia, as dangerous. Charges of "deviation" were met by counter-charges of "revisionism," opportunism, and betrayal of the revolution. Promised nuclear assistance to China ceased; and in 1960 Russian technicians in China suddenly went home, taking papers and plans with them. Fear of Chinese expansion began to grow. This increased greatly after 1964, when China's capacity to produce nuclear weapons was suddenly demonstrated. By 1969, armed clashes began to occur along the Amur River and in Central Asia. Meanwhile, as the split widened, competition for leadership of the world revolution developed. Missions from Peking were sent to support "national liberation movements" throughout Africa and Asia. China presented itself as part of the agrarian, underdeveloped majority of mankind fighting against the urban, industrialized centers of imperialism in the West. As both powers involved themselves in competing to help North Vietnam and to win influence in its war with the United States, China suffered humiliation. After 1965, as American bombing of North Vietnam continued, Peking was unable to change the course of events or to protect an ally just beyond its borders. Other setbacks and failures in China's foreign relations, culminating in the slaughter of the pro-Chinese Indonesian Communist Party after its abortive coup in October 1965, served to turn China inward.

By 1970, the people of China had raised their minimal standard of living and had increased levels of agricultural and industrial production, transportation, electrification, health, and education. Meanwhile, confirmed in great-power status because of its nuclear capacity and facilitated by greater domestic stability at home, Peking's leaders were able to respond more positively in 1971 to efforts by the American government to end the war in Vietnam and to restore diplomatic relations. Gestures of "people-to-people" diplomacy by ping-pong players and newsmen were followed by the admission of the Communist regime to the United Nations and the expulsion of the Nationalists of Taiwan. All agreed that Taiwan was an integral part of China, while the formula for ending the Communist-Nationalist civil war remained unresolved. Thus, what began with the Sino-Soviet split and rivalry over leadership in the Communist world brought the Cold War to its close. President Nixon's dramatic visits to Peking and to Moscow in 1972 profoundly shifted the foundations of great-power relationships. Thereafter, both the Soviet Union and Japan, as well as the United States, entered into more positive policies towards China. How positive these would continue to be will be shaped by the internal problems still faced by China.

"IMPERIAL" JAPAN: 1912–1950

By the early twentieth century, Japan, unlike China, had already achieved a unified modern state and was on the way toward becoming the first nonwestern industrial country. The coming of a new reign (Taisho, 1912–1916) coincided with World War I and its aftermath, at first seeming to auger a period of prosperity and peaceful growth but ending in an atmosphere of increasing anxiety and tension. During this period, when Japan allied itself with the Atlantic Allies (America, Britain and France), its economic and political power grew enormously. The *zaibatsu*, merchant houses whose interlocked industrial, financial, and mercantile strength brought them great wealth and influence, emerged as an aggressive force. The intellectuals, journalists, and writers and teachers, joined businessmen in trying to introduce and expand elements of democracy and personal liberty into government procedures. A law was passed by which the privilege of voting was given to all men over twenty-one years of age. Elections, party politics, and much paraphernalia of parliamentary government grew in importance. Japanese people, exposed to ever more ideas and styles from the West, became more and more involved in currents of an emerging global awareness of a common culture and fashion. Many supported the League of Nations, sympathized with movements of national self-determination, and grew to appreciate music, literature, entertainments and sports of the West.

Depression and Difficulty after 1926 Japan entered a time of great economic and political troubles in the late twenties, soon after Emperor Hirohito came to the throne. From heights of achievement, reform, and prestige, the country fell into a series of crises from which it did not emerge until after its final military defeat in 1945.

Explanations for the sudden end of both prosperity and popular civilian government, together with cessation of friendly relations with former allies, are not simple. Perhaps economic troubles after World War I can be seen as pivotal. Increased advantages, concessions and privileges gained from China were taken away by "allies" at the Washington Conference (1922). Stiff American and European competition ate into Japanese markets. Demands for exports dropped off sharply. The great 1923 earthquake brought misery and destruction to Tokyo and Yokohama. The "crash" of world

markets in 1929, with global depression in its wake, caused severe suffering for millions of poor people, unable to earn enough to eat. For Japan, such profound poverty was unprecedented.

Without adequate natural resources of its own and with a rapidly increasing population to feed, Japan could no longer survive in isolation. Foreign trade was vital—and, as troubles multiplied, leaders looked for ways to bolster trade—to import raw materials, metals, and oil in particular and to export finished products. As world conditions deteriorated, Japan found itself surrounded by a ring of hostile countries, Asian and western. In 1928, Nationalist China tried to conquer and consolidate North China; this included steps to cut off vested privileges held by foreigners. Japan sent troops to guard its interests; the clash that occurred was followed by other incidents.

Radical Militarization and Expansion By 1931, Japan's plight was so desperate that military leaders, looking back to a proud *samurai* heritage, which in past times of crisis had saved the nation from chaos and collapse by imposing strict discipline and firm order, took matters into their own hands. Army officers staged a bomb incident which served as the pretext for launching an invasion of Manchuria, a source of rich raw materials. As its armies swept over Manchuria and on into Mongolia, world powers condemned Japan but were loath to take action. This solution to her problems seemed so easy that further conquest seemed tempting. Meanwhile, inside Japan, young officers set out to seize direct control of government. Not long after the Manchurian Incident, the Prime Minister was assassinated. Other deeds of violence against civilian officials followed. Finally, early in 1936, military units took over all chief offices in Tokyo, summarily killing a number of high ranking ministers. While severe punishment was meted out against the leaders of this "uprising," military men retained virtually full control of the government. Thereafter, step by step, Japan moved steadily deeper into commitments to a policy of war and intensive preparations for war. Attitudes toward China became openly aggressive, and hostile to all who might interfere.

War broke out in 1937, starting with a contrived incident at the Marco Polo Bridge near Peking and ending with Japan's surrender to the Allied Powers in 1945. In actuality, however, deepening involvement in a quagmire of war policies was not unavoidable. Rather, a series of tragic miscalculations led Japan to her terrible defeat. First, it was too late (if ever) to seize and hold North China by a localized war. Nor could China ever again be brought to her knees by the capture of the great port cities along her coasts and inland artery, the Yangtse. Although pushed deep into the interior, China's government did not collapse and her people simply refused to give up. Japanese soldiers, so self-controlled when in their own society, gave way to such mad rapine and murder that even normally apathetic peasants were aroused to implacable fury. Thus, what had begun as a simple "incident," with hopes for quick gains, settled into a protracted and expensive stalemate, with no end in sight.

A second occasion for a fateful choice came after the outbreak of global war. Japan had joined Germany in an anti-Communist pact in 1936. If Japan's allies succeeded in crushing her foes (France, Holland, and Britain) in Europe,

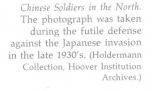

Chinese Soldiers in the North. The photograph was taken during the futile defense against the Japanese invasion in the late 1930's. (Holdermann Collection, Hoover Institution Archives.)

as seemed to be happening, much of the danger to Japan's position in Asia could be eased. But was this really the wisest alternative? Would it not be better to make generous concessions, withdraw troops from China, and come to an accommodation with the United States? By so doing Japan stood to earn splendid economic profits from the war in Europe just as it had done in World War I. Such a move would enable Japan to take a giant step toward constructing an enormous economic empire in Asia without having to pay for costly military campaigns. But for this to be accomplished, much depended upon whether Japan could gracefully withdraw from China without too great a loss of national "face" and whether America could be persuaded to soften its hostility. In the event, both obstacles turned out to be too formidable.

American public opinion, hitherto somewhat apathetic, was much aroused by the war in Europe. Militaristic regimes in both Germany and Japan were seen as posing serious threats to world peace and American security. As America swung more and more aid to a beleaguered Britain, it also moved from verbal protests and refusal to recognize Japanese conquests to outright sanctions. Hard words could be ignored; but the withholding of shipments of scrap iron from the United States and of oil from British and Dutch holdings in Southeast Asia cut into the very vitals of Japan's economy.

On the other side, Japan's military would have to admit that their program of prosperity through conquest had failed. Yet to say so would involve them in a massive shift of national sentiment sufficient to endanger their positions in government. To avoid such an eventuality and such national "loss of face," war with the western democracies seemed inevitable. Also, they reasoned, that so long as Germany succeeded in Europe, Japan would be safe to do as she wished in Asia. Britain was too beseiged and America would not dare to concentrate its strength in Asia so long as Germany remained dangerous. If Germany were defeated, on the other hand, its long death struggles would buy time for Japan to conclude her conquest of China. By harnessing the enormous natural resources and human energies of the huge Chinese empire, to which would be added a maritime domain covering all of Southeast Asia (the whole of which would be dubbed the "Greater East Asia Co-Prosperity Sphere") Japan expected to defend herself from further attack from enemies across the vast oceans, especially if those enemies were wounded and war weary. In short, just as the Mongols and the Manchus had conquered and ruled over China for centuries, so now Japan's leaders wished to ascend the Dragon Throne and, by incorporation, to create the most powerful, populous, and fabulously rich empire the world had ever known.

The attempt to solve her problems by continued resort to armed might required an all-out effort by the entire nation of Japan. Faced with this appalling dilemma, and unable either to think of a dangerous war against a strong alliance of world powers or to compromise so as to satisfy the Chinese, Americans, and Japanese military leaders, Prince Konoe resigned

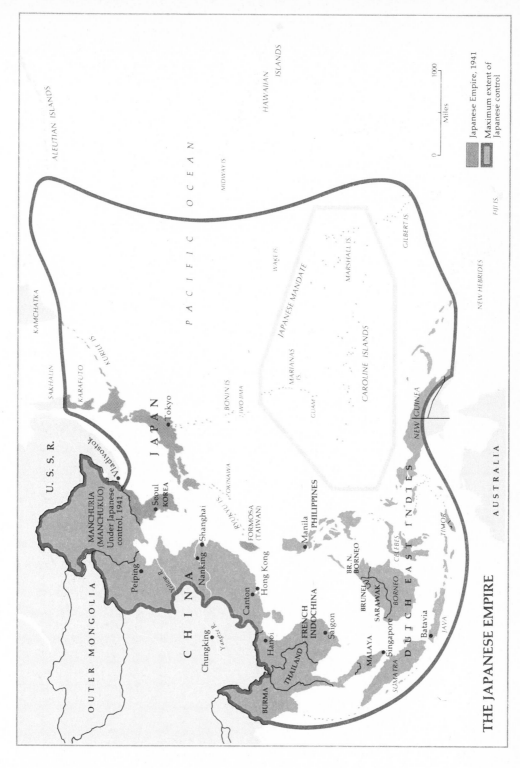

THE JAPANESE EMPIRE

Japanese Empire, 1941

Maximum extent of Japanese control

1000

Miles

0

ALEUTIAN ISLANDS

HAWAIIAN ISLANDS

MIDWAY IS

PACIFIC OCEAN

KAMCHATKA

SAKHALIN

KARAFUTO

KURILE IS

JAPAN
Tokyo

BONIN IS

IWO JIMA

WAKE IS

JAPANESE MANDATE

MARSHALL IS

GILBERT IS

NEW HEBRIDES

FIJI IS

U.S.S.R.

Vladivostok

MANCHURIA
(MANCHUKUO)
Under Japanese
control, 1941

Seoul
KOREA

RYUKYU IS

OKINAWA

FORMOSA
(TAIWAN)

MARIANAS
IS

GUAM

CAROLINE ISLANDS

NEW GUINEA

OUTER MONGOLIA

Peiping

Yellow R.

CHINA

Nanking
Shanghai

Hong Kong

Canton

Manila

PHILIPPINES

BR. N.
BORNEO

BRUNEI

SARAWAK

BORNEO

CELEBES

DUTCH EAST INDIES

TIMOR

AUSTRALIA

Chungking

Yangtze R.

Hanoi

FRENCH
INDOCHINA

Saigon

THAILAND

BURMA

MALAYA

Singapore

SUMATRA

JAVA

Batavia

in October 1941 and turned the reins of government over to General Tojo and his war cabinet. The entire nation was transformed into one enormous, tightly disciplined military machine. All schools, Shinto shrines, radio programs, newspapers, cinemas, and other forms of mass media were harnessed to single-minded expressions of loyalty to the "divine destiny" of Japan as personified in the divinity of its emperor. Every sector of society, whether labor unions, business groups, cultural guilds, religious institutions, or political parties, were expected to do their part to "assist the emperor" in his hallowed task. A monolithic, totalitarian party, called the Imperial Rule Assistance Association, was organized to make sure that this was done. In turning away from such recently constructed political institutions as the Diet and such ideals as democracy and individual liberty, by which the sacred cause of the body politic became paramount and all rival notions were viewed as dangerous, Japan was in some degree returning to a militaristic heritage from its "feudal" age.

Yet, even as they took this direction, many senior leaders in Japan knew that, ringed as Japan would be by a wall of implacable foes, the risks were very grave. Unless a swift victory could be won while Germany was still fighting, and then unless Japan generously sued for a peace with hopes of modest returns from demoralized and desperate foes whose main concern was still to cope with Germany, dangers to Japan would grow and grow. Knowing how weak American, British, and Dutch forces were in the Pacific and how easily lands of southeast Asia could be overrun, so that desperately needed oil and minerals could be obtained, Japan gambled and tied its destiny to the survival of Germany.

Here again the leaders of Japan miscalculated. Most of all, they seriously misread human factors. Counting their own national spirit as superior, they discounted the possibility of such spirit and will in other peoples, whether American, British, Chinese, or Russian. More than that, in their stealthy and swift destruction of the American fleet at Pearl Harbor at dawn on Sunday of December 7th, 1941, by which they won a smashing naval victory and thus cleared the way for their easy conquest of Southeast Asia, they committed a blunder. Any chance of winning a speedy war was lost. American public opinion was awakened and galvanized almost over night into a single-minded determination to completely crush both Japan and Germany. With a swiftness which must have seemed frightening, the Americans rebuilt their fleets, launched air armadas, and sent strong forces across the Pacific. Within six months, at Midway, they stopped Japan; and six months later they began a great, inexorable counter-offensive. Yet, so disciplined and fanatical were the people of Japan that, with a fatalistic stoicism ingrained through centuries, they would doubtless have fought any invasion of their Islands—at a tremendous cost of life. But, after atomic bombs wiped out the cities of Hiroshima and Nagasaki, on August 6th and 9th of 1945, and as the Soviet Union declared war, leaders prevailed over the frantic efforts of die-hard military fanatics and terms of "unconditional surrender" were accepted (August 14th). The emperor himself shattered precedent and

After the Hiroshima Bombing, 1945. A man pushes his loaded bicycle down a path which has been cleared of rubble. On either side of the path, debris, twisted metal, and gnarled tree stumps fill the devastated area. (Stanley Troutman, Acme.)

doubtless prevented bloody resistance by personally announcing the surrender over the radio. Never in all her history had Japan been conquered by foreigners.

THE JAPANESE "MIRACLE"

Resurgent Mercantile Miracle In thirty years of doubling production every decade, Japan has become, after the United States and the Soviet Union, the most productive nation in the world, and one of the most prosperous. Rising from the ashes of catastrophic destruction with spectacular speed, her strength has grown until she is now an economic giant. The resurgence of this country has been one of the "miracles" of modern history, an event that beggars simple explanation. Even more remarkable, in light of Japan's martial history, this has been accomplished wholly by mercantile means and without military power. None can deny American shields and statesmanship have made important contributions. But it was by the energy, skills, and wisdom of Japan's own people that such an achievement was really made possible. How then can one account for such a resurgence? In this complex process, a number of factors deserve emphasis.

First, one must reach deep into the roots of Tokugawa Japan. At that time, national unification removed countless petty restrictions to enterprise and enabled the growth of a single, relatively free economic system. Long generations of uninterrupted peace enabled unprecedented prosperity. Urban industrial and commercial life reached high sophistication. Although the ruling *samurai* class relegated merchants to low status, an expanding money economy brought many *samurai* hopelessly into debt to rich merchants, insomuch that some merchants could amass vast fortunes, marry *samurai* daughters, and patronize the arts and literature as never before. Such developments provided Japan with a highly advanced merchant and cultural community and gave her a remarkable technocratic infrastructure.

Most of all, as in Europe, Japan evolved her own brand of nationalism at a very early stage and to a degree without parallel in Asia. Seeing themselves as a single, unique people, with a common source and a common language, heritage and pride, the Japanese developed an amazingly strong and intricate system of disciplines to reinforce their national consciousness. Two centuries of strictly enforced peace under Tokugawa vigilance left this indelible mark. A docile people meekly followed rules and did as they were told. Countless points of etiquette firmly governed patterns of personal conduct in every sphere of life so as to provide a quintessence of refined harmony and prevent disturbance. Nowhere did proper decorum more tightly regiment a whole people, regardless of class. The very fact that so many millions (then 30, now over 100) had to make do and get along on such small, mountainous, resource-poor islands gave logic to this ethic. When applied to any community or national problem—whether disastrous earthquakes and typhoons or needs of modernization, military conquest, or economic reconstruction—no people could be so galvanized to common purpose and self-sacrificing effort. This "spirit" or "will" or discipline has been truly phenomenal.

Next, one must count a remarkable capacity to learn and, thereupon, to make abrupt, even radical and diametrically opposite turns of direction and policy. With cities burned to ashes, production way down, and shipping gone, Japan did as she had done in 1868 (or 1931). Seeing how worthless had been a policy of prosperity by conquest, she turned her back upon a once hallowed militaristic tradition and the class it represented. Seldom if ever has a people been more disillusioned with its leadership. The very depth of their previous indoctrination when set beside the false information they had been fed, the hatred for Japan found among Asian peoples, and the excesses committed by Japanese troops abroad brought about a traumatic shock. The original Meiji revolution had not, like revolutions in Europe, boiled up from social forces but had been forced down upon the nation by a small, tightly knit and dynamic group of leaders mostly from warrior-gentry (*samurai*) background. But Japan's postwar transformation stands as a mute, profound repudiation of the Meiji approach and represents an extreme turn to far more broadly based movements from merchant, agricultural, and cultural forces coming up from below.

Finally, some benefits emerged from American occupation. For a people steeled to suffer rapine, pillage, and death in last-ditch struggles against an overwhelmingly powerful invasion, the orderly, open, and friendly appearance of occupying forces came as a relief. Common people saw themselves misled and mistaken in their fears. On the other side, free of usual political pressures in America, the carefully constructed plans for Japan, however stern, showed generosity and statesmanship. Every effort was made to provide for complete recovery, reconstruction, and reform. Whatever its failings, the occupation's rational policies for restoration accomplished what was intended. With an almost uncharacteristic radicalness, Americans revolutionized both society and government. Sovereignty was firmly vested in the people. All concentrations of wealth or power that might be dangerous (like the *zaibatzu*) were broken up. A daring and sweeping reformation of the agrarian system vested ownership largely among smaller holders. All these changes were protected by a new Constitution. With much the same unquestioning faith they had shown in their own former leaders, most people accepted what was done by the Americans. They looked to General Douglas MacArthur for leadership and hope. Their hopes were not disappointed. By September 8, 1951, a Peace Treaty was drawn up and signed by forty-eight countries. Eight months later, Japan regained her independence. The emergence of Japan as a powerful ally of the United States reflected new political and economic realities in the world, such as the Cold War and Korean Conflict and such as mutual interdependence and benefit of trade between Japan and the United States.

In 1945, Japan's future looked bleak. With empire gone, economy smashed, more than 70 million people to feed, scarcely any raw materials, production only thirty-seven percent of its prewar level, and punitive actions and reparations to be exacted by Occupation forces, progress seemed impossible. Yet, by 1970, no casual visitor to Japan could not be impressed with what he saw. Signs of good living, political stability, and world-wide influence could be seen on every side. TV antennas, air-conditioners, crowded freeways, jammed commuter trains, and swank clothing speak for themselves. Speeding at 125 miles per hour by the bullet train through a vast industrial belt stretching from Tokyo to Osaka one is aware of Japan's advanced technology, and its ability to provide material comfort for a population which, if trends continue, may be the first country to reach zero population growth. In twenty years, average income has risen from $146 to over $2,000—bypassing that of Austria and England. Indeed, with the third largest economy in the world, surpassed only by the trillion-dollar economy of the U.S. and the 400-billion-dollar economy of the U.S.S.R., but larger than the combined economies of China, India, and much of Southeast Asia, Japan can be said to have experienced its own "revolution," one that has transformed its people, its government, and its place in the world. This "revolution" has been gradual and progressive and altogether peaceful, a transformation altogether different from the radical and violent events with which the term has been more commonly linked in recent times. (Japan's "revolution," therefore, bears a closer resemblance to England's "Glorious Revolution" of 1688 and the gradual and progressive developments that have followed it.)

Economic Growth and Social Transformation Japan's "economic miracle" has inspired the awe of people around the world. A gifted, educationally advanced, highly literate, very hardworking and thrifty people, with great community discipline (or "company commitment") and low personal expectations, was certainly a crucial factor. Another factor was Japan's "starting from scratch" and completely rebuilding her industrial base with the latest developments in plant equipment. Using an existing resource of gifted engineers and scientists, Japan showed that it is much cheaper to buy new technology than to develop it; to spend less on research and development than other countries; and then to beg, borrow, and copy more advanced models from those countries that had made such investments. In this manner Japan created one of the most efficient industrial systems in the world.

Next, Japan struggled with no expensive tax burden for armaments and defense; but rather was able to see her people plough the difference back into growth investment. Again in food production, Japan produced another or a second agricultural revolution. By means of farm subsidies and new technology (fertilizers, insecticides, and light machinery), together with a complete reform of the whole land tenure system, Japanese intensive agriculture became one of the most efficient in the world, insomuch that the country became self-sufficient in rice and grew significant proportions of

Modern-day Assembly Line in Japan. Workers assembling transistor radios at a factory in Osaka. (Paolo Koch, Rapho-Guillumette Pictures.)

her needs in other staples. The fishing industry also developed to the point where it could produce a major portion of the protein needs of the country. Finally, whereas before the war the sign "Made in Japan" had been a symbol of shoddy quality, the excellence of precision craftsmanship in light appliances and tools produced by Japan transformed its reputation.

In short, within a quarter century Japan has become *the* commercial entrepôt *par excellence*. Founded upon multilateral trade in a world without war or protective barriers, in twenty years (1951–1970), her exports have grown from .850 billion to over 25 billion dollars; and her imports, from .974 to some 18 billion dollars. But, in the main, all Japan could offer were the skills and hard labors of her people, so poor is she in raw materials and natural resources. In exchange for fuels (oil, coal), ores (and scrap metals), rubber, natural fibers, and lumber, without which she could not function, Japan has sold the work of many hands, becoming the leading shipbuilder, maker of motorcycles, and producer of fine cameras, radios, calculators, and other light appliances. Without stable conditions of world peace and world trade, Japan's economy would be shattered.

The result of such enormous economic growth has been an equally swift change in the character of Japan's society. Whereas after the Meiji revolution, an ability to limit the death rate through modern medicine and food production brought about a dramatic surge in population growth, population control since 1945 has been equally successful in limiting the birth rate. Through the Eugenics Protection Law of 1948, abortion for economic or personal reasons became legal. Further campaigns of publicity, social pressure, education, late marriage, and unitary families (with an ideal of two children), helped to bring this about. Changes in the status of women, by providing unlimited education and full legal rights (in such matters as marriage and work) were radical in their impact, as typified in an almost complete switch to modern clothing, style consciousness, and commercial fashion. Also, most of the society became urban, in a process of geographic relocation and of commercial-industrial redistribution through an open system of competition for labor. As a result, villages, in which less than twenty percent of the population devoted itself to agriculture, looked outward and became integrated into the larger administrative structures of the country. By 1972, every ninth person lived in Tokyo, and every fourth was employed within the huge Tokyo-Osaka megalopolis. Like London or Paris, in finance, business, education, industry, government, and culture, Tokyo became the throbbing heart of national life.

While in many ways Japan has shared an experience of "future shock" with the rest of the western, industrialized world, she does not seem to have shared the most serious problems of that world. Japan has had no serious drug problem (nor of drink); no serious crime problem; no gun problem (with possession tightly controlled); no serious "poverty culture" (since even the less fortunate have a strong work ethic and hardy fortitude, and try to look middle class); no minority problem (despite some prejudice against backwardness, in the Eta and in Koreans); and, with security mainly provided by the United States, no draft and no wars. Perhaps Japan's most serious problems relate to pollution, parking, crowding, and general anxieties relating to ecology and energy. Intellectual, cultural, and social concerns

Tokyo Central Station. Commuters pass en route to their destinations during rush hour. (International Society for Educational Information, Tokyo.)

provide an atmosphere of heady ferment, but they do not disturb the quiet stability and social strength of the land.

Political Stability and National Security Judged on performance, the parliamentary system of Japan has produced one of the most stable governments in the world. Assured by a skillful blend of centralized, democratic, and technocratic institutions, Japan has maintained the political tradition of remarkable durability so characteristic of the Tokugawa and Meiji periods. One reason advanced for this is that, in basic and crucial issues of domestic tranquillity and foreign defense, Japan has had no major worries because these concerns (and expenses) have been shouldered by America. Certainly assurance of internal prosperity and external peace does increase the prospects for political stability. America has indeed largely helped to supply both these needs, first, by providing a shield of military security and, second, by providing vast markets to help pay for Japan's economic growth. Such help may be considered "artificial" or "contrived," especially if one assumes that sovereignty and interdependence are incompatible. Yet, without the concerted willingness of Japan's society and government to accept such American help, such conditions would not have been possible. Willingness to submit to conditions of close alliance, compliance, and cooperation with the United States—some might even call it subordinate-sovereignty as a "client-state" or "dependency" of the United States, albeit on terms most enlightened and generous—made possible an arrangement of great mutual benefit.

Looked at by stages, this special relationship and political stability can be seen as changing, as a process of evolution from lessening dependence to greater interdependence, if not ultimate independence. During the Yoshida Period (1945–1954) of the Occupation and after the 1946 election, the old prewar parties reemerged and then slowly coalesced into two major groupings. To the right-center were the Liberal, Progressive, and Democratic parties, which became the LDP and continued to hold power; and to the left were Socialist parties, of various shades from extreme radical to reformist. The conservative center, elitist in social background (leadership taken from ranks of generals or professors or established wealth), launched the "miracle" with its programs of technocratic "economism." Like the Meiji *samurai* elite it was distinctly autocratic and oligarchic. During the Second or Hatoyama-Kishi Period (1954–1960), tensions arising from prewar, wartime, and postwar animosities surfaced. It was a time underlying unrest and of sharp conflict between reactionary and radical forces, between conservatives (LDP) and socialists. Seeing a gradual decline in their grass-roots following and organization and being fearful of what riots and radical actions, arising from the hot rhetoric of extreme leftists, might do to the country, successors of Prime Minister Yoshida tried to turn the clock back. They sought to reverse reforms imposed upon the country by SCAP—the Supreme Commander of the Allied Powers, namely, MacArthur. This drift, especially apparent under Prime Minister Hatoyama Ichiro (1954–1956), was evidenced by centralizing control in police (1954), in education boards (1956), in local government (1956), and in attempts to increase military forces and the emperor's status (despite Constitutional prohibitions). Such changes, most of them relatively small, provoked suspicion and unrest. The period became marked with increasing street demonstrations and "confrontation politics." Extreme Socialists, not content with defending the Constitution, wanted much more radical reforms. Matters came to a head in 1960, in struggles over the renewal of the U.S. Security Treaty of 1952. This treaty not only allowed the U.S. to keep military installations (including nuclear weapons) in Japan, but allowed for use of U.S. forces either to maintain domestic order upon request of the Japanese government, or to engage in various foreign ventures in Asia connected with global Cold War politics. As the pitch of protest reached a climax, with special anxiety over Soviet-American tensions and what were seen as tricky tactics of unpopular Prime Minister Kishi Nobusuke, media attacks increased and over 100,000 demonstrators took to the streets, most of them peaceful. Some hoped to see the dawning of a new age of revolutionary politics of mass consciousness. But, with the signing of a new treaty under more agreeable terms, by which nuclear weapons could no longer be kept in Japan nor could bases be used for staging military ventures without prior consultation, tensions subsided and confrontations in the Diet ended. During the Third Period, 1960–1972, political life settled into a quieter routine. Ikeda, the new Prime Minister, sought to give politics a low profile through compromise and concessions. A new generation of leaders, without memories of wartime grudges, no longer tried to reverse the Occupation. Realization of the immensity of Japan's economic power and acclaim from abroad replaced the defeat and gloom of the past with a brighter vision of the future. As a result, inspired by growing confidence and pride, plans to double the economy within a decade were realized within seven years. Under Prime Minister Sato (1964–1972) opposition to the ruling LDP became more fragmented than ever. A new consensus of comfortably established and moderate middle-class voters emerged which, despite student violence in 1969 and a steady leftward drift in policies, favored slow reform of the status quo in order to meet new conditions (as was revealed in opinion polls of 1970).

But by 1970, conditions in the outside world were indeed beginning to change, if not drastically, at least enough to cause an increasing sense of insecurity. A changing balance of world power and particularly of America's role in global affairs, cast shadows over questions of national security and prosperity in Japan. American capacities, especially her self-confidence and international prestige, appeared to have been eroded by the Vietnam War and by more serious internal problems. The great defense shield of America, reinforced by great commercial, cultural, and technical interchanges for a quarter century, seemed to falter. Therefore, whereas from 1945–1954 Japan's foreign policy had been made in Washington and whereas from 1954–1970 talk of independence from Washington had grown, the "shocks" of 1971 and 1972 started a definite process by which the very ground beneath existing structures of international relations began to shift.

Yet, the changes of the 1970's were only belated adjustments to deeper changes in the realities of power. The very growth and dominance of Japan in world trade, generally to the disadvantage of other countries, brought strains to older relationships. Western powers had been in a process of moving out of Southeast Asia for two decades. The re-emergence of Japan's power in the area, begun with war reparations and followed in steady succession by advances in diplomacy, and then in trade, aid, and investment, had become so great that it was beginning to overwhelm small countries. Not surprisingly, animosity and cries of "exploitation" grew up. Similar irritations with America and Europe developed. The American balance of trade tipped more and more to its own disadvantage, made worse by inflation and Vietnam spending and by Japan's protectionist tariff barriers and refusal to revalue the yen. Japanese irritations over American military bases, test-bombing in the Pacific, and continued occupation of Okinawa resurfaced. At the same time, fascination with China, with its changing society and with its potential as a marketplace and source of raw material grew in Japan.[1] Despite a general antipathy to the Soviet Union, due to bitter memories of its attack upon Japan at the close of the war, a similar fascination began to grow over prospects for investment in Siberian development, in return for oil and raw materials.

Thus, the "Nixon shocks" of 1971, which put a ten-percent surcharge upon all imports to America, which allowed the dollar to "float" against other currencies, and which sent President Nixon to Peking and to Moscow in March and July of 1972, served to formalize changes already in the wind. For Japan, the real shocks lay in lack of foreknowledge. Lack of consultation by Washington constituted a slap in the face, a callous disregard of the

---

[1] In 1970, 22% of China's trade was with Japan and only 2% of Japan's trade was with China.

sensibilities of a close partnership. It became clear, therefore, that a time for changing relationships had arrived.

Changes came in quick succession. After nearly a decade in office, Prime Minister Sato resigned. His successor was Tanaka Kakuei, the son of a poor farmer and the first "rags to riches," self-made man to break the elitist hold of generals and graduates in reaching the highest political office of the land. Tanaka came into office armed with great personal vigor and popularity. His own "Tanaka shocks" followed in quick succession. In accordance with agreements already reached, Okinawa was returned to Japan. Diplomatic relations with Communist China were opened; and, since all were agreed that only one China could exist, ties with Taiwan began to be broken. Finally, steps were taken for Japan to provide her own defensive shield by building up its military forces. Thus, Japan's weight was added to the shifting balance of power in the world—balancing new relationships with China against possible Chinese attack upon Soviet power in Siberia. Yet, the same major problem remains. How can Japan maintain good relations, sufficient to provide for her own security under conditions of peace, so that the commerce so essential to her survival can continue?

FURTHER READING   In addition to the general East Asian works and the general works on China and Japan cited at the end of Part XIV, Chapter 3, the following further suggestions are added:

China   Three volumes of readings, which are highly useful, can be recommended here. Edited by F. Schurmann and O. Schell, this trilogy is * Imperial China, * Republican China, and * Communist China (1967). O. Clubb, Twentieth-Century China (1964), as seen through the eyes of an American official of long experience. P'u Yi, From Emperor to Citizen (1964–1965), 2 vols., translated by W. J. F. Jenner, is the autobiography of the last Manchu emperor who survived serving as a puppet in Manchuria and imprisonment by the Communist Party, to become a low official in the People's Republic. H. McAleavy, A Dream of Tartary (1963), also deals with the imperial family in the twentieth century.

H. Isaacs, The Tragedy of the Chinese Revolution (1952), deals with the Communist-Kuomintang break of 1927. More kindly views of Nationalist leadership are found in E. Hahn, The Soong Sisters (1942), and Chiang Kai-shek, An Unauthorized Biography (1955). Chiang Kai-shek, China's Destiny (1947), expresses his own views, even if written by another.

Red Star over China (1944), by E. Snow, brought world attention to Mao for the first time. J. Chen, Mao and the Chinese Revolution (1965), brings the narrative down to 1949. But perhaps the best study, tough and incisive, is that by B. I. Schwartz, Chinese Communism and the Rise of Mao (1951). American failures are well depicted in H. Feis, The China Tangle (1953). More recently, B. Tuchman, in * Stilwell and the American Experience in China, 1911–1945 (1972), has presented us with a very readable narrative. For further convenient survey, one should consult C. P. Fitzgerald, * *The Birth of Communist China* (1966); C. Brandt, B. I. Schwartz, and J. K. Fairbank, * *The Documentary History of Chinese Communism,* (1952). Chai Winberg, *The Essential Works of Chinese Communism* and S. R. Schram, * *The Political Thought of Mao Tse-tung* (1963). T. J. Hughes and D. E. T. Luard, *The Economic Development of Communist China* (1961); R. Hughes *The Chinese Communes* (1960); and R. MacFarquhar (ed.), *The Hundred Flowers* (1960), throw light upon internal debates and upheavals. R. J. Lifton, *Thought Reform and the Psychology of Totalism* (1961), provides us with a psychiatric analysis of revolution.

Finally, *The Sino-Soviet Split* (1964), is documented by W. E. Griffiths; and *The China-India Border* (1964), is given a pro-China treatment by A. Lamb.

Japan On militarism, A. Axelbank, *Black Star Over Japan: Rising Forces of Militarism* (1972), seeks to explain reasons for such tendencies in Japan. R. Benedict, * *The Chrysanthemum and the Sword* (1967), gives us a classic analysis of society before the war. Other important works on Japanese nationalism are: R. Storry, *The Double Patriots: A Study of Japanese Nationalism* (1957), with emphasis on patriotic societies; Y. C. Maxon, *Control of Japanese Foreign Policy: A Study of Civil-Military Rivalry, 1930–1945* (1957), which looks at institutions.

Three works which concentrate on successive phases of Japan's development, from 1912 to 1945, are: A. M. Young, *Japan under Taisho Tenno 1912–1926* (1928), and *Imperial Japan: 1926–1938* (1938), and F. C. Jones, *Japan's New Order in East Asia: Its Rise and Fall, 1937–1945* (1954). R. J. C. Butow, *Tojo and the Coming of the War* (1961), and *Japan's Decision to Surrender* (1954), provide straightforward studies.

Japan's American Interlude, (1960), by K. Kazuo and *Japan—Enemy or Ally* (1948), by M. Ball throw light upon the American Occupation and years immediately after the war. On Japanese politics in the postwar era, R. A. Scalapino and J. Masumi, *Parties and Politics in Contemporary Japan* (1962); W. M. Tsuneishi, *Japanese Political Style: An Introduction to the Government and Politics of Modern Japan* (1966); N. B. Thayer, *How the Conservatives Rule Japan* (1969); J. M. Maki, *Government and Politics in Japan: The Road to Democracy* (1962) are just a few of the clear, excellent, and forceful studies which can be consulted.

Finally, among broad studies relating readers to general developments in Japan, two introductory works are especially useful: E. O. Reischauer, *The United States and Japan* (1965), is a classic, and R. W. Van Alstyne, *The United States and East Asia,* is also handy. T. C. Smith, *The Agrarian Origins of Modern Japan* (1959), and C. D. Sheldon, *The Rise of the Merchant Class in Tokugawa Japan* (1958), serve to provide a foundation for study of more recent economic history. G. C. Allen, *Japan's Economic Recovery* (1958), and R. P. Dore, *Land Reform in Japan* (1959), focus on this development. Also see G. C. Allen, *Japan's Economic Expansion* (1965). H. Kahn, The *Emerging Japanese Superstate: Challenge and Response* (1970), deals with the logic of Japanese growth.

*Books available in paperbound edition are marked with an asterisk.

4 Africa in the Twentieth Century

After 1914, a new source of opposition to colonial rule began to appear among the uprooted workers in urban areas. The simultaneous growth of an urban proletariat and an educated elite in such cities as Lagos and Dakar made inevitable African demands for participation in the power structure. Moreover, religious leaders among Africans used the newly acquired Christian religions to buttress their solidarity with the people in the face of colonial oppression—as, for example, William Wade Harris in Ivory Coast, or John Chilembwe in Nyasaland, who resisted the idea of Africans serving in World War I.

The war had a great impact on Tropical Africa. First, Africans saw the war at first hand, since much against their will, almost 200,000 Africans served in the French army and a lesser number in the British army. Second, the shortage of colonial officials encouraged numerous revolts in remote areas; vast regions of French West Africa, for example, had to be reclaimed from the resistance movement. Third, the war sent home a number of veterans who had seen white Europeans do manual labor, lose battles, and act like human beings no longer on a pedestal. These Africans had a different perspective on European-African relationships and believed they should share in colonial governance, even if in secondary positions. The seeds of nationalism were sown.

The war also brought to an end colonial rule in the four German colonies, which, in accordance with the Versailles Peace Conference of 1919, were awarded to Britain, France, Belgium, and South Africa as mandates of the League of Nations. During the ensuing interwar years, there was a constant stream of propaganda from Germany for the return of her possessions, which did not occur.

The process of decolonization took place peacefully in some areas (West Africa) and involved prolonged military struggle in others (Algeria). The impact of two world wars had weakened Europe's will to rule and depleted the resources necessary to continued domination. Painful as the loss of empire was, the evolution of a modern world made decolonization almost inevitable. Europe's imperial powers left in Africa an important legacy of government, economic structure, social life, and intellectual accomplishment, which transformed the Dark Continent and brought its states into the modern family of nations.

Most apologists for colonial rule in Africa had supposed that Europe's "civilizing mission" would last hundreds of years. This was implicit in such colonial philosophies as Lord Frederick Lugard's idea of the Dual Mandate, which became classic British colonial philosophy in the interwar years. Lugard held that colonizers had a double responsibility—to the white-world traders and settlers *and* to the African peoples that they might experience economic development and prosper, and be so ruled as to be guided into eventual self-government. It was presumed that this would take years of slow, methodical development; but an increasing number of educated Africans began to question this assumption. It was these young men who took over the role of resistance to European rule from the older leaders, who, by the 1920's were either defeated, exiled, pensioned off, or co-opted by the colonial regime. A small number of colonial officials also began to doubt the validity of the "white man's burden," and under the impact of such political events as the Popular Front in France in 1936, a new group of colonial officials and teachers who were socialists or liberal in persuasion came to Africa. These men and the African elites—mainly students fresh from British and French schools and universities—sowed seeds of discontent which sprouted after World War II as a full-fledged nationalist movement.

The world tide of nationalism reached Africa in the mid-1950's and brought release from the imperialistic clutches of Europe. The former Italian

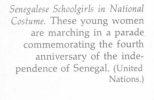

Senegalese Schoolgirls in National Costume. These young women are marching in a parade commemorating the fourth anniversary of the independence of Senegal. (United Nations.)

colony of Libya acquired independence in 1951, the Anglo-Egyptian Sudan, French Tunisia, French and Spanish Morocco in 1956. But the true bellwether of African autonomy was Ghana, in 1957, the century's first Black African state to achieve independence. By 1968, all of Africa was decolonized and free save for the Spanish Sahara on the northwest coast; the minor French Territory of Afars and Isass in the Gulf of Aden; Portugal's holdings; and the administratively anomalous white settlements of Rhodesia and South-West Africa (renamed Nambia by the UN). In the mid-1970's, the British had yet to recognize Rhodesia's unilateral declaration of independence in 1965; and South-West Africa, although placed under UN mandate in 1968, was still being "illegally" administered by the Republic of South Africa—which had become independent in 1910 and a republic in 1961.

EUROPEAN RULE IN THE INTERWAR YEARS

After World War I, despite heavy losses in manpower and resources, European nations (excepting Germany) held on to their colonies; put down uprisings and rebellions; and tried to expand education, improve transportation and communication, and create new markets for such minerals as copper.

The Economy There was much talk of economic development by such people as Albert Sarraut, French minister of colonies, whose *la mise en valeur* policy would transform French Africa into a prosperous trading area. Some of the developmental projects, such as the Office of the Niger, to develop irrigation lands near West Africa's biggest river, failed. The British had better luck in the Sudan on the Nile River with the Gezira Scheme, which concentrated on growing cotton with Sudanese farmers. Roads, ports, railroads, and communication networks were strengthened, but the essential element for economic development, capital, was lacking. The prevailing philosophy was that colonies should pay for themselves (by import and export taxes, licensing, etc.). Some progressive colonial governors, such as George Guggisberg of the Gold Coast, were able to successfully float bond issues in European money markets, but this was the exception rather than the rule. European private investment was centered mostly in the Belgian Congo and the Rhodesias for the development of new copper mines, or in South Africa for burgeoning gold and diamond production. International trading corporations, mainly British, French, or Swiss based, increased their operations in Africa, usually buying agricultural produce such as peanuts, cocoa, cotton, or coffee for market in Europe, and selling European consumer goods to the growing African market.

There was a strange hierarchy in the business world of colonial Africa. World War I had practically eliminated the small European businessman from Africa, and during the interwar period, Lebanese and Syrians in West Africa and Indians in East Africa asserted a dominance over small and middle-sized businesses. In West Africa, this meant that many enterprising African and Creole (French-African) merchants, active since the nineteenth century, were forced out of business or became small traders. Thus, large

European firms maintained a virtual monopoly on wholesale and export-import business, with Orientals handling the middle sectors; only the smallest sector of retail trade was left to Africans.

Education There were several reasons for the expansion in educational facilities experienced by colonial Africa during the interwar years. First, colonial officials were short of European manpower after the blood-letting of the war, and needed more trained African auxiliaries. Second, some colonies (such as Guggisberg's Gold Coast) decided they had a duty to educate more Africans than the missionary schools could handle. This led to subsidies to missions to expand their schools or to the creation of new state schools. Curricula, which had previously been rudimentary, now became patterned after elementary and secondary programs in use in France and Great Britain. It was still necessary to go to France or England for university training—and an increasing number of Africans did so.

Expansion of education proved to be incompatible with the assumptions of indirect rule of the British and policy of association of the French. Education created an African elite that was interested in emulating the colonial rulers and bringing about the modernization of colonies; at first, they did not demand independence, but argued for more jobs within the colonial system. The goals of elites, whether in Senegal, Gold Coast, or Nigeria, where they first appeared, was to participate in the colonial framework on an equal footing with Europeans. They wanted equality of opportunity and were basically reformers, not radicals. Only a few militants in the interwar period called for abolishing colonial rule; it was an indication of the deep-seated inferiority which colonial rule and mission education had bred among the Africans. It took the smashing defeat of France and the helplessness of Britain during World War II to demonstrate to these elites that they could aspire much higher, to total independence.

THE AFRICAN
NATIONALIST
MOVEMENT

Early members of the African-educated elite were assimilated to western education, dress, and life style. Blaise Diagne, Senegal's deputy in the French Parliament for twenty years, and an active participant in early pan-African conferences would not speak against French colonial policy. He held that only France gave social equality to Africans. Joseph Casely Hayford of Gold Coast, lawyer and writer, in 1920 organized the National Congress of British West Africa, which sought to unify English-speaking West Africans. Herbert Macauley, grandson of the first African bishop, Samuel Crowther, organized municipal politics in Lagos and began the African participation in modern party politics. Such men sought to expand western schooling and bring political participation to more Africans. They were models to younger Africans who were influenced by the radical currents of the 1930's such as socialism, bolshevism, and especially pan-Africanism. The first pan-African Congress had been held in Paris in 1919, presided over by Blaise Diagne and organized by W. E. B. Dubois, the brilliant black American scholar and leader. The Paris Pan-African Congress gave notice that black people in America and Africa were concerned with the rights of Africans to self-determination and improvement, and pan-African principles became a basic charter for African activities in the interwar years.

Reformist Efforts   Colonial officials managed to keep a tight rein on colonial politics. In French Africa, radical newspapers and magazines from Europe were censored or seized, lest local Africans become tainted. In Central and East Africa, lack of urban areas—where politics was allowed in microcosm in West Africa—and fewer schools meant a much smaller elite. Political protest often came from millenarian movements or African separatist churches, since it was possible to criticize and preach new doctrines in churches. Many such religious leaders, such as John Chilembwe, Simon Mpadi, and Simon Kimbangu found themselves viewed as threats to the established order and were imprisoned. In South Africa, such African gradualists as John Tengo Jabavu hoped to work with whites, but violence in the labor unions in the 1920's caused the South African government to keep Africans under control and to disenfranchise the elites in the 1930's. Not all resistance to colonialism came from educated Africans. The famous Aba riots of 1929, for example, were caused by angry women in Eastern Nigeria, who refused to be taxed by a warrant chief appointed by the British—this was an area where Lugard's policy of indirect rule did not work.

The cause of the African elites was inadvertently given moral support during the interwar years by world opinion, which was shocked by Italy's invasion of Ethiopia in 1936. Still smarting from the defeat suffered at the hands of Menelik in 1896 at Adowa, the Italians used modern weapons such as tanks and poison gas to attack the hapless Ethiopians. Emperor Hailie Selassie made an impassioned plea for help to the League of Nations, but to no avail, and Mussolini's forces took over Ethiopia for the next five years. Many newspapers in Western Europe and the United States reacted negatively to this last imperial venture in Africa, and Ethiopia became a rallying point for African elites and European liberals to share a common cause. This was the highpoint of imperialism, with only Liberia left as an independent state free of European control. In reality Liberia had become dependent on United States aid and commercial operations such as the vast Firestone plantations.

In Nigeria, the 1930's brought to the fore the Nigerian Youth Movement, which was a pioneering attempt by urban African elites to attract recruits in rural areas throughout Nigeria. The NYM wanted access to jobs, better education, and local control of Nigeria by Nigerians—but within the framework of the British Commonwealth. The emphasis was still reformist; colonially-imposed institutions still had some prestige among educated Africans.

Quest for Independence   The impact of World War II changed these elite movements and urban parties into more broadly based political parties seeking not reform but total independence from the mother country. First, the Atlantic Charter of Roosevelt and Churchill with its promise of self-determination for all peoples (even though this was later modified by Churchill) was held out as a commitment to freedom in French and British areas alike. Second, African troops again served in a world conflict where they saw their European masters humbled—France beaten, Britain almost defeated—and witnessed the speed Japan used in conquering British, French, and Dutch possessions in East Asia. African veterans had returned from World War I enlightened; this time they returned resolved to change their status. Veterans formed the backbone of the parties, caucuses, and action groups that sprang up even before the peace was signed. Third, this war exhausted Europe's resources; it became apparent that countries such as Britain and France were no longer first-rank world powers, having been supplanted by the United States and the Soviet Union.

The Free French of Charles de Gaulle realized change was inevitable and at the Brazzaville Conference of 1944, proposals emerged to change the face of French Africa. All French colonies of North and Tropical Africa were to have deputies in the French Parliament, colonial subjects were to become citizens of the French Union (as the empire was restyled), with voting rights for both men and women. The French plan for bringing more Africans into political participation involved the calculated risk of pure assimilation, under the assumption that this would repay their loyalty and support during the war years and keep them quiet. The French gamble worked for the short term in Africa. (It failed in Indo-China, where Ho Chi Minh and others, who had fought Japanese domination, fought the return of the French.)

The African elites now seized the initiative to organize western-style political parties in each French colony to contest the forthcoming parliamentary elections. These elite parties were soon transformed into mass parties, with keen competition for rural voters. Illiteracy was still the rule in Africa, and often parties were known by their symbols (elephant, tiger) rather than their names. The pent-up energy engendered by the war was thus channeled into internal elections and participation in a broader French state—the Fourth Republic. This contained African ambitions for almost a decade.

In British Africa, one must distinguish between western, eastern, and southern holdings. In West Africa, British governors in Gold Coast and Nigeria gave constitutional governance and more seats on the Legislative Councils of the colonies. But Africans were unhappy because these reforms came from above—that is, from the paternalistic colonial ruler, rather than from the people below. The Africans had learned their lessons well from European textbooks about constitutional democracy. By 1950, both Gold Coast and Nigeria were on the road toward internal self-government. In East Africa, where almost no African elite had arisen because of fewer towns and educational opportunities and the persistence of traditional values, ethnic associations, such as those developed by the Kikuyu people in Kenya, helped to develop a sense of political consciousness; and the Mau Mau uprisings of the 1950's emphasized African dissatisfaction with European land appropriation; and separatist churches continued to be a forum for those interested in politics. In Southern Africa, political participation of black Africans had been limited or denied since, in 1910, the British parliament had formed the independent union of South Africa from the white-settler colony of the Cape of Good Hope, Natal, and the defeated Boer republics. Direct rule by white settlers emerged in Southern Rhodesia in 1923 when Britain took over the territory from the British South Africa Company. This put the black Africans of Rhodesia in the same position of political inferiority as obtained in the Union of South Africa, where, in 1948, apartheid became official policy.

Portugal was generally inspired by British southern African policies for her two big colonies of Angola and Mozambique, although provision was made for "evolved" Africans or mulattoes to become assimilated to Portuguese citizenship in the French manner—few Africans actually qualified, however. The Belgians in the Congo were intent upon educating Africans (in mission schools especially) to become solid workers and they created few secondary schools. Hence there was practically no Congolese elite to become interested in politics. Not until late in the 1950's, with pressure building up elsewhere on the continent, did nationalist movements surface in the Congo.

The Nation-State and Political Parties African nationalists almost unanimously accepted the idea of transforming the European-designed colony into the African nation-state, despite the lack of linguistic unity and the fact that many ethnic groups and old kingdoms were split up by the artificial borders. Identity with the colony became a pragmatic necessity for aspiring political leaders. A good example is the dilemma faced by nationalist leaders in French West Africa, which was composed of eight colonies: Do we strive for one, large, independent country; or do we work for separate independence for each colony? Leopold Senghor, the Senegalese poet-politician, argued for keeping together, while Félix Houphouët-Boigny of the Ivory Coast argued for splitting up. The French tended to favor the latter course, and so the nationalist drive tended to extend downward to the smallest size colony, even eventually to tiny British Gambia, which was no more than land on either side of the Gambia River. Colonial rule had already lent a mystique to boundaries; and, although they may have had no logical explanation in terms of classical European nationalism, they did delineate political units at a time when "units" was what the nationalists needed.

The device the Africans borrowed from Europe for capturing control of new nation-states was the political party, which was first authorized in the interwar period in urban West Africa, spread to countryside after 1945, and was eventually authorized in Central and East Africa. Elites planned and dominated party councils; but they knew strength lay in numbers, and put strenuous efforts into organizing rural clubs and action groups, and mobilizing existing voluntary organizations. The Convention People's Party in Gold Coast, organized by Kwame Nkrumah in 1948, became the archetype

political party. It was based upon a strong party organization, which welded together various voluntary organizations such as labor unions, mutual aid societies, sporting clubs, and so forth; but it was animated by the charismatic personality of Nkrumah. Teacher, student, professor, newspaper editor, and political activist, Nkrumah had lived and studied in the United States and Britain for more than ten years, and had returned to Africa with an idea—a way to force change toward the dream of African independence. He transformed the urban-elite political tradition of Gold Coast into modern mass politics, with slogans, central and regional committees, strikes, and organized protests. In some colonies, such as Uganda and Northern Nigeria, party politics was dominated by traditional chiefs of great prestige, such as the Kabaka of the Ganda and the Sultan of Sokoto; in other colonies, such as Guinea under Sekou Touré, one man emerged as a strong controlling political personality. And in most French areas, one intercolony party, the RDA (Democratic African Rally) emerged to dominate nationalist politics under the direction of Houphouët-Boigny of the Ivory Coast.

THE DECOLONIZATION OF AFRICA The rise of the African nationalist movement, nurtured by growing elites and expanding schools, could not be contained by the large colonial powers. It could only be slowed down as in East and Central Africa, or forcibly restrained as in South Africa, where white supremacy reasserted itself after World War II at the precise moment other colonies were striding toward independence. The goals of Africans were not entirely clear at the outset, since the legacy of seeking participation in empire persisted among older Africans. When the challenge to European hegemony was clear, contingencies had to be worked out by the powers. In the case of Britain, a precedent in freeing India, Pakistan, and Burma from colonial rule meant that as the 1940's and 1950's progressed, an increasing number of colonial officials realized that imperial rule in Africa would have to end, and provision for an orderly transfer of government to African hands became inevitable. African frustration with imposed revised constitutions in West Africa made it apparent that increased African participation in local councils was necessary.

Ghana   Decolonization was foreshadowed by the election, in 1952, of Kwame Nkrumah as Gold Coast Prime Minister—with control over domestic affairs. Nkrumah had a sympathetic colonial governor, Charles Arden-Clarke, with whom to work during the period of transition; and by 1957 Nkrumah was able to hold independence ceremonies in his country, renamed Ghana in honor of the ancient West African empire. Ghana's independence attracted world-wide attention. The first black colony to gain statehood, Ghana had set the stage—free all-black government had become a fact.

The End of French Rule   Pressure was then put upon France. Already, in 1956, with a socialist government in power, France had granted independence to Tunisia and Morocco in North Africa, and also passed the *loi-cadre* authorizing devolution of institutional power from the home government to the African colonies. Then, in 1958, Charles de Gaulle was recalled from retirement as a result of the French army's lack of confidence in the Paris regime. In order to concentrate upon his Fifth Republic constitutional changes, and to cope with the escalation of the Algerian war, de Gaulle decided to liberalize the status of France's possessions in Tropical Africa. He made a personal tour in 1958 and offered them membership in the new French Community, a Gallic version of the British Commonwealth, or independence. All colonies held referendums and such was the depth of assimilation that all voted for the Community save Guinea. There, Sekou Touré, a shrewd trade unionist, convinced his people that independence was too tempting to pass up. French officials were shocked and left Guinea in a huff, tearing out phones and plumbing as they departed. This performance was not enough to forestall the inevitable—other colonies wanting to emulate the bold Guineans—and by the end of 1960, France had liquidated her holdings in Tropical Africa save for the little Territory of Afars and Isass and the French Community faded away.

In North Africa, the two protectorates of Tunisia and Morocco sought independence after World War II, and competing nationalist groups and parties grew up to force France's hand. Although France tendered her protectorate increasing amounts of self-government, the Muslim Tunisian leader Habib Bourguiba suffered exile, jail, and humiliation before the French, in 1956, finally permitted Tunisia to organize its own modern government and let the protectorate expire. Also in 1956, France agreed to let Sultan Mohammed V return from exile, where he had been sent because of his support of nationalist groups. Morocco's French colonists had been equal to their counterparts in Tunisia in opposing independence, but the fact was that with the end of the Indo-China war in 1954, France was immediately plunged into the Algerian conflict later the same year.

Algeria was the principal problem of decolonization in North Africa because France had made it an integral part of the French state—more than a million *colons* lived there who were opposed to change. Some Algerians, such as Ferhat Abbas, were inclined to work for reform and serve in the French Assembly. But younger Algerians, tiring of broken promises and physical repression, took matters in their own hands and organized the *Front de Libération Nationale* (FLN) liberation movement, which began the long (1954–1962) Algerian struggle. The French let Morocco and Tunisia go by 1956 and then moved an army which eventually became a half million men into Algeria for the bitter struggle to retain what was considered to be French soil. It was colonist partisans who, in 1958, created the French government crisis that recalled de Gaulle to power. The general finally concluded that prolonged warfare was self-defeating, and following an overwhelming Algerian referendum vote for independence, he proclaimed Algeria independent in 1962. France thereupon was besieged with hundreds of thousands of *colons* from North Africa who belatedly realized that Algerians henceforth would be proprietors of Algerian land. It was a bitter final curtain to the drama of French imperialism, but it ended the only sustained military action that France had to face during an otherwise orderly period of decolonization.

President Habib Bourguiba of Tunisia. (Courtesy, Embassy of Tunisia.)

The End of British Rule East and Central Africa under British rule faced a peculiar dilemma during the decolonization years. In Kenya and Northern and Southern Rhodesia, white settlers demanded a controlling voice in government. The contest in these areas was three cornered: imperial administration, white settler, and African nationalist. The response of the British Colonial Office was to set up multiracial constitutions, with voting colleges and a restricted franchise. Greater political weight was thereby given to the white community, which was dwarfed mathematically by the blacks. African nationalism finally won out in areas such as Uganda, where there never were many European settlers. But it took the guerilla terrorist activities of the Mau Mau uprisings in Kenya to convince landed British residents that they should abdicate politically to the Africans, who were led by the veteran politician, Jomo Kenyatta. Uganda became independent in 1962, Kenya—with Kenyatta as prime minister—in 1963.

Further south, however, the settlers tried to institutionalize a privileged multiracial society, and in 1953 created the Federation of Rhodesia and Nyasaland. Its chief proponent, Roy Welensky, tried to keep Europeans on top of politics, but pressures from African nationalists forced the Federation to disband a decade later. In 1964, Nyasaland (as Malawi) and Northern Rhodesia (as Zambia) became independent, African controlled nations.

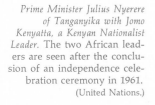

Prime Minister Julius Nyerere of Tanganyika with Jomo Kenyatta, a Kenyan Nationalist Leader. The two African leaders are seen after the conclusion of an independence celebration ceremony in 1961. (United Nations.)

The idea of "one man, one vote" was too powerful to be resisted by most of the new nations and their multiracial voting colleges. But Southern Rhodesia, where conservative extremists won out, remained in white hands. In 1965, Southern Rhodesia declared its unilateral independence from Great Britain, and went the same road as apartheid South Africa. A kind of southern Iron Curtain now came into existence, with Africans still under European dominance south of Rhodesia and the Portuguese colonies.

Tanganyika was a special case. It was a former German colony taken over by Britain as a mandate during the interwar years; after World War II, its political consciousness slowly developed under the tutelage of Julius Nyerere, an honest and effective African nationalist who became Tanganyika's first president when independence came in 1961. He presided over the fusion with Zanzibar Island—the politically dominant power in East Africa in the nineteenth century—where Africans had revolted against their Arab rulers and obtained their independence in 1963. The result of this fusion, Tanzania, became an independent state in 1964.

The End of Belgian Rule   Decolonization became tragic in the Belgian Congo. The Belgians viewed the area mainly in economic terms, and since there were practically no educated elite, persisted in believing their rule would continue. The rapid events after independence in Ghana and Guinea caught the Belgians off guard. In 1957, Congolese Africans were authorized to participate for the first time in municipal elections, but lacked the experience of the West and East African militants in structuring a program of political change. Belgian officials panicked as African nationalism reached high tide on the continent in 1960. When political activity became inevitable, Congolese tended to form political parties on the basis of ethnic groups, since there had not been a cadre of elites to organize nationwide parties, as occurred in Nigeria under the nationalist Nnamdi Azikiwe. Rather, politics now became an ethnic rivalry, and the one man who had a vision of a unified state, Patrice Lumumba, was killed the year after independence in 1961 in mysterious circumstances. The Congo situation was complicated by Moïse Tshombe's desire to have copper-rich Katanga province secede from a strife-ridden Congo, where ethnic groups fought centralists and regionalists. Tshombe's action resulted in a United Nations force being called in to restore order to the Congo, and many African nations saw in Katanga's attempted secession the hand of European business trying to hold on to valuable copper mines. Despite this and later crises, the Congo central government slowly expanded its central rule and kept the peace.

Portugal   In 1972, Portugal had rejected a UN suggestion for consideration of independence for her colonies of Angola, Mozambique, and Portuguese Guinea. But by the end of 1974 the Portuguese dictatorship had been overthrown and a new government came to power that rejected the legal fiction of assimilation that held that all three colonies, plus Sao Tome and Principe, were integral parts of Portugal. The sacrifices and resistance of the African insurgents for more than a decade finally bore fruit, and Portugal recognized the respective movements of national liberation and arranged for an orderly transfer of power. Thus the Portuguese-speaking territories of Africa moved toward independence, leaving Rhodesia, South Africa, and South-West Africa as the only major areas of Black Africa still under white domination. The sun finally set on Europe's oldest African empire.

THE EUROPEAN LEGACY The visible remainder of Europe in Africa is noticeable today to the traveller who visits for the first time: architecture (with a distinctive French, British, or Portuguese bent), roads, railways, ports, languages, telecommunications, European firms and products. But the questions arise, what was the impact of Europe; and what was the impact of modernization, which has affected countries all over the globe? In most parts of Africa, the European colonial interlude brought material advancement and initiated Africa's entry into the modern industrial and commercial world. Yet Liberia, which was never colonized, and Ethiopia, which was only briefly so, also claim to be countries of the modern world. Europe's legacy in Africa then is both tangible and intangible; and part of it is an introduction to the modern world, which Africans might well have gained for themselves without benefit of colonial domination.

Senegalese Girl in Dakar. (United Nations.)

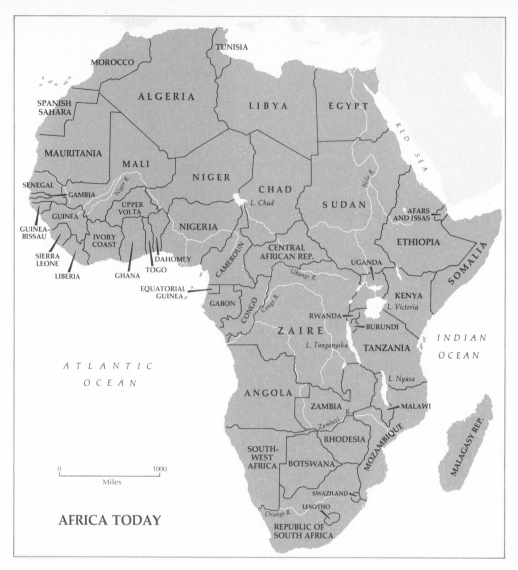

AFRICA TODAY

Less obvious to the traveller is the influence of France on the food Africans eat and of Britain on the clothes they wear; and the impact of a school system that has produced Africans trained in much the same curriculum as Britons, French, and Belgians. Commercial practices, methods of government, bureaucratic organization flow from colonial times. Most African states still retain colonial codes and statutes. Currency denominations (francs, pounds sterling), universities, police and military organization, and party politics owe their inception to European rule.

All of Africa was not Europeanized. A visitor to the countryside will still find traditional families in small villages, pursuing age-old techniques of agriculture and grazing, will discover the continuity of African beliefs and customs, and will occasionally converse with an elderly African born before effective European domination of his country. In North Africa one finds the persistence of Islam, the dominance of Arabic, and the deep-seated permanence of Berber culture. In Tropical Africa, local languages persist, African-modified Islam and many traditional religious beliefs live on—despite the fact many young people are required to study colonial languages, and often in mission schools. Traditional forms of marriage persist and identification with clan, ethnic group, and village is still more important than association with a new nation presided over by leaders in a remote capital. This traditional Africa is still alive and furnishes continuity to the African experience; it has not been destroyed by the European domination, but molded, adapted, and modified.

It is in the cities and towns of Africa where one senses a synthesis between traditional and modern, where the European-inspired veneer is strongest. Here the young and the elites adopt European clothing, work habits, small family size, and occupational goals, and integrate them into their own value systems. One may meet a Wolof from Senegal, who will be quite different from a Wolof of Gambia; same ethnic group, same traditional history, but different colonial experiences: the Senegalese will have French education and clothes, the Gambian will have British education and clothes.

The legacy of Europe runs deep in the government and economy of the new nations; some are linked to the European Common Market by preferential trade agreements, others have regional associations (such as certain French-speaking nations) which continue colony/mother-country relations. Many European businesses continue to operate with a scope reminiscent of colonial days; increased investment characterizes such disparate countries as Kenya and Ivory Coast, Gambia and Cameroun. Charges of neo-colonialism are not without foundation, but how does one draw the line between aid for developing countries and increased commercial speculation? Countries such as Guinea, which declared its independence early (1958), have not prospered economically because of isolation from a strong monetary union, lack of investments, or mistakes in planning. Guinea has relied on "human investments"—her people—but has not matched Zaire (the former Congo), which has also tried to pursue a nonaligned posture. It has been difficult for African nations to pursue their own self-interest, and to many Africans, the world of the 1970's seems strikingly similar to the colonial period, because the economic power that should be theirs is concentrated in foreign hands. Libya and Nigeria, with their vast oil holdings, may become an exception.

Africa has made progress in other areas: the school systems have mostly been decolonized (for example, African history rather than European history is now taught young Africans); Africans have representation in the United Nations; and some African nations enjoy a standard of living much higher than a decade ago.

The most perplexing legacy of Europe remains in the southern extremes

Life in Nigeria. Nigerians paddle past the imposing facade of the Federal Palace Hotel in Lagos. (Terrence Spencer, Camera Press, London.)

of Africa, where in Rhodesia and South Africa, small white-settler groups still control and disenfranchise numerically superior groups of black Africans. The prospect of majority rule for these Africans in their own land is not bright, since the advent of apartheid (the doctrine of separation of races) in South Africa and the white minority government in Rhodesia. Economically, to be sure, blacks in these areas are well off compared to other parts of the continent; but they do not have the right of free association, the vote, participation in political parties, or meaningful access to higher education, and are systematically excluded from the levers of power. It is in these countries that the negative legacy of Europe and her racial prejudices weighs heaviest upon the people and will probably remain for years to come.

Europe conquered Africa, dominated it, and gave both positive and negative aspects of her civilization. The impact is still being felt today by the Dark Continent, which struggles toward self-determination and dignified membership in the family of nations. Africa is almost free of the curious interlude of aggressive imperialism that climaxed European expansion overseas and characterized African history for more than a century.

FURTHER READING Literature on modern Africa is growing more extensive every year. For the colonial period, general works include R. L. Buell, *The Native Problem in Africa* (1965), a fundamental assessment of the 1920's; L. H. Gann and P. Duignan, eds., *Colonialism in Africa, 1870–1960*, in three volumes (1969–1971); and Prosser Gifford and Wm. R. Louis, *Britain and Germany in Africa* (1967) and *Britain and France in Africa* (1972).

Specific works on European colonial rule by colonial governors include Lord Lugard, *The British Mandate in Tropical Africa* (4th ed., 1929), for Britain; and Robert Delavignette, *Freedom and Authority in French West Africa* (1950), for France.

African nationalism can be studied in R. W. July, *The Origins of Modern African Thought* (1968); Hollis Lynch, * *Edward Blyden, Pan-Negro Patriot* (1967); T. O. Ranger, *Revolt in Southern Rhodesia* (1967); James S. Coleman, *Nigeria: Background to Nationalism* (1957); Thomas Hodgkin, * *Nationalism in Colonial Africa* (1956), which is a seminal work still valuable today; David Kimble, *A Political History of Ghana, 1850–1928* (1963), which shows the evolution of African politics in British dominated areas; and G. Wesley Johnson's *Origins of Black Politics in Senegal* (1971), covering the beginnings of African politics in French areas.

Social histories on the transformation of African life under colonial rule are found in the writings of sociologists and anthropologists. For example, Michael Banton, *West African City* (1957); David Brokensha, *Social Change in Larteh, Ghana* (1966); Kenneth Little, * *West African Urbanization* (1965); and Leo Kuper, * *An African Bourgeoisie* (1965), an award-winning study of the black African middle class in South Africa. Special mention should be made of P. C. Lloyd's * *Africa in Social Change* (1969); and Hortense Powdermaker, * *Coppertown: Changing Africa* (1962).

Modern politics during the colonial and decolonization period, examining the play of forces between Europeans and Africans, is found in such works as Martin Kilson, * *Political Change in a West African State* (1966); John Marcum, *The Angolan Revolution* (1959); Amilcar Cabral, * *Revolution in Guinea* (1969); R. I. Rotberg and Ali A. Mazrui, eds., *Protest and Power in Black Africa* (1970); Carl Rosberg and J. Nottingham, *The Myth of Mau Mau* (1966); Edward Roux, *Time Longer Than Rope* (1948); and Kwame Nkrumah, *Ghana* (1957).

For scholarly analyses of modern independent African states see Aristide Zolberg, *One-Party Government in the Ivory Coast* (1964); William Foltz, *From French West Africa to the Mali Federation* (1963); David Hapgood, *From Independence to Tomorrow* (1965), a critical look at Africa's independent leaders; Dennis Austin, *Politics in Ghana* (1970); Claude Welch, *Dream of Unity: Pan Africanism and Political Unification in West Africa* (1966).

Cultural expression of modern Africa can be followed in the beautifully illustrated magazine, *African Arts,* published at UCLA, which publishes African literature, drama, and arts.

*Books available in paperback edition are marked with an asterisk.

PART XVIII

The end of the Second World War brought striking changes to Europe. All the major west European powers were exhausted either from defeat, occupation, or the strain of six years of war. The pre-1939 power balance had been destroyed, and the resulting vacuum filled by two new superpowers, the United States and the Soviet Union, both of which were extra-European entities. The Communist zone was now extended to include nearly half the continent, resulting in an "Iron Curtain" that geographically split Europe right down the middle. With eastern Europe dominated by the Soviet Union, the weakened western powers had to receive assistance and protection from the United States if they did not want to risk a similar fate. There ensued the Cold War, an ideological and economic struggle between the opposing blocs that many feared might continue indefinitely. It was accompanied by an arms race between the United States and the Soviet Union, made more sinister by mass development of thermonuclear weapons in both countries. Though most European powers played no more than minor roles in military preparations, costs of rearmament were a further economic burden for nations attempting to recover from the most devastating of wars.

The worst conflicts were still located in central and east-central Europe, which had always been the major trouble zones of the century. If the Soviet Union was the real victor in the Second World War, the nation to loose the most was Germany; she was deprived not merely of continental hegemony but of her very territorial unity and political sovereignty. The prospect of permanent division of that country into an eastern and a western state posed a grave question for the future. Maintaining control of the satellites was the major internal difficulty of the Communist bloc.

Postwar western Europe lost the position of world leadership held there for several centuries. Two gigantic European wars, with their resultant waste of life and treasure, together with the organized resentment of the Afro-Asian peoples, made it impossible for the weakened powers of western Europe to maintain their colonies. From 1945 through the 1960's the record of European empire was one of continuous retreat. Most colonies were liberated peacefully and with fairly good grace, but some of them were the scenes of bloody wars of colonial rebellion with serious effects on the newly emerging peoples and on the embattled colonial powers themselves.

The most hopeful of the great postwar changes was the progress made by western Europe toward international unity. The sovereign states of the west had at intervals fought and pillaged one another for half a millennium, and the militarist orgies of the twentieth century had come close to wrecking western civilization. The searing experience of the Second World War finally made many Europeans realize that such intense nationalist competition was a fatal anachronism in the modern world, that all of Europe had much to gain from cooperation. Though premature efforts at political federation and military unification proved abortive, large strides were eventually made toward economic integration. Thanks to the aid and encouragement of the United States, economic recovery was rapid from the late 1940's on; and by 1960 a great Common Market of six major continental economic powers was emerging. The other nations also made sizable progress, forming a trade association of their own. Thus, if eastern Europe had been forced to share whatever fate history held in store for the Communist world, western Europe had more happy prospects. Deprived of the burden of world leadership, it was finding new peace, freedom, and prosperity.

LINEAR CONSTRUCTION BY NAUM GABO. (Courtesy The Phillips Collection, Washington, D.C.)

THE RESURGENCE
OF EUROPE
SINCE 1945

LEGACY OF THE PAST

In the 1950's, Europeans began to congratulate themselves about the success of their mid-century recovery from the wreck of the Second World War. Unprecedented heights of economic prosperity and physical well-being were achieved, together with the first genuine measures toward west European unity in modern history. In the eastern Communist sphere, supposed destalinization and the relaxation of tensions augured a more human new era. Within a few more years, social scientists began to talk of a "post-industrial era" for much of Europe, in which the old problems of industrialization had finally been conquered.

By 1975, the future prospect for the remainder of the twentieth century seemed somewhat more sobering. Neither western nor eastern Europe have escaped so easily the burdens of their past, and mature or "late" industrial society has generated new frustrations and imbalances of its own. Little further progress has been made toward west European unity, and the spirit of national exclusiveness still remains strong. Even in western Europe, only a portion of the society lives in an affluent world of advanced industrialization; many pockets of partial or under-development remain. For the most sophisticated sectors, grave challenges have arisen through the scarcity and great cost of fuel and raw materials. The blight of environmental degradation has become almost concomitant with industrial affluence.

In eastern Europe, the legacy of Stalinism has never really been overcome, nor is there any likelihood that it will be during the next generation. The existing Communist power structures are absolutely dependent on totalitarian controls, which not merely eliminate the possibility of personal freedom but retard full economic development as well. With the dissolution of all west European empires, the Soviet Union remains the only major repressive imperialist power in the world. Its leadership shows no indication of relinquishing that status, calculating that Russian power must remain dynamic and expansive abroad lest it grow weak and relaxed at home.

The East Berlin Wall.

MAJOR EVENTS SINCE 1945

1945–   Formation of the United Nations (1945)
            Welfare State in Britain (1945)
            Nationalization of British basic industries (1945–1948)
            Fourth Republic in France (1945)
            Rise of Christian Democrats in Italy; De Gasperi government (1945)
            Potsdam Conference: partition of Germany (1945)
            Communist takeovers in east central Europe (1946–1948)
            Truman Doctrine (1947)
            Marshall Plan (1948)
            Titoist Yugoslavia expelled from Communist bloc (1948)
            Formation of Benelux network (1948)
            Constitution of the Republic of Italy (1948)
            Berlin Blockade (1948–1949)
            Establishment of satellite government in Czechoslovakia (1948)
            Formation of NATO (1949)
            Establishment of West German Federal Republic (1949)
            Establishment of East German Democratic Republic (1949)
            Stalinist purges in Soviet Union and satellite countries (1949–1952)
            Communist triumph in China (1949)
            COMECON organized (1949)
            Formation of Council of Europe (1949)
            Indonesia receives independence (1949)

1950–   Korean War (1950–1953)
            Formation of European Coal and Steel Community (1951)
            Death of Stalin (1953)
            France withdraws from Indo-China (1954)

1955–   Restoration of Austrian unity and independence (1955)
            Khrushchev assumes power; "de-Stalinization" begins (1955)
            Hungarian anti-Communist revolt (1956)
            Suez invasion (1956)
             Russian Sputnik sent into orbit (1957)
            Ghana first colony in Africa to receive independence (1957)
            Common Market (1957)
            Gaullist Fifth Republic in France (1958)

1960–
            Construction of Berlin Wall (1961)
            Cuban missile crisis (1962)
            Beginning of Sino-Soviet split (1962)
            Rumanian Communist declaration of independence (1964)
            Khrushchev deposed as Russian premier (1964)

1965–
            Military coup in Greece (1967)
            General Strike in France (1968)
            Soviet invasion and occupation of Czechoslovakia (1968)

1970–
            Britain Joins the Common Market (1972)

1 Onset of the Cold War, 1945-1953

The Soviet Union was the real victor in the Second World War. Stalin helped Hitler to start the war in 1939, and then, after Hitler turned on him, gained the assistance of the United States and Britain in the complete defeat of his former ally. In this process, Russia seized nearly the entire Nazi empire in eastern Europe.

The goals for which Britain and the United States had theoretically waged the war were stated in their "Atlantic Charter" of 1941, translated by Roosevelt and Churchill into a pledge of national independence and political democracy for victims of the Axis. This very point, however, created a contradiction in the wartime alliance of the foes of Germany, since the Soviet Union, contrary to the principles of the Atlantic Charter, aimed to subordinate the independence of as many European states as possible and recognized as "democracy" only the bureaucratic despotism of the totalitarian police state.

The ostensible reason for Britain's original declaration of war on Germany in 1939 had been to defend the territorial integrity of Poland. But from the very beginning of the subsequent anti-German alliance formed by Britain, Russia, and the United States, Stalin made it clear that he insisted on retaining all the territory seized earlier while he was an associate of Hitler, including the eastern half of prewar Poland. Later, as Russian armies advanced into Poland and other east European countries, it became evident that Stalin planned to dominate the affairs of at least some of these states as well. Ever since its inception in 1917, the Soviet regime had labored to undermine other polities by means of unremitting political struggle (or "cold war," if one prefers) that was only briefly interrupted for four years (1935–1939) in the face of the threat from Nazi Germany. The only logical assumption was, therefore, that Stalin's government would continue to try to expand its power in the postwar period, and that tension and conflict could be reduced only by a realistic program of negotiation over concrete interests and issues.

The leader of the western Allies, the American president Franklin Roosevelt, was essentially ignorant of world politics, which he tended to interpret in terms of domestic affairs and had no interest in educating himself about. Refusing to make any attempt at an objective analysis of the character and goals of the Stalinist regime, the American leadership automatically classified all governments at war with Germany as "peace-loving," and chose to operate on the blind assumption that they were working toward the same goals held by the United States.

At the first wartime conference of the Big Three at Teheran in Persia in 1943, Churchill made efforts to head off complete Russian domination of eastern Europe and urged serious discussion of a postwar settlement. Stalin effectively blocked this, hoping to avoid any negotiations about central and eastern Europe until the Red Army was in control of as much of the eastern half of the continent as possible. Roosevelt was always eager to conciliate "Uncle Joe," as Stalin was sometimes insipidly referred to. The American position was that any possible postwar problems would somehow be automatically, indeed miraculously, resolved by a magical device of international concord and representation to be called the "United Nations." Roosevelt and his advisers believed that Stalin should be placated in every way to make sure that the Russian government would not refuse to join this new international association, the successor of the defunct "League of Nations."

Stalin accurately took the measure of western diplomacy, gauging its timidity, confusion and naiveté. When the final climactic wartime conference of the Big Three was held in the Russian Crimea at Yalta in February 1945, Stalin had his way almost completely. In return for agreeing to join the United Nations, Stalin was allowed to retain all the territorial booty gained as an ally of Hitler. The Baltic states, Finnish Karelia, Rumanian Bessarabia, and all of prewar eastern Poland were incorporated into the Soviet Union. After the collapse of Germany, the Soviet Union also established its own occupation zone in eastern Germany and eastern Austria, the remainder of those two countries being occupied by the United States, Britain, and France.

At the time of the Yalta conference, Roosevelt was exhausted and near death. Within two months he was succeeded as president by Harry S. Truman (1884–1972), who was without experience or training in world diplomacy. One thing on which all American leaders were agreed was that the American public would not stand for further military involvement abroad as soon as the main war was over, and would insist on "bringing the boys home." Therefore, the American government showed complete disinterest in using the enormous power of the United States to bargain explicitly with Stalin about Russian occupation of Poland and other east European countries, where Communist control was steadily being imposed. Though a mood of disillusionment with Communist interpretations of "democracy" and Stalin's good faith began to set in even before Germany collapsed, the American leadership continued to believe that it should not try to do anything direct or concrete to guarantee the independence and integrity of east European countries.

At western insistence, Russia also agreed to enter the war against Japan. As it turned out, after the United States perfected the atomic bomb it did not need Soviet assistance; but in August 1945, Stalin hastened to enter the last two weeks of the conflict with Japan in order to seize some of the fruits of victory. Manchuria was easily overrun, and Stalin then demanded to be given an occupation zone in Japan as well. This was refused, but the Soviet Union gained control of all of Sakhalin island, the Kuriles and the northern half of Korea, fulfilling an old dream of Russian expansionists.

DOMESTIC PROBLEMS OF THE SOVIET UNION

In fact, despite the outwardly imposing growth of Soviet power, Russia was desperately tired and exhausted when the war ended. No country had suffered more than the Soviet Union, and it has been reliably calculated that twenty million Russians lost their lives during the years 1941–1945. One out of every three healthy Russian men between the ages of 20 and 40 was either killed or partially disabled. Casualties were so severe that, despite its greater population, the Soviet Union had fewer men under arms than the United States when the war came to an end.

Moreover, the destruction wrought by the retreating Germans had turned the western part of the Soviet Union into a wasteland. In 1945, the country's industrial output was only half of what it had been before the war. Several years of intense effort were needed to begin to make these losses good, and most of the army had soon to be demobilized in order to fill the labor force. By 1948, Russia only had 2.8 million men under arms. Despite the great growth of the Communist empire, the Soviet Union was much weaker than the United States. This fact was obscured by American miscalculations, the vast geographic scope of the Communist world, and the complete isolation imposed by Stalin.

The Soviet government had found it necessary to relax certain political controls during war time. Traditional symbols of Russian nationalism were emphasized, the Orthodox church was temporarily encouraged, and everyone was led to expect more freedom and higher living standards. Even before the fighting was over, however, Stalin had begun to reimpose the full weight of Soviet totalitarianism. MVD police units followed the Red Army as it reoccupied western Russia, carrying out a thorough purge of the population that had lived under German rule. The population of the forced labor camps again swelled to ten million or more. The minority peoples in the Caucasus and Crimea were herded off to central Asia. In 1946, there was also a thorough shake-up of the Red Army command, and many prominent Russian military leaders were banished to obscure garrisons.

The only direct resistance to the Stalinist regime came in the newly occupied territories of the western Ukraine (formerly Polish). There, thousands of volunteers in the "Ukrainian People's Army" (UNA) held out in forested areas during nearly five years of a guerrilla-type struggle against the Red Army and the MVD. Whole divisions had to be committed to the field against them. A guerrilla revolt is, however, ultimately ineffective against a totalitarian system able to impose complete control and massive terror. Hundreds of thousands of Ukrainians were rounded up and shipped off to labor camps, depopulating parts of the countryside, and the last units of the UNA were suppressed in 1949.

As rigid Stalinist orthodoxy was reimposed, life in the Soviet Union remained harsh and gray. Every effort was bent toward industrial reconstruction; by 1950 output had reached the prewar level and was still rising. This increase, however, was achieved partly at the expense of the peasantry, whom Stalin ground down still further through higher taxes and increased demands for food delivery. Thus the reactionary Communist system of neo-serfdom became more ruthless than ever. Terror had become accepted as a natural reality of life and, except for the western territories, there were no attempts to rebel. The fact that the Soviet regime, despite ghastly blunders, had led Russia to victory in "The Great Fatherland War" gave it a legitimacy in the eyes of some Russians that it had not previously enjoyed. Stalin, however, had few illusions. He was personally convinced that it was the secret police that held the Soviet Union together.

REVOLUTION IN EASTERN EUROPE
The east European lands between Germany and the Soviet Union suffered even more than the west from the Second World War. Twenty-two percent of the pre-1939 population of Poland was killed, and nearly eleven percent of the Yugoslavs perished. Huge displacements of population ensued, as the millions of Germans whose ancestors had lived for centuries in Czechoslovakia, Hungary, and Rumania were expelled and driven to the west. When the western border of Poland was extended to include a large part of what had been eastern Germany, more millions of Germans were forced to leave. At the same time, perhaps as many as five million east Europeans were moving back to their original homes, whence they had been deported to Germany as laborers during the war.

In most east European countries, the government system and major parties had largely been destroyed during the war. The decisive factor in the whole region was the Red Army, but the Russian occupation forces were not so crude as to impose immediately a direct Communist dictatorship over the countries they had overrun. Stalin had made vague promises about respecting democratic forms and could not be sure to what extent the spread of Russian dominion might still be opposed by the West.

At first liberal—though not conservative—parties were allowed to reorganize and independent native leaders were permitted to hold some of the cabinet seats in the governments of all the occupied countries, save Poland. Several elections were held with at least partial freedom, and for some months most east European governments were largely controlled by non-Communist elements. During 1946, formal peace treaties were arranged with the four minor German satellites of the Second World War—Rumania, Hungary, Finland, and Bulgaria. These called for payment of reparations, a limitation of armed forces, and the ratification of territory seized by Russia from Finland and Rumania. Finland alone of these east European states did not have to undergo Red Army occupation and hence managed to retain national independence.

In Poland, Czechoslovakia, Hungary, Rumania, and Bulgaria, pro-Communist officials were placed in charge of the police and armed forces, insuring a Communist monopoly of organized violence. Only in Czechoslovakia and Bulgaria did the local Communist parties have any degree of popular support, and so the future of east European communism could not be left up to elections. A new technique had to be devised to introduce Communist dictatorship behind a facade of coalition government.

For this purpose, the Soviet government defined a new kind of regime—the "People's Democracy." Both Communists and "Progressive" non-Communists were theoretically included, but the former occupied all the key posts. The People's Democracy was a transitional regime through which the countries of eastern Europe were to pass into a fully Communist society. What could not be achieved by popular support was to be attained over a period of several years by police power and the duress of Russian occupation.

Formation of Communist "People's Democracies" Of all the eastern countries, Poland was the most anti-Russian, and underground resistance groups that had fought the Germans continued to battle the Red Army and security police for nearly three years after the war ended. There, the Soviet command did not long dally; it quickly established official Communist control to prevent any independent political activity. Bulgaria was the most pro-Russian of the new satellite countries, and there the Communist party had had some support for nearly thirty years, facilitating a swift and complete transition to complete Communist rule. Rumania was much more anti-Russian and anti-Communist, though Rumanian feeling was partially placated—after the reoccupation of Rumanian Bessarabia by Russia—by the return of territory recently lost to Germany and Hungary. By the end of 1946, Poland, Bulgaria, and Rumania had all been converted into *de facto* Communist dictatorships.

The countries that enjoyed the longest period of tolerance in the transition to "People's Democracy" were Hungary and Czechoslovakia, where non-Communists were allowed to administer much of the government for more than two years. Conditions in the two countries were, however, dissimilar. The Hungarians were intensely nationalistic and extremely anti-Russian. The Communist party had little support and the Soviet Union was blamed for Hungary's recent territorial losses to Rumania. Therefore Russian policy at first exercised relative moderation.

In Czechoslovakia, many people were disillusioned and rather cynical after their experience in the war. Just as many had collaborated with the Germans, many now collaborated with the Russians. Czech leaders tended to look toward Russia as their future protector from a revival of German power. Czechoslovakia possessed the only developed industrial system in east-central Europe, but in the aftermath of the war many poorer voters were sympathetic to Communist economic promises. Therefore the Czechs at first proved less antipathetic to communism than any of their neighbors,

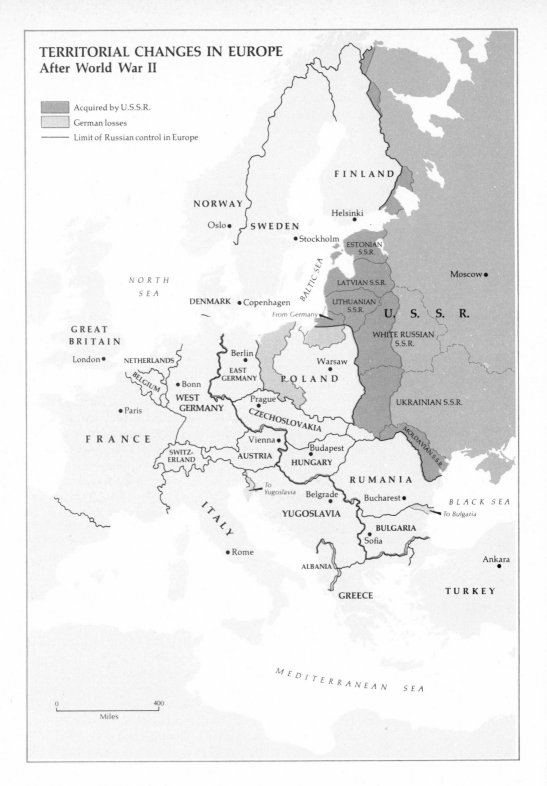

TERRITORIAL CHANGES IN EUROPE
After World War II

Acquired by U.S.S.R.
German losses
——— Limit of Russian control in Europe

FINLAND

NORWAY

SWEDEN

Oslo•

Helsinki•

•Stockholm

ESTONIAN
S.S.R.

Moscow•

NORTH
SEA

DENMARK

•Copenhagen

LATVIAN S.S.R.

LITHUANIAN
S.S.R.

U. S. S. R.

From Germany

WHITE RUSSIAN
S.S.R.

GREAT
BRITAIN

London•

Berlin•

NETHERLANDS

BELGIUM

•Bonn

EAST
GERMANY

Warsaw•

POLAND

WEST
GERMANY

UKRAINIAN S.S.R.

•Paris

Prague•

CZECHOSLOVAKIA

FRANCE

SWITZ-
ERLAND

Vienna•

AUSTRIA

•Budapest

HUNGARY

MOLDAVIAN S.S.R.

RUMANIA

To
Yugoslavia

Belgrade•

BLACK SEA

ITALY

YUGOSLAVIA

Bucharest•

To Bulgaria

BULGARIA

•Rome

Sofia•

ALBANIA

Ankara•

GREECE

TURKEY

MEDITERRANEAN SEA

0   400
Miles

BALTIC SEA

thirty-eight percent of them voting the party ticket in free elections in 1946. On the other hand, the reputation of Czechoslovakia as the most democratic country in east-central Europe and its cultural affinity with the West made it advisable for Communists to proceed slowly. The period of grace in these two countries did not last long, however. In the spring of 1947, the Communists drove all independent leaders out of the Hungarian government. In Czechoslovakia, an anti-Communist reaction set in by the latter part of 1947, and so the Communists seized full control of its government in a bloodless coup early in 1948.

In each satellite country the Communist party, swollen with new members, was renamed and given an innocuous title, but the political monopoly remained the same. Control was exercised from Moscow through a number of channels. First, leaders of the Communist parties in the satellites were usually "Moscovites"; that is, most of them had spent long years of exile in the Soviet Union, where they had become thoroughly reliable. Second, there was a great deal of ideological intercourse between the theorists of the Russian party and the satellite leaders, so that the latter were very sensitive to changes in the Russian line. Third, Soviet diplomatic representatives wielded much influence in the satellite states. Fourth, and ultimately most decisive of all, was the fact that large Red Army detachments long remained on the soil of satellite countries to guarantee obedience. The Russian MVD had direct contact with the secret police of the other Communist lands, and to a considerable degree controlled its sister branches.

RESISTANCE TO COMMUNIST EXPANSION

During 1945–1946, western opinion became increasingly disenchanted with the aims and practices of Stalinist Russia. A Soviet demand in 1945 that it be allowed to annex two provinces of neutral Turkey—which had at no time been associated with Nazi Germany—was rejected, but the wartime illusion about the natural, non-negotiated "cooperation of the peace-loving powers" remained sufficiently strong that no effort was made to contest Russian domination of most of eastern Europe.

The first potential conflict arose in 1946 when Stalin refused to evacuate Soviet troops from Persia after British and American troops had been removed from wartime duties there. A firm stand by the western governments on this occasion, however, led Stalin to withdraw Russian troops from Persia.

A much more serious problem arose a few months later, when Greek Communists launched an armed rebellion against the postwar Greek government in September 1946. This was the only non-Communist regime in the Balkans and the only state in all of eastern Europe that was completely free of Russian influence. The main supporter of the Greek government was Great Britain, whose forces had landed in the Greek peninsula in 1944. By 1946, however, British troops had been withdrawn, and Britain was suffering a postwar economic crisis that precluded further assistance.

The Greek Communists were being supplied and assisted from the new Communist states of Yugoslavia and Bulgaria, with the concurrence and apparently the assistance of Stalin. Should Greece fall, Communist domination of eastern Europe and the Balkans would be complete, opening the way to Turkey and the Middle East.

Any decision to stop the Communist advance inevitably rested with the United States, whose vast superiority in wealth and power made her the natural leader of the western world.

The Truman Doctrine After 1945, American military forces had been rapidly demobilized, but Washington was finally disabused of its mistaken calculations concerning Soviet intentions. Therefore, in March 1947, President Harry S. Truman announced the "Truman Doctrine," under which the United States would "support free people who are resisting attempted subjugation by armed minorities or by outside pressure." Confrontation in Greece marked the official beginning of what would be known for the next quarter-century as the "Cold War." American military missions were sent to Greece and Turkey to train the armed forces of both countries, and military aid was accompanied by substantial economic assistance. Shortly afterward, the tide turned against the Communist forces in the Greek mountains, but this was only the beginning of an extensive program of American activity in many parts of the world to halt the advance of Communist power.

THE
MARSHALL PLAN
The heartland of European civilization, the centers of its main culture and economic vigor, lay in the west, beyond the pale of Soviet power, but the countries of western Europe were slow to recover from the social and economic ravages of war. Indeed, the harsh winter of 1947 provoked a relapse. Production sagged and inflation soared almost out of control. The middle classes had lost much of their remaining savings and the workers were disgruntled by low living standards. Credit, raw materials, and outlets for west European industry were all lacking.

Paradoxically, in the years immediately following 1945, communism had more popular support in western than in eastern Europe. Fear of Russian domination was less immediate among industrial workers in France and Italy, where the Communists had for the first time in the history of any country organized a mass party following in a free competitive society, supported by Communist-dominated trade unions with approximately two million members in each country. In Rome and Paris, Communist ministers participated in coalition governments with liberals and Christian Democrats. As east European coalition governments were turned into Communist dictatorships, there was a fear that the same thing might happen in the west. Belgian Communists had tried to overthrow the postwar Belgian government as soon as it was established, and, after Cold War lines began to be drawn, Communists were ejected from the governments of France and Italy in 1947.

The economic situation of western European countries remained precarious in the extreme. Unless employment and production could be restored, all western Europe would become prey to instability and a balanced

Postwar Refugee Camp in West Germany. Conditions in Germany in 1945–1946 were if anything worse than this picture indicates. The greatest immediate postwar achievement of the German people was simply staying alive during the first two years, when the average ration was only slightly above starvation level.

postwar peacetime economy for the western world would be impossible. Therefore, in June 1948, the United States announced a long-term economic aid program to rehabilitate Europe. Officially named the European Recovery Program (ERP), this became known as the Marshall Plan, in honor of its originator, the American Secretary of State, General George C. Marshall (1880–1959). Since the Soviet Union did not permit the Russian-occupied nations to participate, Marshall Plan aid was given only to the non-Communist West. Within a little over three years it channeled some thirteen billion dollars in loans and shipments into the economies of west European countries. This proved decisive in the sweeping and rapid economic recovery that occurred after 1948.

THE PROBLEM OF POSTWAR GERMANY: DE FACTO PARTITION

The most intractable single problem in postwar Europe was the future of Germany. In the immediate settlement made by the "Big Three" in 1945, Germany was divided into four zones of military occupation (including one for France), with the former capital of Berlin to be similarly divided into four sectors. Located in the middle of the Soviet zone, Berlin could not be entered directly from the western zones, but the Russian government promised free access. Assent was given to the Russian demand that the Oder-Neisse river line serve as temporary eastern boundary between Germany and Polish-occupied territory, though this arrangement was never formally ratified afterward by either the British or American government. Nevertheless, a large section of eastern Germany was lopped off, part of it going to the Soviet Union but the bulk going to Poland as compensation for the latter's eastern losses to Russia. Nine million Germans were forcibly expelled from these territories and had to be moved to the west, and it was further agreed that Germany should eventually pay ten billion dollars to Russia for war reparations.

Military government in Germany lasted four years, until 1949. During the first year, the major problem was simply to keep the population alive, for economic breakdown was general. At least four million Germans had been killed in the war. An even greater number of German soldiers were prisoners in Russia, France, and elsewhere, so that at first the country seemed to be inhabited only by women, children, and old people. There were some fifteen million displaced persons, and regular housing was not available. All these, together with millions of ordinary Germans, lived in cellars and refugee camps. Amid this welter of gloom and stagnation, the western powers soon dropped any ideas of punitive treatment, although, in the beginning rapid German revival was hardly encouraged. The American military government, for example, received orders merely to maintain a level of economic production sufficient to avoid "disease and unrest."

One of the major concerns of the victors was denazification. The principal surviving Nazi leaders were placed before a special international court on war crimes, held at Nuremburg. Documented cases were prepared charging the chief Nazis with having waged aggressive war and having committed "crimes against humanity." Soviet Stalinist judges participated,

The Prisoners' Dock at Nuremberg. The Nuremberg war crimes trial constituted an unprecedented procedure. Designed to enforce an international rule of law, there was inevitably some question as to the objectivity and detachment with which the tribunal operated.

but vetoed any reference to the Nazi-Soviet collaboration in these crimes between 1939 and 1941. Twelve of the major defendants were hanged, seven imprisoned for life, only three acquitted. However, the prosecution and/or reeducation of ordinary Nazis was much more difficult, and in many cases impossible. Mass questionnaires and huge collections of data merely sowed confusion; the proceedings were buried in thirteen million information forms and met passive resistance from the majority of the population. (Similar purges were conducted of fascists and of collaborators in formerly occupied countries of western Europe. The purge was most severe in the Low Countries, and comparatively milder in Italy and France.)

The four occupying powers had originally agreed to follow a joint policy and treat all of Germany as a unit. This soon became impossible in view of the arbitrary and exclusive manner in which the Russians handled their eastern zone. The rule of a Communist political coalition was imposed, and the east German economy was ruthlessly exploited. At the end of 1946, the British and American governments therefore decided to coordinate their zones into a single administrative unit which was also joined by the French zone in March 1948. After that, the Russians refused to participate in the Allied Control Council, and Germany lay completely divided into two zones. Dismantling of German industry had long since ceased in the west, and energetic measures were now taken to encourage economic reconstruction.

Four in a Jeep, Vienna. The Four-Power occupation of Austria was conducted with greater cooperation than in the case of Germany. In Vienna, the Austrian capital, there were for some time integrated patrols of American, Russian, British, and French military police. All four powers then jointly withdrew in 1955, and Austria became a permanently neutral but independent republic.

After the division of the country became complete, the Soviet command closed all land routes to Berlin in order to expel the western powers from their bridgehead in East Germany. When this blockade began in June 1948, Stalin believed that he could soon force the western units out by hunger and lack of supplies. Militarily, the blockade was something of a bluff, for the western powers had full legal right to access and the United States' possession of the atomic bomb gave it total military superiority over the Soviet Union. The American government, however, had decided never to try to intimidate Stalin with the threat of atomic war, and made no attempt to call the Russian bluff. Instead, the western powers operated a giant "air lift" to supply the two million inhabitants of west Berlin with food and fuel throughout the following winter. Three hundred airmen lost their lives, but Berlin was supplied and Stalin's object defeated. He lifted the Berlin blockage in May 1949.

Meanwhile, the western powers had gone ahead with preparations for the meeting of a western German parliament in 1948, to prepare the government and constitution of a united and independent new West Germany. The Russians then established in East Germany the last of the Soviet satellite states, the Russian zone being officially constituted the German Democratic Republic in October 1949. The divided city of Berlin lay right in the middle of this new state, and, due to the four-power provisions governing transportation between sectors of the city, an East German could simply take the subway into the western zone and freedom. In the years that followed, many hundreds of thousands of them did so, resulting in a constant drain on the East German population.

Berlin, Before and After: The Potsdamer Platz, 1945 (   ) and West Berlin's Hansa District, Reconstructed in the 1950's (   ). Berlin became a focus and a symbol of divided post-war Europe. During the 1950's West Berlin was dramatically rebuilt, rising anew from the rubble of 1945, while Communist East Berlin long remained in a shambles.

THE NORTH ATLANTIC TREATY ORGANIZATION

Stalin's abortive effort to drive the western powers out of Berlin increased the fears in western Europe of new attempts to expand Russian power. Therefore, at American urging, a North Atlantic Pact was signed in April 1949. It pledged the United States, Canada, Britain, France, Italy, Belgium, Holland, Luxemburg, Denmark, Norway, Portugal, and Iceland jointly to "Maintain the security of the North Atlantic area" during the next twenty years. Five months later this agreement was put into effect by creation of the North Atlantic Treaty Organization (NATO), providing for an international military force to which each member would contribute. The NATO army was supposed to reach a total of fifty divisions within three years. However, the west European nations found it difficult to keep up with the schedule of contributions. Though Greece, Turkey, and West Germany subsequently joined, NATO never achieved the long-range goal set for it—seventy-five divisions. Nevertheless, the units that were constituted helped to reestablish a balance of power in Europe.

By 1949, lines in the Cold War were fully drawn. Under the sometimes uncertain but economically generous leadership of the United States, western Europe was regaining its vigor and asserting its determination to retain its independence. The Communist empire had reached its limits in 1945–1958, and did not advance beyond that point.

TITOISM AND THE COMMUNIST SPLIT

The only divergence in the general pattern of Russian domination of eastern Europe occurred in Yugoslavia and Albania. In these two countries native Communist movements had seized power by themselves and were not mere creatures of Russian occupation. The Yugoslav Communist chief, Tito, had established his own government while fighting German forces and Serbian royalists during the wartime confusion. This government took over all Yugoslavia after the German retreat in 1945. Having achieved complete power, the Yugoslav Communists moved much more rapidly than the regular Russian satellite states, quickly turning their country into a full Communist dictatorship. In the first years after the war, Tito and his subordinates prided themselves on the creation of a government which resembled the Soviet system more closely than did any other in Europe.

However, the fact that Tito's Yugoslav communism was independent and not based on Russian power made Stalin suspicious and apprehensive, especially after a series of Russian suggestions about state policy were rejected. By the end of 1947, Tito had proposed a new South Slav Communist federation with Albania and the Bulgarian puppet government, which would presumably have placed the latter under Yugoslav rather than Russian influence.

Stalin was determined to quash all spontaneity or efforts at local independence within the Communist world. In June 1948, the Yugoslav Communists were officially ejected from the international Communist organization, the Cominfirm, which Stalin had set up the previous year. He justified this by the largely fraudulent accusation that the Yugoslav leaders had been unwilling to carry out a campaign for the full collectivization of agriculture. Stalin seemed confident that the Yugoslav regime would be unable to stand alone and, frightened by the West, would have to submit to Soviet leadership. Tito himself was shocked by this sudden excommunication, for he had always prided himself on Leninist-Stalinist orthodoxy.

Tito was, however, more than a Communist. He was also the leader of the Yugoslav people, and the split with Russia united them behind him in support of their national independence. The only way for the Yugoslav Communists to justify the existing ideological situation was to take the position that Stalin, not Tito, was the heretic who had deviated from true Marxism. They eventually launched a propaganda countercampaign of their own, emphasizing the "pure," "democratic" Marxism of Yugoslavia compared with the degeneration of the ideology in the hands of the power-hungry, paranoid, "social-fascist" Stalin dictatorship.

To strengthen his hand, Tito began to renew relations with the West. During the first two years after the break, the Yugoslavs continued to mouth the customary Communist foreign policy clichés, dividing the world into categories of "peace-loving" Marxist states and "warmongering" capitalist countries. Gradually, however, Tito and his subordinates came to accept the fact that western aid might be necessary to sustain an independent communism in Yugoslavia. The United States was eager to take advantage of the split in the Communist camp, and supplied Yugoslavia with significant military and economic assistance after 1950.

The Communist dictatorship of tiny Albania took an intermediate position. It was second to none in repressiveness, but feared the domination of the Soviet Union on the one hand and of Yugoslavia on the other. It

Stalinism and the Satellite Countries of Eastern Europe. The Stalin-Tito confrontation was watched with interest by the West. (The New York Times, August 28, 1949.)

WITH APOLOGIES TO WALT DISNEY

refused to support Tito in his quarrel with Russia, maintaining its position as an independent but pro-Stalinist state.

Tito's refusal to serve as Kremlin stooge increased Stalin's suspicion of all satellite Communists, for he was well aware of the role played by national pride and rivalry in east European politics. Between 1949 and 1952 the satellite world rocked beneath a series of mass arrests. The purges were most severe in Bulgaria, Hungary, and especially in Czechoslovakia, where over half a million party members were expelled. Public show trials were held, reproducing the familiar Stalinist spectacle of outstanding Communist leaders confessing imaginary "crimes against the people," preparatory to their own execution. In the process, the satellite Communist parties were reduced by approximately 1,700,000 members, or about one-fourth of their total registration.

The purge extended into the Soviet Union as well. The older Stalin became and the more complete his control, the greater grew his suspicion and fear. By 1950, when he reached his seventieth birthday, he refused to trust anyone. A new wave of mass arrests began in Russia, and even his closest associates were not safe.

SOVIET POLICY IN ASIA AND THE KOREAN WAR

The Soviet Union is an Asian as well as a European power, and Stalin had extended its influence in Asia in 1945. The construction of a Communist satellite in North Korea during the next few years was, however, dwarfed in significance by the complete victory of the Chinese Communist party in China during 1949. From Stalin's point of view, this was a mixed blessing. The Chinese Communists had won their victory on their own; like the Yugoslavs, they were independent.

Indeed, it might have been in an attempt to outflank the new Red China that Stalin enabled the satellite North Korean regime to launch an invasion of South Korea in June 1950. Although the United States government had seemed to indicate that it had no interest in defending territory on the Asian mainland, this blatant attack brought an immediate American response. Supported by the United Nations, an international army, composed mainly of American troops, expelled the North Koreans, then fought a bitter three-year war against Chinese Communist troops who came to their aid. After many hundreds of thousands of casualties, peace was finally made in 1953 on the basis of the approximate prewar demarcation line between North and South Korea.

The Korean War roused Stalin's anxiety all the more because during its course China took the lead as the dominant Communist power in Asia. During 1951 and 1952 the atmosphere in Moscow became increasingly gray and sinister, while policy in the satellites grew even more brutal. Heavy industry and agricultural collectives were emphasized at the expense of living standards, which declined further. As Stalin felt his life drawing to a close, he prepared to tighten the screws in his empire ever more harshly.

SUCCESS AND FAILURE OF THE UNITED NATIONS

Cold war conflict diminished much of the effectiveness of the new organization of nations jointly established by the Allied powers in 1945. Called the United Nations, it was originally composed of members of the victorious anti-Axis coalition, and its fundamental goal was to provide an international rule of law and arbitration to keep world peace. The Charter of the United Nations provided for a General Assembly, in which each member country had one vote (except for the Soviet Union to which the Roosevelt appeasement policy granted three votes). It also established a Security Council, which was to deal with special questions of "international peace and security." In addition, the United Nations organization had as its goal the welfare of citizens throughout the world. A variety of agencies for economic and cultural problems were established as well as a trusteeship program to help the former Italian colonies in Africa prepare for independence.

The United Nations had originally been organized by the "Big Three," and the predominance of the great powers was partially guaranteed by giving five major countries—the United States, the Soviet Union, Great Britain, China, and France—permanent seats on the Security Council; the other six seats were to rotate among the lesser powers. Moreover, it was arranged that no great power could ever be outvoted in the Security Council by giving each permanent member special veto power to kill any proposal it wished. This arrangement has to a considerable extent paralyzed the political activity of the United Nations, for the Soviet Union has often employed its veto to block projects in the Security Council. Significant matters then have to be referred to the General Assembly, where the veto does not exist, but a two-thirds majority is needed for approval. With political accord so difficult to achieve, the main accomplishments of the United Nations lie in programs for health improvement and cultural interchange. Nevertheless, the United Nations does not completely lack practical political utility for, if it cannot solve major problems, it sometimes serves as a moderating influence and has provided impartial arbitration in several disputes among non-European powers. Its boldest act came in 1950, when, after the Russian delegate had walked out in a huff, the United Nations branded North Korea as an aggressor and authorized an international army to roll back its invasion.

THE BALANCE OF AFFAIRS AT STALIN'S DEATH

Stalin died suddenly in March 1953, at the height of his power. During the last eight years of his life, he had become the most influential figure in contemporary history, even more so than Hitler at his prime. The Soviet Union had emerged from the Second World War as one of the two great super-powers on the globe, far and away the dominant state in Europe. Though the Russian standard of living was in some respects almost primitive, Russian power had been extended beyond the farthest dreams of the tsars.

Stalin probably had no plans for armed intervention in western Europe, but obviously intended to extend his influence as far as possible. The totalitarian state could not easily remain in equilibrium, for its internal justification rested on ideological messianism, outward threat, and imperial expansion. The determination of the United States to halt Communist expansion after 1947 had led to a balance of forces in Europe. A stable frontier had been established between the Communist and non-Communist worlds that would last for some time into the future. The weak states of eastern Europe had easily fallen under Russian dominion, but the stronger and more developed countries of western Europe had recovered from the war, reasserted their independence, and achieved bold new levels of national development.

FURTHER READING

Two of the best accounts of the Cold War in paperback are L. J. Halle, * The Cold War as History (1967); and Adam Ulam, * The Rivals: America and Russia since World War II (1971). See also Herbert Feis, The Potsdam Conference (1960), and From Trust to Terror: Onset of the Cold War, 1945–1950 (1970).

*Books available in paperback edition are marked with an asterisk.

In the 1960's, with the rise of the irrationalist left, a current of leftist historiographic revisionism began to develop which blamed American "hostility" and "capitalism" for the Cold War, insisting that all Stalin's aggressive and murderous acts were essentially defensive. Most of this cant is too inane to consider seriously, but the trend did give rise to one or two significant items of scholarship, such as R. M. Freeland, *The Truman Doctrine and the Origins of McCarthyism* (1972).

The Soviet takeover of eastern Europe is best approached through H. L. Seton-Watson, * *The Soviet Bloc* (rev. ed., 1961). For specific countries, see M. K. Dziewanowski, *The Communist Party of Poland* (1959); P. E. Zinner, *Communist Strategy and Tactics in Czechoslovakia, 1918–1948* (1963); and Ghita Ionescu, *Communism in Rumania, 1944–1962* (1964). Czeslaw Milosz, * *The Captive Mind* (1954), is a fascinating exposition of the pressures facing the Polish intelligentsia in the Stalin era. For Tito and the Yugoslav regime, F. Maclean, * *The Life and Times of Josip Broz–Tito* (1957); and Adam Ulam, *Tito and the Cominform* (1952).

Edgar O'Ballance has written a brief account of *The Greek Civil War, 1944–1949* (1966). Germany and Austria under occupation are treated in Eugene Davidson, *The Death and Life of Germany: an Account of the American Occupation* (1959); W. P. Davison, *The Berlin Blockade* (1958); and W. B. Bader, *Austria Between East and West, 1945–1955* (1966). On the Communist political offensive in western Europe, see Mario Einaudi, J. M. Domenach, and Aldo Garosci, eds., *Communism in Western Europe* (1951).

The two major American programs to bolster western Europe are examined in H. S. Ellis, *The Economics of Freedom* (1960), which deals with the Marshall Plan; and Lord Ismay, *NATO: The First Five Years, 1949–1954* (1955). W. R. Harris, *Tyranny on Trial* (1954), gives an account of the Nuremberg war crimes trials. Two useful studies of the early years of the United Nations are E. P. Chase, *The United Nations in Action* (1950); and C. M. Eichelberger, *U.N.: The First Ten Years* (1955).

2 The Soviet World Since Stalin

The Leninist-Stalinist revolution, rather than marking a break with Russia's past, had merely reversed the brief liberal trend of 1860–1917. It had reinforced the dominant pattern of Russian history, which stressed the brutal accumulation and use of power, the enserfment of much of the population, and imperial military expansion.

In 1953, the Soviet Union possessed a great complex of heavy industry, by far the largest in Europe, but it was inefficient, poorly planned, and concentrated on military hardware. Actual living standards compared rather poorly with an underdeveloped southwest European country such as Spain. In some ways, economic development was not as positive as that which had occurred during the final phase of the tsarist regime, when it had been more rational and more oriented toward consumption. The most that could be said for Leninist-Stalinist economic development was that it had achieved at frightful cost the same sort of thing that was already being carried out under freer and less costly conditions before the revolution. The Russian Civil War, for which Leninism had been directly and fully responsible, and the Second World War, in whose coming Stalin had connived with Hitler, had laid waste vast tracts of Russia, requiring herculean efforts of compensation.

Stalin's political system had been a modern bureaucratic form of oriental despotism, in which the chief agent was the Communist party. Here again, rather than being revolutionary, the system was a reversion to the Russian past, to the structure prevailing under Ivan the Terrible. The process of enserfment had begun all over again with the collectivization of agriculture and the huge forced-labor system. Russian culture had been stifled almost altogether.

Despite all the suffering and misery, the Soviet Union was a totally different society from that existing when Stalin came to power. In addition to having created massive new industries, the Russians had developed great cities, were fast becoming an urban society, and had largely achieved literacy.

Hundreds of thousands of trained technical specialists were being turned out by universities and scientific institutes. After the damage of the Second World War had been repaired, living standards slowly began to rise. Russia in 1953 had the potential to begin to live as a modern society, with modest but growing prosperity. All this, however, depended on the government, and whether or not the Leninist-Stalinist system would continue unchanged after Stalin.

THE THAW   Stalin's successors were at first gravely apprehensive about the stability of the regime without the old tyrant who had formed it and dominated it. Once Stalin's iron will was no longer present, they feared the possibility of revolt. On the other hand, there were those who realized that a system of irrational mass terrorism could not be continued forever, that a rigidly centralized totalitarianism would eventually collapse under its own weight.

Since Stalin had been careful never to allow any single lieutenant to hold disproportionate power, no individual leader could immediately assume his position. Collective leadership was exercised by the dominant figures in the Communist party Politburo: Malenkov, a favorite of Stalin's and chief administrator of the government bureaucracy; Molotov, the foreign minister and the leading Stalinist of them all; Bulganin, the minister of defense; Khrushchev, former boss of the Ukraine and now made chief of the party organization; and Beria, head of the police. The least popular was Lavrenti Beria. Hated and feared as a butcher even by many of the Communist faithful, he was a grim symbol of the Stalinist terror. Within three months, the other Russian leaders banded together to relieve Beria of his post as chief of the MVD. He was executed at the end of the year.

The prime minister of the post-Stalin regime was Georgi Malenkov (1902–   ), a plump, talented bureaucrat who had the keenest mind in the group. Even more than other colleagues, Malenkov favored relaxation of government pressure. During the next year, some attempt was made to achieve better relations with the West and relax Cold War tensions. Though Soviet Russia remained a totalitarian police state, penalties were lightened and the hand of the secret police became both less capricious and less obvious. Slightly more freedom was given to Russian writers to say what they thought. In economic policy there was a partial de-emphasis of the pharaonic structure of heavy industry in favor of consumer goods. The newest Five-Year Plan paid special attention to increasing light industry for the benefit of the Russian masses.

These changes during 1953–1954 encouraged unrest among the most discontented inhabitants of the Soviet empire. At the time of Beria's arrest in mid-1953, there were violent anti-Russian demonstrations in East Berlin and other cities of Soviet-occupied Germany, and a temporarily successful revolt was made by prisoners of the dread concentration camp at Vorkuta in the Arctic Circle. The new policies aroused the anxiety of much of the Communist leadership, which feared the situation might get out of hand. Early in 1955, the Politburo forced Malenkov to resign as prime minister, relegating him to a less significant bureaucratic post.

NIKITA KHRUSHCHEV IN POWER

The new Soviet government was officially headed by Marshal Bulganin, the former defense minister, but it later became clear that the true strong man was the secretary of the Communist party apparatus, Nikita Khrushchev. Just as Stalin had risen to power from relative obscurity because of his control of party machinery, so Khrushchev began to achieve the upper hand through his contacts and authority within the party organization. Khrushchev had, however, developed a bitter hatred of Stalin and some of Stalin's methods which he had adroitly concealed while building his own career. By 1955, Khrushchev had become dominant, but he would never be the absolute dictator that Stalin had been. The Communist bosses were determined to retain a considerable degree of collective leadership so as never to revert to one-man tyranny. Khrushchev was thus first among equals and the dominant figure in the government, but not a personal dictator. Also, after the liquidation of Beria, the tactic of assassination of rival or disgraced leaders was abandoned. Banishment from high office or even imprisonment might be imposed, but henceforth there would be no more shootings of leading Communists. The fate of non-Communists remained, of course, another story.

Nikita Khrushchev in 1956. This shows a good-humored Khrushchev making a public address during the first months of his period as top Soviet leader. At times he seemed to have the potential for creating a more humáne form of communism, but his own inconsistencies and the requirements of the Soviet system severely limited his reforms. (Radio Times Hulton Picture Library.)

Khrushchev's personality was quite different from that of the former tyrant. The bald, round, five-foot three-inch Khrushchev was as much of an extrovert as Stalin had been a recluse. He was constantly in the limelight, travelling and making numerous speeches both inside and outside Russia.

Physically tough, he sometimes gave way to drinking bouts from which he always recovered in time to get on with vital business. Bold, self-confident, and crudely frank, he had an explosive temper and on occasion could be quite emotional. Khrushchev had been born a peasant—he was one of the few true plebians among the old Stalinists—and he never lost a crude, down-to-earth sense of humor. Withal, he lacked broad philosophy or statesmanlike training. He had grown up a domestic Stalinist boss, without experience in world affairs. Though he had visionary new ambitions, he lacked constancy and cohesion and, once he assumed central direction, he found it difficult to restrain his impulses. Hence his boastfulness, a tendency to move by fits and starts, frequent changes of pace and mood, the habit of reacting impulsively to events, and the inability to achieve a fully coherent policy.

One of the aims of Khrushchev's government was to moderate and normalize relations with the east European satellites, relaxing pressures slightly and hoping to encourage a more willing collaboration. A formal military alliance, the Warsaw Pact of May 1955, raised the latter to a status of theoretical equality with their Russian master and allowed them more of the appearance (if not the reality) of sovereign power. A rapprochement was worked out with Tito's regime in Yugoslavia, leading to a visit to Belgrade by Khrushchev and other Russian leaders. Though Tito made no concessions, normal relations were resumed.

In July 1955, Soviet leaders met with heads of the leading Western countries for the first time in a decade in a "Summit Conference" at Geneva. This conference produced scant concrete result, but did seem momentarily to relax international tension.

De-Stalinization At the Twentieth Congress of the Communist party, which met in Moscow in February 1956, Russian Communist leaders received their greatest shock in two decades. Khrushchev launched into a full-scale denunciation of Stalin, detailing in long procession some of the crimes of the dead tyrant. He officially rejected the "Cult of Personality" and made Stalin responsible for a great list of tragedies, from the horrors of the 1930's to the split with Yugoslavia. To the relief of the majority of party faithful, he announced that the days of one-man rule and government by terror were over.

Yet here Khrushchev and other Soviet leaders were caught in a dilemma, for by "De-Stalinization" they in no way meant democratization. They wished to avoid the worst excesses of Stalinism while retaining the totalitarian Leninist-Stalinist system. Indeed, from their point of view, they had to retain the Stalinist state, for they themselves were all products of Stalinism and without totalitarian police controls their power would vanish. Hence, De-Stalinization meant, not an end to the secret police, but a curbing of the police's bloody capriciousness, an end to mass murders and wholesale deportations, and a reduction in the scope of the concentration-camp system. The Soviet populace, trained to Stalinism and submissiveness for nearly forty years, could rest a bit easier. In the satellites, however, where most people were both anti-Russian and anti-Communist, the opportunity provided by De-Stalinization had explosive consequences.

THE RESTIVE SATELLITES During the reconciliation with Tito in 1955, Khrushchev had declared that the Russian government recognized the validity of "different paths to socialism" in individual countries. News of the De-Stalinization campaign raised a ferment of excitement. In Poland and Hungary, especially, members of the Communist party were thrown into severe dispute over the course to take. Liberal Communist intellectuals suddenly became outspoken, and, Communist youth organizations openly debated heretical propositions.

Communist "Domesticism" in Poland   The Polish Communist party had an independent tradition of its own. Ruthlessly purged by Stalin in the 1930's, it still retained some sense of unity, and had not been so harshly wracked in recent years as certain other satellite parties. Many members of its Central Committee felt that greater concessions must be made to the people and more authentic leadership provided. A workers' rebellion at the industrial city of Poznan in June, 1956, sharpened this mood. The leading figure of the "national" sector of the party, Wladyslaw Gomulka, had recently been released from prison and was invited to return to meetings of the Polish Politburo. He seemed the best candidate for an authentic, more moderate, Polish Communist chief and it was decided to make him secretary of the Polish Communist party.

Deeply concerned that De-Stalinization in Poland, their most important satellite, might get out of hand, Khrushchev and other Russian officials flew to Warsaw, while Red Army troops were ordered to converge on the Polish capital. There ensued a long day of "sincere, difficult, and bitter" negotiation between the Polish and Russian leaders. Afterward, Khrushchev and his colleagues ordered the Russian forces to retire and acquiesced in the elevation of Gomulka, who became head of the Polish Communist party on October 21. The latter had managed to convince the Russians that he was no Titoist. Polish authorities pledged themselves to stand firmly behind the Warsaw Pact in foreign affairs and maintain strict Communist control at home. They insisted that they claimed only the right of "Domesticism," following the Polish path to socialism, in accord with Khrushchev's De-Stalinization speech. Divergent national patterns that did not split the Soviet bloc and did not diminish the power of the Communist party were reluctantly conceded by the Russian bosses.

The Hungarian Revolt of 1956   The Hungarian revolt, which broke out at the same time, was much more radical and drew Russian attention away from Warsaw. In Hungary, the Stalinists who had controlled the government were divided from liberal elements of the party by a great gulf, and at first only made minor concessions. Opposition among students, workers, and even the party intellectuals reached fever pitch. Exactly two days after

1745   THE SOVIET WORLD SINCE STALIN

Hungarian patriots burning a portrait of Stalin in the streets of Budapest, 1956.

Gomulka's elevation to power in Poland, a popular demonstration broke out in Budapest and soon turned into armed rebellion. Most units of the supposedly reliable Hungarian army joined the revolt, leaving the government helpless. Imre Nagy, leader of the moderate faction in the Hungarian Communist party, was made premier and negotiated the withdrawal of Russian troops still stationed in the country.

The Hungarian revolt was perhaps the only spontaneous popular revolution ever to seize power in an east European country. Contrary to Leninist theory, it was directed against, not for, the Communist party, whose power was completely broken in Hungary. The revolutionaries set about to establish a new democratic regime that would break old ties with the Soviet bloc and adopt a neutral stance in foreign affairs. This the Russians would not tolerate. On November 4, 1956, the Red Army re-entered Hungary in

Hungarian Freedom Fighters Atop a Captured Russian Tank. The doomed Hungarian revolution of 1956, the only spontaneous and direct popular revolution in eastern Europe in the 20th century, dramatically revealed the thirst for freedom smoldering there. It also demonstrated that none of the captive satellite peoples could hope to throw off Russian domination without external assistance.

massive strength to crush the revolution. Despite heart-rending pleas for aid to the western world, no help was forthcoming for Hungary's freedom fighters. Though they managed to hold the frontier open for the escape of some 200,000 people to the west, the Hungarian rebels were completely crushed, and the Communist regime re-established.

THE KHRUSHCHEV ERA

The Russian leaders had never intended that De-Stalinization lead to dissolution of their empire, and so the thaw was followed by a re-freeze. Rigid totalitarian repression was applied in Hungary, and the trend toward moderation in other satellites was temporarily halted. The partial exception was Poland. There the semi-autonomous regime of Gomulka permitted greater cultural freedom than anywhere else in the Communist world. Further attempts to collectivize agriculture were largely given up, and Polish peasants were left free to cultivate their own land so long as they provided the state economy with produce. This mood in Poland lasted only a few years, however. Though a "national Communist," Gomulka was a figure of the old guard and in politics a hard-line authoritarian. Within only a year, new controls were imposed on cultural affairs and there was no further talk of liberalization in Poland.

The Yugoslav regime continued its precarious independence, but Tito affirmed his Communist loyalty by approving Soviet suppression of the anti-Communist revolt in Hungary. The only strong voice to speak up was that of Milovan Djilas, formerly one of Tito's most trusted subordinates and ideologists, who criticized the new elites of Communist dictatorship in his international best seller, *The New Class*. When Djilas refused to be silent, he was sentenced to a term in prison.

A more positive result of the post-Stalin thaw and the restiveness in the satellites was a change in Russian economic policy vis-à-vis the captive countries. Until the death of Stalin, Russia had exploited their economies through discriminatory trade and investment arrangements, and sometimes through wholesale confiscation. After 1953, commercial relations began slowly to be altered to a less exploitative pattern, and the Stalinist drive for heavy industry in the satellites was partially relaxed. More consumer goods were produced and the Soviet Union even began to lend slight economic assistance on a few occasions. The middle and late 1950's were a time of rapidly increasing production and general improvement in living conditions. East Germany achieved an extraordinary rate of industrial development, becoming the greatest economic power in the satellite world. But slowly rising living standards were not enough to reconcile the people of East Germany, who continued to flee into West Berlin by the tens of thousands. In Hungary, the new satellite regime under Janos Kadar attempted a policy of "centrist" totalitarianism. Rigid political and cultural controls were maintained, but serious attention was given to improving economic conditions. The Hungarian people lapsed into resignation, and tried to enjoy whatever meager material pleasures could be offered by the "goulash Communism" that Khrushchev preached.

Communist economic policy was most disastrous in Czechoslovakia. There the population long remained completely submissive to the old Stalinist leadership, which was not shaken up by the Russians. The basic economic problem was that Czechoslovakia already had a developed industrial system to which little could be added by the primitive oriental style of the centralized Communist "command economy." Czechoslovakia had once been the most prosperous country in eastern Europe, but a welter of plans, controls, and red tape began to snarl the productive system. After significant growth in the 1950's, the rate of expansion slowed to less than one percent annually in the years 1961–1963. By that point, the Czech economy was stagnating, and a fundamental readjustment had to be attempted.

The Russian Economy   The Soviet economy continued to make impressive quantitative advances during the 1950's, and annual investment still totaled at least twenty-five percent of the net Soviet income. By 1960, Soviet output in bulk was equal to nearly fifty percent of that of the United States. Khrushchev had already boasted that by 1970 Russian production would surpass that of America and make possible the transition to "true communism," thus eliminating the discriminatory practices of state socialism. Russian economic experts, however, knew better.

Rigid central control, shock tactics, and labor terrorism were not ineffective in establishing a 1930-style heavy industrial complex, but the new demands of the 1960's were more complex. A sophisticated and developed economy relied on careful management, technocratic judgments, and decentralized decisions. Whole new industries geared to electronics and computers were arising that could not be created or managed merely by post-

Stalinist bureaucrats in Moscow and a host of poorly cared for laborers. Moreover, Russian production was far less extensive and efficient than official statistics indicated. First of all, most statistics were falsified from top to bottom as managers tried to give the appearance of having reached impossible goals, since failure to do so made them liable to severe punishment. Secondly, much of Soviet production was planned in terms of sheer bulk quantities that failed to take into consideration actual needs or appropriate uses. Large amounts of goods were sometimes a net loss because they were unusable when produced. Tons of heavy steel plates rusted when finer steel was needed; the latter was inadequately produced because it made a less impressive paper statistic.

Once the early phase of heavy industrialization had finally been completed in Russia, it became more difficult to move rapidly through the latest, more sophisticated, and diversified phases. The rate of economic growth in Russia declined considerably in the early 1960's, as it did in most of the satellites. It became increasingly clear that the Stalinist "command economy" would have to be made more flexible, responsive, and adaptable. The new technological managerial class would have to enjoy greater influence and slightly greater autonomy to make new decisions. It was found that many industrial plants were more productive if given a measure of autonomy and incentive.

This approach found expression in the new managerial tactic of "Liebermanism" (named after a Russian economist who urged it). As it began to be applied to aspects of the economy in the 1960's, "Liebermanism" meant little more than an extremely limited application of the old capitalist principles of industrial autonomy, self-responsibility, and market competition. In fact, as few managerial reforms as possible were instituted, for every step toward partial autonomy of economic factors meant a slight erosion of total state power. Hence the new economic reforms of the 1960's removed some of the obstacles holding back Russian progress, but the very nature of the Leninist-Stalinist system made it impossible to come to grips with the fundamental problem itself. In the complicated new world of computer technology, the Soviet Union seemed to be falling behind rather than catching up.

These facts were not at first appreciated in the West because of the regime's over concentration of resources on such spectacular developments as rocket construction and space launchings. The Soviet Union put the first artificial man-made satellite in orbit around the earth in the autumn of 1957 and later launched the first human into outer space in 1961. Russian propaganda made the most of these accomplishments, and Khrushchev boasted that Soviet nuclear missiles could destroy any country on earth.

In fact, the Soviet system was beset by severe contradictions. The Russians could shoot rockets to the moon, but their highway system at home was primitive. Though the Red Army possessed more heavy tanks than any military force in the world, the average Russian ate meat infrequently. The Soviet Union might control a great satellite empire in eastern Europe, but the population of Moscow suffered under a dehumanizing housing shortage, with entire families still living in a single room. Living standards were rising, but not in proportion to the growth of heavy industry or military hardware, to say nothing of any comparison with even the less-developed countries of the West.

There was not the slightest doubt that ordinary people in Russia would have liked to see the end of the Cold War arms race and expensive space missiles. A Communist Youth newspaper published an anonymous letter on June 11, 1960, which asked,

What do these satellites and rockets do for simple mortals like me? I, for instance, owed 300 rubles before the rocket was launched, and I still owe 300 rubles. . . . There are not enough houses, nurseries, goods, or roads. Say to any worker: "Ivan, if we don't launch this rocket your son Vovik could go to kindergarten, and you would be able to buy an electric iron in the store." I am sure he would say: "For God's sake, don't launch any of those rockets." Rockets, rockets, rockets! Who needs them? To the devil with them and the moon for a while and give me a better dinner instead.

The real Achilles' heel of the Soviet economy was its agricultural system. Collective farming under state control was grossly unproductive, though nearly fifty percent of Russian labor was still tied up in the countryside. After a succession of bad harvests in the late 1950's, it seemed clear that farm output was scarcely keeping pace with population growth. Khrushchev undertook several spectacular changes. Collective farms were increasingly concentrated into big "state farms," and huge new areas of central Asia were brought under cultivation, temporarily increasing total Soviet agricultural acreage by twenty-five percent. In 1958, the machine-tractor stations were decentralized, and later a shake-up was carried out among agricultural directors. Yet none of these changes resulted in significant long-term improvement. The real problem seemed to be in the basic ethos or structure of the state collective farm system. The peasant farm workers lacked the enthusiasm, training, or freedom to raise productivity, irrespective of hypothetical planning. No solution was in sight, for the freeing of farm production would require the loosening of a major cornerstone of the Soviet totalitarian system. Despite the talk of De-Stalinization, the very thought of such liberation was anathema.

Russian Society Russian society after Stalin was dominated by what the Yugoslav Milovan Djilas labeled the "new class," a new Soviet ruling class of high Communist party and state bureaucracy functionaries, that had assumed the place of the old tsarist aristocracy. Despite the nominal goal of communism, the differential in privilege and income—not to speak of power—between the Soviet new class and the ordinary population was actually greater than in the liberal western world. The new class was a direct creation of Stalinism, and though the more arbitrary tactics of the late dictator had been eschewed in the interest of greater security for the new class itself, the Soviet elite understood that their position was based on the totalitarian system, which they were determined to preserve at all costs.

Beneath the ruling new class, there was a new Russian middle class of specialists, engineers, and educated functionaries who held the skilled managerial and operative positions within the Russian economy. This new Soviet middle class was much larger than the old semi-capitalist middle class under Tsarism. Its careers were based not on government and politics, but on economics and education. The new middle-class Russians were mainly concerned with acquiring a larger apartment, eating better food, and planning a more prosperous life for their families. Ordinarily they were not members of the Communist party, for political notions were less important to them than personal goals. Two children were now the norm for middle-class Russian families, just as had been the case for the last generation or two in western Europe.

The ordinary Russian population was of course composed of factory workers and peasant farmers on the collectives. Though living standards rose notably in the 1950's, the pace was not dramatic, and economic rewards were severely gradated according to function. Food by western standards remained poor, usually adequate in quantity but deficient in quality. The worst shortage in Russian life was housing, which remained almost unbelievably cramped and disfunctional. Housing had scarcely advanced over the standards of 1917 and in American terminology most of Russian society lived in "ghetto conditions," though the totalitarian police state assured a lower crime rate.

In the early years of the revolution, Communist ideologists had made much of the liberation of women; as it worked out, women were the sector of society most discriminated against, and in many ways their condition was worse than in the west. Many more Russian women held jobs outside the home than did those in the West, but this was due to economic necessity; two salaries were almost always necessary to support a family minimally. In addition to long work weeks, Russian women were deprived of many of the western conveniences. Hence, after their paid jobs were done, they had to toil long hours standing in food queues, preparing meals by hand, or doing domestic tasks. Child-care facilities were often inadequate. Though there were many more women "doctors" than in the West, most of these were actually medical aids, not fully qualified physicians. Moreover, "equality" for women sometimes meant their employment in heavy repair jobs for which their strength was insufficient. As a result of these manifold strains, the *Kommunist* of Moscow reported in November 1963 that whereas before the Communist takeover Russian women had lived on the average two years less than men, their current longevity in peacetime had declined to eight years less than men. This was exactly opposite to the trend in the West, where women on the average lived considerably longer than men.

Despite the Communist success in institutionalizing their system, many teenagers and young adults showed little identification with the Marxist vision. The rate of juvenile delinquency was rising, as in the industrial West, and sophisticated young people turned their backs on the Bolsheviks in favor of the syncopated musical rhythms of the West. There was a jazz set in Moscow and Leningrad, just as in London and Los Angeles. The Russians even had their own "zoot-suiters," known as *stilyagi*, who paid tourists exorbitant prices for western jazz records and western clothes. Apolitical, self-absorbed youth were strongly condemned by the official press and by Communist groups, but others complained that even the "Young Communists" were in large part composed of careerists and opportunists whose only interest lay in material self-advancement. Khrushchev himself took note of these problems, lamenting that in a "workers' society" the sons and daughters of the educated classes still tried to avoid physical labor. Even the lower classes were not altogether adjusted to their lot, as the high rate of alcoholism among Russian workers testified.

Religion in the Soviet Bloc   The main cultural and spiritual alternative to communism in the Soviet bloc was not liberalism or any other political or material creed but the Christian religion. During the 1920's and 1930's the Communist regime had waged unremitting persecution of the Christian churches, subjecting the leadership of the Orthodox church, suppressing some religious communities, and driving others underground. The official line changed in 1941, when a terrified Stalin rallied support against the German invasion not in the name of communism but on behalf of "Mother Russia," for whom "mother church" constituted a major source of support. Restrictions were later reimposed after the war ended.

The nominal membership of the Russian Orthodox and other churches declined greatly under communism, but a stubborn hard core of the faithful remained. There were further signs of renewal in the 1950's and 1960's, and it became clear that religious belief would not simply die out, even under persecution. In an officially atheistic society, rebellious young people had some interest in turning to a transcendent spirituality in protest and as a logical alternative. In the 1960's, it was calculated that the Orthodox church had about 30 million communicants (in a total Russian population that reached 240 million by 1970). Beyond these, there were other millions of Russians who remained believers but—in order to avoid reprisals—rarely or never attended church. Under Khrushchev, a new wave of persecution was launched against religious organizations, which has continued unremitting. Religiously active people are sometimes sentenced to outright prison terms, their children taken from them to be raised in an atheist environment.

The same conditions prevailed in general in the satellites, though with significant differences in certain countries. The major exception was Poland, which stood out as the most Catholic country in Europe—more so than even Spain or Ireland. Catholicism was fully and deeply identified with Polish nationalism, with the peasant lower classes, and enjoyed some credence among many of the urban workers. Therefore, in Poland the Communist regime largely kept hands off the Catholic church. Though Catholic activities in broader national social and cultural affairs were quite restricted, the church retained its internal autonomy for religious activity.

At the opposite extreme stood tiny Albania, the most backward Communist country in Europe. Its ruthless dictatorship remained the most Stalinist and completely totalitarian in the entire east European Communist world. (Going even beyond the Soviet Union, in November 1967 it ordered the closing of all churches, mosques, and other religious institutions in order to make Albania in law and theory the first completely atheist country in the world.)

CULTURAL PROTEST

New cultural protest was reflected in Russian literature, for after the first post-Stalin "thaw" it was not possible to return fully to the old straitjackets. One of the major themes of the newer Russian literature was mirrored in the title of a mediocre but influential novel published by Vladimir Dudintsev in 1956, *Not by Bread Alone.* The major literary sensation of the decade was the publication abroad in the following year of a long novel, *Doctor Zhivago,* by the distinguished poet Boris Pasternak. This book aroused attention probably beyond its literary merit because it affirmed an absolute standard of individual truth and justice. *Doctor Zhivago* said little or nothing about political ideology, but its individualistic humanism cut across ideological categories and brought a storm of official disapproval. Though Pasternak was universally regarded as the greatest living Russian poet, he was placed under house arrest and virtually forbidden to accept the Nobel Prize for Literature that was later awarded him. Police harassment probably contributed to his death in 1960.

Nobel Prize Winner Alexander Solzhenitsyn. Solzhenitsyn's major work, *The Gulag Archipelago,* was published in the West in 1973 and drew critical acclaim for its unstinting documentation of Soviet political oppression in the thirties and forties. In 1974, impatient with his eminence and embarrassed by his disclosures, the Soviet government made him an unwilling exile in the West. (Gamma Presse Images.)

The greatest figure in post-Stalin Russian literature was not Pasternak but the novelist Alexander Solzhenitsyn, who first came to prominence when Khrushchev permitted the publication of his *A Day in the Life of Ivan Denisovitch* in 1962. This was a sober, stunningly realistic portrayal of life in a Stalinist concentration camp, whose publication the Communist leadership subsequently regretted, since not all the camps have been closed down. During the next ten years, Solzhenitsyn published a series of novels on contemporary and historical themes. The best of them is his trenchant and profound *The First Circle* (1968), a searingly honest and stark but carefully restrained work about Communist and prison-camp society. It is probably the finest Russian novel of the twentieth century. Solzhenitsyn was awarded the Nobel Prize in 1970. Forbidden by the authorities to travel to Stockholm to accept, he wrote an eloquent acceptance speech nonetheless that affirmed the power of free artistic creation, while speaking out against the totalitarian state of the East and the irrational, terrorist elements among the intelligentsia of the West.

During the 1960's, scores of lesser literary figures were speaking and writing their minds. Denied publication, they circulated their mimeographed works among themselves as a means of *samizdat* (self-publication). Culturally isolated amidst a police-controlled and largely submissive society, they persisted even after some of their most eloquent and outspoken colleagues were sentenced to long prison terms at hard labor.

KHRUSHCHEV'S
CLUMSY
SEARCH FOR A
NEW STABILIZATION

As he consolidated his personal power in Soviet government, Nikita Khrushchev began to search for a new formula to achieve global stability that would be in Russia's interests and at least partially defuse the Cold War tension with the United States. This seemed to involve the achievement of stabilization in Germany, with the East German regime recognized and guaranteed in international law. One goal was to establish all of Germany and much of east-central Europe as a "nuclear-free zone" from which atomic weapons would be banned. The Russians hoped to establish a similar nuclear-free zone over China and East Asia, to avoid the danger of atomic competition from China and reduce the danger of conflict there. The end result would be a kind of global understanding with the United States that would reduce overt tensions and military competition, making it possible to concentrate greater attention on domestic development.

Khrushchev was not, however, an experienced or clear-sighted international statesman. He himself had trouble sorting out his own ideas and did not know how to translate them into practice. A lifelong Stalinist *apparatchik* (party-man), his notion of political behavior was basically strong-arm tactics made up of bluster, threats, and bullying. The Russian government held the initiative throughout the late 1950's and early 1960's, but its policy often seemed disconnected and Khrushchev's bluster often frightened and disconcerted western statesmen. When the West responded negatively to his first proposals about Germany, he placed a time limit on a treaty with East Germany and threatened to drive the western powers from Berlin. Thus it was not clear what the new Russian policy of "peaceful coexistence" really meant.

The Berlin Wall East Germany was the most important of the Soviet satellites, but it would never be secure so long as West Berlin remained an open city, enabling masses of East Germans to escape to the West. Within fifteen years, well over two million had fled. Since the western powers adamantly refused to make a deal that would cut off the refugee flow, Communist authorities closed off all transit points between East and West Berlin on August 13, 1961. They quickly built a high wall all around West Berlin, manned by barbed wire, searchlights, watchdogs, and security police with submachine guns.

A Section of the Berlin Wall. A refugee attempting to escape from East Germany captured by Communist police. The "wall of shame" was open testimony to the inability of Communist regimes to compete openly with the West, but served its purpose of stabilizing the East German regime and its economy. Several thousand refugees have attempted to find an escape route through the Wall since 1961. Most have not made it and many died in the attempt.

This was the clearest admission in Communist history that a Leninist-Stalinist state could only exist as a pure police regime behind barbed wire, but it stopped the refugee traffic and stabilized the situation of East Germany. Russian diplomatic pressure against West Berlin then eased, though Khrushchev had failed to get an agreement with the West.

The Cuban Missile Crisis At almost the same time, the Soviet Union acquired its first ally in the western hemisphere when the revolutionary Cuban dictatorship of Fidel Castro officially joined the Soviet bloc in July 1961. The Castro regime had not originally been Communist, but the only organized group and explicit ideology on which Castro could base a totalitarian revolution was that of communism, which he adopted *sui generis* under his personal leadership.

The Soviet leaders gladly accepted alliance with Cuba, for it would give them their first base in the western hemisphere and make possible a new round of military blackmail against the United States. During September and October 1962, Russian technicians worked feverishly to install in Cuba some forty-seven intermediate-range ballistic missiles, capable of carrying atomic warheads.

The American government under President John F. Kennedy responded immediately by declaring a complete naval blockade of Cuba at the end of October 1962. It demanded that the Russian offensive weapons be removed, under pain of an attack on Cuba. The Soviet government quickly gave way, not desiring any atomic showdown, and within a fortnight the missiles were withdrawn.

The sudden Russian backing down after all Khrushchev's confident bluster of recent years surprised many observers, for it amounted to a clear-cut Soviet defeat. This reflected, however, the underlying confusion of Russian policy, continuing Soviet military inferiority, and also the fact that the United States was no longer the sole, or even the main, rival of the Soviet Union.

THE SINO-SOVIET SPLIT — During the 1960's, the main Russian concern in foreign policy was the growing rivalry with Communist China. The Chinese regime, like that of Yugoslavia, was not a satellite. Though the Chinese economy was very backward, the country's immense population provided it with a great potential power base. The Chinese leadership was overtly Stalinist and derided the notion of peaceful coexistence. They refused to subordinate themselves to the Russians, but demanded military and economic assistance and insisted on a more aggressive revolutionary line abroad. The Chinese leaders considered Asia their rightful sphere, and began to indicate their interest in former Chinese borderlands occupied by the Russian tsars. In 1959, the Russians abruptly refused to honor their previous promise to furnish China with information on atomic development; and beginning in 1960, economic aid was sharply curtailed.

The Chinese had begun to maneuver for a position of leadership inside world communism. Their only European ally, however, was tiny Albania, the most thoroughly Stalinist regime of them all, which feared domination both by liberal Communist Yugoslavia and by the main Russian bloc. Meanwhile the Chinese encouraged revolutionary outbursts and guerrilla warfare in southeast Asia and elsewhere, and engaged in a brief border war with India. The Russian leadership invited the Chinese regime to send delegates to an "ideological conference" at Moscow in mid-1963 to try to patch up their differences, but this was a complete failure. By that time the antagonism had become official, and became more intense with each passing year.

THE FALL OF KHRUSHCHEV — While retaining his political hegemony within the Soviet Union, in 1957 Nikita Khrushchev came perilously close to being unseated by a combination of members of the Stalinist old guard, led by Molotov, and more moderate state bureaucrats, led by Malenkov. They resented his showboat style of De-Stalinization, blamed him for letting the Hungarian revolt get out of hand, and considered him too erratic to guide Soviet affairs. In the summer of 1957, the anti-Khrushchev elements mustered a seven-to-four vote in the Soviet Politburo to oust him as party secretary. Khrushchev saved his position by drawing on broader support in the Central Committee to override the decision of the Politburo. This direct appeal to a vote of the broader party elite would have been unthinkable under Stalin. Once Khrushchev's leadership had been ratified, Molotov and Malenkov were both denounced as leaders of "anti-party" groups and banished to unimportant posts.

However, dissatisfaction with Khrushchev's leadership continued to mount among Russian officials. He failed to achieve agreement with the United States, bungled the Cuban missile crisis, and was unable to restore harmonious relations with China. At home, Russian economic growth had dropped to three percent or less in 1963 and was falling well below that of the United States. It had been necessary to raise food prices as much as forty percent, occasioning several bloody riots within the Soviet Union. Moreover, Khrushchev's erratic style led to confusion and extravagance. In a surprise move in October 1964, he was suddenly ousted from his post as Soviet premier, relieved of all duties, and sent into forced retirement on a small country estate outside Moscow.

The group that succeeded Khrushchev emphasized the principle of collective leadership more than had the deposed premier. Key figures were the new prime minister, Alexei Kosygin, and the party secretary, Leonid Brezhnev; both were professional bureaucrats and managers who had worked their way up in the dual party-government apparatus.

The new leaders had not objected to most of Khrushchev's policies so much as to the incoherence with which he pursued them. They made few innovations, and rested on the status quo in Germany. The vague notion of a new deal with the United States was given up. Arab nationalism was exploited as a weapon against western influence in the Middle East but the Soviet Union kept hands off during the brief Arab-Israeli war of June 1967, in which the Russians' Arab protégés suffered disastrous defeat.

After October 1964, Russian policy reverted to maximal encouragement of limited wars by Communist or pro-Communist forces in underdeveloped areas; these were labeled "national liberation" wars. Major support was given the Communist regime in North Vietnam as it sought to expand control over all Indo-China. The military-industries lobby was more powerful in the Soviet Union than in any other major country and obtained great increases in spending, including hundreds of new offensive missiles, an antimissile defense system, and great expansion of the Russian navy.

Relations with China continued to deteriorate, and by the late 1960's there were minor armed clashes on the Russo-Chinese border. Geopolitical analysts talked of conflict between Russia and China as natural and inevitable, and warned of a final military showdown between the two Communist giants for control of the vast Eurasian land mass.

GROWTH OF AUTOMONY IN EASTERN EUROPE

The growth of autonomy increased steadily in some of the east European regimes during the mid-1960's. Yugoslavia remained fully independent;

A Plant Workers' Council Meeting in Yugoslavia. Yugoslavia is the only Communist country to have achieved any degree of workers' autonomy or democracy. Many local factory worker groups are allowed to elect their own leaders and to some extent regulate their own internal economic conditions.

already in the 1950's, it had ended forced collectivization and begun to decentralize the economy, establishing workers' councils to give labor a small voice in industrial management. Under the aging Marshal Tito, Yugoslavia remained an authoritarian Communist regime without political or genuine cultural freedom, but its social and economic policies were the most liberal in the Communist world.

More surprising was the emergence of the Rumanian dictatorship as a de facto independent state. For fifteen years, Rumania had been controlled by a tightly totalitarian regime thoroughly subservient to Russia, but during that period a new generation of native Rumanian leaders was being developed. In 1958, the Soviet government had finally agreed to withdraw Russian troops and after 1961 more pronationalist Rumanian Communists began to take control. On April 22, 1964, the central committee of the Rumanian Communist party declared that it no longer recognized any center of world communism that could define doctrine for or control the affairs of other Communist governments. Under its leader, Nicolae Ceausescu, the Rumanian regime defined a new theory of "socialist nationalism," under which modern nationalism was held to reach its height under a socialist system that brought all sectors of the nation together. The Rumanian regime appealed to national pride for support and planned maximum independent development of Rumanian resources. There was no internal liberalization, however, for unlike Yugoslavia, the system remained totalitarian. The foreign policy of independent Rumania was cautious and clever. Ceausescu assured the Russians of his country's Communist orthodoxy and did not try to withdraw from the Communist bloc, but asserted its complete independence within that bloc.

The most subservient regimes were those of East Germany and Bulgaria. Poland, in fact, marched backward in the 1960's, as its government re-Stalinized. In Hungary, by contrast, the occupation regime of Janos Kadar maintained rigid dictatorship and subservience to Russia, while introducing broad social improvements and a considerably decentralized new economic plan (called the New Economic Mechanism) in 1968.

The most far-reaching break with post-Stalinist tyranny was attempted by the Czech government in 1968. There the reform elements had at long last gained control and soon went far beyond the Rumanian position of mere national independence. The new Czechoslovak government that took office under Alexander Dubcek in March 1968 announced plans to abolish the totalitarian police state altogether and introduce "socialist democracy" that would bring economic decentralization, social freedom, cultural liberation, and even a measure of political freedom.

Neo-Stalinism: The Russian Invasion of Czechoslovakia As the greatest imperialist power in the world, the Soviet Union has had to sustain its imperial hegemony in three different realms: the Russian empire over the captive national minorities within the Soviet Union, its international control over the east European Soviet bloc, and its worldwide role as the supporter of Communist parties and internal subversion on several continents. The latter role was already contested by China and foreign parties had begun to renounce Russian domination. If the Czechoslovak regime were allowed to renounce Communism completely in favor of "socialist democracy," the Russian leaders were convinced that this would begin the disintegration of the entire Soviet bloc, after which reform and liberalization would spread to the Soviet Union itself.

On August 20, 1968, approximately 350,000 Russian troops, assisted by token forces from other satellites, invaded Czechoslovakia. The small Czech forces were ordered not to fight, though for some time the little country united in passive resistance. Such tactics were hopeless before the massive invasion, and Russian party secretary Brezhnev announced the so-called "Brezhnev Doctrine" according to which the Soviet Union had the right to intervene in any other Communist country whenever Communist orthodoxy was threatened. A new puppet government was soon installed and the totalitarian Communist police system reimposed.

THE SOVIET UNION IN THE 1970's By such means the Soviet regime maintained totalitarian orthodoxy throughout the Communist bloc, with the exception of Yugoslavia and the internal independence of the totalitarian nationalist states of Rumania and Albania. Within Russia, nothing more was heard of De-Stalinization. Living standards were slowly rising, but more rapid improvement was ruled out by the insistence of the Communist state on retaining control of nearly all aspects of Communist life.

By 1968, the Soviet Union had lost the leadership of international communism, which as a unified entity had long since ceased to exist. Indeed, it was doubtful that even within the Soviet Union many people still believed in Leninist messianism. The dominant political passion throughout the Communist world, whether in Europe or Asia, was nationalism rather than communism. Such stirrings were also strong within the Soviet Union. According to official statistics, some 7,000 students were expelled from universities and institutes in the Ukraine alone during 1968 for "ideological reasons," chief of which was Ukrainian nationalist sympathies.

There was a widespread mood of dissent among the scientific intelligentsia of Russia, chafing over the continued lack of intellectual liberty. The Soviet Union's leading physicist, Andrei Sakharov, chief inventor of Russia's hydrogen bomb, placed himself at the head of this movement, and made semi-public demands for liberalization despite the danger to his career and his personal freedom. Even within the regime itself, there was a tiny circle of "reform Communists," who circulated a semi-secret *Political Diary* after 1964. They urged a more liberal Communism and reconciliation with the United States, pointing out that whereas only ten percent of the American gross national product went for military expenses, in the more backward Soviet Union nearly one-third of the gross national product was devoted to the armed forces. Yet these voices were isolated among the great submissive and conformist masses of the Russian-inhabited portions of the Soviet Union, where the police state reigned supreme.

Brezhnev and Kosygin on the Reviewing Stand before Lenin's Tomb, May Day, Moscow 1968. The top Soviet leaders stand in the center of the reviewing platform at this annual ceremony. The photo was taken just a few months before the invasion of Czechoslovakia.

By the 1970's, the Soviet regime was essentially a rigid and aging bureaucracy, desperately in need of reforms to open up its technology and economic life, yet unwilling to make real changes for fear of losing power. The regime had lost its revolutionary messianism, but had to retain its expansionist ideology as well as the remaining Cold War tensions with the United States in order to justify the inordinate demands made of its citizens. The growth phase of Russian Communism was at an end, but the old leadership refused to accommodate itself to a more flexible system. Russia regarded its east European empire as vital to its security. Though the Soviet government did not want war, its determination to maintain dominion threatened the possibility of new tensions and military intervention within the Russian bloc. The division of Europe between an independent West and a largely Russian-dominated East seemed likely to persist for some time.

FURTHER READING The most readable biography of * *Khrushchev* is by Edward Crankshaw (1966); see also, C. A. Linden, *Khrushchev and the Soviet Leadership, 1957–1964* (1967). The Russian regime since Khrushchev is treated in J. W. Strong, ed., *The Soviet Union under Brezhnev and Kosygin* (1971).

Two good accounts of the Hungarian revolution of 1956 are François Fejto, *Behind the Rape of Hungary* (1957); and Ferenc Vali, *Rife and Revolt in Hungary* (1961). Kenneth Jowitt, *Revolutionary Breakthroughs and National Development: The Case of Rumania, 1944–1965* (1971), is a case study of the Rumanian system. William Shawcross, *Dubcek* (1970), narrates the Czech liberalization that failed. An acerbic account of the frustrations of Tito's regime is given in N. D. Popovic, *Yugoslavia: The New Class in Crisis* (1968). East Germany after the Berlin Wall has been examined in Welles Hangen, *The Muted Revolution* (1966). For an excellent overview of nationalism and communism in the Balkans, see Paul Lendvai, * *Eagles in Cobwebs* (1969). A. Bromke and T. Rakowska-Harmstone, eds., * *The Communist States in Disarray, 1965–1971* (1972), provides a good survey of recent problems in the Communist states. An extreme interpretation of the Sino-Soviet split is given by H. E. Salisbury, *The Coming War Between Russia and China* (1969).

W. Kolarz, *Religion in the Soviet Union* (1961), describes the persecution and survival of religious groups. Milovan Djilas, *The New Class* (1957), is an outstanding critique by a former top Yugoslav Communist. Andrei Amalrik, *Will the Soviet Union Survive Until 1984?* (1970), is a brilliant critique by a leading internal opponent of the Soviet regime, currently sentenced to hard labor.

*Books available in paperback edition are marked with an asterisk.

3 The Resurgence of Western Europe

Economically, western Europe suffered more severe consequences from the Second World War than from the First. Germany lay crushed, much of Italy was in ruins, and France and Britain had been partially impoverished. There was extensive social dislocation. Prewar political elites were temporarily discredited, and most people no longer considered them able to lead western Europe out of the valley of destruction and into new prosperity. The stage was thus set for sweeping changes in government policy and economics.

EMERGENCE OF THE WELFARE STATE

The major political consequence of the end of the war in northwestern Europe was the growth of the moderate left. Conservative forces were not only held responsible for the prewar depression; in some countries they were also blamed for collaboration with nazism. Moreover, in Britain and France, resistance against Germany had been encouraged by the promise of better conditions at war's end. The main result of this was a change in government policy toward the "welfare state," by which the government itself intervened directly in economic affairs, nationalized certain industries, and provided all manner of welfare insurance and services to ensure at least the minimal well-being of the entire population.

The most dramatic change was the stunning victory scored by Britain's Labour Party over the Conservatives led by Churchill in the general elections of July 1945, just two months after the fighting ended. Desire in Britain for change in domestic policy was so strong that the Labourites won a majority of 195 seats—their first clear-cut electoral triumph and their strongest. The new Labour government of Clement Attlee, which led the country from 1945 to 1951, carried out a remarkable reorganization of economic policy. To improve management and eliminate wasteful competition, the nation's basic industries—coal, electric power, railroads, gas, and steel—were nationalized. Government planning commissions helped coordinate all significant aspects of production. To conserve resources, a regimen of "austerity" was followed until 1952, while hard work and Marshall Plan aid expanded productive facilities. By the end of 1948, industrial production was eighteen percent greater than it had been before the war, exports were up thirty-eight percent, and imports had been reduced by eighteen percent. Two years later, it was possible to cancel further Marshall Plan assistance. Meanwhile, the Labour government created the most complete welfare state legislation known to any large western country. Wartime medical care was expanded into the National Health Service (1946), which provided largely free medical and dental care for the entire population. A new National Insurance Act broadly extended health, old age, and unemployment insurance. An expanding economy and the assistance of state employment agencies provided full employment.

Such social reforms were expensive, and the British became one of the most heavily taxed people of the western world. Steeply graduated income levies and confiscatory inheritance duties tended to equalize income, though some important differences persisted. Government regulation helped ensure adequate distribution of consumer necessities while fostering exports.

Similar policies were to a greater or lesser extent adopted in most of the small countries of northern Europe. Indeed, the social democratic welfare state had been pioneered in Sweden during the 1930's, and the welfare and state interventionist systems in Sweden and Denmark were even more extensive than in Britain. In Norway, Finland, Belgium, and Holland, broad social security programs were also instituted. The predominant political force in northern Europe was the Social Democratic parties, which had largely dropped their earlier Marxist ideology and adopted a philosophy of national reform and social harmony on the basis of a mixed economy—partly public, mostly private, but in key aspects regulated or coordinated by the state.

Thus, the welfare state did not mean socialism. Only selected portions of the economy were nationalized, and in all north European countries from Britain to Finland, the great majority of businesses remained in private

Social Services in Finland. The "Park Aunt" system provides care for children in Finnish parks during winter weather. (Lehtikuva Oy.)

hands. The big change in postwar social democracy compared with prewar liberal democracy was that the government now took responsibility for minimal economic well-being, the coordination of a largely private economy, and the achievement of a certain amount of a social equality.

Social Democracy in France   The pattern in France was slightly different. There too the forces of the left dominated immediate postwar politics and hoped to establish major political and economic changes. However, the major force of the French left was the largely Russian-dominated Communist party. French Socialists were weaker but had adopted a social democratic, rather than Communist, ideology and tended increasingly to cooperate with moderate liberals of the center. France's undisputed national hero, General Charles de Gaulle, the leader of the wartime struggle, served as the first postwar prime minister and hoped to provide strong new leadership. Unable, however, to overcome the manifold divisions in French party politics, a disillusioned and disdainful de Gaulle temporarily retired in disgust in 1946. The new constitution of the French Fourth Republic, adopted that year, closely resembled the political structure of the preceding Third Republic (1871–1940). The executive remained weak, controlled by parliament, and perhaps the most notable change was the extension of the vote to women.

The purge of wartime collaborationists in 1945–1946 injected much bitterness into French affairs, but by 1947 that issue was being forgotten as the moderate left and the center closed ranks against the Communist party and the threat of advancing Russian power in east-central Europe. Communist ministers had participated in coalition governments in both France and Italy since 1945, but they were ejected from the cabinet of each country in 1947. In France, the middle-class status quo soon reasserted itself. By 1948, the balance of forces in the national assembly had returned to much the same pattern as in the 1930's. For the next decade France was governed by shifting coalitions of center parties, moderate conservatives and the Socialists, who espoused the same social democratic programs found in northern Europe.

Between 1945 and 1948, a version of the welfare state, less sweeping than in Britain, Sweden, or Denmark, was instituted in France. New insurance and compensation plans provided basic assistance for more than half the population. As in Britain, some major industries were nationalized—gas and electricity, railroads, coal, airlines, large banking and insurance enterprises, and the largest automobile plants.

One development in France that went beyond the changes in Britain was the organization of a national economic planning agency, the *Commissariat du Plan*, consisting of thirty economic experts and their staff set up under Jean Monnet in 1946. Its powers slowly increased in the years that followed until it was able to control the bulk of French investment, setting new goals and stimulating productive expansion.

By 1950, France, and nearly all of western Europe, was entering a new period of dramatic economic prosperity that encouraged new political and social stability. In 1951, the Conservatives returned to power in Britain, but accepted all the basic features of the welfare state, and outdid the Labourites in the construction of government-financed housing. In most of western Europe, the 1950's were a decade of political continuity and equilibrium, following the deep changes of the 1940's.

CHRISTIAN DEMOCRATIC RULE IN ITALY AND GERMANY

Initially the gravest problems were faced by the two defeated powers, Italy and Germany. After the Nazi and Fascist dictatorships, both countries had to completely reorganize their civic structures. The task was easier in Italy, for fascism had not been truly revolutionary nor totalitarian. Since non-Fascist forces had not been so thoroughly suppressed, and since liberal elements had reversed Italy's alliances in 1943, the reconstruction process had begun in southern Italy even before the fighting ended. In West Germany, national elections and a functioning government were not established until 1948. Postwar Italy quickly regained its sovereignty and signed a final peace treaty with the Allied Powers in 1947. Its terms were light: the only reprisals were the loss of Italy's African colonies and payment of $360 million in reparations to Russia and several Balkan countries. Minor adjustments were made on Italy's northern frontier to make the boundary more equitable to ethnic minorities. The monarchy was abolished by referendum and a new constitution of 1948 established an independent Italy as a democratic, constitutional republic rather similar in government structure to France. Western Germany regained full independence in 1949, but the country as a whole remained divided, the east under Russian domination. Because of this, a regular peace treaty with Germany remained impossible, and West Germany's role in Europe remained clouded and uncertain for years.

The downfall of the dictatorship had completely discredited right-wing forces, and political life was organized in both countries around a major new center party, the Christian Democrats, and the left. The Christian Democrats dominated the governments of both Italy and Germany for the next two decades. They represented the ordinary middle classes which amounted to about forty percent of the total population.

The situation of the left in the two countries was, conversely, altogether dissimilar. In postwar West Germany, the left was represented almost exclusively by the Socialists, who had become a typical west European social democratic party and finally in 1959 renounced the last lingering theoretical vestiges of Marxism. Support for communism was almost nonexistent, for Communism was considered a mortal enemy of German interests and values, whether middle or lower class. It was held responsible for the division of the country and for the totalitarian regime that tyrannized East Germany. In Italy, however, the left was divided between a large Communist party that was often able to garner twenty-five percent of the national vote and a distinctly smaller Socialist group. Italian Communists, like those of France, were permanently excluded from government power after 1947, and became a perpetual opposition party. The Italian Socialists quickly split in half

Alcide de Gasperi. Christian Democrat premier of postwar Italy, De Gasperi provided the leadership for the reconstruction of his country and the beginning of a new era of prosperity. (Italian Cultural Institute.)

between doctrinaire socialist and practical social democrat factions just as they had prior to fascism. For fifteen years, the majority group of doctrinaire Italian Socialists flanked the Communists as an opposition group.

The outstanding leader of postwar Italy was Alcide de Gasperi, head of the Christian Democrats, who served as prime minister from 1945 to 1953. He succeeded in institutionalizing a new democratic system in Italy, maintaining a stable government and constitutional liberties at the same time. With Marshall Plan aid, the Italian economy began to recover very rapidly after 1950, and set new records with each passing year. Growing prosperity served at least momentarily to assuage political and social tensions, but the Christian Democrat majority slipped to a dangerously thin plurality during the course of the 1950's.

The leader of postwar Germany was Dr. Konrad Adenauer, former mayor of Cologne, who became prime minister at the age of 73, and governed for the first fourteen years of the new Federal Republic of West Germany (1949–1963). *Der Alte*—"the Old Gentleman"—was a sincere and honest

Dr. Konrad Adenauer. Prime minister and political father-figure for the new state of West Germany, Adenauer governed for fourteen years (1949–1963) despite his advanced age. Under his aegis West Germany reemerged as the greatest economic power in western Europe. (German Information Center.)

constitutionalist but wielded the German executive power with an iron hand. He presided over the restoration of West German sovereignty; and his own party, resting on the larger German middle classes, enjoyed a much more solid majority than did their Italian counterparts. Germany's economic recovery after 1949 was breathtaking. During the following decade, its growth rate was equaled only by Japan among major industrial powers, and it developed the third most productive economy in the world. The key to postwar West German history thus became the fabled *Wirtschaftswunder*—the "Economic Miracle."

Political conditions were not dissimilar in the second Republic of Austria. The prewar first Austrian Republic had been torn apart by the struggle between the Socialists and the Catholic Christian Social party. These two groups having learned their lesson, the second Republic (established in 1945) was governed by a strict Christian Social-Socialist party coalition—all power and offices divided by *proporz,* i.e., strict cooperative proportionality—and regained its unity and independence in 1955 as a result of the partial detente in the Cold War. Spared further political strife, the new Austria developed as a state bound to neutrality by international law and free to develop its own resources. Austrian economic expansion was not so dramatic as that of Germany, but made steady and impressive gains.

AN END TO WEST EUROPEAN EMPIRE Though the leading nations of western Europe regained prosperity and self-confidence within only a few years after the end of the war, they completely lost the commanding world position they had enjoyed for the past three centuries. All of western Europe was now dwarfed by the two superpowers, the United States and Russia, while the European empires overseas had begun to dissolve before the war ended. Japanese expansion undercut the European position in southeast Asia, but even in countries never threatened by military occupation, the rising tide of domestic nationalism, anticolonialism, and the strain on European resources brought a hasty retreat from imperial responsibility. Within twenty years after the close of the Second World War, nearly all of the overseas empires of western Europe had been dissolved, in some cases reconquered by native peoples, more often voluntarily abandoned by European powers.

Great Britain led the way in this process, which has been described in greater detail in Part XVII. In nearly all cases, Britain granted independence to its far-flung protectorates and colonies without conflict, and remained on relatively good terms with most of the new independent states, many of whom became members of the loose confederation known as the British Commonwealth. Holland abandoned the Dutch East Indies under severe duress, however; and, later, Belgium abruptly pulled out of the Congo to avoid the trauma of rebellion. Even Britain did not fully avoid colonial conflicts, as exemplified by terrorist campaigns in Palestine, Malaya, and Cyprus (and then nearer home in Northern Ireland). The only exception to the whole trend was little Portugal, whose authoritarian leaders considered the colonies of Portuguese Africa vital to the future strength and independence of Portugal itself.

The country most severely affected by the decolonization process was France. Though French leaders were willing to grant greater autonomy to their overseas colonies, the dominant forces in French politics believed that France could not afford to give up such a potentially wealthy region as Indo-China, or an area nearer home such as Algeria, inhabited by nearly a million French-speaking Europeans. The resulting colonial wars for Indo-China (1946–1954) and Algeria (1956–1962) both ended in complete failure, cost a great deal of money, seriously divided French opinion at home, and threatened the very civic institutions of France itself.

Only once did the former west European colonial powers undertake a major new initiative vis-à-vis an African or Asian country. In November 1956, after the Egyptian government arbitrarily nationalized the Suez Canal company, British and French forces invaded the canal zone to reassert their rights and influence in North Africa. This act, which coincided with the Russian invasion of Hungary, was met by severe threats from the Soviet Union and the disapproval of the United States. The British and French governments lost their nerve and withdrew their forces, revealing the impotence of western Europe in any new designs of grand world strategy.

The most serious problem to emerge in the wake of imperial retreat centered about the new Jewish state of Israel, carved by European Jews out of part of the former British protectorate of Palestine. The creation of Israel climaxed the fifty-year old movement of Zionism to create a nationalist state for Jews; but it was realized at the expense of Palestinian Arabs, hundreds of thousands of whom became displaced persons. Israel became the focus of the enmity of surrounding Arab states, who preferred to project their problems onto Israel rather than concentrate on domestic development. To increase its influence, Russia later adopted the Arab cause, but Israel won each of four successive rounds of war with its Arab neighbors (1948, 1956, 1967, 1973). Failure to come to terms over the existence of Israel has left the whole region in an uproar, and helped make the Middle East the second most volatile region in the world, after Southeast Asia.

One result of the colonial withdrawal has been to disprove the old contention that west European imperialism was the source of west European prosperity. The opposite was more nearly true. Free of imperial responsibilities and concentrating primarily on their domestic development, the economic well-being of the former colonial powers has improved more rapidly than ever before.

GROWTH OF WEST EUROPEAN UNITY

The Council of Europe The reduction of west European power and influence made many Europeans feel the need for closer association and cooperation than ever before. One consequence was the formation of the Council of Europe in 1949 by the governments of ten nations: Great Britain, France, Italy, Ireland, the Netherlands, Belgium, Luxemburg, Denmark, Norway and Sweden. They were later joined by Greece, Turkey, Iceland, West Germany and Austria. The Council organization is composed of a Council of Ministers (the foreign ministers of the member nations) and a Consultative Assembly, to which the member states send representatives roughly according to the size of their populations.

This first step toward European confederation has remained largely consultative, however, for the larger countries have feared the loss of sovereign power. Since all decisions must be unanimously approved by the Council of Ministers, each member holds veto power and partly as a result no major new policies have been developed by the Council of Europe.

An attempt to form an all-European army, to be called the European Defense Community and composed of multinational forces under a common command from France, Germany, and the Low Countries, foundered in 1954. The French assembly voted against committing French troops to a force not under French control.

The Schuman Plan and the Common Market Plans for west European economic cooperation have been much more successful than schemes for political and military unity. The first of these was the Benelux agreement, which established a common market for Holland, Belgium, and Luxemburg in 1948. The arrangement proved immensely successful, and ten years later the three countries signed a fifty-year treaty of economic union.

The prolonged stagnation of the 1930's and the miseries of the war had finally taught west Europeans the lessons of economic interdependence they had previously been so reluctant to learn. Two years after the formation of Benelux, a more far-reaching plan for the economic integration of the leading continental countries was introduced by the French economic planners led by Jean Monnet. The British Commonwealth comprised a free trading area; the new Scandinavian Union of Norway, Sweden, Denmark and Finland constituted another in the north; but there was no such coordination between the main west European continental countries. Hence the new Schuman Plan, devised by Monnet's group but named after the French foreign minister, proposed to begin by integrating the production and marketing of coal, iron, and steel in France, West Germany, Italy, and the Benelux nations. These six countries then established the European Coal and Steel Community by treaty in 1951. Over a period of five years, a complete common market for these industries was created within the six member countries, and proved an enormous success, helping to stimulate broad industrial expansion.

From that point, the whole system was expanded in 1957 to establish a European Economic Community (EEC), better known as the Common Market, that resulted eventually in the creation of a complete common trading area among the member countries. The EEC was complemented by the establishment of Euratom, a common arrangement for the development of atomic research and power in western Europe.

The Common Market was just as successful as the preliminary Coal and Steel Community, and was quickly recognized as a major factor in the continuing economic expansion of the late 1950's and 1960's. Seven other countries not part of the Common Market—Britain, Denmark, Norway, Sweden, Austria, Switzerland, and Portugal—had responded with a more limited European Free Trade Association (EFTA) of their own in 1959. This association was much less integrated than the Common Market; and during the following decade leading members of the EFTA, especially Britain, showed increasing interest in joining the Common Market itself. Britain was allowed to become a member in 1972. By that time, the scope of the EEC had extended either directly or indirectly over nearly all western Europe. Altogether, the EEC has proven the most effective venture in international cooperation known to modern Europe.

THE NEW WESTERN EUROPE

Sustained Long-Term Economic Development The quarter-century after 1948 constituted the most remarkable period of sustained long-term economic development in west European history. The Marshall Plan was obviously crucial to its first phase, but the expansion has been continued so long, without the interruption of a full-scale cyclical depression, that analysts have been at a loss for a completely satisfactory causal explanation. Obviously much has been learned from the past and many previous mistakes have been avoided. The ubiquity of economic planning and a Keynesian approach have contributed a direction and coordination that was previously lacking. The new emphasis on international cooperation and both international and intercontinental trade have also been indispensable. Both capital and labor have cooperated in the process—though with some variations and differences—but the role of government has been the most novel of all.

West Germany achieved the "economic miracle" of the 1950's, but the highest growth rates of the 1960's among the larger countries were registered by Italy and by the more backward economy of Spain. Two of the smaller countries, Denmark and Holland, made almost equally dramatic gains. French industrial growth accelerated and has sustained a high rate, while of the major powers Britain has registered the most modest gains. Though Britain has lost ground compared with Germany and France, this has not been because the British economy has stood still but because its rate of expansion was less rapid. The highest standard of living in all Europe is enjoyed by the numerically small population of Sweden, which, after the United States, has the most efficient specialized industrial plant in the world. Throughout Europe, the new prosperity has been based above all on efficient management and a relatively high rate of investment, resulting in growing productivity.

Between 1958 and 1970, per capita income calculated in United States dollars rose as follows:

	1958	1970
United States	2,558	4,756
Denmark	1,101	3,163
West Germany	1,094	3,028
France	1,196	2,906
Belgium	1,154	2,656
Netherlands	845	2,398
Great Britain	1,249	2,175
Japan	302	1,904
Italy	612	1,710
Ireland	578	1,321
Spain	295	790

An Affluent New Society The prolonged prosperity of the 1950's and 1960's drastically altered the texture of west European society. New patterns of mass consumption brought a wave of affluence, not merely for the upper and middle strata, but for much of the working class as well. Items that less than a generation earlier would have been considered luxury goods became articles of common consumption and looked on as ordinary necessities. Leisure-time activities produced major industries in themselves. The amount of time and money invested in sports soared, and a paid vacation of up to four weeks became standard for ordinary workers in most west European countries. For the first time in history, travel became possible, at least to some extent, for ordinary people; and tourism increased enormously. The tourist flow was mainly from north to south, and Italy and Spain were the primary recipients. By 1970, each was visited by more than 20 million tourists per year, the bulk of them from northern and central Europe.

Though the new affluence and mass consumption got under way in the 1950's, they flowered fully only in the 1960's. Washing machines and refrigerators became increasingly common among working-class families, but the new glamor items were television sets and automobiles. These had become standard for the middle sectors, and an increasing percentage of workers came to own them, as well. Their frequency in selected countries as of 1971 is indicated below:

	Automobiles per 1,000 people	Television sets per 1,000 people
United States	432	399
France	245	201
West Germany	234	262
Denmark	219	250
Great Britain	213	284
Holland	200	270
Italy	187	170
Ireland	122	153
Japan	86	214
Soviet Union	12	120

Mobility and informality have shattered much of the old European social patterns. Though class lines are still much stronger than in the United States, the rigid class barriers that existed as late as the 1940's have been steadily dissolving, as the lines between the middle and working classes begin to blur in terms of consumption and life style. In most west European countries taxes and social welfare payments take at least one third of gross income. The result has been at least a partial redistribution of income. An increasing emphasis has been placed on technical achievement, leading some commentators to speak of a "meritocracy" that is replacing the class pattern of nineteenth and early twentieth century society.

In fact, significant differences in income and opportunity continue to exist, but they are considerably smaller than before the 1940's. The number of students in higher education has increased from three to four times and more in most west European countries, but only a very small minority of them come from the working sectors of society. According to one study, the proportion of the age group 20-24 enrolled in higher education in different western countries was:

	1950	1965
Italy	3.7	7.7
Norway	3.3	7.8
Great Britain	4.0	8.5
Denmark	4.5	8.9
West Germany	3.4	8.9

	1950	1965
Sweden	3.7	11.1
Finland	4.2	11.4
Belgium	3.7	14.1
France	4.1	14.1
Netherlands	7.4	14.3
United States	22.0	45.0

In some countries, workers continue to feel the effects of income disparities, which accounts for the strong hold that the Labour, social democratic, and Communist parties still have on the votes of the working strata. The major change, compared with the preceding generation, is that these differences are now argued primarily in technical and economic terms about adjustments in income and benefits. The fundamental structure of a prosperous and expanding society is itself rarely questioned by most of the west European left.

One indication of the relative social harmony that has been attained is the lack of industrial conflict in most of western Europe, with the major exception of Italy, as shown below:

	Days Lost on Strike per 1,000 workers (Annual average, 1965–1969)
Italy	1,574
Ireland	1,350
United States	1,232
Great Britain	294
France	243
Japan	198
Belgium	156
Denmark	110
Holland	12
West Germany	10

Postwar West European Culture   Since 1945, Europe has failed to produce major new cultural achievements in literature, art, or music that are in any way equivalent to its accomplishments in technology or economics. The immediate concerns of postwar artists were stark and rather pessimistic. This mood gave way in the 1950's to further experimentation in new forms that were steadily divested of content. By the 1960's, the literary and artistic intelligentsia had become highly self-absorbed and so devoted to abstract or subjective forms that in many cases they had little of significance to convey to society at large.

Jean Paul Sartre (left); Albert Camus (right). Novelist, philosopher and above all political journalist, Sartre has been the most celebrated, if hardly the most lucid and honest, of post-1945 west European intellectuals. Novelist and essayist, Camus was the leading cultural spokesman of the postwar generation and its most outstanding literary figure prior to his premature death in an auto accident. (Radio Times Hulton Picture Library.)

The most important new literary philosophy in the immediate aftermath of the war was French existentialism, whose chief spokesman was the novelist and essayist Jean-Paul Sartre. To Sartre, existentialism was based on the assumption that man had no essence and no intelligible grasp of transcendance. Truth in itself did not exist, nor did inherent values. Sartre asserted that all human life was a matter of individual human creation, that people created their own truths or values for themselves out of their existences. Life was thus inherently absurd, but people might yet give it meaning through their willpower, through their individual choices in action. This philosophy was remarkably similar to Mussolini's, but Sartre instead embraced Stalinism, asserting that collectivist utopianism was the only higher human value.

Such extravagance was too much for the other major postwar French literary figure, Albert Camus. His allegorical novel, *The Plague* (1947), reaffirmed individual human self-sacrifice and solidarity in the face of disaster and rejected the Sartrian flight from reason. Camus' major historical-philosophical study, *The Rebel* (1951), rejected the coercive, destructive character of modern political revolutions and utopian tyrannies, but emphasized the transforming imperative of continuing moral rebellion to try to reform society. Camus' last works before his premature death sought to recapture traditional human values and regain tranquillity of spirit.

The pessimistic agonizing of existentialism lost its appeal in the 1950's, and after that point no single philosophy or trend played a dominant role. French novelists retreated into pure subjectivism in technique and seemed to lack anything of significance to communicate to their readers. The latest vogue in avant-garde theater was the "theater of the absurd," which sought to dramatize the meaningless and degrading as a higher form of reality. In painting, purely abstract art held sway, but its complete dehumanization deprived it of appeal to society.

The most popular new art form was the postwar cinema, dominated mainly by the Italians and the French. The first vogue was that of stark realism as practiced by the Italians in the late 1940's. This later gave way to the cinema of subtle photographic and psychological technique whose main subject matter in France and Italy during the 1960's was sensuality and self-indulgence, intended to portray either the self-affirmation of the young or the decadence and degeneration of the middle-aged and wealthy. Despite sophistication of technique, the postwar European cinema, like the theater, usually lacked profound content or ability to probe serious aspects of human personality.

In a secular and profane age, art had earlier been held up as a new religion, destined to reveal the potential and goodness of mankind. Contemporary art has not found much goodness in men, however, and, lacking criteria by which to interpret the significance of good and evil, has reveled in portraying the ugly, base, vicious and perverse. Thus, by the 1960's, as Walter Laqueur has written, "western Europe faced a sick avant-garde culture manifested in music and painting, in literature, the theatre and the cinema that encountered scarcely any hostility from a gullible and docile public or from critics so fearful of being called old fashioned that they treated every idiocy seriously."

The intelligentsia of western Europe as a whole revealed many signs of confusion and disorientation. There was no clear sense of a common philosophical or spiritual creed, but instead a desperate search for novel form or shocking expression simply to create something dissimilar to the past. Some young scholars tried to regenerate a form of neo-Marxism as the most extreme expression of modern secular utopianism, though variants of anarchism and extreme self-assertion seemed more congenial to most of the radical members of the literary intelligentsia.

In historical study, the major postwar achievement was the completion of Arnold Toynbee's ten-volume *A Study of History*, in 1954. This was, among other things, an attempt to re-evaluate the place of western civilization in the entire course of world history through detailed analysis of twenty other civilizations on the basis of factors influencing their rise, duration, and decline. Toynbee eventually concluded that there was no reason as yet to conclude that western civilization was fated inevitably to decline and fall like all its predecessors, since it displayed considerable vitality in many different fields. The major question mark, said Toynbee, was whether western civilization had the moral and spiritual stamina necessary to continue and flourish. His judgment was that spiritual, not material strength, had been the determining factor in the vitality of human culture. Ultimately, he warned, the scientific accomplishments of the western world would matter little if its religious basis were entirely lost.

Religion Since the Second World War, the materialistic, secular character of west European life has become even more strongly accentuated. The arrival of the welfare state, in relieving most of the population from the most desperate material cares, did not have the effect of freeing their energies for spiritual pursuits. The leisure time and purchasing power afforded west Europeans during the past generation has been primarily devoted to hedonism. In Scandinavia and England, church attendance has dropped to an all-time low, though the traditional religious communities in the Low Countries have retained greater vitality.

There was some revival of German Protestantism after the close of the war. There the churches had suffered most, and for the first time in German history, nearly all Protestant denominations were represented in one body—the Evangelical Church Council. At first the heroic minority of anti-Nazi pastors dominated the Church Council, preaching a return to theological and ethical rigor. The influence of these reformist elements diminished in the 1950's, however, for economic prosperity seemed to discourage moral introspection. West Germany regained its place as the center of intellectual Protestant theology, but postwar theology itself became increasingly secularized and desacramental, preaching a "demythologization" of religion which seemingly proposed to eliminate its transcendant qualities. Such inquiries became increasingly abstruse and merely another branch of secular metaphysics, with little genuine religious content.

"Christian Democracy" became one of the two most powerful political forces in the immediate postwar period, and was embraced mainly by the Catholic lower-middle classes in Italy, West Germany, France, and the Low Countries. Christian Democracy was, however, a political not a religious movement, designed to establish a new moral and philosophical base for parliamentary liberalism after the wreckage of nazism and fascism.

There was something of a genuine Catholic revival in France and Spain during the 1940's. The defeat of the forces of the left and of liberalism during the Spanish Civil War and the opening round of the Second World War encouraged the reassertion of Catholic influence, strongly stimulated by the regimes of Franco and Petain. In France, Catholic lay societies burgeoned again, reasserting social, economic, and cultural influence; and some of these new organizations have remained a permanent feature of French life since the war.

The major changes in recent years have occurred within the Roman Catholic church. The reign of Pope John XXIII (1958–1963) brought a new and more liberal spirit to the Vatican, culminating in the convocation of an ecumenical council in 1963. Pope John, born of a peasant family, caught the popular imagination by stressing the need for Christian unity, encouraging the relaxation of certain Catholic dogmas, and enabling Catholics to take a more democratic, conciliatory attitude toward social and political problems.

The resulting liberalization of Catholicism has produced the greatest shock waves within the church in four centuries. The use of a variety of new liturgical forms, the fostering of reformist attitudes, an urge to make the church more helpful in social problems, and the questioning of church authority have proceeded apace. This has led to a crisis of religious vocations and a considerable number of resignations from the clergy in certain countries. The liberal movement within Catholicism is most profound in Holland; but even in Spain, cornerstone of Catholic conservatism, large numbers of the younger clergy have demanded change; and in 1973 the Spanish church hierarchy even encouraged separation of church and state.

De Gaulle and the Fifth Republic in France France was the dominant power on the west European continent from the middle of the seventeenth century until 1870, when that position was lost to a united Germany. After 1945, with the total defeat and partition of Germany, France was unable to reassume that role due to her own weakness and the impotence of western Europe compared with the foreign superpowers of the United States and Russia. France did, at least momentarily, regain special influence in the 1960's, but only after weathering years of severe crisis.

The major political problems faced by France during the two decades after the Second World War were not created by internal strife but stemmed from colonial revolt in the overseas French empire. The exhausting struggle to retain Indo-China was finally ended by the brief reform ministry of Pierre Mendès-France in 1954, but soon afterward an even more bitter colonial struggle broke out in French Algeria. This was the more difficult to resolve because Algeria was technically not a colony but a department of France in which resided a million French-speaking Europeans, outnumbered though they were by nearly nine million native Algerians.

The parliamentary system of the Fourth Republic, like that of its predecessor, represented all the main factions of French life and functioned on the basis of multiparty coalitions that normally opted for the status quo. Bold and resolute leadership was the exception, and the more moderate and left-wing forces began to doubt the wisdom of a hard-line policy in Algeria. The *colon* (European colonist) population there was determined to fight to the last, and enjoyed the support of the main sections of the French army, humiliated by the defeat in Indo-China and determined not to lose France's last major holding in the world. As the government in Paris vacillated, militant *colons* and the army forces in Algeria rose in revolt in May 1957, threatening civil war if a firm new national government were not established.

In this desperate situation, the French government and parliament turned to France's undisputed national hero, General Charles de Gaulle, leader of the resistance against Germany in the war. For nearly twelve years de Gaulle had been preparing a return to power under the right conditions, and in extremis the parliament voted him full power to resolve the crisis. De Gaulle's return was accepted by nearly all elements of French politics and he quickly restored discipline in the army.

De Gaulle's goal was, however, not merely to resolve the Algerian problem but to reorganize and strengthen the government of France, preparing the way for a policy of national "grandeur" and the reassertion of French hegemony. To this end, he supervised drafting of a constitution for a new Republic—France's Fifth—whose major new feature was the creation of a strong presidential executive of the American type directly elected by popular vote. The new constitution was overwhelmingly approved by plebiscite, after which de Gaulle was elected the president of the Fifth Republic.

De Gaulle grasped the futility of trying to retain military control over rebellious Algeria. In 1962, he granted Algeria its independence and afterward nearly its entire European population was repatriated to France. Similarly, he presided over the liquidation of the rest of France's African empire as well, for he realized that such territories cost France more than they gained. He hoped to replace political ties by cultural and economic ones.

After strengthening France and freeing it of the colonial burden, he proposed to reassert an independent French foreign policy and establish its political dominance in western Europe. To this end, de Gaulle pulled French troops out of NATO and began construction of France's own nuclear deterrent, called a *force de frappe* (striking force). This was most exiguous in size, approximately equivalent to the atomic payload of one American B-52, and critics dubbed it a "striking farce." De Gaulle was successful in making France's voice the strongest in western Europe, but he was completely unable to carve for France a major independent role in world affairs. The disproportion between France on the one hand and the United States and Russia on the other was too great. De Gaulle became a living anachronism, attempting to re-establish the grandeur of Louis XIV in an age when western Europe played a secondary role and had to depend upon cooperation and unity to prosper. The worst effect of de Gaulle's rule was to retard the process of European unity during the 1960's.

France made great economic progress under the Fifth Republic, and government planning coordinators provided the most effective state economic administration of any of the larger countries of western Europe. The prosperity, however, was not well distributed, and after de Gaulle was elected to a second five-year term, his majority dwindled as larger sectors became disenchanted with a kind of one-man rule.

The blowup finally occurred in May 1968. It began with a university rebellion by students in the Paris area, frustrated by the lack of opportunities for self-assertion and demanding full autonomy within the university and then later by extension for French society as a whole. Though students and workers had few contacts and little in common, the revolt eventually mushroomed into a broad series of labor walkouts that momentarily approached the scope of a nation-wide strike. The workers, however, were demanding little more than higher pay and better fringe benefits.

Charles de Gaulle. De Gaulle in the final, climactic phase of his career, as president of the new executive-dominated Fifth French Republic, 1959 to 1969. (French Embassy Press & Information Division.)

De Gaulle was shaken by the revolt, but reassured by the loyalty of military commanders, decided to hold fast politically while making economic concessions. The French middle classes, fearing a radical upset, once more rallied to him for the third time in a quarter century. New elections gave the Gaullist party a solid parliamentary majority and becalmed the situation. Only one year later, however, after French voters rejected certain minor economic changes by plebiscite, the aged general carried out his threat to retire for good, and passed away two years later.

He had been the most dominant figure in French history since Napoleon. De Gaulle had presided over the restoration of France in 1945 and saved it from civil war in 1957. He ended the colonial nightmare, strengthened its government executive and extended French prestige. Yet he had probably clung to power too long, thus obscuring his earlier achievements. He had delayed needed social and economic reforms, fostered capricious personalistic government, postponed closer European unity, and yet failed to convert France into a new independent major power, something entirely beyond her capacity. His role in French and European history will long be debated.

The Southern Dictatorships: Spain, Portugal, and Greece   The southwestern peninsula states of Spain and Portugal have always been the most anomalous parts of western Europe, partly cut off by geography, economically underdeveloped and shaped by somewhat dissimilar social and cultural patterns. Everywhere else in Europe, right-wing dictatorships had in one way or another fallen under German control during the Second World War and gone down to defeat with Hitler. But in the Iberian peninsula, the Spanish regime of General Francisco Franco and the Portuguese "New State" of Dr. Antonio de Oliveira Salazar had remained neutral and were still firmly in power after 1945.

Since memories of the Spanish Civil War were still strong, Allied leaders largely credited Franco's power to German assistance. Thus a policy of ostracism was imposed on Spain from 1945 to 1948 and the United States and nearly all European governments broke relations with her. The passage of time, however, and the growth of the Cold War changed perspectives. Franco's government appeared much less an aggressive Fascist regime and more a conservative, pluralistic right-wing dictatorship that was staunchly anti-Communist. The ostracism was broken in 1949 and relations with the United States quickly improved, resulting in the signing of a pact of military assistance between the two countries in 1953.

The Franco regime pursued a cautious program of internal liberalization during the 1950's and 1960's, allowing partial freedom of opinion and even a certain degree of dissident political activity, though never on the public level. The economy was liberalized in 1959, largely on the French model of the Fifth Republic, and the 1960's became the greatest boom decade in Spanish history. Per capita income began to climb toward $1,000, lifting Spain out of the category of the "poor" nations for the first time in 300 years.

The regime aimed at and achieved psychological depoliticization and, as the years passed, most Spanish people grew accustomed to a somewhat benign dictatorship. The old opposition lost contact with younger Spaniards and active opposition after the 1940's was comparatively infrequent. In a private scientific opinion poll in 1969, fifty-two percent of Spaniards questioned replied that they preferred the continuation of the present order of things in one form or another rather than face drastic changes.

As Franco grew older, he prepared for the succession to his regime by arranging the eventual restoration of the Spanish Bourbon monarchy. In 1969, Prince Juan Carlos, grandson of the late Alfonso XIII, was designated the eventual heir and successor. Even so, the regime rested primarily on the loyalty of the army and its large state bureaucracy, manned in considerable measure by members of the former Fascist party, the Falange, later rechristened simply the "Spanish Movement."

Despite remarkable economic development, Spain remained the second poorest country in western Europe, still dependent in sizable measure on foreign investment and the tourist trade. Hundreds of thousands still had to seek work in the more developed countries. Though Spain would not continue to grow without participation in the Common Market, the aversion to its government in other countries and continuing weaknesses made it impossible to arrange more than a marginal associate status with the European Economic Community.

Since the mid-1960's, university students have been in almost continual revolt—at least in Madrid and Barcelona—and Basque separatists in northeastern Spain have adopted terrorist tactics. The Spanish Catholic Church has begun to loosen its ties with the regime. As younger priests demand fundamental changes, the hierarchy has moved toward the advocacy of separating church and state.

Somewhat the same general situation has obtained in Portugal, save that the Salazar regime long refrained from any marked encouragement of economic development, leaving Portugal the most backward country of western Europe. During the past fifty years there has been little disturbance of the continuity of Portuguese rural life, and altogether Portuguese society has known less change than any other in Europe.

The most unique feature of Portugal in the second half of the twentieth century has been its determination to maintain its three major colonies in Africa. Salazar's government opposed the common trend of western Europe and held its ground against major rebel movements in Angola, Mozambique, and Portuguese Guinea. The predominant concern was not so much profit from the colonies as the conviction that the loss of these territories would reduce Portugal to insignificance in the world and undermine the future of the regime at home.

Salazar suffered a stroke near the end of 1968 and died a year later. He was replaced by Dr. Marcello Caetano, like Salazar, a former university professor, but also leader of the liberal faction within the government. From 1968 to 1974, Caetano maintained the basic features of the authoritarian system in Portugal while encouraging modest features of political liberalization and placing greater emphasis on economic development.

During these years, the rebel movements in Portuguese Africa grew in intensity, and Portuguese military frustration steadily mounted. The whole operation became enormously expensive for the poorest country in western

Europe. Slowly, the younger officers of the Portuguese army, called on to lead the African campaigns, began to turn against the Portuguese government system, blaming it for both the African debacle and the backwardness of Portugal itself. In a bloodless coup in April 1974, the Caetano government and the whole regime was overthrown by the army. A new left-liberal cabinet led by a general took power and established full civil liberties with the promise of democratic elections soon afterward. Negotiations were begun with certain of the African rebels and the end of the old Portuguese colonial empire was near at hand, soon to leave the Soviet Union as the only militarist-imperialist power in the world. However, the establishment of a stable new democratic political system in Portugal promised to be a difficult undertaking.

The social and economic structure of Greece is in general similar to that of Spain and Portugal. Between 1944 and 1948, Greece was wracked by a civil war between left and right somewhat analogous to the earlier Spanish Civil War. As in Spain, the anti-leftist forces won with the benefit of foreign assistance. But, whereas Franco was bolstered by the Fascist tide of Germany and Italy, Greek anti-Communists were backed by the liberal democracies of Britain and the United States. From 1948 to 1967, Greece was therefore ruled by a liberal constitutional monarchy similar to those in western Europe during an earlier generation. During that period Greece, with American assistance, enjoyed more rapid economic development than Portugal and almost as much as Spain. Its parliamentary system, however, was divided between several quarreling factions ranging from right to left and in the mid-1960's dissidence became more extreme.

In 1967, as the balance of power began to swing toward the moderate left, hard-line elements of the army intervened and bloodlessly established a military dictatorship. When the king himself tried to take over power from the military a few months later, he was forced into exile. Greece thus joined Spain and Portugal in the ranks of south European right-wing dictatorships. For several years Greece enjoyed new economic prosperity accompanied by political calm.

By the early 1970's, however, political discontent began to increase as the military regime failed to extend civil liberties or prepare for a return to parliamentary rule. An abortive effort in July 1974 to engineer the union of the east Mediterranean island republic of Cyprus with Greece ended in disaster, as Turkish forces seized the northern half of Cyprus to protect the Turkish minority there. The resulting outcry in Greece shattered the military government, and parliamentary government returned, though on a shaky basis.

Thus by 1974 Spain remained the only right-wing authoritarian country in southern Europe, though the unity and prosperity of the new Greek and Portuguese governments was quite uncertain. Despite Spain's continuing economic growth, its own long-range political future is clouded and its political structure prevents closer integration with the world of the west European liberal democracies.

RECENT CHANGES AND FUTURE PROBLEMS

By the 1960's, sociologists affirmed that the most developed parts of western Europe had, together with the United States and a few other countries, already entered a "post-industrial society." The old problems of basic industrialization and mass education had been conquered, and the nineteenth-century class society had been transformed by the welfare state and affluence into a mass consumer society dominated by technology and a managerial technocracy. The new problems, no longer related to achieving subsistence, were those of environmental decay, as nearly all west European cities were filled with traffic jams and enveloped in smog, while industrial wastes befouled rivers, lakes, and the very ocean itself.

At the same time, there was talk of growing "alienation" and boredom, especially among the young. Most people no longer had any significant

Willy Brandt. The leading public figure in West Germany since Adenauer, Brandt first came to fame as mayor of beleaguered West Berlin and then took over as West Germany's first Social Democrat premier in 1969. A spy scandal forced him to resign in 1974 after he had devoted great energy to improving relations with the Communist world. (German Information Center.)

religious faith or commitment, and the older mores and social values seemed to some to be less relevant to a technological society. Sweden, once praised as the most progressive of all social democracies, began to be denounced by critics as a system of "democratic totalitarianism" under perpetual Socialist rule, a land where direct individual freedom was increasingly restricted by statist direction.

Affluence, of course, was strictly a relative measurement and much of the theorizing about "postindustrialism" was premature. If nearly all of western Europe had been raised above the level of extreme want by the 1960's, only a minority of the population was truly affluent. In the new age of extreme materialism and secularism, the bulk of society was ever eager for further steady increases in the living standard, and this led to new demands.

The left in Europe had become moderate and social democratic, but still stood for new social and economic changes that would promote greater government control, more social equality, and higher incomes for workers. As the fear of communism and Russian imperialism receded, the moderate left once more gained greater strength in the larger countries where the left had lost power in the late 1940's or 1950's.

The trend began with Italy's "opening to the left" in 1962, when the Christian Democrats broadened their governmental base by forming a new coalition with a reunified Italian Socialist party. Two years later, thirteen years of conservative dominance in Britain came to an end as Labour won the elections of 1964, and remained in power for the next six years. In 1965, the Christian Democrat majority also sagged in Germany. A two-party coalition of Christian Democrats and Socialists was formed to govern Germany in 1966. After the elections of 1969, the Christian Democrats were ousted from the government of Germany for the first time in the postwar period, as the Socialists managed to establish a modest majority with the aid of the small German liberal party (FDP). The leftist protest vote in France rose during the late 1960's, and, four years after the resignation of de Gaulle, a Socialist-Communist coalition barely missed gaining a majority in the French elections of 1973.

Serious problems loomed ahead in the 1970's. Not much progress had been made toward genuine west European unity, the role of the United States overseas was being reduced, and the Soviet Union made steady gains in military power while west Europe remained militarily weak. Though a public opinion poll early in 1973 showed that two-thirds of west Europeans still thought that the United States was their best foreign friend and the most honest and trustworthy country abroad, the new attitude was one of greater independence even if not greater power or security.

The Economic Crisis of the Mid-1970's The assumption of post-industrial affluence and freedom from want proved fallacious. Some time after 1970 the great postwar economic boom began to come to an end, especially for Italy and Britain. It had been based on American credit, relatively cheap labor, low-priced raw materials and oil, large export markets, and sometimes inadequate internal investment. In the 1970's these factors began to be at least partially reversed.

The result by 1974 was soaring inflation, extreme financial deficits, oil-price gouges, and international shortages which created severe problems for all industrial nations. Italy was pushed to the edge of government bankruptcy and Britain was not far behind. The dream of the 1960's was being ruined because of poor leadership, inefficient organization, extreme worker demands, and political cowardice and disunity. The revolution of rising expectations has led to a psychology that constantly demands more and more while seeking to work and produce less and less. The very conditions of prolonged prosperity may serve to create economically destructive or counterproductive attitudes.

The remainder of the 1970's will be a time of severe testing. Major adjustments must be made by European states that will determine their security and prosperity for the last quarter of the twentieth century. Even more than in the past, they must act in concert with each other and with the United States. Hedonistic consumerism must give way to a new spirit of cooperation, solidarity and self-sacrifice. Political and economic leaders must find the courage to make difficult decisions that are adjusted to economic need. Peace and prosperity can no longer be taken for granted.

FURTHER READING

The best single-volume history of postwar Europe is Walter Laqueur's *Europe Since Hitler* (1970). The problems of European unity and cooperation may be approached through L. N. Lindberg and S. A. Scheingold, *Europe's Would-Be Policy* (1970); and two studies by F. R. Willis, *France, Germany and the New Europe, 1945–1963* (1966), and *Italy Chooses Europe* (1971).

Ernest Watkins, *The Cautious Revolution* (1950), treats the coming of the British welfare state. The two basic books on French politics since the war are Philip Williams, *Crisis and Compromise: Politics in the Fourth Republic* (1964), and Williams and M. Harrison, *Politics and Society in De Gaulle's Republic* (1971). Social and economic problems are studied in Stanley Hoffman, * *In Search of France* (1963); and John Ardagh, * *The New French Revolution* (1968).

The best survey of postwar West Germany is Alfred Grosser's *Germany in Our Time* (1971). Elizabeth Wiskemann, *Italy Since 1945* (1971), is a brief summary. Fuller political studies are Norman Kogan, *A Political History of Postwar Italy* (1966); and Giuseppe Mammarella, *Italy Since Fascism* (1966). Stanley G. Payne, * *Franco's Spain* (1967), summarizes Spain in the 1950's and 1960's. Roland Huntford, *The New Totalitarians* (1971), returns a negative report on statist Sweden under the Social Democrats.

Jacques Ellul has written a trenchant critique of *The Technological Society* (1965). Two major aspects of the arts are set forth in Maurice Nadeau, *The French Novel Since the War* (1967); and Roger Manvelle, *New Cinema in Europe* (1970). The cultural hysteria of the 1960's is analyzed in Christopher Booker, *The Neophiliacs* (1969).

*Books available in paperback edition are marked with an asterisk.

INDEX

velopment of, 1771; in German Confederation, 1134, 1263; government, 1190–1191; invaded by Germany, 1584; political development in, 1209; Treaty of Versailles, 1480; war with German Confederation, 1197

Depression, 1095, 1152, 1207, 1249, 1319, 1330, 1398, 1434; causes of, 1247; the Great, 1493–1495, 1551–1553, 1557, 1561, 1565, 1585. *See also* Crash

Derby, Lord, 1191, 1194, 1195–1197

Descent of Man, The (Darwin), 1263

De-Stalinization, 1744, 1759

Destra Storica, 1298

Dharma, 1384

Diagne, Blaise, 1704

Dickens, Charles, 1184

Dictatorship, 1190, 1203, 1213, 1468, 1515, 1530, 1559, 1780–1782; Bolshevik, 1501; communist, 1727, 1736, 1755–1756; by consensus in China, 1674; French, 1155; military, 1155, 1191, 1486, 1782; Nazi, 1540; presidential, 1200; Spanish, 1573, 1780–1781

Diem, Ngo Dinh, President, 1658

Diet, Confederate, 1133

Diplomacy: classical school of, 1063; postwar problems of, 1486–1492

Disease, 1152

Disraeli, Benjamin, 1118, 1175, 1191, 1195–1197, 1283–1284

Divine Mandate, 1651

Djilas, Milovan, 1747, 1750

Doenitz, Admiral Karl, 1604

Dole, 1155, 1551, 1552

Dollfuss, Engelbert, 1545

Don Carlos of Portugal, 1212

Doré, Gustave, 1060

Dostoevsky, Fyodor, 1312–1313

Drama, "Theater of the Absurd," 1775

Dravidians, 1369

Dreyfus (Captain Alfred) case, 1295–1296

Dubois, W. E. B., 1704

Dual Mandate, the, 1702

Dual Monarchy, 1334

Dubcek, Alexander, 1759

Du Cayla, Madame, 1123

Dudintsey, Vladimir, 1753

Dulles, John Foster, 1658

Duma, the, 1321

Dupleix, Joseph, 1378

Dutch, the, 1079, 1393; in Southeast Asia, 1395–1396

Dyarchy, 1626–1627

Dynamo, development of, 1179

Dzhvgashvili, Josif. *See* Stalin, Joseph

East Africa, 1418, 1429

East Asia, 1403–1416

East Germany, 1734, 1754, 1755

East India Company: British, *see* British East India Company; Dutch, 1373

East Indies, Dutch, 1363

Ebert, Friedrich, 1531, 1536

Economic development, 1770–1771

Economic theory, 1100–1102, 1249

Economics: failure of classical, 1100; Keynes' "new," 1495; the liberals in, 1069; "Natural Law" of, 1247

Economy: deterrents to growth of, 1089; expanding, 1243–1249; government intervention in, 1248–1249, 1473, 1495, 1543, 1648; international, 1245–1247; Japan's growth of, 1695, 1698; planned, *see* Five-Year Plans; Four-Year Plans; post World War I, 1485, 1492–1495; Russian, 1312; wartime, 1597, 1601

Ecumenical Council (1963), 1776

Education, 1060, 1335, 1412; in Africa, 1704, 1715; compulsory, 1284, 1294; elementary, 1128, 1294; for family planning, 1640; higher, 1772; influence of westernized forms, 1622–1623, 1625; as a political issue, 1208; prevalence of, 1144, 1179, 1279; public, 1144, 1206, 1211, 1284, 1308. *See also* Learning, Universities

Egypt, 1076, 1078, 1081; European occupation of, 1419

Einstein, Albert, 1269

Eisenhower, Dwight D., 1604

Eisenstein, Sergei, 1511

Electrical power, 1245; first commercial use of, 1179

Emigration, 1089, 1250, 1298, 1315, 1493

Emigrés, 1072, 1120

"Ems Dispatch," 1229

Encyclicals, 1263, 1566

Engels, Friedrich, 1182

England, East Indian trade of, 1374; population of, 1099; transport, 1086, 1092. *See also* Britain; British Empire

English East India Tea Company, *see* British East India Company

Enlightenment, the, 1058

Entente (*Entente Cordiale*), 1446–1447

Equality, 1211, 1305, 1622

Erzberger, Matthias, 1535

Estates General, in Sweden, 1210

Estonia, 1485, 1591

Ethiopia, 1364, 1418, 1431, 1569, 1713; invaded by Italy, 1429, 1569, 1705

Euratom, 1770

Europe: economic cooperation, 1769–1770; ethnic and economic boundaries ignored, 1483; first step toward confederation, 1769; Nazi domination of, 1590, 1597–1600; political geography revised, 1067, 1215, 1477, 1481; western, eastern, and central regions, 1058

European coal and steel community, 1770; concert, 1188

European Economic Community (EEC), 1770, 1781

European Free Trade Association (EFTA), 1770

Evangelicalism, 1171

Evolution, 1179; theory of, 1263–1264

Existentialism, 1774

Expeditions: British-French reach Peking, 1193; to the East, 1392

Extraterritoriality, 1409

Fabian Society, 1254–1256

Factories (trading post), 1374

Factory Acts, 1117, 1194, 1195

Factory system (industrial), 1060, 1088, 1090, 1097–1098

Faidherbe, General Louis, 1426

Falange, the, 1781

Falloux Law, the, 1206

Family, restructured in China, 1674–1675

Famine, 1152, 1506, 1507, 1518

Faraday, Michael, 1179

Farben, I. G., 1248

Farmers, in Russia, 1516

Farming: freehold, 1209, 1223; improved technology of, 1095

Fascism, 1434, 1436, 1526–1528, 1597; in Italy, 1526–1531, 1765

Faust (Goethe), 1172

February Patent, 1234

Federation of Rhodesia, 1711

Ferdinand I (King of Naples), 1074–1075, 1129, 1130

Ferdinand I of Saxe-Coburg (Tsar of Rumania), 1348

Ferdinand VII (King of Spain), 1074, 1075, 1212

Ferdinand the Good [the Simple] (Emperor of Austria), 1141, 1163, 1166

Feudalism, in Japan, 1413, 1415

Speransky, Michael, 1144–1145, 1148, 1149
Spice Islands, 1393
Spice trade, 1373
"Spirit of Locarno," the, 1434
Sri Lanka (Ceylon), 1369; independence of, 1651
SS (Nazi), 1541
Stadion, Count, 1166
Stäel, Madame de, 1171
Stalin, Joseph, 1512–1514, 1516, 1520–1521, 1724, 1736, 1752
Stalinism, 1516–1524, 1725–1726
Stambolov, Stefan, 1348
Standard of living, 1060, 1099, 1179, 1520, 1639, 1771–1772
Stankevich, Nicholas, 1150
Stanley, Henry M., 1424
State, German deification of the, 1178
State Council (Russia), 1145
States-General (Netherlands), 1208
Statuto, the (Sardinian), 1168, 1216
Stavisky Affair, 1557
Steam power, 1089, 1090, 1091–1092, 1202; in ships, 1179
Steamships, 1179, 1394
Steel and steel production, 1243–1244, 1287, 1332, 1645
Stein, Baron Karl, 1069, 1135
Stendhal, Marie Henri Beyle, 1183
Stephenson, George, 1092
Stock exchange: collapse of, 1493–1494; in London, 1094; in Vienna, 1338
Stolypin, Peter, 1321–1323
Storm and stress, period of, 1171
Storm Troopers, 1534, 1538, 1540, 1541
Stowe, Harriet Beecher, 1184
Straits Convention, 1083
Stresemann, Gustav, 1489, 1491
Strike(s), 1114, 1195, 1292, 1773; general, 1259, 1320, 1472, 1531–1532, 1550–1551; London Dock, 1253; right to, 1203; in Russia, 1319, 1320, 1324; sit down, 1558; sympathy, outlawed, 1551
Struve, Gustav von, 1158
Struve, Pyotr, 1323
Study of History, A (Toynbee), 1775
Sturm und Drang, 1171
Subhas Chandra Bose, 1633
Submarines, 1464–1467, 1597, 1604
Sudan, 1428–1429; independence of, 1703
Sudetenland, 1575–1578
Suez Canal, 1394, 1419; crisis over, 1768
Suffrage, 1116, 1120, 1122, 1126, 1190, 1208, 1236, 1282, 1284; in Austria, 1234, 1341; in England, 1109, 1110,

1195–1197; in France, 1190, 1199–1200, 1294, 1764; in Germany, 1231; in Hungary, 1335; in Italy, 1216, 1298, 1299; in Japan, 1684; in Norway, 1210; in Prussia, 1223; restricted, 1190, 1209, 1210, 1212, 1216, 1298, 1305; in Russia, 1305, 1321, 1507, 1521; Scandinavian, 1209, 1210; secret, 1347; in Spain, 1212; in Switzerland, 1211; three-class system of, 1347; unequal, 1234, 1341; universal, 1156, 1190, 1200, 1208–1211, 1231, 1294, 1299, 1341, 1344, 1347, 1521, 1561; for women, 1209, 1210, 1218, 1252, 1549, 1764
Suffragettes, 1252
Suharto (General/President of Indonesia), 1655, 1656
Sukarno (President of Indonesia), 1654–1657
Sumatra, 1373, 1389, 1650
Summit Conference at Geneva, 1744
Sun Yat Sen, 1410, 1661–1664
Supply and demand, law of, 1100, 1114
Sweden, 1209, 1561, 1763, 1771; government, 1190–1191; political development of, 1210; received Norway, 1067; Switzerland, 1211, 1561; political structure and development of, 1210; regained independence, 1067; Republic of, 1191
Syllabus of Errors (Pius IX), 1262, 1329
Syndicalism, 1258–1259
Syria, 1081, 1553

Taaffe, Count Edward, "Iron Ring" of, 1338–1339
Taff Vale decision, 1290
Tagore family, 1623
Taiping Rebellion, 1410
Taiwan, 1409, 1672
Talleyrand-Périgord, Charles Maurice de, 1066, 1067, 1126
Tamerlane, 1367
Tamil, 1369
Tanaka Ka Kuci, Prime Minister, 1699
Tanganyika, 1425, 1712
Tariffs, 1111, 1117, 1136, 1295, 1330, 1549; internal, 1135; movement toward reduction of, 1245; preferential, 1555; as revenue, 1407; treaties for, 1136, 1203; spread of, 1249
Taxation, 1543; indirect, 1485, 1628
Taylor, A. J. P., 1141
Tchaikovsky, 1313

Technology, 1523–1524; adaptation of science to, 1179; advances in, 1086–1092, 1244; agricultural, 1095; Great Britain's supremacy in, 1086–1087; industrial, 1090–1091; maritime, 1374; military, 1587, 1605
Teheran peace conference, 1606, 1724
Telford, Thomas, 1091
Terrorism, 1317, 1319, 1320, 1502, 1625, 1725–1726
Textiles, 1089, 1645; in British economy, 1087; production of, 1087, 1089, 1090. See also Cloth, manufacture of
Thailand, 1389, 1390, 1395, 1396, 1400
Theology, 1171, 1567; and Darwinism, 1264–1265; postwar, 1776
Thermodynamics, 1179
Thiers, Adolphe, 1083, 1126, 1128, 1293
Thieu, General Nguyen, 1659
Third Reich, 1434; acquires Austria, 1575; acquires Czechoslovakia, 1578; acquires France, 1585; acquires Memel, 1579; moves into the Balkans, 1593–1594
Third Section of the Imperial Chancery, 1148
Thistlewood, Arthur, 1113
Tibet, 1369, 1406, 1409
Tilak, B. G., 1626
Tisza, Colomon, 1335
Tito, Marshal, 1601, 1735–1737, 1744, 1747
Togo, 1553
Togoland, 1425
Tojo, General, 1690
Tokugawa period, 1413
Tokyo, 1414, 1695
Tolstoy, Leo, 1312
Tonkin, 1409; Gulf of, Resolution, 1659
Totalitarianism, 1517, 1523, 1663, 1664; communism, fascism, and nazism compared, 1545–1546
Touré, Samori (African king), 1431
Towns, population of, 1099
Toynbee, Arnold, 1775
Trade, 1373, 1392; African, 1422, 1431, 1703; commodities, 1374, 1391, 1394, 1407; "country," 1374; importance of to Japan, 1685, 1695; Indian, 1646; the merchant company, 1373–1374; monopoly, 1407; restraints on, see Tariffs; in Southeast Asia, 1391, 1394, 1398; the Zollverein, 1135–1136. See also Commerce
Trade routes, 1373, 1393
Trade Union Act, 1114

1 2 3 4 5 6 7 8 9 0